MOTOR CONTROL
AND LEARNING

THIRD EDITION

MOTOR CONTROL AND LEARNING

A Behavioral Emphasis

Richard A. Schmidt, PhD

Failure Analysis Associates, Inc.
and
University of California, Los Angeles

Timothy D. Lee, PhD

McMaster University

Human Kinetics

Library of Congress Cataloging-in-Publication Data

Schmidt, Richard A., 1941-
    Motor control and learning : a behavioral emphasis / Richard A.
Schmidt, Timothy D. Lee. -- 3rd ed.
        p.   cm.
    Includes bibliographical references (p. 423) and index.
    ISBN 0-88011-484-3
    1. Movement, Psychology of.   2. Motor Learning.   I. Lee, Timothy
Donald, 1955-   . II. Title.
    BF295.S248   1999
    152.3--dc21   98-15263
                                                                          CIP

ISBN: 0-88011-484-3

Acquisitions Editors: Richard D. Frey, PhD and Judy Patterson Wright, PhD; **Developmental Editor:** Marni
Basic; **Assistant Editor:** Henry V. Woolsey; **Copyeditor:** Joyce Sexton; **Proofreader:** Erin Cler; **Graphic
Designer:** Nancy Rasmus; **Graphic Artist:** Angela K. Snyder; **Cover Designer:** Jack Davis; **Illustrator:** Mic
Greenberg; **Printer:** Edwards Brothers

Printed in the United States of America   10   9   8   7   6   5   4   3

Human Kinetics
Web site: http://www.humankinetics.com/

United States: Human Kinetics, P.O. Box 5076, Champaign, IL 61825-5076
1-800-747-4457
e-mail: humank@hkusa.com

Canada: Human Kinetics, 475 Devonshire Road, Unit 100, Windsor, ON N8Y 2L5
1-800-465-7301 (in Canada only)
e-mail: humank@hkcanada.com

Europe: Human Kinetics, P.O. Box IW14, Leeds LS16 6TR, United Kingdom
+44 (0)113-278 1708
e-mail: humank@hkeurope.com

Australia: Human Kinetics, 57A Price Avenue, Lower Mitcham, South Australia 5062
(08) 82771555
e-mail: humank@hkaustralia.com

New Zealand: Human Kinetics, P.O. Box 105-231, Auckland Central
09-523-3462
e-mail: humank@hknewz.com

CONTENTS

PREFACE

Most of us have marveled at one time or another about how highly skilled performers in industry, sport, music, or dance seem to make their actions appear so simple and easy, performed with incredible efficiency, smoothness, style, and grace. Like the first two editions (Schmidt 1982, 1988), this edition of *Motor Control and Learning: A Behavioral Emphasis* was written for those who would like to understand how it is that these performers can achieve such artistry while we, as beginners in a similar task, are clumsy, inept, and unskilled. This book was written particularly as a textbook for university or college undergraduate and graduate students taking courses in human performance or motor learning, primarily in fields such as kinesiology, psychology, or physical education. Students in other fields such as the neurosciences, physical and occupational therapy, biomedical or industrial engineering, and human factors (ergonomics) should also find the concepts contained here to be of interest, as movement behavior is a part of all of them. And for those who are (or are becoming) practitioners in these fields, the principles of motor behavior outlined here should provide a solid basis for tasks such as designing human-machine systems, developing training programs in sport or industry, or teaching progressions in dance or music.

The emphasis of the text is behavioral. That is, the primary focus is on movement behaviors that can be observed directly and on the many factors that affect the quality of these performances and the ease with which they can be learned. In this sense, the book has strong ties to the methods and thinking of experimental psychology. Yet, at the same time, the book focuses on the neurological and mechanical processes out of which these complex movement behaviors are crafted. Brain mechanisms that allow the detection of errors, spinal cord processes that are capable of generating patterns of skilled activities in locomotion, and various biomechanical constraints that act to determine the nature of our movement behaviors are all important if we are to understand high-skilled performance. This blending of behavioral, neurophysiological, and biomechanical analysis reflects the fact that the fields of motor behavior and motor learning, movement neurophysiology (or motor control), and biomechanics are rapidly moving together toward the shared understanding of complex movement behaviors.

This edition of the text retains the same goal of presenting an up-to-date review of the state of knowledge in movement control and learning, and it does so with a format that is similar to that of the previous editions. We have directed considerable effort toward including the most recent knowledge from a number of rapidly developing subfields, and each of the chapters has been revised extensively in light of these newer concepts. In addition to including more than 450 references to work published since the last edition, we have also strived to pay homage to some of the important early research developments in the various areas, and many of these are highlighted in sidebars throughout the book.

Some chapters from the previous edition have been reduced, combined with other chapters, or otherwise shortened in order to reduce complexities in the text without sacrificing its in-depth coverage or the richness of its concepts. And we have expanded certain chapters and sections to present new, exciting areas of research that have emerged since the previous edition. Perhaps this is evident most prominently with the addition of a new chapter on coordination (chapter 8)—reflecting the growth of a topic area that was given only a few pages of discussion 10 years ago.

Many new practical examples from areas such as human factors, sport, therapy, and music illustrate these concepts and contain concrete suggestions for practical application. As before, the revised text reflects a logical progression, so that later chapters build upon concepts presented in earlier chapters, with the final result being a consistent, defensible framework of ideas about skills. Having such a framework, or point of view, is important for those who wish to use the information presented here, both so that contributions to new applications may be made and so that the design of continued skills research is aided.

The book is divided into three parts. Part I provides an introduction to research and fundamental concepts that are important to understanding motor behavior. The first chapter, a brief history of the field, is followed by a presentation of methods in movement research in chapter 2, focusing on various paradigms and statistical techniques used in the study of movement behavior. In chapter 3 the human is regarded as a processor of information, and we focus on the many ways that information is dealt with in motor behavior. The concept of attention is the focus of chapter 4, with particular emphasis on the role of attention in motor behavior.

Part II deals with motor control. Chapter 5 views motor control from a closed-loop perspective, in which the sensory contributions to movement control are examined, with particular emphasis on new research regarding the role of vision. In chapter 6, the focus shifts to contributions of the central nervous system to movement control, with emphasis on motor programs and the generalized motor program. Some principles of "simple" motor behavior are presented in chapter 7, together with a discussion of theoretical concepts that integrate the central and sensory contributions to movement control. Chapter 8

presents a discussion of the factors involved in movement control that make coordination both easy and difficult to achieve. The final chapter in this part includes a discussion of factors that determine skill differences among people, with emphasis on important themes about abilities and the prediction of skills.

Part III deals with the acquisition of skill, or motor learning. Chapter 10 concentrates on some special methodological problems for studying learning. The effects of practice, the structure of the practice session, and the many variables under the control of a teacher, coach, or therapist are discussed in chapter 11, while feedback contributions to learning are included in chapter 12. In both of these chapters, much new information is covered that demands important changes in our understanding of the processes involved in practice and the ways in which these impact on learning. Various theoretical treatments of motor learning are presented in chapter 13. And finally, chapter 14 deals with the factors associated with the retention and transfer of skills.

Throughout the long process of this revision there were a number of people who provided very highly valued input. Judy Wright, Marni Basic, and Rick Frey of Human Kinetics provided considerable feedback and encouragement for this major revision. Andrea Swanson helped with the references and the author index, and Erin Lanktree translated the sections that appear in the boxed text on page 217. And we called upon a number of colleagues to read and critique certain chapters. The many suggestions made by the following people were invaluable in making the necessary revisions: Jack Adams, Romeo Chua, Digby Elliott, Nikki Hodges, Jim Lyons, Matt Heath, Jason Murdoch, Jen Richardson, Stephan Swinnen, Seijiro Tsutsui, Chuck Walter, and Laurie Wishart. The final manuscript is much better as a result of all their efforts, and we are grateful.

CREDITS

Figure 1.2
Reprinted, by permission, from Gelfand, I.M., Gurfinkel, V.S., Tomin, S.V., and Tsetlin, M.L., 1971, *Models of the Structural-Functional Organization of Certain Biological Systems*, Cambridge, MA: MIT Press, v.

Figure 1. 3
Reprinted, by permission, from Weinberg, R.S., and Gould, D. 1995, *Foundations of Sport and Exercise Psychology*, Champaign, IL: Human Kinetics, 12.

Figure 2.4
Reprinted, by permission, from Chapanis, A. 1951, "Theory and Methods for Analyzing Errors in Man-machine Systems," *Annals of the New York Academy of Sciences, 51,* 1181.

Figure 2.9
Adapted, by permission, from Brown, I.D., 1962, "Measuring the 'Spare Mental Capacity' of Car Drivers by a Subsidiary Auditory Task," *Ergonomics, 5,* unknown.

Figure 2.10
Reprinted, by permission, from Plagenhoef, S., 1971, *Patterns of Human Motion: A Cinematographic Analysis*, New York: Prentice Hall, 42.

Figure 2.13
Journal of Motor Behavior, 32, 302, 1991. Adapted with permission of the Helen Dwight Reid Educational Foundation. Published by Heldref Publications, 1319 Eighteenth St., N.W., Washington, D.C. 20036-1802. Copyright © 1991.

Figure 2.14
Reprinted from Carnahan, H., "Eye, Head and Hand Coordination During Manual Aiming." In L. Proteau and D. Elliott (Eds.), *Vision and motor control,* Copyright 1992, Page 42, with permission from Elsevier Science.

Figure 2.15
Reprinted, by permission, from Carter, M.C., and Shapiro, D.C., 1984, "Control of Sequential Movements: Evidence for Generalized Motor Programs," *Journal of Neurophysiology, 52,* 792.

Figure 2.17
Reprinted, by permission, from Schmidt, R.A., Zelaznik, H.N., Hawkins, B., Frank, J.S., and Quinn, J.T., 1979, "Motor-output Variability: A Theory for the Accuracy of Rapid Motor Acts," *Psychological Review, 86,* 427.

Figure 3.6
Reprinted from Hyman, R., 1953, "Stimulus Information as a Determinant of Reaction Time," *Journal of Experimental Psychology, 45,* 192.

Figure 3.8
Adapted, by permission, from Simon, J.R., and Rudell, A.P., 1967, "Auditory S-R Compatibility: The Effect of an Irrelevant Cue on Information Processing," *Journal of Applied Psychology, 51,* 302.

Figure 3.9
Reprinted, by permission, from Klapp, S.T., and Erwin, C.I., 1976, "Relation Between Programming Time and Duration of the Response Being Programmed," *Journal of Experimental Psychology: Human Perception and Performance, 2,* 596.

Figure 3.10
Reprinted from Sperling, G., 1960, "The Information Available in Brief Visual Presentations," *Psychological Monographs, 74,* 498.

Figure 3.11
Reprinted from Peterson, L.R., and Peterson, M.J., 1959, "Short-Term Retention of Individual Verbal Items," *Journal of Experimental Psychology, 58,* 198.

Figure 3.12
Reprinted, by permission, from Adams, J.A., and Dijkstra, S., 1966, "Short-Term Memory for Motor Responses," *Journal of Experimental Psychology, 71,* 317.

Figure 4.2
Reprinted, by permission from Schneider, W., and Shiffrin, R., 1977, "Controlled and Automatic Human Information Processing: I. Detection, Search, and Attention," *Psychological Review, 84,* 20.

Figure 4.4
Adapted, by permission, from Davis, R., 1959, "The Role of 'Attention' in the Psychological Refractory Period," *The Quarterly Journal of Experimental Psychology, 11,* 215.

Figure 4.5
Adapted, by permission, from Davis, R., 1959, "The Role of 'Attention' in the Psychological Refractory Period," *The Quarterly Journal of Experimental Psychology, 11,* 215.

Figure 4.6
Reprinted, by permission, from Greenwald, A.G., and Schulman, H.G., 1973, "On Doing Two Things at Once: Elimination of the Psychological Refractory Period Effect," *Journal of Experimental Psychology, 101,* 74.

Figure 4.8
Adapted, by permission, from Pashler, H., 1993, "Doing Two Things at the Same Time," *American Scientist, 81 (1),* 52.

Figure 4.9
Reprinted, by permission, from Posner, M.I., and Keele, S.W., 1969, "Attentional Demands of Movement," In *Proceedings of the 16th Congress of Applied Physiology, Amsterdam,* Amsterdam: Swets and Zeitlinger.

Figure 4.10
Reprinted, by permission, from Posner, M.I., and Keele, S.W., 1969, "Attentional Demands of Movement," In *Proceedings of the 16th Congress of Applied Physiology, Amsterdam,* Amsterdam: Swets and Zeitlinger.

Figure 4.11
Adapted, by permission, from Tipper, S.P., Lortie, C., and Baylis, G.C., 1992, "Selective Reaching: Evidence for Action-centered Attention," *Journal of Experimental Psychology: Human Perception and Performance, 18,* 893, 896.

Figure 4.13
Reprinted from Mowrer, O.H., 1940, "Preparatory Set (Expectancy): Some Methods of Measurement," *Psychological Monographs, 52 (233),* 12.

Figure 4.14
Reprinted from Drazin, D.H., 1961, "Effects of Foreperiod, Foreperiod Variability, and Probability of Stimulus Occurrence on Simple Reaction Time," *Journal of Experimental Psychology, 62,* 45.

Figure 4.15
Reprinted, by permission, from Posner, M.I., Nissen, M.J., and Ogden, W.C., 1978, "Attended and Unattended Processing Modes: The Role of Set for Spatial Location." In H.L. Pick and I.J. Saltzman (Eds.), *Modes of Perceiving and Processing Information,* Hillside, NJ: Lawrence Erlbaum, 149.

Figure 4.16
Journal of Motor Behavior, 9, 107, 1977. Adapted with permission of the Helen Dwight Reid Educational Foundation. Published by Heldref Publications, 1319 Eighteenth St., N.W., Washington, D.C. 20036-1802. Copyright © 1977.

Figure 4.18
Journal of Motor Behavior, 10, 173, 1978. Adapted with permission of the Helen Dwight Reid Educational Foundation. Published by Heldref Publications, 1319 Eighteenth St., N.W., Washington, D.C. 20036-1802. Copyright © 1978.

Figure 4.19
Adapted, by permission, from Apter, M.J., 1989, *Reversal Theory: Motivation, Emotion, and Personality,* New York: Routledge, 18.

Figure 5.6
Journal of Motor Behavior, 17, 229, 1983. Adapted with permission of the Helen Dwight Reid Educational Foundation. Published by Heldref Publications, 1319 Eighteenth St., N.W., Washington, D.C. 20036-1802. Copyright © 1983.

Figure 5.7
Adapted, by permission, from Whiting, H.T.A., Gill, E.B., and Stephenson, J.M., 1970, "Critical Time Intervals for Taking in Flight Information in a Ball-catching Task," *Ergonomics, 13,* 269.

Figure 5.8
Adapted, by permission, from Savelsbergh, G.J.P., Whiting, H.T.A., and Bootsma, R.J., 1991, "Grasping Tau," *Journal of Experimental Psychology: Human Perception and Performance, 17,* 317 and 321.

Figure 5.9
Reprinted, by permission, from McLeod, P., and Dienes, Z., 1996, "Do Fielders Know Where to Go to Catch the Ball or Only How to Get There?" *Journal of Experimental Psychology: Human Perception and Performance, 22,* 538.

Figure 5.10
Reprinted, by permission, from Lee, D.N., and Aronson, E., 1974, "Visual Proprioceptive Control of Standing in Human Infants," *Perception & Psychophysics, 15,* 230.

Figure 5.11
Reprinted, by permission, from A. Shumway-Cook and M.H. Woollacott, 1995, "Motor Control: Theory and Practical Applications," *Cook Motor Control:* 53.

Figure 5.13
Reprinted, by permission, from Dewhurst, D.J., 1967, "Neuromuscular Control System," *IEEE Transactions on Biomedical Engineering, 14,* 170, © 1967 IEEE.

Figure 5.14
Adapted, by permission, from F.M. Henry, 1953, "Dynamic Kinesthetic Perception and Adjustment," *Research Quarterly for Exercise and Sport* 24: 177.

Figure 5.18
Reprinted, by permission, from Angel, R.W., and Higgins, J.R., 1969, "Correction of False Moves in Pursuit Tracking," *Journal of Experimental Psychology, 82,* 186.

Figure 6.3
Reprinted, by permission, from Rothwell, J.C., Traub, M.M., Day, B.L., Obeso, J.A., Thomas, P.K., and Marsden, C.D., 1982, "Manual Motor Performance in a Deafferented Man," *Brain, 105,* 523.

Figure 6.5
Reprinted from *Biophysics, 11,* Shik, M.L., Severin, F.V., and Orlovskii, G.N., "Control of Walking and Running by Means of Electrical Stimulation of the Mid-Brain," p. 757, Copyright 1966, with permission from Elsevier Science.

Figure 6.10
Reprinted, by permission, from Slater-Hammel, A.T., 1960, "Reliability, Accuracy and Refractoriness of a Transit Reaction," *Research Quarterly for Exercise and Sport, 31,* 22.

Figure 6.11
Reprinted, by permission, from Polit, M.H., and Bizzi, E., 1979, "Characteristics of Motor Programs Underlying Arm Movements in Monkeys," *Neurophysiology, 42*, 191.

Figure 6.17
Reprinted from Armstrong, T.R., 1970, "Training for the Production of Memorized Movement Patterns," *Technical Report, 26*, 35.

Figure 6.18
Adapted from Shapiro, D.C., 1977, "A preliminary Attempt to Determine the Duration of a Motor Program," In D.M. Landers and R.W. Christina (Eds.), *Psychology of Motor Behavior and Sport* (vol. 1), 21, Champaign, IL: Human Kinetics.

Figure 6.19
Reprinted, by permission, from Terzuolo, C.A., and Viviani, P., 1979, "The Central Representation of Learning Motor Programs," In R.E. Talbott and D.R. Humphrey (Eds.), *Posture and Movement*, 115, New York: Raven.

Figure 6.21
Reprinted, by permission, from Shapiro, D.C., 1977 March, *Bilateral Transfer of a Motor Program*, paper presented at the annual meeting of the American Alliance for Health, Physical Education and Recreation, Seattle, WA.

Figure 7.2
Reprinted, by permission, from Fitts, P.M., 1964, "Perceptual-Motor Skills Learning," *Categories of Human Learning*, 258.

Figure 7.3
Adapted from Fitts, P.M., 1954, "The Information Capacity of the Human Motor System in Controlling the Amplitude of Movements," *Journal of Experimental Psychology, 47*, 385.

Figure 7.4
Journal of Motor Behavior, 8, 120, 1976. Reprinted with permission of the Helen Dwight Reid Educational Foundation. Published by Heldref Publications, 1319 Eighteenth St., N.W., Washington, D.C. 20036-1802. Copyright © 1976.

Figure 7.5
Reprinted, by permission, from Schmidt, R.A., Zelaznik, H.N., Hawkins, B., Frank, J.S., and Quinn, J.T., 1979, "Motor-Output Variability: A Theory for the Accuracy of Rapid Motor Acts," *Psychological Review, 86*, 425.

Figure 7.6
Reprinted, by permission, from Schmidt, R.A., Zelaznik, H.N., Hawkins, B., Frank, J.S., and Quinn, J.T., 1979, "Motor-Output Variability: A Theory for the Accuracy of Rapid Motor Acts," *Psychological Review, 86*, 427.

Figure 7.8
Reprinted, by permission, from Schmidt, R.A., Zelaznik, H.N., and Frank, J.S., 1978, "Sources of Inaccuracy in Rapid Movement," *Information Processing in Motor Control and Learning, 197*.

Figure 7.9
Journal of Motor Behavior, 12, 50, 1980. Adapted with permission of the Helen Dwight Reid Educational Foundation. Published by Heldref Publications, 1319 Eighteenth St., N.W., Washington, D.C. 20036-1802. Copyright © 1980.

Figure 7.10
Reprinted, by permission, from Schmidt, R.A., Zelaznik, H.N., and Frank, J.S., 1978, "Sources of Inaccuracy in Rapid Movement," *Information Processing in Motor Control and Learning, 196*.

Figure 7.11
Journal of Motor Behavior, 12, 86, 1980. Adapted with permission of the Helen Dwight Reid Educational Foundation. Published by Heldref Publications, 1319 Eighteenth St., N.W., Washington, D.C. 20036-1802. Copyright © 1980.

Figure 7.13
Reprinted, by permission, from Schmidt, R.A., and Sherwood, D.E., 1982, "An Inverted-U Relation Between Spatial Error and Force Requirements in Rapid Limb Movements: Further Evidence for the Impulse-Variability Model," *Journal of Experimental Psychology: Human Perception and Performance, 8*, 165.

Figure 7.14
Reprinted, by permission, from Schmidt, R.A., and Sherwood, D.E., 1982, "An Inverted-U Relation Between Spatial Error and Force Requirements in Rapid Limb Movements: Further Evidence for the Impulse-Variability Model," *Journal of Experimental Psychology: Human Perception and Performance, 8*, 167.

Figure 7.16
Reprinted, by permission, from Rack, P.M.H., and Westbury, D.R., 1969, "The Effects of Length and Stimulus Rate on Tensionn in the Isometric Cat Soleus Muscle," *Journal of Physiology, 204*, 44 and 45.

Figure 7.22
Adapted, by permission, from Meyer, D.E., Abrams, R.A., Kornblum, S., Wright, C.E., and Smith, J.E.K., 1988, "Optimality in Human Motor Performance: Ideal Control of Rapid Aimed Movements," *Psychological Review, 95*, 343.

Figure 7.23
Adapted, by permission, from Meyer, D.E., Abrams, R.A., Kornblum, S., Wright, C.E., and Smith, J.E.K., 1988, "Optimality in Human Motor Performance: Ideal Control of Rapid Aimed Movements," *Psychological Review, 95*, 345.

Figure 8.1
Reprinted, by permission, from Schneider, D.M., and Schmidt, R.A., 1995, "Units of Action in Motor Control: Role of Response Complexity and Target Speed," *Human Performance, 8*, 34.

Figure 8.2
Reprinted, by permission, from Schneider, D.M., and Schmidt, R.A., 1995, "Units of Action in Motor Control: Role of Response Complexity and Target Speed," *Human Performance, 8*, 34.

Figure 8.3
Reprinted, by permission, from Schneider, D.M., and Schmidt, R.A., 1995, "Units of Action in Motor Control: Role of Response Complexity and Target Speed," *Human Performance, 8*, 38 and 40.

Figure 8.4
Reprinted, by permission, from Schneider, D.M., and Schmidt, R.A., 1995, "Units of Action in Motor Control: Role of Response Complexity and Target Speed," *Human Performance, 8*, 46.

Figure 8.5
Reprinted, by permission, from Goodale, M.A., and Servos, P., 1996, "Visual Control of Prehension." In H.N. Zelaznik (Ed.), *Advances in Motor Control and Learning*, Champaign, IL: Human Kinetics, 87.

Figure 8.6
Reprinted from *Human Movement Science, 9*, Marteniuk, R.G., Leavitt, J.L., MacKenzie, C.L., and Athenes, S., "Functional Relationships Between Grasp and Transport Components in a Prehension Task," p. 158, Copyright 1990, with permission from Elsevier Science.

Figure 11.9
Adapted, by permission, from Lee, T.D., and Magill, R.A., 1983, "The Locus of Contextual Interference in Motor-skill Acquisition," *Journal of Experimental Psychology: Memory and Cognition, 9,* 739.

Figure 11.10
Reprinted, by permission, from Lee, T.D., Wishart, L.R., Cunningham, S., and Carnahan, H., 1997, "Modeled Timing Information During Random Practice Eliminates the Contextual Interference Effect," *Research Quarterly for Exercise and Sport, 68,* 103.

Figure 11.11
Adapted, by permission, from Hird, J.S., Landers, D.M., Thomas, J.R., and Horan, J.J., 1991, "Physical Practice is Superior to Mental Practice in Enhancing Cognitive and Motor Task Performance," *Journal of Sport & Exercise Psychology, 13(3),* 286 and 287.

Figure 11.12
Adapted from Armstrong, T.R., 1970, "Training for the Production of Memorized Movement Patterns," *Technical Report, 26,* 15.

Figure 12.2
Reprinted from Bilodeau, E.A., Bilodeau, I.M., and Schumsky, D.A., 1959, "Some Effects of Introducing and Withdrawing Knowledge of Results Early and Late in Practice," *Journal of Experimental Psychology, 58,* 143.

Figure 12.3
Journal of Motor Behavior, 24, 192, 1992. Adapted with permission of the Helen Dwight Reid Educational Foundation. Published by Heldref Publications, 1319 Eighteenth St., N.W., Washington, D.C. 20036-1802. Copyright © 1992.

Figure 12.4
Journal of General Psychology, 7, 245-260, 1932. Reprinted with permission of the Helen Dwight Reid Educational Foundation. Published by Heldref Publications, 1319 Eighteenth St., N.W., Washington, D.C. 20036-1802. Copyright © 1932.

Figure 12.6
Reprinted from Bilodeau, E.A., and Bilodeau, I.M., 1958, "Variable Frequency Knowledge of Results and the Learning of Simple Skill," *Journal of Experimental Psychology, 55,* 379.

Figure 12.8
Reprinted, by permission, from Bilodeau, I.M., 1956, "Accuracy of a Simple Positioning Response With Variation in the Number of Trials by Which Knowledge of Results is Delayed," *American Journal of Psychology, 69,* 436.

Figure 12.9
Reprinted, by permission, from Lavery, J.J., 1962, "Retention of Simple Motor Skills as a Function of Type of Knowledge of Results," *Canadian Journal of Psychology, 16,* 305.

Figure 12.10
Reprinted from *Human Movement Science, 9,* R.A. Schmidt, C. Lange, and D.E. Young, "Optimizing Summary Knowledge of Results for Skill Learning," page 334, © 1990, with kind permission of Elsevier Science—NL, Sara Burgerhartstraat 25, 1055 KV Amsterdam, The Netherlands.

Figure 12.11
Journal of Motor Behavior, 26, 274, 1994. Reprinted with permission of the Helen Dwight Reid Educational Foundation. Published by Heldref Publications, 1319 Eighteenth St., N.W., Washington, D.C. 20036-1802. Copyright © 1994.

Figure 12.12
Reprinted, by permission, from Swinnen, S.P., Schmidt, R.A., Nicholson, D.E., and Shapiro, D.C., 1990, "Information Feedback for Skill Acquisition: Instantaneous Knowledge of Results Degrades Learning," *Journal of Experimental Psychology: Learning, Memory, and Cognition, 16,* 712.

Figure 12.13
Journal of Motor Behavior, 8, 280, 1976. Reprinted with permission of the Helen Dwight Reid Educational Foundation. Published by Heldref Publications, 1319 Eighteenth St., N.W., Washington, D.C. 20036-1802. Copyright © 1976.

Figure 13.1
Reprinted from Snoddy, G.S., 1926, "Learning and Stability," *Journal of Experimental Psychology, 10,* 11.

Figure 13.2
Reprinted, by permission, from Crossman, E.R.F.W., 1959, "A Theory of the Acquisition of Speed Skill," *Ergonomics, 2,* 157.

Figure 13.3
Reprinted, by permission, from Fleishman, E.A., and Rich, S., 1963, "Role of Kinesthetic and Spatial-Visual Abilities in Perceptual Motor Learning," *Journal of Experimental Psychology, 66,* 9.

Figure 13.4
Reprinted, by permission, from Ackerman, P.L., 1990, "A Correlational Analysis of Skill Specificity: Learning, Abilities, and Individual Differences," *Journal of Experimental Psychology: Learning, Memory and Cognition, 16,* 887.

Figure 13.5
Adapted, by permission, from Ackerman, P.L., 1988, "Determinants of Individual Differences During Skill Acquisition: Cognitive Abilities and Information Processing," *Journal of Experimental Psychology: General, 117,* 299.

Figure 13.6
Journal of Motor Behavior, 4, 149, 1972. Reprinted with permission of the Helen Dwight Reid Educational Foundation. Published by Heldref Publications, 1319 Eighteenth St., N.W., Washington, D.C. 20036-1802. Copyright © 1972.

Figure 13.7
Adapted, by permission, from Schmidt, R.A., 1982, "The Schema Concept," In J.A.S. Kelso (Ed.), *Human Motor Behavior: An Introduction,* 227.

Figure 13.8
Adapted, by permission, from Schmidt, R.A., 1982, "The Schema Concept," In J.A.S. Kelso (Ed.), *Human Motor Behavior: An Introduction,* 229.

Figure 13.9
Adapted, by permission, from Schmidt, R.A., 1982, "The Schema Concept," In J.A.S. Kelso (Ed.), *Human Motor Behavior: An Introduction,* 230.

Figure 13.10
Reprinted, by permission, from Pew, R.W., 1966, "Acquisition of Hierarchical Control Over the Temporal Organization of a Skill," *Journal of Experimental Psychology, 71,* 768.

Figure 13.12
Reprinted, by permission, from Vereijken, B., Whiting, H.T.A., and Beek, W.J., 1992, "A Dynamical Systems Approach to Skill Acquisition," *The Quarterly Journal of Experimental Psychology, 45A*, 327.

Figure 13.13
Journal of Motor Behavior, 24, 136, 1992. Adapted with permission of the Helen Dwight Reid Educational Foundation. Published by Heldref Publications, 1319 Eighteenth St., N.W., Washington, D.C. 20036-1802. Copyright © 1992.

Figure 14.3
Reprinted from Fleishman, E.A., and Parker, J.F., 1962, "Factors in the Retention and Relearning of Perceptual Motor Skill," *Journal of Experimental Psychology, 64*, 218.

Figure 14.4
Reprinted from Neumann, E., and Ammons, R.B., 1957, "Acquisition and Long Term Retention of a Simple Serial Perception Motor Skill," *Journal of Experimental Psychology, 53*, 160.

Figure 14.5
Adapted, by permission, from Elliott, D., and Madalena, J., 1987, "The Influence of Premovement Visual Information on Manual Aiming," *The Quarterly Journal of Experimental Psychology, 39A*, 546.

Figure 14.6
Reprinted, by permission, from Adams, J.A., and Dijkstra, S., 1966, "Short-Term Memory and Motor Responses," *Journal of Experimental Psychology, 71*, 317.

Figure 14.7
Adapted, by permission, from Rosenbaum, D.A., Weber, R.J., Hazelett, W.M., and Hindorff, V., 1986, "The Parameter Remapping Effect in Human Performance: Evidence from Tongue Twisters and Finger Fumblers," *Journal of Memory and Language, 25*, 713.

Figure 14.8
Journal of Motor Behavior, 1, 33, 1969. Adapted with permission of the Helen Dwight Reid Educational Foundation. Published by Heldref Publications, 1319 Eighteenth St., N.W., Washington, D.C. 20036-1802. Copyright © 1969.

Figure 14.9
Reprinted from Adams, J.A., 1961, "The Second Facet of Forgetting: A Review of Warm-Up Decrement," *Psychological Bulletin, 58*, 260.

Figure 14.10
Journal of Motor Behavior, 3, 7, 1971. Adapted with permission of the Helen Dwight Reid Educational Foundation. Published by Heldref Publications, 1319 Eighteenth St., N.W., Washington, D.C. 20036-1802. Copyright © 1971.

Figure 14.11
Reprinted from Lewis, D., McAllister, D.E., and Adams, J.A., 1951, "Facilitation of Interference in Performance on the Modified Mashburn Apparatus: I. The Effects of Varying the Amount of Original Learning," *Journal of Experimental Psychology, 41*, 53.

PART 1

INTRODUCTION TO MOTOR BEHAVIOR

This first part introduces the field of motor control and learning. In chapter 1 the area is described, and the important distinctions separating motor control and learning from other, related fields of study are made. Then, a brief history of the field is given, showing how knowledge about movements from psychology and physical education, as well as from the neurosciences, has recently been combined. The second chapter deals with the various scientific methods used for studying motor skills. Here, we explain the tools of motor behavior research, focusing on the various ways in which motor behavior can be measured. Chapter 3 presents the information-processing approach, which is fundamental to understanding how humans think and act. The last chapter in this section describes how attention influences motor behavior.

EVOLUTION OF A FIELD OF STUDY

Understanding Movement
    A Behavioral Level of Analysis
    Emphasizing Movements
    Potential Applications

Origins of the Field
    Early Research
    Postwar Research
    Motor Control Today

Summary

Movement is truly a critical aspect of life. Without movement, we could not feed ourselves, we could not reproduce, and we would not survive. Life as we know it would not be possible without the capability to move. Our capacity to move is more than just a convenience that enables us to walk, play, or manipulate objects; it is a critical aspect of our evolutionary development, no less important to understand than is the evolution of our intellectual and emotional capacities. In fact, ethologists (those who study animal behavior) assert that our highly developed cognitive capacities evolved so that we could make the movements essential to survival—the construction of shelter, the making of tools, and communication. Surely the study of movement needs no further justification than its significance in terms of the evolution of humankind.

Movement takes many forms. Some forms can be regarded as genetically defined (inherited, or "self-differentiated" according to developmental biologists), such as people's control of their limbs or the ability of the centipede to simultaneously keep track of all those legs. Other examples are the "scratch reflex" of dogs or the rapid blink of the eye in response to a sudden puff of air. Here, the patterns of action appear to be determined by genetic makeup and/or through growth and development, and these actions appear to be quite stereotyped across members of the same species. A second class of movements can be thought of as "learned"—for example, those involved in controlling an automobile, operating a typewriter, or performing a triple-twisting somersault. These learned movements are often termed *skills*. They do not seem to be inherited, and mastering them requires long periods of practice and experience. Guthrie (1952) perhaps provided the best definition: "Skill consists in the ability to bring about some end result with maximum certainty and minimum outlay of energy, or of time and energy" (136). Skills are especially critical to the study of human behavior, as they are involved in operating machines in industry, controlling vehicles, preparing meals, playing games, and so on. Skills and genetically defined movements can both be very simple (e.g., snapping fingers or blinking eyes), or they can be very complex (e.g., pole-vaulting).

This book is about all these kinds of movements, whether they be primarily genetically defined or learned through practice. In particular, we will be concerned with how these various movements are *controlled*—how the central nervous system is organized so that the many individual muscles and joints become coordinated. We will also be concerned with how sensory information from the environment, the body, or both is used in the control of movement and how such information allows a person to select a movement. The scientific field of study that addresses these issues is known as *motor control*—the study of the control of movements in humans and animals.

In this book, we will add one important aspect to motor control that is often not included—the study of how movements are *learned*, that is, how movements are produced differently as a result of practice or experience. Indeed, we believe many of the movements already mentioned are made up of a complex combination of genetic determinants coupled with modifications made through practice or experience. Understanding how movements are learned is the major concern of a field of study called *motor learning*. We see no good justification, however, for separating the study of motor learning from the study of movement or of motor control in general, as this artificial separation inhibits the understanding of both issues. For these reasons, as the title reveals, the subject matter of the book is motor control *and* learning.

Understanding Movement

How can knowledge and information about movement be acquired? A logical way to proceed would be to study some relevant aspect of the movement-control process using scientific methods. But which processes should be examined? One possibility would be to focus on the nature of biochemical interactions that occur within cells as individuals move. Or we could focus on the cell itself, asking how cells interact with each other in the control of movement. In a similar way, we could consider groups of cells, such as a whole muscle, the spinal cord, or the nerves, and ask how these relatively more complex structures are involved in movement control. Another possibility would be to focus on the movements of the freely moving animal or human, concentrating on the factors that determine movement accuracy, the choice of movement, or the patterns of action. Along the same lines, we could study movement in an even more global context, asking about the role of movement in society, the choice of certain skilled occupations or sports, movement in groups or teams, and so on.

Clearly, there are various ways to consider the same phenomenon. They have been termed *levels of analysis,* and analogous levels are present in any area of scientific concern. Illnesses, for example, can be considered at levels that range from the biochemical determinants of disease through the effects of disease on entire societies. Because these various ways of considering a single problem are so diverse, a given scientist will usually focus on one, or at most two, of these levels of analysis.

A Behavioral Level of Analysis

The focus of this text is primarily at the behavioral level of analysis. The major goals will be to understand the variables that determine motor performance proficiency and to understand the variables that are most important for the learning of movement behaviors. Also of interest is how such information can be used in the solution of certain practical problems such as those involved in the design of equipment that humans must control, in the selection of individuals for occupations, in the teaching of skills in sport and industry, and in rehabilitation.

This behavioral level of analysis, however, is more interesting and complete when combined with two other fields of study, each representing a deeper level of analysis. *Biomechanics* concerns the mechanical and physical bases of biological systems. Certainly in order to understand movement we must understand something of the body itself, with all its joints, levers, and associated mechanical characteristics. Also related to the study of movement, *neurophysiology* concerns the functioning of the brain and central nervous system and the ways in which they control the contractions of muscles that move the limbs. The study of movement will be attacked at various levels of analysis—the behavioral level and the levels of biomechanics and neural control.

Emphasizing Movements

In considering movements, especially skills, it is often difficult to isolate a movement from its environment. In driving a car, for example, there are the coordinated actions involved in changing gears (clutch, accelerator, shift lever, etc.) as well as the movements of steering. These parts of the skill are the means through which the driver *affects* his or her environment. But skills are also *affected by* the environment. For example, whether or not the road turns or whether snow is present influences the driver's movements of the vehicle controls. Such reciprocal relations between the environment and the individual make it very difficult to pinpoint the various determinants of motor behavior, because the interaction of the many motor control and environmental factors is extremely complex and difficult to study with experimental procedures.

The approach taken in this text is to focus on these mutual interactions between the environment and the motor system. A large portion of this approach deals with the behavior and capabilities of the motor system to produce movements, studied more or less independently of the role of sensory or environmental information. But at the same time, the role of environmental information such as vision, and the ways in which it is processed and used to guide movements, will be an important concern. In any case, we will deliberately try to downplay skills in which the quality of the *movement* components per se is almost irrelevant to the outcome (such as in playing chess).

In deciding which skills to include in our field of study, it is helpful to consider the probable limiting factors in the performance. In the chess example, intellectual decision making seems to be the important factor and should not be included in this treatment. In a 26-mile marathon, or in weight lifting, as other examples, the factors seem to be more closely related to cardiovascular fitness and strength, respectively—also not within the confines of the present field of study. We will emphasize most strongly skills in which the focus is on the capabilities to use environmental information in the complex control of the limbs.

Potential Applications

Given an understanding of some of the processes underlying the control of movements, where can these principles be applied? High-level sports, games, and athletic events come to mind as areas for application, as these activities often involve the same kinds of processes that are studied in the area of motor control and learning. But potential generalizations should not be limited to these kinds of activities. Many apparently genetically defined actions such as walking and maintaining posture are under consideration here. How these movement capabilities, when disrupted by injuries or stroke, can be improved via treatments emphasizing the learning of *new* movement patterns—the subject matter of physical therapy—is also an application area. Many industrial skills, such as using a lathe, typing, woodcarving, and handwriting, are of critical importance to this field of study. Artistic performances, such as the playing of musical instruments, the creation of a painting, or the production of a dance, are certainly under the heading of motor behavior as treated here. The evocation of sounds, whether they be from the vocalist in an opera or from the student learning a new language,[1] is also a motor task, as the sounds are controlled by muscular activity of the vocal apparatus in ways analogous to the control of the hands and fingers of the skilled typist. The potential applications for the principles discovered in the field of motor control are present in nearly every aspect of our lives.

Origins of the Field

In an examination of the early research on movement and learning, it will be evident that the field, as we know it today, emerged from two isolated bodies of knowledge. These two areas are (a) the branch of neurophysiology primarily concerned with the neural processes that are associated with (or are causes of) movements, with only slight reference to the movements themselves, and (b) the branch of psychology and related fields primarily concerned with high-level skills with very little reference to the neurological mechanisms involved. For nearly a century, these two fields developed knowledge at different levels of analysis but with little mutual influence. Only toward the end of the 1970s did the two fields begin to come together. For the reader interested in more detail on these historical developments, see Irion (1966), Adams (1987), and Summers (1992).

Early Research

Some of the earliest motor skills investigations were done around 1820 by the astronomer Bessel (cited by Welford, 1968) as he tried to understand the differences among his colleagues in recording the transit times of the movements of stars. This skill involved estimating the time required for the image of a star to move through the crosshairs of a telescope. Bessel was interested in the processes underlying this complex skill, as well as in why some of his colleagues estimated accurately and others could not.

Considerably later, studies were made of the visual contributions to hand movements in localizing targets (Bowditch & Southard, 1882). Leuba and Chamberlain (1909) studied the accuracy of limb-positioning movements; Fullerton and Cattell (1892) examined force reproducibility; and Judd (1908) studied transfer of learning with dart-throwing tasks. An important trend was established by Bryan and Harter's (1897, 1899) work on receiving and sending Morse code; periods of no improvement (plateaus) between segments of improvement were identified, and considerable debate about the existence and interpretation of these plateaus was to continue for some decades (e.g., Book, 1908/1925; Keller, 1958). Galton (see Boring, 1950) studied the relationships among strength, steadiness, and body configuration in over 9,000 British males and females; Book (1908/ 1925) examined typing skills for very large samples of subjects ranging widely in ability and age. Retention of skills over long intervals of no practice was an important theme, and typing was a convenient way to study it (e.g., Bean, 1912; Swift & Schuyler, 1907). A remarkable series of studies on the retention of typing skill was initiated by Hill, Rejall, and Thorndike (1913), showing savings in the relearning of typing skill after two consecutive 25-year periods of no practice (Hill, 1934, 1957).

One of the earliest systematic approaches to the understanding of motor skills was conducted by Woodworth (1899), who sought to identify some of the fundamental principles of rapid arm and hand movements. This work, together with that of Hollingworth (1909), uncovered principles still being discussed by motor skills researchers. There was also some research, published in German and French, that is virtually forgotten today. Work on such topics as memory for movements, speed-accuracy trade-offs, and phase transitions in bimanual movements were studied in Germany and in France during the middle and late 1800s. A summary of this research is provided by Worringham (1992).

A major influence of the time was that of Thorndike (1914), who was concerned with processes underlying the learning of skills and other behaviors. His Law of Effect, which continues to have its influences in psychology, states that responses followed by a reward tend to be repeated. Responses that are not followed by a reward (or that are punished) tend not to be repeated. This idea formed the cornerstone for much of the theorizing about learning that was to follow in this century. Thorndike was also a pioneer in the area of individual differences, in which the focus is on the differences among individuals over practice (see chapter 9).

Most of the work mentioned here originated from the field of psychology, and much of the field of motor behavior today is the legacy of this early thinking and research. But the early research, which is similar in method to at least some of today's work, marked a severe break in tradition from the pre-1900 views of behavior. The pre-1900 research often involved *introspection*, including subjective self-reports of feelings that were unobservable. Skills were studied only because they were thought to provide "access to the mind." As the century turned, there was a shift to more systematic and objective approaches to the study of skills. And, of equal importance, skills were beginning to be studied because investigators wanted to know about the skills themselves.

Toward the end of this period, there was a slight increase in the number of studies conducted on skills. Some of these concerned handwriting proficiency, ways in which practice sessions could be structured to maximize motor learning, and whether or not skills should be "broken down" into their components for practice. Skills research placed greater emphasis on industrial applications (Gilbreth, 1909; Stimpel, 1933). So-called time-and-motion studies analyzed production-line assembly movements; such research became the target of criticism by workers because of the strict standards of performance it imposed on them. There was rising interest in the most efficient ways to perform tasks such as carrying mortar and shoveling coal and in methods of improving the conduct of work in extremely hot environments. Some early theories of learning were published (e.g., Snoddy, 1935), and work by physical educators interested in sports and athletic performances emerged (e.g., McCloy, 1934, 1937). An interest in factors associated with

growth, maturation, and motor performance began to surface; and studies by Bayley (1935), Espenschade (1940), McGraw (1935, 1939), and Shirley (1931) led the way to the formation of the subarea that we now call *motor development* (see Thomas, 1997 for a historical review).

The evolution of the study of the physiological or neural bases of movement paralleled work in the motor behavior area during this period, but without much formal contact between the fields. The characteristics and contraction properties of muscle tissue were a topic of early study by Blix (1892–1895) and Weber (1846; see Partridge, 1983), who identified "springlike" properties of muscle that have only recently been "rediscovered." Jackson conducted early investigations of the neural control of movement in the 1870s, well before the advent of electrophysiological techniques that were to revolutionize the field. But what led to the development of various electrophysiological methods was the discovery by Fritsch and Hitzig (1870) that the brain is electrically excitable. These methods gave rise to studies by Ferrier (1888) that investigated the responses in the cortex to artificial movements, as well as to the work by Beevor and Horsely (1887, 1890) investigating sensory and motor areas of the brain.

One of the more important influences in the neural control area was the work on reflexes at about the turn of the century by Sherrington and his coworkers. Sherrington studied and classified the major responses to stimuli presented to the extremities, and he believed that most of our voluntary movements resulted from these fundamental reflexes. Sherrington is credited with the creation of a number of classical concepts of motor control, most of which are still in our thinking today. For example, he first talked of *reciprocal innervation*, the idea that when the flexors of a joint are activated, the extensors tend to be automatically deactivated, and vice versa. Also, Sherrington coined the term *final common path*, which referred to the notion that influences from reflexes and sensory sources, as well as from "command" sources from the brain, eventually converge at spinal levels to produce the final set of commands delivered to the muscles. Indeed, Sherrington's early writings (e.g., Sherrington, 1906) are still interesting reading today (see also a tribute to his work by Gallistel, 1980).

Sherrington was one of those involved in research on various sensory receptors associated with the perception of movement. Various sensory receptors were identified, such as the Golgi tendon organ that was thought to signal changes in muscle *tension,* and the muscle spindle that was thought to be involved in the perception of muscle *length* and hence joint position. Sherrington coined the term *proprioception,* which refers to the sense of body position and orientation thought to be signaled by the various muscle and joint receptors together with receptors located in the inner ear.

Somewhat later, scientists conducted research on various brain structures. Herrick (1924) proposed numerous hypotheses about the functions of the cerebellum, many of which seem at least reasonable today. Also, patients with accidental cerebellar damage were studied (e.g., by Holmes, 1939) in an attempt to pinpoint some of the movement-control deficits associated with this structure. Other brain structures, studied in patients with various kinds of brain damage, became subjects of interest (Adrian & Buytendijk, 1931).

Early neural control research mainly involved very simple movements. Indeed, experimenters sometimes isolated nerve-muscle preparations, or used animals with various degrees of experimentally induced spinal cord damage; here the concern about movement was usually secondary to interest in the neurological processes. When movements were studied, the movement was often not considered in much detail; and measures of the speed, accuracy, or patterns of movement were usually missing from these reports. The motor behavior work, on the other hand, typically involved very complex actions (e.g., typing, telegraphy) but with very little concern about the underlying neural or biomechanical mechanisms that controlled them.

An exception to this general separation of the neural control and motor behavior areas is found in the research of two important physiologists in the 1930s and 1940s. During this period, Nikolai Bernstein and Erich von Holst published a number of seminal papers that have had a significant impact on motor control theorizing today. Unfortunately, many scientists involved in the study of movements, from both behavioral and neural control areas, were mainly ignorant of the contributions made by Bernstein and von Holst until

translations of their work appeared in English— Bernstein's work had been published in Russian, von Holst's in German. Their early papers reappeared in English in the late 1960s and early 1970s (see Bernstein, 1967, 1996, and Whiting, 1984; von Holst, 1937/1973, Gallistel, 1980). Thus, while the two areas were being blended in Russia and Germany, these trends were not seen in the United States or England, where most of the work on movement was being conducted. Ironically, it was the translation of this work many years later, and the attention that it received (e.g., Turvey, 1977), that served as a significant catalyst to the merging of the neural control and motor behavior areas.

Postwar Research

World War II had profound effects on the world, and it is not surprising that it also had major effects on movement research. One of the earliest and most direct effects can be traced to the need to select the most suitable people for pilot training, which resulted in the creation of the U.S. Army Air Force's Psycho-Motor Testing Program initiated by Arthur Melton in the early stages of

Figure 1.1.　Nikolai A. Bernstein (1897–1966).

the war (see Melton, 1947 for a description of some of this work). Important studies were conducted on underlying motor, perceptual, and intellectual abilities as they related to the selection of pilots and other military personnel (see chapter 9). Similar studies were conducted in England. In addition, scientists studied gunnery, physical training in the heat and cold, vehicle control, and many other issues that related to combat performance.

When the war ended in 1945, the prevailing attitude in the United States was that the efforts related to selection and training of military personnel should not be abandoned. Consequently, this research continued for many years; some of these programs still exist today. The military research effort was sustained by Arthur Melton's creation in 1949 of the U.S. Air Force Human Resources Research Center, which carried on many of the wartime programs but also expanded to include studies of more general interest. A major contribution of this program was Fleishman's work on individual differences and abilities (e.g., Fleishman, 1965). The wartime programs, devoted to personnel selection and motor abilities, had not resulted in the success in pilot selection that had been anticipated. Researchers began to realize that training—not selection—was perhaps more important to the development of proficient pilots. Hence, much attention was directed toward procedures for teaching motor skills, the transfer of motor skills from one activity to another, and the retention of skills (chapter 14).

In addition to the formal laboratories that were supported by defense funds, research relevant to the military was given increased federal funding. This funding, in the form of contracts, grants, and training programs, was responsible for a great shift of attention among psychologists toward motor behavior research. The directions imposed by federal funding agencies had, and continue to have, a profound influence on the behaviors studied and the research questions asked. The area of motor behavior was important at the time, and a great deal of funding was directed toward it, convincing a large number of psychologists to become interested in this area of research.

A second major influence in the creation of that boom in motor behavior research in the postwar period was the emergence of various theories of learning, most notably that of Hull (1943). In scientific inquiry, theories generally provide an organization of the conceptual issues and findings as well as strong suggestions for future research. Theories stimulate and provide focus for the research of others, and Hull's theory was no exception. His was a general learning theory, applying to animals and humans and to verbal and motor behavior, and it was often tested with motor tasks. A major emphasis of the theory was the fatigue-like process associated with long practice periods. The theory attempted to explain how fatigue and recovery processes combined to determine the learning of motor skills. Thus, a large number of scientists worked with motor tasks to investigate Hull's predictions. Most of this work has relevance to the structuring of practice sessions (see chapter 11) or to the effects of fatigue on performance and learning. Hull's theory later proved to be an inadequate account of the processes and variables that determine motor learning and performance. However, theories like Hull's provide strong directions for research and contribute experimental data for use by future generations, even though the original theory may be shown to be inadequate.

As the complexity of machines increased in this period and industrial methods became more complicated, it became obvious that many machines were exceeding the capabilities of humans to operate them effectively. For example, a number of serious airplane accidents that were initially attributed to "pilot error" were eventually traced to the way in which the instruments and controls in the cockpit were arranged (Chapanis, 1965; Fitts & Jones, 1947; Schlager, 1994). Thus, shortly after the war, there emerged a study of man-machine interactions, variously termed *human factors, ergonomics* (in England), or *engineering psychology* (a subarea of industrial psychology). The guiding concepts were that humans were an important link in most of the machinery involved in industry, and that such machinery must be designed with humans in mind. This thinking, while it began in the military, is now seen in automobile design (lighting, suspension, steering), the organization of assembly lines and workspaces, the design of home appliances, and many other areas (Sanders & McCormick, 1993; Wickens, 1992).

This period also saw a great deal of experimental effort in England. One of the most important contributions was by Craik (1948), who proposed that we consider the brain as a kind of computer in which information is received, processed, and then output to the environment in the form of overt actions of the limbs. An important part of this general idea is the notion of *central intermittency*, according to which the human is seen as responding in discrete bursts rather than continuously, as it might appear. Craik's idea paved the way for other English psychologists such as Welford, who in 1952 proposed the still relevant *single-channel hypothesis* (see chapter 4) associated with the *psychological refractory period*—the delay in response to the second of two closely spaced signals. Also, a great deal of work was done in ergonomics, on training and conditions of practice, and on hand movement control, particularly with respect to anticipation and timing (Poulton, 1950).

The ideas about central intermittency and the analogies of the brain to the computer were accompanied by similar new directions in psychology and related fields. One of the new ideas was represented by Wiener's (1948) book *Cybernetics*, which outlined an information-processing basis for human behavior. Also, Shannon and Weaver's (1949) *The Mathematical Theory of Communication* established important principles of information processing that later led to systematic attempts to study the motor system in terms of its capabilities and limitations in processing information.

In keeping with the information-processing basis for behavior suggested by Craik and others, Fitts (1954) presented some now famous fundamental relations among characteristics of hand movements—their movement time, their movement extent, and their accuracy (see chapter 7). This formulation, which has since come to be known as Fitts's Law, was an early attempt to apply mathematical and information-processing principles to the understanding of human movements, and it suggested that more complex limb control could be understood by future application of such methods and thinking. Even as a young man, Fitts was regarded as one of the future leaders in this area, but he died unexpectedly in the mid-1960s before his full potential could be realized.

In the middle of this postwar period, a great deal of motor behavior research was being conducted—enough that Robert and Carol Ammons, themselves researchers in this area, created a

Figure 1.2.   Paul M. Fitts (1912–1965).
Reprinted from Gelfand, Gurfinkel, Tomin, and Tsetlin, 1971.

journal in 1949 entitled *Perceptual and Motor Skills*. The journal now publishes both motor and nonmotor research, but during its early years it served as a major outlet for motor behavior work. In addition, the *Research Quarterly*, a physical education research journal, and the *Journal of Experimental Psychology* published a great deal of motor behavior research during this period.

Toward the end of the postwar period, the number of psychologists interested in motor behavior research gradually declined, while the number of physical educators interested in these problems strongly increased. The psychologists' lack of interest may be attributed to decreased federal support for motor behavior research, disillusionment with Hull's theory, and increasing interest in other types of human behavior such as verbal learning and memory. This trend reached its peak in the mid-1960s when an "academic funeral" sponsored by Ina and Edward Bilodeau was held at Tulane University. Renowned motor behavior psychologists gathered to hear the last rites and to bid each other farewell as each moved on to other related topics in psychology. The eulogies were recorded in a volume entitled *Acquisition of Skill* (Bilodeau, 1966), which describes well the attitude of the times.

Motor behavior research was dead, or so the psychologists thought; but they did not consider a man named Franklin Henry, trained in psychology and working in the Physical Education Department at Berkeley, who had a continuing interest in motor behavior research. Fittingly acknowledged as the father of motor behavior research in physical education, he advocated an approach using psychological techniques, laboratory tasks, and careful measurement. Unlike the psychologists, though, he used whole-body activities (as well as the psychologists' traditional fine-motor tasks) in his research, and many of these tasks included very rapid motor actions representative of activities in sports and games. Henry educated many doctoral students who subscribed to his general method and point of view as they assumed positions in physical education departments during the college growth boom of the 1960s. Many of these disciples created PhD programs and trained more students in this basic tradition, with the result that Henry's influence became pervasive by the 1970s and continues today. With the leadership of A.T. Slater-Hammel, these new motor behavior scientists organized the North American Society for the Psychology of Sport and Physical Activity (NASPSPA); the Canadian Society for Psycho-Motor Learning and Sport Psychology soon followed. These groups flourished in the 1970s. During this period, two books devoted strictly to motor behavior and motor learning were published, one in England (Knapp, 1963) and one in the United States (Cratty, 1964). Many more (including the first two editions of this book) followed.

Not all psychologists of the period were bored with motor behavior research. Fitts and Peterson (1964) presented influential experiments on limb movement accuracy; Bilodeau and Bilodeau (1961) and Adams (1964) wrote needed reviews of motor behavior research; Adams (1968) wrote a theoretical treatment of the role of sensory feedback in movement learning; and Keele (1968) wrote an

Figure 1.3.   Franklin M. Henry (1904–1993).
Reprinted from Weinberg and Gould, 1995.

often quoted review of motor control. But these were the exceptions. As the 1970s approached, the cluster of scientists in physical education and (to a limited extent) psychology began to evolve in new directions. Posner and Konick (1966) and Adams and Dijkstra (1966) presented seminal articles dealing with short-term memory for movements. Henry and his students (e.g., Henry & Rogers, 1960) were interested in motor programs; Posner (1969) studied attention and movement control; Pew (1966) examined practice and automaticity; and Adams (1971) initiated a return to theorizing about motor learning. These emphases provided strong leadership for the motor behavior area in the 1970s.

As in the early period, the neural control and motor behavior scientists were oblivious to each other, but important contributions were being made in neural control that would later be influential in joining the two areas. One of the more important contributions was the work on muscle-spindle mechanisms by Merton (1953; Marsden, Merton, & Morton, 1972), to be discussed in chapter 5. While the specific mechanisms proposed by Merton now appear to be incorrect (Houk, 1979; Smith, 1977), Merton's original ideas about automatic regulation of movement are reasonable in very general terms. Merton was one of the first to measure movements *and* neurophysiological processes in the same investigation, creating a beginning for a blend of behavior and neurological emphases that was seen later.

At about the same time, a great deal of research was devoted to the sensory receptors associated with movement perception and kinesthesis. Skoglund (1956) published a classic paper showing that the various receptors in a joint capsule appear to be activated only at certain specific joint angles, suggesting that these receptors have a large role in the perception of joint position. This point of view is currently being seriously questioned, as newer data suggest that the joint receptors operate only at the extreme range of movement. This debate is discussed in more detail in chapter 5.

Numerous studies on the nature of muscle and its contractile and mechanical (i.e., springlike) properties were also completed during these postwar years, and these studies attracted the attention of contemporary researchers in motor behavior and motor control (Rack & Westbury, 1969). These physical characteristics of muscle and of the motor apparatus were utilized by scientists in the Moscow laboratories who were following the earlier traditions of Bernstein. The extensive work on movement control by this group, originally published in Russian and thus generally unknown to American and British researchers, attracted a great deal of attention through various translations (e.g., Gelfand et al., 1971; Kots, 1977). This research has special relevance for the control of locomotion and provides important links between the neural control mechanisms and behavioral principles. But despite these efforts, by 1970 almost no association existed between the behavioral scientists interested in more global and complex skills and the neurophysiological scientists interested in simple movements and neural control.

Motor Control Today

The 1970s brought massive changes in the field of movement control and learning. The strict stimulus-response (S-R) orientation that had such a strong foothold during most of the century was overshadowed by the cognitive information-processing approach, arising in large part from the impact that Neisser's (1967) *Cognitive Psychology* had on the field of experimental psychology in general and (later) on motor behavior in particular. The move toward cognitive psychology was a reaction to oversimplified S-R theories of behavior; and ideas about internal and mental and motor processes, together with many methods and paradigms for understanding them, took the place of such theories. Perhaps more than anything else, Neisser's book popularized the study of processes such as response selection and movement programming, whose existence must be *inferred* from the behaving individual rather than being directly observed.

Influenced by cognitive psychology, the motor behavior field seemed to undergo a transition from a *task orientation*, which focuses primarily on the effects of variables on the performance of certain motor tasks, to a *process orientation*, which focuses on the underlying mental or neural events that support or produce movements (Pew, 1970, 1974b; Schmidt, 1975b, 1989a). Humans were considered processors of information, and it was necessary to understand how movement information is coded and stored, how actions are represented in memory, and how information about errors is processed so that learning can occur.

Led by such researchers as Adams and Dijkstra (1966) and Posner and Konick (1966), the process orientation helped to create the area of *short-term motor memory*—the study of the processes underlying the memory loss in simple movements over short periods of time. Many studies were conducted in this area during the late 1960s and early 1970s (see chapter 14). Studies were also completed on information-processing activities during the learning of simple motor tasks (see chapter 12).

More importantly, theorizing returned to motor behavior and learning, a style of inquiry that had been relatively dormant since the failure of Hull's (1943) theory. Adams sparked the interest in theory when he presented a feedback-based theory of verbal learning (Adams & Bray, 1970), followed the next year by a similar theory devoted to motor learning (Adams, 1971). Pew (1974a) returned to the old idea of a movement *schema* (Bartlett, 1932)—the abstract hypothetical structures responsible for movement control and evaluation, to be discussed in chapter 13. And, one year later, the schema theory for the learning of simple motor skills was presented (Schmidt, 1975b). Together, these theoretical ideas have generated a great deal of interest in motor skills, as is made evident later in the text.

Figure 1.4. Jack A. Adams (b. 1922).

The motor behavior field not only changed its direction, but also grew rapidly during the 1960s and 1970s. Formal courses of study in universities flourished, and new journals appeared. In 1969, Schmidt founded the *Journal of Motor Behavior*, which was closely followed in 1972 by the *Journal of Human Movement Studies*, created by the English motor behavior scientist John Whiting. A review journal entitled *Exercise and Sport Sciences Reviews* was created in this period, and it devoted a major portion of its space to motor behavior research. And the psychological journals (e.g., *Journal of Experimental Psychology, British Journal of Psychology*, and *Ergonomics*, to name a few) continued to publish some motor behavior research. As the field grew, motor behavior textbooks proliferated. More than 30 textbooks written subsequent to Knapp's (1963) and Cratty's (1964) initial books, as well as a large number of chapters in edited volumes on more specific topics, are currently available.

Also, the 1970s were the beginning of a long-needed merger between the neural control and the motor behavior scientists. Many people were trained formally in both motor behavior and neural control, and these people completed the bridge between the two levels of analysis. More and more behavior-oriented scientists are asking questions about movement control and making increased use of various electrophysiological and biomechanical techniques to understand the functions of the central nervous system in movement. The neural control scientists are shifting from studies that examine only the neural mechanisms to studies investigating these mechanisms during complex movements. Much of this latter work is done with animals, principally monkeys and cats. Records from electrodes implanted in the brain, spinal cord, or muscle are taken while the animal is engaged in motor activity. Representing this approach are Grillner and his colleagues (1972, 1975) and Smith and her colleagues (1986), who studied locomotion in cats; Evarts (1972, 1973), who studied a number of separate brain structures in monkeys; and Houk (1979) and Granit (1970), who studied the gamma motor system in monkeys and humans. Recent important work by Georgopoulos (1995) using monkeys and by Bizzi (e.g., Bizzi et al., 1995) with frogs has specified more precisely the brain and spinal neuronal correlates that underlie complex motor activity. Jeannerod has also made comparative analyses of monkey and human brain areas involved in grasping (e.g., Jeannerod et al., 1995).

The essential feature of all this work is the strong attempt to find an association between movement behaviors and neurological processes in order to provide a more complete understanding of how movements are controlled. This marks a refreshing change from the earlier research in which the movements per se were hardly considered. The surfacing of the association between motor behavior and motor control resulted in several reviews written toward the end of the 1970s, such as those by Brooks (1975, 1979, 1986), Grillner (1975), Wetzel and Stuart (1976), and Gallistel (1980). Behaviorists and neurophysiologists have both participated in a number of recent scientific meetings, and the results have often appeared in edited volumes (e.g., Stelmach & Requin, 1980, 1992; Swinnen et al., 1994).

An additional change has occurred recently— one far more subtle than those just mentioned. The field of motor control is acquiring an independent identity rather than remaining a mere blending of two different fields. It is becoming a field of study in its own right, complete with its own journals and methods for asking research questions and collecting data. Such methods involve the use of sophisticated techniques for recording and analyzing movements, such as electrophysiological recordings, cinematographic and three-dimensional analyses, measurement of the kinematics of movement, and advanced methods for examining the involvement of brain structures, integrated with the more traditional techniques for studying learning (e.g., Corcos, Jaric, & Gottlieb, 1996).

The influence of Bernstein (and others) has resurfaced in the writings of a number of scientists who conduct motor control research (e.g., Greene, 1972; Kelso, 1995; Kugler & Turvey, 1987; Reed, 1988; Turvey, 1977). According to Turvey (1990), Bernstein's legacy resulted in two rounds of theorizing and experimentation. The first round dealt with the degrees of freedom problem—how a system with many independent parts could be controlled without the need for an executive "decision maker." The second round extended Bernstein's thinking on coordination and the degrees of freedom problem to a search for laws and principles of self-organization. Much of this work uses physical biology as its basis. The dynamic pattern perspective (e.g., Kelso, 1995) suggests that coordinated movement evolves over time as a function of the interaction between the body parts, and between the body parts and the physical world. Also associated with this view are the ideas that perception and action are functionally inseparable—that understanding the motor system depends on understanding the physical principles of our actions and how they interact with biological functions. Advocates of these traditions show a reluctance to use cognitive-psychological styles of inquiry with hypothetically defined brain structures such as memory, motor programs, schemas, and the like. This approach has added a considerably different emphasis in the attempt to understand motor behavior.

The late 1970s and early 1980s were also characterized by a general decline in interest in *motor learning*, with a corresponding increase in issues of movement control or human performance. This was unfortunate, because the issues involved in learning have perhaps the most practical applicability to training, physical therapy, and teaching in general. But recently we have seen renewed interest in learning, sparked in part by counterintuitive findings about variations in practice scheduling (Shea & Morgan, 1979; Lee & Magill, 1983b; Magill & Hall, 1990); these developments are described in chapter 11. Also, new findings and thinking have renewed research interest in the role of knowledge of results and feedback for learning (Salmoni, Schmidt, & Walter, 1984; Schmidt, 1991), described in chapter 12.

In this brief historical sketch of motor control and motor learning, we have reviewed some of the important changes in scientific thinking and communication during this century. Earlier, a number of distinct fields related to movement existed, with separate journals and scientific meetings, little formal or informal contact, and infrequent cooperation. Today we are seeing the integration of issues from physical biology, neurophysiology, biomechanics, experimental and applied psychology, physical education, and kinesiology. These efforts are supported by new journals and interdisciplinary cooperation to form the emerging field called *motor control and learning*.

Summary

This text is fundamentally concerned with movements of human beings. Some of these movements are probably genetically defined while others are *skills*, requiring practice or experience. Even though most of the field of human behavior is concerned in one way or another with movement, in this text we focus primarily (but not exclusively) on those movements in which cognitive involvement is relatively slight, and for which the nature of the movement itself—rather than the choice of the movement from already learned alternatives—is the primary determinant of success. We will focus on movements that do not have heavy concentration on cardiovascular endurance or strength, as these activities seem to be more closely aligned with other fields of study. Finally, the focus is on many different movements that fall within the categories mentioned, such as those in musical performance, in work in industry, and in sports and games, as well as in walking.

The field of movement control and learning, viewed from a historical perspective, emerged from separate but parallel fields of motor behavior and neurophysiology. Both fields showed steady growth through the beginning of World War II, then increased in growth and sophistication after the war and through the 1960s and 1970s. The two fields, however, were largely separated until the early 1970s, when they began to share common problems and methods. Today, we have a new field of motor control and learning with its own subject matter (movements), research methods, and journals.

Notes

[1] Learning the rules (grammar) of language would probably not be of much relevance for the area of motor control, but learning to make the guttural sounds involved in German or the nasal sounds inherent in French could logically be included in the area of motor control (MacNeilage, 1970).

METHODOLOGY FOR STUDYING MOTOR PERFORMANCE

A major goal of this book is to present not only relevant principles and theories about the nature of motor performance and control, but also the research evidence that supports (or, in some cases, refutes) these principles and theories. In evaluating this evidence, it will be necessary to understand something of the methods of this research and the ways in which the motor behaviors are measured, so that the relevance of the evidence to the particular principle or theory in question can be more effectively established. Later in the book (chapter 10), we focus on the methods and paradigms used specifically in the study of motor *learning*.

Classification of Behavior

In any field of study, the objects under investigation are usually classified according to some scheme or framework in order to simplify discussion. The field of motor behavior is no exception. Classification of movements and motor tasks is important for two fundamental reasons. First, in the research literature on motor behavior and control, various terms are used to describe the tasks and movements. These terms must be understood if we are to communicate about the field. The second reason is that the laws of motor behavior seem to depend on the kinds of performances under consideration. That is, the relation between certain independent and dependent variables is often different for one kind of task or behavior as compared to another. Without classi-

fication, the laws of motor control would be far more difficult to understand.

Classifications of Motor Skills

Movement behaviors have been classified in various ways. Two important classification schemes refer to the discrete/continuous/serial dimension, which is based on the particular *movements* that are made, and the open/closed dimension, which is determined by the perceptual attributes of the task.

Discrete, Continuous, and Serial Skills

Discrete movements are those with a recognizable beginning and end. Kicking, throwing, striking a match, and shifting gears in a car are examples (figure 2.1). The end of the movement is defined by the skill in question, not arbitrarily by the time at which an observer ceased examining it as would be the case for swimming or jogging, for example. Discrete skills can be very rapid, requiring only a fraction of a second to complete (e.g., kicking, blinking an eye), but they can also require considerable time for completion, as in writing your signature. They can also be quite cognitive in nature. A common laboratory task is to press one of four buttons when one of four lights comes on, the problem being for the subject to decide which button goes with which light. Thus, the decision about which button to push is paramount, and the "how" of pushing the button is clearly secondary in importance. While many discrete skills

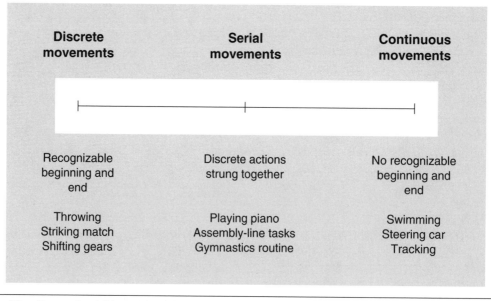

Figure 2.1. The discrete/serial/continuous classification for motor behavior.

have large verbal-cognitive components, there are certainly examples of discrete skills that are highly "motor" as well.

Continuous movements, defined as those that have no recognizable beginning and end—with behavior continuing until the movement is arbitrarily stopped—are at the opposite end of the continuum (in figure 2.1). Examples are swimming, running, and steering a car. Continuous tasks tend to have longer movement times than do discrete tasks (they might even continue all day). This, however, is not to be taken as basic to their definition.

A common class of continuous skills, both in everyday experience and in the laboratory, consists of tracking tasks. The tracking task is characterized by a pathway (track) that the individual is to follow and a device that the person attempts to keep on the track via certain limb movements. In steering a car, for example, the track is the road, and the device is the car. A very common laboratory example involves two dots on a computer monitor. One of the dots is moved by the experimenter (or by the computer), and it can move in either a predictable or an uncertain way on the screen. The second dot is moved by the subject via a hand control, and the subject's task is to keep the two dots aligned.

There are basically two kinds of tracking tasks: *pursuit* and *compensatory*. In pursuit tracking, experimenter-produced actions of the target and the subject's own movements are both displayed. A real-world example is steering a car. In compensatory tracking, the experimenter-produced variations in the track are combined with the subject's movements to produce a *single* displayed value, and the subject's goal is to maintain this value at some constant location. Practical examples of compensatory tracking are often seen in aircraft instruments, such as the glide slope indicator; here the difference between the proper altitude and the actual altitude is displayed, and when the dial is in the middle of the screen, the pilot's altitude is correct. Compensatory tracking tasks are almost always more "difficult" than pursuit tracking tasks, particularly if the behavior of the track is irregular and unpredictable.

Tracking tasks also vary in terms of the aspect of the display that the subject controls. The most simple is the *zero-order*, or positional, display. If the subject moves the handle from one position to another and then stops, the indicator on the dis-

play moves a proportional amount and also stops; that is, the handle movements control the position of the pointer. In a *first-order*, or velocity control, movement of the handle causes changes in velocity of the pointer. Moving the handle farther in one direction causes the velocity of the pointer to increase in the same direction, and stopping the handle movement off center results in a constant velocity of pointer movement. Finally, in a *second-order* task, the movements of the control produce changes in the pointer's acceleration. Keeping the handle centered produces zero acceleration, but moving the handle to a new position off center accelerates the pointer in the same direction. Each of these kinds of tracking tasks is used in research, and there are real-world examples of each in various control systems (see Poulton, 1974 for more details).

One final type of tracking task is *step tracking*. In this task, the track "jumps" from one fixed location to another, often unpredictably, and the subject's task is to move the control as quickly as possible to correct this sudden change in the track's location. Step-tracking tasks can be either pursuit or compensatory in nature.

Serial movements are neither discrete nor continuous, but rather seem to be made up of a series of individual movements tied together in time to make some "whole" (see figure 2.1). Examples are starting a car, filling and lighting a pipe, and many tasks on production lines in industry. Such tasks may require many seconds to complete, and they may appear to be continuous, although they might have discrete beginnings and ends. Serial tasks can be thought of as a number of discrete tasks strung together, with the order of the actions being important.

Open Versus Closed Skills

Environmental predictability during the performance provides another basis for classifying movement skills (Poulton, 1957). *Open skills* are those for which the environment is constantly (perhaps unpredictably) changing, so that the performer cannot effectively plan the entire movement in advance (figure 2.2). A good example is seen when a hockey player has a breakaway. While skating toward the goalie, the player may make a general decision about whether to go left or right, but the final decision will depend a lot on what the goalie does. Another example is driving on a busy freeway. Although you may have to make a general plan about what you want to do, such as pass another car, your precise plans must be left flexible enough to deal with unexpected actions of other drivers. Success in open skills seems to be determined by the extent to which the individual is successful in adapting the behavior to the changing environment. Often this adaptation must be extremely rapid, and the effective responder must have many different actions at his or her disposal.

Closed skills, for which the environment is predictable, are at the other end of the continuum shown in figure 2.2. An environment may be predictable because it is perfectly stable—for example, the environment in which one performs skills like archery, bowling, or signing one's name to a check. A predictable situation can also arise when the environment is variable but the changes are very predictable or have been learned as a result of practice; examples are juggling and industrial production-line tasks. Here, the essential feature is that the environment for the next few seconds or so is essentially predictable, so that the movement can be planned in advance. Of course, some skills have environments that are semi-predictable, and these can be classified somewhere between the ends of the open/closed continuum in figure 2.2. Farrell (1975) has provided additional distinctions that help us to classify movements on this dimension. The observation that open skills seem to require rapid adaptations to a changing environment, whereas closed skills require very consistent and stable performances

in a predictable environment, raises interesting questions about how the two classes of skills might best be learned and taught. Should the methods for teaching open and closed skills be different? Do different individuals perform better in one of these skill classes or the other? Are the laws of performance different for the two kinds of skills? Evidence suggests that the answer to these questions is yes, and we will discuss these issues in more detail in later chapters.

Basic Considerations in Measurement

A fundamental issue in any science concerns how the behaviors of the objects of study are measured, and motor behavior is no exception. We are often faced with operationalizing *skill* so that we can assign numerical values to certain performances based on the quality of the movements. Scientists must be able to measure the degree of skill exhibited by a performer in scientifically acceptable ways. Some of the criteria for good measurement systems are (a) the objectivity of the system, (b) the reliability (or stability) of the measuring system, and (c) the validity of the system.

Objectivity

The term *objectivity* is important in measurement because of the scientific demand that observations be subject to public verification. A measure-

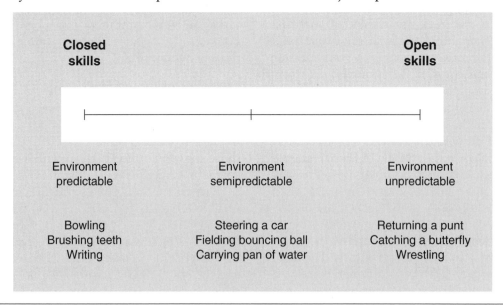

Figure 2.2.   The open/closed continuum for motor behavior.

ment system is objective to the extent that two observers evaluating the same performance arrive at the same (or very similar) measurements. Using a tape measure to determine the distance a javelin was thrown yields very similar results regardless of who reads the tape. By comparison, evaluation of performances such as diving, gymnastics, and figure skating is more subjective—although elaborate scoring rules, complete with certification tests for judges, help make it more objective. From the point of view of research in motor behavior, it is important to use performances in the laboratory for which the scoring can be as objective as possible, and this necessarily limits the usefulness of tasks such as figure skating for providing an understanding of motor behavior in general.

A second aspect of objectivity is related to the *sensitivity* of the measuring device to changes in the skill of the performer. How high did the girl jump when she set the school record in the high jump? The record books report that she jumped 5 ft 6 1/2 in. But it is more accurate to say that she jumped *at least* 5 ft 6 1/2 in. The measurement system for the high jump (and for the pole vault) indicates only whether or not the bar was knocked off during the jump, and it is possible that the successful jumper cleared the bar by six inches. In such situations, the scoring system is *insensitive* to the variations in the performer's actual level of skill.

In this example, the scale of measurement itself was acceptable in sensitivity; in fact, we often see track meet officials measuring the height of the bar very carefully, perhaps to the nearest 1/4 in. However, sometimes the scale of measurement itself is lacking in precision. Often, continuous measures are artificially categorized, as in hit/miss scoring for basketball and golf putting. For these examples the details of the movement, together with information about the performer's skill level, are lost in the oversimplified measurement method. Such methods make it more difficult to determine whether an individual has improved on the task with practice, or to identify which of two individuals is the more skilled performer—both of which may be critical questions in the study of movement.

Reliability

A second aspect of the measurement system that is important to motor behavior is *reliability*, the

extent to which the measurement is *repeatable* under similar conditions. A lack of reliability can result from random technological error, such as the stretch in measuring tapes, errors in clocks, and errors in reading instruments. These errors, while they might seem to be important sources of unreliability, probably contribute very little to unreliability as long as a quality recording apparatus is used. The most important source of unreliability manifests itself when the performer does not perform the same action twice in exactly the same way. Some of these intrasubject variations are caused by momentary changes in the internal state of the subject (degree of attention, fatigue, or boredom, for example), while others are caused by systematic changes, such as alterations in strategy and the like. Both of these factors tend to obscure the constructs that scientists are attempting to measure.

Experimenters seek to minimize these sources of variability through experimental control in the testing situation. Researchers typically use tape-recorded instructions to subjects to eliminate variability in what and how information is presented; they use testing rooms that are either silenced or sound-deadened; subjects are tested one at a time to eliminate variability due to another person's presence in the room; and the entire experimental session is often quite formal and impersonal. This is the primary reason motor behaviorists tend not to measure skills in everyday settings—at a ball game or on an industrial production line, for example. In these situations, the environment is not well controlled; there are many sources of variation from other players or workers, from changes in the score of the game, from the level of proficiency of opponents, from day-to-day changes in the weather, and so on. Primarily for reasons of experimental control, motor behavior tends to be most profitably studied in the laboratory, away from these sources of variability. To be sure, this makes the situation less natural and more artificial, and the measures we take are not quite as directly related to practical situations; but the alternative of studying skills during a game seems particularly hopeless.

The procedures that have been mentioned can reduce variability in experimental settings. But even when the task is well learned and simple, when the experimental situation is well controlled, and when the subject is trying to do well, there is a great deal of variability because biological systems are inherently unstable. Experimentally, the best method for countering this type of variability is to record many observations of the "same" behavior on the same subject, taking the average of a large number of measurements under essentially identical conditions. With this procedure the variations in the subject's performance tend to "average out," raising the reliability of the measurement system, so that the mean of a large number of observations more closely represents the construct being measured.

Validity

Another aspect of the measurement process is *validity*, the extent to which the test measures what the researcher intends it to measure. An important aspect of validity (called *construct validity*) is the extent to which the measures taken actually reflect the underlying construct of interest. We would be reasonably comfortable with a 10 min typing test to operationalize typing skill, but we would perhaps be less comfortable with a measure of finger-tapping speed to assess typing skill. There are, on the other hand, situations in which validity does not seem to present much of a problem. One of these involves what are often called *face valid* tests, which are so obviously measures of the concept of interest that they usually are not questioned. For example, if we wish to determine which member of a group of individuals has most skill in javelin throwing (a construct), we might have them all throw the javelin as a standardized test.

Another class of measurement situations in which the importance of validity is minimal is in experiments on motor learning (Schmidt, 1989). In these situations, an arbitrary task is created that represents a motor performance novel to the subject, and the experimenter studies how the subject attempts to learn it or what variables influence that learning. The particular constructs being measured (e.g., balance, timing, movement speed) frequently are not important to the experimenter, because the primary focus is on the variables that affect performance and learning generally.

Measuring Motor Behavior

In the field of motor behavior and control, measurement can be approached in three different ways. At the most general level, we can describe how well a movement achieved some environmental goal that was inherent in the task (e.g., whether or not a target was struck). Here the emphasis is on the outcome of movement. At a more specific level, we may be concerned with quantifying the actual movements the person made. In this case, the focus of analysis is describing the movement itself. The third level of analysis, which will be dealt with only occasionally in this book, entails the study of the central nervous system (including the brain) prior to and during the production of movement. At this level, researchers are interested in the neural activities involved in planning and executing movements.

Describing the Outcome of Movements

The first aspect of measurement in motor behavior is the quantification of the extent to which a given movement achieved the goal that was intended or instructed. For example, did the movement result in striking the target, or was the movement made at the right time? Such measures generally concern the movement in relation to some object or to another performer in the environment, although some movements (e.g., modern dance, diving) may not be so closely associated with other environmental elements. The achievement of such environmental goals can be assessed in three fundamental ways—through measures of (a) error, (b) speed, and (c) movement magnitude.

Measures of Error for a Single Subject

Many performances require the subject to do something with minimum error; thus the performance measures actually represent some form of accuracy score. The goal of accuracy can be imposed in many ways; for example, subjects can be asked to move with a certain amount of force, hit a certain spatial target, move at a certain speed, or perform some act at a particular time (e.g., hitting a baseball). A correct force, distance, speed, or time can be defined that is the subject's target; then deviations of the subject's performances with respect to this target are measured. At the most crude level, the performances can be scored as hit/miss, or right/wrong, as in shooting a basketball or judging which of two lifted weights is heavier. The accuracy score can be refined by dividing the possible outcomes into hit/almost hit/miss, or by dividing a target for dart throwing into 10 or more zones, for example. But motor performance is complex, and more sophistication in the measurement of accuracy is required.

In the discussion that follows, assume that a single performer is striving for accuracy in arriving at some target (e.g., a force, a speed, a location in space) and that the movement outcomes can be placed along some measurable dimension (e.g., kilograms, centimeters per second, centimeters) as in figure 2.3. Let the correct value along this dimension—the target—have the value T. The values that the performer actually achieves are abbreviated by x_i, where i is a subscript notating a particular trial (i.e., the ith trial). For example, x_{23} is the score on the 23rd trial. In the simple formulas that describe these fundamental statistical accuracy scores, the symbol Σ means "the sum of." For example, Σx_i means to add up all of the values x_i, where i ranges progressively from 1 through n, where n = 5 in the following example:

$$\Sigma\, x_i = x_1 + x_2 + x_3 + x_4 + x_5$$

In the following explanation, assume that the target (T) is 100 units and that the individual does not always achieve this target score. In figure 2.3 there are five scores: 93, 103, 99, 105, and 96 units for trials 1 through 5, respectively.

It is obvious that no single trial will be very effective in describing the subject's behavior, as the scores possess a great deal of variability. One solution, therefore, is to combine these scores to achieve a more representative measure of the subject's capability. In the study of motor behavior, researchers have typically focused on five methods for combining scores. Each has a slightly different meaning in terms of the performer's capability. These methods are described in the next sections as (a) constant error, (b) variable error, (c) total variability, (d) absolute error, and (e) absolute constant error.

Constant Error (CE)—Computation. The first statistic to be considered as a measure of the subject's accuracy is the *constant error (CE)*, which measures the average error in responding. Its formula is

$$\text{Constant Error} = \Sigma\, (x_i - T)\, /\, n \qquad (2.1)$$

where x_i is the score on trial i, T is the target, and n is the number of trials the subject performed. It is very easy to compute this measure from table 2.1, which can serve as a work table for computing all of the statistics presented in this section on error measures. The trial numbers are listed in column A; the scores obtained (x_i) are given in column B. All other values in the table are computed from these initial values.

To compute the CE, the numerator calls for finding the difference between each of the scores on the test (x_i) and the target (100); these remainders are shown in column C, headed $(x_i - T)$. It is important to notice that for CE, the *sign* (+ or –) of the difference is retained in this column. Next, the summation sign calls for adding values for each of the trials (in this case for each of the five trials), and this sum is presented at the bottom of column C (–4.0). Then the formula calls for dividing by n, the number of movements, in order to get the average CE over trials. The final CE score is –4.0/5, or –0.80.

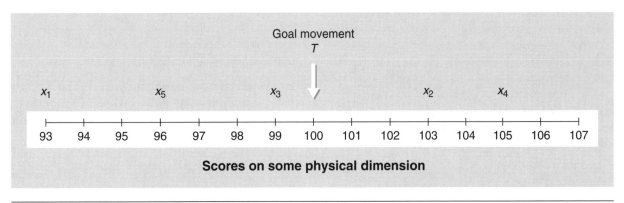

Figure 2.3. An arbitrary measurement scale, showing locations of a target (T) and of five hypothetical movement attempts $(x_1, \dots, x_5)$.

Table 2.1   Work Table for Computing Various Components of Response Error

A Trial	B x_i	C $(x_i - T)$	D $(x_i - M)$	E $(x_i - M)^2$	F $(x_i - T)^2$	G $|x_i - T|$
1	93	–7	–6.2	38.44	49	7
2	103	+3	+3.8	14.44	9	3
3	99	–1	–0.2	0.04	1	1
4	105	+5	+5.8	33.64	25	5
5	96	–4	–3.2	10.24	16	4
Sum	496	–4.0	—	96.80	100	20
Mean	99.2	–0.80	—	19.36	20	4
Square root	—	—	—	4.40	4.47	—

Interpretation of Constant Error.   The CE score of –0.80 indicates that on the average, the subject fell slightly short of the target (by .80 units). Notice that the CE is given in units that represent the amount of *deviation,* sometimes called *bias.* One could also ask for the subject's scores *on the average* by consulting the mean for column B. Thus, the average score was 496/5 = 99.2 units, meaning that the subject fell short of the target by 99.2 – 100 units, which is also –0.80 units. The CE represents the average magnitude of the movement and measures the direction of the errors on the average.

While a measure of average error might, at first, seem satisfying to students as a measure of accuracy, notice that the value computed for the subject (–0.80) was far smaller than the error for any of the single movements that contributed to the average. The movements were scattered a great deal, with the center of movements being roughly the target that was the goal. What the CE does not consider is this amount of scatter, variability, or inconsistency in performance of the movements. Consider a second hypothetical subject with scores of 99, 99, 99, 99, and 100. These scores represent a very small scatter but would result in precisely the same CE score as for the subject we have just been considering. For this reason, the variable error is used to describe this aspect of the subject's inconsistency.

Variable Error (VE)—Computation.   The variable error (VE) measures the *inconsistency* in movement outcome. It is the variability of the subject about the mean movement and is calculated by the formula

$$\text{Variable Error} = \sqrt{\Sigma\,(x_i - M)^2 \,/\, n} \quad (2.2)$$

where x_i and n are defined as in the previous example. The M is the subject's average movement, measured in the same units as the scores for the task, so that for this example the M has the value of 99.2 units. To compute the VE for this subject, use table 2.1 once again. Notice that the formula indicates first to compute the difference between the performance score and the subject's own mean (M), so the first step is to compute the subject's M. Computed in the previous section, the M for these movements was 99.2 units. Now, the values in column D of table 2.1 represent the differences between the scores on the trials and 99.2. For example, 93.0 – 99.2 equals –6.2, the first entry in column D. The next instruction from the formula is to square each of these values, and these squared values are given in column E. Next, obey the summation sign and add the squared values, the sum of which (96.80) is shown at the bottom of column E. Then divide by the number of cases to get 19.36 and take the square root to arrive at the final answer of 4.40 units.

Interpretation of Variable Error.   The VE reflects the variability or inconsistency in movements, as can be seen from the "ingredients" in the formula. The important feature is the difference between the subject's score on each trial and his or her own average score. Thus, if one subject always moves very consistently, the VE will tend to be small. If the subject always receives the same score, even though it is not the correct one (such as 99), then the VE will be zero. This is so because the subject's average score will be 99, and the difference between each of the scores and the average will always be zero as well.

Thus VE does not depend on whether or not the subject was close to the target, since it is the measure of spread about the subject's own average. To illustrate, the VE for the set of scores 43, 53, 49, 55, and 46 achieved while aiming at a target of 100 units will be precisely the same (4.40) as that calculated in the previous example. (These five new values were achieved by subtracting 50 from each of the raw scores in table 2.1).

Using Constant Error and Variable Error.   An additional aspect of error scores is important from the point of view not only of research but also of practical application. Compare two archers: Archer A has a large VE and small CE, whereas Archer B has a small VE and large CE. This situation was described years ago by Chapanis (1951) and is illustrated in figure 2.4. (Actually, the measurement of error scores in two dimensions is more complicated than this [Hancock, Butler, & Fischman, 1995]. For our purposes, however, it is clear that the average performance of Archer A is near the origin [0,0] but inconsistent, whereas Archer B is clearly biased away from the origin, but quite consistently so.)

From the data presented in figure 2.4, who should be regarded as the more skilled archer? The answer is Archer B, the person with a small VE who is highly consistent. The reason is that consistency is far more important than bias for

this skill. If Archer B's sights had not been aligned properly, then we might expect the type of performance seen in figure 2.4. Once Archer B's sights were properly aligned, we would expect performance to be accurate *and* consistent. However, there is no simple change in the sights that will make Archer A accurate and consistent.

The study of motor learning will show that the measure of error that is most sensitive to the effects of practice is consistency (VE); bias (CE) often changes quickly in the first several trials and remains near zero thereafter, even after years of practice. There are some situations, however, in which CE is preferred to VE; but these are specialized applications. Thus, these two measures of error, CE and VE, seem to represent two distinct aspects of performance. But sometimes it is more desirable to have a measure of "overall error" that combines both these performance indicators, rather than using these separate measures of accuracy and variability.

Total Variability (E)—Computation.   The total variability around a target (or error) for a set of movements (labeled E by Henry, 1975, and sometimes called *root-mean-square error*) can be thought of as the measure of "overall error" in moving (see also Chapanis, 1951). E can be defined as the square root of the sum of VE² and CE², or when expressed as E²:

$$E^2 = VE^2 + CE^2 \qquad (2.3)$$

E can also be computed directly from the formula:

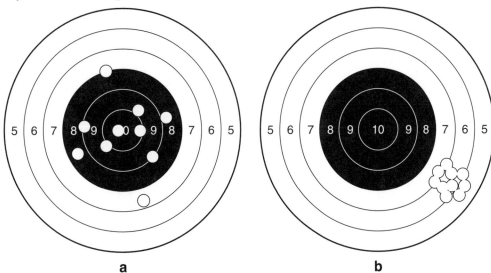

| | **a** | | **b** |

Figure 2.4.   Distribution of archery shots. Archer A has a small CE and large VE. Archer B has a large CE bias, but a small VE. Reprinted from Chapanis, 1951.

$$\text{Total Variability} = \sqrt{\Sigma\,(x_i - T)^2 / n} \qquad (2.4)$$

where x_i, T, and n are defined as before. To apply the formula, we can use table 2.1 again. Notice that the major "ingredient" is the difference between the score x_i and the target, and this difference (with the sign included) is given in table 2.1, column C—the same values used to compute CE. Next, square each of these values; these squared values are given in column F. The summation sign then says to add the squared values, and the sum (equal to 100) is given at the bottom of column F. Next, divide by n (5), which results in a value of 20; then find the square root, so that the final value for E is $\sqrt{20}$, or 4.47.

Interpretation of Total Variability. The total variability, E, is the total amount of "spread" of the movements about the target, and so it represents a kind of overall measure of how successful the subject was in achieving the target. The key to understanding this formula is the expression in the numerator $(x_i - T)^2$. E is based on the sum of a group of squared differences, where each difference is the amount by which the subject missed the target. This is in contrast to the VE, where the numerator $(x_i - M)^2$ represented the deviations from the *subject's own average*, not necessarily the target. In many cases, because CE tends to be very close to the aimed-for target, E and VE come to represent very similar aspects of the subject's movements. But because E represents accuracy with respect to the target, a number of writers recommend E (e.g., Henry, 1975) as the best combination measure of overall error.

Absolute Error (AE)—Computation. A statistic closely related to the total variability (E) is absolute error (AE), which can also be thought of as a measure of overall accuracy in performance. It is the average *absolute deviation* (without regard to direction) between the subject's movements and the target, and its formula is:

$$\text{Absolute Error} = \Sigma\,|x_i - T| / n \qquad (2.5)$$

where x_i, T, and n are defined as before. The vertical bars (| |) are the symbol for "absolute value of" and mean to take away the sign of the difference inside *before* summing.

To compute AE, refer again to table 2.1. The first step is to compute the values for the numerator terms, and this is done in column G, headed $|x_i - T|$. Notice that each of the values in this column is the score for the target (in this case,

100), subtracted from the score received by the subject on that trial, with the sign removed (i.e., with the absolute value taken). The summation sign Σ is an instruction to add up these values from 1 to n (recall that n is 5 in this example), and the sum is given at the bottom of column G as 20. The next step is to divide by the number of trials included ($n = 5$), and so the final answer is 4.0.

Interpretation of Absolute Error. In providing an interpretation of the AE, it will be helpful to consider the ways in which it is similar to E. First, notice that the numerator is essentially the same for the two statistics, each numerator having a difference between the obtained score (x_i) and the target as the major "ingredient." Second, the values for E and AE (4.47 and 4.0, respectively) are very similar; the two values will be equal only in special circumstances but will be very close in most situations. Third, both of the formulas involve methods for eliminating the sign of the difference between the score and the target; for the AE, the method is to take the absolute value, while for E, the method is to square the values in the numerator.

Which Is Better, Absolute Error or Total Variability? The AE is a very "logical" measure to use to describe the subject's overall accuracy in a task because it is sensitive to the extent to which the subject was "off target." It was used far more commonly than E in the early research, and it was used for many different applications. A controversy, however, has been raised about the use of AE (Schutz & Roy, 1973). AE can be shown to be a complex combination of CE (accuracy or bias) and VE (variability), and it is difficult to be certain of the relative contribution of each. Because of the relation among E, CE, and VE (namely, $E^2 = VE^2 + CE^2$), E can be shown to be an exact combination of the variability and bias and thus is preferred to AE. The tendency today, when a researcher wishes to present a combined measure of accuracy and variability, is to prefer E, for two reasons: first, E measures essentially the same component of movement as AE, and second, E is more easily interpreted since it represents a simple combination of CE and VE. However, we will use AE a great deal in this text, because much of the earlier research was done using only this measure.

Absolute Constant Error ($|CE|$). One final measure of accuracy is merely a transformation of constant error, CE:

Absolute Constant Error = |CE|

Thus, for a single subject, the absolute constant error (|CE|) is just the absolute value of the CE, which is simply .80 in the present example. Be careful to note, however, that |CE| is not calculated in the same way as AE.

Interpretation of Absolute Constant Error. The situation sometimes arises (e.g., Newell, 1976a) in which approximately half the subjects in a group have positive CE scores while the other half have negative CE scores. However, if one characterizes the average bias for this *group* of subjects, the positive and negative signs will tend to "cancel" each other out. This could give rise to the misleading conclusion that the average bias for the group was nearly zero when in fact every subject in the group showed a bias of considerable size. In this case, it is useful to also compute |CE|, which tells the researcher the amount of bias for each subject without regard to its direction and will not be subject to this "canceling" effect of the positive and negative CEs. In recent years, in cases in which group data have been the focus of a researcher's experiment, there has been a trend to report |CE| (as the measure of accuracy) along with VE (as the variability score) (see Schutz, 1977, for more statistical details).

Relationships Among the Error Scores. One way to evaluate the relative contributions of the various measures of error is to consider the following cases. At one extreme, when CE is very large (the extreme is the situation in which all the person's movements lie on one side of the target), then the absolute error (AE), the total variability (E), and the constant error (CE) all tend to measure the same component of responding—the bias or directional deviations of the errors. In the following case, the target is again 100, but Subject 1 produces five movements--80, 90, 85, 82, and 87, all considerably short of the target. Table 2.2 gives the measures of error for this subject. Notice that the statistics E, CE, AE, and |CE| are all around 15, but that the VE is very much lower at 3.54. This suggests that when the CE is large in either direction, the measures of overall error tend to represent the bias, and VE alone measures the variability.

Now consider Subject 2 in table 2.2. This subject has the same spread of outcomes as Subject 1, but with much less bias. We obtained these scores

by adding 15 to each of Subject 1's scores to get Subject 2's scores: 95, 105, 100, 97, 102. Table 2.2 gives the error measures of this set of scores. Now notice that the measures of overall error tend to be very close to the VE, all around 3. The CE, however, is now nearly zero. Here the overall error measures represent the variability of the movements (VE), exactly the opposite of the situation with Subject 1.

Therefore, when CE is large in either direction, the measures of overall error (E and AE) tend to represent the amount of bias in the measures. When CE is small, E and AE tend to represent the amount of variability (VE) in the scores. When CE is intermediate in value (with some bias, but with scores falling on both sides of the target), the measures of overall error represent both the bias and the variability. This should make clear why simply examining overall error statistics does not provide a very complete picture of performance.

Other Measures of Accuracy. There are many tasks in the motor behavior literature that cannot be scored so simply. A task for which accuracy is important is the *tracking task;* in this case, performance is ongoing, thus preventing the computation of a discrete performance error. A common tracking task is the *pursuit rotor,* shown in figure 2.5a. There are many varieties, but all have a target (usually a small circle) that is embedded in the surface of a turntable-like structure that rotates at various speeds. The subject holds a stylus in the preferred hand and attempts to keep its tip in contact with the target as the turntable rotates. A trial might last from 10 s to 1 min, and performance is scored in terms of the amount of time in the trial that the subject maintained contact with the target. The performance measure is usually called *time on target (TOT)* and can range from zero (if the subject never touched the target) to the

Table 2.2 Error Measures for Two Hypothetical Subjects on an Accuracy Task

	E	CE	VE	AE	|CE|
Subject 1	15.61	−15.2	3.54	15.2	15.2
Subject 2	3.55	−0.2	3.54	3.0	0.2

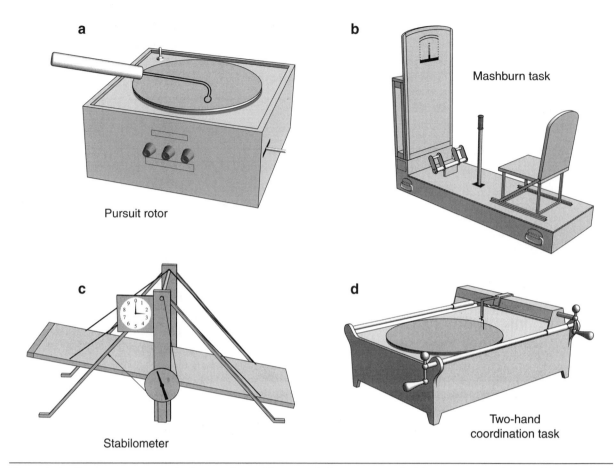

a

Pursuit rotor

b

Mashburn task

c

Stabilometer

d

Two-hand
coordination task

Figure 2.5.   Four movement tasks frequently used in motor behavior research: (a) pursuit rotor, (b) Mashburn task, (c) stabilometer, and (d) two-hand coordination task.

duration of a trial (if the subject was always in contact with the target). Time on target is a complex combination of bias (if the subject is consistently behind the target, for example) and variability (if the subject is alternately ahead of and behind the target).

Other common variations of tracking tasks are shown in figure 2.5. The *complex-coordination task* (or *Mashburn task*) is shown in figure 2.5b. It was designed to simulate certain features of airplane controls. The control panel contains three double rows of lights. One row of each pair is controlled by the movements of the subject (left-right and forward-backward movements of the stick, and right-left movements of the pedals), while the other row of each pair is controlled by the experimenter. The subject attempts to match the experimenter-determined lights with appropriate movements of the controls. The task is scored in terms of the number of correct matches that can be achieved in a trial of fixed duration.

The *stabilometer* is shown in figure 2.5c. The standing subject attempts to keep an unstable

platform level; the scores denote either time in balance or the number of times the platform edge touches the floor (indicating extreme loss of balance) during a trial of perhaps 30 s. The number of times a stylus touches the sides of a maze is another example of this kind of measure. Figure 2.5d shows the *two-hand coordination task*, in which the subject attempts to follow a target by moving a pointer with two crank handles. One handle controls the right-left movement, and the other controls the forward-backward movement, much as in the "Etch-a-Sketch" toy. The score is again TOT, or the amount of time in a trial that the subject was over the target. All these measures, including TOT, are measures of *overall* error, and they tend to confound the bias with variability in performance.

In each of the foregoing examples, the experimenter does not keep a record of the subject's actual behavior, although critical events are recorded. There are other tracking tasks for which a continuous record of the movements of the subject and the target is kept. From these data a measure of overall accuracy, the root-mean-square

(RMS) error, can be computed. (Notice that RMS error is analogous to E, described earlier. Both are root-mean-square deviations of the behavior from some target, computed on successive "trials.")

Essentially, the RMS error is based on taking small "slices" of time and measuring the deviation of the subject's line from the target at each of these times, as shown in figure 2.6. This can be done every second (or more frequently) over the entire course of a 20-s trial, providing 20 measures of error. To compute the RMS error, square each of these deviations from the track, add up the squared deviations (20 of them), divide by the number of measures (20), and then take the square root, giving a measure of the amount of deviation over the course of the trial. Root-mean-square error in each of these cases represents essentially (but not exactly) the area between the subject's movements and the target, as shown by the shaded portions of figure 2.6. As with TOT, the RMS error is a measure of overall error and is sensitive to both the bias and the variability in performing.

Measurement of Time and Speed

The second fundamental way of assessing skills is by measurements of speed. Basic to this idea is the assumption that the performer who can accomplish more in a given amount of time, or who can produce a given amount of behavior in less time, is the more skillful. These two kinds of measures are essentially the same, since a time measure (time/unit) can easily be converted to a speed measure by taking the reciprocal; that is, $1/$(time/unit) = units/time, which is a measure of speed. Both speed and time measures have been used a great deal in motor behavior research. Reaction time and movement time are common examples, described next.

Reaction Time. Reaction time (RT) is a measure of the time from the arrival of a suddenly presented and unanticipated signal to the *beginning* of the response to it. In the RT paradigm shown in figure 2.7, the subject is given a warning signal, and after a randomly determined foreperiod (perhaps ranging from 1 to 5 s), the stimulus is presented. Thus the subject is prevented from anticipating when (temporal anticipation) the stimulus will arrive. Sometimes "catch trials," in which the stimulus is not presented at all, are used to prevent anticipation. Also, subjects can be prevented from anticipating which movement to make (i.e., spatial or event anticipation) through the use of two or more choices, so that the proper response is signaled by the stimulus (e.g., red light means move left, blue light means move right); this is termed the *choice-RT* method. Reaction-time measures are common in many sport settings; an example is the interval between the starter's gun and the first movement in a swimming race. Reaction-time measures are also studied extensively in the laboratory as measures of information-processing speed.

One variation of the RT method is to partition RT into its "central" and "peripheral" components (Weiss, 1965). Figure 2.7 shows a hypothetical electromyographic (EMG) trace taken from a muscle involved in the movement to be made (EMG indicates the electrical activity in a muscle). During a substantial part of the RT, the EMG is

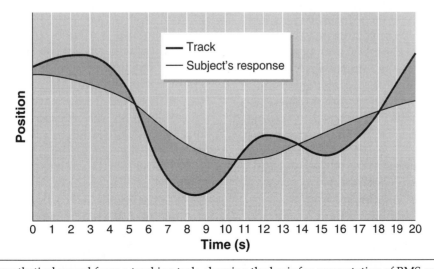

Figure 2.6. Hypothetical record from a tracking task, showing the basis for computation of RMS error.

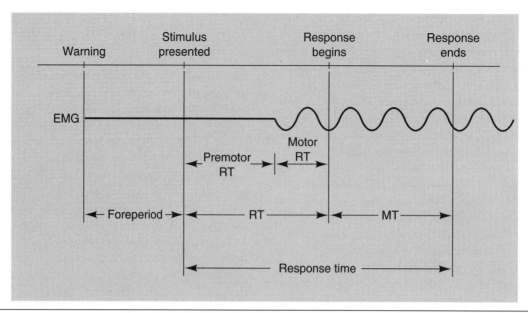

Figure 2.7. Critical events involved in the RT paradigm. (The upper trace is a hypothetical EMG record taken from the relevant muscle.)

silent, indicating that the command to move the finger has not yet reached the finger musculature. Then late in the RT, the muscle is activated, but no movement occurs for 40 to 80 ms. The interval from the signal to the first change in EMG is termed *premotor RT* and is thought to represent central processes involved in making the response (e.g., perception, decisions). The interval from the first change in EMG to finger movement is termed *motor RT* and represents processes associated with the musculature itself. Such methods are useful in gaining information about the location of the effect of some independent variable on RT (e.g., Fischman, 1984).

Reaction-time measures are very common in research on skills, for two basic reasons. First, RT measures are components of real-life tasks (e.g., sprint starts). A more important reason (which we will amplify in chapters 3 and 4) is that RT presumably measures the time taken for mental events, such as stimulus processing, decision making, and movement programming. These two motivations for using RT measures differ considerably. In the first case, RT is a measure studied for its own sake; in the second case, RT allows the researcher to understand the kinds of mental processes that lead to movement (e.g., Posner, 1978). Regardless of the motivation, the measurement of RT is the same.

Movement Time. Movement time (MT) is usually defined as the interval from the initiation of

the response (the end of RT) to the completion of the movement (figure 2.7). Clearly, MT can be just about any value, ranging from a few milliseconds for a very quick movement to several weeks if the movement is jogging from Los Angeles to Chicago. Some sport skills have minimal MT as a goal (e.g., time to cover 100 m, or time for a quarterback to "set up" for a pass), and MT is used a great deal in skills research as a result of its overall external validity in these practical settings. Sometimes researchers use RT and MT tasks together in the same response, as in requiring the subject to lift a finger from a key and move to a button as quickly as possible after a stimulus.

The sum of RT and MT is termed *response time* (figure 2.7). Research has consistently shown that very different processes or abilities are required in reacting quickly as opposed to moving quickly once the reaction is over, and this has justified separating response time into RT and MT. What is frequently called "brake reaction time" in driver education tests is really response time, because it consists of the time used to initiate the foot movement from the accelerator pedal plus the time required to move the foot to the brake pedal.

Often when measures of speed are used, the degree of accuracy in the task is not taken into account. A well-known phenomenon in motor behavior is the *speed-accuracy trade-off*, meaning simply that when performers attempt to do something more quickly, they typically do it less accurately. In most measures of speed, therefore, accuracy requirements are kept to a minimum so that speeding up the movement (which is the major goal for the subject) does not seriously affect accuracy. In some situations, though, measures of speed are confounded with measures of accuracy, and the speed with which the subject performs is dependent on the amount of error he or she is willing to make or the amount of error the experimenter will tolerate. Such trade-offs are particularly troublesome for experimenters, because it is not always clear to subjects how much error will be tolerated, and experimenters are unsure about how to interpret an independent variable that produces increases in speed but decreases in accuracy. Methods based on the theory of signal detection (e.g., Swets, 1964) have been developed to solve this problem, but they are not used very often in motor behavior research, and they will not be described here (see Wickens, 1992, for more details on signal detection analyses). One solution to this problem is to hold accuracy constant by various experimental techniques so that a single dependent variable of speed can be assessed. Or speed can be held constant, via instructions, so that accuracy can be assessed (e.g., Quinn et al., 1980; Schmidt et al., 1979).

Measures of Movement Magnitude

A third way of measuring skills is by the *magnitude* of behavior that the performer produces, such as the distance that a discus was thrown or the amount of weight that was lifted. These measures have particularly important applications to sport settings, as many sports use such measures as the primary determinants of success in the activity. Surprisingly, these measures are not used much in motor behavior research, as the scientists apparently believe that skills are more easily assessed by measures of accuracy or speed. One exception, though, is the Bachman (1961) ladder-climb task (figure 2.8) using a specially constructed ladder. At the beginning of, say, a 30-s trial, the subject begins to climb the ladder without skipping rungs until balance is lost and the subject topples over. The subject quickly returns to the starting position and begins climbing again, and so on until the trial has been completed. The score is the number of rungs accumulated in a given trial. A variant of the task is to climb as high as possible in a single attempt.

Figure 2.8. The Bachman ladder-climb task.

While it might seem that the tasks whose goals are maximum movement magnitude are considerably different from those requiring speed or accuracy, their fundamental determinants may not be all that different. At first glance, producing maximum movement magnitude would seem simply to be a matter of generating more force. But these skills certainly require precise timing of the forceful contractions and accurate coordination among the various participating limbs. Therefore these precise muscular activities might be essentially the same as those required in tasks that seem to necessitate only accuracy. Of course, inconsistency (in terms of VE) in these processes will degrade performance, and such inconsistency is probably related to the VEs that are seen in the outcomes of simpler tasks.

Measurement of Secondary Tasks

There are instances in both practical and research settings in which none of these basic methods of measurement will be sensitive to differences in skill among individuals or to differences in skill caused by some independent variable. Generally these situations involve tasks for which differences in performance are not evident because they are well learned (driving a car down an open road), or involve tasks that do not "tax" the motor system very much because they are so simple (drinking a glass of water without spilling). How are skills assessed in such situations?

One method is to use some measure of *critical incidents*. In the driving example, accident rate might be used as a measure of skill; with pilots, "near misses" (midair near-collisions) might be used. But these techniques are difficult to utilize in the laboratory because (fortunately) such critical events occur so infrequently. A more useful technique is to employ some sort of secondary task, performed simultaneously with the primary task, as a measure of the skill in the *primary* task. For example, Brown (1962) used a verbal task in which the individual was presented with eight-digit numbers at 4-s intervals. Each number contained seven of the same digits as the previous one, and the subject's task was to detect the digit that was different and to provide a response. Errors were counted as omitted responses, incorrect responses, and late responses.

Figure 2.9 shows the scores obtained when only the verbal task was performed, as well as the scores obtained when this task was performed by subjects who were driving under various conditions. The mean percentage of correct responses when the verbal task was performed alone was 90.6%. When the task was performed during driving in quiet residential areas, the mean percentage dropped to 83.8%. And when the task was performed in heavy traffic conditions, the percentage again dropped, to 79.5%. Yet it was very difficult to see any differences in vehicle control in light and heavy traffic, largely because driving is so well learned by most people. This secondary task provided evidence about the difficulty of the driving conditions when the driving task itself would not have provided such a measure. Other experimenters have used RT tasks (e.g., Kerr, 1975) and measures of finger-tapping regularity (e.g., Michon, 1966). In these cases, the implication is that these tasks require some of the subject's *limited capacity* to process information; presenting the secondary task simultaneously with the primary task requires the use of some of this capacity, and lowers the performance on the secondary task in relation to the amount of capacity demanded by the primary task. (See chapter 4 for more on this assumption and general method.)

Rather than a task, secondary *physiological* measures of effort can be used during the performance of a main task. One technique is to measure pupil diameter by photographic techniques. Pupil dilation is associated with circumstances in which effort, arousal, or information processing is demanded (e.g., Beatty & Wagoner, 1978; Kahneman, 1973). Similarly, measures of heart rate, heart rate variability, oxygen consumption (as a measure of overall effort), or even EMG from the muscles of the forehead (to indicate the level of concentration) can be used, depending on the particular situation. Some promising neurophysiological techniques have also emerged, such as the recording of *event-related potentials* from the scalp. One such potential has been called *P300*, as it occurs as a positive voltage about 300 msec after the presentation of a stimulus (Duncan-Johnson & Donchin, 1982). The latency of the P300 and the magnitude of its amplitude appear to be highly correlated with RT, thus providing an unobtrusive way to measure processing activities. In all these cases, these secondary measures become the focus of the investigator, especially when the main task does not provide sensitive measures of the subject's performance.

A variation of this technique is to use a secondary task as a distractor in order to increase the overall "load" on the performer. Normally, fatigue may not have any obvious effect on the well-learned task of driving. However, if the driver is required to perform a simultaneous mental arithmetic task, then large differences between fatigued and rested driving may be seen. The major interest is in the performance of the main task, and the secondary task has increased the

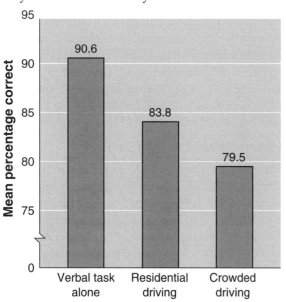

Figure 2.9. Mean number of correct digit detections alone and during driving in various experimental conditions.
Adapted from Brown, 1962.

sensitivity of the measurement system for the main task. However, care must be taken with these techniques, as Brown (1962) has shown. When truck drivers were fatigued, their performance on the secondary digit-detection task actually increased, suggesting that they were devoting less capacity to the driving task and over-compensating by devoting more capacity to the secondary task. While these techniques can be somewhat tricky to use, they have served well in a number of situations—mainly for continuous, highly learned tasks.

Describing Characteristics of Movements

Countless methods could be employed to describe movements, depending on the characteristics of the movement that were of interest to the observer. At the most fundamental level, one can use verbal descriptors to characterize movement. For example, movements have been described in dance notation created by Laban (1956) and in terms of units of work behavior called "Therbligs" in industrial time-and-motion studies. Another way is to illustrate movement with photographs, as was done over a century ago by Muybridge (1887, 1989) using series of still photos (see the boxed text below), or with videotaped or computer-generated graphics. Such methods are of some use in describing or illustrating the basic forms of movement, but have limited value in detailed assessments of performance. In this section we focus on *kinematics,* a branch of mechanics in physics that involves the description of "pure" motion without regard for the forces and masses that produced the motion. The devices that can be used to collect this information are also widely varied, and we will describe some of the most common of these.

Movement Kinematics

As applied to movement behavior, kinematic measures are those that describe the movement of the limbs, the entire body, or both. The locations of various parts of the body during the movement, the angles of the various joints, and the time relations between the movement in one joint and the movement in another are examples of the many ways movements can be recorded.

Location. Perhaps the most common of the kinematic methods entails recording the locations of the limbs during a movement. Early in the history of motor behavior and biomechanics, researchers used cinematography to record movements. Often the subject being filmed wore tape markers over certain landmarks (e.g., the wrist or

Eadweard Muybridge's Movement Photographs

Probably the very first photographic analysis of human and animal locomotion was published by Eadweard Muybridge in 1887. Muybridge's methods involved an automated sequence of timed still photographs, linked together by electronic signals such that motion was studied by examining the changes from one sequence to the next. He used 36 separate shutters, arranged so that three different angles could be photographed simultaneously, positioned at the side, front, and rear of the subject. At each angle a series of 12 shutters was electronically arranged to open in a timed sequence after a manual signal had been sent to the first shutter. The length of the time intervals was determined by Muybridge on the basis of the speed at which the subject performed the activity (e.g., picking up an object vs. running at full speed).

In all, Muybridge published 781 plates (each plate being a series of 36 photographs of the subject). The subjects were both humans and animals. Humans of all ages, normal and disabled, performed actions such as walking, running, jumping, skipping, lifting objects, and hammering. Many of the humans were photographed in the nude, providing rather explicit and unabashed details of body actions. Animals from a wide range of species were photographed in various natural and contrived settings. Muybridge's series of still sequence photographs remains as a magnificent legacy in the history of human and animal motion analysis.

ankle) so that the locations of these body parts could be studied frame by frame. Figure 2.10 shows an example in which the locations of the ball of the foot, the ankle, the knee, the hip, the wrist, the elbow, and the shoulder are plotted during a jumping motion from a squatting position (Plagenhoef, 1971). These positions on successive frames were separated by nearly fixed periods of time, so a graph of the position of the landmark against time could be generated from the data.

An example of this type of graph is seen in figure 2.11, taken from Wadman et al. (1979). For now, consider only trace A, which represents position. This trace, read from left to right, represents an arm movement of about 17 cm. The movement began where the trace leaves the horizontal axis. The largest amplitude (about 20 cm) was achieved about 125 msec after the movement started, and then the limb stabilized its position at the final location.

But examining the location of a limb in space may mask some of the more subtle factors that determine its control, and for this reason motor

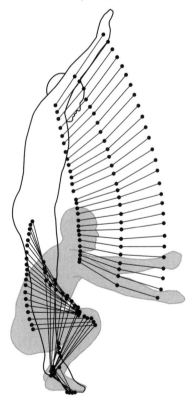

Figure 2.10.   A person jumping upward from a squat, showing one form of film analysis in which the positions of various landmarks are plotted as a function of time. Reprinted from Plagenhoef, 1971.

behavior researchers often examine variables that can be derived from location information—velocity and acceleration.

Velocity.   Trace B in figure 2.11 is a record of velocity of the movement at each moment in time, placed on the same time scale as the positional trace for easy comparison. The velocity trace was determined by computer, which read in the position information from the potentiometer and then calculated the slope or inclination of the line at each moment. The slopes (called derivatives) of the positions at each moment in time yield the velocities at corresponding moments, representing *the rate of change in position*. Then this information is output onto the same record as the position information. Such a trace is useful here in showing that the maximum velocity (V_m) was about 2.7 m/s and that the maximum velocity occurred at about 75 ms through the movement. Also shown are a gradual increase in velocity until the peak velocity (the midpoint of the movement) is reached and then a decline toward the end. Such a trace gives a more complete description of the movement than does positional information alone.

Acceleration.   Trace C in figure 2.11 is a record of the acceleration at each moment of time. This record was also obtained by the computer, which calculated the slope or inclination of the velocity curve at each moment. The slopes of the velocities yield the accelerations and represent *the rate of change in velocity*. This output is plotted along with the other two traces on the same time scale. Initial acceleration lasts about 100 ms until the acceleration trace returns to zero. Then there is a deceleration (a negative acceleration trace) that lasts for about the same length of time. Also, the peak velocity of the movement is achieved at the point at which the acceleration changes to deceleration (where the acceleration curve crosses the zero baseline).

These kinematic variables, with simultaneous recording of position, velocity, and acceleration as a function of time, provide a reasonably complete picture of these movements. Scientists often search for changes in these kinematic variables when certain independent variables are changed—for instance, instructions to the subject or the size of a target to which the person is moving. Examples of this kind of research are provided later in the text.

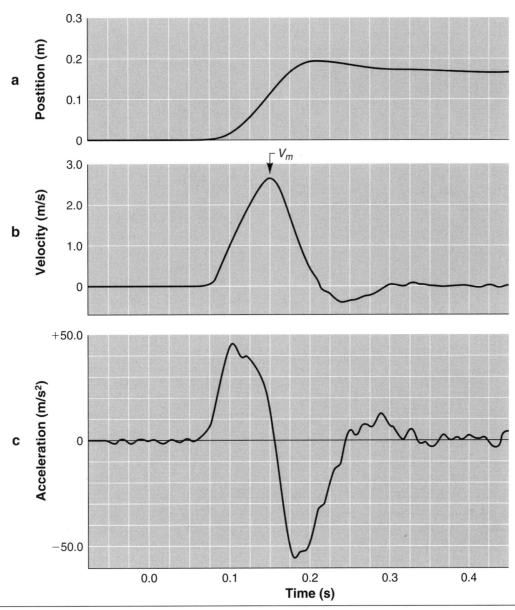

Figure 2.11. Position, velocity, and acceleration traces representing a rapid 17-cm elbow extension movement. Reprinted, by permission, from Wadman, W.J., Denier van der Gon, J.J., Geuze, R.H., and Mol, C.R., 1979, "Control of Fast Goal-Directed Arm Movements," *Journal of Human Movement Studies, 5,* 5.

Coordination Kinematics. In chapter 8 we will focus on movement coordination—how the actions of one body part are controlled together with the movements of another body part. Many types of coordination exist, such as the coordination of two or more joints in one limb (as when reaching for a cup) or of different limbs simultaneously (as of the arms and legs while walking), or even more subtle coordinations (such as in talking while breathing). For movements that are *oscillatory,* one measure of coordination is to describe the *temporal phasing* between the two body parts.

Consider the simple action of tapping two fingers on a table. Suppose we plotted the dis-

placement records of the up-and-down tapping cycles of the right finger along the abscissa and the left finger along the ordinate. Plotted separately, each would be represented as a back-and-forth, overlapping straight line along its respective axis. However, to assess how these two fingers are coordinated, the time records of one finger can be plotted relative to those of the other finger. At any point in time, the position of the left hand and the position of the right hand can be presented as a data point on the graph. When the points are combined over time they produce one continuous trace, as illustrated in the two examples in figure 2.12 (see also Winstein &

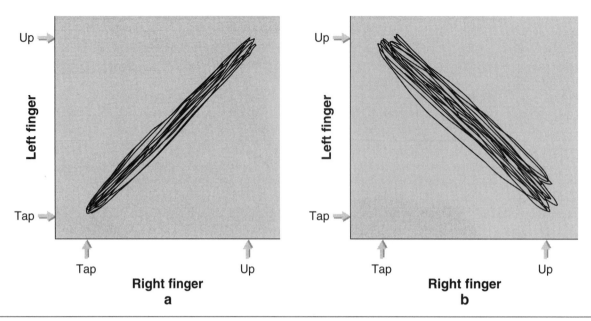

Figure 2.12.   Sample displacement plots of two fingers moving simultaneously. In-phase coordination (a); anti-phase coordination (b).

Garfinkel, 1989). In figure 2.12a, the two fingers tap the table at approximately the same time, are at maximum height above the table (in the "up" position on the graph) at about the same time, and seem to be moving within their respective cycles at about the same time—the coordinated motions are *simultaneous*. The example in figure 2.12b illustrates *alternate tapping*—one finger taps the table at about the same time that the other finger reaches maximum height, then vice versa. This figure illustrates just two of the types of temporal coordination patterns that exist between oscillators (see chapter 8).

A quantitative measure of temporal coordination can also be made by considering the displacements of each cycle over time. This is represented in figure 2.13 in two ways. In figure 2.13a, displacement is plotted over time—position A represents the finger at the time of a tap, position B is about halfway up, position C represents the "up" point, and position D is halfway back down again. Figure 2.13b represents the same data by plotting these displacements against their velocities (called a *phase plane* representation). Now positions A and C represent zero velocity, and positions B and D are the maximum upward and downward velocities. The value of phase plane representations is that the position of each finger at any point within its cycle can be described as a phase angle (ϕ) describing the progress through a cycle, or a circle containing 360 degrees. Since

the phase planes of each finger can be determined independently, the measure of coordination is simply the difference between the phase angle for the left finger (ϕ_L) and the phase angle for right finger (ϕ_R). This measure is called *relative phase*.

From figures 2.12a and 2.13, it is clear that at any one time, the two phase angles are about the same. That is, when both fingers are "down," each phase angle is 0°; when both fingers are "up," each phase angle is 180°, and so on. Thus, the relative phase ($\phi_L - \phi_R$) will always be around 0° whenever a sample is measured. This simultaneous pattern of relative phasing is often called moving *in-phase*. For figure 2.12b, notice that the temporal phasing of the one finger is always about opposite to that of the other. That is, when one phase-angle cycle is at 0°, the other is at 180°; then when the first is at 180°, the other has reached 360°. The relative phase for this series of estimates produces an average relative phase of about 180°, which is sometimes called moving in an *anti-phase* pattern.

But notice also that there is some variability in the plots presented in figure 2.12. Thus, researchers often calculate the standard deviation of these relative-phase estimates in order to supplement the description of a pattern's average relative phase with an estimate of its *stability*. Both the mean and standard deviation will be used to describe important features of coordination in chapter 8.

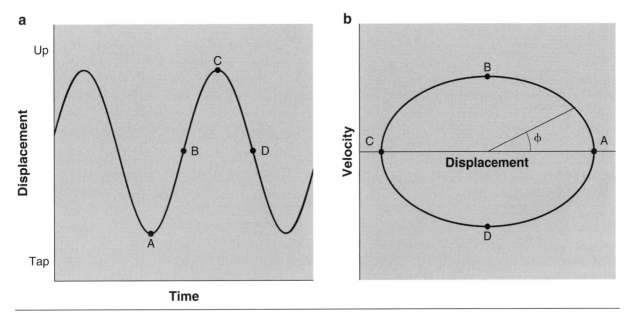

Figure 2.13.   Cyclical movement of a finger's displacement relative to time (a) and relative to its velocity (b). Adapted from Burgess-Limerick, Abernethy, and Neal, 1991.

Measurement Devices

Recording the positions of the body parts—and the *changes* that these undergo during movement—has a long history that has recently included many developments with advanced computing technology. Devices for recording movement kinematics can be placed into two general categories: direct methods and imaging methods (Winter, 1990).

Direct Methods.   Body position information can be acquired directly through various methods. For example, a goniometer is a hinged device that, when strapped to the side of a body joint, will physically change in angle along with changes in the joint angle. Most goniometers are wired with potentiometers that will send voltage information, which is proportional to the joint angle, that can be accumulated and analyzed by a computer. Potentiometers are also used in many other direct-measurement devices, such as apparatuses that are physically moved by the subject. Many other types of direct-measurement techniques also exist—graphics tablet and virtual reality technology being two of the more recent developments that have been used in motor behavior research (e.g., Chua & Elliott, 1993).

Imaging Methods.   Muybridge (boxed text on page 31) could probably be credited with initiating the analysis of human movement through imaging techniques. High-speed cinematography introduced a way to capture images of moving limbs very rapidly. However, frame-by-frame analysis methods were tedious ways of examining changes in locations over time. Fortunately, technology has introduced more automated ways of performing this analysis. Such instruments have relieved the scientist of the time-consuming job of reading locations from each frame of film. The cost of such analysis systems was prohibitive for many years. However, computer systems that analyze such data are now more powerful and much cheaper, and the use of these measurement techniques has become very common in recent years.

Today the most common imaging devices use *video* and *optoelectric* methods. Video methods are straightforward, as movements can be captured on relatively inexpensive videotape using VHS and 8-mm formats. Typically, the subject being recorded wears pieces of tape or fluorescent "markers" that can easily be seen on film and later digitized for analysis. For optoelectric methods, tiny light bulbs (called light-emitting diodes or LEDs) are attached to the subject on various body parts. Light-sensing devices then detect and record the locations of the body parts during the movement.

Figure 2.14 illustrates an optoelectric analysis of changes in the wrist and elbow during the throw of a ball (from Carnahan, 1993). The wrist joint angle was inferred from LEDs placed on the knuckles, wrist, and elbow; the elbow joint angle was inferred from wrist, elbow, and shoulder

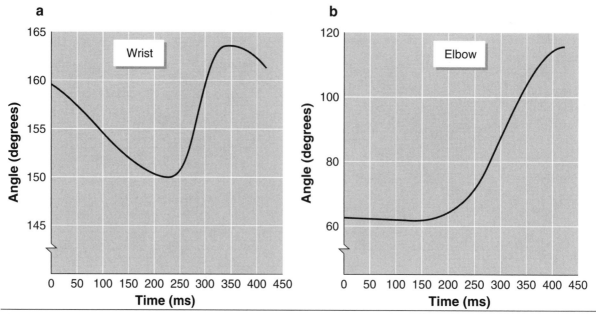

Figure 2.14.   Optoelectric analysis of wrist and elbow displacements over time.
Reprinted from Carnahan, 1992.

LEDs. Comparing the changes in the wrist and elbow angles over time reveals a clear description of what happened during the throw: the elbow stayed at the same angle while the wrist flexed, and then both extended at approximately the same time. Imagine now what would have happened if changes in the shoulder angle had also been included—more complete description of the throw would have emerged.

Carnahan (1993) provides a nice overview of the advantages and disadvantages of these video and optoelectric devices, and these are summarized in table 2.3. The video system provides more flexibility but gives up some precision in the analyses of movement kinematics. Optoelectric systems have limited usefulness outside of the laboratory but can provide very precise analyses of movement.

Electromyography

Another common method for describing movement characteristics is to measure the involvement of a muscle in a movement by recording the electrical activity associated with contraction. The simplest method is to attach (with adhesive collars) recording electrodes to the skin surface over the involved muscle and to have this weak signal amplified and recorded on a polygraph recorder or computer for later analysis. Occasionally subcutaneous electrodes are used; the electrode is placed just under the skin but above the muscle belly. Or a small wire electrode can be embedded *within* the muscle so that electrical activity in small portions of the muscle can be recorded.

Table 2.3   Comparing Video and Optoelectric Imaging Devices

Video

- Slow sampling rate
- Ability to record movements over a wide work space
- Relatively inexpensive
- Variation in precision of measurement
- Forgiving if markers are temporally blinded from view (due to extrapolating procedures)

Optoelectric

- Fast sampling rate
- Limited work-space area in which movements can be performed
- Expensive
- Very precise measurement
- Not forgiving if LEDs cannot be sensed (if blocked from sensor)

A recording using surface electrodes, taken from a study by Carter and Shapiro (1984), is shown in figure 2.15. Subjects were asked to perform a four-phase movement involving rotation of the right wrist, and the record at the top of the figure shows the clockwise (supination) and

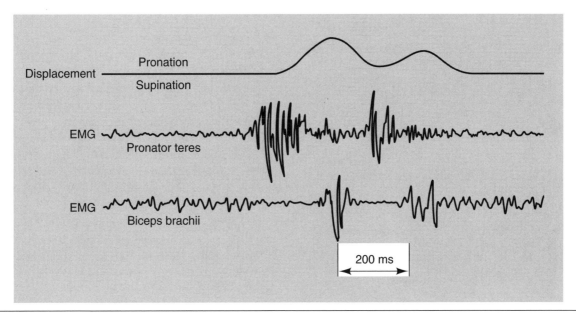

Figure 2.15.   A typical EMG tracing taken during a movement.
Reprinted from Carter and Shapiro, 1984.

counterclockwise (pronation) movements. The EMGs are from the pronator teres muscle, which acts as the pronator (counterclockwise) , and the biceps muscle, which acts as the supinator (clockwise). Once the movement begins, one sees marked activity in the various muscles; the activity is dependent on the particular action being performed. The biceps is the first muscle to act, throwing the wrist into supination; then the biceps is turned off and the pronator acts to brake the action and reverse it; then the biceps brakes and reverses that action, and so on. These records describe the *temporal patterning* of the movement segments. Also, information about the intensity of contraction is provided by the amplitudes in these records, with larger EMG amplitudes being generally indicative of larger forces. However, while there is good relation between EMG amplitude and force under static, controlled conditions within a given muscle, many situations arise that can degrade this relation, so that the amount of force produced is usually not accurately reflected by the amount of EMG being produced.

A record of transformed EMG activity, taken during a rapid elbow extension (from Wadman et al., 1979), is depicted in figure 2.16. A number of changes were made in the raw EMG signals before they were recorded. First, the EMGs were *rectified;* that is, the negative voltage values were given positive signs so that the resulting record would be positive. (Notice that figure 2.16 has two such records, with the biceps record inverted

so that the two patterns can be compared more easily.) When the EMG is rectified, the pattern of electrical activity can be seen more readily than with the raw signals shown in figure 2.15. Second, these records were *averaged* for a number of similar movements, mainly so that the important patterns of contractions could be seen over and above the trial-to-trial variations. These patterns are more reliable than are those for a single trial.

Such records are useful in that they provide one kind of description of what the central nervous system "tells" the muscles to do. In the example shown, it appears that the triceps muscle contracted for about 100 ms; then it turned off and the biceps muscle contracted for about 50 ms; and then the triceps muscle came on again for another burst of about 100 ms. These records are even more helpful if they are superimposed on other records of kinematic information, such as those shown in figure 2.15, so that the changes in the muscle actions can be associated with the actions of the limbs.

Measures of Brain Activity

The most recent advances in measurements have been the various methods of measuring brain activity. Their use in describing the brain activity that underlies motor performance is just in its infancy, and there is considerable promise for more. Each of the techniques has advantages and disadvantages, although changes in methodology are occurring at a rapid pace, and many of the

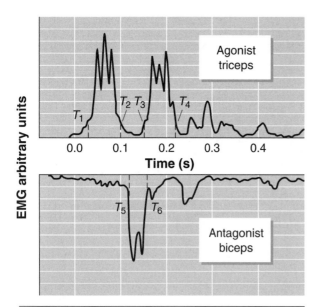

Figure 2.16. Rectified and averaged EMG signals from the triceps and biceps muscles during a rapid elbow extension.

Reprinted, by permission, from Wadman, W.J., Denier van der Gon, J.J., Geuze, R.H., and Mol, C.R., 1979, "Control of Fast Goal-Directed Arm Movements," *Journal of Human Movement Studies, 5*, 10.

current disadvantages may be overcome in short order.

Electroencephalography (EEG) has been around the longest, although improvements in the techniques have been slow. Another type of encephalography, known as magneto-encephalo-graphy (MEG), has been developed more recently and holds considerable promise. Both techniques have the advantage of working very quickly, providing indications about mental events that occur briefly. However, their capacity to allow inferences about localized anatomical structures is significantly less than that of other, albeit slower methods (Gevins et al., 1995; Wikswo, Gevins, & Williamson, 1993).

In contrast, positron emission tomography (PET), single-photon emission computed tomography (SPECT), and magnetic resonance imaging (MRI) techniques provide much more detailed information about the localization of brain structure and activity. The major disadvantage of these techniques is that sustained activity of the performance over a fairly long period of time (30–50 s) is required in order to complete the recordings. Nevertheless, research in motor behavior using continuous activities has been done, and these findings are encouraging for future research (Remy et al., 1994; Winstein, Grafton, & Pohl, 1997).

Empirical Equations

An important process for evaluating the outcomes of various experimental procedures begins after the main performance measures are generated from the experiment. This process involves determining the relationship between some independent variable and a dependent variable on the basis of the empirical data. One important kind of relationship is linear. In a graph, the dependent variable plots essentially as a straight line with the independent variable.

In figure 2.17 we have plotted data from an experiment by Schmidt et al. (1979), for which the error in hitting a target with a handheld stylus is plotted as a function of the average velocity of the movement. A quick examination of the plot in figure 2.17 indicates that the relationship between these two variables is essentially linear. A line has been placed through the points that seems to represent their general direction, and this line is called the *line of best fit*. The actual placement can be done accurately by various statistical techniques (e.g., regression) or can be done "by eye" for a rough approximation.

The goal in this section is to express this line of best fit in terms of what is known as an *empirical equation*, a kind of shorthand that enables us, with but two numbers, to convey information about a linear relationship for an empirically determined set of data points. These two numbers also will have special meaning in terms of various theories; that is, these numbers will be measures of certain hypothetical constructs. We begin with the general equation for a line:

$$Y = a + bX \qquad (2.6)$$

In this equation, Y represents the values on the y-axis (error), X represents the values on the x-axis (average velocity), and a and b are constants (figure 2.17). The constant a is termed the y-intercept, and it refers to the value of Y when the line crosses the y-axis; here the value is about 2 mm. The constant b is called the slope and refers to the amount of inclination of the line. The slope can be *positive* (upward and to the right, as in this example) or *negative* (downward to the right), associated with either positive or negative values of b. Once these values are specified from a given set of data, the empirical equation can be written that describes the linear relation between values of X and Y.

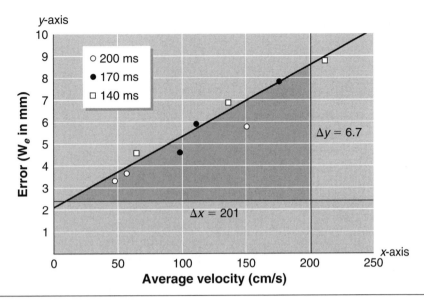

Figure 2.17. Graphical method for determining constants for linear empirical equations. Reprinted from Schmidt, Zelaznik, Hawkins, Frank, and Quinn, 1979.

Computation of Constants

The computation of the constants needed for the empirical equation is simple. After the line of best fit has been applied to the data points, extend it leftward until it crosses the y-axis and read off the y-intercept, or a. In the data shown in figure 2.17, a equals 2.08 mm.

Next, draw two lines, one perpendicular to the y-axis and one perpendicular to the x-axis, forming the shaded triangle as shown. The length of the line forming the base of the triangle will be called ΔX, and the length of the line forming the side of the triangle will be called ΔY. The symbol Δ means *change in*; measures of the changes in Y and the corresponding changes in X (201 cm/s) can be seen. Then, the slope of the line is defined as

$$b = \Delta Y / \Delta X \qquad (2.7)$$

That is, the slope is defined as the change in Y divided by the corresponding change in X. Here, the slope (b) is computed as $6.7/201 = +.033$. The interpretation of this slope is that each time the value of X increases by 1 cm/s, there is a .033-mm increase in the Y value (error).

Uses of Empirical Equations

The slope and intercept are the only two values needed to determine the linear relationship. Putting the slope and the intercept together into the general equation for the line, we have the empirical equation for these data:

$$Y = 2.08 + .033X$$

Having been provided the calculated values of a and b found by a person in California, someone in Munich can reconstruct the line of best fit by using the linear equation. This is done by picking any two arbitrary values of X (say, 50 and 250 cm/s) and calculating the values of Y for these values of X:

$$Y = 2.08 + .033 (50) = 3.73 \text{ mm}$$

$$Y = 2.08 + .033 (250) = 10.33 \text{ mm}$$

Then, on a new graph, these data points ($X = 50$, $Y = 3.73$; and $X = 250$, $Y = 10.33$) can be plotted, and the line in figure 2.17 drawn between them. Thus, saying that the intercept was 2.08 and the slope was .033 can convey a great deal of information about the experiment to someone who does not have access to the nine actual data points.

In addition, this relation can be used to predict *new* values of error before they are found. If we wanted to choose a velocity value so that the error was only 5.00 mm, we could take the empirical equation and substitute the value of the error as follows, then solve for the value of the velocity:

$$5.00 = 2.08 + .033X$$

$$X = (2.08 - 5.00) / (-.033)$$

$$X = 88.48 \text{ cm/s}$$

Thus, if we wanted the error to be about 5 mm, we would use a velocity of about 88 cm/s. Having an empirical equation makes it possible to predict this result without actually having to go into the laboratory.

Interpreting Empirical Equations

In addition to the benefits provided by empirical equations in terms of description of experimental results and prediction of new findings, the values of the constants *a* and *b* often have special theoretical meaning, depending on the nature of the data collected and the kind of independent variable studied. In the present example, the meaning of the constant *a* (the intercept) is related to the amount of error for the slowest movement possible, and thus the intercept seems to represent a kind of "background" or "baseline" error. On the other hand, the value of the slope *(b)* refers to the amount of *increase* in error as the velocity increases, and it represents the "difficulty" of the task. For example, if another task had had a slope larger than .033, we would know that the second task was more difficult than the first one. In this and other similar situations to be discussed later, the slope and intercept describe two distinct features of the task or the subject's behavior.

Summary

Motor behavior can be classified according to several dimensions, such as *continuous/serial/discrete*, referring to the extent to which the movement has a definite beginning and end, and *open/closed*, referring to the extent to which the environment is predictable. Most of the tasks used in motor control work fall into one or another of these basic categories. In measuring movement, attention is devoted to a measure's *objectivity* (the extent to which two independent observers achieve the same score), its *sensitivity* to changes in skill, its *reliability* (the extent to which the score is repeatable), and its *validity* (the extent to which the test measures what the experimenter wants it to measure).

The outcome of movements in terms of the environmental goal can be measured in essentially three ways: in terms of errors, speed, or magnitude. There are many ways to measure errors in movement; chief among these are *constant error* (a measure of average error or bias), *variable error* (a measure of consistency), *total variability* (a measure of overall error), and *absolute error* (also a measure of overall error). Each of these error measures has a different meaning and is used in different aspects of the measurement process. Measures of speed are used when accuracy is less important and when rapid actions are critical. Measures of magnitude are used when the *amount* of behavior is critical. A fourth but related measure is based on the analysis of simultaneous secondary tasks, providing a measure of the spare capacity of the performer after he or she has devoted attention to a primary task.

Movements can be measured in many ways, but common methods involve the calculation of kinematic variables (position, velocity, acceleration) and the recording of the electrical activity from muscles (EMG). Two methods used to assess kinematics, *video* and *optoelectric*, are commonly used, although each comes with its own advantages and disadvantages. Studies of brain activity are also becoming increasingly popular, and their use in motor behavior research is only in its infancy. *Linear empirical equations* provide a description of a linear relationship between a dependent and an independent variable. The parameters of the equation can be easily estimated, and they provide a means by which the relationship can be used to predict new facts before they are found.

CHAPTER 3

HUMAN INFORMATION PROCESSING

Human functioning in the environment can be conceptualized and studied in many ways; one of the most popular is based on the fundamental notion that humans are processors of information. It is assumed that information is available in the environment, that the individual accepts the information into various "storage systems" called memory, and that the information is "processed." The term *processed* means that the information is coded, that its code may be changed from one form to another, that the information may be combined with other information, and so on. In this chapter we discuss information processing as it relates to human motor behavior (see also Marteniuk, 1976).

The Information-Processing Model

The information-processing model of functioning begins with the input of information from the environment through one or more of the sense organs and then considers what happens to this signal (or what the signal causes to happen) once inside the system. A "black box" model of the process is shown in figure 3.1. The individual is considered to be the box, and information enters into the box from the environment. This information is then processed in various ways until eventually it is output as observable motor activity. This model prevailed in the stimulus-response (S-R) tradition (see chapter 1), in which researchers were primarily concerned with the relationship between what went into the box (the information, or stimuli) and the output (the response). With the emergence of *cognitive psychology*, however, interest in the processes that occur *within* the box has increased. Obviously, this is an abstract way to study human behavior because it focuses on processes and events that are not directly observable. Knowledge about these processes is inferred from the overt behavior of the human under various experimental conditions.

Why not investigate these internal processes directly rather than make inferences about them? This is simply not possible, because the neural processes and their locations in the brain are not well understood. Adequate knowledge and techniques for studying complex human phenomena such as perception, decision making, and response planning are not currently available. However, through use of the cognitive-psychological per-

Input
(Signals)

Processing
(The human)

Output
(Motor response)

Figure 3.1. The simplified information-processing model.

spective, the internal events can be studied in a variety of ways.

Some of these approaches focus on the nature of the structure into which the information "flows," and some focus on the changes in the nature of the information as it proceeds through the system. Perhaps the most common approach is to consider the temporal aspects of information processing, concentrating on the duration of these various processes. This basic *chronometric approach*, as it is termed (see Posner, 1978), makes considerable use of the reaction-time (RT) method, whereby the chief measure of the subject's behavior is the interval between the presentation of a stimulus and the beginning of the response (i.e., RT).

Of course, many different information processes occur during RT; but if the experiment is designed properly, so that the durations of most other processes are held constant, one can usually infer that an increase in RT caused by some experimental variable was caused by the lengthening of the duration of a *particular* process. This chapter presents many examples of this type of research and thinking.

Three Stages of Information Processing

Although the notion that there are separate stages or processes between a stimulus and a response has been popularized by the relatively recent cognitive-psychological viewpoint, the general concept of stages of processing is quite old (see boxed text below). This thinking, coupled with more recent efforts from cognitive psychology (e.g., Sanders, 1980; Schweickert, 1993; Sternberg, 1969), has led to the view that various processing stages can be define and that these processes can be either *serial* (sequential) or *parallel* (simultaneous) in nature.

The Nature of Serial and Parallel Processing

Imagine an automotive plant as a model of information processing, as in figure 3.2. Some stages

Donders's Stages of Processing

Over a century ago, the Dutch physician Donders (1868/1969) made the first attempts to measure the time required to complete certain thought processes. Donders assumed the existence of a series of separate, nonoverlapping stages of processing between a stimulus and a response. The notion was that the processing that occurs in stage 1 is different from the processing that occurs in stage 2, and that stage 2 processing cannot begin until stage 1 processing is completed. Donders studied this idea using three RT methods that differed in systematic ways.

In the simplest method, termed the *a*-reaction task, the subject was presented with a single, unanticipated stimulus that required a single response (e.g., pressing a key using the right hand in response to the illumination of a red light). This reaction task is often termed the *simple*-RT task. In a more complicated task, termed the *c*-reaction task, a subject was presented with two different light stimuli and asked to respond by pressing a key with the right hand if a specific stimulus was illuminated. For example, if the two stimuli were red and blue, then the task might be to respond if the red stimulus was illuminated but to *not* respond to the blue stimulus. This reaction task is sometimes called a *go/no-go* RT task. In the *b*-reaction task, the subjects were again presented with more than one stimulus and asked to make specific responses to specific stimuli. For example, a red light might require a key press with the right hand whereas a blue light would require a left-hand response. This reaction task is often called a *choice*-RT task.

Donders's logic was that among the three RT tasks, the next more complicated task required an additional processing stage to be completed before a response could be made. The *c*-reaction task was more complicated than the *a*-reaction task because a subject had to discriminate between two possible stimulus alternatives in *c* whereas no discrimination was required in *a*. Because both tasks have the same requirements for movement choice, Donders argued that any differences between the RT for *c* and the RT for *a* would reflect the additional processing required for the stimulus-discrimination stage of processing.

Perhaps more important to motor behavior, Donders argued that any difference between the RTs for the *c*- and *b*-reactions was attributable to a stage that involved the selection of a response. Notice that the *c*-reaction and the *b*-reaction both involved the same element of stimulus discrimination. However, the *b*-reaction had the added requirement that one of two possible response alternatives must also be selected.

Later thinking and research, most notably by Sternberg (1969), identified a number of flaws in Donders's *subtractive method* (see Massaro, 1989, for an excellent analysis of Donders's and Sternberg's logic and methods). But even so, Donders's basic idea that the duration of stages could be examined by subtracting the RTs in various conditions was remarkable, given the time of his work, and served as the foundation for more modern analyses of human information processing.

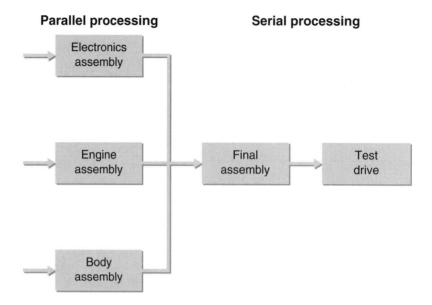

Figure 3.2.   Examples of serial and parallel processing in an automobile assembly plant.

occur at the same time in different places, such as the fabrication of the electronics, the assembly of the engine, and the assembly of the body. But at some time during the overall process, these components combine to complete the final assembly stage. After final assembly, imagine a test-drive stage, in which the drivers search for problems before the car is sent to the dealers, yet another stage. This simple analogy contains an example of parallel processing with respect to the electronics, engine, and body assembly stages, and an example of serial processing with respect to the final assembly and the test-drive stages. Thus, this system has both serial and parallel processing, but at different times in the total sequence. In human behavior, many have thought that the total RT has various stages, some of which can be performed in parallel and some of which are performed serially.

At least three stages can be proposed that intervene between the presentation of a stimulus and the evocation of a response (see figure 3.3). First, the individual must sense that a stimulus has occurred and identify it. This stage is frequently called the *stimulus-identification stage*. Second, after a stimulus has been properly identified, the individual must decide *what* response to make. The decision can be to do one of a number of actions, or the stimulus can be ignored in favor of no action at all. This stage is usually called the *response-selection stage*. Finally, after the

response has been selected, the system must be prepared for the appropriate action and must initiate that action. This stage is frequently called the response-initiation stage, but we will use the more inclusive term *response-programming stage* to represent the preparations of the motor apparatus and the initiation of the action. More detailed discussion of these stages is presented in the remainder of the chapter.

First, we offer a word of caution about the usefulness of this kind of RT approach. What does the analysis of events that occur in an RT paradigm have to do with throwing a baseball, playing a video game, or anything besides RT? The application to common skills is possible under a number of assumptions. For example, assume in driving a car that stimuli from the environment (vision of the road, horns honking) and from the driver's body (acceleration, vibrations) enter the information-processing system as input, as shown in figure 3.3. As each stimulus is input, it is processed, leading to a response or not. Thus, the driver can be thought of as an information-processing channel to which information is continually presented and out of which come responses. Driving a car does not appear to have much in common with the RT task, but the assumption is that the processes within the individual are the same. This assumption could be wrong, and many (e.g., Turvey, 1977) think that it is.

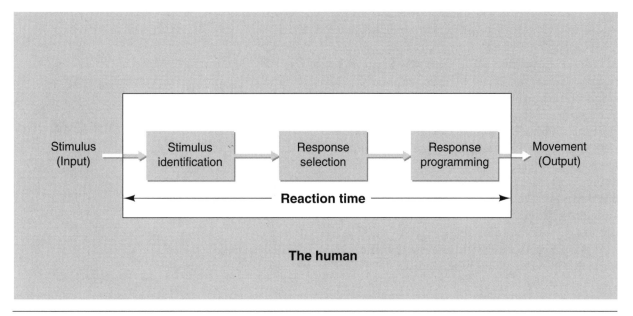

Figure 3.3. An expanded information-processing model.

Stimulus-Identification Stage

Think of the stimulus-identification stage as beginning with an environmental stimulus that must be detected; this stimulus information must then be identified or recognized as a part of a pattern. These two substages are considered in the following sections.

Stimulus Detection

When an environmental stimulus acts on the body (e.g., light entering the retina of the eye or sound entering the ear), it must be transformed into the code of neurological impulses that are sent toward the brain. The stimulus is presumably processed further at each level of analysis until the stimulus *contacts memory*, meaning that some aspect of the stimulus is aroused, such as its name or an attribute with which it has been associated in the past (e.g., its red color, such as with a stop sign). As we shall see, considerable processing must occur in order for the stimulus to arouse the proper associate in memory, rather than improper associates or all possible associates. Scientists working in this area have assumed that the variables affecting the stimulus-identification stage relate to the nature of the stimulus that is presented. For example, a variable called *stimulus clarity*, which refers to "sharpness" of the stimulus, has been used. With increased clarity, the overall RT is shorter, and this change is attributed to the increased processing speed in the stimulus-identification stage. A variable called *stimulus intensity* (the brightness of a light stimulus or the loudness of a sound stimulus) also affects encoding in these RT tasks.

Pattern Recognition

In more realistic tasks, the stimuli that enter the system are seldom unitary as they are in RT tasks, and we must usually extract a pattern or feature from the stimuli presented. Often these patterns have to do with such things as the shape of a face or where a baseball is going, how fast it is traveling, and what kind of spin has been put on it. Some of these pattern detections are genetically defined (e.g., related to survival). Others may depend heavily on learning, such as recognizing the pattern of movements of a defensive team in American football.

Important studies of chess players demonstrate the influence of learning on pattern detection (deGroot, 1965; Chase & Simon, 1973). In one such study, deGroot asked chess masters and good-to-average chess players to reconstruct the locations of the chess pieces in a half-finished game after viewing the board for 5 s. As one might imagine, the chess masters were far superior to the good-to-average players. It could be argued that the superiority of the chess masters in this task was not necessarily evidence that they had learned to remember chess patterns, but rather that they were superior in their inherent perceptual ability. This last hypothesis is doubtful, however; when the chess pieces were placed on the board in random fashion, the chess masters and the average players were about equal in their ability to relocate the pieces. One interpretation is that the processes in the stimulus-identification stage were improved in the masters through years of experience in game situations.

Analysis of such static situations seems important to many activities; but even more important from the point of view of motor behavior is an ability to extract patterns of movement from the environment. In many situations, how the environment changes from moment to moment will determine which action is most appropriate.

A great deal of information is contained in the movement of the visual field, and it seems clear that an individual can use this information to provide an unequivocal analysis of movements in an environment or of the environment's movements. Gibson (1966), for example, refers to "optical flow patterns," which are the patterns made up of the rays of light that strike the eye from every visible part of the environment (see figure 3.4). As the individual and/or the environment moves, the angles of these rays change to allow the subject to extract a pattern of movement from the changing visual array. For example, you *know* that a ball is coming directly toward your eye if the rates of change of the angles of the rays of light from all edges of the ball are the same. This *looming* can elicit strong avoidance reactions even in children and young animals that have presumably never been hit in the eye, suggesting that these kinds of pattern recognitions may be genetically defined. We will discuss in more detail these various aspects of visual information processing in chapter 5.

These interpretations are important for many fast-action sports and games. Patterns of opponent position or action arouse meaningful responses that lead to fast action in highly skilled players, while they may go nearly unnoticed by novices (for reviews see Ericsson, 1996; Starkes & Allard, 1993). For example, certain patterns of linemen and backfield movement in American football mean that the play will be a run to the right side, and an effective response to this action by the defensive player often depends on recognizing such a pattern quickly and accurately. Pattern recognition in athletic preparation has been given more attention lately as a means for potential improvement in sport and industry.

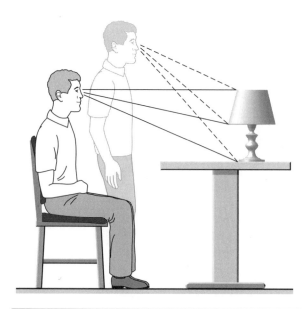

Figure 3.4. Optical arrays vary as the location of the observer changes in the environment.

Response-Selection Stage

At the end of the stimulus-identification stage, the individual presumably has analyzed the information in the stimulus input and now has a basis for "knowing" what happened in the environment. In the next stage, response selection, the subject decides what response to make. A baseball outfielder must make rapid decisions about whether to attempt to field a hit ball in the air or after it bounces, what direction to move in to catch it, and what to do with the ball if it is fielded successfully. Such decisions are important and apply to a wide variety of activities in sport, industry, driving, and so on.

Number of Stimulus-Response Alternatives

For over a century (since Donders's contribution, described in the boxed text on page 43), scientists have believed that the processing of information relevant to the selection of a response requires more time when there are a larger number of alternatives. The idea is that if increasing the number of alternatives causes an increase in the choice RT, then the increased RT is associated with changes in the way the information was processed in the response-selection stage.

In the choice-RT paradigm, the subject might be presented with four stimulus lights and instructed that one of the four will be illuminated on a particular trial. Each of the four lights is associated (via instructions from the experimenter) with one of four different responses (e.g., pressing one of four buttons located under the four fingers of the right hand). The task is to press the appropriate button as quickly as possible after the stimulus light comes on. Usually subjects are not able to predict exactly when the stimulus will occur and are thus prevented from initiating the response in advance. The time from stimulus to response will be sensitive to the speed of the processing responsible for the selection of the appropriate finger.

One of the earliest studies addressing this question was done by Merkel in 1885 (described by Woodworth, 1938). The digits 1 through 5 were assigned to the fingers of the right hand, and the Roman numerals I through V were assigned to the fingers of the left hand. On any given set of trials the subject knew which, from the set of 10 stimuli, would be possible (e.g., if there were 3 possible stimuli, they might be 3, 5, and V). Merkel studied the relationship between the number of possible stimuli/responses and the choice RT. His basic findings are presented in figure 3.5, which plots the choice RT against the number of stimulus-response (S-R) alternatives. As the number of alternatives increased, so did the time taken to respond to any one of them. The relationship between choice RT and the number of alternatives was curvilinear. Note, for example, that as the number of alternatives was increased from 1 to 2, the increase in choice RT was about 129 ms,

whereas when the number of alternatives was increased from 9 to 10, the increase in choice RT was only about 3 ms. Further, notice how long the RTs were with 10 alternatives (over 600 ms). When one considers that in high-level baseball, the ball can travel from the pitcher to the plate in as few as 460 ms (Hubbard & Seng, 1954), it is clear that the lengthened RT will have important implications for the performance of certain rapid skills.

This relationship between number of alternatives and choice RT has been studied a great deal since Merkel made his original observations. The overall conclusion has not changed, although there have been some refinements in technique and much additional theorizing about the causes of the relationship. The most widely known findings and explanations of the effect were apparently determined by two people at about the same time—Hick (1952) and Hyman (1953). The relation they discovered between the number of S-R alternatives and RT has since been termed Hick's law, or sometimes the Hick-Hyman law (Keele, 1986; Proctor & Dutta, 1995).

Hick's Law. Hick (1952) and Hyman (1953) studied the relationship between RT and the number of S-R alternatives in much the same way as Merkel had, using various numbers of lights that were associated with an equal number of keys to be pressed when the appropriate light appeared. As Merkel found, choice RT increased as the number of possible S-R alternatives increased. The RT values, as well as the overall shape of the function, were consistent with Merkel's findings in figure 3.5. However, what Hick and Hyman discovered was that choice RT appeared to increase by a nearly constant amount (about 150 ms) every time the number of S-R alternatives *doubled*. This suggested that the relationship between the choice RT and the logarithm of the number of S-R alternatives should be linear. The interpretation was that the logarithm of the number of S-R alternatives was a measure of the amount of information that had to be processed, suggesting that more alternatives required more processing.

The formal relation that has come to be known as Hick's law states that the choice RT is linearly related to the Log of the number of stimulus alternatives. In equation form,

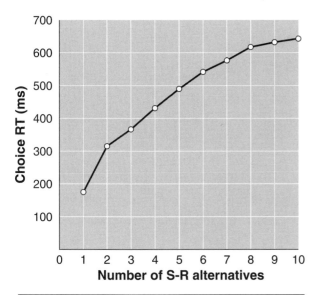

Figure 3.5. Choice RT as a function of the number of S-R alternatives. (Data from Merkel 1885, as cited by Woodworth 1938).

$$\text{Choice RT} = a + b[\text{Log}_2 (N)] \qquad (3.1)$$

where N is the number of S-R alternatives and a and b are the empirical constants. Notice that equation 3.1 is somewhat different from the "typical" linear equation discussed in chapter 2, where $Y = a + bX$; but if X equals $[\text{Log}_2 (N)]$, then equation 3.1 means that choice RT is linearly related to $\text{Log}_2 (N)$.

The data from four subjects in Hyman's (1953) study are presented in figure 3.6; the data of interest at this point are the open circles, indicating experiments in which the number of S-R alternatives was varied. In each case, there was a strong linear trend between the amount of information [or $\text{Log}_2 (N)$] and choice RT. The empirical equation for each subject is shown on that subject's graph; for example, for Subject G.C., the intercept (a) was 212 ms and the slope (b) was 153 ms. Notice that these "constants" from the empirical equations were considerably different for different subjects. Nevertheless, in each case the RT was linearly related to the amount of stimulus information.

That the relationship between the choice RT and the logarithm to the base 2 of the number of alternatives should be so clearly linear is of considerable interest in its own right. A linear relationship is the most simple of relationships, and scientists become excited about the possibility that complex behaviors of human beings can be described by such simple expressions. But of even more importance is one interpretation of this relationship: that the time required to make a decision about a response is linearly related to the amount of information that must be processed in coming to that decision.

Measuring Amount of Information. Up to this point, the term *information* has been generally used to mean signals from the environment telling us about the state of the outside world. Scientists who study information processing, however, use the term more restrictively: in this context, information refers to the amount of *uncertainty* that has been *reduced* by a signal that was presented. If during a walk in the rain your friend

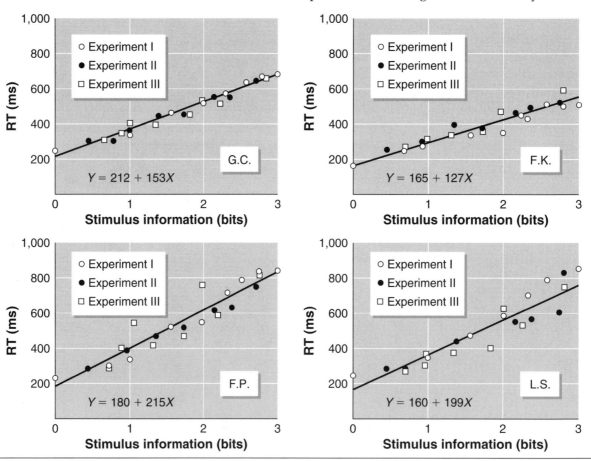

Figure 3.6. Choice RT as a function of stimulus information.
Reprinted from Hyman, 1953.

says that it is raining, that "signal" conveys little information because there was little original uncertainty available to be reduced further. But if he says that it is raining in the Sahara desert, that signal conveys a great deal of information because (a) there is low probability that it is raining there and (b) you had no previous knowledge that it was raining there. Thus, the amount of information *transmitted* is affected by both (a) the amount of uncertainty prior to the signal's being presented and (b) the amount of reduction of uncertainty.

Generally speaking, the amount of information *(H)* is given by a simple equation:

$$H = \text{Log}_2 (1/P_i) \qquad (3.2)$$

where P_i is the probability that a given event *(i)* will occur. As the probability of an event *(P_i)* decreases, the amount of information conveyed by a signal describing that event increases; this is why a signal about a rare event (it is raining in the desert) carries more information than a signal about a common event (it is raining in Eugene, Oregon).

The amount of information contained in a signal is measured in *bits* (short for *bi*nary dig*its*). One bit is defined as the amount of information necessary to reduce the original uncertainty by half. For example, your friend tells you that she is thinking of one of four people in your family, and she wants you to guess who it is. If there are two males and two females in your family, and your friend also tells you that it is a female she is thinking of, she has reduced the number of possibilities (and hence your uncertainty) from four to two (that is, by half). The statement that the person is a female has conveyed 1 bit of information. (The same logic is used in the board game, Guess Who? The best strategy is to ask questions that will eliminate as many of the incorrect alternatives as possible.)

Interpreting Hick's Law. Now we will connect the notion of reduction of uncertainty to the logarithm involved in Hick's law. First, the logarithm to the base 2 of some number *N* [abbreviated Log₂ *(N)*] is defined as the power to which the base 2 must be raised in order to obtain that number. For example, the $\text{Log}_2 (8)$ is 3, since 2 must be raised to the third power to obtain 8 ($2^3 = 2 \times 2 \times 2 = 8$). Other examples are shown in table 3.1. Notice that as the number of original times *N* is doubled (say from 4 to 8, or from 8 to 16), table 3.1 shows

that the Log₂ of the number increases by 1 in each case. In an RT situation, if *N* is the number of equally likely S-R alternatives, resolving the uncertainty about *N* was defined earlier as requiring $\text{Log}_2 (N)$ bits of information. In terms of Hick's law, we can say that choice RT is linearly related to the amount of information needed to resolve the uncertainty about *N* S-R alternatives. Stated differently, every time the number of S-R alternatives is doubled, the amount of information to be processed is increased by 1 bit, and the time required for choice RT is increased by a *constant* amount.

To this point, we have considered only the circles in figure 3.6 (Hyman, 1953, experiment 1); in that experiment, the number of S-R alternatives was varied in order to change the amount of information to be processed. In Hyman's experiment 2 (filled circles), the amount of information was varied by changing the probability of the stimulus. Remember, as the event becomes less probable, having to process a signal about it conveys more information, as in equation 3.2. When information was increased by decreasing the stimulus probabilities, RT again increased linearly. In experiment 3, Hyman varied information by changing the sequential dependencies (the tendency for a given event to be followed predictably by another). The effect was to make a particular stimulus more or less probable, and the squares in figure 3.6 also show a linear relationship between information and RT. If this interpretation is correct, the response-selection stage can be thought of as being involved in reducing uncertainty about alternative responses when a given stimulus is presented.

Table 3.1   Relation Between Number of Alternatives (*N*) and the Log₂ (*N*)

Number (*N*)	Log₂ (*N*)
1	0
2	1
4	2
8	3
16	4
32	5
64	6
128	7
256	8

Interpreting the Intercept and Slope. How should we interpret the intercept (*a*) and the slope (*b*) in Hick's law? From the earlier discussion of empirical equations (chapter 2), recall that the intercept (*a*) was that value of RT associated with $\text{Log}_2(N) = 0$, or the value of RT when the line crossed the RT axis. In the data from various subjects in Hyman's (1953) study (figure 3.6), the average of these intercepts was 179 ms (mean of 212, 165, 180, and 160 ms). Also, recall that when $\text{Log}_2(N) = 0$, the value of *N* must be 1 (table 3.1), denoting a situation with only one alternative, in which there is no uncertainty about what to do. Consequently, it has been reasonable to interpret the intercept of Hick's law as a measure of the overall "speed" of the perceptual and motor system exclusive of any time required for decision about which response to make. To this basic 179-ms time, then, is added the time to make additional decisions about choice when there is more than a single stimulus and response.

Also from Hyman's (1953) data, the slopes of the relation ranged from about 127 ms/bit to 215 ms/bit for the various subjects (figure 3.6). Remember that the slope (*b*) is a measure of the amount of inclination of the line, the amount of increase in choice RT as $\text{Log}_2(N)$ is increased by one unit (1 bit). So, with 1 additional bit of information there were from 127 to 215 ms of additional choice RT. Thus, the slope is the "speed" of decision making by the response-selection stage of processing. Seen in this way, the slope and intercept measure two different underlying processes in human performance.

The practical implications of the slope are important and probably obvious. For games in which rapid reaction is important, if the player can double the number of likely alternatives for which the opponent must prepare (and the opponent cannot anticipate them), then the player increases by 1 bit the amount of information that must be processed in order to respond, and thereby increases by a constant amount the opponent's choice RT in initiating the appropriate response. These kinds of effects are seen in most of the fast ball games, as well as in reaction situations involved in driving a car, performing various industrial tasks, and so on.

Qualifications to Hick's Law. Whereas Hick's law does hold very generally over a wide variety of situations and people, a number of other variables have to be taken into account in order to accurately predict choice RT, and a few situations exist in which the law does not appear to hold at all. The key variable is the subject's *familiarity* with responding to a particular stimulus by means of a specific response. These familiarity effects have been studied in various ways, most notably by examining (a) practice or experience with the task and (b) the nature of the relationship between the stimuli and the associated responses.

In one of the first studies to investigate the role of practice in relation to Hick's law, Mowbray and Rhoades (1959) used a two- and four-choice RT task and found, as had been observed previously by many researchers, that in early practice the four-choice task showed a much slower choice RT than did the two-choice task. However, their study is unique in that they provided their subjects with an incredible 42,000 trials of practice! After this amount of practice, the four-choice RT was reduced to a level essentially equal to that of the two-choice RT. Thus, the slope of the choice-RT function between 1 and 2 bits (two and four alternatives) was reduced by practice, eventually becoming essentially zero. Similar findings were also reported by Seibel (1963).

Another set of data that can be similarly interpreted was generated by Mowbray (1960). When the task involved digit-naming (the number of possible digits was varied, and the RT was measured by a voice microphone), increasing the number of possible digits to be named did not increase the choice RT. Because there is no reason to believe that the relation between the numeral 4 and the vocal response "four" should be genetically determined (such names and numerals are probably arbitrary), the interpretation is that the names of digits are so highly practiced that the association between the digit and the name is nearly direct, not requiring further reduction in uncertainty (see also Fitts & Seeger, 1953; Hellyer, 1963).

Similar findings of essentially zero slope for highly overlearned S-R relationships were provided by Leonard (1959). In this study, choice RTs with one, two, four, and eight alternatives were examined, but the situation was quite different from those studied earlier. The subjects placed their fingers on the appropriate number of keys and were instructed to press as quickly as possible on the key that vibrated. The relationship between the stimulus (vibrations) and the response (pressing that finger on the key) was very direct. As the number of S-R alternatives increased from two to eight, Leonard found no further increase in choice RT. That is, the slope of the line was zero. When the finger was vibrated, the relation between it and the response was so direct that no additional time was required for decision making (see also Keele, 1986, for a good review).

These findings illustrate the importance that the relationship between the stimulus and response can have to response selection. The exceptions to Hick's law suggest that highly overlearned S-R relationships can *facilitate* response selection when multiple alternatives are available. In the next section we examine how this same influence of S-R familiarity can also have *detrimental* effects on response selection.

Stimulus-Response Compatibility

The relationship between a stimulus and a response was given the term *stimulus-response compatibility* (or simply, S-R compatibility) in 1951 by Small (see Small, 1990), and refers to the extent to which the stimulus and the associated response are connected in a "natural" way. Although S-R compatibility effects have been studied in a wide variety of ways (Hommel & Prinz, 1997; Proctor & Reeve, 1990), the most common and strongest of these effects involve variations of the method shown in figure 3.7. When a subject is asked to respond to one of two lights by pressing one of two keys with the fingers, the *ensemble* is said to be *spatially* S-R compatible if the lights and keys are organized in a direct way. In figure 3.7, configuration A is compatible because the left light

requires the subject to press the left key. Conversely, configuration B is less compatible (is "incompatible") because the left light calls for the subject to press the right key, and the right light calls for the left key. The typical result in this type of experiment is that subjects respond faster and make fewer errors in spatially compatible S-R ensembles than in incompatible ones (e.g., Fitts & Deininger, 1954; see the review in Proctor & Van Zandt, 1994).

Why do these response-selection effects occur? One possibility is that the right limb responds to the right light faster than to the left light because of some anatomical or neural advantage. If this is so, then imagine what would happen if a subject used crossed hands in the experimental setup. In such a situation the left key would be pressed with the right hand and the right key would be pressed with the left hand. Now condition A is compatible with respect to the spatial mapping of the stimulus and the key to select (as before), but incompatible with respect to the mapping of the stimulus and hand to select (i.e., the *right* stimulus is responded to with the right key, but using the *left* hand). The situation for condition B is reversed. There is still a spatial incompatibility between the stimuli and keys (as before), but now the stimulus and the hand to select are compatible (i.e., the *right* stimulus is responded to with the left key, using the *right* hand).

Are S-R compatibility effects dependent on the spatial relationship between the stimulus and the key or between the stimulus and the effector used to make the response? Findings from

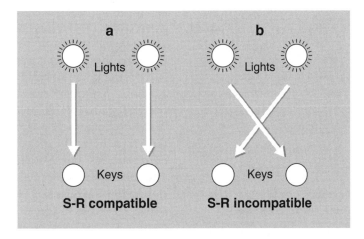

Figure 3.7.   S-R compatibility is defined by the relationship between the stimuli and the responses to which they are associated.

experiments that have addressed this question (Anzola et al., 1977; Wallace, 1971) reveal that it is the spatial compatibility between the stimulus and the response key that is crucial: regardless of which hand is used (i.e., crossed or uncrossed conditions), performance is better in the spatially compatible conditions (ensemble A in figure 3.7) than in spatially incompatible conditions (ensemble B in figure 3.7).

The influence of S-R compatibility on response selection can also be seen when the spatial dimension of the stimulus is *irrelevant* to response selection. In an early demonstration of what was to become known as the *Simon effect*, subjects were asked to respond by pressing a right key whenever the auditory stimulus "right" was presented via earphones, and by pressing the left key when the word "left" was presented (Simon & Rudell, 1967). Some of these auditory stimuli were presented to the left ear and some to the right ear. However, note that regardless of the ear to which the stimulus was presented, subjects were to respond to the content of the message; the spatial location (ear) to which the message was sent was irrelevant. The findings revealed that the irrelevant (spatial) feature of the stimulus had a profound effect on response selection. As can be seen in figure 3.8, choice RT was faster when the message of the signal and the response were compatible with the spatial origin of the stimulus. These findings, along with others reported since Simon

published his initial series of studies, suggest that there is *interference* in selecting a response when the irrelevant stimulus is incompatible with the response. The spatial dimensionality of the stimulus tends to attract the response toward it and must be inhibited before the correct response can be selected (see also Simon, 1969a, 1969b, 1990).

Although the spatial layout of the S-R ensemble has a critical effect on response selection, this appears to be only a partial explanation of what is going on here (Umiltà & Nicoletti, 1990). For example, choice RT to the stimulus word "right" or to a rightward-pointing stimulus arrow is faster when the subject responds with a button press with the right hand or with the word "right" in comparison to what occurs with incompatible relationships (e.g., McCarthy & Donchin, 1981; Weeks & Proctor, 1990). Thus, even *nonspatial* stimuli and responses seem to have dimensions that produce compatibility relationships affecting response selection. Together, these findings suggest that the response-selection stage is susceptible to compatibility effects when the relationship between the set of stimulus alternatives and the set of response alternatives has a learned association. Interference is likely to occur when the response is inconsistent with the learned association (Proctor & Van Zandt, 1994).

Compatibility and Complex Actions

When people respond to stimuli that require *complex* actions, the issue of S-R compatibility and response selection seems to be related to the *intentions* of the action. For example, Rosenbaum et al. (1990) describe the common act of a waiter who reaches for an upside-down glass in order to pour water into it. The waiter's initial hand position is awkward because the hand is inverted to pick up the glass. However, when the glass is turned upright, the hand is in the correct holding position. The response initially selected by the waiter "trades off" an awkward early posture in order to achieve a posture that is much better suited to filling the glass with water. In this case, compatibility between the stimulus (the glass) and the waiter's response (initial hand posture) is defined not in terms of the initial interaction, but rather in terms of the efficiency of the intended final position. As seen in experimental demonstrations of this effect, selection of the initial position that maximizes the efficiency of the hand's posture upon movement completion is initiated

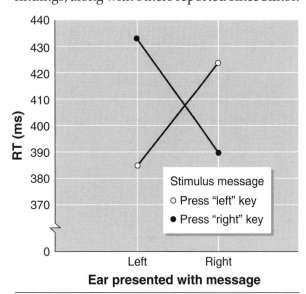

Figure 3.8. The Simon effect—the irrelevant stimulus (which ear receives the message) interacts with the information content of the message.
Adapted from Simon and Rudell, 1967.

faster than selection of a position that is less efficient at the end of the action (Rosenbaum et al., 1992). Thus, for more complex actions, S-R compatibility effects may influence the response-selection stage in terms of the information that is specified about *how* an action is to be performed, rather than simply about where to move.

Response-Programming Stage

Once the person has identified the stimulus and selected the response, the organization and initiation of an action must be accomplished. After response selection, the task is to translate this abstract idea into a set of muscular actions that will achieve the response. These processes are thought to occur during the *response-programming stage*. Like the processes in the earlier stages, the events occurring in response programming are probably very complex—requiring that some program of action be called from the performer's memory, that the program be prepared for activation, that the relevant portions of the motor system be readied for the program (called *tuning*), and that the movement be initiated. It is helpful to view the response-programming stage as the final set of processes that allows the individual to communicate with the environment, just as the stimulus-identification stage is viewed as the first stage that allows the environment to communicate with an individual.

Information about the response-programming stage has been developed relatively recently in comparison to research regarding the other two stages. Not until 1960, when Henry and Rogers performed an experiment on the nature of the movement to be produced in RT situations, did conceptualization about the response-programming stage begin.

The Henry-Rogers Experiment

Henry and Rogers (1960) studied the nature of the movement to be made using a simple-RT paradigm, in which the subjects knew on any given trial which response was to be made. In various series of trials, Henry and Rogers had the subjects make different movements while keeping the stimulus for the movement, as well as the response alternatives, constant. The first movement involved merely lifting the finger from a key a few millimeters and had essentially no accuracy requirement. For the second movement, the subject lifted the finger from the key and moved approximately 33 cm forward and upward to grasp a tennis ball suspended on a string, which stopped a timer measuring movement time (MT). The third movement involved a second suspended ball mounted 30 cm to the right of the first ball. The subject lifted the finger from the key, moved forward and upward to strike the first ball with the back of the hand, moved forward and downward to push a button, and then moved forward and upward again to strike the second suspended ball. Remember, the stimulus and response alternatives of these three movements were exactly the same (so that the processing speed in the stimulus-identification and response-selection mechanisms should also be the same); the only variation was in the nature of the *movement*. The primary measure, as before, was the RT, or the interval from stimulus onset until the movement began.

Henry and Rogers's data from adult men and women are presented in table 3.2. The medium-complexity movement (single-ball grasp) resulted in a 36-ms longer RT than did the simpler finger-lift response. The most complex movement (double-ball strike) resulted in an additional 13-ms increase in RT over that for the single-ball grasp. Because the stimuli were not changed for the different movements, these data suggest that the increased RT as the movements were increased in complexity was due to an increased amount of time required to program the movement in some response-programming stage. Henry and Rogers's original idea was that more complex motor commands, such as would be necessary to control the limb through several movement reversals and to produce grasping and striking actions, would require more brain centers to be coordinated, in turn requiring more time for all of this neurological complexity to be organized during RT. In slightly modified form, this idea still has a great deal of support (see Christina, 1992; Henry, 1980; Klapp, 1996).

Table 3.2 RT and MT as a Function of the Complexity of the Movement

Movement	RT (ms)	MT (ms)
Finger lift	159	—
Single-ball grasp	195	95
Double-ball strike	208	465

(Adapted from Henry and Rogers 1960.)

What is going on in the Henry and Rogers experiment? The obvious conclusion is that RT increased as the *complexity* of the movement to be made increased. But what was actually involved in making the movement more "complex"? The careful reader will notice a number of factors that came into play in this regard. Relative to the finger-lift task, the double-ball-strike task involved additional movement parts, increased accuracy demands, and longer movement durations (and perhaps other factors). Research conducted since this pioneering experiment suggests that all of these factors may have played a role in producing the results seen in the Henry and Rogers experiment.

Number of Movement Parts and Reaction Time. Results similar to the Henry and Rogers (1960) data have been found in a number of replications of their study and implicate the addition of movement parts as the primary reason for the increase in RT (e.g., Christina, 1992; Fischman, 1984). Corroborating evidence can also be seen in experiments using different tasks. For example, Sternberg et al. (1978) observed that the latency in speaking the first word of a sequence increased by about 10 ms for each word that was added to the sequence (i.e., response strings of 1, 2, 3, 4, or 5 words), and by 5 to 15 ms for additional letters to be typed (see also Canic & Franks, 1989).

Movement Accuracy Effects on Reaction Time. At the same time as Henry and Rogers (but quite separate from them), Paul Fitts (see chapter 1) was investigating movement complexity effects as well, using aiming tasks that varied in target distance and accuracy demands. Although Fitts's primary concern related to the ongoing movement (as revealed by MT; see chapter 7), he also found that RT increased slightly as task difficulty increased (Fitts & Peterson, 1964). Findings that RT increases as the target size is decreased (making accuracy demands more difficult) have since been reported in a number of experiments by Sidaway and his colleagues (e.g., Sidaway, Sekiya, & Fairweather, 1995).

Movement-Duration Effects on Reaction Time. In addition to complexity and accuracy demands, the movements studied by Henry and Rogers (1960) varied in at least one other important respect, their *duration*. From Henry and Rogers's data (table 3.2), notice that the more

complex movement required much more time to produce (465 ms) than the simpler one (95 ms). This observation has led various scientists to conjecture that the duration of the movement to be produced might be a major variable in the response-programming stage.

Klapp and Erwin (1976) asked subjects to make 10-cm movements of a slide along a trackway, with goal MTs of 150, 300, 600, or 1,200 ms. The number of actions and accuracy demands of the movement were held constant, but the duration of the response was varied. As the response duration increased, the RT to initiate the response increased as well (see figure 3.9), especially when the response durations were below 600 ms. Similar effects were reported by Rosenbaum and Patashnik (1980), who varied response duration measured by the time that a button had to be depressed, and by Quinn et al. (1980), who varied the MT for aiming responses of a stylus to a target (see Klapp, 1996, for a review).

Response Complexity and Motor Programming

The effect of movement complexity on RT is remarkably robust, and it occurs both when the person knows the movement in advance (simple RT) and when the movement is indicated by the stimulus (choice RT) (see Klapp, 1995, 1996). Regardless of the variations in method and movements, the effect of movement complexity on RT has been interpreted as relating to the time neces-

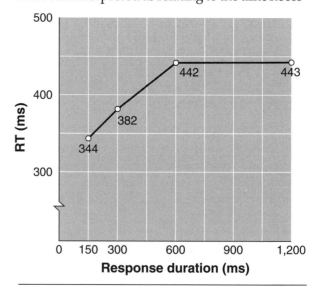

Figure 3.9. RT as a function of the duration of the response.
Reprinted from Klapp and Erwin, 1976.

sary to prepare the movement during the response-programming stage of RT. Despite nearly 40 years of research on this topic, the ideas of Henry and Rogers about the process of movement organization during the motor programming stage remain remarkably valid today.

Memory

So far, our focus has been on what happens to information as it enters the system and is processed, eventually leading to a response. Information must be retained (some would use the word *stored*) for future use, much as information is stored in a computer. The systems that presumably hold the information for future processing are collectively called *memory.*

Memory is one of the most controversial and highly debated topics of information processing (e.g., see articles in the January 1991 issue of the *American Psychologist*). Researchers tend to conceptualize ideas and experimental methods according to particular theoretical *frameworks,* and these vary greatly among psychologists. We will briefly present one of these frameworks. However, the interested reader should consult the many books on this topic for more complete discussions (e.g., Anderson, 1995; Roediger & Craik, 1989).

Memory is a consequence of information processing. When previously processed information influences current information processing, then we assume that memory is the reason. Indeed, when viewed this way, it is obvious that everything we do is influenced by memory. The current state of our skills and knowledge reflects previous information processing. Thus, there seems to be no doubt that memories exist. Rather, the debate among psychologists concerns (1) *how* memory affects the performance of our daily activities and (2) what form or *nature* best describes these memories.

Direct Versus Indirect Influences of Memory

Many researchers believe that memory influences our daily activities in two rather distinct and separate ways. Memory has a *direct* influence when there is a deliberate attempt to recollect past experiences for the purpose of facilitating current information processing (e.g., Richardson-

Klavehn & Bjork, 1988). For example, when saying hello to someone on the street, people usually try to address the person by name. However, one of life's awkward moments occurs when you cannot recall the name. In this case, there is a failure to directly recall a specific memory as a purposeful and explicit means to solve a problem (addressing the person by name). Terms such as memory *search* and *retrieval* of information describe conscious attempts to use memory in a direct way.

Memory can also have an *indirect* effect on information processing. For example, in typing a letter to a friend one may attempt to recall certain things to write about; however, the actual production of the letters on the computer screen involves coordinated actions of the two hands. In this case, the memory for past experience in typing is having an indirect impact on the ability to carry out this activity. You do not need to specifically recollect when you last typed, or even when you learned to type, in order for the memory of the skill to influence your performance. The memory of the skill is incidental to using it—one does not have to be conscious that memory is being used in order for it to influence performance. Motor skill can be described mainly in terms of an indirect memory influence.

Since this book is about the learning and control of motor skills, our interest in memory is in how it impacts current information processing indirectly. Ironically, however, much of what is known about memory comes from experiments in which subjects were asked to recall or recognize information in a direct manner. In the remainder of this chapter, then, we will describe a rather traditional distinction that psychologists have made between various memory systems, customarily labeled *short-term sensory store (STSS)*, *short-term memory (STM)*, and *long-term memory (LTM)*. In the last chapter of the book ("Retention and Transfer"), we focus on the indirect influences that memory for motor skill has on our daily activities.

Short-Term Sensory Store

The most peripheral memory influence is thought to involve a process that serves to hold massive amounts of information for a brief period of time. When information is presented to the system, the short-term sensory store accepts it without much recoding and then loses it rather quickly as new information is added. Just as the redness of a burner on an electric stove fades when the burner is turned off, the information in the short-term sensory store is thought to fade or *decay* with the passage of time. Such a system can be proposed for each of the stimulus modalities—vision, touch, audition, kinesthesis, and so on.

Some of the earliest and strongest evidence about short-term sensory store comes from the work of Sperling (1960). Sperling presented a matrix of three rows of four letters each on a tachistoscope, a device for presenting visual information very briefly and under controlled conditions. The matrix was presented for 50 ms so that the subjective impression was a bright flash of the letters. In addition, one of three tones was presented, indicating which row of four letters the subject was to recall. The tone could be presented 100 ms before the letter matrix was flashed on, simultaneously with the letter matrix, or 150, 300, or 1,000 ms after the matrix appeared.

In figure 3.10, the number of letters recalled is plotted as a function of the temporal location of the tone. When the tone was presented before the letters, the recall was about 3.3 letters (out of 4). When the tone was presented 150 ms after the letters, recall was only about 2.3 letters. When the tone was presented after a full second, recall was only about 1.5 letters.

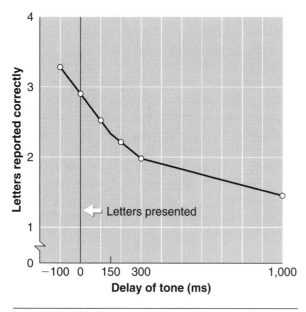

Figure 3.10. Number of items correctly recalled as a function of the delay of the tone indicating which row should be recalled.
Reprinted from Sperling, 1960.

The concept is that all of the letters are delivered by the flash to short-term sensory store, where they are stored briefly. However, the subject does not know which of the rows to attend to until the tone is presented. If the tone is presented immediately, the letters are still available and the subject recalls them. But if the tone is delayed, the letters in short-term sensory store have begun to fade and the subject cannot report as many of them. This evidence suggests that (a) the short-term sensory store was capable of holding all the information presented to it (because the subject could report any of the letters in the row if the tone was presented immediately) and that (b) the short-term sensory store loses information very rapidly with time.

On the basis of later experiments, the information in short-term sensory store is thought to have a maximum duration of about 1 s, with a more practical limit of about 250 ms. Also, it involves rather *literal* storage of information, in that the stimulus is recorded in the same way it came into the system in terms of both spatial location and form; this is analogous perhaps to how film records images that enter the lens of the camera (see table 3.3).

Short-Term Memory

Short-term memory is thought to be a storage system for information delivered either from short-term sensory store or from long-term memory. It has a limited capacity and a relatively short duration, and it is thought of as a kind of "workspace" for processing (Atkinson & Shiffrin, 1971).

Peterson and Peterson (1959) and Brown (1958) provided evidence for this kind of system that was to have a strong influence on research in memory for the next two decades. Basically, Peterson and Peterson provided subjects with a single *trigram* (three unrelated letters), then removed the letters, and had the subjects count backward by threes from a three-digit number until recall of the trigram was requested from 0 to 18 s later. The backward counting was intended to prevent the subject from rehearsing the trigram during the retention interval. Thus, all the subject had to do was remember the trigram while counting backward for up to 18 s.

Peterson and Peterson's results are shown in figure 3.11, where the probability of successfully

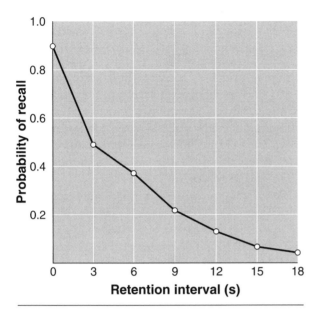

Figure 3.11. Probability of correct recall of a single trigram as a function of the retention interval. Reprinted from Peterson and Peterson, 1959.

recalling the trigram is graphed as a function of the length of the retention interval. When the recall was nearly immediate, the probability of recall was about .90; but when the retention interval was increased only by a few seconds, there was a marked decrease in the recall. This persisted until, at 18 s, almost no trigrams could be recalled. The evidence suggests the existence of a memory system that loses information rapidly (in about 30 to 60 s) unless the information is *rehearsed* in some way.

A major difference between short-term memory and short-term sensory store (table 3.3) relates to capacity. Previously we mentioned that the capacity of short-term sensory store was very large, essentially limitless. However, on the basis of experiments in which subjects have been asked to remember as many members of a list of items as they can, evidence suggests that short-term memory has a capacity of only about 7 (plus or

minus 2) items (Miller, 1956). This conclusion, however, depends on the definition of an "item." Sometimes subjects group separate items into larger collections, so that each collection may contain 5 "items" of its own; this process has been termed *chunking* (Miller, 1956). The idea is that if there are 88 letters to remember (e.g., the letters in the first sentence in this paragraph), it would be difficult to remember them without rehearsing them. But by chunking the letters into larger, more meaningful groups (words or sentences), one can recall the items more easily. In this sense, the capacity of short-term memory is thought to be seven chunks. Ericsson, Chase, and Faloon (1980) showed that after 175 days of practice with a technique for chunking effectively, a subject was able to increase the capacity of short-term memory from 7 to 79 items! Nonetheless, there were probably only about seven chunks or groups of items held in storage at any one time.

Another distinction between short-term memory and short-term sensory store (table 3.3) is in the nature of the coding processes. In short-term memory, coding is considered abstract. For example, stimuli are given names, and the separate stimuli are often combined in various ways to produce chunks that can reduce the number of separate items in short-term memory. Although many theories of short-term memory do not directly say so, the implication is that short-term memory is related to consciousness; those things in short-term memory are essentially things of which we are consciously aware.

In a motor analogue of verbal short-term memory, Adams and Dijkstra (1966; Posner & Konick, 1966) asked blindfolded subjects to move a slide along a trackway until it struck a fixed stop that defined a criterion position. Then the subject moved back to the starting position to wait for the remainder of the retention interval (from 10 to 120

Table 3.3   Characteristics of the Three Memory Systems

Attribute	Memory system		
	STSS	STM	LTM
Storage duration	Less than 1 s	1 s to 60 s	Seemingly limitless
Type of coding	Very literal	More abstract	Very abstract
Capacity	Seemingly limitless	7 ± 2 items	Seemingly limitless

s), after which the subject attempted to move the slide to the criterion position with the stop removed. The absolute error in recalling the position increased sharply as the retention interval increased from 10 to 60 s and changed very little thereafter (figure 3.12). These findings closely paralleled the early findings of Brown (1958) and Peterson and Peterson (1959) in that nearly all the forgetting of the position occurred within the first 60 s, which is interpreted as the approximate upper limit for retention in short-term verbal memory. More about short-term motor memory studies is presented in chapter 14.

Long-Term Memory

When items are practiced (or rehearsed), which of course requires information-processing activities, they are in some way transferred from short-term storage to long-term storage, where they can be held more permanently and protected from loss. An example is learning a new phone number. The first time you hear it, you are likely to forget it quickly if you do not rehearse it. Repeated practice results in the number's being transferred to more permanent storage. In some cases, this storage is indeed permanent—can you remember what your home phone number was when you were a child?

Long-term memory, of course, provides the capability for making movements that have been

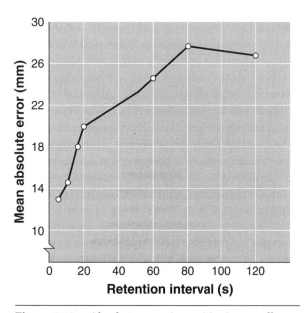

Figure 3.12. Absolute error in positioning recall as a function of the retention-interval length.
Reprinted from Adams and Dijkstra, 1966.

practiced before. Some of the variables that appear to determine retention of well-learned acts will be discussed in chapter 14. For now we can say that practice leads to the development of better and stronger long-term memory for movement and that these memories are often present after many years. Riding a bicycle is the most often cited example, as people appear to be able to ride acceptably well after 40 years or more with no intervening practice.

Another major distinction between long- and short-term memory relates to the amount of information that can be held (table 3.3). Most argue that short-term memory has a functional capacity of about seven chunks, whereas long-term memory must have a very large capacity indeed. In the motor realm, the analogue of well-learned facts and principles is well-learned movements, and the functional capacity of long-term motor memory must also be very large if it is capable of retaining all of the movements that humans typically perform on demand.

Summary

A great deal about the way we move can be understood by considering the human as an information-processing system that takes in information from the environment, processes it, and then outputs information to the environment in the form of movements. Using the concepts of subtractive logic initiated by Donders (1868/1969), *stages of processing* can be defined through the use of RT methods. The first stage, called *stimulus identification*, concerns the reception of a stimulus, preliminary preconscious analyses of features, and extraction of patterns from the stimulus array. Variables like stimulus clarity and stimulus intensity affect the duration of processing in this stage. A second stage, called *response selection*, concerns the translation or decision mechanisms that lead to the choice of response. The duration of this stage is sensitive to variables such as the number of S-R alternatives and S-R compatibility (the extent to which the stimulus and response are "naturally" linked). The final stage, called *response programming*, is associated with changing the abstract idea of a response into muscular action. The duration of this stage is related to variables affecting the response, such as response complexity and response duration.

Parallel to the ideas about stages of processing are concepts about information storage systems, or memory. Motor skills use memory in an indirect way, although much of what we know about memory involves directed remembering. In a common framework, memory can be thought of as consisting of three memory compartments: a *short-term sensory store*, capable of storing a large amount of literally coded information for perhaps a second; a *short-term memory*, capable of storing only about seven (plus or minus two) abstractly coded items for perhaps 30 s; and a *long-term memory* capable of storing very large amounts of abstractly coded information for long periods of time.

ATTENTION AND PERFORMANCE

Attention has always been a topic of major interest to psychologists and motor behavior researchers alike. Over 100 years ago William James (1890), one of the earliest and most renowned experimental psychologists, wrote:

> Everyone knows what attention is. It is the taking possession by the mind, in clear and vivid form, of one out of what seem several simultaneously possible objects or trains of thought. Focalization, concentration, of consciousness are of its essence. It implies withdrawal from some things in order to deal effectively with others. (403–404)

Types of Attention

But *does* everyone know what attention is? As Norman (1976) and Moray (1970) have pointed out, many different definitions of attention exist, and people use the term in a variety of ways. Inherent in James's statement, however, are a number of features of the phenomenon that are considered important.

One of these is the notion that attention is *limited:* we can attend to only one thing at a time, or think only one thought at a time. In terms of motor behavior, we seem strongly limited in the number of things we can do at a given time, as if some "capacity" would be exceeded if too much activity were attempted. Another important feature is that attention is selective: we can concentrate on one thing or on something else. These various concepts that have been used to describe attention are briefly reviewed in the next sections.

Attention and Consciousness

Early in the history of research on human performance, as implied by James's (1890) statement, attention was linked to the notion of consciousness, which is defined roughly as "what we are aware of at any given time." However, the term "conscious," and in particular the concept of *unconscious behavior,* fell out of favor during the growth of behaviorism after the turn of the 20th century. The measurement of consciousness was troublesome because at that time the only way to understand what was "in" subjects' consciousness was to ask them to introspect, or "search their own minds," and this was far too subjective

for the behaviorists' approach to accumulating data and theorizing.

In recent years, however, the concept of consciousness has seen a resurgence in popularity among psychologists and neuroscientists (Cohen & Schooler, 1997; Posner & Peterson, 1990). Methods of cortical measurement (see chapter 2) have allowed scientists to observe patterns of brain activity, revealing much more objective types of information than had previously been available through methods of introspection (Chalmers, 1995). Consciousness has also been linked to the concept of *controlled versus automatic* processing (discussed later in this chapter). Performance on direct versus indirect memory tests (Roediger & McDermott, 1993), and the use of process-dissociation measures (Jacoby, Yonelinas, & Jennings, 1997), suggest an independence between conscious and unconscious influences on behavior. For example, automatic (unconscious) processing appears to be preserved well in older adults whereas controlled (conscious) processing is quite susceptible to decline with aging. Performance errors such as *action slips* (Norman, 1981) are explained as situations in which an unconscious or automatic action has not been successfully inhibited or counteracted by conscious, controlled processing (Hay & Jacoby, 1996; Reason, 1990; Reason & Mycielska, 1982).

Attention as Effort or Arousal

Another way to operationalize the notion of attention is based on the idea that when people perform attention-demanding tasks such as balancing a checkbook or diving in competitive swimming, they are expending mental *effort* that is revealed in various physiological measures. For example, Kahneman (1973) and Beatty (Beatty & Wagoner, 1978) have used pupil diameter, measured by special techniques that do not interfere with eye movement, as an indirect measure of attention. When the subjects are asked to perform various memory tasks, pupil diameter increases when the subject is under pressure to provide an answer, with the increase being larger for more difficult tasks. Similarly, it is useful to consider attention as reflected by various physiological measures of arousal, a dimension indicating the extent to which the subject is activated or excited. Kahneman (1973) used physiological measures of skin resistance (a weak current passed between two electrodes on the skin decreases with increased arousal) and heart rate as indirect measures of the attention demand of various tasks.

Attention as a Capacity or Resource

A more recent concept suggests that attention involves a *limitation* in the *capacity* (or resources) available to handle information from the environment. If activity A requires attention, then some (or perhaps all) of this "pool" of limited capacity must be allocated to its performance or control. Because the amount of this capacity is thought to be limited, some other activity B that requires this capacity will interfere with A. Interference could be demonstrated in many ways: (a) B could suffer in performance speed or quality while A was relatively unaffected; (b) B could be unaffected while A suffered; (c) both A and B could suffer together; or (d) B could be prevented from occurring altogether while A was in progress. These patterns of interference could presumably tell us something about the nature of the limitations in capacity.

Interference as a Measure of Attention

Thus, there has been a shift from the position that attention is related to consciousness to the idea that attention is some kind of limited capacity for processing information. Furthermore, the operational definitions have changed so that attention is defined in terms of the interference between two tasks performed simultaneously. If two tasks can be performed as well simultaneously as individually, then at least one of them does not require attention, or a portion of the limited capacity; we would say that at least one of them was automatic and did not require attention. On the other hand, if one task is performed less well when it is combined with some secondary task, then both tasks are thought to require some of the limited capacity. In this instance, both tasks are *attention demanding*. Also, over time, this interference criterion became the critical test of whether or not a certain task "required attention." Although this test for attention has achieved popularity in recent times, it is not really new; before the turn of the century, Welch (1898) examined the decrement in maximum gripping force to determine whether or not other simultaneous tasks (reading and calculations) required attention.

Structural Interference and Capacity Interference

But tasks can interfere with each other for a variety of reasons, only some of which would be interpretable as interference due to limitations in some central capacity (attention). To confront this problem, researchers have defined two kinds of interference. *Structural interference* results when two physical (or perhaps neurological) structures are the source of the decrement. For example, the hand can be in only one place at a time, and interference between handwriting and dialing a telephone with the same hand would be due, at least in part, to this kind of limitation, and not necessarily due to a limitation in some central capacity. Also, the eyes can be focused at only one signal source at a time, and thus two simultaneous visual signals presented in widely different locations could suffer in processing speed because of this structural limitation. On the other hand, when one can reasonably rule out the possibility that structural interference between two tasks is occurring, then a *capacity interference*—or a decrement in performance due to some limitation in central capacity (i.e., attention)—is inferred. For example, there is some evidence that both kinds of interference may be involved when someone uses a cellular telephone while driving. A handheld telephone appears to produce more interference than a hands-free telephone during activities such as dialing (Briem & Hedman, 1995), suggesting a structural interference effect. However, the two types of telephones increase the likelihood of an automobile accident by about the same amount when conversations have been ongoing (Redelmeier & Tibshirani, 1997), supporting a capacity-interference interpretation.

Selective Attention

Very closely related to the limited-capacity view is the concept that we can *allocate* attention to different inputs or tasks. Selective attention can be either *intentional* or *involuntary*, depending on how a specific allocation has been achieved (Eimer et al., 1996). Intentional selection occurs when we voluntarily choose to attend to one source of information (e.g., listening to the radio) while excluding or inhibiting attention to other sources (e.g., the television or someone talking to us). An involuntary selection usually occurs as a response to an external stimulus—for example, when you suddenly pay attention to a loud or pertinent sound (e.g., the sound of two cars colliding). Selective attention is readily observed in the dual-task situations already described. Directing attention toward activity A may reveal deficits in the performance of task B, although no performance deficit is observed for A. However, by shifting the attention to activity B, you may observe that activity A is now the one that suffers and that performance of B is very good.

Theories of Attention

If attention is defined as, or measured by, the degree of interference between two tasks, the focus turns to which kinds of tasks do and do not interfere with each other, and under which conditions these patterns of interference could be expected to occur. More importantly, most of the everyday tasks we perform can be thought of as collections of processes involving stimulus input and encoding, response selection and choice, and motor programming and movement control. The fact that two complex tasks interfere with each other (or do not) might not be very meaningful by itself, because it would not be clear what the cause of the interference was or where in the information-processing activities the interference occurred (Jonides, Naveh-Benjamin, & Palmer, 1985). Did both tasks require action selection activities at the same time, or did both require movement programming at the same time? As a result, simpler laboratory tasks are used in this research so that the various processing stages can be more easily identified and studied. The following theories of attention attempt to explain the patterns of interference found in the various tasks, using various hypothetical structures and processes.

Single-Channel, Filter Theories

The early theories of attention (e.g., Broadbent, 1958; Deutsch & Deutsch, 1963; Keele, 1973; Norman, 1969; Treisman, 1969; Welford, 1952; see also B. Kerr, 1973), while different in detail, had some important features in common. They all assumed that attention was a *fixed* capacity for processing information and that performance would deteriorate if this capacity was approached or exceeded by the task requirements. These were single-channel theories of *undifferentiated capac-*

ity, in that attention was thought of as a single resource that could be directed at any one of a number of processing operations. The theories differed, though, in terms of the kinds of information processing that required attention. Welford's theory assumed that all the processes required attention; in other words, the human could be regarded as a single information channel that could be occupied by one and only one stimulus-response operation at a time (see figure 4.1, line 1). Of course, if only one operation can be done at a time, then any task attempted at the same time as another will be blocked, representing a rather severe source of interference. For this reason, processing in the single channel is defined as attention demanding, on the basis of the interference criterion described earlier.

Weaker versions of the single-channel theory, denying that all the stages of processing required attention, moved the location of the single channel to later in the sequence of processing. Thus, these other theories (Broadbent, 1958; Deutsch & Deutsch, 1963; Keele, 1973; B. Kerr, 1973; Norman, 1969; Treisman, 1969) presumed that early stages of processing were done without attention but that attention was required at the later stage(s) of processing. Processing without attention implies *parallel processing*, such that a number of separate signals can be processed simultaneously without interfering with each other. For example, processes that translate sound waves into neurological impulses in the ear, and those that change mechanical stimuli into neurological activity in the movement receptors in the limbs, can occur together, presumably without interference. In other words, these theories assumed that peripheral information processing occurs simultaneously and without interference, but they differed with respect to the stages in which the interference occurs.

Broadbent (1958) and Deutsch and Deutsch (1963) theorized that a kind of *filter* is located somewhere along the series of stages of information processing (see figure 4.1, lines 2 and 3). According to these theories, many stimuli can be processed in parallel and do not require attention prior to reaching the filter. When the filter is reached, however, only one stimulus at a time is processed through it (the others being "filtered out"), so that the information processing from then on is sequential, requiring attention in the single channel. Which of the stimuli are filtered

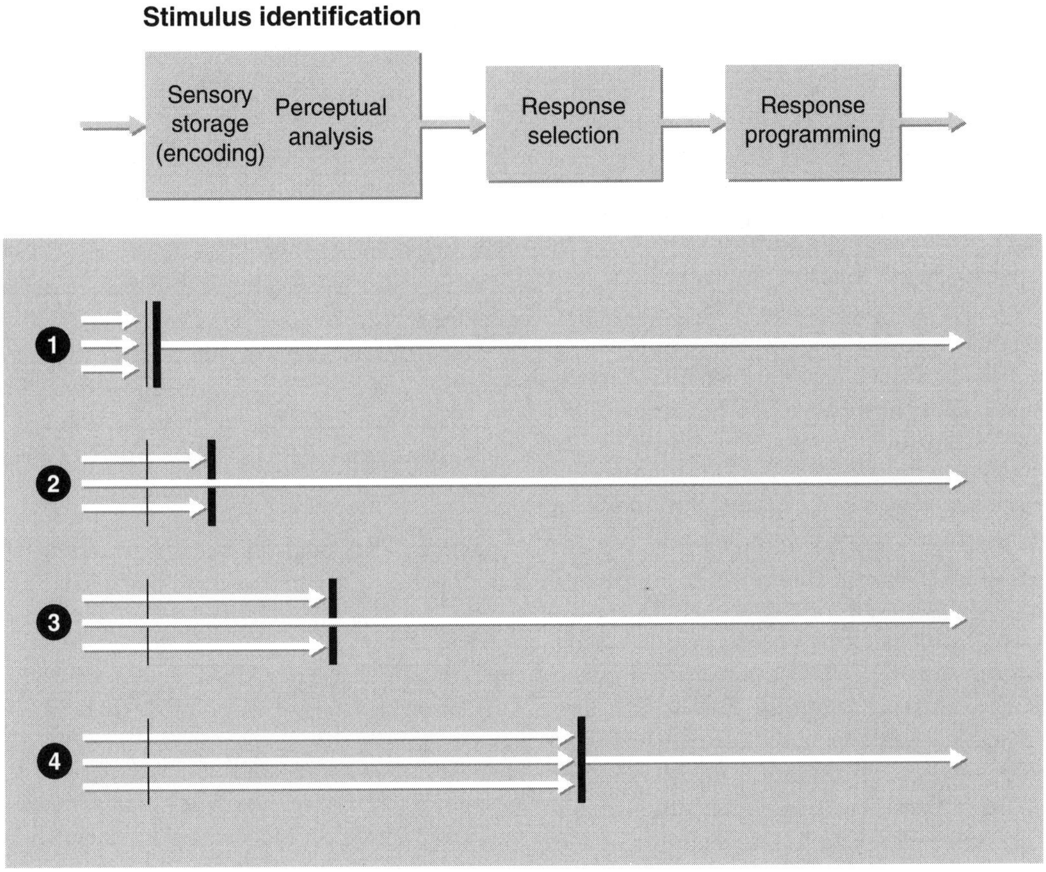

Stimulus identification

Figure 4.1.   Utilization of attention in various stages of processing, according to various theories. (Line 1 represents the original single-channel theory, [Welford 1952]; line 2 represents Broadbent's [1958] filter theory; line 3 represents the Deutsch and Deutsch [1963] and Norman [1969] theories; and line 4 represents Keele's [1973] theory.)

out and which one is processed further into the single channel presumably depend on which activity the subject is engaged in, which stimuli are expected, and which are relevant to the task in question.

Figure 4.1 shows the locations of the proposed filter for these two theories. The sensory storage stage is considered the most "peripheral," involving the translation of the physical stimuli into neurological codes. The perceptual analysis stage involves the process that abstracts some preliminary, simple meaning from the stimuli (e.g., perception of right angles, of verticality). (Notice that the stages labeled *sensory storage* and *perceptual analysis* can be readily combined to yield the stimulus-identification stage discussed in chapter 3.) Broadbent viewed perceptual analysis and later stages as requiring attention, while Deutsch and Deutsch, Treisman, and Norman saw perceptual analysis as being automatic (i.e., not requiring attention), with later stages requiring attention. Thus, these theories are similar, but

they differ with respect to where the proposed filter is located in the chain of processes.

Keele's (1973) theory of attention places the bottleneck even later in the sequence of stages than the Deutsch-Deutsch theory. According to Keele's concept, information processing is parallel and attention-free through the stimulus-identification and response-selection stages. At this point, *memory contact* is made, in which certain associates of the stimuli are activated, such as items in related categories, items closely associated with the stimulus, or even certain aspects of early preparation for a movement that is to be triggered by the stimulus. In this view, because all such stimuli contact memory at about the same time, selective attention must determine which of these memory contacts are to receive further processing. These subsequent operations, such as memory searches, rehearsal, recoding, or readying a movement for production, are attention demanding, according to Keele. If two such processes are required at the same time, decrements in performance will occur. Thus, in figure 4.1, Keele's view is represented as line 4, indicating that processing can be in parallel and without interference through response selection, with subsequent operations requiring attention.

Flexible Allocation of Capacity

In contrast to filter theories, an argument presented by Kahneman (1973) was that the capacity for attention can change as the task requirements change. For example, as the difficulty of two simultaneous tasks increases, more capacity becomes available and more of it is used in processing. Eventually, when task requirements for processing two streams of information begin to exceed maximum capacity, decrements occur in one or more of the simultaneously presented tasks; that is, interference occurs. Kahneman's theory also differed from the earlier views by suggesting that parallel processing could occur in all of the processing stages, but with some demand on attention at the same time. Kahneman's view that the amount of allocated attention is not fixed creates a number of difficulties for certain secondary-task techniques for measuring spare capacity (see chapter 2), which assume that capacity is fixed.

More recent theories of attention have focused on issues of flexibility in information processing. For example, rather than assuming that processes requiring attention can deal with only one stimulus at a time, more recent theories suggest that these resources can be shared by parallel processing. How they are shared is presumably a function of the relative importance of the tasks, their relative difficulty, and other factors. Trade-offs between proficiency in two simultaneous tasks have been discussed by Norman and Bobrow (1975), Posner and Snyder (1975), and Navon and Gopher (1979).

Multiple-Resource Theories

Some researchers have argued that attention should not be conceptualized as a single resource, but rather as *multiple pools* of resources, each with its own capacity and each designed to handle certain kinds of information processes. In this view, resources for selecting the finger to make a movement and resources for selecting the movement of the jaw to say a word are separate. Hence, these two operations could coincide without in-

terference (e.g., McLeod, 1977; Navon & Gopher, 1979; Wickens, 1976, 1980, 1992).

Similarly, Shaffer (1971) and Allport, Antonis, and Reynolds (1972) argued that attention can be devoted to separate stages of processing at the same time. Such a position is inconsistent with fixed-capacity theories, in which the processing was thought to be confined to a single stage of processing although one or more separate operations might be able to be performed in parallel. These views help to explain skill in complex tasks such as typing and sight-reading of music, for which attention is thought to be devoted to input (sight-reading) and output (finger movements) stages at the same time.

Action-Selection Views of Attention

In all of the viewpoints about attention that have been described, the basic assumption has been that information-processing activities require some kind of capacity (or "fuel") in order to occur. Decrements in performance result when various activities compete for this capacity. Recently, however, researchers interested in attention have begun to question the validity of this fundamental assumption. Scientists such as Neumann (1987, 1996; see also Allport, 1987, 1993) have criticized the various resource theories and presented a view that is considerably different.

Neumann argues that when an animal or human has a certain momentary intention to obtain some goal (e.g., to run, to drink), many stimuli received at this time are processed in parallel in the early stages—the final product of this processing being the selection of a certain action. Then, *as a result* of this selection, certain processes are *prevented* from occurring, or can occur only with great difficulty. Thus in Neumann's view, interference between two simultaneous tasks occurs not because attention (as a resource) is needed in order to perform various processes; rather, it occurs *because* an action has already been selected, and these other processes are completely or partially blocked. Thus, *selection* is the most basic and fundamental process of attention, not resources or capacity.

This theory has an interesting ecological aspect, in that if a particular action is important (and is selected), then it would seem critical that other possible actions be prevented, at least for a while until the original action has run its course. The selected action requires certain subprocesses or structures for its completion, and preventing some other action from using them would ensure that the selected action would, in fact, have a good chance of being completed and of having its goal fulfilled. As we will see in the next sections, this theory is consistent with the general finding that very little interference occurs in processes related to stimulus processing, with most of the interference between tasks occurring in stages related to the planning or production of movements.

Attention and Patterns of Interference Among Tasks

It is certainly beyond the scope of this text to do a thorough analysis of the extensive literature documenting the patterns of intertask interference. For our purposes, however, some generalizations about the nature of these patterns, as well as about the situations in which the most and least interference seems to be produced, will enable us to have a reasonable insight into the nature of attention at least as it relates to the selection and control of movement.

Sensory Information Processing

In this section, we examine the nature of sensory information processing, with particular focus on the extent to which information processing of a number of signals can occur in parallel and without interference. Understanding these capabilities for parallel processing helps us understand the role of attention in these early stages of processing.

The Stroop Effect

A very interesting and powerful effect that helps us understand the processing of sensory information is the so-called *Stroop effect,* named after the psychologist who first identified the phenomenon (Stroop, 1935). Since this classic article appeared, more than 700 articles on the effect have been published (MacLeod, 1991). For example, Keele (1972) had subjects respond to the ink colors red, yellow, green, and blue by pressing the appropriate one of four keys as quickly as possible after the color was presented (a four-alternative, choice-reaction time [RT] task). In one condition of the experiment, various irrelevant symbols such as ± or √‾ were printed in the color to which the response was to be made. In

another condition, the colors were printed as letters that spelled the name of a color; however, that name was different from the color of the ink in which the word was printed. For example, the word "RED" was written in green ink, and the subject was to respond with the "green" button, ignoring the fact that the word spelled was "RED." Even though in both conditions the color of the ink was the relevant stimulus, the latter condition produced slower RTs than did the first condition in which the color-irrelevant forms were used. This finding, that the meaning of the word interferes with the naming of the color in which the word appears, represents the basic Stroop effect (many variations exist; see MacLeod, 1991).

Why should an irrelevant dimension of the display (the words) interfere with the RT to the color of the ink? Why cannot the subject simply focus on the color of the ink and ignore the word that the letters spell? The most plausible interpretation is that the color of the ink and the word itself represent two simultaneously presented stimuli. Both are processed together during stimulus identification, and both arouse some meaning (i.e., they contact memory) about the nature of the stimulus and the response to be produced. Because these two stimulus events require different responses (e.g., pressing the "green" button in response to the color, versus pressing the "red" button in response to the meaning of the word), Keele argues that the source of interference is in response competition and that it arises during a stage in which the movement itself is chosen or organized. But the fact that both stimuli (the color and the word) achieved *memory contact* approximately together implies that the processing of the two patterns in stages prior to response selection must have been simultaneous. This line of evidence suggests that the processing in stimulus identification occurs in parallel and without attention.

The Cocktail Party Problem

Another important method for addressing questions about sensory information processing is called the *dichotic listening paradigm.* In a typical dichotic listening experiment, the individual is presented (via headphones) with a different message in each ear. Usually the subject's problem is to ignore one of the messages and to concentrate on (and later report about) the other. Much has been learned about the kinds of information that can or cannot be ignored. A message that cannot be ignored (while another message is attended to) implies that the to-be-ignored message is being processed through the stimulus-identification stage whether the individual tries to ignore it or not, perhaps without attention being required for that processing.

The dichotic listening paradigm is a formal way to study the "cocktail party problem" described by Cherry (1953). At large, noisy parties, attending to one conversation while ignoring the many other conversations is often quite difficult. But, with intention, the various potentially "interfering" conversations can be tuned out. Situations occur, however, in which information in these unattended messages cannot be ignored, such as when your name is spoken.

The findings from the dichotic listening paradigm led to the suggestion that all of the auditory stimuli are processed through stimulus identification in parallel and without attention, and that some mechanism operates to prevent attention from being drawn to unwanted sources of sound. The mechanism, called *selective attention* by some, is such that when the sound is relevant or pertinent to us (e.g., our name or the sound of a car's horn), the stimulus is allowed to "pass through" for additional processing and attention. It is as if stimuli from the environment had entered the system simultaneously and had been processed to some superficial levels of analysis, with only those relevant (or pertinent) to the individual being processed further. Of course, this further processing will usually require attention (but see the next section), implying that two such activities cannot be done together without interference. Like the evidence from the Stroop effect, the evidence from these observations argues against the early-selection models of attention presented in figure 4.1.

Automatic and Controlled Processing

Whereas a number of "early" processes (stimulus encoding, feature detection, and so on) can apparently be conducted in parallel and without attention, it is clear that other processes prior to choosing an action cannot. For example, if you are asked to detect whether the name of your home town has a *t* in it, various mental operations are required in order for you to come to the answer, and common experience tells you that performing them would be detrimental to a number of other tasks that might be called for at the same time (e.g., remembering your friend's phone

number). This kind of processing is what Schneider and Shiffrin (1977) have called *controlled processing*. This kind of processing is (a) slow; (b) attention demanding, in that other similar tasks interfere with it; (c) serial in nature; and (d) strongly "volitional," in that it can be easily stopped or avoided altogether. But Schneider and his colleagues (Schneider, Dumais, & Shiffrin, 1984; Schneider & Fisk, 1983; Schneider & Shiffrin, 1977) have also argued for another class of information processing: *automatic processing*. This form of information processing is qualitatively different from controlled processing; it is (a) fast; (b) not attention demanding, in that other operations do not interfere with it; (c) parallel in nature, with various operations occurring together; and (d) not "volitional," in that processing is often unavoidable (Underwood & Everatt, 1996).

Schneider and his colleagues have studied these processes using a variety of "memory search" tasks. In one example, Schneider and Shiffrin (1977, experiment 2) gave subjects two types of comparison stimuli. First, subjects were presented with a memory set, which consisted of one, two, or four target letters (e.g., *J D* represents a memory-set size of two). After the presentation of the memory set, they received a frame that could also be composed of one, two, or four letters (e.g., *B K M J* represents a frame size of four). If either of the two letters in the memory set was presented in the frame (as *J* is in this example), the subject was to respond by pressing a "yes" button as quickly as possible; if none of the letters from the memory set was in the frame, a "no" button was to be pressed. Subjects practiced under one of two conditions. In *varied-mapping* conditions, on some blocks of trials a given letter in the frame would be a target, and on other blocks of trials it would not be a target. Thus, seeing a *J* in the frame, for example, would in one block of trials lead to a "yes" response and in another block lead to a "no." On the other hand, with *consistent-mapping* conditions, a given letter in the frame was either always a target or never a target, leading to a consistent response when it was detected (i.e., either "yes" or "no," but never mixed responses in different blocks of trials).

Figure 4.2 shows results for the "yes" responses from these conditions after considerable practice for a memory-set size of four. The varied-mapping condition (open circles) shows a strong effect of the frame size, with RT increasing

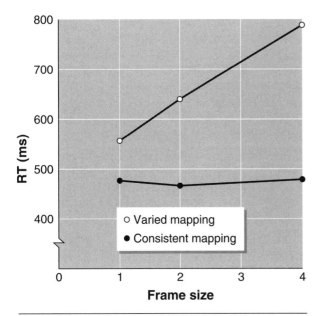

Figure 4.2.   RT to detect target letters in a letter matrix of one, two, or four letters (frame size) for varied- and consistent-mapping conditions; more letters to be searched led to no increase in RT for the consistent-mapping condition, suggesting automatic processing.
Reprinted from Schneider and Shiffrin, 1977.

approximately 77 ms/item in the frame. On the other hand, this effect was virtually absent in the consistent-mapping condition. Both early in practice and later in practice for the varied-mapping conditions, search of the frame for a target letter seemed to be slow, serial, and strongly influenced by the number of items to be searched; this kind of processing typifies controlled processing. But after much practice with consistent-mapping conditions, the processing was much faster, appeared to be done in parallel, and was not affected by the number of items to be searched; this is typical of automatic processing. In other experiments using very similar tasks, Schneider and Fisk (1983) reported that after considerable practice with consistent-mapping conditions, subjects could do these detections simultaneously with other secondary tasks without interference. However, sometimes these detections became unavoidable, as if they were triggered off without much control. One subject told of interference with her usual schoolwork after being in the experiment; an *E* (a target letter in the experiment) would unavoidably "jump out" of the page and distract her.

For various reasons, however, the concept of automaticity is not perfectly clear. One problem is that if a process is to be truly automatic, then *any* other simultaneous task should be possible without interference. Neumann (1987), in a review of this topic, argues that no information-processing activity has been shown to be interference free across all secondary tasks. Whether or not interference is seen—as well as the amount of interference—seems to depend on the nature of, or the relationship between, the two tasks (McLeod, 1977; Schmidt, 1987). Second, the findings of Schneider and colleagues of no effect of "resource costs" (i.e., frame size in figure 4.2) sometimes show a small positive slope for the consistent-mapping conditions, which suggests that they are not completely interference free. Recent thinking suggests that automaticity may better be thought of as a *continuum* (MacLeod & Dunbar, 1988; Underwood & Everatt, 1996). Certain information-processing activities are attention free with respect to *certain kinds* of secondary tasks, and the problem is then to define which kinds of tasks will and will not interfere with what other kinds of tasks (Neumann, 1987). Various theoretical models have been developed that expand this view of automatic processing as a continuum, such as from memory-retrieval (Logan, 1988) and parallel distributed processing perspectives (Cohen, Dunbar, & McClelland, 1990).

The study of automatic processing, and of the ways in which it is developed with practice, has strong implications for understanding control in skills. Many processes in skills, such as the detection of individual letters or words as you read this sentence, or the recognition of patterns of activity in a game, can with extensive practice become faster and more efficient. Such gains in skilled situations are of course extremely important, in that information-processing loads are reduced so that the performer can concentrate on other aspects of the situation (e.g., the meaning of a poem, strategy of a game), processing is much faster, and many processes can be done in parallel. On the other hand, such automatic processing can occur only with some cost, which is often seen when attention is drawn to the wrong place (distraction) or when an inappropriate movement is triggered (e.g., you respond to your opponent's "fake" in tennis).

Interference and Response Production

Whereas the general findings are that many "early" stages of information processing can be done in parallel and without much interference from other stimulus tasks, the situation appears to be distinctly different with respect to the organization and initiation of movements. Research studies from various sources point independently to the view that only one movement can be initiated at a time. We turn next to these various lines of evidence for single-channel processing during these "late" stages of information processing.

Psychological Refractory Period

Probably the most important evidence on this issue emerges from the *double-stimulation paradigm,* in which the subject must respond to two closely spaced stimuli each of which requires a different response. An example of this paradigm is illustrated in figure 4.3. The subject is presented with a sound (Stimulus 1, or S_1) that calls for a response by the right hand (Response 1, or R_1). Somewhat later, a light is presented (S_2) that requires a response by the left hand (R_2). The two stimuli are presented in different modalities and require responses by different hands (to minimize structural interference). The stimuli are usually separated by at least 50 ms, and they may be separated by as long as 500 ms; that is, the second stimulus could, in some situations, come well after the response to the first stimulus. The separation between the onsets of the two stimuli is called the *stimulus onset asynchrony (SOA).* Further, the arrival of the signals is usually random, so that the subject cannot predict the occurrence of a given stimulus (either S_1 or S_2) on a given trial. Thus, both stimuli must enter the information-processing system and be processed separately.

Experimenters have been interested in the RT to the second of the two stimuli (RT_2) because it provides an indication about how the processing of the second stimulus has been affected by the processing of the first. The critical comparison is between RT_2 when preceded by S_1 versus RT_2 when S_1 is not presented at all; that is, the "control RT_2" is a measure of RT_2 when the subject does not have S_1 presented at all. Using this method, experimenters have shown repeatedly that the response to the second of two closely spaced stimuli is considerably longer than RT_2 in the control condition. Apparently S_1 and R_1 cause a great deal of interference with the processing of S_2 and R_2. This important phenomenon was discovered by Telford (1931), who named it the *psychological refractory period (PRP).*[1] The findings from Davis (1959), presented in figure 4.4, are typical. In this example, S_2 followed S_1 by an SOA of 50 ms. The control RT_2 (RT for S_2 in separate trials in which S_1 was not presented) was 124 ms. However, when S_2 followed S_1, the RT_2 was 258 ms—about twice as long as the control RT_2. Thus, the presence of S_1 and R_1 caused a marked increase in RT_2. In other studies, the amount of increase in S_2 caused by S_1 and its processing can be 300 ms or more (Creamer, 1963; Karlin & Kestenbaum, 1968), making the RT for the second stimulus around 500 ms!

Another important result in studies of refractoriness is the effect of the length of the SOA on R_2. Figure 4.5, also containing data from the Davis (1959) study, plots the values of RT_2 for various values of the SOA, which ranged from 50 ms to 500 ms. Notice that because the RT_1 was about 160 ms in this data set, all the SOAs greater than or equal to 200 ms occurred when the second stimulus was presented after the subject had responded to the first (see also figure 4.4). In figure 4.5, we see that as the SOA was increased from 50 ms to 300 ms, RT_2 progressively shortened, until there was no delay at all (relative to the control RT_2 shown

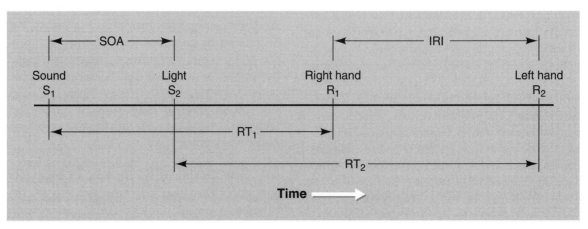

Figure 4.3. The double-stimulation paradigm (SOA = stimulus onset asynchrony, IRI = interresponse interval).

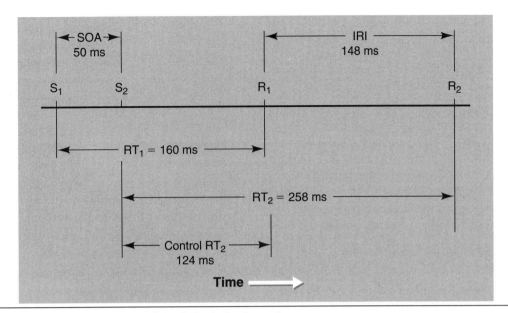

Figure 4.4.   An early demonstration of psychological refractoriness.
Adapted from Davis, 1959.

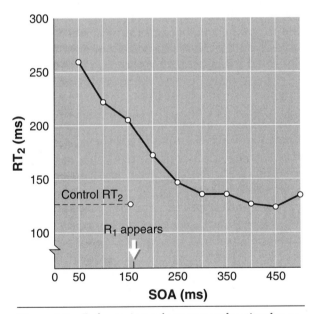

Figure 4.5.   Refractoriness decreases as the stimulus onset asynchrony (SOA) increases.
Adapted from Davis, 1959.

in the figure) with longer SOAs. The most important points from figure 4.5 are that (a) the delay in RT_2 decreased as the SOA increased and (b) there was considerable delay even though R_1 had already been produced (i.e., at SOAs of 200 ms or more).

One major exception to this generalization about the effect of the SOA should be mentioned. If the second signal follows the first one very quickly, with an SOA as short as, say, 10 ms, then the two signals are apparently dealt with as a single, more complex event. This is called a *grouping* effect. The two signals elicit the two responses at about the same time but with a slightly greater RT for both than if only one of the responses had been made to a single stimulus (see Welford, 1968).

The Single-Channel Hypothesis

A major contribution to the understanding of human information processing in motor tasks was made in 1952 when Welford proposed the *single-channel hypothesis* to account for the well-known findings about psychological refractoriness (see figure 4.1). In the original version of the theory, Welford hypothesized that if S_1 entered the single channel and was being processed, then processing of S_2 had to be delayed until the single channel was cleared. This was a strict serial-processing model, because S_1 and S_2 would not be processed together.

How does this theory "work" to explain psychological refractoriness such as that seen in figures 4.4 and 4.5? Referring back to figure 4.4, S_2 was presented 50 ms after S_1, and RT_1 was 160 ms. Thus, there was $160 - 50 = 110$ ms of RT_1 remaining when S_2 was presented. According to the single-channel hypothesis, S_2 processing must be delayed until the channel is cleared, and thus the actual RT_2 will be the control RT_2 plus the 110-ms delay. Note from the data that the control RT_2 was 124 ms, which makes the estimate of RT_2 in the double-stimulation situation $124 + 110 = 234$ ms.

If you look up the obtained value of RT_2 (258 ms) given in figure 4.5, you will see that the estimate (234 ms) is fairly close. Thus, the duration of RT_2 was thought to be the control RT_2 plus the amount that RT_2 overlapped with RT_1 or

$$RT_2 = \text{Control } RT_2 + (RT_1 - SOA) \quad (4.1)$$

It can be seen in figure 4.4 and equation 4.1 that as the size of the SOA increases, there is less overlap between the two RTs, and the predicted value of RT_2 decreases. This accounts for the finding that the RT_2 decreases as the SOA increases, as shown in figure 4.5 and in other research (Welford, 1968).

Evidence Against the Single-Channel Hypothesis

While the original single-channel hypothesis accounts for some of the data, a considerable amount of evidence has suggested that the theory is not correct in its details. According to the single-channel hypothesis, RT_2 lengthened as a direct function of the amount of overlap between RT_1 and RT_2, as can be seen in equation 4.1. The first concern was that even when there was no overlap between RT_1 and RT_2 (that is, when S_2 occurred after the subject had produced a response to S_1), there was still some delay in RT_2. Look at figure 4.5. When the SOA was 200 ms, so that S_2 occurred 40 ms after R_1, there was still some delay in RT_2 (about 50 ms) that did not disappear completely until the SOA had been lengthened to 300 ms. How can there be refractoriness, according to the single-channel view, when the RT_1 and RT_2 do not overlap at all?

Welford (1968) suggested that after R_1 is produced, the subject directs attention to the movement, perhaps concentrating on the feedback from R_1 to confirm that the movement was in fact produced correctly before processing S_2. Thus, according to Welford's view, attention was required after the response, which delayed RT_2, as did the attention produced during the response.

But this explanation could not solve other problems. In the double-stimulation paradigm, as the SOA decreases, say, from 150 to 50 ms (in figure 4.4), the overlap between the two stimuli increases by exactly 100 ms; now, the single-channel model assumes that the delay in RT_2 is a direct function of this overlap, so the model predicts that RT_2 should be increased by exactly 100 ms in this example. Generally, the increase in RT_2 in these situations has been much smaller than

expected on the basis of the model (Davis, 1959; Kahneman, 1973; see Keele, 1986, for a review). These effects are probably attributable to the fact that some processing of S_2 was being completed while S_1 and its response were being processed, which is strictly contrary to the single-channel hypothesis.

Moderating Variables in Psychological Refractoriness

Various factors act to change, or modify, the effects just seen in double-stimulation situations. Some of these variables are practice, stimulus or response complexity, and stimulus-response (S-R) compatibility (see also Pashler, 1993, 1994).

Effects of Practice. Practice has marked effects on the exact nature of the delay in RT_2 in this paradigm. Gottsdanker and Stelmach (1971) used 87 sessions of practice, 25 min each, in the double-stimulation paradigm for a single subject. They found that the amount of delay in RT_2 was steadily diminished from about 75 ms to 25 ms over this period. But the delay was never quite eliminated, suggesting that refractoriness might have a "real" structural basis in the information-processing system.

Complexity of Stimulus 1. Karlin and Kestenbaum (1968) found that the delay in RT_2 was strongly affected by the number of choices involved in RT_1. For an SOA of 90 ms, when S_1 was a simple RT (one stimulus, one response), the amount of delay in RT_2 was approximately 100 ms. However, when the first response was a two-choice RT, the delay was approximately doubled, so that RT_2 was over 500 ms. A five-choice S_1 produced an even larger delay, increasing RT_2 to about 630 ms (Keele, 1986). Because increasing the complexity of S_1 affects its processing time according to Hick's law (chapter 3), the magnitude of the delay in RT_2 apparently depends on the duration of processing for S_1.

Stimulus-Response Compatibility. An important moderating variable is S-R compatibility, or the relationship between the stimuli and responses to be made (see chapter 3). Greenwald and Schulman (1973) varied the compatibility of the first response (S_1-R_1). In a compatible condition, S_1 was an arrow pointing to the left or right, and R_1 was a hand movement in the indicated direction. In a less compatible (or less "direct") condition, S_1 was the visually presented word "left" or "right," and R$_1$ was again the manual response in the indicated direction. Thus, reading the word "left" or "right" required transformations from the stimulus to the response that were less "natural" than seeing the arrows (see chapter 3). In both conditions, S$_2$-R$_2$ was the same; S$_2$ was the number 1 or 2 presented auditorily, and R$_2$ was the vocal response "one" or "two." Figure 4.6 gives the results; C refers to the control RT$_2$ with no S$_1$ or R$_1$ required. When S$_1$-R$_1$ was not directly compatible (open circles), RT$_2$ was lengthened considerably and refractoriness increased as the SOA decreased, as we have seen before (figure 4.5). But when S$_1$-R$_1$ was compatible (closed circles), there was no lengthening of RT$_2$ at any of the SOAs. If the compatibility among the stimuli and responses is very high, the usually devastating effects on the first signal and its response can be reduced or even completely eliminated.

Implications of Refractoriness for Practical Situations

We have seen that the second of two closely spaced reactions can suffer considerably in processing speed, and this fact can have important practical implications. For example, in many games, players "fake" an opponent by displaying the initial parts of one response (e.g., a slight movement to the right) followed quickly by another response (e.g., a movement to the left) that is actually carried to completion. If an opponent

attempting to follow this player responds to the first move, a full RT (about 150–200 ms) will be required, plus the added delay caused by refractoriness, to *begin* to respond to the second move. Thus, RT to the second move could be as long as 500 ms (see Creamer, 1963; Karlin & Kestenbaum, 1968), which is a very long time in fast ball games such as basketball, hockey, lacrosse, and soccer. But this is not the only problem. If the player has "taken the fake," then he or she not only will suffer a delay in the RT to the "real" movement, but also must overcome the momentum that the first movement has produced—plus make up any distance that may have been traveled in the wrong direction (see also figure 4.16).

An apparent principle of faking is that the actual move should follow the fake by sufficient time that the second move is treated separately rather than being grouped with the first one. Thus, the SOA should probably be around 50 ms or longer. Also, the second move must not follow the fake by so long an interval that the refractory effects of the first response have dissipated—probably not more than 250 ms (see figure 4.5). It would be interesting to study the most effective fakes in sport to discover whether the most effective SOAs correspond with estimates from experimentation. It is possible that such intervals are a part of natural actions in other species. Watch a rabbit being chased by a dog. The rabbit runs with unpredictable directional changes,

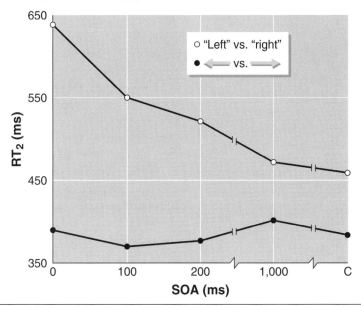

Figure 4.6. RT to the second of two closely spaced stimuli at various stimulus onset asynchronies (SOAs) as a function of the S-R compatibility of the first reaction; the compatible arrow stimuli produced no refractoriness for the second reaction. Reprinted from Greenwald and Schulman, 1973.

probably using intervals between directional changes that are highly effective in confusing the dog. Refractoriness might be an important survival mechanism in animals other than humans.

Separation Between Responses

Evidence about refractoriness suggests that the perceptual-motor system has difficulty responding to closely spaced stimuli, and that responses must therefore be separated considerably in time. How closely in time can two responses be produced, provided that they are not grouped and produced simultaneously? Kahneman (1973) examined this separation—called the *interresponse interval (IRI)* in figure 4.3—as it is affected by bringing the stimuli closer to each other in time. In figure 4.7, we have plotted some of the data from Smith's (1969) study, as Kahneman (1973) did. Stimulus onset asychronies were 50, 150, 300, and 500 ms, and the separations between responses that resulted from these intervals are plotted.

As the SOA decreased (moving leftward on the graph), the interval between the two responses decreased, but only to a certain point. It appears that no matter how small the interval between stimuli, provided they are not grouped and emitted simultaneously, approximately 200 ms occurs between responses. This is a most important result.

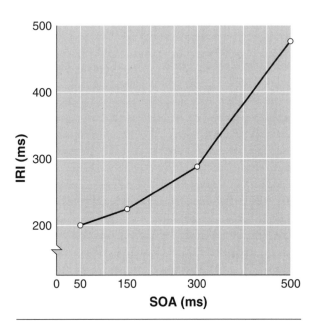

Figure 4.7. The relation between the interresponse interval (IRI) and the stimulus onset asynchrony (SOA). (Data from M.C. Smith 1969; adapted from Kahneman 1973).

This finding suggests that if a signal "gets into" the information-processing stages up to a certain point, a response to it is generated. If another stimulus is presented soon afterward, indicating that the system should do some *other* action, the second action must wait for at least 200 ms before it can be initiated. To explain this phenomenon, some writers (see Welford, 1968) have suggested the idea of a "gate" that "slams" 50 ms after S_1 to prevent a second signal from entering the information-processing mechanisms and interfering with the response to the first signal. If a second signal comes before this point, the first and second signals are processed together as a unit, and the two responses are grouped.

Skilled piano players can produce many movements of the fingers in which the separation between movements is far less than 200 ms. How do they do this? We will discuss this issue in detail in chapter 6, but for now we can say that the system can prepare a "response" to a given stimulus that in itself is complex and involves many movements in rapid succession. The "response" that is planned by the response-programming stage is still one response, but it has many parts that are not called up separately. This can be thought of as *output chunking*, whereby many sub-elements are collected into a single unit, called a *motor program* (Keele, 1973; Schmidt, 1976a). Also, according to this general view, these programmed outputs occur in discrete "bursts" separated by at least 200 ms. These discrete elements are difficult to view directly, however, because the muscles and limbs smooth out the transitions between elements, giving the impression that we respond continuously.

It is fortunate that S_2 cannot get into the system to disrupt the preparation of a response to S_1. When preparing a response to a dangerous stimulus, subjects will be successful only if they can process the information and produce the movement without interference from other conflicting signals. Consequently, rather than seeing refractoriness only as a "problem" to be overcome by the motor system in producing rapid-fire actions, we can also view refractoriness as protective. It tends to ensure that responses to important stimuli are appropriate and complete. This is consistent with Neumann's (1987, 1996) view of attention as discussed earlier, according to which interference can be the result of an action's having been selected.

Finally, a single channel does seem to exist, contrary to the conclusion drawn earlier in the section about the single-channel hypothesis. But the single channel does not appear to apply to all stages of processing as the 1952 version of the theory stated. Rather, it appears that parallel processing can occur during the early stages of information processing and that a single channel is properly placed during the stages in which decisions occur about the response to be made. Pashler (1993, 1994) has presented persuasive evidence suggesting that the response-selection stage (which, for Pashler, includes response programming) represents the bottleneck where single-channel processing occurs. According to the model in figure 4.8, the processing regarding what response to make and how the response is to be made can be done for only one stimulus at a time. Further processing of the second of two closely spaced stimuli is put on hold until the response selection and programming for the first stimulus are complete. This version of the single-channel hypothesis appears to have considerable support.

Attention and Interference During Movement

To this point, we have examined only the processes present during the RT, which, of course, take place prior to movement. But one can conceptualize a "stage" of processing, following response programming, in which the individual carries out the movement and keeps it under control. Strictly speaking, it is not a stage in the

sense of the other three stages, as it does not occur during RT. Nevertheless, it is important to consider the attentional characteristics of these processes.

In thinking about our own skilled movements, we are perhaps left with the impression that skills require conscious awareness for their performance. We must be careful with these analyses, though, because we cannot be sure whether it is the movement itself that requires awareness or the programming and initiation of future movements (e.g., in a dive, when to "open up" to enter the water). We are in a weak position for determining the extent to which movements themselves require consciousness when we use only the methods of introspection.

On the other hand, sometimes it seems that a particular movement is performed automatically, especially when it is a part of a well-learned sequence (e.g., a part of a dance routine). People that routinely drive a car with a standard transmission sometimes find, when driving an automatic transmission car, that they attempt to depress the "clutch" at a stop sign even though the car has no clutch pedal. Only after having made this movement do you typically realize that you have produced it. Have you ever found, in buttoning your shirt and daydreaming sleepily about the upcoming day's activities, that the buttoning activities continue even though a particular button might be missing? These examples, plus others that you can think of, suggest that not all movements require attention for their performance, while some seem to require considerable attention.

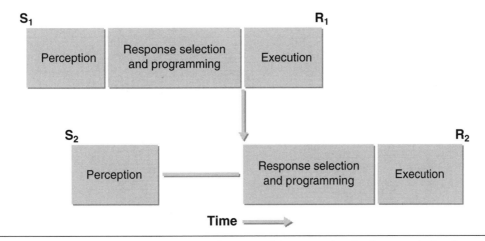

Figure 4.8.   Pashler's bottleneck theory. Response selection and programming for the second stimulus must wait until the selection and programming of the first response is complete.
Adapted from Pashler, 1993.

When a movement requires a great deal of attention, what parts of the movement are involved? As we mentioned earlier, attention could be devoted to the response-programming stage for future elements in a long sequence. Attention also could be devoted to other aspects of the environment. In driving, for example, the movements themselves are carried out with minimal attention; instead, attention is directed to traffic patterns. Another possibility is that we pay attention to our movements to control them, to carry out any necessary corrections. We will consider some of these questions in the following sections.

Secondary-Task Interference

An early tool for evaluating the role of attention in simple movements involved *secondary* tasks, as discussed in chapter 2. The subject performed a *primary* task for which the attention demand was of interest. But the subject was also occasionally presented with another task. These secondary tasks have been of two types. *Continuous* secondary tasks are those that are performed during the duration of the performance of the primary task. Examples include tasks that impose limited motor demands and emphasize cognitive processing (such as repeatedly subtracting 3s from a three-digit number or counting the times the letter *e* is presented during a message through headphones), or tasks that involve considerably more motor skill (for reviews see Abernethy, 1988; Ogden, Levine, & Eisner, 1979). When both the primary and secondary tasks include motor skills, the subject is required to coordinate the performance of each. This entails a very special

type of processing that has attracted a tremendous amount of research interest in recent years. We describe research on *coordination* in chapter 8.

The other type of secondary task used in attention research is the discrete secondary task. A stimulus, called a probe, is presented at various times or places in the performance of the primary task, and a quick response to the probe is made with an effector not involved in the main task. The probes are often auditory, and the response may be either manual or oral. This method has often been called the "probe technique."

The Probe Technique

This secondary-task method assumes a fixed attentional capacity, as illustrated in figure 4.9. If the capacity required for the primary task is low, as in the diagram on the left, then the capacity remaining for processing the probe stimulus will be relatively large, and the probe RT will be fast and accurate. If the primary task is very demanding, as illustrated on the right side of figure 4.9, then little of the spare capacity will remain for the probe stimulus; its processing will be slow. Thus, in the earlier work of this kind, it was assumed that the duration of the probe RT could give an indication of the attention requirements of the main task.

In an early study by Posner and Keele (1969), subjects made 700-ms wrist-twist movements of a handle through 150°, attempting to move a pointer to either a large or a small target area. The experimenters presented probe signals at various points throughout the movement—at the start or at 15°, 45°, 75°, 105°, or 135° of handle movement. The probe RTs are plotted as a function of their

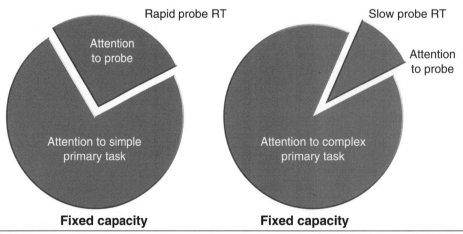

Figure 4.9. Assumptions of the probe-RT task: with fixed total capacity, attention to the probe decreases as the complexity of the primary task increases.
Reprinted from Posner and Keele, 1969.

location within the movement in figure 4.10. The horizontal line represents the no-movement control probe RT (i.e., RT in the absence of a primary task). First, the finding that the probe RTs were always larger than the corresponding values of the no-movement probe RT was taken as evidence that the movements generated interference. Next, probe RT showed a U-shaped function; there was a marked slowing of the probe RT at the beginning of the movement, with somewhat less slowing at the end. This finding suggests that interference from the movement is strongest at the beginning, that a relatively interference-free portion is near the middle, and that interference is produced near the end again, perhaps from control in positioning the pointer accurately in the target zone. This later suggestion is supported by the fact that the probe RT increased as the target size decreased, as if more precise positioning is somehow more interfering (see also Ells, 1973; Salmoni, Sullivan, & Starkes, 1976). Another of Posner and Keele's (1969) experiments used a blindfolded movement to a stop, in which essentially no target accuracy was required; the movement was analogous to pushing a door closed. In this example, increased probe RTs were found only at the beginning, as in figure 4.10; there was no increased probe RT at any later point in the movement, implying that the movement produced no interference once it was initiated.

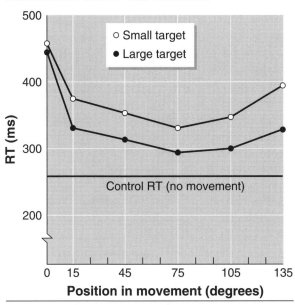

Figure 4.10.   Probe RT elicited at various points in movements to large and small targets.
Reprinted from Posner and Keele, 1969.

The probe technique has been used in a number of ways in attempts to assess the "attentional workload" involved in performing various jobs (Ogden, Levine, & Eisner, 1979) and in sport activities such as catching a ball (Populin, Rose, & Heath, 1990; Starkes, 1987), shooting a pistol (Rose & Christina, 1990), and receiving tennis and volleyball serves (Castiello & Umiltà, 1988). Although these studies have revealed a number of interesting findings, they need to be interpreted cautiously, as suggested in the next section.

Problems With the Probe Method

There are a number of problems with the probe-RT paradigm and in interpretation of the results of these experiments. First, the method assumes a fixed, unitary capacity, which is, of course, contrary to Kahneman's (1973) views and contrary to the idea of pools of resources discussed earlier. Second, McLeod (1977, 1980) has identified a number of other difficulties. One of these was shown in his finding that a probe RT with a manual response was interfered with by a simultaneous tracking task, whereas a probe RT with a vocal response was hardly influenced (see also Greenwald & Schulman, 1973; figure 4.6). If the probe RT actually measures some general, "spare," undifferentiated capacity (attention), why was more of this capacity available when the only change was in the nature of the movement to be made in response to the probe? Such evidence makes it doubtful that any such undifferentiated, spare capacity exists.

We now believe that changes in probe RT indicate something about the particular pattern of interference between whatever processes are involved in the primary task and the processes involved in the *particular* probe task chosen. These experiments tell us that various movement tasks require many of the same processes that auditory-manual probe tasks do, *not* that some undifferentiated capacity is or is not used. Conversely, findings that the probe RT is not elevated by the primary task do not necessarily mean that the primary task is automatic; rather, they indicate that the particular processes needed in this probe-RT task are not also involved in *that* movement task. Of course, other probe-like tasks could probably be found that *would* interfere with the primary task (Neumann, 1987); if so, this would force us to conclude that the primary task is not automatic after all.

What has usually been meant by the statement that some task can be performed "automatically" is that it can be performed without interference from other mental tasks involving (conscious) information-processing activities. This fits with our subjective experiences about "automatic" movements that are done without consciousness. But, as has been said previously (Neumann, 1987; Schmidt, 1987), it is probably best to think of automaticity *with respect to* some other simultaneous secondary task(s). Thus, a given task might be automatic with respect to doing a probe-RT task, but might not be automatic with respect to reading aloud.

Interference Among Hand Movements

Consider next a situation in which the subject plans two movements in advance and tries to execute them simultaneously. You are probably well aware of the difficulty in rubbing your stomach with one hand while patting your head with the other (or vice versa). Of course, doing either of these tasks by itself is easy for most of us; but when we attempt them together, the two hands are particularly difficult to control, and a great deal of mental effort seems to be required. In another example (Klapp et al., 1985), it is particularly difficult to tap a regular rhythm with your left (nonpreferred) hand while tapping as quickly as you can with your right (preferred) hand. Such effects are not limited to these clever little demonstrations. In many piano performances, the two hands must perform with different rhythms for a short while, and most pianists claim that this is one of the most difficult aspects in these pieces. *Rubato* involves the gradual speeding or slowing of one hand with respect to the other, also considered to be a very advanced technique in piano playing (Peters, 1985b).

In these examples, the two tasks are internally generated and are usually not "driven" by any obvious environmental signal. It would thus seem that not all of the interference we observe among tasks has to do with the processing of environmental stimuli leading to a response. Rather, an additional source of interference might have to do with the control of the limbs per se. Although it is tempting to attribute an attentional "overload" explanation to these and related effects, the issue is much more complex. In fact, we devote an entire chapter to the problems of

simultaneously coordinating the actions of two or more effectors later in the book (chapter 8).

Action-Centered Interference

A different approach to the examination of interference effects during movement has been introduced by Tipper, Lortie, and Baylis (1992). This experimental approach relates to the everyday problems of interference that one encounters when reaching for an object in a cluttered environment, for example reaching for a paper on a desk that has other papers scattered on it, or reaching for a particular piece of fruit in a basket of fruit (Castiello, 1996). The questions of interest relate to how interference effects are produced by the potentially distracting objects in the environment.

The task for subjects in the Tipper, Lortie, and Baylis (1992) studies was to respond to the illumination of a light by pushing one of the buttons located on a table directly in front of them. As illustrated in figure 4.11, the buttons were arranged in three rows of three buttons each, and near every button were two lights—a red light indicated that its button should be pushed, and a yellow light indicated a distractor (nontarget) button that was to be ignored. When no distractor lights were illuminated at the same time that a target light appeared, response time was very fast. However, on some trials, a yellow light was illuminated at the same time that a target light appeared. The critical issue addressed by Tipper, Lortie, and Baylis was whether the distractors would affect response time to reach the target button, and if so, which distractors would have the largest effects.

Two sets of results are presented in figure 4.11. On the left are the findings for a layout in which the hand was moving away from the front of the table (the "start position") to contact a target in the middle row (one of the filled boxes). In this condition as compared to a no-distractor (ND), control condition, only the distractors in the *front row* (FR) interfered with response time. When distractors appeared in the back row (BR), the response time was almost the same as in the no-distractor, control condition. In a powerful experimental manipulation, Tipper, Lortie, and Baylis were able to reverse this pattern of findings by having movements start at the back of the table and move toward the subject (arrangement at upper right of figure 4.11). In this configuration as compared to no-distractor conditions, targets in

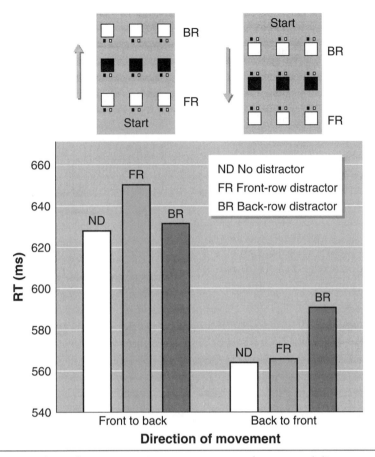

Figure 4.11.   Action-centered interference in various arrangements of targets and distractors. Adapted from Tipper, Lortie, and Baylis, 1992.

the middle row were now unaffected by distractors in the front row, but were severely interfered with by distractors in the back row. In both spatial arrangements, interference was large when the distractor was located *between* the start and end points of the movement, but not when it was located "beyond" the target.

These and related findings (e.g., Howard & Tipper, 1997; Meegan & Tipper, in press; Pratt & Abrams, 1994) have been interpreted to suggest that attention and interference during movement are highly dependent on the nature of the action. The "amount" of interference produced by a particular distractor changes as a function of its relation to the intentions of the movement at any given time. This view suggests a rather radical departure from interference effects during movement as implied by various capacity views of attention. Rather, the findings support Neumann's (1996) view that the nature of the selected action drives attention and determines which potential factors will or will not cause interference.

Anticipation

So far in this chapter, we have discussed the difficulties performers have in responding to generally unanticipated stimulus information. The processing speed, as measured by RT, tends to be slow, indicating that humans have severe limitations in information processing. The problem with this line of thinking, though, is that RT is usually studied in highly unrealistic situations. One important component of these situations is that the subject is seldom allowed to *anticipate* environmental information. In fact, experimenters go to elaborate lengths to prevent the subjects from anticipating. "Catch trials," in which the stimulus is sometimes withheld, are often used; choice-RT tasks are often employed, preventing the subject from knowing *what* stimulus is going to occur; or foreperiods are randomized so that the subject cannot predict *when* the stimulus will arrive. Clearly, under these conditions, humans find information processing very difficult indeed.

But in just about every "real" skill, suddenly presented and unexpected stimuli are the exception rather than the rule. Of course, unexpected events do sometimes occur—and sometimes we even try to make them occur (e.g., faking in sports); but most of the stimuli to which we respond in most of our daily activities are very predictable. During walking or driving, the stimuli emerge from a generally stable environment that allows us to preview upcoming events with plenty of time to do something about them. And when a signal does arrive, it is often not a discrete event, but rather a pattern of sensory information that unfolds before us. Gibson (1966) has emphasized that visual information is really an *optical flow* of signals, from which the performer detects important future environmental events (see chapter 5 for a discussion of this idea).

Poulton (1957) has described three apparently different kinds of anticipation. One obvious type is *receptor anticipation,* in which the performer detects the upcoming events with various sensory receptors. However, the performer must also estimate how long his or her *own* movement will take, and must allow for this interval in initiating the actions (e.g., batting in baseball) so that some critical aspect of the movement occurs at the proper time; this is *effector anticipation,* because the effector's duration must be predicted. Finally, Poulton describes *perceptual anticipation;* here the environmental events are not viewed directly, but they are still predictable because the performer has had a great deal of practice with them. In the next sections, we consider important principles of performers' capability to anticipate.

Spatial, or Event, Anticipation

One way in which performers can anticipate future activities is by knowing what kinds of stimuli are going to be presented and what kinds of responses will be required. This class of anticipation is called *spatial,* or *event,* anticipation. In an experimental study of these processes, Leonard (1953, 1954) and Jeeves (1961) used an apparatus that had trackways arranged as spokes of a wheel. Subjects were asked to move repeatedly from the center position to the ends of the spokes and back again as quickly as possible. If the next spoke was indicated only after the subject had arrived at the center position, subjects could not anticipate which movement to make next, and performance

was slow, jerky, and labored. But if subjects were informed about the next trackway when they were at the outside of the previous one, they could plan the next movement in advance while they were moving toward the center. Overall, performance was smoother, less jerky and labored, and of course more rapid. Analogous effects were found by Leonard (1953), whose subjects used advance information to effectively reduce a six-choice RT task to a three-choice task, with associated gains in speed as would be expected from reducing the number of S-R alternatives (Hick's law, chapter 3). Many other experiments lead to a similar conclusion (Schmidt, 1968).

Some experimenters have sought to determine what kinds of information about the upcoming *movement* can be used in advance and how much time can be "saved" by using it. Using the *precuing technique,* Rosenbaum (1980, 1983), Goodman and Kelso (1980), Zelaznik and Hahn (1985), and others have examined tasks in which various aspects of the response could be specified in advance, leaving other aspects unspecified until the stimulus actually arrived; the stimulus then provides the remainder of the information to produce the action, as well as the "go" signal. For example, Rosenbaum (1980) used a task in which the movement was to be made (a) with the right or left hand, (b) toward or away from the body, and (c) to a target that was near to or far from the starting position—an eight-choice RT task ($2 \times 2 \times 2 = 8$ alternatives). Rosenbaum found that providing advance information about any one of the three movement features (arm, direction, or extent) reduced the RT by about 100 to 150 ms. Apparently, when the subjects had this advance information they could engage in processing before the stimulus arrived, thus "saving" processing time during RT. There seemed to be a greater advantage in receiving information about which arm was to be used (150-ms reduction in RT relative to the no-precue condition) as compared to information about the extent of the movement (100-ms reduction), suggesting that the situation is somewhat more complex than simply reducing the number of alternatives from eight to four. Klapp's (1977b) work, using a different paradigm, makes a similar point.

One way to think of these effects is illustrated in figure 4.12. If the subject receives advance information about a certain feature of the movement, some of the processing operations normally done

No advance information

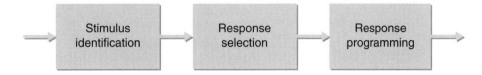

Advance information available

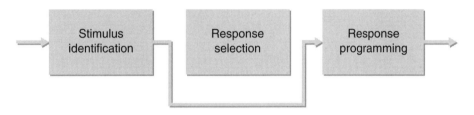

Figure 4.12. Bypassing the response-selection stage by processing information in advance.

during RT can be done in advance, and can be "bypassed" when the reaction stimulus finally arrives. If sufficient information is given so that all the aspects can be selected in advance (e.g., knowing arm, direction, and extent in Rosenbaum's situation), then one can think of "bypassing" the entire response-selection stage. The work of Rosenbaum and others suggests that portions of response programming can be done in advance as well. It is also interesting to note in Leonard's (1953, 1954) and Jeeves's (1961) studies that advance information allowing partial or complete selection of upcoming actions was presented while the subject was already moving to the center position. This result should not be particularly surprising, but it does show that one movement can be planned while another is being executed.

Temporal Anticipation

The evidence just reviewed on spatial anticipation suggests that the performer can, by knowing some specific information about the response to be produced, eliminate (bypass) or at least shorten some of the stages. This shortening of RT is rather modest, though, and the responder still has difficulty processing environmental stimuli quickly. The evidence presented in the next sections suggests that if the person can anticipate *when* the stimulus is going to arrive, rather large reductions in RT can be made. Under the proper circumstances, the performer can *eliminate* RT altogether!

Foreperiod Regularity

Imagine that the subject is in a simple-RT situation (one stimulus and one response) and that there is a warning signal followed by a foreperiod, the end of which is the stimulus onset. Foreperiods may be regular (e.g., always 3 s), or they may be variable and unpredictable (e.g., 2, 3, or 4 s in some random order). It seems obvious that a regular foreperiod will result in the shortest RTs. If the foreperiods are constant and very short (e.g., less than a few seconds), evidence shows that the subject can respond essentially *simultaneously* with the stimulus after some practice (provided that the subject knows which response to produce). Quesada and Schmidt (1970) showed that the average RT with a constant 2-s foreperiod was only 22 ms! It seems likely that the person anticipated the temporal onset of the stimulus and began the response processes before the stimulus came on so that the overt movement was made at about the same time as the stimulus. The rule seems to be that if the foreperiods are both regular *and* short, *and all* aspects of the response to be made are known in advance, then the subject can (with practice) perform the needed processes in advance and emit the response simultaneously with the stimulus. This has been termed *early responding* in the literature because the response is triggered before the stimulus actually arrives.

On the other hand, when the foreperiod is regular but very long (a few seconds or more), and various features of the response are known in advance, subjects apparently cannot shorten RTs to zero even with extensive practice. Under these conditions, Mowrer (1940) found RTs of about 230 ms. The RTs in these situations with long but regular foreperiods seem to be similar to those in which the foreperiod is short but irregular (thus preventing an early response). When the foreperiods are long (e.g., 12 s), early responding is prevented because the subject cannot anticipate the *exact* stimulus onset when it is so far in the future. This occurs because the internal "timing" of short durations is much less variable than for long durations. Attempts to anticipate the stimulus onset following a long foreperiod result in too many early responses (by a second or so), which is usually not tolerated by the experimenter. All the subject can do is engage in *preparation* and respond very quickly when the stimulus does arrive.

Foreperiod Duration

In simple-RT situations, there is a great deal of evidence that irregular foreperiods averaging about 1 s produce shorter RTs than do longer ones of 2, 3, or 4 s (e.g., Klemmer, 1956; Welford, 1968). This effect seems to be quite small, however, and it is overshadowed by a larger effect that is apparently related to when the subject expects the signal. In these latter situations, the fastest RT is not associated with the shortest foreperiod as would be expected from Klemmer's results, but rather with the most probable foreperiod or, if the foreperiods are all equally probable, with the center of the range of foreperiods (Aiken, 1964; Mowrer, 1940; Poulton, 1974). Mowrer (1940) had subjects respond to tones presented every 12 s, but he occasionally presented tones at greater or less than 12-s intervals. The data in figure 4.13 show that the shortest RTs were at the interval that was most expected (12 s), and that longer and especially shorter intervals resulted in slower RTs. It appears that as the end of the expected foreperiods draws near, the subject begins to prepare for the stimulus and response. Because maintaining a prepared state is effortful, this readiness begins to increase only when the first of the group of stimuli is expected, reaches a maximum at about the center, and declines toward the end. Presumably, the subject is most expectant for the signal when it is presented with an average foreperiod, and the RT is somewhat faster as a result.

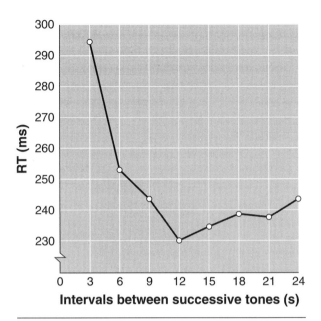

Figure 4.13. Minimum RT occurs at the most probable inter-stimulus interval.
Reprinted from Mowrer, 1940.

Aging Foreperiods

A notable exception to the findings on foreperiod duration is seen in experiments in which *no catch trials* are provided (i.e., trials in which the stimulus never arrives; e.g., Drazin 1961; Rothstein 1973; Salmoni, Sullivan, & Starkes 1976). Drazin's data are shown in figure 4.14, where the RT is plotted against the average foreperiod duration. Here there were variable foreperiods and no catch trials, and the RT decreased as the stimulus was presented later and later in the group of foreperiods.

At first, this result seems to be contradictory to the earlier conclusion that a stimulus presented at the center of the foreperiods elicits the most rapid RT (Aiken, 1964; Mowrer, 1940). The critical difference is that the studies by Drazin (1961), Rothstein (1973), and Salmoni, Sullivan, and Starkes (1976) did not employ catch trials. Without catch trials, the subject can become increasingly expectant for the stimulus as the foreperiod "ages" toward the last possible time of stimulus presentation.

Consider an example with four possible foreperiods (1, 2, 3, and 4 s) and no catch trials. Note that when only 0.5 s of the foreperiod has elapsed, the probability that the signal will appear at the 1-s point is one in four (.25). After the 1-s interval has passed without the signal being presented, the probability that the signal will arrive at 2 s has increased to one in three (.33), and

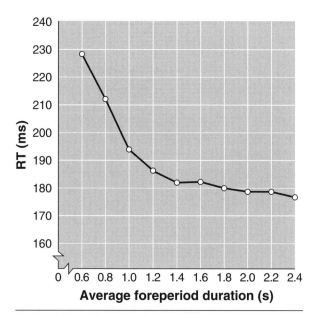

Figure 4.14. The aging foreperiod effect.
Reprinted from Drazin, 1961.

so on, until beyond the passage of 3 s the probability of the signal's arriving at 4 s increases to 1.0. Thus, the subject has a basis for becoming increasingly expectant as the foreperiod "ages."

Temporal and Spatial Anticipation: Implications

Essentially, anticipation is a *strategy* to reduce the time, or even the stages, of processing that would normally be involved in responding to an unanticipated stimulus. For this reason there are a number of situations in which attempts are made to either prevent or enhance anticipation. For example, the starter in a sprint race prevents early responding by using an unpredictable foreperiod, requiring the athletes to wait for the signal before initiating the response (see boxed text on page 84). On the other hand, the dance instructor or the drill leader in the military uses predictable foreperiods so that all the performers can respond simultaneously with the first count and with one another. Dance instructors use a count that has the first 1-2-3-4 presented without action, and the pupils know that the first action must begin with the "1" of the second 1-2-3-4. Drill leaders issue a command (e.g., "Column left") to provide the soldiers with event predictability and then at a very predictable time will give another command—"March!"—that is the stimulus to perform the action; a good unit will respond as a single person right on command.

These concepts are also seen in American football, in which the quarterback provides a set of signals for his teammates just before the ball is snapped. The basic idea is for the quarterback to enable his team to anticipate and begin moving before the opposition can do so. From the principles discussed in the previous sections, the signal count should be predictable (allowing temporal anticipation), with each team member (but not the opposition) knowing which signals are to be used. This allows temporal anticipation for one team, but forces the opposition to be delayed by at least one RT before responding. The signal caller should be careful to avoid the aging foreperiod effect, as an alert defense could predict the onset of the "go" signal with increasing certainty as the count "ages," since the rules do not allow for catch trials.

Benefits Versus "Costs" of Anticipating

The previous sections have described benefits to performers when they correctly anticipate temporally or spatially. However, in both the outside world and in motor behavior, the adage that you don't get something for nothing holds equally well, and there are necessarily "costs" of various kinds that result from anticipating.

What happens if we anticipate incorrectly, as happens when the batter anticipates a curve ball but receives a fastball, or the boxer expects a blow from his opponent's left hand but receives one from the right hand? LaBerge (1973) and Posner, Nissen, and Ogden (1978) used a method of estimating some of the costs of anticipating incorrectly, called the *cost-benefit analysis*.

In the method used by Posner, Nissen, and Ogden, the subject fixated on the center of a screen and received one of three precues. One second after the precue, a signal would come on at one of two locations on the screen (which could be seen without an eye movement), and the subject's task was to lift the finger from a key as rapidly as possible after stimulus onset. Only one response was ever required (lifting a single finger from a key) regardless of which stimulus came on. One of the precues was a plus sign, presented on one-third of the trials, indicating that either of the two signals could come on with equal probability (these were called *neutral-precue trials*). On the remaining two-thirds of the trials, however, the precue was an arrow pointing to the left or to

Foreperiods and False Starts in Sprinting

A rare event occurred in the 1996 Summer Olympic Games—a sprinter false started *twice* and was disqualified from the 100-m final. In the second of his fast starts, British sprinter Linford Christie appeared to explode out of the blocks with an excellent and legal start. A moment later the start was ruled invalid because Christie had apparently "jumped the gun." His RT, as indicated by the time from the starter's signal until the sudden rise in force of his foot against the blocks, was faster than the 100-ms minimum RT allowed by Olympic standards. Some arguments were raised at the time that such standards place too fine a constraint on what might otherwise be an exceptional performance. Was this a fair judgement? You make the call!

The starter's goal in the sprint is to have all the athletes reacting to the sound of the gun. For this reason the starter attempts to *prevent* anticipations by using variable foreperiods and by sometimes aborting a start when the foreperiod ages too long (a type of catch trial). What the starter observes in the sprint is forward movement of the athlete in relation to the sound. When that movement occurs before or coincides with the sound, it is easy to infer that the athlete has anticipated, and awarding a false start is obvious. What is more difficult, however, is determining whether a movement that occurred very soon after the signal could have resulted only from anticipation. In other words, how fast is too fast?

In this and the previous chapter we have discussed numerous experiments in which simple RT has been optimized under various experimental constraints. Typical minimum, simple RTs range from about 130 ms to 200 ms or so. But consider that these RT values have been achieved under very controlled experimental conditions with responses involving very simple movements (such as finger lifts). The sprint start entails a much more complex coordination of effectors, involving more complex motor programs; consequently an even longer RT, not a shorter one, might be expected. Still, one could argue that the RTs of world-class sprinters might be expected to be better than that of the average subject in an RT experiment. However, though sprint training does improve many speed-related factors, there is only so much that can be shaved off the stages of processing involved in simple RT. The minimum of 100 ms as an acceptable RT sprint start is a conservative criterion that still leaves plenty of time for anticipation (perhaps up to 100 ms). Anything faster is most likely due to anticipating. Christie was almost certainly guilty of a false start.

the right, and it meant that the signal would be presented on the side of the screen to which the arrow pointed. However, this precue was correct only 80% of the time. On the remaining 20% of the trials, the subject was "tricked," with the signal arriving on the side of the screen opposite to the direction indicated by the arrow. Those trials in which the signals arrived on the side indicated by the arrow were called *valid-precue trials,* while those in which the arrow pointed away from the eventual signal were called *invalid-precue trials.*

The RTs to the valid and invalid conditions, as well as to the neutral precue, are shown in figure 4.15. When the precue was valid, with the signal arriving where the subject expected it, there was a 30-ms *benefit* relative to the neutral-precue condition in which the subject had no information to predict where the signal would arrive. However, when the signal was presented in the location opposite to that indicated by the arrow (invalid), the RT was increased and there was a 40-ms *cost* of anticipating the direction incorrectly. Notice that this cost involves only the detection of the signal, because the response was always the same. But what are the costs involved in actually *moving* incorrectly?

Schmidt and Gordon (1977) used a two-choice RT task in which the subject had to produce a

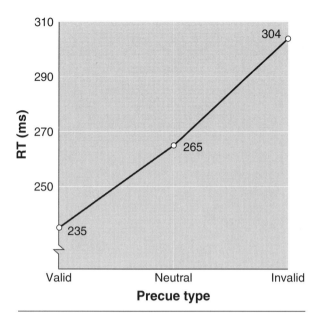

Figure 4.15. The cost-benefit analysis: RT as a function of type of precue.
Reprinted from Posner, Nissen, and Ogden, 1978.

correct amount of force on a lever in a direction indicated by a signal light. In one series of trials, the right and left signals were presented in random order, and subjects could not successfully anticipate the direction of the upcoming response. But in another series, the signals were presented in an alternating order, and the subjects would develop strong spatial anticipation about the next response. In this alternating series, however, a few signals were embedded that were opposite to the direction expected; that is, the series would be R, L, R, L, R, R, for example, where the subject was expecting the last R to be an L.

On those trials for which the subject was anticipating one direction but was presented with the unexpected signal, there were errors about 64% of the time. The effect is shown in figure 4.16. These subjects had a rapid RT (144 ms, on the average), moved in the incorrect direction (i.e., left) for 144 ms, and only then reversed direction to *begin* to move in the correct direction.[2] Falsely anticipating appears to be a major cause of this kind of error.

Next, if the subject was anticipating left but the right signal came on, and the subject did avoid making an error, then the RT was somewhat longer (276 ms) than it would have been if the person had not been anticipating at all (235 ms). Thus, inhibiting an already planned (incorrect) movement does require time

(276 − 235 = 41 ms). This can be thought of as the cost of anticipating incorrectly and is very similar to the 40-ms cost found by Posner, Nissen, and Ogden (1978; figure 4.15). Interestingly, though, in the Schmidt and Gordon study (1977), there was an 83-ms benefit (i.e., 235 − 152) of anticipating correctly, which is somewhat larger than benefits found by others (see figure 4.15).

However, more important is the finding that people actually *moved* in the incorrect direction on a majority of the trials (64%) in which they were falsely anticipating. They did not *begin* to move in the correct direction for 288 ms (144 + 144 ms; see figure 4.16). This was *compounded* by the fact that the person now had farther to go to reach the correct target, so that target arrival was delayed even longer. And, in having to move farther to the target, an errant performer is less accurate in hitting the target, because the error in hitting a target is roughly proportional to the movement distance (chapter 7). When we put together all these negative aspects of making an error, it is clear that the cost of anticipation can be quite high.

Many theoretical questions arise from these data on error production, but a major importance of these findings is in their application to various common activities. A tennis player anticipating that a shot will be hit to her left moves to the left, only to experience that sinking feeling when the ball is hit to her right. The defensive lineman in American football expects to be blocked to his left so leans or moves to his right, only to find that he is now being blocked to his right, making the task a very easy one for his opponent who was going to block him in that direction anyway. Effective coaching techniques should employ the notion that anticipating has certain benefits and costs—and that one should determine whether or not to anticipate in a certain situation by weighing the probable gains against potential losses. In many situations, the benefit of correctly anticipating might be very small compared to the cost of a false anticipation (e.g., when a driver anticipates what another driver may do). In other cases, the reverse is true. Obviously, these factors will depend on the particular activity, as well as on the particular situation (e.g., the score of the game, position on the field).

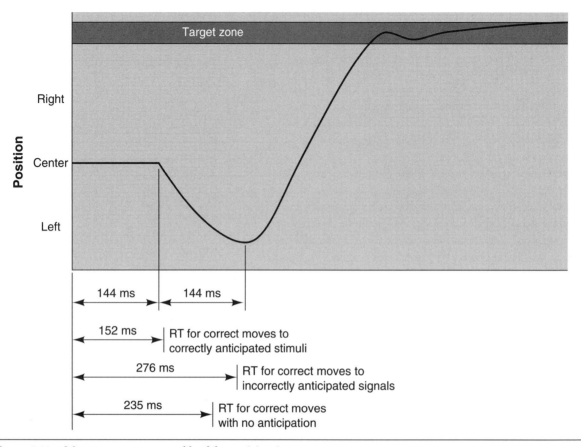

Figure 4.16. Movement error caused by false anticipation.
Adapted from Schmidt and Gordon, 1977.

Attention, Arousal, and Anxiety

We shift emphasis slightly at this point to discuss some important aspects of human performance related to arousal and anxiety and their relationship to ideas about attention. Anxiety is common, as in an important game or match or when we are threatened with harm in some way. How do high-anxiety conditions affect the processing of information necessary for successful performance?

Consider this true story. An airline pilot, with over 20,000 hours of flying experience, returned to San Francisco after an all-night flight from Hong Kong. He drove home to Oakland (20 miles away), slept for a few hours, and drove to the local airport to check out his private plane for a flight. With his family of three aboard, he left for a destination a few hours away, watched an automobile race there, and late at night began the return flight. At about 2:00 A.M. he radioed that his heater was not working and that he was above a layer of clouds over the Oakland airport. A pilot with his experience would, in this situation, be expected to perform a relatively lengthy (20- to 30-min) instrument approach

through the clouds to the airfield, but instead he radioed that he was looking for a "hole" in the clouds, presumably to avoid the instrument approach. The plane crashed a few minutes later after a wing broke off, killing all aboard.

What happened? We might guess that the pilot was very fatigued from the overseas flight, from the two other flights that day, and from the car race; he was also cold. The fatigue and cold led to a bad decision to find a "hole." Also because of the fatigue, the pilot may have been handling the plane badly, perhaps becoming disoriented and diving too steeply through the "hole," and the wing failed. Similar examples come from underwater diving, as pointed out by Norman (1976) and Bachrach (1970):

A woman enrolled in a diving course but lacking experience, was reported to have ... drowned while diving for golf balls in a twelve-foot [pool]. When her body was recovered, she was wearing her weight belt, and, in addition, was still clutching a heavy bag of golf balls. (122)

Again, something went wrong. Perhaps fatigue and cold led to panic. What effects do anxiety and panic have on information processing in these situations, causing people to abandon highly practiced techniques and resort to the skill level of an inexperienced beginner? We consider some possible answers to these questions in the next few sections.

Arousal and Anxiety Defined

Arousal and *anxiety*, along with related terms such as *stress* and *motivation*, all generally refer to states of activation that differ along a number of dimensions. Someone who is "psyched" or "pumped up," or otherwise in a highly energized state of activation, may be referred to as highly aroused or in a state of high anxiety. Gould and Krane (1992) suggest that arousal and anxiety refer to two distinct concepts that can be distinguished in terms of how they are manifested. Arousal refers mainly to a person's physiological level of activation. Assessments of arousal levels are usually done using respiratory, cardiovascular, biochemical, and electrophysiological techniques (Hackfort & Schwenkmezger, 1993). In contrast, Gould and Krane define anxiety in terms of the *affective* domain—the emotional and cognitive impact of arousal, such as nervousness or tension. Anxiety is typically measured at the *behavioral level* (such as obvious signs of trembling or avoidance-type behaviors) or at the *cognitive level*. This latter approach often uses self-report questionnaires, such as the Competitive State Anxiety Inventory-2 (Martens et al., 1990) and the Sport Anxiety Scale (Smith, Smoll, & Schutz, 1990), which have been designed specifically for use with athletes.

Two distinctions are often made in discussions of anxiety. *State anxiety* is assessed by questions such as "Are you worried about your performance *now*?" Of course, state anxiety can vary from minute to minute and from task to task. A second kind of anxiety is *trait anxiety*, which is a measure of the individual's *general* tendency toward worry or anxiety. It is assessed by questions such as "Are you *usually* worried about your performance?" This general tendency should not fluctuate very much from moment to moment or from task to task; it is a stable characteristic of the person. Those individuals who are classed as high trait-anxious are those who tend, under the specific conditions of a task or test situation, to become highly anxious. That is, high trait-anxious people tend to be the most state-anxious on a given motor task.

Arousal, Anxiety, and Performance

How do arousal and/or anxiety influence performance? This relationship has been characterized in a number of ways, each with some supporting evidence. We review each of these briefly in the next sections (more in-depth analyses are presented in Gould & Krane, 1992; Weinberg & Gould, 1995; Zaichkowsky & Takenaka, 1993).

The Inverted-U Principle

One of the oldest and certainly one of the most interesting aspects of arousal and performance was discovered by Yerkes and Dodson (1908) in studying the learning of brightness discrimination in mice. They found that increased intensity of electric shocks delivered to the mice increased performance, but only up to a point. Beyond this point, further increases in the intensity of the shock seemed to impair performance. If the shock was arousing, then there appeared to be an optimum level of arousal; that is, the relationship between shock intensity and performance followed an inverted U-shaped function (see figure 4.17). The principle has been called the Yerkes-Dodson law, after its originators, or, more commonly, the *inverted-U principle* (Duffy, 1962).

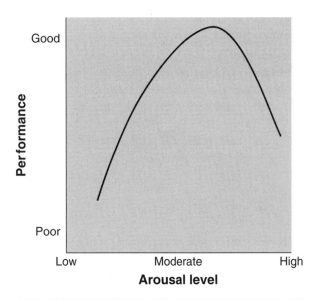

Figure 4.17. The inverted-U relation between arousal and performance.

Weinberg and Ragan (1978; see also Klavora, 1977; Martens & Landers, 1970; Sonstroem & Bernardo, 1982) have provided evidence for this phenomenon in movement behavior. They asked college males to throw tennis balls at a 5-cm target, 6.1 m away. After 10 trials of initial practice, the subject was asked to fill out a questionnaire, and he then received one of three feedback statements. In the High Stress condition, the subject was told that 90% of the population of college males would have performed better than he did. In the Moderate Stress condition he heard that 60% of the population would have had better performances than his. In the Low Stress condition, the subject was told that only 30% of the population was better at throwing. Because the subjects were also told that this task was an important indicator of success in most sport tasks involving throwing (which is not actually correct, as we shall see in chapter 9), such (false) statements about their level of performance were expected to be arousing to differing degrees. Indeed, arousal data indicated that this was the case.

In figure 4.18 are the throwing scores for the subjects in these three stress conditions. Increased arousal from the Low Stress to the Moderate Stress condition produced strong gains in performance, but further increases in arousal in the High Stress condition produced a decrease in throwing proficiency relative to that in the Moderate Stress condition. Consistent with the

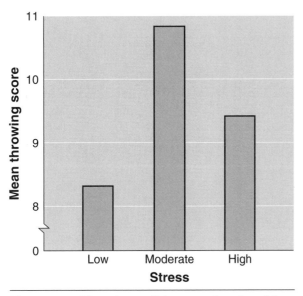

Figure 4.18. Throwing proficiency as a function of three stress conditions.
Adapted from Weinberg and Ragan, 1978.

inverted-U principle, there was a clear optimal level of arousal for the performance of this motor task.

The inverted-U principle clearly suggests that there is no simple relation between the level of stress and the quality of performance. How often do coaches and sportscasters suggest that an athletic performance was very good because the athlete or team was "up" for the game (see Nideffer, 1976)? The common belief seems to be that the more "up" we are, the better we perform, which is not usually the case. Actually, there is rather strong evidence that, while the inverted-U principle has *some* explanatory power, the relation between arousal, anxiety, and performance is much more complex. Although the principle has come under criticism in recent years, the fundamental concept of an optimal arousal-performance relationship has remained central to alternative views, which we examine next.

Zones of Optimal Functioning

One of the limitations of the inverted-U principle is the lack of sensitivity to the wide fluctuations in arousal that can occur within and between individuals and to the ways in which these relate to performance. Thus, Hanin (1980, 1989) proposed that for each individual there exists a *zone* (or bandwidth) defining a range of arousal levels within which the individual's performance is optimized. Although similar in concept to the inverted-U principle, the hypothesis argues that optimal functioning does not always occur at a moderate level of arousal—that instead it can be within a range of high arousal for one performer, yet within a range of low arousal for another performer (Hackfort & Schwenkmezger, 1993). Similarly, zones may be specific to task and environmental characteristics as well. Recent studies of athletic performances by track and field athletes have provided some support for the hypothesis (e.g., Turner & Raglin, 1996).

Catastrophe Hypothesis

Other theorists have suggested that the inverted-U principle is too limiting as a descriptor that relates arousal (or anxiety) and performance (Hardy, 1990; Jones, 1990; Neiss, 1988). Two of the problems that have been suggested are (a) that performance is not related to arousal in just a *unidimensional* way and (b) that the relation between arousal and performance is not always linear. As an alternative, Fazey and Hardy (1988) suggested that improvement in performance is related to a complex interaction between increases in a physiological arousal component and cognitive anxiety (such as worry), but only up to a certain point. Performance is hypothesized to suffer when cognitive anxiety extends beyond a certain point, although not in a gradual decline as predicted by the inverted-U principle. Rather, the prediction is that there will be a *catastrophic impact* on performance that is abrupt and nonlinear. Although there is intuitive appeal for the hypothesis (Gould & Krane, 1992), the supporting evidence is probably best considered as preliminary at this point (Hardy, 1990).

Reversal Hypothesis

A rather different view of arousal and performance is presented in the reversal hypothesis (Apter, 1984). This view, which has been used by Kerr (1990) to explain sport performance, is based on how one *interprets* the hedonic tone of his or her own arousal level. For some individuals, increases in arousal can be interpreted in a positive way (the person is said to be in an *arousal-seeking* or *paratelic* state). However, for other individuals, the same level of arousal can be interpreted in a negative way (the person is said to be in an *arousal-avoidance* or *telic* state). As illustrated in figure 4.19, increases in arousal will have an impact on the individual in terms of how that person interprets the change. However, reversal theory goes on to predict that increases in

arousal can result in a shift in the individual's state: what a person had viewed as exciting can suddenly be viewed from a highly anxious state. These ideas offer a promising approach for understanding not only between-individual differences, but also the way the changes within a person can accompany factors such as learning (Gould & Krane, 1992). For example, what a person might once have considered terrifying (such as skydiving or rock climbing) may produce feelings of high excitement after success has been achieved (Kerr, 1990). By the same token, failures may reverse these states in the opposite direction. Like catastrophe theory, however, these ideas require further empirical examination.

Attentional Mechanisms and Arousal

What attentional mechanisms play a role in the relationship between arousal and performance? Various possibilities exist, such as the cue-utilization hypothesis suggested by Easterbrook (1959), as well as the concepts of perceptual narrowing and hypervigilance.

Easterbrook's Cue-Utilization Hypothesis

According to this viewpoint, the individual is assumed to take in cues, from the environment or from his own movements, that aid in future performances. In a game situation, such cues might be the movements of opponents, the movements of teammates, patterns of play, the time remaining

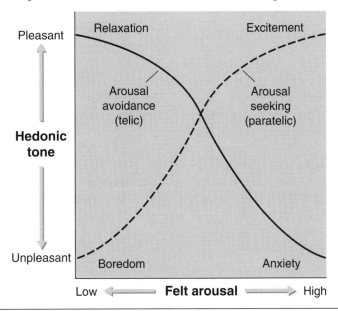

Figure 4.19. The reversal hypothesis of the changing felt states under arousal conditions.
Adapted from Apter, 1989.

in the game, and so on. When the arousal level is low, there are presumably many cues available for performance, but some of these are irrelevant. The *selectivity* of the cues is poor during low arousal. With an increase in arousal to moderate levels, there is a reduction in the number of cues used, with a shift to those cues that are more relevant to the task performance. As an optimal level of arousal is approached, the most effective combination of attention to relevant cues and minimal inclusion of irrelevant cues seems to exist. However, when the arousal level is further increased, there is a further restriction in the range of cues used; many relevant cues are not included, and performance deteriorates. This may have occurred with both the pilot and scuba diver discussed earlier.

Perceptual Narrowing

The Easterbrook view of cue utilization is very similar to the idea of *perceptual narrowing* described by Kahneman (1973) and others. With this notion, increased arousal causes increased narrowing of the attentional focus, with a progressive elimination of input from the more peripheral aspects of the environment. The term *peripheral* need not refer to events that are actually "in" the periphery (e.g., in peripheral vision), but it refers to events that are relatively improbable. It just so happens that, with vision, events that are expected are usually in our central vision (because we direct our gaze toward them), and events that are improbable occur in peripheral vision.

In addition to the reduced range of cues that can be attended to as arousal increases, there is an increase in the number of shifts in attention to different input sources. Some researchers (e.g., Kahneman, 1973) have referred to this effect as increased *distractibility*. Thus, high levels of arousal are likely to cause the individual to direct attention to many different sources from moment to moment, with some of these sources providing irrelevant information and causing the relevant signals to be missed. Apparently, the individual must discriminate between relevant and irrelevant cues during performance, and one effect of high arousal is deterioration in the quality of such discrimination.

Increased narrowing of attentional focus and increased distractibility to irrelevant cues seem to be common with many different sources of arousal. For example, the arousal from working in loud, continuous noise or vibration, from increased motivation to succeed or fear of failing, from certain activating drugs, and from very hot or cold environments seems to cause similar shifts in attention. In addition, certain depressive drugs such as alcohol appear to cause such narrowing effects even though these are not caused by increased arousal. Mildly intoxicated drivers appear to perform effectively with respect to cues and responses that are common and relevant, but they do not respond effectively to an unexpected signal such as a child running from between two parked cars.

Considerable evidence is available to support the notion of perceptual narrowing in a variety of tasks (see Kahneman, 1973). In an interesting and practical setting, Weltman and Egstrom (1966) studied novice scuba divers in air, in a controlled water tank, and in the ocean. The divers performed two main tasks (arithmetic and a dial-detection task), and the response times to a light stimulus presented in peripheral vision in the diving masks were measured. As the subjects were moved from the air to the tank to the ocean conditions, large (300% to 400%) increases in time to detect these peripheral signals were found, whereas the performance of a main task done in central vision was hardly affected. The focus of attention was clearly narrowed with increased stress.

Hypervigilance, or Panic

When the stress conditions become more severe, the responses of human performers can be even more disrupted. A classic example involves the many cases that have been documented about the so-called problem of *unintended acceleration* (Schmidt, 1989b, 1993). In the typical case, a driver starts an automatic transmission car, then before putting the car into drive or reverse intends to put his or her foot on the brake. Once the gearshift is engaged, the vehicle begins to accelerate wildly and usually does not come to rest until crashing, with a reported complete failure of the brakes. Many of these accidents have involved actions lasting 9 or 10 s, and some even 40 s. Later investigations almost inevitably reveal that the driver had pressed the accelerator instead of the brake, but (more surprisingly) had *kept* the accelerator pressed to the floor for the entire period! For what seems to be an "eternity" in terms of our earlier analyses of motor skills, the driver had failed to choose a number of alternative actions (e.g., shift to neutral, turn off the engine, apply the hand brake). It is as if the driver were "frozen" (Schmidt, 1989b, 1993).

Such situations often stem from what Janis, Defares, and Grossman (1983) call *hypervigilance* or what one might loosely term panic. The contributing conditions seem to be a sudden and intense stimulus, a potentially life-threatening outcome, and a situation in which time to take an appropriate action is quickly running out. All of these seem to be present in most cases of unintended acceleration. The individual appears to freeze, perhaps because attention is so narrowed that no alternative actions are considered. It could also be that many alternatives are considered but that, because of the increased distractibility, none is considered long enough for a solution to be initiated; the individual dithers until it is too late. These situations, in which completely inappropriate actions are taken by people under stress, are not as rare as they might appear, as evidenced by analyses of numerous vehicle accidents (Perel, 1976). Further, they might also occur in highly stressful sport events, industrial tasks, and so forth, with outcomes that are much less dramatic or not so easily analyzed.

Summary

Even though attention has had a long history of thought in psychology, we are still unclear about its nature, the principles of its operation—indeed, even its definition. Many theorists think of attention as a single, undifferentiated, limited capacity to process information; others argue that attention is really a number of pools of capacity for separate kinds of processing. The capabilities to perform various tasks together is presumably limited by these capacities; therefore, attention demand is usually estimated indirectly by the extent to which tasks interfere with each other. Processing sensory information (or performing other processes early in the sequence) can apparently be done in parallel, with little interference from other tasks. But processes associated with response selection, and particularly response programming and initiation, interfere greatly with other activities.

Characteristics of attention play an important role in motor performance. Psychological refractoriness—the delay in responding to the second of two closely spaced stimuli—is taken as evidence that some single channel, or bottleneck, in processing exists in the response-selection or response-programming stage. Other evidence, using secondary probe techniques, suggests that attention demands are highest at both the initiation and termination stages of movements. Recent evidence suggests a more radical view, that attention is determined by the demands of action.

Some of the stages of processing can apparently be bypassed by anticipation. Providing both spatial and temporal predictability allows early responding, whereas providing other information leads to increased readiness and faster response.

Performance is influenced by arousal, and several hypotheses have been suggested to explain this relationship. The mechanisms that appear to limit performance under stress are related to the decrease in cue utilization and the failure of decision-making processes.

Notes

[1] In a way, this label is unfortunate. The original idea was that the delay in the subject's response to the second of two closely spaced stimuli was analogous to the delay found when a single nerve fiber is electrically stimulated twice in rapid succession in physiological experiments. If the second stimulus is very close to the first (within 5 ms), no response at all will be recorded from the second stimulus. This effect has been termed the refractory period, meaning that the nerve was insensitive to additional stimulation while it "recovered" from the effects of the first stimulus. These neuronal processes have little to do with the psychological refractory period, as the time courses are much longer in the behavioral work (e.g., 200 ms).

[2] There is no particular significance to the finding that (a) the RT to the beginning of the error and (b) the interval from the initiation of the error until the initiation of the correct move both happened to be 144 ms on the average.

PART 2

MOTOR CONTROL

The human motor system is a very complex whole with many interacting pieces, processes, and mechanisms, and to attempt to successfully understand the entire system would be extremely difficult. For this reason, scientists generally study in isolation various parts of the system, or various modes of control—fundamentally different ways in which the system's parts can work together—and examine them somewhat independently. In chapter 5, the focus is on the role of sensory information; we shall consider the ways in which information from the environment influences, or even determines, movement behavior. In chapter 6, we examine the central control and representation of action, in situations in which sensory influences do not have a particularly strong role. Chapter 7 deals with various laws and models regarding the control of relatively "simple" movements. This analysis is extended in chapter 8 to more complex tasks involving the coordination of more than one effector. This part ends with a discussion in chapter 9 of factors that tend to make individuals differ from each other in their skilled behaviors.

SENSORY CONTRIBUTIONS TO MOTOR CONTROL

One of the ways in which motor control is achieved relies heavily on the concept that we use *sensory* (or *afferent*) *information* to regulate our movements. This can be information that tells us about the state of the environment or about the state of our own body. A way to think about how sensory information is used in the control of action is to consider the moving human as a type of *closed-loop* system. As discussed in the boxed text on page 97, a closed-loop system depends heavily on the involvement of particular types of sensory information as it executes its function. Such sensory information, when discussed in the context of closed-loop motor control, is often termed *movement-produced feedback*, or simply feedback, implying that the sensory information to be considered is the result of performed actions. Of course there are many other forms of sensory information that are not associated with the performed movements, and these are usually considered under the more general heading of sensation and perception. In this chapter we discuss the various kinds of sensory information that can be used in the control of movement.

The various sources (or receptors) of sensory information that are available during movement are traditionally classified into three groups (Sherrington, 1906). Perhaps the least important for our purposes is the class of receptors called *interoceptors.* They tell us about the states of our internal organs, such as with "hunger pains," and have questionable relevance for motor behavior. The remaining two classes of receptors are divided according to whether they provide information about the movement of objects in the environment *(exteroceptors)* or information about our own movements *(proprioceptors).* The roots *extero* and *proprio* refer to events outside one's body and events in one's own body, respectively.

Vision

Certainly the most critical receptor for supplying information about the movement of objects in the outside world is the eye. Thus, we begin our discussion with the richest feedback information for motor control.

How Vision Provides Information

Subjectively, we all know that darkness critically impairs the performance of many tasks, although we also know that vision is not essential for all motor performances. People who are blind learn to move in the environment with remarkable facility, although they are at a large disadvantage in many situations. In terms of human performance, vision provides information about the movements of objects in the environment for subsequent motor behavior, and much of motor control is involved in tailoring our behavior to meet these visually determined environment demands.

Two Visual Systems

Concerning vision as an exteroceptive system (for detecting events in the outside world), recent evidence and theorizing argue for the existence of two visual systems. The lines of evidence to support these different systems come from a wide range of levels of analysis, using various techniques and subjects in the research. Indeed, even the names for the two systems differ markedly, with such proposed dichotomies as cognitive versus motor vision, explicit versus implicit vision, object versus spatial vision, and overt versus covert vision (Bridgeman, 1996). We will refer to the two systems as *focal vision* and *ambient vision* (after Trevarthen, 1968).[1]

Focal Vision.   This visual system is the one we are all most familiar with subjectively. It has to do with events mainly (but not exclusively) in central (i.e., focal) vision, and its accuracy (acuity) is degraded by decreasing levels of illumination. Focal vision is concerned with visual events about which we are (or will be) aware, and thus it is strongly linked to consciousness. One of its main functions is to answer the question "*What* is it?" when visual stimulation is received. Some theorists (e.g., Bridgeman, 1996) call focal vision "cognitive vision" because it seems to make important contributions to many cognitive tasks (e.g., reading).

Ambient Vision.   A second visual system is called *ambient vision.* Unlike focal vision, ambient vision is apparently available for the entire visual field, including both central and peripheral locations. Decreasing illumination (to a point) does not have important effects on its acuity, and information from ambient vision can be used without conscious awareness. One of its main functions is to answer the question "*Where* is it?" when visual stimulation is received. Bridgeman (1996) calls

Closed-Loop Control Systems

One way of *modeling* motor control has been to consider sensory control of action in ways analogous to mechanical systems control. *Closed-loop* systems are important in many situations, especially those that require a system to "control itself" for long periods of time (see chapter 6 for a discussion of *open-loop* systems). A diagram that illustrates how a simple closed-loop system works is shown in figure 5.1. First, input all about the system's goal is provided to a *reference mechanism.* In a home heating system, for example, the system goal might be a thermostat setting of 68°, with the overall goal being the achievement of this temperature in the house. Next, the reference mechanism samples the environment that it is attempting to control to determine what the temperature actually is. This information from the environment is usually termed *feedback.* The reference mechanism then compares the value of the goal to that of the sample obtained from the environment, and an *error* is computed, representing the difference between the actual and desired states. The error is information that is given to an *executive level,* where decisions are made about how to reduce the error toward zero. If the error is large enough, instructions are sent to the *effector level,* and a mechanism that has some effect on the environment is activated—in this case, the heater. The heater raises the temperature of the room, and this raised temperature will be periodically sampled. When the difference between the actual and desired temperatures is zero, the executive level shuts off the heater. In such a way, the heater cycles between being on and off as a function of the actual value of the room temperature and thus maintains the system goal. Such systems are termed *closed-loop* because the loop of control from the environment to decisions to action and back to the environment again is completed, or closed.

How does this model of the closed-loop system correspond to the human motor system? For now, think of the reference of correctness and the executive level as being contained in the stages of information processing, so that the system can receive and process feedback information following the stimulus-identification stage, and then program instructions to the musculature to reduce the error in the response-programming stage. Instructions are then given to the effector level, usually thought of as the muscles or as a program of action that actually controls the muscles. Then, the information from the various muscle, joint, and tendon receptors, as well as from the eyes, ears, and so on, is sent back to the reference mechanisms for analysis, and decisions about future action are again made.

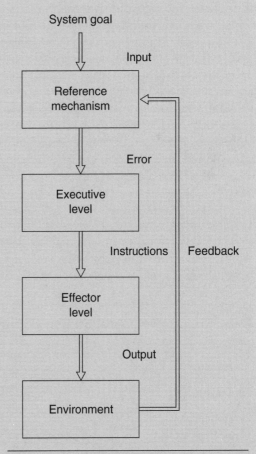

Figure 5.1. The elements of the typical closed-loop control system.

ambient vision "sensorimotor vision," because localizing features in the environment provide information for movement behavior and control. The features that distinguish between focal and ambient vision are listed in table 5.1, using categories suggested by Owens (1985).

Evidence for the Two Visual Systems

Classifying things is easy; however, before a classification is accepted, scientists usually demand strong evidence that it facilitates understanding. It is desirable to have a *double dissociation*, in which, for this example, the effect of some independent variable on the focal system is *opposite* to the effect of the same variable on the ambient system; this is one of the strongest lines of evidence that there are fundamentally two kinds of visual systems. With use of this logic, the evidence for the two visual systems is quite strong.

Double Dissociations in Behavioral Studies. Bridgeman, Kirch, and Sperling (1981) used an induced-motion paradigm, in which small movements of a surrounding background in a given direction made it appear that a fixed target element within it moved in the opposite direction. Under these conditions, subjects said that the (actually stationary) target moved about 2.5° of visual angle, which is a measure of the bias received by the focal (conscious) system. Bridgeman, Kirch, and Sperling then suddenly extinguished the target and background, and the subject's task was to quickly move a mechanical pointer to the last location of the target, a measure of the ambient (sensorimotor) system's accuracy. These pointing movements were largely unaffected by the movement of the background. In this study, the conscious perception of the target's position was biased by the movements of the

background, but the information given to the motor system for pointing was not. Another experiment used the reverse procedures: here, the target was actually moved, and the background was moved in the opposite direction by such an amount that the subject perceived (consciously) that the target was stationary. When the target and background were extinguished, the pointing tended to be to the actual location of the target, not to the position that the subject perceived consciously.

This is a double dissociation: the moving background altered the conscious perception of the fixed target position but not the pointing direction, and the altered actual position of the target (whose location was perceived as fixed because of the moving background) did not bias the pointing direction. These results suggest that our (conscious) perception of the target location can be biased by the movement of the background, but that the motor system receives other information that is not biased by the moving background.

Double Dissociations in Brain-Injured Patients. Evidence for the separate functioning of two visual systems has also been found in patients who have specific damage to parts of the brain that are involved in the processing of visual inputs. For example, patients who have a type of brain injury called *optic ataxia* are able to recognize an object, but cannot use this same visual information to accurately guide their hand to the object (Perenin & Vighetto, 1988). In contrast, a type of disorder called *visual agnosia* results in an inability to recognize common objects, yet subjects are able to use the object's visual information to make accurate grasping actions (Goodale & Milner, 1992; Goodale et al., 1991). This double dissociation is the same type as the

Table 5.1   Two Visual Systems: Some Distinguishing Features

Feature	Focal vision	Ambient vision
Retinal locus	Central retina only	Full retina
Visual field	Central vision	Central/peripheral
Low illumination	Degraded	No effect
Awareness	Conscious	Nonconscious
Function	What is it?	Where is it?

(Adapted from Owens, 1985.)

one described in the previous section. Together with other behavioral and neurophysiological evidence, these findings suggest that the specific visual systems have selective *functional* significance for the processing of visual information, perhaps based on evolutionary factors (Milner & Goodale, 1993).

One interpretation of these results is the two visual systems hypothesis, according to which focal vision is used for consciousness, and ambient vision is used mainly for movement control. The ambient system presumably participates in the pickup of environmental information about the locations of objects near us, can receive this information from both central and peripheral vision, and can be used nonconsciously by the motor system in the control of actions. It is a strange and exciting possibility that when we move about, we are responding to visual information we are not aware of!

Visual Information About Time-to-Contact

Another important issue related to the general topic of how visual information is provided has to do with the nature of the visual display itself. In many everyday activities we must process dynamic information—visual information that is changing, sometimes at a very rapid rate. For example, in passing another automobile we are bombarded with various sources of visual inputs that change at different rates: the stationary environmental information that we drive past (such as road signs), the car that we are passing, the car that is coming rapidly toward us in the other lane, and the information within our own car that is travel-

ing at the same speed as ourselves. All these sources of information represent visual cues that we must accurately perceive in order to execute a safe pass.

Considerable research in motor behavior has been directed at a subset of skills involved in the perception of dynamic visual information. Many of these skills are used in ball games and require *interceptive* actions such as catching or striking. The moving object provides various types of information, such as its position in space and the way that position is changing (in the case of a pitched ball in baseball). However, probably the most important and frequently studied information source relates to the temporal prediction about *when* the object will arrive, called time-to-contact (T_c) information.

An important view regarding how T_c is perceived was formulated by Lee (1980, 1990; Lee & Young, 1985), and relates quite closely to the concept of *visual proprioception* and to the work of James Gibson (1966, 1979). Consider an object, such as a ball, that is moving directly toward your eye, as shown in figure 5.2. If the angles of the light rays from the edges of the ball (i.e., α_1 and α_2) are increasing at the same rate (with respect to straight ahead), this specifies that the ball is moving directly toward your eye. Such information, called looming, usually provides strong avoidance reactions that appear to be nearly "automatic," or at least difficult to inhibit. But in addition, Lee's work shows that these changes tell us about the amount of time remaining until contact will be made (Lee, 1976, 1980, 1990; Lee & Young, 1985).

In figure 5.2, the edges of the ball cast a retinal image of size A, which increases as the ball comes

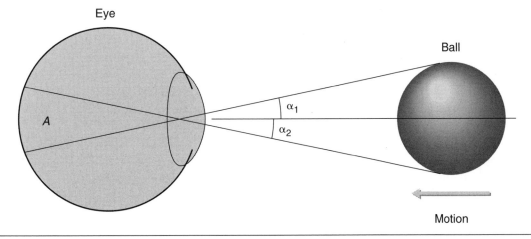

Figure 5.2. Diagram of a ball approaching an eye, showing the size of the image (*A*) it projects on the retina; at any moment, the time until contact is proportional to tau, which is directly proportional to the retinal size *A* divided by *Å*, the rate of change of *A* (i.e., tau = *k A/Å*).

Visual Proprioception

Figure 5.3 illustrates one of James Gibson's concepts about how changes in head position contribute to changes in the angles of light rays entering the eye (Gibson, 1966, 1979). The pattern of rays experienced is called the *optical array*, and it provides a unique specification of the location of the eye in space. The changes in the optical array when the eye is moved from one place to another are called the *optical flow*, implying that the visual environment "flows past us" as we move around. An important point is that the particular patterns of flow specify distinct kinds of movements with respect to the environment. For example, if the angle between the light rays from two sides of an object is constant over time, this specifies that you are not moving with respect to that object. If the angle between these rays is increasing, then you are moving toward the object; if it is decreasing, you are moving away from the object. Also, if the angles from the two sides of an object (with respect to straight ahead) are increasing at the same rate, the eye is moving toward the center of the object (e.g., you are walking toward a picture on the wall). In conditions in which the angles from both sides of an object are changing in the *same* direction, if the rate of increase in the angle of the rays from the right side of the object is greater than the rate of increase from the left side, and continues in this way, you will pass the object so that it is on your right side.

The optical flow generated as you move in the environment also tells you about the *environment itself* in ways that could not be achieved if you were stationary. For example, imagine looking out the window at two telephone poles as illustrated in figure 5.3. Which of them is closer? The question is difficult to answer if you remain still, because the poles appear to be nearly the same thickness and height. But if you move your head sideways you can tell immediately. You will notice that one of the poles seems to "move more quickly" as you change head position. This, of course, is the same as saying that the angles of the rays received from on object have changed more quickly (α_1 in the figure) than did those from the other (α_2), implying that Pole 1 is closer than Pole 2. Thus, the visual system, through movement of the entire head or body, can provide rich information about the nature of the environment.

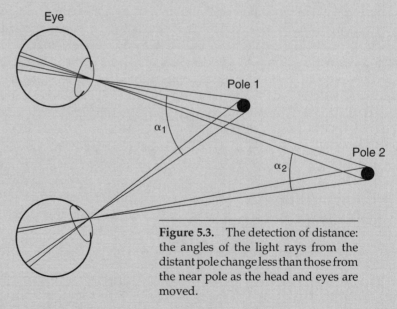

Figure 5.3. The detection of distance: the angles of the light rays from the distant pole change less than those from the near pole as the head and eyes are moved.

In this view, vision is not merely an exteroceptive sense, passively providing information about the environment. It is also a proprioceptive sense telling us about our own movements. As well, vision is dependent on movement in some situations for informing us about the environment. In this way, vision and movement are very closely and reciprocally linked. Excellent discussions of this basic idea are found in Gibson (1966, 1979) and Lee (1980; Lee & Young, 1985), the latter showing relevance to many situations, including sport-related motions and bird flight.

closer; also, the more rapidly the ball approaches, the faster the image will be expanding. Let's abbreviate this rate of expansion occurring at some moment (or the derivative of A with respect to time) as $\dot{A}$, where the dot means the "rate of change." Lee defines the term "proportionate rate of expansion" as simply the rate of expansion $\dot{A}$ divided by the size of the retinal image A ($\dot{A}/A$), which is a measure of the rate of change at some moment as a proportion of the size of the retinal image A. Lee (1976) showed that the reciprocal of this ratio, or $A/\dot{A}$, is directly proportional to T_c. This is true regardless of the size of the object, the velocity at which it travels, or its distance from the eye. That is,

$$T_c = \text{tau (or } \tau) = k\, A/\dot{A} \qquad (5.1)$$

where k is an arbitrary proportionality constant. In other words, T_c is proportional to the reciprocal of the proportionate rate of expansion of the retinal image. This makes common sense. At a given distance, an object has a retinal size of A; the rate of change in the object's retinal image ($\dot{A}$) will be larger the faster it is traveling. This makes the denominator in equation 5.1 larger and hence tau smaller, indicating that there will be less time until the object contacts the eye.

One potential limitation of the tau concept is that the velocity of an approaching object must be constant in order for tau to specify T_c. Thus tau will overestimate the T_c for accelerating objects and underestimate T_c for decelerations. To resolve this issue, Lee et al. (1983; Lee & Reddish, 1981) suggest that actions are based on the latest tau value possible. Theoretically, the most important point is that a relatively simple transformation of optical flow allows the specification of important temporal events in the environment, and does not depend on the perception of either distance or velocity cues. In a later section we will see how ideas regarding T_c have been used to explain various features of motor control.

Time to Process Visual Feedback

Consider someone who is working at night in a toolshed, striking the head of a nail with a hammer or swinging a heavy ax with both hands to split wood for the fireplace. Suddenly, as the tool comes down on the object, the electrical power to the shed goes off and all the lights go out. What is the fate of the swinging action that had been

initiated and that it is now too late to stop? Questions like these have been addressed by experimenters for over a century, using various theoretical approaches.

Moving to Stationary Targets

The initial estimate of the time required to process visual feedback was provided almost a century ago by Woodworth (1899). The research was motivated by his view that aiming movements comprise a two-stage process. In the *initial-impulse* phase (also called a *ballistic* or *programmed* movement phase), he argued that subjects send an impulse to the hand that drives the limb toward the target (much more will be discussed about this type of control strategy in chapter 6). Once the movement is under way there is an opportunity to correct any error in the intended path of the limb (which Woodworth called the *current-control* phase), whereby the subject can use visual feedback to *home in* on the target, making fine adjustments as needed. However, this second phase of the movement should occur, according to Woodworth, only if there is sufficient time to process the error arising from the analysis of the visual feedback. Thus, Woodworth reasoned that aimed movements with vision should be more accurate than those made without vision *only if* there is sufficient time to process the visual feedback. On the other hand, movements made faster than visual feedback would be expected to result in target dispersions that are equally inaccurate for both blind and sighted aims. The critical question then is, how much time is required to process visual feedback? This question has been addressed a number of times using more or less the same experimental method as Woodworth's. Therefore, we will examine the Woodworth (1899) study in some detail.

The Woodworth (1899) Study.   To address the question of how much time is required to process visual feedback, Woodworth asked his subjects to make back-and-forth movements of a pen with the goal that each movement be equal in length to the one preceding it. A strip of paper moved underneath the subject's pen at a constant velocity; thus a record of the previous movement could be used as the target for the next and could also be used later to calculate measures of error. Subjects performed with their eyes open or closed and moved at varying rates of speed (paced by a metronome at speeds of 200 to 20 cycles/min—involving movement times per cycle that ranged from 300 ms to 3 s, respectively). However, aiming was done only in one direction; the return movement was made to a physically restricted stop. Thus, the values of available time to process visual feedback from the stop to the intended target were about half of the total cycle time, or between 150 and 1.5 s (Carlton, 1992).

The average errors (similar to absolute error [AE]; see chapter 2) in the eyes-open and eyes-closed conditions are illustrated by the open and filled circles in figure 5.4. On the left side of this figure (short movement times [MTs]), the eyes-open and eyes-closed conditions produce equivalent average error. The critical point in the graph occurs when these conditions begin to depart in average error. As figure 5.4 shows, the departure point of the vision condition from the average of the eyes-closed condition (represented by the dotted line) occurs between movements of 215-ms duration and movements of 250-ms duration. That is, movements with times of 250 ms or more could benefit from the availability of vision, but movement with durations of 215 ms or less could not. Notice that, for this task, the estimate of the time to process visual feedback seems to be about the same as in responding to a visual stimulus in a *choice*-reaction time (RT) task.

Keele and Posner (1968). Although Woodworth's study is still considered a landmark in

motor control research, it did contain some peculiarities. The repetitive, back-and-forth nature of the task meant that subjects had to aim at the target and to prepare to reverse the movement at about the same time, making the role of vision more complex than in an aimed movement that terminates at the target, such as hitting a nail with a hammer. As well, the nature of the task required subjects to try to match the previous movement they had made; the target was more ambiguous than is our hammer/nail example (Meyer et al., 1990, describe other peculiarities).

In another well-known experiment, Keele and Posner (1968) overcame these problems by using a discrete-task version of Woodworth's research strategy. They trained their subjects to move a stylus to a small target about 15 cm away. Knowledge of results about MT was provided and, in separate sessions, subjects were trained to move as closely as possible to assigned MT goals (150, 250, 350, and 450 ms). On certain randomly determined test trials the experimenters turned off the room lights when the subjects left the starting position, so that the entire movement was made in the dark.

Figure 5.5 illustrates the probability of missing this target as a function of the vision condition and the *actual* MT. In the 150-ms MT condition (the actual MT was 190 ms), about as many target misses were recorded when the lights were on (68%) as when the lights were off (69%). As the

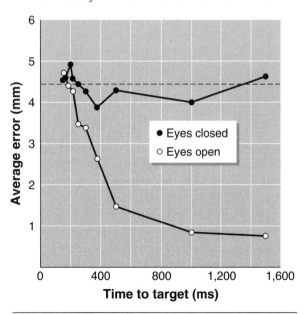

Figure 5.4. Aiming errors in moving to targets with the eyes open and closed.

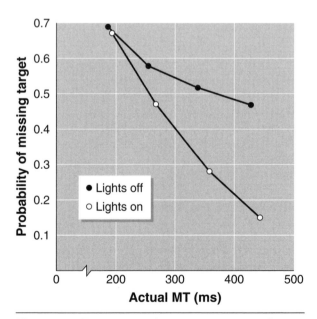

Figure 5.5. Target misses during movements with room lights on and off.

MTs increased, an advantage emerged when the room lights were on, consistent with the view that vision could be used when sufficient time was available for detecting and correcting errors. Nevertheless, despite the changes in the design of their study, Keele and Posner's estimate of the time required to process visual feedback information (between 190 and 260 ms) was very similar to the estimate suggested by Woodworth (1899).

Visual Feedback Uncertainty. But *uncertainty* about whether or not visual feedback would be available on a trial seems to have played an important role in the experiment of Keele and Posner (1968). In their methodology the room lights went off unexpectedly on some trials, the order being determined randomly. Perhaps if subjects knew in advance that vision would or would not be available, their attention might be focused more appropriately, and the estimate of the time to process visual feedback might be considerably less than in situations in which subjects are "surprised" by the presence or absence of vision. If the subject never could count on having the lights on, then a strategy employing vision might be avoided in favor of an alternative strategy. The unpredictability of vision in Keele and Posner's study may have forced the subjects to ignore vision, and thus the estimates of visual processing time in their study may have been too large.

Zelaznik, Hawkins, and Kisselburgh (1983) and Elliott and Allard (1985) performed experiments similar to the Keele and Posner study except that under some circumstances the subjects knew in advance when vision would or would not be available. Elliott and Allard (experiment 1) manipulated vision by using blocks of trials in which the room lights were either left on or were turned off at *random* (as in Keele & Posner) or in a *blocked* order (so that an entire series of trials was done either with or without vision). For movements made as fast as possible (225 ms), the availability of vision improved target aiming accuracy only when trials were blocked; no differences were found between vision and no-vision conditions when the trials were randomized (i.e., when visual feedback availability could not be anticipated).

Zelaznik, Hawkins, and Kisselburgh (1983) also found that visual feedback could be used more quickly on predictable trials than when it was presented randomly. The findings from their third experiment are illustrated in figure 5.6. In

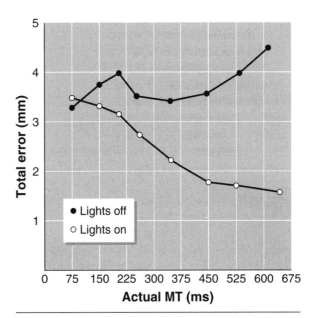

Figure 5.6. Target accuracy (total variability, E) in a stylus-aiming task as a function of MT and lighting conditions.
Adapted from Zelaznik, Hawkings, and Kisselburgh, 1983.

this study, all trials were conducted in a blocked (predictable) order. No advantage for the availability of visual feedback was found when MTs were about 75 ms; however, clear differences were present at MTs of about 150 ms. These data suggest that vision, when its presence can be expected, can be used in far less time than the minimum suggested by Woodworth (1899) and by Keele and Posner (1968), perhaps with visual processing times as short as 100 ms. In other experiments, Zelaznik, Hawkins, and Kisselburgh showed that the advantage for the lights-on condition remained even if the procedures were reversed so that the lights were off initially but would come on suddenly.

Other studies support the contention that the visual processing estimates obtained by Woodworth (1899) and Keele and Posner (1968) were rather conservative. By preventing visual feedback of the initial 75% of the distance to the target, Carlton (1981a) found that vision could be used in 135 ms (see also Carlton, 1979, 1981b; Spijkers & Lochner, 1994). Smith and Bowen (1980) showed that distorted or delayed visual information caused disruptions in movement accuracy when the MTs were only 150 ms, also suggesting that visual processing time was far faster than had been previously measured. Similar results were reported by Elliott and Allard (1985, experiments 2 and 3). Perturbations of the position of a visual stimulus also result in very fast movement corrections, with initiations begun in about 100 ms (Paulignan, MacKenzie, Marteniuk, & Jeannerod, 1991; Pélisson et al. 1986), although perturbing its size necessitates considerably longer processing times (Paulignan, Jeannerod, MacKenzie, & Marteniuk, 1991). Reviews of this research by Carlton (1992) and Glencross and Barrett (1992) include discussion of a number of other related studies. When all this evidence is taken together, it suggests that no single, *absolute* estimate of the time to process visual feedback is likely to be correct.

Intercepting Moving Targets

Hitting a nail with a hammer is just one example of how vision is used in motor control; the object is stationary and the human acts to make contact with the object (defined as a "closed" skill in chapter 2). Now consider another class of skills in the situation in which the environment changes during the action (called "open" skills in chapter 2). We have already seen an example of the role of vision in this situation; the work of Paulignan, MacKenzie, Marteniuk, and Jeannerod (1991) showed that if a stationary object *changed* position, then vision of this perturbation could be used in as little as 100 ms. It may be the case, then, that processing visual information about *moving objects* involves a different process (Pélisson et al., 1986).

An early study by Whiting, Gill, and Stephenson (1970) appears to support this argument. A ball was dropped from a 3-m height to an angled trampoline-like spring, which bounced the ball another 3 m toward the subject, who attempted to catch it. Trials were conducted in a completely darkened room, and a small bulb inside the ball could be lit for periods of 100, 150, 200, 250, or 300 ms after it hit the trampoline. With a ball flight time (from the point when the ball left the trampoline until the catch was attempted) of 400 ms, these viewing times left the subject without sight of the ball for periods of 300, 250, 200, 150, or 100 ms prior to hand contact, respectively. The proportion of balls caught in each of the vision conditions is presented in figure 5.7. Although performance under the best condition was not as good as in a control condition in which all the room lights were on[2] (represented by the dotted line in figure 5.7), Whiting, Gill, and Stephenson found that catching performance improved as each delay became smaller—even when the 150 and 100 ms-before-contact conditions were compared! Thus, one conclusion is

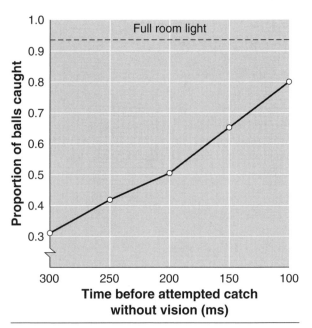

Figure 5.7. Number of balls caught in full room light and in conditions in which lights have been extinguished prior to attempted catch.
Adapted from Whiting, Gill, and Stephenson, 1970.

that visual information of the ball flight could be used in at least 100 ms to improve catching performance (see Savelsbergh & Whiting, 1996, and Savelsbergh, Whiting, & Pijpers, 1992, for reviews of related experiments).

One potentially confounding factor in the Whiting, Gill, and Stephenson study was that the length of the viewing period *covaried* with the amount of time without vision; the longer the time with vision the less time without it, and vice versa. An experimental approach that allows these factors to be independently examined uses *stroboscopic* conditions. The stroboscopic conditions are simulated with the use of goggles that can be alternately opened and closed by a signal from a computer to provide periodic "snapshots" of visual information. Using this method, Elliott, Zuberec, and Milgram (1994) examined the independent contributions of the length of time that the goggles were open, the length of time that vision was not available, and the relative frequency with which the open and closed periods were alternated. Interestingly, Elliott, Zuberec, and Milgram found that the most important contribution to catching performance was *not* the amount of time that vision was available, but rather the time *between* the visual snapshots of the ball (i.e., the length of time without vision). Subjects could perform well with as little as 20 ms of available vision of the ball as long as no more than 80 ms intervened between snapshots (see also Assaiante, Marchand, & Amblard, 1989), although longer periods without vision updating can support performance during aiming at stationary targets (Elliott, Chua, & Pollock, 1994). These findings do not constitute rejection of earlier estimates of the minimum time to process visual information. Rather, they serve to reject the idea that a minimum amount of *continuous* visual information is needed, and suggest that visual information can be processed *intermittently,* with use of very short durations of information.

Arguments can be raised that experimental occlusion of vision is not a natural approach to examining the speed of visual processing. In other words, the lights in our toolshed example do not go out very often. Critics of this approach have used a number of alternative paradigms in which the use of visual feedback information is inferred from the adjustment (homing in) actions that occur during the preparation for object contact. For example, Bootsma and van Wieringen (1990) found that expert table tennis players could use visual information about the moving ball to adjust their forehand drive in the last 105 to 156 ms of ball flight (depending on the individual). Estimates ranging from 50 to 135 ms were reported by Lee et al. (1983) in a task that required subjects to jump to hit a falling ball. Longer estimates for responding to changes in the path of a ball after a perturbed bounce have been found (about 190 ms in McLeod, 1987; 150–190 ms in Carlton, Carlton, & Kim, 1997). However, the longer delay times in these two studies may be attributable to the unexpectedness of the change in flight path and the larger objects that were being manipulated (a cricket bat in McLeod, 1987; a tennis racket in Carlton, Carlton, & Kim, 1997).

Interpreting the Evidence

It seems that vision, under various conditions, can be processed for motor control considerably faster than our usual estimates of RT to a visual stimulus. One interpretation of these differences in visual processing time estimates is that the various experimental conditions influence *strategic* differences in the ways that subjects prepare for specific types of visual information. For example, Glencross and Barrett (1992) suggest that under some situations, subjects may make *deliberate* errors (e.g., undershooting the target) in the

initial movement phase in order to reduce the uncertainty of the information specified by the visual feedback (see also Barrett & Glencross, 1989; Carlton, 1981a). With use of this strategy, the *amount of information* to be processed in the visual display is reduced because the direction of the corrective action is known in advance.

Another interpretation is related to the hypothesis of two visual systems proposed by Trevarthen (1968) and discussed earlier in the chapter. Presumably, much of the visual information for movement control is handled by the ambient system, which is thought to be nonconscious and spatially oriented (Bridgeman, Kirch, & Sperling, 1981; Pélisson et al., 1986). However, various experimental manipulations of visual feedback-processing time may call into use the focal visual system (review table 5.1). Thus, it may be that the motor control studies using stationary stimuli have forced the subjects to use the (slower) focal system, which is not the system they would normally use in "real" environmental skill situations. What is clear is that the time to use visual information changes as a function of the characteristics of the target and the intentions of the movement (Carlton, 1992). In the next sections we describe other evidence related to the role of vision in motor control.

Vision and Anticipatory Actions

Situations in which the movement goal involves an interaction with a *changing* environment include cases where either the subject or the environment (or an object in the environment), or both, are moving. For example, in ball sports, in which the performer must *intercept* a moving object, there are times when the performer must stand still and intercept a moving object (as in batting a ball) or must move to intercept a ball in flight (as in catching a forward pass in American football). Activities such as locomotion and driving a car are examples of situations in which the motion of the individual provides a changing visual array. In all cases, information about the changing environment is used to prepare *anticipatory actions* that allow people to complete the task (such as catching a ball or avoiding objects in their path). The issue that we deal with in greater detail next concerns how these actions become specified by the changing environment.

Interceptive Control

Most of the research on the role of vision during interceptive activities has involved a moving object, such as in catching or striking a ball. According to Savelsbergh and Whiting (1996; Savelsbergh, Whiting, & Pijpers, 1992), the primary use of vision is to specify information about (1) *when* to intercept an object—in particular, temporal information about T_c, and (2) *where* to go to intercept it—information about the spatial characteristics of the ball flight. Research suggests that the visual system specifies these types of information in different ways.

Temporal Information. As mentioned previously in the chapter, there now appears to be considerable evidence that T_c is likely specified by tau (Lee et al., 1983; but see also Abernethy & Burgess-Limerick, 1992). An experiment by Savelsbergh, Whiting, and Bootsma (1991) illustrates how tau is used to specify *when* to carry out the hand actions required to grasp a moving ball.

Subjects were positioned with their elbow on a table and their wrist locked into a position such that a ball that swung on a pendulum would come directly into contact with the subject's palm. The only task was to time the "catch" of the ball with a grasping action; there was no spatial uncertainty. Savelsbergh, Whiting, and Pijpers used balls of two sizes (5.5 and 7.5 cm in diameter), although the most important ball used was a third one that was 5.5 cm but was covered with a balloon that could be inflated to 7.5 cm. Once the ball was released, the balloon *deflated* from 7.5 to 5.5 cm over the period of the ball flight (which was about 1.7 s).

A plot of the apparent change in relative size of these objects in figure 5.8a illustrates how tau might be perceived by the subject under conditions of a constant ball size (A) and with the deflating balloon (B). As the balls (A) approached the subject, the retinal image increased in size about 1,200%; the retinal image of the deflating balloon (B) expanded only about 500% after the initiation of the balloon's trajectory. In addition,

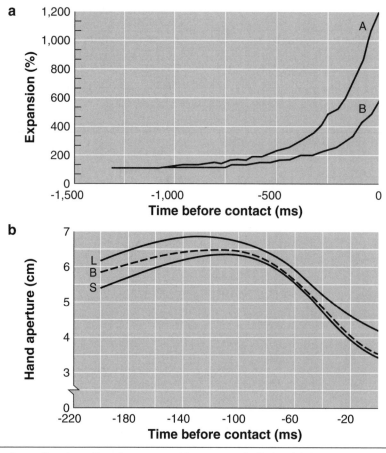

Figure 5.8. Temporal coordination of hand aperture with apparent ball size. (a) Apparent rate of expansion during ball flight (A = constant ball size, B = balloon). (b) Hand aperture changes prior to contact (L = large ball, B = balloon, S = small ball).

Adapted from Savelsbergh, Whiting, and Bootsma, 1991.

the rate of expansion for the balls was considerably faster than for the balloon. In response to this changing visual array, the average apertures of the hand changed as subjects prepared to catch the moving objects during the final 200 ms, as illustrated in figure 5.8b. Throughout the final 200 ms of ball flight, the hand aperture was larger in anticipation of catching the large ball (L) compared to the small ball (S). But notice the changes in the hand aperture over this same period for the deflating balloon (B). At 200 ms before contact, the hand prepares for the deflating ball with an aperture whose size is between that of the large and the small ball; and as the balloon decreased to the size of the small ball, the hand aperture did as well. What made this finding even more compelling were the postexperiment interviews, which indicated that none of the subjects was aware of the deflating properties of the balloon: the scaling of hand aperture to the moment-to-moment size of the deflating balloon had apparently occurred without conscious awareness.

These findings illustrate both how T_c is revealed to the subject by the optic expansion of the visual flow, and how the catching actions of the subjects were scaled in anticipation of intercepting the object with a temporally precise grasp. However, as cautioned by Abernethy and Burgess-Limerick (1992), the fact that this experiment and others (e.g., Lee, Lishman, & Thomson, 1982; Savelsbergh et al., 1993) provide evidence *consistent* with tau does not rule out the possibility that T_c can be specified in other ways as well (see also Cavallo & Laurent, 1988; Smeets et al., 1996; Stewart, Cudworth, & Lishman, 1993; Tresilian, 1995, 1997; Wann, 1996).

Spatial Information. One of the most difficult tasks faced by outfielders in baseball is judging where to go to catch a batted ball; it is not uncommon, even among the most highly skilled, for an outfielder to run in to catch a ball, only to reverse and run backward. What information is used to make the judgment?

McLeod and Dienes (1993, 1996), following earlier work by Chapman (1968; see also Michaels & Oudejans, 1992; Todd, 1981), suggest that a fielder uses the angle of elevation (α) of gaze between the fielder and the ball as the key information for making decisions about *where to go* to intercept the ball. The sequence of illustrations in figure 5.9 describes McLeod and Dienes's (1996) analysis. Figure 5.9a shows how α is computed in

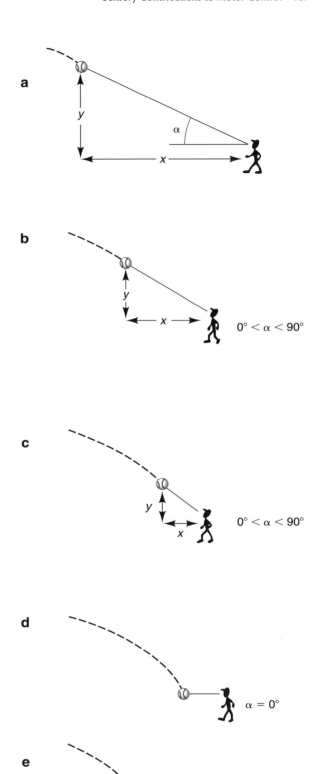

Figure 5.9. How a fielder uses the angle of elevation of gaze to decide whether to run forward or backward to catch a ball.
Reprinted from McLeod and Dienes, 1996.

relation to a fielder in baseball or cricket. Given the path of the ball in figure 5.9a, the fielder determines that movement toward the ball (to decrease x) is required before the ball hits the ground (as y approaches 0). The fielder's forward movement is depicted in figure 5.9, b and c (further decreasing x), as the ball falls to the ground (further decreasing y). In so doing, the fielder always keeps the angle of gaze (α) between 0° and 90°. If the angle of gaze ever becomes 0° (i.e., $y = 0$ and $x > 0$), then the ball will land in front of the fielder (figure 5.9d). Likewise, if α ever equals 90° (i.e., $x = 0$ and $y > 0$), then the ball will go over the fielder's head (figure 5.9e). But how does the fielder use this information to make the catch?

Chapman (1968) predicted (and the prediction was confirmed in experiments by McLeod & Dienes, 1993, 1996; Michaels & Oudejans, 1992) that the fielder will arrive at the correct place to catch the ball if the fielder's running speed is adjusted in order that the *acceleration* of the tangent of α is *zero*. Contrary to Chapman's prediction, however, fielders do not run at constant velocities; rather they accelerate and decelerate their running speed as necessary based on updated samples of angular gaze (α) in order to keep the acceleration of tan α at zero (McLeod & Dienes, 1996). Of course, this strategy does not guarantee that the fielder will always make the *catch*, only that the fielder will be in the right position to try to catch the ball.

Controlling Whole-Body Actions

The work by McLeod and others represents just a small part of a much larger research field dealing with the control of balance. Early thinking about postural control tended to focus on mechanisms that are seemingly obvious contributors to the skills, such as the vestibular apparatus in the inner ear. The receptors are sensitive to deviations from the vertical, to the orientation of the body in space, and to the accelerations applied to the head when the body is moved. All these aspects of balance possibly could be signaled by these receptors.

A second class of processes for the control of balance includes the various receptors associated with the joints and muscles. These processes will be discussed in more detail later in this chapter, but for now consider that the system is organized to maintain given angles (or muscle lengths) for the joints associated with a particular position. When the body begins to lose equilibrium, the

movement of the joints away from the balanced position can be sensed by the joint receptors, or perhaps by the stretch of the spindles in the muscles that control the joint. Also, there could be tactile sensation from the feet or toes indicating loss of balance. Each of these receptors, alone or in some combination, could conceivably provide the input necessary in order for the person to sense a loss of balance and could provide a basis for initiating a correction. Nashner and McCollum (1985) have conducted experiments in which the balance of the subject is unexpectedly disrupted during standing or walking, and have observed that compensations are produced as a result of these perturbations (for reviews, see Shumway-Cook & Woollacott, 1995; Woollacott & Jensen 1996). It is clear that the structures in the muscles and joints are the major receptor mechanisms.

Vision and Balance.   A third source of feedback about balance was emphasized by Lee (e.g., see Lee, 1980 for a review). Earlier in this chapter we discussed the concept of visual proprioception, noting that it tells us where our eyes (and therefore, our head and body) are in space and how they are moving (if they are) via analysis of the patterns of optical flow received from the surrounding surfaces and elements in the environment (boxed text on page 100). Could vision be involved in the control of balance? One common finding, as pointed out by Lee (1980), is that people who are blind are generally less stable in posture than are sighted people, with the former swaying more when they stand. Also, sighted people sway more when they have their eyes closed. All this suggests that vision has an important role in balance.

But more convincing evidence for this assertion comes from some of Lee's experiments (Lee & Aronson, 1974). Lee used a "moving room" apparatus whereby a person stood on a stationary floor in a three-sided "room" with walls that could be moved backward and forward as a unit without movement of the floor. The effect of this wall movement on the posture and sway of the subject was studied. The general arrangement is shown in figure 5.10. With small children as subjects, moving the wall a few centimeters toward the subject caused loss of balance, resulting in a rather ungraceful sitting response and great surprise on the part of the child. Moving the walls away from the subject caused a drastic forward lean, which resulted in a stumble or a fall. When

Figure 5.10.   Experimental apparatus and paradigm for the "moving room."
Reprinted from Lee and Aronson, 1974.

adult subjects were studied, the effect was less drastic, but increases in sway, in phase with the direction of the wall movement, could be seen.

How can these effects be explained? Remember, the floor of the room was fixed, so that the movements of the walls could not have exerted *mechanical* influences on the position of the subjects. The mechanisms associated with the joint angles and muscle lengths, as well as the vestibular apparatus, also were not directly affected. The most reasonable explanation is that moving the wall toward the child changed the optical array. If the child was using the form of the optical array as a source of feedback. that signaled posture and balance, he or she could have interpreted the changed visual array as a loss of balance and produced a compensation in the opposite direction as a result. The walls appearing to move closer to the eye would, if the room were "normal," provide an optic array signaling that the person was falling forward, and a compensation to move backward would be expected. This is just what Lee found: moving the wall toward the subjects caused them to fall backward (see also Nashner & Berthoz, 1978).

Vision and Locomotion.   The role of vision during walking and running also seems to be greatly influenced by the optic flow of information. We walk down busy streets and through crowded

corridors and rarely bump into things or people. We walk on surfaces that have different textures and give them very little attention. But obviously we depend on vision to locomote through the environment. Is vision in this context used in the same way as discussed in the previous sections?

One way of answering this is to consider the activity of jogging along a path next to a stream. In this case the placement of the feet with each step is much more critical than, say, on the smooth surface of a running track; to avoid injury, the jogger's goal is to try to step on ground points that indicate good footing and to avoid unstable footings (such as tree roots and loose debris). If the jogger is running at a constant velocity, then how is stride length altered in order to selectively step on good ground footings?

Several potential solutions to this question were tested in an experiment by Warren, Young, and Lee (1986). Two experienced athletes ran at a constant velocity on a treadmill. At various times certain visual objects appeared on the treadmill, and the runner's task was to try to step on these visual cues by altering stride lengths as appropriate. Inspection of the running kinematics revealed that almost all the variations in stride length were attributable to changes in the *vertical impulse* applied at takeoff. A change in the vertical impulse will alter the amount of time that the lead leg spends in the air; thus, with velocity constant, the stride length will also change. According to Warren, Young, and Lee (1986), the vertical impulse necessary to achieve a specific distance is determined by the tau values of the takeoff and target point. The *tau gap* ($\Delta\tau$) is the difference in the values of T_c between the takeoff point of the first foot placement and the targeted landing spot of the second foot placement ($\tau_2 - \tau_1$). Since the runner is moving at a constant velocity, the tau gap directly specifies the time and hence the length of the stride required to get from the first to the second target, which can be altered by the vertical impulse against the ground by the takeoff leg (see also Hollands et al., 1995; Patla, 1989; Patla et al., 1989; Warren & Yaffe, 1989).

Of course, vision supplies much more than T_c information about how to walk without colliding with objects. Environmental cues provide information about *how* we must accommodate our actions. For example, in walking through *apertures* such as doorways there is a critical ratio between aperture clearance and shoulder width with a value of 1.3: for any value lower than this critical ratio, humans will rotate their shoulders in order to increase the effective passage width (Warren & Whang, 1987). A critical value also appears to be evident when we step over obstacles, and there is evidence that the leading leg uses a greater clearance difference if the obstacle is fragile (Patla et al., 1996). Many more examples are possible. However, the main point here is that vision is used in complex ways in order that we may locomote through the environment safely and efficiently (Patla, 1997).

Audition

Another of the senses traditionally classified as exteroceptive is hearing, or audition. Certainly, audition has a strongly exteroceptive role, informing us about the nature of movements in our environment—the direction of approach of a bicyclist in the dark, the sound of the starter's gun, and so on. But at the same time, like vision, audition can tell us a great deal about our own movements. As we all know, most of the movements we make in the environment produce sounds, such as the sound of footsteps when we are jogging or the sound of our own speech. The nature of these sounds, then, provides us with a great deal of information about our actions—for example, crunching sounds tell us about the kind of terrain we are jogging on, or beeps from the telephone tell us whether or not we are dialing correctly.

To some extent, audition and vision are very similar, providing both exteroceptive and proprioceptive information. For example, while flying in a dark cave, bats use acoustic information to orient themselves; sounds from objects (exteroceptive feedback) and from their own movements (exproprioceptive feedback) provide information for orienting them within the cave. Unfortunately, there has been very little research regarding how bats and humans use audition in motor control. One recent exception is a study by Lee (1990) in which he hypothesizes that bats can determine T_c by using tau in exactly the same way as described earlier—except that tau is based on the acoustic flow field rather than the visual flow field. However, there is a need for further research on this hypothesis and on the role of audition in motor control in general (see also Jenison, 1997).

Proprioceptors

In the next section we review the set of sensors that provide proprioceptive information (or kinesthesis) about the movement of the body. Although they do not seem to be as salient for movement control as vision, these sensors are fundamental in their importance for closed-loop control (Abbs & Winstein, 1990). In the first section we briefly outline their anatomy and function, and later we describe their role in motor control.

Vestibular System

Located in the inner ear are sensors that provide information about movements of the head. One aspect of head movement that is critical for motor control is its orientation with respect to gravity, that is, whether the head is upside down, tilted, and so on. Such information is provided by two small structures located in the inner ear, the *saccule* and *utricle*, that signal information about the orientation of the head to the line of gravity. If the head is spinning (e.g., in a somersault), they provide information about the rate and direction of spin. Located near the utricle and saccule are three fluid-filled half circles, called the *semicircular canals*. Because the canals are oriented in each of the major planes of the body (frontal, sagittal, horizontal), these structures are in a position to sense particular directions of movement, as well as rotation. All these vestibular structures contain thick fluid that moves when the head position is changed. The movement of the liquid bends tiny hairs that send information to the central nervous system about the movements of the head. As one might imagine, these structures are important in balance, as well as in movements for which the individual requires information about forces and accelerations applied to the head (e.g., flying a plane, doing a somersault; see Kelly, 1991, for further discussion).

Muscle Receptors

There are two main types of receptors that provide complementary information about the state of the muscles. The *muscle spindle* is located in the fleshy part of the muscle body and is most active when the muscle is *stretched*. The *Golgi tendon organ* is located in the junction between the muscle and tendon and is most active when the muscle *contracts* (Gordon & Ghez, 1991).

Muscle Spindles

Between the fibers of the main muscles of the body are small spindle-shaped (cigar-shaped) structures that are connected in parallel with the muscles so that they become stretched when the main muscle is stretched. Figure 5.11a shows that the spindle consists of three main components: small muscle fibers called *intrafusal fibers* that are

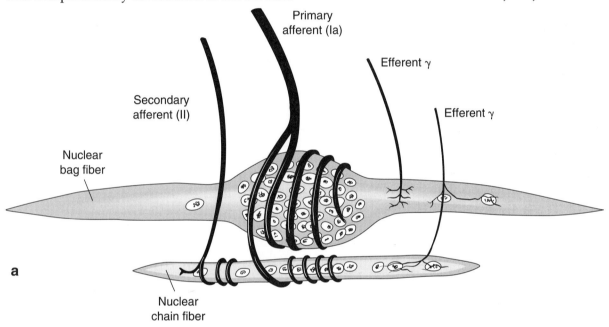

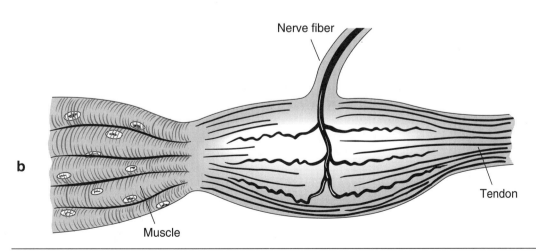

Figure 5.11.   Muscle receptors. (a) Muscle spindle; (b) Golgi tendon organ.
Reprinted from Shumway-Cook and Woollacott, 1995.

innervated by *gamma (γ) efferent (motor) neurons and type Ia and II afferent neurons.*[3] The intrafusal fibers are made up of two types, bag and chain fibers, the polar ends of which provide a tension on the central region of the spindle, called the *equatorial region.* The sensory receptors located here are sensitive to the length of the equatorial region when the spindle is stretched. The major neurological connection to this sensory region is the *Ia afferent fiber,* whose output is related to the length of the equatorial region (position information) as well as to the rate of change in length of this region (velocity information). The spindle connects to the alpha motor neurons for the same muscle, providing excitation to the muscle when it is stretched. This is the basis for the so-called stretch reflex discussed later in this chapter. Thus, the spindle appears to have a strong role in movement regulation (Vallbo, 1974).

There has been a great deal of controversy about what the spindle actually signals to the central nervous system (see Gandevia & Burke, 1992, and commentaries). A major conceptual problem in the past was that the output of the Ia afferent that presumably signals stretch or velocity is related to two separate factors. First, Ia output is increased by the elongation of the overall muscle via elongation of the spindle as a whole. But, second, the Ia output is related to the stretch placed on the equatorial region by the intrafusal fibers via the gamma motor neurons. Therefore, the central nervous system would have difficulty in interpreting changes in the Ia output as being due to (a) changes in the overall muscle length with a constant gamma motor neuron activity, (b) changes in gamma motor neuron activity with a constant muscle length, or perhaps (c) changes in both (see Muscle Spindles and the Gamma Loop, later in this chapter). Another problem was that there was no strong evidence that the Ia afferent fibers actually sent information to the sensory cortex of the brain, where other sensory events were thought to be registered. This was suggested by Gelfan and Carter's (1967) research on humans undergoing operations involving wrist tendon repair under local anesthetic only. When the muscles were passively stretched and the subjects were asked what they felt when the tendon was pulled, they usually reported no sensations or sensations that were inconsistent with the direction of tendon pull. Primarily for these reasons, an older view

held that the muscle spindles were not important for the conscious perception of movement or position.

Data from Goodwin, McCloskey, and Matthews (1972) and others (Rogers, Bendrups, & Lewis, 1985; Sittig, Denier van der Gon, & Gielen, 1985a) have helped to change this point of view. In these studies, subjects had a rapid vibration applied to the biceps tendon at the elbow. The blindfolded subject was asked to "track" the passive movements of the vibrated arm with corresponding movements of the other arm; thus, the subject had to perceive where the right arm was and match that (consciously felt) position with movements of the left arm. The vibration of the tendon produces a small, rapid, alternating stretch and release of the tendon, which affects the muscle spindle and distorts the output of the Ia afferents from the spindles located in the vibrated muscle.

Goodwin, McCloskey, and Matthews (1972) found as much as 40° misalignment of the vibrated arm with the unvibrated arm. The interpretation was that the vibration distorted the Ia information coming from the same muscle, which led to a misperception of that limb's position and hence to improper decisions about the positioning of the opposite limb. The argument, then, is that this information from the Ia actually did reach consciousness and that the Ia was the basis for knowing the limb's position. (To control for the possibility that the vibration merely influenced the structures in the joint capsule, the authors placed the vibrator over the triceps tendon; the misalignment occurred in the opposite direction, much as would be expected if the perception of the Ia output from the triceps muscle were being disrupted.) Such evidence supports the idea that the muscle spindle provides information about limb position and velocity (Sittig, 1986; Sittig, Denier van der Gon, & Gielen, 1985a, 1985b)—quite a different view from that held earlier. There is still some question whether or not the spindle is sufficiently sensitive to detect small positional changes, and thus it may be only one of a number of sources for detecting position (see Kelso & Stelmach, 1976).

Golgi Tendon Organs

The other receptor for muscle information is the Golgi tendon organ. These structures are tiny receptors located in the junction where the muscle "blends into" the tendon (figure 5.11b). They seem to be ideally located to provide information about tension in the muscles, because they lie in series with (i.e., between) the force-producing contractile elements in the muscle and the tendon that attaches the muscle to the bone.

The Golgi tendon organ has been shown to produce an *inhibition* of the muscle in which it is located, so that a stretch to the active muscle would cause the same muscle to decrease its tension somewhat. Also, the finding that a very large stretch of the muscle (near physiological limits) appeared to be required to induce the tendon organ to fire led to speculation that the sensor was primarily a protective device that would prevent the muscle from contracting so forcefully that it would rupture a tendon.

However, the work of Houk and Henneman (1967) and Stuart (e.g., Stuart et al., 1972) has provided a different picture of the functioning of the Golgi tendon organ. First, anatomical evidence revealed that each organ was connected to only a small group of from 3 to 25 muscle fibers, not to the entire muscle as had been suspected. Thus, the various receptors were sensing forces produced in different parts of the muscle. Moreover, there were only a few (up to 15) different motor units[4] represented in the muscle fibers attached to a single tendon organ, so that the tendon organ now appeared to be in a very good position to sense the tensions produced in a limited number of *individual* motor units, not in the whole muscle. This work has also shown, contrary to the earlier beliefs, that the tendon organs can respond to forces of less than .1 g (Houk & Henneman, 1967). Such evidence suggests that the Golgi tendon organs are very sensitive detectors for active tension in localized portions of a muscle, in addition to having the well-known protective function discussed earlier (see Jami, 1992, for further discussion).

Joint Receptors

The joints of the various limbs are surrounded by a sheath called a joint capsule, which is primarily responsible for holding the lubricating fluid for the joint. Embedded within the joint capsules are different kinds of receptor cells (Ruffini endings, pacininan corpuscles) known as the *joint receptors*. They are located primarily on the parts of the joint capsule that are stretched most when the joint is moved, originally leading investigators to believe that these receptors were involved in the perception of joint position. By studying the cat hindlimb, Skoglund (1956) found individual re-

ceptors that were active at very specific locations in the range of limb movement (e.g., from 150° to 180° of joint angle for a particular cell). Another cell would fire at a different set of joint angles, and so on. Presumably, the central nervous system could "know" where the limbs were by detecting which of the joint receptors were active.

These conclusions have been seriously challenged, however (see Kelso & Stelmach, 1976, for a review). A number of investigators (e.g., Burgess & Clark, 1969) have found that only a small proportion of the joint receptors fire at specific angles; rather, most of the joint receptors tend to fire near the extremes of the movement in a joint. Further, other researchers have found that the nature of the firing pattern is dependent on whether the movement is active or passive (Boyd & Roberts, 1953) and is dependent on the direction of motion of the joint (see Smith, 1977). The fact that the firing pattern of the joint receptors is dependent on factors other than the simple position of the limb has dimmed enthusiasm for the hypothesis that the joint receptors are the means by which the system determines joint positions.

Cutaneous Receptors

Other receptors related to movement perception are located in various places in the skin. Although such receptors can signal many separate states of the body, such as pain, pressure, heat, cold, or chemical stimuli, the important ones for movement control are those receptors that signal information about touch and, to some extent, deep pressure. In addition, pain sensations are certainly information for specific kinds of movement behaviors.

Different kinds of cutaneous receptors exist: some close to the surface and others much deeper, some in glabrous (hairless) skin and others particular to hairy skin. One of these, called the pacinian corpuscle, is located deep in the skin and is stimulated by deep deformation such as would be produced by a blow or heavy pressure. Other kinds of receptors in the skin include the Meissner corpuscles, Merkel's disks, Ruffini's corpuscles, and "free" nerve endings. The last provide especially strong signals when hairs on the body are deformed by light touch, as they are located close to the hair follicles. Near the surface of glabrous skin (such as that of the lips and the palms of the hands) there is a particularly strong concentration of Meissner corpuscles and Merkel's disks. The fingertips have one of the highest concentrations of cutaneous receptors on the body and provide information about the surfaces of objects through touch (Martin & Jessell, 1991).

Input to the Central Nervous System

The major pathways for transmitting signals from the periphery to the brain are the spinal tracts, located alongside the vertebrae that make up the spinal column. There are 8 cervical, 12 thoracic, 5 lumbar, and 5 sacral vertebrae, defining a number of *segments* of the spinal cord. Except for the input from the structures in the head and neck (for our purposes here, mainly from the eyes, ears, and vestibular apparatus, entering through one or more of the 12 cranial nerves), the input to the central nervous system is through bundles, called roots, that collect and guide the input to the spinal cord at each segment. Each segment serves a particular region of the body.

Input from the various receptors comes together in the periphery into *spinal nerves*, collections of individual neurons (both sensory, or afferent, and motor, or efferent) that carry information toward and away from the spinal cord. These nerves branch into two roots near the cord, called the dorsal (posterior, or back) and *ventral* (anterior, or front) roots, where they contact the spinal cord separately. At this point, there is almost complete division of the neurons into afferent (or sensory) neurons, which enter via the dorsal roots, and efferent (or motor) neurons, which leave the cord via the ventral roots. Once inside the cord, the afferent neurons can either *synapse* (connect) with other neurons whose cell bodies are in the central gray matter, or travel to higher or lower levels in the cord or to the brain in one of the many tracts that form the white matter adjacent to the gray matter.

Ensemble Characteristics

Proprioception enables us to tell with remarkable accuracy where our limbs are and how they are acting, but how do the various receptors mentioned in the previous sections contribute to our motor control capabilities? An important concept is that any one of the receptors in isolation from the others is generally ineffective in signaling information about the movements of the body. This is so because the various receptors are often

sensitive to a variety of aspects of body motion at the same time. For example, the Golgi tendon organs probably cannot signal information about movement, because they cannot differentiate between the forces produced in a static contraction and the same forces produced when the limb is moving. The spindle is sensitive to muscle length, but it is also sensitive to the rate of change in length (velocity) and to the activity in the intrafusal fibers that are known to be active during contractions; so the spindle confounds information about position of the limb and the level of contraction of the muscles (force). And the joint receptors are sensitive to joint position, but their output can be affected by the tensions applied and by the direction of movement, or by whether the movement is active or passive (Paillard & Bruchon, 1968).

As a solution to this problem, many have suggested that the central nervous system combines and integrates information in some way to resolve the kind of ambiguity in the signals produced by any one of these receptors (e.g., Wetzel & Stuart, 1976). Producing an *ensemble* of information by combining the various separate sources could enable the generation of less ambiguous information about movement (Gandevia & Burke, 1992). How the central nervous system does this, and which sources of information are most strongly represented in which situations, are important questions for the future. We turn now to the ways in which these various sources of sensory information contribute to movement control.

Proprioception and Motor Control

The closed-loop ideas presented earlier have been considered in human performance in various ways, but one of the more common is to think of the closed-loop system as a system that contains conscious decision making. (Of course, as discussed earlier, this does not rule out the possibility that other embedded closed-loop systems do not involve consciousness.) It is useful to consider the executive level of this system as consisting of the information-processing stages discussed in the previous two chapters. This idea is illustrated in figure 5.12. An original command for action, such as an external stimulus or an internal self-generated "go" signal, starts the action by progressing through the stimulus-identification, response-selection, and response-programming stages, eventually leading to evocation of the movement commands to the muscles. This portion of the closed-loop model is similar to that involved in an open-loop system.

The difference becomes apparent, however, when one considers the actions *subsequent* to this first aspect of the movement. First, a *reference of correctness* is generated that will serve as the standard against which the feedback from the performance is judged. This reference of correctness can be thought of as a representation of the feedback qualities associated with moving correctly; it is analogous to the value to which you set your thermostat in your home heating system or to the compass heading for the automatic pilot of a ship. The reference of correctness represents the state of the feedback associated with the correct movements of the limbs during the intended action; it specifies *a goal to be achieved.*

According to the model presented in figure 5.12, muscle contractions cause the limbs and

body to move, producing changes in the environment as a result. Each of these effects generates information. The contracting muscles and the movement of the body produce sensations from the various receptor systems described earlier. Then, via the reference of correctness, the system can compare the feedback it receives with the feedback it expects to receive. If the two sources of feedback are the same, the implication is that the movement is correct and that no adjustments are necessary. But if a difference exists between the feedback received and the reference, then an error is signaled and a correction is required.

Influence of Movement Duration

Closed-loop models such as the one in figure 5.12 are conceptualized in essentially two ways, depending on the nature of the motor skill. For rapid movements, feedback provides a basis for knowing whether a movement produced is correct or not. For example, after a golf ball is hit, the sensations from the swing are available in memory

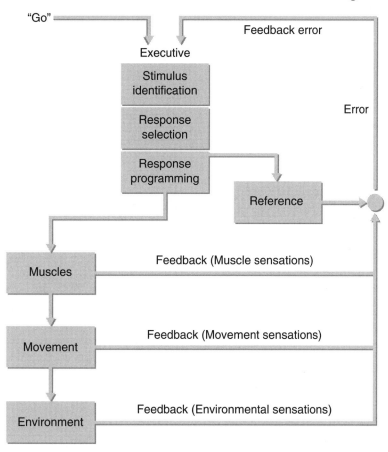

Figure 5.12.   The expanded closed-loop model for movement control.

for a brief period of time and can be analyzed. A professional golfer probably will be able to tell a great deal about the direction and distance of the golf shot just from the feel and sound of it. A second way in which the closed-loop ideas in figure 5.12 are used concerns the control of ongoing movements. These kinds of models have obvious relevance to continuous skills, such as steering a car down a highway. Think of the reference as evaluating the set of sensations associated with moving at a particular speed or with maintaining a certain distance behind another car. If one of these goals is not met, the feedback received and the reference do not match, and an error is fed back to the executive level to compute a correction. Thus, these closed-loop models view the control of a car on a highway as a series of corrections that keep the vehicle safely on the road.

Control of Long-Duration Movements

The closed-loop model presented in figure 5.12 has been very useful for describing certain kinds of movements. The model seems to have the most relevance for tasks that require a great deal of time, because the processes involved in the analysis of the error information are ongoing and relatively slow. Also, the model best relates to movements in which something is *regulated* at some constant value, such as keeping the car at a particular speed by monitoring the speedometer or keeping the airplane on the proper glide path when guiding it onto the runway. These are called *tracking* movements (chapter 2), and they constitute an important class of motor behavior. Tracking tasks have received considerable study, much of this work having been directed to problems in vehicle control, gunnery, and the like. An excellent review of the research on tracking was provided by Poulton (1974) and has been updated by Hammerton (1989) and Wickens (1992).

There are many different mathematical and physical models of tracking behavior; the major differences relate to how the system uses feedback information and how the system initiates a correction when errors are detected. The most important generalization from this research is that if the models are used in computer or mechanical *simulations* of the human (in which the device is controlled in ways analogous to those in figure 5.12), these nonliving devices "come alive" to behave in ways nearly indistinguishable from their human counterparts. For example, when we perform a laboratory tracking task, approximately 200 ms

elapses between the appearance of an error and the initiation of a correction back toward the center of the track. Such lags and the character of the correction can be mimicked very well, and the statistical agreement between the actual and simulated movements is good for this kind of task. This evidence does not prove that humans actually track this way, but the agreement between theoretical predictions and data is very strong, and alternative theories cannot boast of similar success.

Changing the Reference of Correctness

We can extend this idea somewhat (as Adams, 1971, 1976a, 1977, has done) to account for how the individual makes a limb movement such as would be involved in sawing a board or in reaching for a mug of beer. Here, the reference of correctness is not a single state as in the earlier examples, but rather a set of states that is changing at each moment in time. Thus, at each moment in time the reference of correctness would have a different specification for position of the limb. Because the reference is constantly changing, it can be matched against the feedback from the moving limb, which is also changing as the movement progresses, so that errors in the movement's *trajectory* can be detected and corrected. This kind of mechanism is the basis for Adams's (1971) theory of learning, according to which the subject learns a set of references of correctness that the closed-loop system is to "track" during the movement. We will have more to say about Adams's ideas later in the book when we discuss learning theory (chapter 13).

But these kinds of models have serious limitations. Engineers can design robots and other machines to behave in this way, using what they call *point-to-point computation* methods. The position of the limb at each point in space and at each time in the movement is represented by a reference of correctness, and the system can be made to track this set of positions across time to produce an action with a particular form. But the system must process information very rapidly, even for the simplest of movements. All these references of correctness must be stored somewhere, creating difficulties when we realize that each of the points will be different if the movement begins from a slightly different place or if it is to take a slightly different pathway through space.

Engineers have generally found that these methods are very inefficient for machine (robot) control; such findings have led many motor behavior researchers (see Greene, 1972; Kelso, 1995; Turvey, 1977) away from these kinds of control processes to explain human skills. But there is still the possibility that the system might operate in this way at certain times or for certain skills that demand very high precision (e.g., threading a needle or slicing a loaf of bread). Also, such a mechanism might serve as the basis for *recognizing* errors at various places in the movement as it is carried out, without actually being the basis for control. After a tennis stroke the performer could say that the elbow was bent too much on the backswing, and thus have the basis for making a correction in the movement on the next attempt. Finally, the possibility exists that the system might make use of reflexive mechanisms (without using the information-processing stages), or mechanical mechanisms (Bizzi et al., 1982), to hold itself on the proper track; these possibilities are discussed later.

A compromise view is that only *certain positions* in the movement are represented by references of correctness. One view is that feedback from the movement when it is at its endpoint is checked against a reference of correctness; then corrections are initiated to move the limb to the proper position. These views of motor control hold that the limb is more or less "thrown" in the direction of the endpoint by some kind of open-loop control and that the limb then "homes in on" the target by closed-loop control. Here, the actual trajectory of the limb is determined by how the limb is "thrown," in combination with mechanical factors such as gravity and friction. In this view, the trajectory is not determined by point-to-point computation as a purely closed-loop system might explain it.

Control of Rapid Movements

One of the most important points to have emerged from the evidence presented in chapters 3 and 4 was that the information-processing mechanisms, which lie at the very heart of the closed-loop system in figure 5.12, require a great deal of *time* in order for stimuli to be processed to yield a response. So far we have assumed that each error signal the system receives must be processed in these stages and that the response (a correction) can follow only after all the stages of processing have been completed. Thus, a correction is seen in the same way as for any other response to a stimulus. It requires a great deal of time and attention.

But there is a problem. In the closed-loop models such as that shown in figure 5.12, rapid actions do not provide sufficient time for the system to (a) generate an error, (b) detect the error, (c) determine the correction, (d) initiate the correction, and (e) correct the movement before a rapid movement is completed. The left jab of champion boxer Muhammad Ali is a good example. The movement itself was about 40 ms; yet, according to our estimates, visually detecting an aiming error and correcting it during the same movement should require about 150 to 200 ms—the time necessary to complete the activities of the stages of information processing. The movement is finished before the correction can begin. For this reason, the closed-loop models of movement behavior do not seem to be well suited for explaining rapid movements.

This and other limitations to the closed-loop models will be raised again in chapter 6. For now, suffice it to say that the closed-loop mechanisms involving the stages of processing appear to have a very difficult time explaining rapid movements. Because these models have much credibility with respect to very slow movement and posture and have little with respect to rapid movement, it is possible that there are essentially two fundamentally different kinds of movements: fast and slow. We return to this distinction in chapter 6.

Reflexive Closed-Loop Control

In considering closed-loop control of movement, we dealt only with the kind of closed-loop model in which the determination of the correction was produced by conscious information-processing mechanisms. What about the possibility that the central nervous system contains closed-loop mechanisms that do not require any attention? Many examples are possible, such as the control of body temperature and the regulation of breathing during sleep. In this section we discuss evidence that these nonconscious mechanisms are involved in the control of voluntary movements as well.

Latencies of Corrections

An experiment by Dewhurst (1967) is representative of a number of studies on this problem. The subject was asked to hold the elbow at a right angle to support a light weight attached to the hand. The subject could monitor the performance in this simple task through vision of a dot on an oscilloscope screen that provided information about the angle of the elbow. The experimenter recorded the position of the arm together with the rectified electromyographical (EMG) activity in the biceps muscle as the subject performed. Unexpectedly the weight attached to the hand was increased, and naturally the hand began to move downward. After a brief period, the subject increased the EMG activity to the biceps muscle, which increased its force output and brought the limb back to the right-angle position.

Given that the lowered arm represents an error in performance that can be corrected, how much time will elapse before the increase is seen in the elbow flexors' EMG? If the subject must process the visual and/or kinesthetic feedback from the arm through the information-processing stages, there should be no increase in biceps EMG for approximately 150 to 200 ms.

Figure 5.13 shows the essential results. The weight was added at the point in time indicated by the arrow, and the limb began to move downward immediately. The records show a small burst of EMG about 30 ms after the weight was added and a larger irregular burst beginning about 50 ms afterward. Just after this second burst of EMG, the limb began to move back to the target position. This change in EMG represents a clear correction

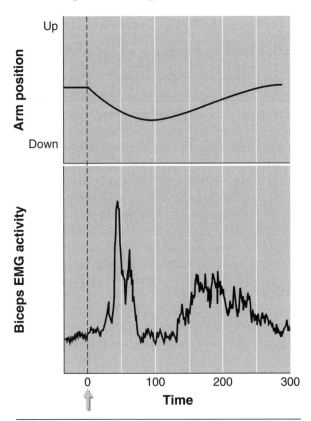

Figure 5.13. Movement and rectified EMG record showing the latencies of two reflex-based corrections.
Reprinted from Dewhurst, 1967.

for the added weight, yet this correction was initiated far more quickly than can be explained by an attentionally based, closed-loop process as shown in figure 5.12. Rather, the correction is thought to be due to the operation of reflexes in lower, probably spinal, levels in the central nervous system.

Consciousness and Reflexive Corrections

Another aspect of reflexive corrections for errors, aside from their apparent rapidity, is that they might not require attention as other corrections seem to. Evidence for this notion was provided in a study by Henry (1953), in which subjects had to regulate the force they applied to a handle. The basic arrangement is shown in figure 5.14. The standing subject (blindfolded in the actual experiment) is pushing against a handle attached to a mechanical device that could continuously alter the position of the handle. The arrangement was such that if the subject was not pressing against the handle, the handle would move forward and backward unpredictably. But there was a spring placed between the machine and the handle so that by modulating the force produced at each moment, the subject could maintain the handle in a constant position.

Henry used three conditions. In one condition, the subject's task was to keep the *pressure* against the handle fixed by varying the position of the handle. When the handle pushed against the subject, the correct response was to "ease up," so that the tension was held constant. In the second condition, the subject was to compensate for the changing pressures exerted by the handle so that a constant *position* of the handle was maintained, but with constantly changing pressure exerted. A third condition was used to assess the conscious *perception* of change; the subject attempted to hold the arm immobile, reporting through a left-finger movement when a change in the pressure exerted by the apparatus was sensed. The pressure changes were different for different segments in the testing period, and Henry could obtain an estimate of the amount of change required for conscious perception of change.

Henry (1953) found that the "threshold" force needed for an appropriate adjustment depended strongly on *what* the subject was asked to control. When the subject was asked to report a conscious change, a force of .559 dynes was required for detection. But when the subject was asked to respond to changes in *tension*, a force of only .296 dynes was successfully detected and responded

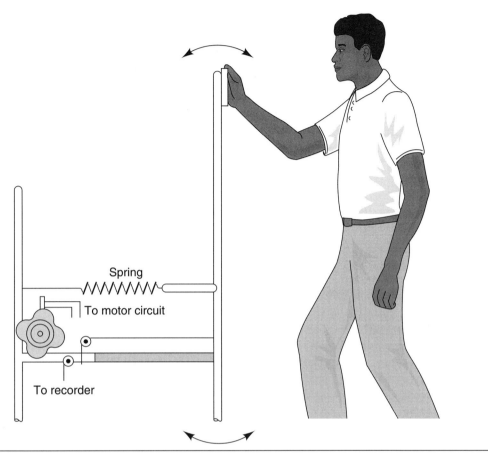

Figure 5.14.   Apparatus and general arrangement in Henry's experiment.
Adapted from Henry, 1953.

to by the muscular system; apparently, subjects were responding to forces too small to be detected consciously. Even more striking was the finding that position changes associated with a force change of only .029 dynes produced successful modifications in movement control. Thus, the motor system, in holding a constant *position* against the apparatus, could respond to a change that was considerably less (i.e., .029 versus .559) than the change necessary for conscious awareness. In the constant-pressure condition—and particularly in the constant-position condition—the motor system was responding to stimuli that were too small to be detected consciously. These adjustments were apparently made without the subject's awareness.

Experiments like the ones just described show two important things about movement control. First, studies like Dewhurst's (1967; see also Houk & Rymer, 1981; see Lee, Murphy, & Tatton, 1983, for a review) show that the corrections for suddenly presented changes in position can be initiated far more rapidly than the earlier 200-ms estimates, with correction latencies of 30–80 ms. This kind of result suggests that the information-

processing stages, at least as shown in figure 5.12, are not involved in these actions, as the stages require far too much time for processing. Second, the data from Henry (1953) and others show that subjects can make adjustments for changes in position—and perhaps for changes in tension—that are so small that the subject cannot perceive them consciously. These data also suggest that the stages of information processing are not involved, because at least some of these stages are thought to entail conscious processing and attention in the sense discussed in chapter 4. Both of these lines of evidence suggest that these kinds of corrections are produced via reflexive mechanisms that do not concern the stages of processing.

Muscle Spindles and the Gamma Loop

The mechanisms responsible for the effects just described probably involve the muscle spindle, the small, cigar-shaped structure located between and in parallel to the main fibers of the skeletal muscles (review figure 5.11a). The (simplified) neurological connections of the spindle to the spinal cord are illustrated in figure 5.15. Recall

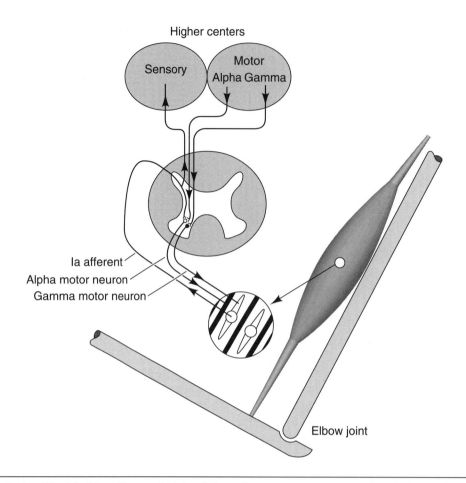

Higher centers

Sensory

Motor
Alpha Gamma

Ia afferent
Alpha motor neuron
Gamma motor neuron

Elbow joint

Figure 5.15.   A simplified "wiring diagram" of the alpha and gamma motor systems in relation to the spinal cord and higher centers.

from figure 5.11a that the small intrafusal muscle fibers are innervated by efferent neurons (gamma motor neurons) that emerge from the ventral (front) side of the cord. When activated by the central nervous system, they cause the intrafusal fibers to contract somewhat, which distends the central sensory region of the spindle. When so distended, the Ia afferent fibers emerging from this area fire more rapidly, and this information is delivered to the dorsal side of the spinal cord through the dorsal roots. The information from the Ia afferent is sent to essentially two places: to the alpha motor neurons in the same muscle and also upward to various sensory regions in the brain. Finally, notice that the alpha motor neurons are innervated by two separate sources. There is innervation from higher motor centers in the brain as well as innervation by the Ia afferent from the spindle. This is a very simplified description; for example, although we have shown only one such circuit here, many of them operate together at the spinal cord level.

As mentioned earlier, when the muscle is stretched, the spindle stretches with it, and the sensory region of the spindle causes the Ia afferent to fire more rapidly, delivering information about muscle stretch to the central nervous system. However, the Ia afferent feeds back to the alpha motor neuron, in that when the Ia afferent is firing more because of a stretch it tends to increase the firing rate of the alpha motor neurons; this causes the same muscle that was stretched to increase its force output and oppose the effect of the stretch.

This process is the basis of what has been called the *monosynaptic stretch reflex*. An example of this reflex is experienced when the patellar tendon is struck lightly just below the kneecap with the knee flexed. The resulting "knee-jerk reflex" is caused by the rapid stretch of the muscle, which stretches the spindle, which increases the firing of the Ia afferent transmitted to the cord where it increases the alpha motor neuron firing rate, which causes the muscle to contract. This is an *autogenetic reflex*, because it causes an action in the same muscle that was stimulated. The loop time, or the time from the initial stretch until the extrafusal fibers are increased in their innervation, is about 30 ms in humans. Because this 30-ms value corresponds with the latency for the first burst of EMG shown in the Dewhurst (1967) experiment (see figure 5.13), this monosynaptic mechanism is probably responsible for this first compensation for the added weight.

Notice that the activity in the Ia afferent is determined by two things: (a) the length and the rate of stretch of the extrafusal muscle fibers and (b) the amount of tension in the intrafusal fibers, which is determined by the firing of the gamma efferent fibers (figure 5.15). Both alpha and gamma motor neurons can be controlled by higher motor centers, and they are thought to be "coordinated" in their action by a process termed *alpha-gamma coactivation* (Granit, 1970; Rothwell, 1994). Notice that the output to the main body of the muscle (through the alpha motor neuron) is determined by (a) the level of innervation provided directly from the higher centers and (b) the amount of added innervation provided indirectly from the Ia afferent.

This information may explain how Dewhurst's (1967) subjects responded so quickly to the added weight. When the subject was holding the weight steadily, a coordinated pattern of innervation to the alpha and gamma motor neurons produced just enough tension in the muscle to hold the elbow at a right angle. Now, when the weight was added, the muscle was stretched, the spindles' sensory receptors were distended, and the additional Ia afferents' firing caused a stretch reflex that tended to increase the activity in the main muscle, all within 30 ms. All this activity occurs at the same level of the spinal cord as did the innervation of the muscles in the first place, and no higher centers were involved in this 30 ms loop. This helps explain why Henry's (1953) subjects were able to make corrections for position that they could not even perceive; some of the corrections for changes in position occur in the spinal cord, without the conscious involvement of the information-processing stages.

Control of Muscle Stiffness. The monosynaptic reflexes have been known for many years (Lee et al., 1983, for a review), but their function in movement is still debated. An early view was that the spindles were responsible for the control of muscle length in posture. They seem particularly well suited to this role, because when an animal sways, the muscles supporting the skeleton are stretched and reflex compensations occur quickly without requiring the animal's consciousness. But the spindle seems also to be related to the control of muscle *stiffness*, which is probably very important in the control of posture and other movements. Stiffness, which is one of the measures used to describe the characteristics of elastic materials, is defined in terms of the amount of tension increase required to increase the length of the object by a certain amount. Engineers define stiffness more precisely as the change in tension divided by the resulting change in length. If a spring is very stiff, a great deal of tension is needed to increase its length by a given amount; for a less stiff spring, much less tension is required. This is important because the muscle seems to provide a compliant (springy) interface between the performer and the environment.

While maintaining posture, it may be that the muscles supporting the skeleton are contracting under the influence of the gamma loop just described. This is conceptualized in figure 5.16, which shows a bone being supported by two opposing muscles producing force. As the system is perturbed, causing the bone to move downward, the muscle on the right side of the diagram is lengthened slightly, causing the stretch reflex described earlier. Perhaps even more important, because the contracting muscle is a "springy" substance, more tension is produced in it by purely *mechanical* means as its length increases. Furthermore, this change in tension is *instantaneous*, just as the change in tension in a spring would be if it were stretched. Such increases in tension have the effect of opposing the perturbation, bringing the system back to the original position. Nichols and Houk (1976) have provided evidence that the muscle spindle is responsible for the maintenance of muscle stiffness when the muscle is stretched, so that it can continue to act as a spring in the control of posture and similar movements (see also Houk, 1979; Houk & Rymer, 1981).

This kind of reflexive adjustment is applicable to situations other than those in which the limbs are being held in a static position. Numerous investigations have shown that these processes seem to keep an ongoing movement on course.

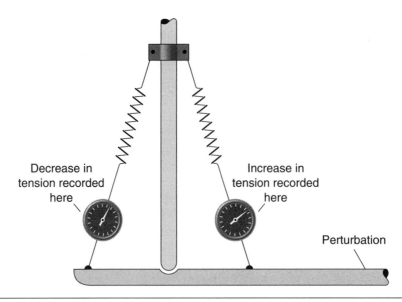

Figure 5.16.   Muscle-spring model with gauges for measuring tension in the "tendons" as a perturbation is applied.

For example, Marsden, Merton, and Morton (1972) had subjects move the last joint of the thumb back and forth in time to a metronome. At an unpredictable time, the movement of the thumb was resisted. The result was an additional burst of EMG within 30 ms of the perturbation. It is impressive that this occurred at any location or time in the thumb's cycle at which the perturbation was applied. Similar findings have been shown in the breathing cycle by Sears and Newsom-Davis (1968). When the resistance to air flow was suddenly changed at various places in the cycle, the EMG in the intercostal muscles (which control the rib cage volume) increased in activity with a latency of 30 ms, regardless of when in the cycle the resistance to air flow was changed. Nashner and Woollacott (1979) have shown similar findings for the situation in which the ankle joint is unexpectedly altered during normal walking. One interpretation of these findings is that there is a reference of correctness that "moves with" the overall movement, so that at any time in the movement the limb's desired location can be specified (Schmidt, 1976a). Thus it may be that the muscle spindles are able to provide information about whether the limb is in a position different from that specified and can induce reflex-based corrections if it is not.

Long-Loop Reflexes.   Have another look at figure 5.13. In addition to the monosynaptic reflex activity (the EMG activity that began with a latency of about 30 ms), there is another kind of activity responsible for the more sustained burst that occurred about 50 ms after the weight was added. This activity also occurs too rapidly to be explained by stages of information processing, yet it is apparently too slow to be accounted for by the monosynaptic stretch reflex. The early burst at 30 ms was very brief and did not result in much actual increase in force, whereas the burst at 50 to 80 ms was larger, more sustained, and probably resulted in the force changes necessary to actually move the limb back to the horizontal position. The response to muscle stretch with a latency of 50 to 80 ms has been termed the *long-loop reflex* (also called the *functional stretch reflex*).

Figure 5.15 shows how the long-loop reflex fits into the overall picture of segmental limb control. When the spindle is stretched and the Ia afferent is increased in its activation, the information is fed back to the spinal cord where it activates the alpha motor neuron and then is sent to higher segmental levels and/or to the brain. The Ia is integrated with other information in sensory and motor centers in the brain that can initiate a more complete response to the imposed stretch. Because the information travels to a higher center to be organized, the reflex requires more time. The 50–80 ms loop time for this activity corresponds with the additional distance that the impulses have to travel, which involves more than one synapse.

Something appears to be regained, however, with the loss in time. First, the EMG activity from the long-loop reflex is far stronger than that involved in the monosynaptic stretch reflex. Second, because the reflex is organized in a higher center, it is more *flexible* than the monosynaptic reflex. For example, Evarts (1973) has shown that if the subject in a task similar to Dewhurst's (1967) is told to resist the stretch, a burst pattern like that in figure 5.13 occurs. If the subject is told to "let go," so that when the weight is added the subject simply lets his or her arm be moved by it, the second burst (presumably due to the long-loop reflex) nearly disappears but the first burst is unaffected. It appears that *prior instructions* can change the response to a given stimulus (the added weight) so that the reaction is appropriate for the particular situation. The monosynaptic reflex, residing at a very low level in the spinal cord, is probably not capable of being modulated by prior instructions (or to any great degree). It is fortunate that we are constructed in this fashion, as there are situations in which we must resist very strongly when perturbations occur. Other situations arise in which a very strong resistance would mean a serious accident; in skiing over bumps, for example, failing to "let go" would result in a very stiff leg musculature when a very compliant (springy) one would be more desirable.

Other Reflexes

Many reflexes can be elicited in humans, and some scientists have suggested that these reflexes play important roles in movement control. For example, Fukuda (1961) collected a number of photographs of athletes, dancers, and other performers in specific situations, such as the base-ball player shown in figure 5.17 who is jumping and stretching his gloved hand high in the air to catch a ball. In this example the position of the head is such that it can elicit the *tonic neck reflex*, which is often seen in infants. When the head is turned to the left, the left arm becomes extended and the right arm curls up alongside the neck. Fukuda's observations, illustrated in examples from baseball among others, suggest that built-in reflex patterns can perhaps be basic components of various skilled actions in adult motor behavior. In support of Fukuda's argument, if one turns the head toward the hand doing a force-production task, there is an increase in force as compared to when the head is turned away (Hellebrandt et al., 1956; Shea, Guadagnoli, & Dean, 1995). This argument would suggest that turning the head supposedly activates the tonic neck reflex

Figure 5.17. A baseball player reaching for a ball, showing a pattern resembling the tonic neck reflex.
Adapted from Fukuda, 1961.

that provides a reflex-based facilitation of the alpha motor neurons on the same side of the body.

It is interesting to think about the possible role of the various reflexes in the control of behavior such as catching a ball, but the evidence about this role is very slim. In the baseball example, it is possible that the player is in this position because he is merely looking at and reaching for the ball, not because the reflexes are producing the classic tonic neck pattern. It is certainly a suggestive set of findings, but the crucial evidence is lacking to link these reflexes as observed in isolation and in childhood directly with the movement patterns seen in adults. A review of the possible role of reflexes in movement is provided by Easton (1972, 1978).

Triggered Reactions

So far, we have seen three distinct processes leading to increased EMG in response to perturbations such as an added weight. There are the monosynaptic stretch reflex (30–50 ms latency), the long-loop reflex (or transcortical stretch reflex, 50–80 ms), and of course the voluntary RT response discussed in chapter 4 that begins at about 120 ms in Dewhurst's (figure 5.13) study.[5] Crago, Houk, and Hasan (1976) argue, however, that there is yet a fourth kind of response to the added weight that falls between the 50–80 ms long-loop response and the voluntary RT latency. They call these responses *triggered reactions:* prestructured, coordinated reactions in the same or in closely related musculature that are "triggered" into action by various receptors. Such reactions have latencies of from 80 to perhaps 200 ms and are far more variable than the latencies of the faster reflexes. Presumably the triggered reaction is like a "fast" RT, perhaps bypassing some of the stages of information processing because the reaction to the stretch is stereotyped, predictable, and well practiced. The performer does not have to spend much time in processes like response selection and programming, and the reaction is just "triggered off" almost as if it were automatic (see Schmidt, 1987).

What evidence is there for this kind of control? Crago, Houk, and Hasan (1976) have shown that portions of the response to an unexpected stretch perturbation were faster than RT (as we have seen before), but also that the latencies increased as the number of stimulus-response alternatives was increased from one to two; here, the perturbation was always a flexion (i.e., a one-choice task) or it could be either a flexion or extension (i.e., a two-choice task). We usually think of processes involved in resolving choice as being "located" in a response-selection stage (Hick's law, chapter 3); these results suggest that, unlike the monosynaptic stretch reflexes, the responses might be mediated in some way by the stages of information processing. Perhaps some of the processes are bypassed, leading to latencies shorter than "normal" RT latencies. Two lines of evidence have

strengthened our belief in these triggered reactions, discussed next.

Wineglass Effect

Suppose you are washing dishes and raise an object to check its cleanliness—for example, holding the stem of an expensive wineglass between your fingertips. If the glass begins to tip or slip (because of the wet surface), a common reaction is to increase the grip of force with your fingers to stop it. Using a laboratory analogue of this basic idea, Johansson and Westling (1984, 1988, 1990; Westling & Johansson, 1984) have studied in detail the motor reactions to stimuli indicating loss of grip, asking subjects to lift small objects (having various surface roughness) between the fingers and hoist them with an elbow flexion. The stimuli indicating that the object is slipping are a set of tiny vibrations in the skin of the fingers, which we detect through cutaneous receptors; yet the response to a slip is a contraction of muscles (located in the forearm) that has the effect of tightening the grip on the object. Thus, in this paradigm, the stimulus does not *directly* affect the muscles that make the response as they did in the Crago, Houk, and Hasan (1976) example previously discussed (i.e., the response is not autogenetic).

Johansson and Westling (1984, 1988) found that after the onset of a slip (measured by vibration sensors in their apparatus), subjects showed an increase in the EMG in muscles responsible for finger gripping force, and with a latency of only about 80 ms (see also Cole & Abbs, 1988). These reflexes were fast enough to prevent a noticeable movement of the object, and often the subject did not even know that a slip had occurred. Sometimes, several of these slips/catches were seen in a single lift of the object, each with very short latencies. In addition to the increase in gripping forces, there was at the same time a corresponding *decrease* in the EMG in the elbow flexors, as if the system were "trying" to reduce the slippage of the object by decreasing its upward acceleration. All this resulted in a beautifully coordinated response to the slipping, which was evidenced in a number of joints—not just in the structures directly affected by the stimulus. The reaction was very fast, was probably nonconscious in nature, and seemed to have the overall "purpose" of reorganizing the system slightly to complete the action successfully (i.e., lifting without dropping). These extremely fast coordinated responses fit perfectly into the category termed triggered reactions by Crago, Houk, and Hasan (1976).

Speech Perturbations

Another example of triggered reactions was provided by Abbs and Gracco (1983; Abbs, Gracco, & Cole, 1984) and by Kelso et al. (1984). In Abbs's work, the subjects were asked to utter nonsense syllables such as /afa/ and /aba/. Try /aba/, for example; the lips must first be open to make the initial vowel sound, and then they must come together briefly to make the stop consonant /b/. In their experiments, Abbs, Gracco, and Cole (1984) would occasionally perturb the lower jaw with a small downward force pulse that prevented the lip from coming up to make contact in its normal position, and the EMG from the musculature in the *upper* lip and its position were measured. When the perturbation was applied, there was an increased EMG in the upper-lip musculature, which moved the upper lip downward, all with a latency of about 25–70 ms. Notice that, as in the wineglass example, this is not an autogenetic response, because the response to the stimulation does not occur in the stimulated muscle; and it seems to be organized with the "purpose" of completing the *action* of making the proper sound (which required lip closure for success). Furthermore, the reaction seems to be dependent on practice, as it is difficult to argue that the making of the particular sound

/aba/ is genetically determined; this feature of susceptibility to practice might be yet another distinguishing characteristic of these triggered reactions.

Servo Action

Both the wineglass and the speech examples present some difficulty regarding (at least simple) servo control for these skills. In servo control, we have usually thought that some error signal is processed so that the musculature can be brought back to a particular state (usually a position) that is being regulated (box on page 97). But in both of these examples, the stimulus has resulted in a fast, coordinated set of reactions that does not have this regulatory role; in fact, in the speech example, the positions of the muscles were systematically *different* from those in the normal, unperturbed trials. These examples suggest a process by which the response to the perturbation has the function of ensuring that a particular *action,* with a particular environmental goal, is carried out properly. Of course, completing the action does not necessarily imply having the limbs in the same (normal) positions, as actions can usually be done in a variety of ways. The system is somehow "smart" enough to find another way to do it when a perturbation is received. The available evidence is summarized briefly in table 5.2, showing that triggered reactions fit in with the other kinds of responses to environmental stimuli discussed here.

Table 5.2 Four Kinds of Responses to Environmental Stimuli During Movement, and Some of Their Differing Characteristics

Response type	Loop time (in ms)	Structures involved	Modified by instructions	Affected by number of choices
Myotatic reflexes (autogenetic)	30–50	Spindles, gamma loop, same muscles	No	No
Long-loop reflexes (autogenetic)	50–80	Spindles, cortex or cerebellum, same muscles	Yes	No
Triggered reactions (not autogenetic)	80–120	Various receptors, higher centers, and associated musculature	Yes	Yes
Reaction time (not autogenetic)	120–180	Various receptors, higher centers, any musculature	Yes	Yes

Feedforward Influences on Motor Control

In this section we will consider evidence that the motor system operates with a feedforward control mode, defined as the sending of some signal "ahead of" the movement that (a) readies the system for the upcoming motor command and/or (b) readies the system for the receipt of some particular kind of feedback information. Such processes appear to occur frequently, and we will consider a few examples.

Saccadic Eye Movements

Numerous situations exist in which the idea of feedforward control appears to be involved in the production and evaluation of human behavior. One of the earliest notions of feedforward control concerned the mechanisms of visual perception after the eye made a *saccade*—a very rapid, jerky movement of the eyes from one position to a new position. Of course, the light patterns falling on the retina are different before and after the saccade. But how does the person know whether (a) the eye moved in a stable world or (b) the world moved, with the eye remaining stationary? The pattern of stimulation (optical flow pattern) on the retina could be exactly the same in both cases.

The answer suggested by von Holst (1954), Sperry (1950), and others (e.g., Gallistel, 1980) was that the visual perceptual system was informed about the upcoming movement of the eye ahead of time, so that the pattern of changed visual input could be evaluated properly. This advance (feedforward) information has been termed *corollary discharge*, or *efference copy*, by these authors (see also Evarts, 1973, and Kelso, 1982, for reviews).

The idea is that a "copy" of the motor (efferent) command to the eye muscles is also sent to some other location in the brain, where it is used to evaluate the incoming visual signals and to "correct for" the fact that the image on the retina is about to move. Thus, the individual has perceived the environment as being stable and "knows" that the eye has moved. How such a system works is the subject of much debate, but many scientists have argued that some such mechanism must exist in order for the individual to interpret incoming visual signals correctly.

Efference Copy in Limb Control

The efference-copy mechanism appears to have a parallel in the control or evaluation of limb movements. First, as pointed out by Evarts (1973), there is neurological evidence that information destined for the muscles is also sent to places in the brain that are primarily sensory in nature. Perhaps the purpose of such activities is to "tell" the sensory system what was ordered by the motor system and to ready it for receipt of the feedback. Thus, the idea of efference copy is much like the establishment of the reference of correctness against which the feedback signals will be compared. One component of this feedforward must simply be the knowledge *that* the person moved voluntarily, so that the person can distinguish feedback from movement as due to active motion versus passive motion.

Related to this example is the well-known heightened kinesthetic sensitivity when the subject is moving *actively* versus passively (Brodie & Ross, 1985). Do this experiment. Take a few different grades of sandpaper, and rank them in terms of roughness by rubbing them with the index finger (eyes closed). First, actively move your finger over the surfaces. Then have someone hold your finger and move it over the surface in the same way, but without your active muscular involvement. You will find that your perception of roughness is much impaired when you are moved passively. Why? One answer is that when the motor system sends the commands to move actively, it also sends an efference copy of the commands to sensory areas in the brain to enable the feedback to be evaluated properly. But when the finger is moved passively, no motor commands are issued to the muscles, hence there is no efference copy, and thus the "same" feedback signals from the finger are not perceived so accurately (for further evidence and discussion, see Lederman & Klatzky, 1997).

Preparatory Postural Reactions

Consider a situation in which a standing subject awaits a signal to raise the arm quickly from a relaxed position at the side to a position in front of the body, as if to point straight ahead. According to earlier discussions about such actions, the commands for the shoulder muscles are generated after a RT of about 200 ms or so. But if the subject is standing in balance, a sudden movement of the arm forward and upward will cause a shift in the person's center of gravity, and balance will be lost unless some compensation is provided along with the action itself. When is such compensation produced?

Belen'kii, Gurfinkel, and Pal'tsev (1967; see also Cordo & Nashner, 1982) recorded the EMG activity from the support muscles of the legs as well as the prime moving shoulder muscles in this action (performed as a RT task). After the stimulus came on, the first signs of EMG activity occurred in the large muscles in the back of the leg (biceps femoris) on the opposite side of the body from the intended action—and these changes occurred about 60 ms *before* any EMG could be seen in the shoulder muscles. The actions of the EMGs in the legs could not have been caused by an imbalance resulting from the movement of the arm, because these changes occurred before the first EMG changes in the shoulder occurred and even longer before any movement in the shoulder occurred. It is possible to consider these changes as an example of feedforward control, in which the motor system sends commands to the spinal levels associated with the leg musculature prior to the arm action, the purpose being to "ready" the legs so that the body does not lose balance when the arm finally moves.

Alternatively, the changes in the patterns of EMGs in the legs prior to action could be considered as a part of the coordination of the entire action, beginning with change in the legs. W. Lee (1980), using this same action, has shown that the temporal aspects of the EMGs are quite closely linked, with the various muscles acting in the same order and with a nearly constant pattern of action for various trials (see chapter 8 for more evidence related to the processes involved in coordination).

Detection and Correction of Errors

What role does feedforward information play in the detection and correction of errors? Since it is information that a movement was ordered and is a record of the kinds of commands that were sent, efference copy can be thought of as a kind of "feedback"—except that it does not come directly from the action produced, but rather from the commands that will result in that action. If you ask a friend to call your home phone while you look on, then you "know" that the phone at home is ringing even though you cannot hear it directly. Knowing that your friend has placed the call is almost as reliable as hearing the telephone ring.

If efference copy could, in this general way, be evaluated as a kind of sensory information, then the idea is that it can be evaluated against a reference of correctness just as feedback can be evaluated. If the subsequent analysis of the efference copy in relation to this reference indicated that there was going to be an error, a correction could be initiated and a new movement command could be sent. This has the advantage of initiating the correction much more quickly than would be the case if feedback from the movement was evaluated; and the correction could even be given before the errant movement was initiated, or at least before the movement could "do much damage" in the environment.

Various experiments appear to provide evidence for such processes. For example, Angel and Higgins (1969) used a step-tracking task in which the target would move suddenly in discrete steps to the left or right; the subject's task was to follow the target movement with appropriate limb movements. When the subject is highly motivated to minimize RT, the person will occasionally move in the wrong direction, reverse the move, and then move rapidly to the correct target. Figure 5.18 is a diagram of a typical corrected trial, showing the incorrect initial movement (beginning at point B) and the subsequent correction (beginning at point C). Interestingly, the correction times, measured as the interval from the beginning of the incorrect movement until the beginning of the correction (from B to C in the figure), were as short as 90 ms. The subjects could not have been processing movement feedback from proprioception or vision in order to detect the error, because the correction for the false move was made more rapidly than could be accounted for by the usual feedback-processing mechanisms. Perhaps the subjects were using a central feedback loop based on efference copy as a basis for initiating these corrections (but see also Schmidt & Gordon, 1977). However, the issue of how people use feedforward information to detect and correct errors is far from settled, and more work is needed for an understanding of these processes.

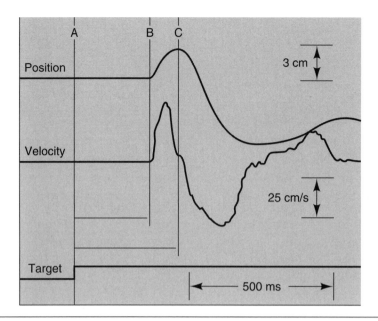

Figure 5.18.   Position (top) and velocity (center) traces showing an error with "rapid" correction toward the target. Reprinted from Angel and Higgins, 1969.

Summary

Closed-loop systems involve the processing of feedback against a reference of correctness, the determination of an error, and a subsequent correction. The receptors for the feedback supplied to closed-loop systems are the eyes, ears, and vestibular apparatus, as well as the Golgi tendon organs, the muscle spindles, the joint receptors, and touch receptors in various places in the skin. All these sources provide input to the central nervous system, and then the information is presumably combined for the purpose of analysis of movement.

Vision provides the richest source of information for closed-loop control. Vision can be used in a variety of ways, providing information about errors in movement as well as providing predictive information so that potential errors can be anticipated and avoided. Closed-loop control models seem to have their greatest strength in explaining movements that are very slow in time or that have very high movement accuracy requirements. Tracking tasks are most obviously related to closed-loop processes. These models have difficulty explaining the kinds of corrections seen in very rapid movements, however, and this fact leads to the suggestion that two fundamentally different kinds of movements exist: slow and fast. However, strong evidence exists for closed-loop *reflexive* control in limb move-

ments. Most of this work suggests involvement of the muscle spindle and the gamma loop, but other receptors are involved as well. Such reflexive corrections can be classified as (a) the monosynaptic stretch reflex (latency = 30–50 ms), (b) the long-loop or transcortical stretch reflex (latency = 50–80 ms), (c) the triggered reaction (latency = 80–120 ms), and (d) RT (latency = 120–180 ms or longer).

Feedforward control models involve the delivery of information to some other part of the system to "prepare it" for incoming sensory information or for an upcoming motor command. Thus feedforward information serves an important role in error detection and correction, often occurring in anticipation of the error.

Notes

[1] Another classification of visual systems is that of static versus kinetic vision (Paillard & Amblard, 1985). Static vision is concerned with identifying the location of static or slow-moving objects in central vision, whereas kinetic vision is concerned with movement of peripheral objects. It is not clear whether the two classes overlap or represent two distinctly different dimensions.

[2] Performance in the various vision conditions may have reached a ceiling level. Thus, direct comparison to performance in the control condition with full room lighting is problematic

because of the richer sources of contextual cues provided, which appear to be particularly important for reducing spatial errors (Montagne & Laurent, 1994). Whiting et al. also noted that subjects used a different catching strategy in the full room lighting condition whereby they would move with the ball and delay their attempts to make the catch, thereby gaining themselves an additional 100 ms or so of ball flight information.

[3] The root "fusal" means fusiform or spindle shaped; so intrafusal fibers are muscle fibers within the spindle, and the extrafusal fibers are those outside the spindle—that is, the fibers of the muscle in which the spindle is embedded. The greek letter gamma (γ) refers to the spindle system (the intrafusal fibers are thus innervated by the gamma motor neurons; the alpha motor neurons innervate the extrafusal fibers). The term *Ia* refers to the fact that the sensory (afferent) fiber emerging from the spindle is a large type I afferent, and the *a* refers to the fact that this fiber comes

from the spindle (type Ib fibers come from the Golgi tendon organs). Type II afferents are smaller in diameter than the type I afferents.

[4] A motor unit is defined as an alpha motor neuron and all of the muscle fibers that it innervates. In humans, the number of fibers supplied by one alpha motor neuron might vary from a few (in muscles requiring fine control—in the hand, larynx, eyes) up to several thousand (in muscles requiring only gross control—in the trunk). There could be from a few to several hundred motor units in any one muscle.

[5] This 120-ms value in figure 5.13 is considerably shorter than the typical RT latency discussed in chapters 3 and 4. But in figure 5.13, the latency is measured by the EMG change, whereas in chapters 3 and 4 the RT is measured with respect to the movement, which usually occurs with an additional delay of at least 50 ms.

CENTRAL CONTRIBUTIONS TO MOTOR CONTROL

The focus in the last chapter was primarily on the role of sensory mechanisms, and motor control was considered as a closed-loop system (boxed text on page 97). In contrast is an open-loop system, in which the instructions are structured in advance and are executed without regard to the effects that they may have on the environment. That is, the behavior of the open-loop system is not sensitive to feedback. A diagram of a typical open-loop system is shown in figure 6.1. The executive and effector mechanisms can be thought of in the same way as for the closed-loop system in figure 5.1, but the feedback loop and the reference of correctness are missing. The executive is "programmed" to send certain instructions at particular times to the effector, and the effector carries them out without the possibility of modification if something goes wrong.

A good example of an open-loop system is the traffic signal at a major intersection. The pattern of red and green lights is controlled from a program that handles this sequence without regard to moment-to-moment variations in traffic patterns. If there is an accident or if traffic is particularly heavy, there can be no immediate modification in the pattern because there is no feedback from the traffic conditions back to the executive. Even though the program for the traffic lights is inflexible, we should not get the idea that it must be simple. The program can be structured so that the north-south street has a 20% longer green-light duration than the east-west street during rush hours, with this relation being altered in midday when the traffic pattern changes. But the only way that modifications in timing can occur

is to have the programmer structure them into the program in advance. In this chapter, we emphasize the open-loop processes and central representations involved in motor control, for which sensory influences play a less dominant role.

Open-Loop Processes

One of the earliest explanations of movement control was the response-chaining hypothesis (sometimes called the reflex-chaining hypothesis) proposed by the 19th-century psychologist William James (1890). The basic idea is illustrated in figure 6.2. James assumed that a movement began by an external or internal signal's causing a muscular contraction. This contraction generated sensory information (which he termed *response-produced feedback*) from the muscles, from the movements that the contracting muscles produced, or from both. This feedback, which James regarded as stimulus information (just like that from any other stimulus such as light or sound), served as the trigger for the next contraction. This second contraction then produced its own response-produced feedback, which triggered the third contraction, and so on until all the contractions in the sequence were completed. The feedback could come from various sources (e.g., spindles, joint receptors, or even vision or audition), and it could trigger responses in the same or in different limbs. With such a mechanism, James could explain how certain actions appear in the proper order in skill, as the chain ensured that the second contraction did not occur before the first one. Also, James thought that this mechanism could account for the *timing among* the various contractions so important for skilled actions; such timing (or *phasing*, as it is now called) would be determined by the temporal delays in the various sensory processes and could be relatively consistent from response to response to produce stereotyped actions. Although such a model seems appropriate for serial tasks (starting the car, buttoning a shirt), there is no conceptual reason why the model could not explain discrete actions, such as speech and throwing, by assuming that the responses triggered are the contractions of individual motor units. Viewed in this way, the response chain shown in figure 6.2, which consists of four units of behavior, might last only 100 ms, or it might continue for a few seconds.

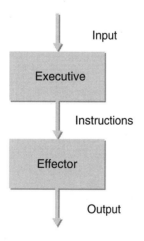

Figure 6.1. The elements of the typical open-loop control system.

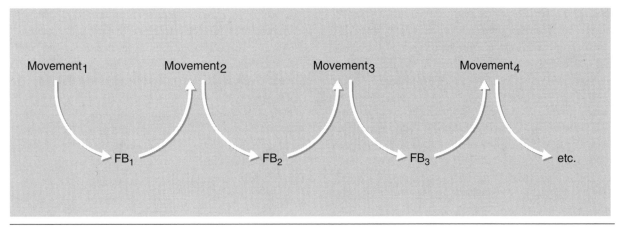

Figure 6.2.   The response-chaining hypothesis. (The response-produced feedback from earlier portions of the action serves as a trigger for later portions.)

James (1890) had recognized that when *skilled* movements were produced they did not seem to require much consciousness for their control. Under the response-chaining hypothesis, movements could be viewed as requiring attention only for the initiation of the first action, with the remainder of the actions being run off "automatically." Also, in James's view of *learning* motor skills, the acquisition of the associations between a given feedback event and the next action is the fundamental basis for improvement in skill.

The response-chaining hypothesis is really a variant of an open-loop control mode, in spite of the presence of feedback. Remember that in a closed-loop system, the executive level is acting on the *error* that is produced, and such errors are computed as the difference between the actual state and the desired state defined by the reference of correctness. In the response-chaining hypothesis, though, there is no reference of correctness against which feedback is compared, and feedback simply serves as the trigger for the next act in the sequence. It is open-loop because the original stimulus sets the chain in motion, and the remainder of the events are determined by the learned associations between feedback and the next act in the sequence. Also, open-loop movements cannot be modified if something goes wrong or if the environment changes, as is the case for a closed-loop model.

One way the response-chaining hypothesis can be tested is to examine the role of sensory information in the production of movement. Of course if the sensory information is eliminated (or delayed or degraded in quality), then the result should be a loss of skill, or even paralysis,

because the *trigger* mechanism has been disrupted. In the next sections, we review some evidence about feedback degradation in relation to this hypothesis.

Deafferentation

There are both temporary methods for interrupting the flow of sensory information into the spinal cord (e.g., the blood pressure cuff technique, the injection of local anesthetics) and permanent *deafferentation* procedures. From the previous chapter, recall that nearly all of the afferent input to the cord entered through the dorsal roots on the posterior side of the cord. In an operation called a *dorsal rhizotomy*, the back of the animal is entered surgically, and the muscles are carefully moved to expose the dorsal roots. Then, at the particular spinal level of interest, the dorsal roots are cut, essentially preventing any sensory information from reaching the cord in the future. This procedure can be done at a single spinal level or at multiple levels, with cutting at each successive level progressively eliminating more and more of the animal's sensations from the periphery. The operation can be done unilaterally or bilaterally, eliminating the feedback from one or both sides of the body. These procedures have been performed on mice, cats, monkeys, and other species in order to study the movement control that results in the deafferented state.

While normally these procedures are limited to animal experiments, a number of examples of deafferented humans have also been reported. Lashley (1917), in a study we will describe in detail later, assessed a patient with a gunshot wound to the lower spine. The lesion had the same effects as surgical deafferentation, and it left the motor innervation of the subject intact. Also, patients with complete or near-complete loss of sensory information due to degenerated afferent pathways (sensory *neuropathy*), but with intact motor systems, have made significant contributions to this area of knowledge by volunteering to perform in a variety of experiments (e.g., Gordon, Ghilardi, & Ghez, 1995; Rothwell et al., 1982; Sanes, 1990; Teasdale, Forget, Bard, Paillard, Fleury, & Lamarre, 1993). Finally, Kelso, Holt, and Flatt (1980) have studied arthritic patients who have had the joints of the fingers replaced with artificial ones. This operation removes the joint and the joint capsule in which the joint receptors are located. Thus, while this is not really a deafferentation procedure in the strictest sense, it does provide a situation in which there is disrupted feedback from the moving limb.

Early Deafferentation Studies

One of the earliest investigations using surgical deafferentation was conducted by Sherrington (1906). He severed the dorsal roots in a monkey so that only the sensations from a single forelimb were lost, with the remainder of the body having normal sensory feedback. A major finding was that after recovery from surgery the monkey never used the limb, keeping it tucked against the chest and using the other limbs to eat and ambulate. For decades, this finding was regarded as support for the response-chaining hypothesis, because eliminating the feedback seemed to eliminate movement altogether, as it should if the hypothesis is correct.

But Sherrington's conclusions were later challenged by a number of separate lines of evidence. On the one hand, considerable research was completed on the control of locomotion in lower organisms such as fish, snakes, frogs, insects, and birds (for reviews of this early work, see Grillner, 1975; and Pearson, 1976). Some of this research involved severing the afferent (sensory) pathways for various segments of the animal's system, and the conclusions generally were that movements are not seriously disrupted. For example, Wilson (1961) deafferented locusts, stimulating the insect electrically with a pulse near the head region, and wing movement patterns resembling flying resulted. The patterns were decreased in amplitude and frequency as compared

to normal flight patterns, but clear rhythmic activity nevertheless continued.

Why were the locust's movements so well accomplished, when Sherrington's monkey did not move the deafferented limb at all? Could it be that monkeys are fundamentally different from the lower species in terms of their motor systems? This is probably not the answer, as studies subsequent to Sherrington's on humans and monkeys have tended to show that movement is not strongly interrupted by deafferentation. For example, Lashley (1917), in his study of the patient who had received a gunshot wound to the spine rendering the legs deafferented, asked the patient to perform various positioning movements without vision. While sitting on the edge of an examination table, the patient was asked to extend the knee to 45°, and the error in producing the movement was compared to that of a "normal" control subject. Lashley found that the deafferented subject and the normal subject could do the positioning task about equally well.

How can the apparently contradictory findings of Sherrington and Lashley be reconciled? One possibility is that the deafferented monkey *chose not* to use the affected limb, which is quite different from saying that the monkey *could not* use it. You know how it feels when you sleep on your arm the "wrong way," or when your jaw is "frozen" after a trip to the dentist; the sensation is strange and unpleasant, and we probably would not use these effectors in these situations unless it was important to do so.

Later Deafferentation Studies

In a series of studies, Taub and his colleagues (see Taub & Berman, 1968, or Taub, 1976, for reviews) and Bizzi (e.g., Polit & Bizzi, 1978) examined this question by using surgical deafferentation affecting various portions of monkeys' bodies. When Taub and Berman's monkeys had both forelimbs deafferented and had recovered from the operation, they were able to move the limbs *nearly* normally: activities such as climbing, swinging, eating, and grooming were different only in minor ways from those of the normal animals. The deafferented monkeys did, however, show some deficiencies in very fine manipulations such as would be required to pick up a small piece of food. Perhaps this is related to the role of the spindle and the gamma loop in these movements (see chapter 5; also, Frank, Williams, & Hayes,

1977). The conclusion to be drawn from these studies is that feedback from the moving limb is not *essential* for movement, but that it undoubtedly aids movement in most situations.[1] However, these findings do call into question the reflex-chaining hypothesis that claims the necessary involvement of feedback in the normal conduct of movement.

Deafferentation in Humans

Provins (1958) studied the role of joint receptors from the fingers by injecting anesthetic directly into the joint capsule. Although the movements of the finger could not be felt by the subject, there was nevertheless a strong capability to move; but the accuracy suffered somewhat compared to that in the condition without the anesthetic. Very similar findings were obtained by Kelso (1977; Kelso, Holt, & Flatt, 1980) in studies involving the joint afferents from the hand. When the feedback from the joint afferents was blocked either by the cuff technique (Kelso, 1977) or in patients who had artificial finger joints (Kelso, Holt, & Flatt, 1980), little or no loss in movement-positioning accuracy occurred without vision. Of course, all these studies involved normal afferent feedback from the muscle spindles located in the finger muscles in the forearm, and it could be that this was the source of feedback that allowed the accurate control. All these studies imply that the joint afferents are not essential for movement, as is often believed (e.g., Adams, 1977).

Using an anesthetic block of the gamma loop and other pathways from the right arm in humans, J. Smith (1969; Smith, Roberts, & Atkins, 1972) found that dart-throwing and grip-strength tasks were only minimally disrupted by this kind of deafferentation. Although some impairments in performance occurred, the most important point is that the movement could be produced even though feedback was not available from the moving limb.

Many studies have been done using the cuff technique popularized by Laszlo (1967). In a series of studies using such tasks as rapid finger tapping, handwriting, aiming, and positioning, impairments in performance under the cuff conditions were found; but the movements, although impaired, still could be produced, contrary to the expectations from a response-chaining hypothesis (see also Chambers & Schumsky, 1978; Kelso, Stelmach, & Wannamaker, 1976; Laszlo & Bairstow, 1979).

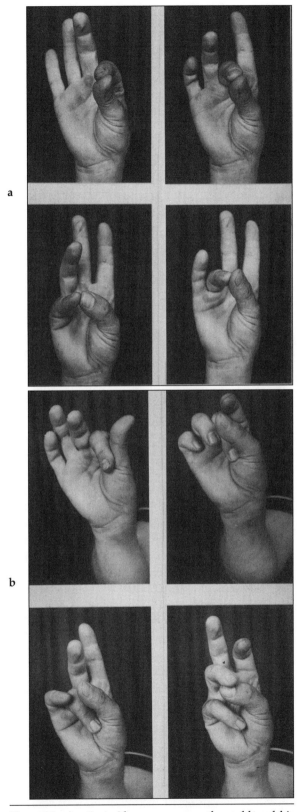

a

b

Figure 6.3. A patient with sensory neuropathy could touch his thumb and fingers without vision quite well early in the sequence (a), but performance is disrupted markedly after 30 s (b). Reprinted from Rothwell, Traub, Day, Obeso, Thomas, and Marsden, 1982.

Recent studies using patients with sensory neuropathy have reached similar conclusions, although these individuals often have severe difficulties in performing many activities of daily living. For example, the patient studied by Rothwell et al. (1982) reported that he had trouble feeding and dressing himself and could not hold a pen in his hand. Yet figure 6.3a illustrates that he could control his hands to sequentially touch the thumb to each fingertip without visual feedback. The later photos shown in figure 6.3b reveal that this activity could not be maintained for very long, however; performance had deteriorated considerably after 30 s, when these photos were taken. From the perspective of the response-chaining hypothesis, sensory neuropathy patients demonstrate remarkable capabilities to perform skilled actions (Sanes et al., 1985).

Implications for the Response-Chaining Hypothesis

Even though work with various kinds of deafferentation has shown that feedback from the responding limbs is not necessary in order for actions to occur, the evidence was often taken incorrectly to mean that feedback in general is *never* used in movement control. The deafferented animals were not completely normal in their movement, especially when the fine control of finger action was required. Also, it is possible, as Adams (1971, 1976b) has said, that other kinds of feedback (e.g., vision) could be substituted for the lost sensations in the deafferented animal. And finally, there are many cases in which feedback is almost certainly used in movement, such as those that we discussed in chapter 5. On strict experimental grounds, the evidence does not really say that the response-chaining hypothesis is incorrect. But the fact that movements can occur without any movement-produced feedback at all strongly indicates that the response-chaining hypothesis is not a very complete account of movement control. Other mechanisms of motor control will have to be used to explain the available evidence.

Central Control Mechanisms

Motor control mechanisms that explain how movements can occur in the absence of sensory feedback are required in order to deal with the evidence just described. In the next sections the role of sensory processes will be more or less reduced in prominence. Keep in mind, however, that various mechanisms of motor control can be isolated for study in the various paradigms, although none seem to operate independently during most everyday activities. It is important for students to understand these mechanisms, but the real problem in understanding motor behavior is to appreciate how these processes work together toward smooth, elegant, and energy-efficient performance (see also Cruse et al., 1990).

Central Pattern Generators

Grillner (1975; Grillner & Wallén, 1985; Grillner et al., 1991; see also Marder & Calabrese, 1996) has reviewed considerable evidence about the control of locomotion and gait in a variety of species. One important set of studies concerns "spinal" preparations in cats and other animals. The spinal cord is cut at a level below the brain so that the higher centers cannot influence lower ones, and often the cord is deafferented below the level of the cut as well. If the prepared cord is then stimulated, it can be shown to display a definite *periodicity* in terms of the activity in the efferent fibers emerging from the ventral side of the cord. Thus, the spinal cord itself is seemingly capable of producing a rhythm that can be present even without feedback from the limbs. With reference to gait patterns, it has been thought that these rhythms in the cord first activate motor neurons that are to go to the flexors of the leg, then activate motor neurons to the extensors, then activate the flexors again, in a pattern more or less like the one that would be displayed in locomotion. Apparently, the spinal cord has complex neural circuitry that is capable of producing these oscillations. These circuits have come to be called *central pattern generators*.

A schematic diagram of how such a spinal generator might be structured is shown in figure 6.4. Many alternatives exist, and the mechanism illustrated in figure 6.4 is only one simple possibility. In this mechanism there could be a neural network in the cord made up of four neurons (the cord undoubtedly uses many more). With a stimulus from some higher center (a chemical or electrical signal in the spinal animal), Neuron 1 is activated, which activates Neuron 2, and so on, until Neuron 4 activates Neuron 1 again. This continuous cycling process would go on indefinitely or until some other process turned it off. Now, imagine that Neuron 1 also synapses with a neuron that drives the flexor muscles and that Neuron 3 also synapses with one that drives the extensor

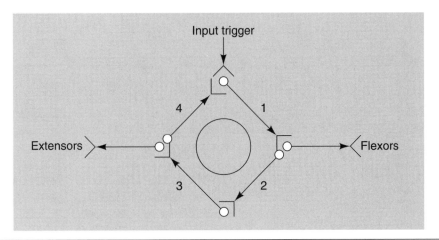

Figure 6.4.   A simple possibility for the connections of interneurons forming a central pattern generator.

muscles. Every time Neuron 2 is activated by Neuron 1, the neuron to the flexors is activated too; the same is true for Neuron 3 and the extensors. Every time around this continuous circle, a burst of the flexors and a burst of the extensors occur, and the bursts occur at opposite points in the cycle. This basic concept of simple oscillating circuits helps to illustrate how a neural network could be expected to produce rhythmic patterns of activity such as gait in animals.

To show that the spinal cord has some slow rhythmic capability is interesting, but to what extent is this activity involved in gait control? A very important surgical preparation in cats has allowed considerable insight into this process. This preparation is called the mesencephalic (midbrain) preparation, or the *Shik preparation* after its originator (Shik, Orlovskii, & Severin, 1968). In this situation, the cat receives a cut of the spinal cord in the midbrain; this totally severs the lower levels of the cord from the higher centers (thought to be responsible for perception and consciousness). The cerebellum, the small structure behind the midbrain, is left intact, connected to the spinal cord side of the cut. In this state, the cat is unable to sense any stimulation from the body (because the afferent pathways to the cortex are severed) and is unable to perform voluntary movements of the legs. Shik, Orlovskii, and Severin supported the cat above a treadmill, as shown in figure 6.5.

A number of important observations have come from this preparation. First, when stimulated with a brief electrical current or a chemical called L-dopa at the level of the cut, the animal on a moving treadmill began to produce stepping movements that resembled normal locomotion in cats. This stepping continued for some time after the stimulus was turned off. As the treadmill sped up, the cat walked faster, even trotting or galloping. It appears that some spinal generator(s) for walking must be turned on by some higher source (thought to be located in the midbrain in the intact cat) and that, once initiated, the pattern of flexion and extension continues without further involvement from the higher centers. Because the mesencephalic animal cannot sense the activity occurring in its limbs, such stepping activity must be independent of the animal's perception of the activity.

As it turns out, a stimulus from the higher center in the midbrain is not the only way to initiate the spinal generators for stepping. Using the same apparatus, Shik and Orlovskii (1976) studied the cat's behavior when the treadmill was turned on. At first, the legs would trail off behind the animal; but then suddenly the animal would initiate stepping, with the total pattern of activity generated as a unit. As the treadmill increased in speed, the animal would walk faster, with minor differences in the pattern of activity from that observed in the normal cat, except for some unsteadiness. As the treadmill further increased in speed, the cat would suddenly break into a trot pattern. Occasionally the cat could be made to gallop. (Remember, there is no control from the higher centers and no stimulus from higher levels in the cord to turn on the spinal generators.) These results indicate that the afferent input from the feet and legs, which are at first dragged by the treadmill, is sufficient to initiate the stepping. Once the pattern generators are turned on, the speed of the oscillation appears to be controlled by the rate at which the treadmill

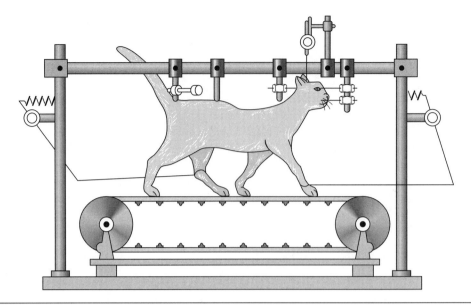

Figure 6.5. Mesencephalic (midbrain) cat supported on a treadmill as used in the study of spinal mechanisms in gait. Reprinted from Shik, Severin, and Orlovskii, 1966.

moves the cat's feet. When the cat's feet are being moved so rapidly by the treadmill that a walk pattern is no longer effective in keeping up, the afferent information presumably triggers a new pattern—the trot. An analogous set of findings has been produced by Smith and her colleagues (Carter & Smith, 1986; Smith, 1978; Smith et al., 1986).

As a result of this evidence, as well as the evidence reviewed by Grillner (1975), several models of gait have emerged. The general features of these models are shown in figure 6.6. The box in the center of the diagram represents a central pattern generator, and it can be turned on or off by higher centers in the midbrain. In some cases, this higher level input appears to be but a single pulse that will turn on the generator, with no further higher level activity necessary in order for the oscillator to continue to operate. In other cases, a continuous input (not necessarily a rhythmic one) appears to be necessary, with the action in the generator continuing only so long as the tonic input is on. The neurons that are capable of turning on spinal generators to produce a total pattern of activity are called *command neurons* (see Kupfermann & Weiss, 1978).

The activity in the generator can also be turned on by sensory input. While the generator is operating, the activities in the flexor and extensor muscles are coordinated, and feedback from the responding limbs also can serve to modify the output; this is shown by the two-way arrows from the various muscles to the spinal generator.

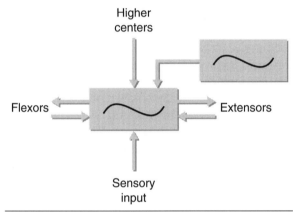

Figure 6.6. Spinal-generator model for gait, showing input to oscillators from sensory sources, from higher centers, from other oscillators, and from moving limbs.

And, finally, a number of spinal generators are thought to exist, perhaps one for each of the four limbs in the stepping cycle of the cat, so that the operation of the separate oscillators must be coordinated (coupled) by interneurons—neurons residing wholly within the cord. Thus, in the diagram a connection is shown from another oscillator to indicate this kind of control.

A number of important concepts emerge from this work on pattern generators. First, for the control of gait and other stereotyped actions in a variety of species (e.g., tail-flipping/escape reactions in lobsters, grooming in mice), strong evidence exists that these patterns are controlled by "prewired" pattern generators that can handle most of the details of the actions. They can be turned on by a variety of sources of stimulation, and they can continue until they "run down" or are stopped by some other source of input. While the basic pattern is quite stereotyped, in "higher" animals (cats), extensive modification of the basic pattern is possible, either from higher centers to make the whole pattern more rapid or more forceful, or from lower feedback sources (e.g., from the leg or foot) that serve to alter the particular pattern of force applied to conform to variations in terrain. And, finally, these pattern generators do not require the conscious awareness of the animal in order to operate. Once initiated, they can apparently continue without involvement of the higher centers. However, in the operation of these generators during running, for example, attention seems to be required, perhaps to evaluate the upcoming terrain or to keep the oscillator running.

Reflex Involvement in Locomotion

Throughout the history of motor skills research, considerable debate has centered on the role of reflexes, and our discussion about genetically defined activities such as locomotion would be incomplete without considering their involvement (see also chapter 5). Some of these diverse viewpoints are presented in the following sections.

Maintaining the Original Pattern

An older notion of control in locomotion was that the patterns of limb action *consisted* of fundamental reflex activities (e.g., Easton, 1972). This was somewhat different from the reflex-chaining hypothesis in that the component reflexes were thought to be the identifiable, genetically defined patterns that we see so often in infants, whereas the reflex-chaining hypothesis involves any chained activity—even those that are learned. A good example of these genetically defined reflexes is *reciprocal inhibition*, whereby the flexors of a joint tend to be automatically inhibited when the extensors are activated. With the *crossed-extensor reflex*, the extensors of one knee are activated when the flexors of the opposite knee are called into action. When we step on a tack, the flexors in the affected leg take the weight off the tack, while the extensors in the opposite leg help to prevent falling. Another example is the *tonic neck reflex*, in which turning the head to the right causes facilitation in the arm flexors on the left and in the arm extensors on the right.

That these reflexes exist is not in question. They are especially easy to identify in infants, and

they have been used in the diagnosis of various neurological disorders. But to say that gait and other movement behaviors *consist* of the various reflexes implies a model in which the motor system is always *reacting* to peripheral stimulation. A more reasonable viewpoint, based on the evidence on central pattern generators, is that reflexes ensure that the pattern of activity specified by the central pattern generator is carried out effectively in the face of unexpected changes in the environment. The muscle spindle and gamma systems seem to fill this role. One function of the gamma system is to maintain muscle stiffness (i.e., its springlike properties) in the face of various unexpected changes in muscle length (Nichols & Houk, 1976). If an animal steps on a patch of ground that is higher than expected, the "springy" muscles allow extensors to yield without collapsing, maintaining a smooth gait. The view is that reflexes are *prepared* to operate if the system is perturbed but do not have a particularly important role under normal circumstances (Grillner, 1975).

Reflex-Reversal Phenomena

An important variation of the concept of triggered reactions (discussed in chapter 5) is the concept of reflex reversals described in relation to locomotion by Forssberg, Grillner, and Rossignol (1975). In the locomoting cat, when a light touch or a weak electrical shock is applied to the top of the foot during the flexion portion of the swing phase of the gait cycle (i.e., the time at which the animal is lifting the foot in preparation for the swing forward), an abrupt increase occurs in the flexion response (with an extension response in the opposite foot), as if the cat were trying to avoid an obstacle (such as a rock) that would cause it to trip. (This crossed-extensor pattern is not voluntary, as it can be shown to exist in the mesencephalic cats described earlier; thus, the response is spinal in origin.) However, when the *same* stimulus is applied to the foot during the phase of the gait cycle in which the foot is on the ground (stance phase), essentially no reaction, or perhaps a slight extra extension, takes place in the stimulated foot—a response *opposite* that shown in the swing phase of the step cycle. Because the same stimulus causes two different patterns of action depending on the phase of the stepping cycle, this effect has been termed the *reflex-reversal phenomenon*. Usually a reflex is thought of as a *stereotyped response* caused by a particular stimulus. Yet the evidence cited indicates that the response to the stimulus depends on the location of the limb in the stepping cycle and is not simple and stereotyped. Thus, a simple view of reflex control cannot explain these effects.

This kind of evidence has been explained (e.g., Grillner, 1975) by assuming that the spinal generators for locomotion, in addition to providing efferent commands to the relevant musculature, also provide feedforward signals to other locations in the cord that serve to modify the actions of various reflexes. The sense of this control is that if the pathways to the extensors of the right leg are being activated (during the stance phase), then the reflex that would serve to lift the leg in response to a tap is inhibited by the central generator, but is activated when the flexors are activated (in the flexion phase). In this way, the pattern generators involve the already structured reflex pathways so that they contribute maximally to the animal's overall movement goals (see also Hasan & Enoka, 1985).

These reflex reversals have also been found in research on the motor control of speech (Abbs & Gracco, 1983; Abbs, Gracco, & Cole, 1984; Kelso et al., 1984). Subjects in the study by Kelso et al. said simple sentences, such as "It's a /baez/ again" or "It's a /baeb/ again," and received an unexpected downward perturbation to the jaw during the target syllable /baez/ or /baeb/. When /baez/ was to be spoken, a perturbation to the jaw evoked a rapid compensation in the tongue muscles but not in the lip, whereas the same perturbation during /baeb/ produced the reverse pattern—a compensation in the lip but not the tongue; and this compensation occurred on

the *first* trial. As in the work on locomotion, the same stimulus (here the jaw perturbation) produced rapid responses (about 30-ms latency) that were very different depending on the action being produced (i.e., the specific word). But, unlike the locomotion findings, these speech modifications were probably learned, as it is difficult to imagine how this capability could have been a part of an inherited pattern as was the case for locomotion. These rapid adjustments seem to serve the general purpose of ensuring that the overall *goal* of the particular movement being attempted at the time is maintained, with the modifications necessarily being different for different movement goals (Schmidt, 1987).

The "Smart" Spinal Cord

Early in the thinking about motor control, the spinal cord tended to be viewed as a "freeway" that simply carried impulses back and forth from the brain to the peripheral receptors. Gradually, as many spinal activities were isolated and studied (e.g., Sherrington, 1906), the spinal cord came to be regarded as considerably more complex. The evidence that the spinal cord contains central pattern generators for gait and other movements continues to point toward the cord as a complex organ where much of the motor control is structured. Further, evidence suggests that the spinal cord is responsible for considerable integration of sensory and motor information, as shown by the following example.

Figure 6.7 shows a frog making a wiping response to a noxious stimulus placed on the "el-

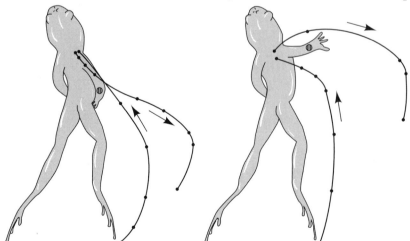

Figure 6.7.   In the spinal frog, the hindlimb response to wipe an acid stimulus from the "elbow" is aimed to various elbow positions without the involvement of voluntary control from the cortex.
Reprinted with permission from Fukson, O.I., Berkinblit, M.B., and Feldman, A.G., 1980, "The Spinal Frog Takes Into Account the Scheme of its Body During the Wiping Reflex," *Science, 209*, 1261. Copyright 1980 American Association for the Advancement of Science.

bow." Fukson, Berkinblit, and Feldman (1980; Berkinblit, Feldman, & Fukson, 1986), like others before them, showed that the frog is capable of performing these hindlimb responses when spinalized (i.e., with a transection that separates the cortex from the intact spinal cord). The response always begins with a movement of the toe to the region of the shoulder area, followed by a rapid wiping action that is aimed at the elbow. It is interesting that the animal can use sensory information from one part of the body (the elbow) to trigger an action pattern in some other part (the hindlimb), even when spinalized. What is of more interest, however, is that the animal produces different wiping movements depending on the location of the elbow at which the response is aimed. That is, the central pattern generator for this response appears to be modified in its action depending on the sensory information from the forelimb about the position of the stimulus—the cord "knows" where the limbs are. Remember, the frog had no cortical involvement in this response, and thus no awareness of the limbs' actions, so this integration of sensory information was done at very low levels, perhaps completely within the spinal cord. Such observations indicate that the spinal cord is a very "smart" organ indeed.

Another example, from the work of Smith et al. (1986) on spinalized cats, is particularly impressive. When a piece of tape was placed on the cat's hind paw, a stereotyped paw-shake program was initiated in which the cat lifted the foot and shook it violently for about 10–13 cycles, apparently for the purpose of shaking the tape loose. Of course, because of the spinal section, this stereotyped program must have been initiated through peripheral stimulation from the foot and controlled by the spinal cord. But even more remarkably, the spinal cat could walk on the treadmill (another program) and shake the paw at the same time, triggering the paw shake when the limb was in the swing phase of locomotion, and turning it off when the foot was on the ground in support. Somehow the spinal cord, without the help of a higher center, "knew" how to coordinate these two actions simultaneously to achieve the double goals of removing the tape and walking without falling.

Human Skills

The evidence and ideas just presented support the concept of a central control mechanism. How-ever, these results on locomotion must not be generalized too far. First, they were produced in animals, and it is not clear whether humans have similar kinds of control in their locomotion, although we might expect that they would. More importantly, the movements studied in the cat are probably genetically defined and "prewired." To what extent are motor programs for movements like throwing a football structured in the same way? Are there programs in the spinal cord that can handle the production of a football pass if they are activated by a pulse from the midbrain, or do programs that are not genetically defined have some different origin? These questions are difficult to answer, as almost no research with animals has used tasks or skills that we could consider learned, or that are not genetically defined.

One hypothesis is that the control of learned and genetically defined actions is fundamentally the same, but no good evidence is available on this question. Instead, we turn next to evidence about the role of central control mechanisms—*motor programs*, specifically—that has been generated in behavioral studies with humans.

Central Control of Rapid Movements

Consider a very rapid limb movement in which the pattern of action is initiated and completed in less than 100 ms. There have been many examples of movements like this in sport, such as the bat swing in baseball (100 ms) and boxer Muhammad Ali's left jab (40 ms). Because these discrete tasks are so highly represented in our everyday activities, they have been studied in laboratory settings in an attempt to understand how they are controlled. A laboratory study might involve beginning with the elbow in one position and then rapidly extending it so that the hand comes to rest at or near a target 30 cm away. Although this movement at first appears to be very simple, the kinds of neurological activities associated with it are elegant and complex.

Although many examples could be presented, one in a study by Wadman et al. (1979) makes the point particularly well. Figure 6.8 is a record from such a set of movements. The electromyograms (EMGs) from the triceps (the agonist) and the biceps (the antagonist) are shown. The "raw" EMGs from the muscles have been *rectified*, meaning the

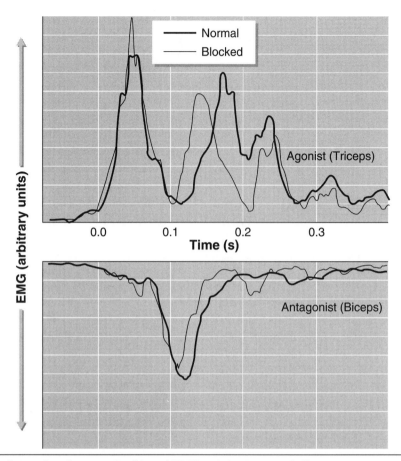

Figure 6.8. Agonist (triceps) and antagonist (biceps) EMG activity in a rapid elbow extension action.
Reprinted, by permission, from Wadman, W.J., Denier van der Gon, J.J., Geuze, R.H., and Mol, C.R., 1979, "Control of Fast Goal-Directed Arm Movements," *Journal of Human Movement Studies, 5,* 10.

negative swings of the EMG signals have been changed to positive values; and the area "under" this set of positive values is plotted. The occurrence of peaks in the rectified EMGs represents periods of heightened activity in the muscle in question. Also, the record for the biceps (the antagonist) has been turned "upside down" so it can be compared to the triceps record.

Figure 6.8 shows a pattern of EMG activity common in many investigations using fast movements. A distinct three-burst EMG pattern is evident. A burst of the agonist (triceps) muscle occurs first, and then the agonist is turned off and the antagonist (the biceps here) is turned on, presumably to bring the limb to a stop. Then, near the end of the response, the antagonist muscle is turned off and the agonist comes on again, probably to cause the limb to be clamped at the target, dampening the oscillations that could be produced. This pattern seems to be degraded somewhat, or even absent, if the movements are slow (Desmedt & Godeaux, 1979).

A question of interest for these kinds of actions is how the motor system "knows" when to turn off the triceps activity and turn on the biceps activity. This question can be extended to apply to skills for which many muscles come on and off at particular times, such as in pole-vaulting and swimming. The closed-loop account of movement behavior (figure 5.12) involving the stages of information processing could account for these features of the movement by indicating that the system monitors the position of the limb (perhaps by sensing the joint angle) and waits until the limb is at some particular position before turning off the triceps and turning on the biceps. That is, the system could use the feedback from the responding limb to trigger the end of activity in one muscle and initiate activity in the other.[2] However, a number of fundamental difficulties arise with this idea about the control of actions, as discussed next.

The Degrees of Freedom Problem

One difficulty for the closed-loop model, and for any other model that holds that the contractions of the various muscles are handled by direct commands from higher centers, was raised by the Russian physiologist Bernstein, writing in the 1940s (translated in 1967). Bernstein's idea was that if the information-processing system were involved in the production of all the decisions about each of the muscles participating in a motor act, then it would be difficult to imagine all of the mental work involved in producing a simple act like that shown in figure 6.8. The fundamental concern is that the system has too many *independent states* that must be controlled at the same time. These independent states are called *degrees of freedom*. Each joint is capable of moving independently, having at least one degree of freedom that must be controlled in an action. Actually, some joints have two degrees of freedom, such as the shoulder that can (a) allow the hand to move in a half sphere with the elbow "locked" and (b) rotate the shaft of the arm, independently. This problem is compounded because each joint has a number of muscles acting on it, and each of these muscles is made up of hundreds of motor units that also must be controlled. All this would lead to an almost impossible situation for the central nervous system if it had to control all these degrees of freedom separately by conscious decisions (see also Greene, 1972; Whiting, 1984).

In searching for answers about how we control movement, a good question is, "How can the very many degrees of freedom of the body be regulated in the course of activity by a minimally intelligent executive intervening minimally?" (Kugler, Kelso, & Turvey, 1980, p. 4). The idea is that an executive level should not be thought of as having much responsibility for the control of the many degrees of freedom; there are simply too many degrees of freedom for even an intelligent executive to control and yet still have capability left over to do anything else.

On other grounds, for many years scientists have thought that *actions* are controlled, not the individual degrees of freedom such as muscles or motor units. When we perform an action, we seem to be aware of the goal of the movement, its global action pattern, and its effect on the environment; but we are hardly aware at all of the particular muscles used and are never aware of the particular motor units involved. Therefore, if the executive does not have the responsibility for controlling the degrees of freedom, how *are* the many degrees of freedom controlled, and how

can the elegant, skilled organizations among the muscles and joints be achieved?

This general question has been of fundamental concern since scientists began to think about movement skills. One solution has been to postulate a structure, subordinate to the executive, that can account for the particular organization required among the separate degrees of freedom. These theoretical structures, called *motor programs* by many (e.g., Brooks, 1979, 1986; Keele, 1968, 1986; Keele, Cohen, & Ivry, 1990; Lashley, 1917; Schmidt, 1975b, 1988), have the capability to strongly influence the activity of the many independent degrees of freedom so that they act as a single unit. If this temporary organization can be imposed on the system, then the problem for the executive will have been simplified so that only a single degree of freedom will have to be controlled. In other words, the executive level is thought to control the selection of a motor program to ready it for action and to initiate it at the proper time. Once under way, the program controls the individual degrees of freedom, and in this sense the executive is freed from the task.

This kind of solution to the degrees of freedom problem sounds very simple—in fact, too simple. Explaining how all the degrees of freedom are controlled by inventing some theoretical structure does not really answer the question of control at all. The question of exactly how the various degrees of freedom are constrained still must be addressed. The debate about the nature of this reduction in controllable degrees of freedom—in terms of what variables are controlled, when, and how—represents a truly fundamental problem for researchers in motor control. We will consider some of these questions in this chapter and again in chapters 7 and 8.

Agonist-Antagonist Patterning

Another argument against the idea that some executive level *directly* terminates the triceps burst of EMG and initiates the biceps burst (figure 6.8) is related to the time available for generating these events. The information-processing stages require considerable time in order for an environmental stimulus to begin to produce some new response, such as the offset of the triceps EMG and the onset of the biceps EMG. Although this model might be acceptable for very slow movements, if the action is very fast (as in this example), the movement will have been finished before one of these stimulus-to-response processes can be completed. Something else must be involved in the activation of the various muscle groups.

This argument, however, does not rule out the possibility that the patterning has been influenced by reflexive adjustments, handled at lower levels in the motor system. As discussed in chapter 5, such processes are far faster than those involved in the stages of processing, and they might be rapid enough to account for the control entailed in these very fast actions. A number of models based on lower level reflex control have been proposed (e.g., Adamovich & Feldman, 1984; Feldman, 1986), and considerable debate has centered on this question. Some available data, however, seem to suggest that these models are not correct either.

The Wadman et al. (1979) experiment had an additional condition that we have not yet described. When the subject had become accustomed to the apparatus and movement task, on particular trials the lever was unexpectedly locked mechanically at the starting position so that no movement of it could occur. Figure 6.8 shows the EMG patterns available from these "blocked" trials, superimposed on the patterns from the "normal" trials. For approximately 110 ms after the initial agonist EMG burst, the two EMG patterns were nearly identical, with only minor modifications in the patterning afterward. The most important feature of figure 6.8 is that the onset of the antagonist (biceps) EMG occurred at a normal time on these "blocked" trials. If this antagonist EMG onset was due to reflexive involvement, perhaps via processes associated with joint movement, then the antagonist onset would surely have been disrupted or prevented when the movement was blocked. Magill et al. (1987) and Shapiro and Walter (1982) obtained similar results for fast movements. Using considerably slower movements, however, Angel (1977) found that the antagonist EMG disappeared when the movement was blocked; perhaps enough time was available here for higher levels to interrupt the sequence. On balance, the data suggest that reflex control cannot explain the EMG patterning seen in these quick movements. In our opinion, this is one of the strongest lines of evidence to suggest that quick movements are prestructured centrally and "run off" as a unit.

From the research on deafferentation discussed earlier comes a second line of evidence against the hypothesis that the pattern of EMG bursts is determined by reflexive control. Because all afferent information from the limb is eliminated, deafferentation produces a situation in which no reflexes from the muscles or joints can operate to control the limb. Yet, as we have seen, animals with surgical deafferentation and humans with temporary deafferentation can move reasonably well under these conditions. Other examples cited by Grillner (1975) are walking and running in cats; ambulation, climbing, feeding, and grooming in monkeys; swimming in fish; and "slithering" in snakes. The fact that these movements are slightly impaired probably means that feedback helps to make those actions more smooth or precise but is not their primary cause.

Producing Modifications in Rapid Movements

In the next sections we examine some of the evidence about the performer's capabilities to *change* a movement once it has been initiated. This information is related closely to the findings presented in chapter 4 (e.g., psychological refractoriness), and the two kinds of findings seem to blend well to provide a picture of what happens during the course of a rapid action.

Anecdotal Evidence

Evidence from personal experience is quite difficult to interpret, for the strong possibility exists that what we think we do is not what actually occurs, leading to a false picture of movement-control processes. Even so, some of our common observations guide us to experiments in which the ideas can be studied more carefully.

Long after his work with the wounded patient, Lashley (1951) provided an example of a skilled pianist playing a piano with a broken key that could not be depressed. As the pianist played a string of notes, the attempts to press the broken key did not interrupt the series of actions at all. In fact, only after the entire sequence was completed did the individual notice and remark that the key was broken. This suggests that the actions do not appear to be structured with feedback to "verify" that a certain finger movement has been made before the next one is commanded. The feedback appeared to be only minimally involved in the production of the movement sequence (see also Gordon & Soechting, 1995). Another example is buttoning a shirt, which sometimes continues in its fine detail even if a button is missing. Again, feedback from the fingers is probably not critically involved.

The British psychologist Bartlett expressed similar views about the performance of certain ball sports. Bartlett (1958) suggested that the "launching" of an action signals a *point* (or *region*) *of no return*—beyond which attempts to modify the action are largely unsuccessful. These ideas are interesting, but they are not based on solid data that document the time course of events within the human information-processing system. In the next sections, we describe some experiments in which these issues were examined.

Initiation of Movement Modifications

Henry and Harrison (1961) presented one of the first experimental analyses of these questions. They asked subjects to begin with a finger on a key located at their hip and, at a "go" signal, to move the arm forward and upward to trip a string located in front of their right shoulder. They were instructed to do this as quickly as possible. The simple reaction time (RT) in these control trials was 214 ms on the average, and the movement time (MT) was slightly shorter, at 199 ms. On some trials, a second light would come on, indicating that the subject should *avoid* tripping the string or at least begin to slow the limb as quickly as possible. The "stop" signal could come on at one of four times: 110, 190, 270, and 350 ms after the "go" signal. Figure 6.9 shows the timing of the essential details of the experiment, indicating where the stop signals could come on within the

RT and MT intervals. Henry and Harrison measured the time taken to begin to decelerate the limb after the "stop" signal was presented.

Only when the "stop" signal was given at the 110-ms location (the earliest of the presentation times) was there a tendency for the subjects to start to slow the movement before it had been completed. But the more interesting feature of these data is the subject's response in the 190-ms condition. Notice here that the "stop" signal came on 24 ms before the movement even started, and yet the movement was carried out without interruption. That is, a signal presented before the movement was not effective in modifying that particular movement, even when the movement lasted for 199 ms (see also Gao & Zelaznik, 1991).

If the information-processing stages are too slow to be involved in the details of a particular action, and segmental reflexive control is not involved either, then the question is, what does produce these patterns of action? The best theory to have been proposed at this point is that these movements are *preprogrammed*, structured in advance, and run off as a unit without much modification from events in the environment. An additional interpretation is that, once some internal "go" signal is issued, the action occurs and cannot be stopped, like pulling the trigger on a gun. When the (external) "stop" signal was presented 104 ms before the overall response was to begin, the response began anyway, and an additional 110 ms or so was required to even begin to stop it.

Logan has performed many of the recent experimental analyses using this "stop-signal" paradigm (see Logan, 1994, for a review). In one of these studies, skilled typists were asked to type phrases as rapidly as possible, but to stop their

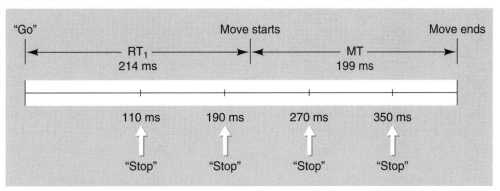

Figure 6.9. A timeline showing the critical events in the Henry-Harrison experiment. ("Stop" signals were presented at various times after an initial "go" signal.)
Adapted and reproduced with permission of authors and publisher from: Henry, F.M., & Harrison, J.S. Refractoriness of a fast movement. *Perceptual and Motor Skills*, 1961, 13, 351-354. © Southern Universities Press 1961.

typing if they heard a stop tone (Logan, 1982). In general, Logan found that the typists produced one to two additional letters after the stop tone was provided (about 200 ms of MT), regardless of the specific position within the word at which the tone was presented. However, several exceptions were notable—one being the word "the." Logan (1982) found that typists would almost always produce the entire "the" *and* the space afterward, and that this occurred even when the stop signal was provided on the last letter of the previous word. Given that "the" is the most frequently used word in the English language (Kucera & Francis, 1967), typists have probably developed a very highly overlearned motor program for typing it—one that is difficult to inhibit from executing in its entirety once the internal "go" signal has been issued.

At what point in the RT to a signal are we committed to action? An experiment by Slater-Hammel (1960) helps to answer this question, as well as supporting some of the other points just made about movement programming.

Inhibiting an Anticipatory Movement

Slater-Hammel (1960) asked subjects to watch a sweep timer that made one revolution per second and to respond by lifting a finger from a key to stop the clock at the moment when the timer reached "8" (i.e., 800 ms after it started). The subject could not, of course, wait until the clock hand had actually arrived at "8" before initiating the movement, because the finger lift would be far too late. So the subject's task on these trials was to anticipate the movement of the clock hand, together with the lags in the information-processing and neuromuscular systems, so that the finger was lifted at precisely the correct time. Slater-Hammel added an interesting condition, however. Occasionally and unpredictably, the clock hand would stop before it reached "8." If this happened, the subject was instructed not to lift the finger from the key—that is, to do "nothing." The clock hand could stop any time from 200 ms to 750 ms after it started—representing points of the clock face very near the "8" (e.g., 50 ms before) or quite some time before the "8" target point. Slater-Hammel studied the capabilities of successfully *inhibiting* the movement as the amount of time before "8" was varied experimentally.

Figure 6.10 presents the probability of successfully inhibiting the finger lift as a function of the

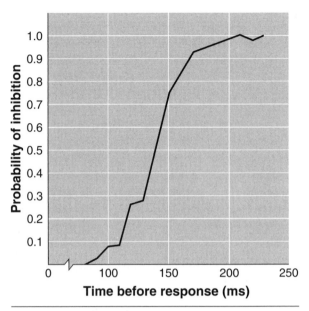

Figure 6.10. The probability of successfully inhibiting an anticipated finger lift as a function of the interval before the critical event.
Reprinted from Slater-Hammel, 1960.

time before "8" that the clock hand stopped. If the clock hand stopped 250 ms before "8," the subject should have had no trouble inhibiting the movement; and, conversely, if the clock hand stopped only 50 ms before the clock reached "8," the subject should never have been able to inhibit the movement. That is essentially what Slater-Hammel found. But notice that as the time before "8" decreased from about 170 ms, the probability of successfully inhibiting the movement decreased sharply, with the probability being about .5 when the interval before "8" was 146 ms. Another way to state this finding is to say that if the clock hand stopped 146 ms before "8," the subject could inhibit the response successfully only half the time.

Another important finding was that although this 50% point occurred at 146 ms before "8," Slater-Hammel's subjects responded a little late on the average (constant error = +22 ms). This occurred because the natural tendency when one does this task, knowing that the sweep hand might stop unexpectedly, is to wait as long as possible before committing oneself to action. Subjects tend to be *positively biased* on these trials as a result. Therefore, to estimate the time required for inhibition, we add the 22 ms to the 146 ms and obtain 168 ms as an estimate of how long before the anticipatory response the inhibition could not occur.

A number of important interpretations may be made from this thinking. First, the finding that the subject could not inhibit a movement once it was internally planned and initiated supports the observations made about the Henry and Harrison (1961) study and the typing of the word "the" shown by Logan (1982). Apparently, once the subject is *committed* to action, the movement occurs even when some signal is presented in the environment indicating that the action should not be performed. In the Henry and Harrison example, the action was already under way when the stop signal was presented, with the movement *continuing* without much interruption. In the Logan and the Slater-Hammel examples, however, the movement had not yet been started when the signal to inhibit occurred, but the movement was *initiated* anyway if this signal occurred beyond a certain point. As mentioned in chapter 4, inhibiting preplanned actions requires time and attention, and these data support this idea. Students do this experiment in the laboratory sections of our motor behavior courses; they *see* that the clock hand has stopped, but their hand responds anyway. The feeling is that they do not have control over the hand, where "they" refers to "their consciousness." The point of no return appears to represent the point at which "control" of the hand has been transferred, with the hand now subservient to the motor program instead (Osman, Kornblum, & Meyer, 1990; see also De Jong et al., 1990).

Programming Rapid Movements in Advance

In chapter 3, we introduced the idea that in a response-programming stage the person selects, organizes, and initiates a program of action that will produce a series of muscular activities resulting in an action. According to this model, the program must be structured completely, or almost completely, before the movement can be initiated, and very little modification will occur in the movement for the next few hundred milliseconds or so. One important line of support for this hypothesis is the evidence that certain variables related to the "complexity" of the movement to be made (i.e., the number of limbs or movement segments), or to the MT of the action, tend to affect the time between stimulus and the beginning of the movement (i.e., the RT; Henry &

Rogers, 1960). More complex rapid movements or those that have longer MTs tend to produce longer RTs (Christina, 1992; Klapp, 1996). It has not been possible to explain how these effects could occur except by the hypothesis that the movement is programmed in advance, with these variables affecting the duration of the stage necessary for completing this preprogramming (Schmidt, 1972c; Schmidt & Russell, 1972).

There are, however, some exceptions to this evidence. If a quick movement is made in a *simple-RT* situation (one stimulus, one response), and if the subjects are highly motivated, sometimes no increase in RT is seen as movement complexity is increased (e.g., Klapp, 1977a). In this situation, because there is no uncertainty about the nature of the movement to be made, the person can presumably preprogram all the details of the movement in advance and then simply wait for the reaction signal to trigger the action. If so, then the extra time for advance planning of the more complex action will not be seen in RT, as these processes have already occurred by the time the reaction signal appears. This evidence is of course consistent with the programming viewpoint, but it indicates that people are flexible in terms of when they program a movement—either before or after the reaction signal—depending on a number of other factors.

Limitations in Processing Speed

The evidence presented in the previous sections has strong implications for how we think about the control of fast actions. First of all, a model in which the information-processing stages are involved in the moment-to-moment regulation of action must be incorrect, because these stages are too slow and limited in capacity to accomplish the necessary processing. As a result, it has been postulated that hypothetical structures such as motor programs handle the details of this control. Evidence suggests that the details of control are not determined by low-level reflexive activities, but rather are structured centrally and run off as the movement unfolds, with reflexive activities playing a regulatory role.

Therefore, at least two levels can be distinguished in the motor system: (a) an executive level (including the information-processing stages) for selecting, organizing, and initiating a complex pattern of muscular activities and (b) an effector level (motor programs and muscular system) for actually controlling or producing the patterns as they unfold. We can further distinguish these two levels by examining two distinct types of errors that can occur in performance, which we describe later in the chapter.

Motor Program Issues

So far we have discussed three lines of evidence that provide support for the notion of motor programs. First, feedback processing is slow, so that at least rapid movements will be completed before the feedback can be returned to the stages of processing and a correction determined and initiated. Some central structure seems to be handling the details of the movement in the meantime. Patterns of EMGs were unaffected for 100–150 ms after an unexpected mechanical block of the movement, supporting the view that at least this portion of the movement was controlled by central programming. Second, movements appear to be planned in advance, as evidenced by the fact that RTs increase with movement "complexity," suggesting that a response-programming stage requires more time to plan as complexity increases. Third, deafferentation studies showed that movement is possible (although degraded somewhat depending on the type of behavior) in the absence of feedback from the moving limb, implying that some central mechanism was at least partly responsible for movement organization and control.

These arguments have led to the idea of a motor program as a prestructured set of central commands capable of carrying out movement essentially open-loop. According to the original notion, which dates back to thinking by James (1890) and Lashley (1917), and more recently to Henry and Rogers (1960), Keele (1968), Schmidt (1976a), and Brooks (1979), movements are centrally structured with only a very minimal role for sensory information in movement control, at least until sufficient time has elapsed that the central information-processing mechanisms can generate and initiate modifications. An early and very clear implication for an open-loop central control mechanism was suggested by Lashley when he said that "an effector mechanism can be pre-set or primed to discharge at a given intensity or for a given duration, in independence of any sensory signals" (p. 123). Although Lashley did

not use the term "motor program," this quote serves as a suitable definition for an extreme view of the concept (see also Keele, 1968).

We have already presented evidence, however, that such a view can explain only a limited set of movement situations, as many examples can be cited in which feedback processes seem to interact with open-loop processes in the production of movement. A more reasonable approach to motor programming is to ask *how* the sensory processes operate together with the open-loop processes to produce skilled actions.

Sensory Information and Motor Programs

The next sections deal with various functions of feedback in movement control. These functions operate before a movement, during a movement, and after a movement.

Prior to the Movement

One of the major roles of sensory information is probably to provide information about the initial state of the motor system prior to the action. Consider this simple example: you must know whether you are standing with your left or right foot forward in order to initiate a walking pattern (Keele, 1973). The spinal frog (figure 6.7) requires sensory information from the forelimb in order to direct the hindlimb to the elbow during the wiping response. Such information is presumably provided by afferent feedback from the various proprioceptors, and it would seem to be critical for the selection of the proper action. These processes were argued in chapters 2 and 3 to be very important for open skills, for which the nature of the environment is unpredictable or constantly changing.

Polit and Bizzi (1979), using deafferented monkeys, showed that when the initial position of the shoulder changed prior to the elbow action, a systematic error in pointing to the target position occurred. This is understandable from figure 6.11, because changing the shoulder angle as shown necessarily affects the *elbow angle* (from θ_1 to θ_2) required for pointing at a target in a given position in space. If the monkey programmed a given elbow angle, then the *equilibrium-point mechanism* (chapter 7) would achieve that angle, and the arm would not be pointing to the proper target. These monkeys did not learn to point to

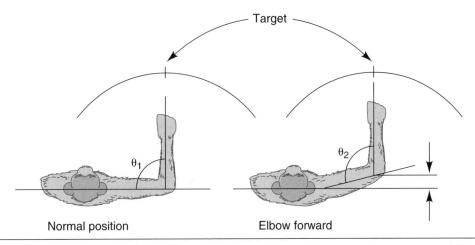

Figure 6.11.   In pointing to a target, the equilibrium point of the elbow is dependent on the angle at the shoulder. Reprinted from Plit and Bizzi, 1979.

the target, even after considerable practice. By contrast, normal, intact monkeys learned in a few trials to compensate for the shifts in the shoulder position. The interpretation is that the intact animals had feedback from the shoulder joint and could adjust the angle at the elbow to compensate for the felt change in the shoulder angle. Thus, these data suggest that to point to a position in space, feedback about the initial positions of the joints is required if the environment is not perfectly predictable.

Another role of afferent information involves what has been called *functional tuning* by a number of authors (Fitch, Tuller, & Turvey, 1982; Turvey, 1977). Recall that the spinal apparatus and resulting limb strength could be affected by changing the head position, much as would be expected on the basis of the idea that the tonic neck reflex was involved in the action (Hellebrandt et al., 1956). In this example, afferent information from the neck presumably adjusts the spinal mechanisms prior to action, thereby facilitating or inhibiting them. But a more compelling reason for assuming that premovement tuning must occur is related to some simple facts about the nature of the motor apparatus. In figure 6.12 are two diagrams of a hypothetical rapid movement. In both cases, the movement involves flexion of the elbow a distance of 45°, beginning with the arm straight. In figure 6.12a, the upper arm is positioned 45° to the vertical, so that a flexion of the elbow will result in the forearm's being horizontal at the end. In figure 6.12b, the upper arm is 45° above horizontal, so that the forearm will be vertical at the end. The same command signal delivered to the biceps muscle group will not "work" in both situations, for two reasons. First, a force is required to hold the forearm against gravity at the target position in the first situation, but not in the second. Second, more force is required to move the forearm against gravity in the first example relative to the second. A logical conclusion from this simple example is that the motor system must "know" where the shoulder position is prior to the action so that the command to the elbow flexors can produce the required 45° movement. How this happens is not entirely clear, but *that* it happens seems to be very clear.

Consider another complicating factor for the motor system to have to cope with in producing a movement. Figure 6.13 is a schematic diagram of the muscle attachments involved in a simple movement. This time, imagine that the movement is an extension movement in which the elbow is to be moved through 45°. Notice that the triceps muscle, which is the primary elbow extensor, is attached to the humerus in two places (internal and external heads) and to the scapula of the shoulder area (the long head). Thus, the triceps muscle performs two actions when it contracts: it extends the elbow and it tends to extend the shoulder joint, pulling the humerus back. Therefore, when the triceps is contracting to produce the 45°-movement, one of the muscles that flexes the shoulder must contract so that the shoulder joint is stabilized and only the elbow moves. Thus, during this simple extension movement, the motor system must "know" that there is a two-jointed muscle involved and produce some compensatory stabilization. The amount of stabilization will be dependent on the shoulder angle, because of the length-tension relation (chapter 7).

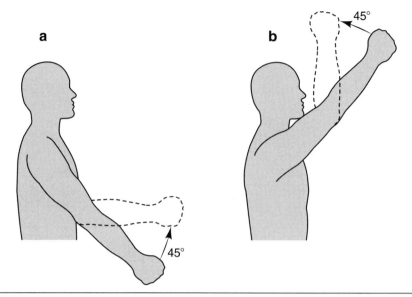

Figure 6.12.   Two 45° elbow flexion movements that appear to require different commands for the action and different forces at their endpoints because of the effects of gravity.

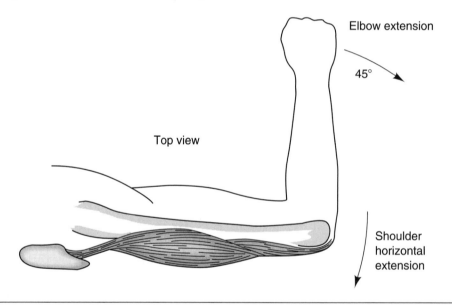

Figure 6.13.   Complexity in a 45° elbow extension movement caused by the fact that the triceps muscle both extends the elbow and horizontally extends the shoulder.

The picture that emerges from these observations is that a "simple" 45°-movement of the elbow joint is not really all that simple in terms of the motor system. In addition, other complicated aspects of the muscle need to be considered by the motor system, such as the nonlinear relationship between the muscle force and limb velocity, together with aspects of the contraction process that make the motor system very difficult to predict and control (Partridge, 1979, 1983). Yet our nervous system controls our limbs beautifully in these "simple" situations. How it does so is exciting to ponder.

During the Movement

One role that feedback seems to have in movement production is a monitoring function, whereby the feedback from the movement is taken in and processed but not necessarily used in the control of the action unless something goes wrong. It is probable that a long string of actions dealing with finger movements in piano playing is programmed and carried out open-loop. Feedback from the fingers is returned to the central nervous system for analysis, as if the central nervous system were "checking for" errors. If no errors appear, then the feedback is ignored. But if the feedback indicates that an error has occurred, attention can be directed to that feedback source, and an appropriate correction may be initiated. Reflexive corrections may also be generated, as discussed in chapter 5.

A second way to view feedback is that it may be intricately involved in the physical control of the limb. We mentioned a number of examples of this in the preceding chapter. The possibility exists that a constantly changing reference of correctness is specified by the gamma motor neurons to the muscle spindles and that their actions result in a continuous set of corrections to keep the movement on the proper course. The feedback could be involved in the determination of the end location of a movement if the reference of correctness were set for this position. And in repetitive movements, the feedback from early segments of the sequence can provide adjustments for the later segments.

Following the Movement

Extensive feedback is also delivered to the central nervous system after a movement. Such information can be evaluated, presumably, by the stages of information processing in order to determine the nature of the movement just made. Information about whether or not the move achieved the environmental goal, as well as about its smoothness, its level of force or effort, or its form or style, is derived from feedback. A major role for such information is in the adjustment of the movement on the *subsequent* trial, perhaps to reduce the errors made on the previous trial. As such, this information has a considerable relevance to the acquisition of skills, as discussed in the final part of this book dealing with motor *learning* (chapters 12 and 13, in particular).

Types of Motor Program Errors

Various theories or viewpoints about motor control processes have been attempts to integrate ideas about the role of feedback with open-loop concepts. These ideas are presented in the next sections. The first task will be to define two distinct types of errors that the motor system can make, each of which uses feedback in distinctly different ways.

When a person makes a rapid movement, there are really two goals (Schmidt, 1976a). First, there is an environmentally defined goal, such as chang-

ing gears in a standard transmission car or doing a somersault from a diving board. A second goal (or subgoal) can be defined in terms of the muscular activities required to produce the desired outcomes in the environment. For example, a person must contract the muscles in the arm and torso in one of a limited number of ways in order to change gears smoothly, and only certain patterns of muscular activity will result in a somersault. Essentially, how to generate this subgoal is the problem facing the performer.

This subgoal can be considered as a pattern of action that is structured in both space and time. Thus, such a pattern of action will determine where a particular part of the body will be at a particular time after the movement starts. If this spatial-temporal pattern (the subgoal) is produced accurately, then the environmental goal will have been achieved. Of course a number of different patterns of action can be used that will result in the overall goal of changing gears (relating to how the clutch is contacted, which fingers are used to grip the gearshift, the velocity of leg and arm actions, etc.), but each of these must be produced accurately in order for the overall goal to be achieved.

Errors in Program Selection

Given the assumptions about the spatial-temporal goal, the first kind of error that the person might produce can be defined as an error in *program selection*. This kind of failure to achieve the environmental goal results from the performer's choice of action. This can happen in a number of ways (Reason & Mycielska, 1982). First, the person can produce the wrong pattern of action: for example, moving right when a left move is appropriate, or moving when it might be important to stand still. Second, an error in selection can occur if the person chooses an appropriate program (e.g., a bat swing pattern when a bat swing is required) but the spatial-temporal pattern that has been defined turns out to be inappropriate. For example, the bat swing could be too high or too low, or too early or too late, because of unexpected changes in the ball's flight. Because all these decisions about where and when to swing—as well as all the contractions that occur in the swing—must be defined in advance, the performer will have made an error because he selected the wrong pattern to produce. Another way to see this is to note that if the person had produced a pattern with a little higher bat location and a slightly earlier swing, the results could have been a home run instead of a miss.

How does a person make a correction for an error in program selection? According to the evidence presented earlier, the person must issue a *new* motor program, as the "old" one will not achieve the goal in the environment. Hence, the information-processing stages must be re-initiated, a new program must be selected in the response-selection stage, and it must be programmed in the response-programming stage; and all these stages are relatively slow. The result is that a new pattern of action in a rapid motor skill usually cannot be selected before the movement has been completed, and the movement will be in error. If the movement has a somewhat longer MT, however, then it is possible that a correction for an error in selection can occur.

Errors in Program Execution

An error in program execution is fundamentally different from an error in program selection (Schmidt, 1976a). An error in execution can occur if the person produces a program of action appropriate for the environment, but some unexpected event occurs that disrupts the movement. This can happen, for example, if the contractions specified by the motor program are not quite achieved by the muscles, perhaps because of inconsistencies in the spinal cord where it is determined which (and how many) motor units are to be activated. Or in a tennis game on a windy day, a perfectly programmed and timed swing will be slowed by an unexpected puff of wind. If you picked up a milk carton that you thought was nearly full but that really was nearly empty, you could smash the carton into the top shelf of the refrigerator.

These influences do not make the *originally* intended movement pattern incorrect, as some compensation that will achieve the originally planned spatial-temporal goal will still result in the achievement of the environmental goal. Thus, the correction for an error in movement execution may not require a new motor program, as the original pattern of action defined by the "old" program will be correct if the motor system can compensate for the unexpected environmental influences. This implies that because the system does not have to select a new motor program,

the correction for an error in execution does not require all the stages of information processing and will be far more rapid than correcting for an error in program selection.

What is the evidence for this kind of correction, and is the correction for error in execution fundamentally different than that for an error in selection? Consider the example from Dewhurst (1967; figure 5.13) presented in the preceding chapter; recall that the subject was instructed to hold a weight with the elbow at right angles. When the weight was suddenly changed, a correction followed in the biceps EMG within about 30 ms, and a more sustained correction followed in about 50 to 80 ms. The corrections were far faster than can be explained by the production of a new program of action; hence it seems reasonable to believe that the original program of action was in some way modified. More importantly, the person did not have to select a new program of action to compensate for the added weight, as the "old" spatial-temporal goal was still appropriate. The goal as stated before the weight was added was "Hold the elbow at right angles," and the goal afterward was the same; the subject seemed only to require additional muscular tension in order to continue with the "old" goal. Thus, it appears that the corrections served the purpose of maintaining the *original* pattern of action and did not result in the generation of a new one. As a result, the corrections had a far shorter latency than would be expected if it had been necessary to produce a new pattern (see chapter 5 for other examples).

What about the role of consciousness in corrections for errors in selection? As you will recall from chapter 5, Henry (1953; figure 5.14) asked subjects to try to maintain the position of a lever in response to unexpected changes in the pressure it exerted against the hand. He showed that subjects were able to compensate for changes in position that were some 20 times smaller than changes they could consciously detect. The subjects were responding to changes in position that they could not perceive—that is, they were responding *unconsciously*. Also, Johansson and Westling (1984; Westling & Johansson, 1984) showed that if subjects began to lose grip on an object held between the fingers, compensations could be made in approximately 30 ms, apparently without conscious awareness. In these examples, the person did not have to select a new program of action when the stimulus occurred, because the original pattern of action was still acceptable. Force changes within the context of this pattern of behavior were required, however, to maintain the movement's overall goals. These were accomplished very quickly and without awareness, and can be thought of as corrections for errors in execution.

Program Selection Errors Versus Execution Errors

Table 6.1 summarizes some of the fundamental features of these two kinds of errors, listed so that their differences can be seen more easily. These differences are important, because without testable distinctions between these error categories it would make little sense to consider these classes separate (see also classifications of reflex responses in chapter 5 for a similar analysis, especially table 5.2).

From the table, we can see that the latencies of the two kinds of corrections are quite different; the selection errors require 120–200 ms or more in order for a correction to begin, and the execution errors are corrected far more quickly, in 30–50 ms. Also, a new spatial-temporal goal is needed to correct an error in selection, whereas the original pattern of action can continue while an error in execution is being produced. We know that selecting and initiating a new movement program (needed to correct an error in selection) require attention and consciousness in the sense defined in chapter 4 and that this process will interfere greatly with certain other (cognitive) processes attempted at the same time; hence only one such correction can be done at a time. Correcting for an error in execution, on the other hand, is automatic with respect to cognitive information-processing activities, and many such corrections could pre-

sumably be done at the same time without interference—some in the arms, some in the legs, and so on. Hick's law clearly applies when one is correcting for errors in selection (chapter 3), with the latency increasing as the number of possible corrections increases. For errors in execution, on the other hand, the number of possible errors is probably not a factor, and so Hick's law would not be expected to apply.[3] All these differences, taken together, clearly argue that corrections of motor program errors are of at least two fundamental types.

Triggered Reactions

The classification scheme in table 6.1 is more than two decades old now (Schmidt, 1976a, 1983), and newer research suggests it may be somewhat too simple to account for all the evidence. One good example involves triggered reactions, as discussed in chapter 5. We saw that triggered reactions were faster than RT, did not seem to require conscious processing, and did not seem to involve the selection of a new movement program—all of which would at first glance seem to place them into the category of corrections for errors in execution. But the notion of errors in execution implies that the correction serves to bring the limbs back on the original *trajectory* after a perturbation, with the spatial-temporal goal being the particular trajectory originally selected (Cooke, 1980). Yet the evidence on triggered reactions shows that the response to various perturbations is a *new* pattern of action, with a trajectory fundamentally different from the one that was occurring before the stimulus. When a given perturbation was applied, we saw altered lip and tongue trajectories in human speech (Abbs, Gracco, & Cole, 1984; Kelso et al., 1984), new hindlimb trajectories in cat locomotion (Forssberg, Grillner, &

Table 6.1   Characteristics of Corrections for Errors in Selection and Execution

Characteristic	Selection	Execution
Latency of correction?	120–200 ms	30–50 ms
Old spatial-temporal goal OK?	No	Yes
New program selected?	Yes	No[a]
Attention required?	Yes	No
More than one at a time?	No	Yes
Hick's law apply?	Yes	No?

[a] Provided that the deviation from the spatial-temporal goal is not very large. (Adapted from Schmidt 1983, 1987.)

Rossignol, 1975), and different, coordinated patterns of elbow and finger movements in lifting tasks (Johansson & Westling, 1984; Westling & Johansson, 1984), all with very short latencies.

It is tempting to suggest that triggered reactions ensure that the *original goal* of the action is achieved—not necessarily that the *original trajectory* of the limbs is achieved. This notion implies that a particular trajectory of the limbs is not always as important as it appeared earlier. Of course, there are many ways in which the motor system can achieve a particular environmental goal; and when perturbed, the system seems to shift from one of these alternatives to another, with a very short latency. This combination of features seems to suggest that triggered reactions fall somewhere between correction for errors in execution and correction for errors in selection, sharing features of both categories, or perhaps forming a third category. It may be that when the perturbation is small, a correction for an error in execution can occur to bring the limbs back on the target trajectory; if the perturbation is somewhat larger, a triggered reaction is produced that selects another trajectory, but without the need for reprogramming the movement using the stages of information processing; and if the perturbation is even larger, a correction for an error in selection is generated, which of course involves the stages of processing. Certainly, more work is needed to clarify this issue.

Modern Motor Program Viewpoints

From the previous sections it is clear that there is considerable evidence for a central open-loop mechanism, structured before the movement is initiated, that serves to organize and control limb movements in coordinated actions. Yet substantial evidence also suggests that feedback from the responding limbs can, through a variety of mechanisms, modify the movement in various ways. Some of the lower level reflex activities serve to keep the movement "on track," and triggered reactions and "reflex reversals" alter the trajectory quickly while maintaining the overall movement goal. Also, feedback from the touch receptors in the skin can modify the ways in which the gamma loop functions in movement control (Merton, 1972).

Hierarchical Levels of Control

This large body of evidence suggests a centrally

organized structure that is capable of handling most of the details of the actions but is also very sensitive to movement-produced sensory information from a variety of sources. One way to view this blending of open- and closed-loop functioning is to consider a hierarchical control, in which a higher order, open-loop control structure has "under" it a set of closed-loop processes that ensure the movement's intended goal in the face of various perturbations. If a signal appears in the environment indicating that the higher order program is no longer relevant, the highest levels in the system (the stages of processing) become involved in stopping it, or perhaps in initiating a different program. But if smaller perturbations occur that do not involve an alteration in the fundamental movement goal, these can be handled by lower levels in the hierarchy, presumably while the original higher level program continues to operate. This is a classic example of a closed-loop system embedded within an open-loop system.

These thoughts lead to a modified, less restricted definition of a motor program, one that is in keeping with the literature on feedback process yet retains the essential feature of the open-loop concept: the motor program is an abstract representation of action that, when activated, produces movement without regard to sensory information indicating errors in selection. Once the program has been initiated, the pattern of action is carried out for at least one RT even if the environmental information indicates that an error in selection has been made. Yet during the program's execution, countless corrections for minor errors can be executed that serve to ensure that the movement is carried out faithfully. Grillner (1975) has said essentially the same thing with respect to the control of gait:

> Perhaps it is useful to regard the relevant reflexes as *prepared* [italics added] to operate but without any effect as long as the movement proceeds according to the set central program. At the same instant when the locomotor movements are disturbed (small hole, a slippery surface, etc.) the reflexes come into operation to compensate. (p. 297)

This idea is similar in many ways to the concept of a *coordinative structure* discussed by Greene (1972), Fitch, Tuller, and Turvey (1982),

Turvey (1977), and Berkinblit and Feldman (1988). In both the motor program and coordinative-structure concepts, the many degrees of freedom in the musculature are reduced by a structure or organization that constrains the limbs to act as a single unit. Also, both notions involve the tuning of spinal centers, corrections for errors in execution, and freedom of the executive level from the details of what occurs at lower levels in the motor system.

Multilevel Hierarchical Control

Greene's (1972) point of view emphasized the hierarchical nature of motor control. He suggested that at the highest levels of the system, the global aspects of the movement are represented in the form of a goal (e.g., shoot a basket). The control is passed down through progressively lower levels until all the particular decisions about which motor units to fire are defined at the muscle level. The higher levels in the system do not have any direct control over muscle contractions; they have control only over adjacent levels of control that eventually result in those contractions. This idea is related to the motor program view in which only two levels exist—an executive and a program or effector. Greene's view suggests that there are more than these two levels.

Along these lines, the highest level specifies what Greene called a "ballpark" movement, which would result in any of a number of movements that were "in the ballpark" for the goal to be achieved. As the system passes control to lower levels, the individual details of the actions are defined by the initial conditions of the limbs, the posture of the performer, the relations with respect to gravity, and a host of other factors of which the highest level of the system is not aware. These lower functions then determine the ultimate movement that will result, on the basis of these lower level interactions with feedback, tuning, and other factors. In short, the "ballpark" movement becomes increasingly well specified at each lower level in the motor system.

Some Problems With the Motor Program Notion

The advantage of the motor program notion as a theory of movement control is that it provides order to a large number of separate findings, such as the inability to use certain kinds of feedback and the kinds of corrections that can and cannot be made. But the ideas about programs that have been stated so far have other logical drawbacks that must be considered. The next section deals with two of the most important: the *storage problem* and the *novelty problem*.

The Storage Problem

Given that an animal can produce a motor program "on command" and initiate it, *how many* such programs must the organism have at its disposal in order to move as it does? Recall that a motor program is thought to result in commands to muscles that define a particular pattern of action. In this view, if the pattern is to be changed (e.g., from an overhand to a sidearm throwing pattern), then a totally new program must be produced. Imagine all the ways to produce a throwing action, each of which must have a separate program.

MacNeilage (1970) pointed out this problem in the context of speech production. According to programming theories of speech, each sound (called a *phoneme*) that a human can produce is governed by a separate program; in order to speak, we simply string together these separate programs in a way that follows the "rules" of intelligible speech. This solution seemed to be a good one—since there are only about 44 sounds in English, then we should require only 44 programs. The difficulty is that the actions of the mouth, jaw, tongue, and so forth for a particular sound are different depending on the sound that precedes it. That is, to make the sound of a *t*, the musculature must make one of two different movements depending on whether the word is "eat" or "boat," as you can easily discover for yourself when you say these two words and note the actions of your own tongue. Thus, the 44 programs for tongue movement for the various sounds must now be multiplied by the number of different sounds that could precede these sounds. Furthermore, the movements of the vocal musculature depend on the sound that *follows* the sound in question. This notion of *context-conditioned variability* led MacNeilage to estimate that a very large number of programs must be stored in memory in order for us to speak as we do. Considering all the various accents, inflections, and combinations, as well as any foreign-language sounds, he estimated that about 100,000 programs would be required for speech alone.

It is possible that the brain *can* store 100,000 programs for speaking, of course, as long-term memory has a very large capacity. But when we consider the number of ways in which we move other than for speech, and the interaction of previous and subsequent states for each of these movements, there would have to be a nearly countless number of programs in long-term memory.

This postulation seems unwise for several reasons. First, many mechanical or electronic control systems have this storage problem, and it is crippling to them; examples are libraries that have to cope with tons of paper and computer systems that have to store programs for every kind of computation. They simply run out of room. A second reason is related to the belief that our motor system evolved in such a way that it was simple to operate and efficient in terms of storage. To store a complex program for every movement is not a simple and elegant way for a system to have developed (e.g., Schmidt, 1975b; Turvey, 1977). There must be a better way to conceptualize the storage of motor programs.

The Novelty Problem

The next concern about motor programming is related to the storage problem, but it takes a slightly different form. The basic issue is how we make *new* movements. Consider a movement like this: beginning in a standing position, jump up from both feet, touching your head with the right hand and your leg with your left hand before you land. Certainly, most of us could do this on the first try. If you had never done that particular movement before and if the action required a program for its execution, then where did the program come from? It is difficult to assume that the program was genetically defined (as walking might be), because such an action does not seem particularly essential. And you could not have learned it through practice, as this was the first time that you produced this action. A logical dilemma arises about motor programming for novel movements.

The same sort of problem exists for more common skills. If you were to study a series of 50 shots in tennis, examining the fine details of the feet, hands, and body, you would probably find that no two movements were *exactly* the same. This is compounded by the fact that the ball never has exactly the same velocity, the same location on the court, or the same height. Therefore, it is unlikely

that any two tennis strokes could be exactly the same. If no two shots are exactly the same, then the programs must also be different. Thus, according to this analysis at least, every shot is "novel" in the sense that it has never been produced in exactly that way before. When you make a movement, you do not simply repeat a movement that has been learned earlier.

On the other hand, a given golf or tennis stroke is certainly very similar to strokes that you have made previously. For example, some people have a certain (but very odd) style of hitting a golf ball that is characteristic of them and no one else. And your favorite touring professional's style is easily recognized. Thus, it is not fair to say that every golf stroke is absolutely new, as considerable practice and experience have led to the production of that action, and this experience tends to make the actions somewhat similar—characteristic of the individual.

Writing more than a half century ago, Bartlett (1932) made the following observation about tennis strokes: "When I make the stroke I do not, as a matter of fact, produce something absolutely new, and I never repeat something old" (p. 202). His point summarizes the issues in this section very well. When making a stroke, you do not make a movement that is absolutely new, because that movement will depend on your past learning. But you do not exactly repeat an old movement either, as any particular movement will be slightly different from all the others that you have made. In this sense, the stroke is considered novel.

One weakness of the earlier ideas about motor programming is that they do not explain how the individual can produce a novel movement or how a movement such as a particular tennis stroke is somehow slightly different from all earlier ones. If our theories about movement programs are to have an application to everyday motor behavior, then they must be able to explain these common phenomena.

The Need for Revision

These two rather persistent problems—the storage problem and the novelty problem—pose rather severe limitations for the motor programming idea as it has been stated previously. One solution has been to introduce a modification to the fundamental programming notion, one that retains all the attractive aspects of programming that have been discussed but that also provides a solution to the two problems identified. This kind of thinking led to Schmidt's idea (1976a) that a motor program should be considered as *generalized*.

Generalized Motor Programs

The idea of a *generalized motor program* is that a motor program for a particular class of actions is stored in memory and that a unique pattern of activity will result whenever the program is executed. In order for the program to be executed, certain *parameters* must be supplied to the program that define how it is to be executed on that particular trial. Because the program's output in terms of movements of the limbs can be altered somewhat according to the parameters chosen on a particular trial, the program is said to be generalized. Before describing how such a system might operate, it will be helpful to consider an example of a generalized program for a different application.

A Computer Model

Perhaps the best example of a generalized program comes from computer science. In this field, many different statistical programs do common statistical procedures. Consider a program that calculates means and standard deviations. Such a program is generalized so that it can produce output for various numbers of subjects and for various numbers of scores per subject. In order to run the program, you must specify certain *parameters*—in this case the number of subjects to be used and the number of scores per subject. Once these are specified, the program can be executed for this particular example.

How does this kind of program solve the storage and novelty problems? First, the storage problem is reduced because, for this class of computing problem, only one program needs to be stored in the system; and this one program can accommodate a wide variety of combinations of number of subjects and number of scores. For example, if the number of subjects can range from 1 to 100,000 and the number of scores can range from 1 to 1,000, there is the potential to run this program in 100,000 $\times$ 1,000 different ways—100,000,000 combinations!

With respect to the novelty problem, notice that the program for means and standard deviations can produce results for combinations of subjects and scores that it has never been used for previously. One simply specifies the proper parameters, and the program is executed perfectly. In this sense, the generalized program provides one kind of solution to the novelty problem.

Invariant Features

A motor program is thought to be responsible for the production of a pattern of action, expressed in both space and time. When patterns of action are examined carefully, we see that various aspects of them are easy to change while other aspects remain almost completely fixed from movement to movement. It is not always obvious which aspects of the movement are fixed and which are easily changed; but examining the movement in certain ways, or with certain theoretical biases, can reveal these features (Schmidt, 1985).

A classic example of ways in which movements demonstrate both fixed and modifiable features is one of our most common movement patterns, *handwriting*. This demonstration was presented many years ago (independently) by Lashley (1942; Bruce, 1994) and Bernstein (1947; reproduced in Keele, Cohen, & Ivry, 1990 [their figure 3.5]), and more recently by Merton (1972) and Raibert (1977). All these demonstrations suggest basically the same thing. Figure 6.14 is a reproduction of the handwriting samples published by Lashley (1942). Two right-handed, blindfolded subjects wrote the words "motor equivalence"[4] normally (with the right hand), with the nondominant (left) hand, and with either hand attempting to produce a mirror image of the words (these have been reversed in the figure to appear as normal). The subject represented in figure 6.14a even wrote the words with the pencil held by the teeth.

These handwriting samples are obviously different in various ways. They are of different sizes and show an increased "shakiness" in some cases. The speed with which a word was produced was probably not the same either. But in all samples for each individual there are many remarkable similarities. A certain "style" is seen in all of them, such as the little curl at the start of the *m* for the subject in figure 6.14a and the way the downstroke of the *q* is made for the subject in figure 6.14b. Some aspects of these written words appear to be invariant, even when the effector used or the size or speed of the writing was changed. What is invariant is the spatial-temporal pattern, or the shapes of the letters. Lashley noted:

a   b

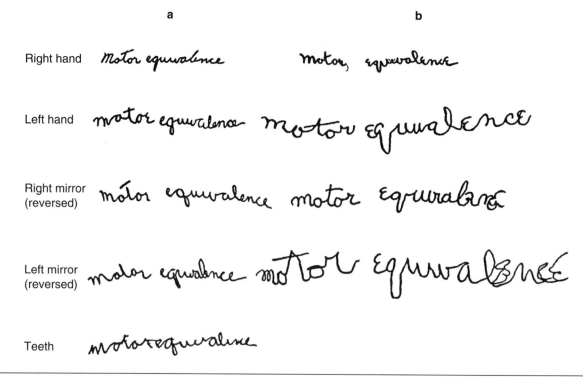

Figure 6.14. Examples from two subjects writing the words "motor equivalence" with different effectors.

In spite of the clumsiness, the general features of the writing, individual differences in the forming of letters and the like, are characteristically maintained. The mechanics of writing is a sequence of movements in relation to bodily position, not a set pattern of special groups of muscles. (1942, p. 317)

Although the meaning of these demonstrations has been called into question (Latash, 1993), the conclusion that something in the performer's memory is common to all these handwritten words has been supported by more in-depth analyses (Wright, 1990). Some abstract structure expressed itself, regardless of the variations in handwriting speed or size or in the limb or muscles used to write the words. Schmidt (1976a) theorized that those features that are invariant, and that in some ways are *fundamental* to these written words, are structured in the motor program; those aspects of the movement that are relatively superficial (speed, effector used) are thought to be parameters of the program. Remember the computer analogy: the way in which the means and standard deviations are calculated is invariant and fundamental to the program—the numbers of subjects and scores are not, and

are parameters of the program. This handwriting example seems to be showing something similar.

If these observations are correct, how can the structure of the motor program be conceptualized so that the invariant features of handwriting are held constant across a wide variety of other changes? In the next section, we consider one possibility that appears to have abundant evidence to support it—the *impulse-timing hypothesis*.

Impulse-Timing Hypothesis

One straightforward viewpoint about the structure of motor programs is the *impulse-timing hypothesis*. The fundamental idea is that the motor program provides pulses of motor neuron activity to the relevant musculature. These pulses produce patterns of contractions in the muscles that can be seen in EMG records or in records of force produced. The amount of force produced is related in a complex way to the amount of neurological activity, and the duration of the force and its temporal onset are determined by the duration of the neurological activity and the time of its occurrence. The major role of the motor program is to "tell" the muscles when to turn on, how much force to use, and when to turn off. Thus the motor program ultimately controls force and time.

Impulses

The combination of force and time generates an *impulse*. A common principle in physics is that the amount of movement produced in a limb is determined by the force(s) acting on it and the time over which the force acts; this product of force and time is called the impulse. Therefore, the impulse-timing hypothesis really means that the motor program controls impulses—bursts of force spread out over time to the appropriate muscles.

In figure 6.15 are three hypothetical, idealized records of the forces produced by a muscle over the time that this muscle is acting on the limb. At each moment of the contraction, the muscle is producing a different force against the bone; the resulting curve in figure 6.15 is called the *force-time curve—* a record of the force produced over time. The impulse is the shaded *area* under the force-time curve. From mathematics, this area is frequently called the *integral*, or *the integral of force over time*.

In the figure, notice that the impulse (the area of Impulse A) can be reduced in half by changing the amplitude of the force for a given amount of time (Impulse B), or by changing the duration of the impulse for a given amplitude (Impulse C), or both. From physics, the velocity of the limb (beginning at rest) after the impulse has ended its action will be directly proportional to the size of the impulse. Thus, Impulses B and C in figure 6.15 would theoretically produce the same velocity at the end of their respective actions (because their areas are equal). And the velocity of the limb with Impulse A would be twice as large as for the other two, because its area is twice as large. In this view, the motor program controls a feature of muscular contraction that is known to be a direct cause of movement—impulses.

If it is correct that the motor program determines impulses, it is reasonable to assume that the motor program is capable of producing a group of impulses, each one in a different muscle group and each one at a different time, resulting in a pattern of activity that produces a skilled movement. Remember, producing impulses in muscles is really nothing more than defining the time of onset and offset of the relevant contractions, as well as their forces. Once these are defined, the movement is defined. Even so, defining these impulse sizes and durations should not be seen as simple, because many factors must be considered by the central nervous system, as discussed earlier (see figures 6.12 and 6.13).

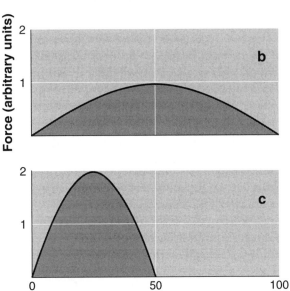

Figure 6.15. Hypothetical impulses seen as the area under force-time curves. (Impulses B and C have half the size that A does, but B is achieved by halving the force with time constant, and C is achieved by halving the time with force constant.)

Invariant Features and the Impulse-Timing View

Given a model of impulses patterned in time to produce a skill, what features of the action must remain invariant? What aspects of these impulses are the same from one handwriting sample to another, and which of them can vary while maintaining a given pattern of activity?

Order of Events. One aspect of the pattern shown in figure 6.14 that seems not to vary is the sequence or *order* of events (Lashley, 1951). In each sample, some event occurred before some other event in making a letter or word, and this order was fixed for all of the samples. We assume that the order of muscular contractions for this sequence of events is fixed in general. A basic assumption of the impulse-timing model of motor programming is that the program has an invariant order of the various elements structured in it.

Notice that this is not the same as saying that the order of *muscles* contracting is fixed in the program. Why? The muscles that produced the writing with the teeth are certainly different from those that produced the writing with the hand, and yet the sequence and the pattern were the same. Clearly, the motor program does not have the order of muscles in it; rather it seems to order the *actions*.

Phasing.   A second aspect of the program that is thought to be invariant is the *temporal structure* of the contractions, usually termed *phasing*. The temporal structure of a series of events (in this case, a series of actions) can be measured in a number of ways, but one of the most common is to evaluate the structure in terms of relative time. In figure 6.16 are hypothetical examples of records taken from two similar actions. This particular record has EMGs in it, but the record could have been defined in terms of movements of the limbs, the forces produced, or other characteristics that cap-

ture in some way the nature of the movement produced. The muscles whose EMGs are shown were chosen because they act at different times in the movement sequence. The sequence begins with a strong burst of EMG from Muscle 1; then Muscle 1 appears to be turned off and Muscles 2 and 3 are activated, with Muscle 2 ceasing its activity before Muscle 3 does. How can this temporal pattern of events in these three participating muscles be described?

One method is to measure the durations of the various elements within the sequence. Shown in the figure are two similar movements, but one of them (Movement 2) has a longer MT than the other. If these two records are evaluated with respect to the durations of the relevant contractions (EMGs), then interval *a* can be defined as the duration of the contraction of the muscles in the entire action, interval *b* is the duration of contraction of Muscle 1, interval *c* is the duration of contraction of Muscle 2, and interval *d* is the duration of contraction of Muscle 3. One way to

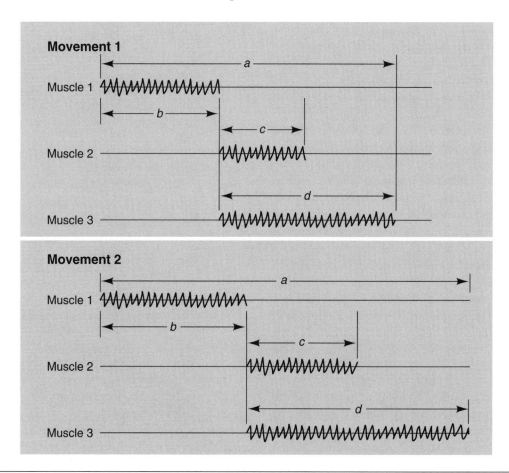

Figure 6.16.   Hypothetical EMG records from two similar movements differing only in MT. (Phasing, or relative timing, is defined by the ratios of the EMG durations among various muscles, e.g., *b/c*, *c/a*, and so on.)

evaluate the temporal structure of these events is to produce ratios of these various times. The sequence for Movement 1 has a ratio of interval *c* to interval *d* of 1:2, or .50. That is, interval *d* is twice as long as interval *c*. Also, interval *b* is one and one-half times as long as interval *c*, making their ratio 1.5:1, or 1.5. Similar ratios can be computed for any two intervals in the sequence.

Another common ratio is that of an element in the sequence relative to the overall length of the sequence. For example, in the Movement 1 sequence the ratio of interval *d* to the overall length of the sequence (interval *a*) appears to be about .60; thus, Muscle 3 is contracting for about 60% of the entire movement.

The fundamental idea of these ratios is this: the temporal structure is measured by (or characterized by) the values of these ratios. If all the ratios are the same in two separate movements, then the temporal structures are the same. Thus, any two movements with the same order of contractions (perhaps that shown in figure 6.16) and the same ratios of muscle action to total MT (e.g., .45, .30, and .60 for Muscles 1, 2, and 3) have the same temporal structure (phasing). Further, these two movements are assumed to be produced by the same motor program.

Movements 1 and 2 in figure 6.16 have this characteristic. The proportion of total MT for each muscle is the same in the two movements, even though the *amount* of time that each muscle is contracting is different for the two movements. Movements 1 and 2 are thought to be governed by the same motor program, because their phasing is the same. If two movements have different phasings, then they are governed by different motor programs.

Relative Force. A third important feature of generalized motor programs is *relative force*, which simply means that the amounts of force produced by any two muscles remain in constant proportion from movement to movement. If in Movement 1, Muscle 1 produced 2 kg of peak force and Muscle 2 produced 4 kg, the ratios of these two forces would be 1:2, or .50. In another movement using the same program, these proportions should be the same, but perhaps with forces of 2.5 kg for Muscle 1 and 5 kg for Muscle 2. The ratio remains 1:2, or .50.

This feature of the movement sequence would seem to remain invariant for the patterns of hand-writing in the examples in figure 6.14. This can be seen in two ways. First, in this kind of model, the height of a given letter is determined in part by the amount of force applied to the limb during the impulse applied by the motor program. But the heights of the letters remain in almost constant proportion as the various letters in a given sentence are considered. For both subjects in Lashley's example, the *t* is always about twice the height of the *o* that follows it. The forces that produced these letter heights may have been in constant proportion in the sequence as well.

The Phonograph Record Analogy

It is sometimes helpful in understanding motor control theories to consider a *model* that has many of the same features as the theory. A good model for the generalized motor program is the standard phonograph record. On the record, structured as invariant features, are three things. First is the order of the events, specifying that the drumbeat comes before the guitar, and so on. Next is the phasing structured in the record. Think of phasing as the rhythm, so that the time between any two events on the record divided by the total record time is a constant. For phonograph records, the ratios between the times of occurrence, or the durations, of any two events are always fixed. Also, the relative force is fixed. For example, the first drumbeat may be twice as loud as the second one.

What is on the record is a code that is translated into sound when the record is played on a given stereo system. It is helpful to visualize motor programs as records, because in many ways they behave the same, and the similarities allow us to visualize the motor program more vividly.

But we know that the record can be played in various ways to produce different sounds. It can be played rapidly or slowly, loudly or softly, with the treble or bass turned up, and so on. Yet a given song can still be recognized because the pattern of the sounds produced is invariant, even though some of the superficial features of the pattern may have varied. The actual muscles that produce the action (here, the particular speakers that will be driven) are certainly not on the record, because the record can be played on any stereo system. In the next section, we discuss some of these more superficial features of movements. These aspects of movement are considered to be *parameters*.

Parameters of Generalized Motor Programs

Motor program theorists have argued that there are a limited number of parameters that can be applied to a generalized motor program. Some of the parameters for which there is strongest evidence are an overall duration parameter, an overall force parameter, and a muscle-selection parameter.

Overall Duration Parameter

The basic idea of an overall duration parameter is that while the motor program contains phasing and sequencing information, it can be run off slowly or rapidly depending on the overall duration parameter assigned, just as increasing the speed of the phonograph turntable speeds up the entire sequence of sounds as a unit.

Initial evidence for an overall duration parameter is found in an unpublished study by Armstrong (1970b). Subjects were asked to learn to move a lever through a particular spatial-temporal pattern. Figure 6.17 shows a tracing of the position of the lever as a function of time in the 4-s movement. Armstrong noticed that when the subject made the movement too rapidly, the entire sequence was made too rapidly, as if the entire movement record was "compressed," with all parts of the movement being shortened in the *same proportion*. Although Armstrong did not

compute the proportions suggested in figure 6.17, a critical test of the idea is that the time between peak 1 and peak 2 divided by the time for the entire movement is about the same in the two movements shown in the figure. Such findings gave initial insight into the possibility of an underlying generalized motor program, with an overall speed parameter that retained the invariant phasing in the movement pattern (see Pew, 1974a for an early discussion of this work).

Following Armstrong's (1970b) and Pew's (1974a) suggestions, Summers (1975) and Shapiro (1977, 1978) examined similar questions in tasks in which the experimenter could instruct the subject to change the overall speed intentionally, rather than incidentally as Armstrong had done. Shapiro's paradigm involved practice at a task in which precise spatial-temporal patterning of pronation/supination of the wrist was required. Thus, to be successful the subjects had to make a series of actions defined in both space and time. The temporal structure of the action for Shapiro's (1977) study is shown in figure 6.18. The proportion of the total MT (which was 1,600 ms) occupied by each of the nine wrist-twist segments is plotted as the line marked with open squares. After considerable practice, Shapiro asked her subjects to speed up the movements but to keep the pattern the same; the pattern of proportions for these "compressed" trials is shown as the line with filled circles in figure 6.18. Notice that the

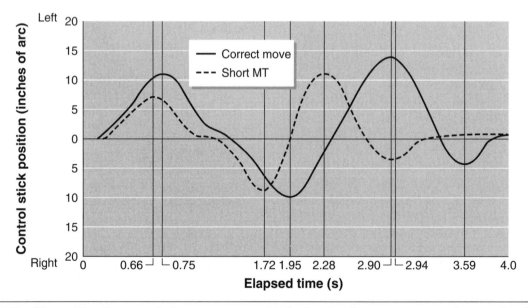

Figure 6.17.   The position-time record of an arm movement task, showing the correct move and a move in which the overall MT was too short.

Reprinted from Armstrong, 1970.

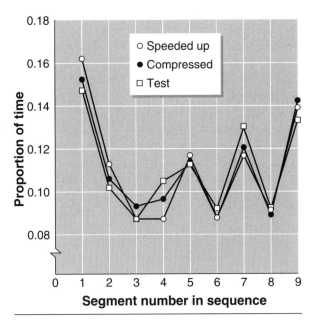

Figure 6.18. Proportion of total MT required to traverse each segment in a wrist-twist movement. (Normal trials had a goal of 1,600 ms; compressed trials were sped up using the same phasing; speeded-up trials were sped up while subjects attempted to ignore the earlier-learned phasing.)
Adapted from Shapiro, 1977.

proportions of time from segment to segment were almost exactly the same for the test trials and the "compressed" trials, but that the MT in the latter was decreased to 1,300 ms, on the average. Essentially, Shapiro showed that the subjects could decrease the time of this well-learned movement sequence as a unit, keeping the phasing in the movement (defined by the proportions) constant. This again suggests that a movement-duration parameter can be applied to some fundamental program so that the given pattern can be sped up as a unit.

Even more remarkable was another finding that both Summers (1975) and Shapiro (1977, 1978) obtained. They asked their subjects to make the movement as rapidly as possible and to *ignore* the phasing that they had learned in the earlier practice trials. In figure 6.18, the line with open circles represents these "speeded-up" trials; again, the pattern of proportions was almost identical to that for the normal trials. Subjects were able to speed up the movements, but they were apparently unable (or at least unwilling) to do so with a different phasing (see also Carter & Shapiro, 1984; Verwey & Dronkert, 1996).

There are other examples. Terzuolo and Viviani (1979) studied the typing of various words, examining the phasing characteristics. Figure 6.19 is a

diagram showing various temporal records in typing the word "trouble." In figure 6.19a, the time of occurrence of each of the letters is plotted for 27 different trials. Each horizontal row of dots represents the time of occurrence for each letter for one trial. The trials are presented in the same order in which they occurred in the experimental session, and no recognizable pattern of phasing appears in them. In figure 6.19b, though, the trials have been reordered so that the trial with the shortest overall MT (845 ms) is at the top, and the trial with the longest MT (1,218 ms) is at the bottom. Notice that the onset times of the various letters "line up" on the sloped lines, as if the longest trials were simply "stretched" versions of the shortest ones. And, in figure 6.19c are the same data, but the time of occurrence of each letter is now expressed as a proportion of the total MT. Notice that the relative time of occurrence of a given letter in the word "trouble" is almost constant from attempt to attempt.

Similar findings have been produced by Shaffer (1980, 1984) in a study of typing and piano playing, as well as by Roth (1988) using an overarm throwing movement. All these data support the notion that a given overall sequence can be sped up or slowed down as a unit while the constant phasing in the sequence is maintained. These data suggest that all the different instances of typing the word "trouble" in figure 6.19 were produced by the same motor program but with a different duration parameter.

One more type of research paradigm has provided evidence that is important to consider. A series of studies by Wulf and colleagues used a research strategy in which variables that are known to affect learning produced different effects depending on what was learned or measured (much more will be described about learning variables in chapters 12 and 13). This strategy attempts to look for patterns of *dissociations* in learning, such that a particular learning variable has different effects on the learning of relative timing as compared to overall duration. These studies have shown that reducing the frequency of augmented feedback enhances the learning of relative timing (Wulf & Schmidt, 1989; Wulf, Lee, & Schmidt 1994; Wulf, Schmidt, & Deubel 1993), but has either no effect or even a degrading influence on learning to scale absolute duration (Wulf & Schmidt, 1996). Similarly, practice that encourages movement variability facilitates the

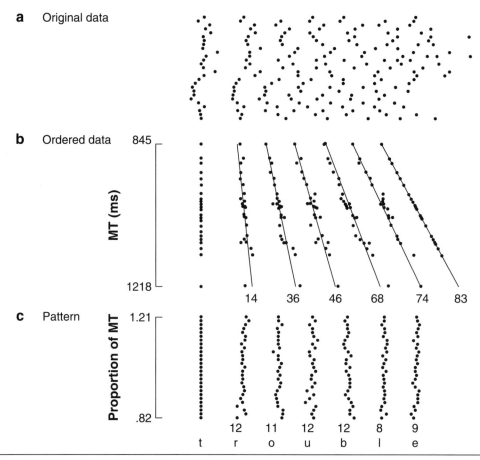

Figure 6.19. Temporal structure in typing the word "trouble." (a) Words are shown in the same order in which they were originally typed; (b) the same words are ordered in terms of their overall MT; (c) the letter durations are expressed as proportions of overall MT.
Reprinted from Terzuolo and Viviani, 1979.

learning of relative timing, but not the scaling of absolute duration (Wulf & Lee, 1993; Wulf & Schmidt, 1994b, 1997). Together, these findings support the separability of parameters and the invariant characteristics of timing skills.

Overall Force Parameter

A second parameter proposed for implementing a generalized motor program is an overall force parameter that modulates the amounts of force produced by the participating muscles. The force parameter is involved with determining how forcefully the relevant muscles will contract when they are recruited by the program. The evidence is weak that such a parameter is actually present, but logically a force parameter is included in the model.

Pew (1974a) described, as an example, a post office in which a conveyer belt carried small packages to an employee to be sorted. The person picked up the package and, with a "set shot" that might be considered good form for a basketball player, tossed the package into one of about 15

equidistant bins for later delivery. This package-sorting "system" required a number of processes on the part of the performer. First, because the bins were equal distances from the person, the final velocity (as the package left the hand) of each of the packages needed to be approximately the same in order for each package to reach its bin, regardless of its weight. But a package with a larger mass will require the application of more force at a *given* duration in order to achieve the desired terminal velocity. Thus, the performer must choose a force parameter that can be applied to the generalized "set shot" program. Presumably, the person would pick up the package, heft it to determine its mass, and then select a force parameter for the generalized program that would achieve the proper goal. The program can be run when the force and duration parameters have been selected.

Another example that supports the concept of an overall force parameter comes from Hollerbach (1978). Figure 6.20 shows the acceleration tracings from a subject writing the word "hell" two

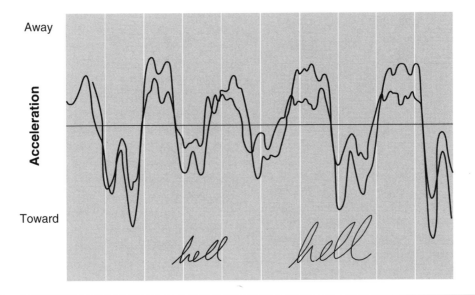

Figure 6.20.   Vertical accelerations produced in writing the word "hell," with one word having twice the amplitude of the other. (The tracings show a remarkable degree of temporal agreement, with systematic differences in amplitude of acceleration.)

times, one word being twice the size of the other. The accelerations are, of course, directly proportional to the forces that the muscles are producing during the action. The tracings have the same temporal pattern, yet the accelerations in the tracing for the larger word are uniformly larger than those for the smaller word. It appears that the forces applied to the pen were simply increased while the original temporal pattern was maintained. Of course, increasing the force leads to increased distance that the pen travels; hence, the word is larger with the same spatial-temporal pattern. Similar interpretations can be made from a study of handwriting by Denier van der Gon and Thuring (1965), who showed that when the friction of the pen on the writing surface was increased, a systematic decrease in the writing size resulted but with no change in the pattern of letters produced.

In the examples just cited, the overall force parameter applies to the participating muscles proportionally, maintaining the relative forces applied to the limb proportionally. This concept is very much like the overall duration parameter, which is applied to the sequence as a unit. A less restrictive view is that the force parameter can be applied to various actions in the sequence without affecting other actions in the body. For example, carrying a heavy backpack would seem to require that more force be applied to the muscles that operate against gravity in walking, but the

muscles that cause the foot to move through the air in the swing phase would not need to have extra force applied to them. Perhaps a force parameter is selected that applies only to those aspects of the program that require extra force. However, this idea has the disadvantage of requiring the motor system to do more "computing" in order to move.

Interaction of Duration and Force Parameters

There is a further argument with respect to the necessity for a force parameter, but it is less obvious than the one just given. Consider a movement in which you begin with your elbow straight, flex the elbow to 90°, and then extend it to the straight position again, completing all of the movements in an overall MT of 300 ms. The motor program presumably determines the phasing of the biceps, the cessation of the biceps and the initiation of triceps (for the reversal), and the contraction of the biceps to bring the movement to a stop. Now consider what would happen if you simply decreased the duration parameter of the program without changing a force parameter. Selecting a shorter duration parameter would cause the program to move through the biceps-triceps-biceps sequence more rapidly while keeping the forces produced by these muscles constant. What will happen to the movement? Because the impulses will be shorter in time, the impulse will be smaller, and the limb will not have moved as far in the time allowed for biceps activity, and thus the movement will reverse itself short of the 90° position. Decreasing a duration parameter while holding a force parameter constant results in an inappropriate movement in terms of its extent.

One possible remedy is to choose the duration parameter so that the overall MT is correct, and then to choose an overall force parameter that will be sufficient for the limb to actually move to 90° before reversing itself (Schmidt et al., 1979). If the force parameter is too large, the movement will go too far in the proper amount of time; if the force parameter is too small, the movement will not go far enough. Thus, with this view, movement distance for a given program is determined by a complex combination of duration and force parameters. Clearly, duration and force parameters must complement each other. The selections of the force and speed parameters are not independent, as the particular value of the force parameter will depend heavily on the chosen duration parameter.

Muscle-Selection Parameter

In the analysis of the handwriting examples shown in figure 6.14 (from Lashley, 1942), we argued that the muscles for the particular action could not be stored "in" the motor program, because the same program produced movements in entirely different limbs. Thus, the sequential ordering embedded in the motor program is considered to be *abstract* with respect to which specific joints and muscles are to be added during the *implementation* of the program. In this case, it is reasonable to think of the specification of muscles (or joints) as another parameter of the motor program.

Additional evidence for this view comes from numerous experiments using a *bilateral-transfer* paradigm. For example, Shapiro (1977) used a wrist-twist task similar to that described earlier, having subjects practice this sequence with the right hand for 5 days. Then she asked the subjects to make the same movements with the left hand, which had never been used for this pattern before. She found a pattern of activity shown in figure 6.21, in which the well-practiced right-hand pattern is indicated by the open circles and the novel left-hand pattern is indicated by the closed circles. The two patterns are nearly identical, and the case can be made that the program that was generated by practice with the right hand could be produced with the left hand. Further evidence for the preservation of sequence

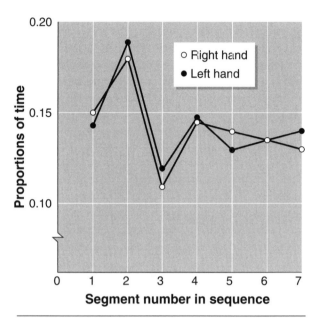

Figure 6.21. Proportions of total MT required to traverse various movement segments in a wrist-twist task. (The pattern is similar for the practiced right hand and for the unpracticed left hand.)
Reprinted from Shapiro, 1977.

learning during transfer to different effectors has been shown by Keele, Jennings, Jones, Caulton, and Cohen (1995; see also Jordan, 1995; Keele, Cohen, & Ivry, 1990).

The Phonograph Record Analogy (Again)

Earlier we presented the analogy between a motor program and a phonograph record, with information about order, phasing, and relative force structured "in" the motor program to define a given pattern. To complete the analogy, add the ideas about parameters just discussed. The overall duration parameter is analogous to the speed of the turntable. When the record turns more rapidly, the overall duration of the record's activity decreases, but the phasing of sounds remains invariant. Next, the overall force parameter can be thought of as the volume control, whereby the same pattern of action can be produced either loudly or softly. This is very much like writing in small or large letters with the pattern of the writing remaining the same. Muscle-selection parameters are analogous to the operation of speakers. If you have one set of speakers in one room and another set elsewhere, you can choose which ones will play the music. If the speaker is analogous to an effector, then this is an example in which the same pattern is produced in two different set of "muscles."

Changing Parameters and Programs

Additional evidence supporting the generalized motor program comes from experiments in which some aspect of the movement has to be changed during the movement. For example, Quinn and Sherwood (1983) had subjects make elbow flexion or extension movements, following through past a switch near the end, such that the time from the beginning of the movement to the switch was 400 ms. Occasionally an auditory signal, administered in different blocks of trials, would instruct the subject to either (a) move faster or (b) reverse the movement. The findings, similar to those from earlier studies in this same general paradigm (Gottsdanker, 1973; Vince & Welford, 1967), showed that the latency of the corrections (the interval from the auditory stimulus until the first EMG change) was 100 ms shorter when the movement had to be sped up than when it had to be reversed. Theoretically, with a reversal, the subject has to stop running a given program and select, parameterize, and initiate a different one that will reverse the movement. However, when the movement is sped up, the existing program can be retained, and only a reparameterization must be done (e.g., with adjusted overall duration and force parameters); the stages involved in program selection and initiation can be bypassed.

Roth (1988) has shown that these principles hold for sport skills studied in the laboratory. For example, the RT to change a tennis ground stroke to a lob (presumably requiring a different program and different parameters) was estimated to be about 600 ms, whereas the RTs to change the direction or length of the ground stroke (presumably requiring only new parameters) were estimated to be about 200 ms less. Analogous results were provided for table tennis and volleyball skills, suggesting that the difference between program *plus* parameter selection versus only parameter selection is general across a variety of movement behaviors.

Concerns About Invariant Relative Timing

The generalized motor program theory was first proposed over 20 years ago, and there have been numerous empirical and theoretical examinations of its predictions since then. In general, the theory has held up well. However, as with all theories, some data and analyses do not provide support.

The most contentious issue with regard to generalized motor programs has been the concept of *invariance*, especially as it relates to relative timing. We argued earlier that in order for a timed segment to be considered invariant, its proportion of time, relative to the total duration of the activity, must be constant over a series of separate executions of the program. But have another look at the phasings for each letter of the word "trouble" that are illustrated in figure 6.19c (from Terzuolo & Viviani, 1979). Although the relative durations for each letter show rather consistent phasings, there are still some deviations. The questions that arise are these: Are these deviations meaningful? And how do you decide whether they are or not?

Statistical Invariance

A qualitative answer is to draw a straight line through the center of the data points plotted in figure 6.19c (this has already been done with the absolute timing data in figure 6.19b). If the data were perfectly invariant, then all the individual data points would fall exactly on vertical lines— and the more they fall off the line, the weaker is the evidence for invariance. In reality, there is very little chance that motor behavior will ever show true, perfect invariance. Therefore, the question is how much deviation from perfection can be tolerated before we begin to *reject* a description of the data as being invariant.

A partial solution to this debate was provided by Gentner (1987). He proposed two statistical methods for assessing relative invariance in a set of data. One method, called the *constant-proportion* test, uses statistical *regression* to assess whether or not a set of ordered phasings has a slope that deviates from zero. The amount of invariance is indicated by expressing relative time as a linear function of the total time. If there is a systematic increase or decrease in the relative proportion accounted for by a segment, then the slope of the regression line will deviate significantly, either positively or negatively from zero, indicating that the relative timing of the segment was not invariant across different absolute durations.

The other approach proposed by Gentner (1987), called the *interaction* test, uses the statistical method of *analysis of variance*. Basically, the method is an analysis showing whether the timing of components that make up the action, combined with other experimental factors (such as instructions to go slow or fast), results in variances that are additive or interactive. Additive (or main) effects in the *absence* of interactions suggest that the component's relative timing does not change as a function of the other conditions in the experiment—that is, that the timing of the components is invariant across the levels of the other factor(s). The presence of interactions, however, suggests that specific invariances (as indicated by the factors that are interacting) do not exist.

Gentner's (1987) analysis provided an objective, statistical solution to the problem of assessing invariance. Using these methods, Gentner reanalyzed some previously published data sets and found that, while some studies continued to support invariant relative timing, many others did not. More recent experiments, using the methods suggested by Gentner, have also produced evidence that is weighted heavily against perfect statistical invariance (Burgess-Limerick, Neal, & Abernethy, 1992; Maraj et al., 1993; Wann & Nimmo-Smith, 1990; but see also Franks & Stanley, 1991).

Do these statistical tests constitute rejection of the idea that relative timing can be invariant? The answer is unclear. Several questions can be raised from a statistical point of view, such as (1) the appropriateness of accepting the null hypothesis when significant effects are not found (which would be evidence in support of invariance) and (2) the level at which to set the cutoff point for the rejection of the null hypothesis. Gentner suggested that a level of $\alpha = .05$ is appropriate; however, a case could be made for more or less stringent levels.

Central Versus Peripheral Invariance

Heuer (1988, 1991) has raised another important issue to consider. He suggested that even in the absence of *measured* invariance, there may still be *central* invariance. Heuer's argument uses as a basis the Wing and Kristofferson (1973a, 1973b) distinction between central and peripheral timing. The idea is that the timing observed at the output or peripheral level is a combination of a central mechanism that periodically triggers an effector into action and the motor delays (such as neural delays and muscle recruitment) that occur following a central trigger. Heuer (1988) demonstrated that, given a central timing signal with perfect invariance in relative timing, a variable motor delay can result in an absence of invariance at the peripheral level.

Thus, perhaps because of complexities in the muscle properties in fast movements (e.g., Heuer

& Schmidt, 1988; Gielen, van den Oosten, & ter Gunne, 1985; Zelaznik, Schmidt, & Gielen, 1986), it is possible that invariance at the level of the generalized motor program might not be detected by searching for invariances in motor output. Perhaps this issue will be resolved only by future research analyzing the brain potentials of action prior to movement output. We will return to the discussion of invariant relative timing when we discuss how the system regulates the coordination of two or more activities at the same time (in chapter 8).

Summary

The response-chaining hypothesis proposed by James (1890) was the first open-loop theory for motor control. It held that each action in a sequence is triggered by the movement-produced feedback from the immediately preceding action. Research on the role of feedback in movement performance under various deafferentation conditions has tended to show that sensation from the moving limb is not *essential* for motor performance, although it contributes to the smooth control of many actions. Thus, the response-chaining hypothesis cannot be universally correct, as it states that feedback from the responding limb is required for the control of a movement sequence.

Motor control scientists have three reasons for believing that movements are controlled by programs: (a) the slowness of the information-processing stages, (b) the evidence for planning movements in advance, and (c) the findings that deafferented animals and humans can show only slight decrements in skill. This is not to say that feedback is not used in movement. Feedback is used (a) before the movement as information about initial position, or perhaps to tune the spinal apparatus; (b) during the movement, when it is either "monitored" for the presence of error or used directly in the modulation of movements reflexively, and (c) after the movement to determine the success of the response and contribute to motor learning.

The earlier definition of motor programs as structures that carry out movements in the absence of feedback was found to be inadequate to account for the evidence about feedback utilization during movement. Also, problems were associated with the requirement for storage of many different motor programs (the *storage problem*) as well as with the means by which the motor program could create a novel action (the *novelty problem*). For these reasons, the motor program is thought of as *generalized*—containing an abstract code about the *order of events*, the *phasing* (or temporal structure) of the events, and the *relative force* with which the events are to be produced.

These generalized motor programs require *parameters* in order to specify how the movement is to be expressed. Such parameters are the *overall duration* of the movement, the *overall force* of the contractions, and the *muscle* (or limb) that is used to make the movements. With such a model, many different movements can be made with the same program (reducing the storage problem), and novel movements can be produced through selection of parameters that have not been used previously (reducing the novelty problem).

Notes

[1] Four of Taub's monkeys were reexamined 12 years after their surgery, and all revealed considerable functional reorganization of the brain structures responsible for sensory representation (Pons et al., 1991). Thus, it seems that motor and sensory systems may have both short- and long-term methods for adapting to the loss of peripheral feedback.

[2] This view could also be related to the reflex-chaining hypothesis. The difference is that the closed-loop model would have the feedback evaluated against a reference of correctness, whereas the reflex-chaining view would have the feedback from the movement trigger the next action directly.

[3] The generalizations that errors in execution can be corrected (a) without interference from other similar corrections and (b) with latencies unaffected by the number of possible corrections have not been studied carefully and should be considered with caution.

[4] Lashley probably had a good reason for choosing these particular words to be written; the term *motor equivalence* refers to the idea that different effectors can be used to achieve the same goal.

Principles of Simple Movement

In this chapter we focus on the fundamental principles that pertain to various movement variables and some theoretical ideas that have emerged from them. Such principles are critical to any science, as they describe the relationships among measures of the objects under study about which scientists will theorize. As such, the basic laws in motor behavior may be seen as analogous to the fundamental principles of physics. The simple laws relating the mass, velocity, and acceleration of objects when forces are applied to them (the principles of mechanics), for example, have served as the cornerstone of the physical sciences, and hence they deserve a special status. In the same way, the field of motor behavior has analogous principles that are somehow fundamental to all the rest: principles that describe, for example, such things as the relationship between the speed at which a limb moves and its resulting accuracy, or the relationship between movement distance and movement time.

Whereas a neat set of simple, elegant principles can be stated for the various branches of the physical sciences, we should not expect something similar for the behavioral sciences, or for motor control in particular. For a number of reasons, in motor control we find far fewer statements possessing sufficient generality and supporting evidence to have attained the status of a "law." One reason is that the motor control principles have been far more difficult to discover, based as they are on data from biological systems that are more variable ("noisy") and complex than the physical systems. Often the relationships are not obvious, and must be "teased out" of background noise or variability in order to be seen. The situation is complicated further by well-known differences among people (termed *individual differences,* chapter 9), which seem to suggest that different laws should exist for different individuals or for different classifications of people (children vs. adults, for example). Even so, these motor control principles describe well many separate sets of data and generalize to a variety of practical situations, and thus represent statements of fundamental knowledge about skilled performance.

One of the most common occurrences in activities of daily living is known as the *speed-accuracy trade-off*. Common sense tells us that as we move more rapidly, we become more inaccurate in terms of the goal we are trying to achieve.

For example, trying to type too fast or pour a glass of milk too quickly generates annoying mistakes; the old adage "haste makes waste" has been a long-standing viewpoint about skills. As we will see, however, the speed-accuracy trade-off exists in different forms for different types of movement tasks; the principles of speed-accuracy trade-offs are specific to the goal and nature of the movement tasks.

Three specific types of trade-offs are presented in this chapter. These relate to situations in which spatial and/or temporal accuracy are the primary demands of the movement. Principles of movement control that relate to these trade-offs will be presented later in the chapter.

Fitts' Law: The Logarithmic Speed-Accuracy Trade-Off

The first class of speed-accuracy trade-off functions occurs in situations in which the goal is to move a limb (or other "effector") as quickly as possible to achieve a target, doing so with a minimum number of errors. Such is the goal in tasks like typing and other forms of data entry.

Early Research

The first major attempt to study scientifically the relationship between a movement's speed and its accuracy probably came from Woodworth, who published a voluminous manuscript full of experiments on movement control in 1899. This work was far ahead of its time in terms of both the ideas presented and the techniques used. Woodworth proposed that aiming movements are made up of an *initial-adjustment* phase that propels the limb toward the target in an open-loop fashion (chapter 6) and a *current-control* phase based on visual feedback that causes the limb to "home in" on the target (chapter 5).

At the time his experiments were conducted, sophisticated electronic recording techniques were not yet available, and methods had to be used that were practical and yet provided the precision necessary to answer the questions addressed by Woodworth. The tasks used by Woodworth involved simple repetitive line-drawing movements to a target; the movement speed was varied by changing the frequency of a pacing metronome. Studies were done with various distances, with the right and left hands, and with the eyes closed and opened in an attempt to uncover some of the fundamental relationships between speed and accuracy. Generally, Woodworth found that accuracy decreased as the movement speed increased, that the left hand was less accurate than the right hand, and that the decrease in accuracy with increased speed was greater when the eyes were open than when closed. Most of his results have not, in general terms at least, been contradicted since. Fifty-five years after Woodworth, the nature of this speed-accuracy relationship was described as a formal mathematical law by Paul Fitts (1954).

Fitts' Research

In 1954, Fitts published a systematic analysis of the relationship between speed and accuracy that has become one of the landmark publications in the history of motor behavior research (Kelso, 1992). In the *Fitts paradigm* (or *Fitts task*), a subject is to tap a handheld stylus alternately between two target plates as rapidly as possible for a period of time (e.g., 20 s). The two targets are usually rectangular and oriented as shown in figure 7.1, with the long dimension perpendicular to the line between the two targets. Both the width of the targets *(W)* and the amplitude of the movement between them *(A)* can be altered from condition to condition, producing a large number of possible combinations of *A* and *W*. The task is scored as the number of taps (regardless of whether they are correct) in 20 s, but

subjects are cautioned to limit errors (misses) to no more than about 5% of their movements. A more general view of the experimental setup is shown in figure 7.2.

Fitts' Law Defined

Fitts found that the relationship between the amplitude *(A)* of the movement, the target width *(W)*, and the resulting average movement time (MT) was given by the following equation:

$$MT = a + b[\text{Log}_2 (2A/W)] \qquad (7.1)$$

where MT is the *average* movement time for a series of taps, computed as the trial duration (20 s) divided by the number of taps completed in that time. For example, a 20-s trial duration divided by 50 taps in the trial yields 20/50 = .4 s/tap, or 400 ms/tap as the average MT.

The Fitts equation has the general form of a *linear* equation $(Y = a + bX)$, where Y is average MT, X is $\text{Log}_2 (2A/W)$, and a and b are empirical constants. (Review the section on linear empirical equations in chapter 2 and the discussion of Hick's law in chapter 3.) Therefore, a graph in which average MT is plotted against $\text{Log}_2 (2A/W)$ should be linear (a straight line).

The data from one of Fitts' original experiment are presented in figure 7.3. The values of *A* and *W* were varied experimentally by changing the arrangement of the target board (as in figures 7.1 and 7.2) for different blocks of trials, and the

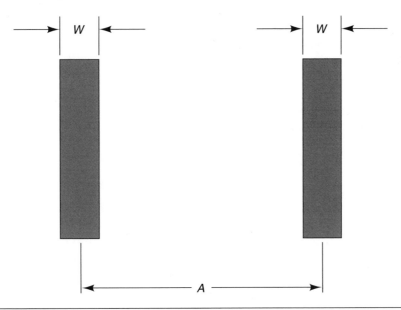

Figure 7.1. The Fitts' paradigm. (The performer taps a stylus alternately between two targets of width *W* separated by a distance *A*.)

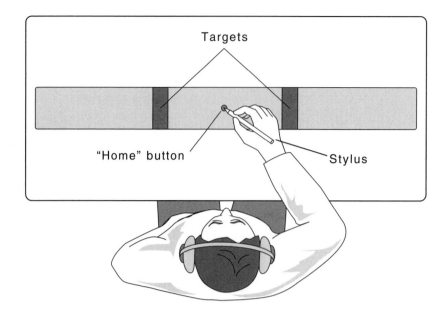

Figure 7.2. A subject performing the Fitts tapping task.
Reprinted from Fitts, 1964.

resulting MTs were measured after subjects had received some practice at the particular tasks. Figure 7.3 illustrates the average MTs as a function of Log_2 $(2A/W)$, where each of the latter values is computed by taking the values of A and W, dividing them, and looking up the value of the Log_2 $(2A/W)$ in the Table of Logarithms (see appendix). For example, one data point in figure 7.3 has a target amplitude (A) of 4 in. (10.2 cm) and a target width (W) of 1/4 in. (.64 cm). Thus, the value $2A/W = 2(4)/.25 = 32$. Now, from consulting the table in the appendix, the Log_2 $(32) =$ 5.0. (The Log_2 of a number is the power to which the base 2 must be raised in order to reach that number; i.e., $2^5 = 32$.)

So for the various combinations of A and W shown, the average MTs lie almost perfectly on a straight line, except perhaps for the leftmost three data points representing movements that were very rapid. Notice, for example, that two conditions for which the Log_2 $(2A/W) = 6$ have target widths of 1/2 and 1/4 in. and amplitudes of 16 and 8 in., respectively. Yet these two conditions had virtually identical MTs. You can see similar situations with the other data points plotted for a given value of Log_2 $(2A/W)$, such as 3, 4, and 5.

Interpreting Fitts' Equation

What does it mean that the Log_2 $(2A/W)$ plots linearly with the average MT in the Fitts task? First, notice that the value of Log_2 $(2A/W)$ seems to determine how much time was required for

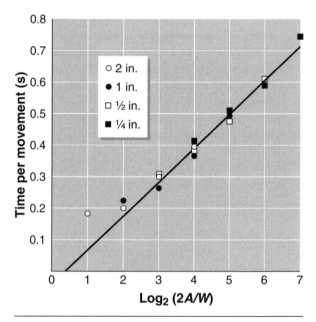

Figure 7.3. Average MT as a function of the ID ($Log_2[2A/W]$).
Adapted from Fitts, 1954.

each of these movements, so this value seems to be related in some way to how "difficult" the particular combination of A and W was for the subject. For this reason, Fitts called this value the *index of difficulty (ID)*. Thus, in Fitts' terms, the "difficulty" of a movement was related jointly to the distance that the limb moved and to the narrowness of the target at which it was aimed.

In fact, the relationship is even more restrictive than this, as the "difficulty" of the movement is theoretically the same for any combination of A and W that has the same *ratio*. Doubling A and doubling W at the same time result in a value of $2A/W$ that is the same, and hence the same value of $Log_2(2A/W)$ and the same predicted average MT. Another way to say this is that the average MT is linearly related to the ID, where ID = $Log_2(2A/W)$; MT = $a + b$(ID).

Next, the values a and b are the empirical constants—they are required in order that the mathematical equation of the line actually fit the observed data from the experimental setting. The constant a is the *intercept*, referring to the value of MT where the line of best fit crosses the MT axis. Here, the intercept is the value of MT when the ID is zero. But what does it mean to say that a movement has "zero difficulty"? This has been a serious problem for the understanding of the ideas surrounding the Fitts task (see Welford, 1968 for a more thorough discussion). For our purposes, a movement with "zero difficulty" is one with a ratio of $2A/W$ of 1.0 (because $Log_2(1)$ = 0). Therefore, the intercept refers to the situation in which the amplitude is one-half the target width, which results in targets that are over-lapping, so that the subject's task of tapping "alternately" from one target to another actually involves tapping up and down as quickly as possible, with essentially no accuracy requirement.

The constant b is the *slope*, and is far more straightforward in its interpretation. Here, the slope refers to the added MT caused by increasing the ID by one bit (*bi*nary digi*t*; refer to chapter 3). In this sense, the slope refers to the sensitivity of the effector to changes in the ID. This can be seen more easily in figure 7.4 from Langolf, Chaffin, and Foulke (1976), where the results from a number of different movement situations using the Fitts task are plotted. Notice that the slope increased progressively as the limb used was changed from the finger, to the wrist, to the arm. The data from this experiment suggest that the larger and more cumbersome limbs (the arms) are more sensitive to the changes in the ID than are the fingers, which can be controlled more precisely. Differences in the slopes of the Fitts equation have also been shown in many other variables. For example, higher slopes in the Fitts equation are typically found in older adults, suggesting that the impact on average MT of higher IDs is greater for older adults than for younger adults (Goggin & Meeuwsen, 1992; Pohl, Winstein,

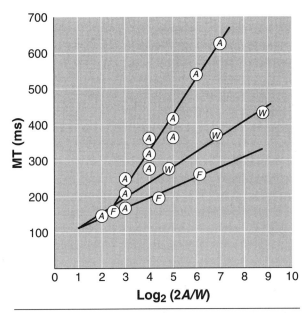

Figure 7.4. The Fitts relationship holds for finger (F), wrist (W), and arm (A) movements, but with systematically different slopes.
Reprinted from Langolf, Chaffin, and Foulke, 1976.

& Fisher, 1996; Walker, Philbin, & Fisk, 1997; Welford, Norris, & Shock, 1969). In contrast, the slope of the Fitts equation can be reduced considerably with practice: B. Kelso (1984) found that the slope was reduced to nearly zero following 40,000 trials conducted over 20 days of practice. Thus, the slope of the Fitts equation represents an interaction of ID with the "controllability" inherent in the independent variable (e.g., limb used, age, or skill level). However, it is important to keep in mind that even though the slopes and the MT values are different under various conditions or with various subjects, Fitts' Law still holds for any one of these. That is, the average MT for any given limb still plots linearly with the ID, but with different values of b.

Next, why is a Log term in the equation, and why is the Log given to the base 2? When the idea was originally published, the interpretation was based on a dominant theme of the day—the *information theory* of communication (Shannon & Weaver, 1949). Recall the discussion of Hick's law of choice reaction time (RT) in chapter 3; the equation of that relationship also had a Log_2 term. The $Log_2(N)$, in which N was the number of equally likely stimulus-response alternatives, was a measure of the amount of *information* (in bits) required to resolve the uncertainty about N alternatives. The Log_2 term in Fitts' Law can be seen in a similar way: $2A/W$ is related to the number of possible *movements,* and the Log$_2$ ($2A/$ W) is the information required (in bits) to resolve the uncertainty among them. Generally speaking, the original interpretation of Fitts' Law was that the system is a processor of information and that when the movement is made more "difficult" by either an increase in the amplitude or a decrease in the target width, more information has to be processed in order to generate a movement that will arrive at the target. Because the amount of information that the human can process per unit of time (i.e., the rate of processing in bits/s) is limited (chapter 3), the individual compensates for a difficult combination of *A* and *W* by increasing the MT, thereby enabling the completion of the necessary processing. According to Fitts, this is why making the movement more difficult requires more MT.

The Speed-Accuracy Trade-Off

Fitts' Law implies an inverse relationship between the difficulty of a movement and the speed with which it can be performed. Increasing the difficulty (ID) decreases the speed (i.e., increases the MT). One way to think about this is that the individual in some way "trades off" speed against accuracy, and this trade-off is done so that the rate of information processing is held constant. In addition to this strict view in terms of the constancy of information processing, people presumably have some control over their strategy in moving. They can move very quickly at the expense of being less accurate or they can move very accurately at the expense of being slower. In this way, Fitts' Law has been fundamental in describing the *speed-accuracy trade-off,* or the performer's capability to change the control processes so that speed and accuracy are kept in some balance. Fitts' Law describes the nature of this balance very well.

Subsequent Research on Fitts' Law

The Fitts task is a rather strange movement situation, and some have felt that the particular configuration of alternate tapping is not very representative of many real-life tasks (e.g., Schmidt, Zelaznik, & Frank, 1978). Can the fundamental principle of Fitts' Law be applied to other, more "natural" movement situations? Fitts and Peterson (1964) showed that the principle can be applied to a single-aiming task in which a stylus is aimed at a target in a single, discrete move. The subject's task was to make a single move as quickly

and accurately as possible to a target of fixed amplitude (*A*) from the home position and with a given target width (*W*). In discrete moves, people appear to trade off speed for accuracy in much the same way as they do for continuous, cyclical movements (but see Guiard, 1993, 1997). Other research since the time of Fitts' original work has extended his ideas in a number of different ways.

Generality of Fitts' Law

Since the publication of Fitts' Law, investigators have studied it in a variety of contexts, revealing that the principle shows remarkable generality. For example, in addition to holding for young adults, the Fitts relationship holds well for children (Hay, 1981; Schellekens, Kalverboer, & Scholten, 1984) and for older adults (Goggin & Meeuwsen, 1992; Pohl, Winstein, & Fisher, 1996; Walker, Philbin, & Fisk, 1997; Welford, Norris, & Shock, 1969). Although Fitts' Law was initially based on movements of the upper limbs, the principle has been found to hold when different effectors are compared, such as the foot, arm, hand, and fingers (Drury & Woolley, 1995; Langolf, Chaffin, & Foulke, 1976); when movement tasks are conducted underwater (R. Kerr, 1973, 1978); when the movements required are so small that they must be viewed under magnification (Langolf, Chaffin, & Foulke, 1976); and even when tasks are only imagined and not actually produced (Decety & Jeannerod, 1996).

Fitts' Law also applies in the context of everyday activities. In Fitts' (1954) original work, subjects placed disks over pegs, where *A* was the distance between the pegs and *W* was the clearance (or tolerance) between the size of the hole in the disk and the diameter of the peg. With ID defined in this way, the Fitts equation predicted MT very well. Movement time effects also follow Fitts' Law when one compares tasks in which subjects point at, reach, and grasp objects of different sizes (Bootsma et al., 1994; Marteniuk et al., 1987). As well, Fitts' Law successfully describes the positioning movements of various computer-input devices such as keys (Drury & Hoffmann, 1992; Hoffmann, Tsang, & Mu, 1995), joysticks (Card, English, & Burr, 1978), computer mice (Card, English, & Burr, 1978; Tränkle & Deutschmann, 1991), and head pointing devices (Andres & Hartung, 1989; Jagacinski & Monk, 1985). An excellent review by Plamondon and Alimi (1997) documents many other demonstrations of Fitts' Law.

Modifications to the Fitts Equation

Modifications to the basic Fitts equation have been tried in an attempt to achieve a better *fit*—which refers to the amount of variance in the experimental data that can be explained by the equation. Modifications to the definition of the ID by Welford (1968; Welford, Norris, & Shock, 1969) provided a slightly better fit, as too did a consideration of the width of the effector that was being moved into the target area (Hoffmann & Sheikh, 1991). In contrast to the logarithmic relationship between A and W proposed by Fitts, an exponential relationship described in terms of a *power law* was suggested by Kvålseth (1980), where

$$MT = a(A/W)^b \qquad (7.2)$$

Numerous other modifications to the Fitts equation are discussed by Plamondon and Alimi (1997). And, while many of these have served to improve the overall fit, it should be kept in mind that Fitts' Law often explains over 90% of the variance in many data sets. Thus the improvement in accuracy gained by changes to Fitts' equation is relatively small.

Importance of Fitts' Law

It may not be obvious why so much attention has been paid to a single principle of motor performance. There appear to be several reasons. First, as we have seen so often, human motor behavior is complex and is challenging to understand. Because of this, it is very difficult to provide precise mathematical descriptions of behavior that are generally applicable. Yet the Fitts principle does just that, and Fitts created it when almost no precise mathematical work was being done in motor behavior. Second, the principle appears to relate to many different situations and to a number of variations of the original Fitts task. Thus the principle appears to represent some fundamental relationship that governs many kinds of motor behavior. Third, since the publication of Fitts' Law, no investigations have shown it to be fundamentally incorrect, although there now exist alternative ways of dealing with the relation between speed and accuracy. One way is to change the temporal and spatial accuracy demands of the task. We describe these effects in the next sections.

Lastly, one of the most powerful motivations for scientists working toward an explanation is the existence of a well-established principle or law—one that has survived the test of time and has been shown to be applicable to a wide variety of situations or kinds of subjects. Fitts' Law certainly meets these criteria. Thus, one natural outgrowth of this work was an attempt to understand the movement-control processes that produced the particular relations described by Fitts' Law. That is, people began theorizing about why Fitts' Law occurs. We have already mentioned viewpoints based on information theory, whereby the ID was taken by Fitts (1954) to be a measure of the amount of information needed to resolve the uncertainty about the movement. However, dissatisfaction with this theoretical perspective led researchers to propose alternative ways of explaining the kinds of speed-accuracy trade-offs that Fitts and others had observed in their data. These theoretical perspectives are dealt with in later sections of this chapter.

The Linear Speed-Accuracy Trade-Off

From the previous section, it is clear that the Fitts paradigm involves a somewhat complicated movement situation that is not typical of many everyday tasks. With use of an alternative approach, the Fitts paradigm was changed to allow examination of the speed-accuracy effects in tasks that required a single, aimed movement—one requiring mainly *preprogrammed* movements.

The Single-Aiming, Constrained Movement Time Paradigm

The revised paradigm used rapid single-aiming movements of a stylus from a starting position to a target 10 to 60 cm away (Schmidt, Zelaznik, & Frank, 1978; Schmidt et al., 1979). But rather than have subjects move as quickly as possible, as did Fitts and Peterson (1964), experimenters required subjects to complete the movement in a particular *goal movement time (MT)* specified by the experimenter. As well, the movements were aimed at a small target line that did not change in width *(W)*. Thus, both timing accuracy *and* distance accuracy were required of subjects. Performance of the goal MT was achieved by giving feedback after each trial about whether the movement was too fast or slow. Only those movements that conformed to the goal MT (i.e., movements that were ±10% of the MT goal) were used for analysis.

One experiment used movement amplitudes (*A*) of either 10, 20, or 30 cm and MT goals of 140, 170, and 200 ms, so that nine different combinations of *A* and MT were performed by subjects in separate sessions. Errors were measured as the within-subject standard deviation (SD) of the movement amplitudes, which defined the "spread" or inconsistency of movements aimed at the target (see chapter 2). In keeping with the Fitts tradition, these errors are termed *effective target width* (W_e), and they define the effective size of the "target" the subject is using when moving with a particular MT and *A*. Notice also that this paradigm is different from the Fitts paradigm because W_e is the dependent variable, with *A* and MT being the independent variables; in the Fitts paradigm, MT is the dependent variable, and *A* and W_e are the independent variables.

Figure 7.5 shows a plot of W_e for the various combinations of *A* and MT. There was a clear increase in variability as *A* increased, with the effect being almost linear for the various MTs studied. Also, W_e increased systematically for any given movement distance as the MT decreased. Both increasing *A* with MT fixed, and decreasing MT with *A* fixed, resulted in increases in average velocity (in cm/s). Thus we can see these data as another example of the principle that increasing movement velocity decreases spatial accuracy (as in Fitts' Law), but this time for very rapid movements.

This speed-accuracy trade-off can be seen somewhat more easily in figure 7.6, where the W_e in figure 7.5 have been replotted as a function of the average velocity, *A*/MT. Now the relationship between W_e and *A*/MT is nearly *linear* across a range of movement velocities, and most of the individual data points fall reasonably close to the line of best fit. Thus, the data in figure 7.6 can be expressed in terms of a linear equation in which

$$W_e = a + b\,(A/\mathrm{MT}) \qquad (7.3)$$

For the data in figure 7.6, the value of *a* (the intercept) was 2.12 mm, and the value of *b* (the slope) was .033. Notice that for very different amplitudes and movement times, but with the ratio of *A* and MT about the same, the W_e was also about the same.

These effects have been produced in a number of separate experiments using various tasks—even in eye movements (Abrams, Meyer, & Kornblum, 1989; Patla et al., 1985). It appears that this linear speed-accuracy trade-off effect is stable enough for some to name it a law of rapid actions (e.g., Flach, Guisinger, & Robison, 1996; Keele, 1986; Sanders & McCormick, 1993).[1]

Relationship to Fitts' Law

The variables in the single-aiming paradigm are essentially the same as those in the Fitts paradigm (but used slightly differently, as we have seen);

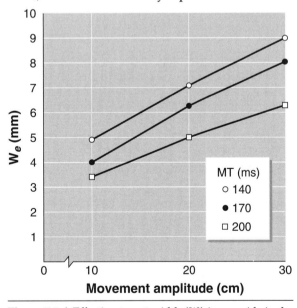

Figure 7.5. Effective target width (W_e) in a rapid single-aiming task as a function of the MT and movement distance.
Reprinted from Schmidt, Zelaznik, Hawkins, Frank, and Quinn, 1979.

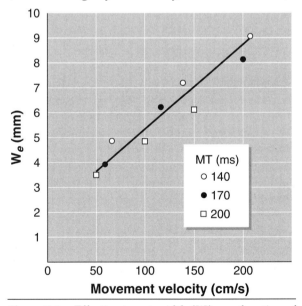

Figure 7.6. Effective target width (W_e) as a function of the average velocity (*A*/MT).
Reprinted from Schmidt, Zelaznik, Hawkins, Frank, and Quinn, 1979.

and yet the speed-accuracy trade-off is considerably different—*logarithmic* in the Fitts paradigm, and *linear* in the single-aiming paradigm. What are the crucial conditions responsible for producing these two different trade-off functions? Two hypotheses related to the key differences between the paradigms have been suggested.

Feedback Hypothesis

Remember that the linear speed-accuracy trade-off has been found using single-aiming movement tasks in which the total MT is very brief—probably less than the amount of time required to detect that an error has been made and to issue a correction (e.g., 200 ms or less in the Schmidt et al., 1979 data in figures 7.5 and 7.6). One obvious hypothesis is that the logarithmic trade-off occurs for movements that are at least partially governed by *feedback-based corrections* (e.g., the Fitts task), whereas the linear trade-off occurs for tasks that are entirely *preprogrammed.* In this view, the two trade-off functions are not to be seen as "competitors," but rather as functions that describe different emphases on movement control—open- versus closed-loop.

This does *not* mean that Fitts' Law holds for movements with long MTs and that the linear trade-off holds for movements with short MTs. Whereas MT is certainly a factor in determining whether a movement will or will not be preprogrammed, the hypothesis is that MT provides a *lower limit* for feedback control; that is, movements with very short MTs cannot be under closed-loop control. However, movements with long MTs could be under open-loop control, provided that the environment is stable, the task is well learned, errors are not too "costly," and so on. Under these conditions, Shapiro (1977, 1978) has shown that skills with MTs as long as 1,600 ms can be under program control, and Zelaznik, Shapiro, and McColsky (1981) found that 500-ms movements showed a linear trade-off. If so, then the linear speed-accuracy trade-off could exist for movements with durations that are far longer than those typically found in the Fitts paradigm.

Movement Time Goal Hypothesis

Another obvious difference between the paradigms that produce the logarithmic and the linear speed-accuracy trade-off is the intended goal MT. The single-aiming paradigm uses *controlled MTs* (i.e., MT goals that are longer than minimum MTs), whereas in the Fitts paradigm the MT goal

is to be as fast as possible while maintaining a high accuracy rate. Some have suggested (Meyer, Smith, & Wright, 1982; Wright & Meyer, 1983) that requiring the subject to achieve a particular MT goal results in a linear speed-accuracy trade-off. Some evidence favoring this view has been reported by Zelaznik et al. (1988), who found that a relaxation of the *precision* demands in matching the MT goal diminished the strength of the linear speed-accuracy relationship.

What effects might the MT goal have on the motor control processes in these two paradigms? Although the control mechanisms will be the focus of discussion later in this chapter, it is important to note at this point that the single-aiming, MT-goal paradigm encourages subjects to adopt a noncorrected, single-impulse control strategy whereas the ballistic (minimized MT) goal requirements of the Fitts task often result in one or more corrective actions (Meyer, Abrams, Kornblum, Wright, & Smith, 1988; Meyer et al., 1990). Impressive support for this hypothesis was provided in a clever experiment by Carlton (1994) in which corrective submovements were examined in two movement tasks. Subjects produced a 400-ms goal MT in one task (timed task), and moved as fast as possible in the other (ballistic task). For each subject, the dispersion of 95% of the aimed movements in the timed task was used to manufacture the target plate used in the ballistic task—a within-subject measure of variability in one task (W_e) being used to determine the size (W) of the target for that subject in the other task. With the spatial accuracy demands of each task now closely equated, Carlton found that the ballistic task condition resulted in corrective submovements on 93% of the trials, whereas corrections occurred on less than 20% of trials in the timed task. This difference in the frequency of corrective submovements between the two tasks is even more impressive when one considers that the timing task was performed about 90 ms *slower* than the ballistic task: if MT were the sole determinant of corrective submovements here, then presumably there should have been more time available for a correction to occur in the timed task.

Thus, it appears that both the feedback and the MT-goal hypotheses have some support. More importantly, though, the two converge on a similar issue regarding the difference between the linear and logarithmic speed-accuracy trade-offs.

A linear trade-off seems to occur in movement tasks that encourage a preprogrammed, open-loop control process; a logarithmic trade-off occurs in the performance of tasks that encourage closed-loop, corrective processes. The nature of these control strategies will be described in more detail later.

The Temporal Speed-Accuracy Trade-Off

Certainly the view is widespread that when we do things faster, we do them less precisely, and there is considerable evidence to support it. However, the evidence that we have considered so far describes the trade-off that occurs in reference to *spatial* accuracy. What happens when the focus is on *temporal* accuracy? We will deal with these situations next.

Anticipation-Timing Tasks

In tasks requiring anticipation and timing, such as hitting a baseball, the individual must monitor the environmental situation (the flight of the ball) and decide when to swing so that the bat arrives at the plate at nearly the same time as the ball. In chapter 4 we mentioned that these tasks require both *receptor anticipation* of the ball flight and *effector anticipation* of one's internal movement processes. Errors in *timing* result if the bat arrives earlier or later than the ball. What is the effect of increasing the speed (decreasing the MT) of the limb or bat on errors in timing?

Early research on this topic (Schmidt, 1967, 1969c) required subjects to move a slide along a trackway so that it would "hit" a target moving rapidly at right angles to the trackway (see figure 7.7), with a follow-through permitted. Accuracy in this task was measured in terms of errors in time—either early or late with respect to the target arrival. Subjects were asked to make a movement that was of "maximal" speed or of "moderate" speed, and four movement distances (15, 30, 45, and 60 cm) were used.

In table 7.1, the absolute errors in timing are given as a function of the movement distance and the movement speed instructions. Notice that the absolute error in timing (for any movement distance) was uniformly smaller (20% on the average) for the "maximal" instruction than for the

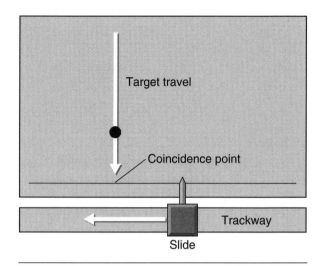

Figure 7.7. A coincident-timing task (top view). (A target on a belt moves directly toward the subject, who attempts to move the pointer so that the two "coincide" at the coincidence point.)

"moderate" instruction. Thus, when the person was performing the task more "violently," with a smaller MT and larger movement velocity, the timing accuracy in these conditions *improved*. Such findings seem to contradict the notion of the speed-accuracy trade-off.

At least two explanations for these effects are possible. First, when the person moved the handle more rapidly, the movement was initiated when the target was closer to the coincidence point than was the case when the movement was slower. That is, the subject waited longer before initiating the rapid movement. This may have provided a more accurate estimate of when the target would arrive at the coincidence point—that is, receptor anticipation, which would permit a more precise estimate of when the person should initiate the movement.

A second explanation is that the rapid movements themselves were more consistent than the slower moves. The variable error (the within-subject SD as discussed in chapter 2) of the MTs (see table 7.1) was about 44% less for the rapid movements than for the slower ones. Thus a second feature of fast movements is more *temporal stability* from trial to trial than for slower movements. This can be seen as an advantage for effector anticipation: the person can predict with greater accuracy when the limb will arrive at the target if the movement is rapid because the trial-to-trial variability in the movement's travel time is smaller.

Table 7.1   MT, Absolute Error in Timing, and Variable Error in MT as a Function of Movement Distance and Instructions in a Timing Task

| Movement distance | Movement speed instructions | | | | | |
| | Maximal | | | Moderate | | |
	MT	AE	MT VE	MT	AE	MT VE
15 cm	76	20	3	139	24	9
30 cm	123	23	7	209	27	13
45 cm	144	25	7	253	30	12
60 cm	206	28	9	274	41	13
Averages	137	24.0	6.5	219	30.5	11.7

Note. AE = absolute error; MT VE = variable error of MT; all measured in milliseconds. (Adapted from Schmidt 1967, 1969c.)

Movement-Timing Tasks

Newell et al. (1979) performed a number of experiments on the temporal consistency of movement, and they provided perhaps the best documentation of the effects of MT. They used a ballistic timing task in which the subject moved a slide along a trackway. The initial movement started a timer, and passing a switch along the trackway stopped it. The major independent variable was the MT. The investigators used a number of MTs (ranging from 100 to 1,000 ms) and a number of movement distances (ranging from .75 to 15 cm) presented in various combinations.

The primary dependent measure of interest was the variable error in timing (VE_t), or the within-subject SD of the MTs about the subject's own mean, taken to be a measure of timing consistency. The VE_t values from experiment 1 of Newell et al. (1979) are provided in table 7.2 for various values of MT. For the 5-cm movements, the inconsistency in movement timing increased markedly as the MT increased from 100 to 1,000 ms (VE_t increased from 10.8 to 125.7 ms). The effect was the same for the 15-cm movements, with VE_t increasing from 9.0 to 91.2 ms. Thus, it appears that this effect is similar to the effect seen in anticipation timing (Schmidt, 1967, 1969c); a smaller MT, given the same distance, produces *improved* movement-timing consistency.

An even more interesting feature of these findings is the suggestion that the timing error is *proportional* to the MT. In the fourth line of table 7.2 are the VE_t values divided by the MTs, multiplied by 100 to convert them to percentage val-

ues. If the VE_t is proportional to MT, then the VE_t/MT% values will be similar for any MT from 100 to 1,000 ms. Indeed, this is essentially what happened, as the VE_t/MT% values were 10.8%, 14.9%, and 12.6% for the 5-cm movements and 9.0%, 8.6%, and 9.1% for the 15-cm movements.

This effect of MT can perhaps be thought of as one that follows from the generally held view that short intervals of time are "easier" to estimate or produce than are long intervals of time. To illustrate, do this simple experiment. First, take a stopwatch and, without looking, estimate 1/2 s (500 ms) by pressing the button and releasing it at the appropriate time. Record the actual time for each of 10 trials. Now, do the same task again but use a target interval of 1 s (1,000 ms). You should find that the shorter interval is much "easier" to produce accurately in that you are much closer, on the average, to the target interval with the 500-ms task than with the 1,000-ms task. And, if you had calculated VEs for your performances, your VE for the 1,000-ms task should be roughly twice that for the 500-ms task. The processes responsible for determining the duration of the intervals are variable, and they seem to be variable in direct proportion to the *amount* of time that is to be produced. Because the movements in the Newell et al. (1979) experiments were, in effect, based on processes that take time, it is reasonable that they should have been variable in time in nearly direct proportion to the amount of time that they occupied.

There is considerable evidence that, generally speaking, the VE_t (or inconsistency) in the production of some interval of time tends to be a

Table 7.2   Errors in Timing as a Function of Movement Distance and MT

	MT (ms)					
	100		**500**		**1,000**	
Distance (cm)	5	15	5	15	5	15
Velocity (cm/s)	50	150	10	30	5	15
VE_t (ms)	10.8	9.0	74.6	42.8	125.7	91.2
VE_t/MT%	10.8	9.0	14.9	8.6	12.6	9.1

(From Newell et al. 1979.)

nearly constant proportion of the amount of time to be produced, at least within broad limits. For example, Michon (1967) found essentially this effect with rhythmic tapping at different rates; Gottsdanker (1970) found the effect for RT (with subjects with long RTs having greater within-subject VE_t of their own RTs); and Schmidt et al. (1979) found these effects for aiming tasks in which the MTs were controlled. This well-documented finding is an apparent contradiction to the speed-accuracy principles described previously in this chapter. Here, increasing the speed (by decreasing the MT) produces increases in accuracy in *timing*, whereas earlier we showed that increasing the speed resulted in diminished *spatial* accuracy.

Temporal Consistency of Impulses

The idea that a movement duration becomes more consistent as the MT decreases suggests that the durations of the particular muscular actions causing them become more consistent as well. Schmidt, Zelaznik, and Frank (1978) and Schmidt et al. (1979) studied this problem by having subjects make rhythmic back-and-forth movements of a lever in time to a metronome. The subject exerted forces (and their timing) with a strain gauge on the handle. There were four different MTs (200, 300, 400, and 500 ms/movement), and the concern was the variability in the duration of the force bursts (i.e., impulses) produced by muscular action during these movements. The results of this experiment are illustrated in figure 7.8, where the within-subject variability in impulse duration is plotted against the MT imposed by the metronome. The strong proportional relation found between these two variables is certainly in keeping with the data presented in the previous section about movement durations as a whole.

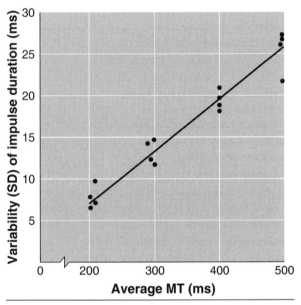

Figure 7.8. Variability in impulse duration as a function of the MT.
Reprinted from Schmidt, Zelaznik, and Frank, 1978.

Temporal Consistency and Movement Velocity

The MT is not the only factor that strongly affects the VE_t; the movement's velocity (i.e., the movement distance divided by the MT, usually in cm/s) has a very strong influence as well. Refer to table 7.2 (Newell et al., 1979) and consider the VE_t for the various values of movement distance—either 5 or 15 cm. Notice that for a given MT (e.g., 100 ms), the movement with the smaller movement distance, and hence the lower movement velocity, has a slightly higher VE_t (10.8 ms for the 5-cm movement, 9.0 ms for the 15-cm movement). This effect is even stronger for the 500-ms and 1,000-ms movements in the same table; the movement with the higher velocity had a smaller timing error, even when the MT was held constant.

To see this effect expressed another way, examine the $VE_t/MT\%$ values presented on the bottom line of table 7.2. Because the division by MT theoretically "cancels out" the effects of MT per se on the timing error (these two variables are nearly proportional), any changes in $VE_t/MT\%$ as a function of movement velocity must be due to something *other than* MT. Here, the movements with the longer movement distance (and hence the greater movement velocity) have smaller $VE_t/MT\%$ values. For the three MTs, these values were about 9% for the 15-cm movements and from 10% to 14% for the 5-cm movements. Increasing movement velocity made the movements more consistent.

Newell et al. (1980) studied these velocity effects more thoroughly than Newell et al. (1979) had in the earlier paper (see Newell, 1980 for a review). Various movement distances (ranging from 1.5 to 67.5 cm) and MTs (ranging from 100 to 600 ms) were used in combination, producing a set of velocity values that ranged from 5 cm/s to 225 cm/s. The timing consistency (VE_t) was studied as a function of these variations in velocity, and we have converted these data to the $VE_t/MT\%$ measure so that they can be compared to the findings in the previous section (see table 7.2). The 1980 Newell et al. data (experiment 3) are shown in figure 7.9, where the $VE_t/MT\%$ is plotted against movement velocity. As the velocity increased, the errors in timing decreased markedly at low velocities, and decreased more gradually with further increases in velocity. Similar effects have been seen in experiments involving wider ranges in velocities and distances (Newell et al., 1993; Jasiewicz & Simmons, 1996). This *velocity effect* is yet another example of the temporal speed-accuracy trade-off.

An interesting application of these findings relates to baseball: as a batter swings "harder" (with a smaller MT and/or a larger movement distance), the errors in timing should tend to decrease, not increase. Note that this prediction is for errors in *timing* and does not relate to errors in *spatial* accuracy; we will consider these issues in more detail later in the chapter.

To this point in the chapter we have presented three relatively different ways in which speed and accuracy are related: two of these ways pertain to spatial trade-offs and one pertains to a temporal trade-off. Theoretical explanations of these effects, however, have largely concentrated

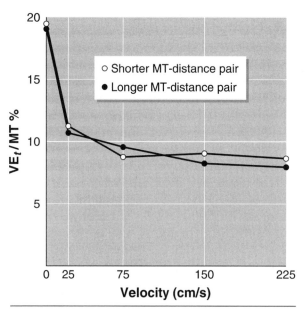

Figure 7.9. VE_t (expressed as $VE_t/MT\%$) as a function of the movement velocity. (Dividing VE_t by MT theoretically "cancels out" the effect of MT on errors.)
Adapted from Newell, Carlton, Carlton, and Hilbert, 1980.

on the spatial trade-off, and two general perspectives have dominated much of the thinking. These perspectives correspond in general to the topics discussed in chapters 5 and 6. With regard to the generation of an impulse to propel a limb toward a target, one perspective has been to consider the importance of *central* contributions. The other perspective has been to examine how *corrective* processes contribute to the speed-accuracy trade-off. In the following sections we describe the major ideas that have been suggested within these general theoretical approaches.

Central Contributions to the Speed-Accuracy Trade-Off

Keele (1981, 1986) has suggested that central processing of rapid aiming movements can be classified under two broad categories. In one category, the thinking is that central commands specify the *distance* that must be traveled to reach a target. Distance programming is assumed by models of impulse variability, whereby the agonist and antagonist muscles produce bursts of force that propel a limb a specific goal distance. The other general class of models assumes a programming of commands that specifies a target's *location*. Location programming is assumed by a class of models that specify equilibrium-tension ratios between agonist and antagonist muscle groups.

Impulse-Variability Theory

A number of the principles related to the linear speed-accuracy trade-off form the basis for impulse-variability models of movement control. Two principles are of critical importance: (a) the variability in the *duration* of a muscular contraction is directly proportional to the duration, and (b) the variability in *force* applied is an increasing function of the force to approximately 65% of maximum, with a leveling off or slight decrease thereafter. The reason these principles are of such importance is that they define the variability in the two dimensions of the *impulse*—the primary determinant of what the limb will do when muscles attached to it are activated. The notion of the impulse, that is, the forces produced over time, was discussed in chapter 6 (review the section on the impulse-timing hypothesis). So if, as we have argued earlier, the impulse is a critical determiner of action, and variability in impulses is a critical determiner of the variability in action, then an analysis of the variability of the components of the impulse (variability in force and variability in duration) should allow considerable insight into the sources of errors in movement control. There was early modeling of these phenomena (Schmidt, Zelaznik, & Frank, 1978; Schmidt et al., 1979), and revisions of the same idea were provided later by Meyer and colleagues (Meyer, Smith, & Wright, 1982; Meyer et al., 1988).

Force-Variability Principles

In this section we consider factors that produce variability in the amount of force generated by the activation of the motor program. This is an important issue for the understanding of processes underlying skillful behavior. All that the muscles can do to bones is to exert force on them, with this application being adjustable in terms of amount of force or in terms of the temporal onset and duration of that force. Complex patterns of force produced *during* a particular contraction are presumably also under the control of the motor system. If the activation sent to the muscles is preprogrammed, then any factors causing the amount of force to deviate from the intended amount of force will cause the movement to deviate from its intended path or fail to meet its goal. Put simply, *muscular forces produce movements, and variability in muscular forces produces variability in movements.*

Schmidt and colleagues (Schmidt, Zelaznik, &

Frank, 1978; Schmidt et al., 1979) began a series of studies concerning the relationship between forces involved in quick, preprogrammed movements and their within-subject variability, and these findings are described next. In relation to slower movements, there has been some interest in these questions for over a century (e.g., Fullerton & Cattell, 1892; see Newell, Carlton, & Hancock, 1984 for a review), although the theoretical orientations of this earlier work were considerably different from present interests.

The initial question addressed in the studies by Schmidt and colleagues was what the relationship might be between the amount of force that was produced and the resulting within-subject variability in that force. For example, why did an aiming movement with twice the amplitude (MT constant) have approximately twice the error in hitting a target (e.g., Woodworth, 1899)? In order to produce a movement of twice the amplitude, the generalized motor program should remain the same, but the overall force parameter would be increased so that the limb would travel twice the distance in the same MT (see chapter 6). Could it be that when the forces in the limb are increased so that the limb can travel farther, the variability in this force is increased as well, making the output of the movement more variable? This was the hypothesis.

Moderate Force Levels.   The subject's task was to produce quick "shots" of force against an immovable handle. Attached to the handle was a strain gauge that sensed the amount of force applied; this information was sent to an oscilloscope so that the subject could see the force levels. A zero-force level was indicated at the bottom of the oscilloscope screen, and increasing force applied to the handle would move the dot upward on the screen. Subjects attempted to produce ballistic "shots" of force that would peak exactly at a target location on the screen, the goal being to produce the same force on each trial. The peak force and the within-subject variability (SD) of the peak forces were measured, and subjects were asked to produce different amounts of force during separate series of trials.

In figure 7.10, the SD in peak force is plotted as a function of the amount of force the subjects were asked to produce. A clear linear relationship between force and its variability was found. From a number of other experiments, force and force variability were found to be

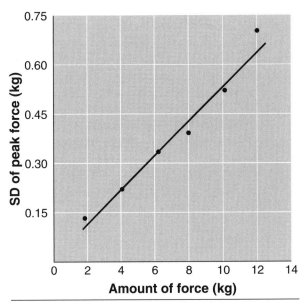

Figure 7.10. Variability in peak static force as a function of the amount of force to be produced.
Reprinted from Schmidt, Zelaznik, and Frank, 1978.

linearly related in situations in which the forces were much smaller than indicated in figure 7.10 (40 g elbow flexion measured at the wrist) and in which they were as large as 65% of the subject's maximum (Newell & Carlton, 1985; Schmidt, Zelaznik, & Frank, 1978; Schmidt et al., 1979; Sherwood & Schmidt, 1980).

These results were from static (isometric) contractions, though, and it was not clear that such relationships would occur in actual *movements*, in which the muscle shortens as it is producing force against the bone. Sherwood and Schmidt (1980) examined this issue in an experiment in which forces were recorded during a simple ballistic timing movement. Again, a linear relationship between force and force variability was found, suggesting that this principle had a strong role in movements. These data certainly supported the speculation that as the amount of force was increased in order, for example, to move farther in the same MT, the variability in force would increase in nearly direct proportion, leading to increased variability in the movement outcome—in this case, in hitting a target accurately.

Near-Maximal Force Levels. Will the linear relationship between force and force variability continue to hold as the forces are increased even further? This is an important question, as many of the skills performed by athletes have very high force requirements, such as those for the forces in the quadriceps muscles generated during a foot-

ball punt for distance. With such large forces, one might expect that there would be no "room" for variability near the performer's maximum. If the subject actually did produce the theoretical maximum on every trial, there would be no variability (because the SD of a set of constant values is zero). Thus, as the maximum force is approached, one could imagine a point of maximum force variability (perhaps near the middle of the range in force capability) and a gradual decline in force variability (i.e., more consistency) as the forces were increased further. With this reasoning, an inverted-U function should exist between force variability and force across the total range of forces available to humans.

In figure 7.11 are the data from experiment 4 of Sherwood and Schmidt (1980), in which the forces were increased to very near the subject's maximum. The figure shows the variability in peak force as a function of the level of force produced, as before. But in this case a maximum point occurred in force variability, with a strong tendency for decreasing force variability as the forces were increased further. The peak force variability occurred, on the average, at about 65% of maximum force for these subjects, with the largest force examined being about 92% of maximum.

Inverted-U or Negatively Accelerating Functions? Some controversy has developed with regard to this inverted-U function. Newell and Carlton (1985, 1988; Carlton & Newell, 1988; Newell, Carlton, & Hancock, 1984) have criticized the procedures used to obtain this inverted-U result, on the grounds that the *time* to peak force was not controlled in these experiments. They showed that larger peak forces tend to be associated with a longer time to achieve peak force, and they argued that this should have the effect of producing an artificial inverted U at high force levels. In a subsequent experiment in which the time to peak force was held strictly constant, Sherwood, Schmidt, and Walter (1988) showed that the inverted-U function was no longer as pronounced as indicated in figure 7.11. Thus, perhaps rather than an inverted-U function, the relation between force and force variability follows a curvilinear, *negatively accelerated* function. Beyond about 65% of maximum force, force variability tends to increase at a decreasing rate, leveling off somewhere near the maximum force capabilities (or perhaps decreasing very slightly—Sherwood, Schmidt, & Walter, 1988).

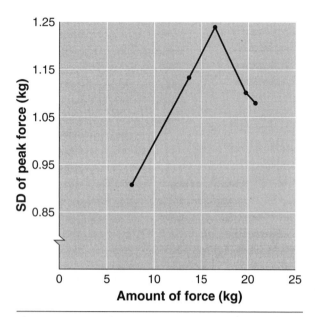

Figure 7.11.   Variability in peak dynamic force as a function of force produced including near-maximal force values. Adapted from Sherwood and Schmidt, 1980.

The theoretical modeling of force summation characteristics by Ulrich and Wing (1991), however, suggests that both the inverted-U *and* the negatively accelerated functions may be correct in certain situations. Although space does not allow a presentation of their assumptions, for our purposes the argument is that *force units* (mechanically independent motor units) are summated in parallel over time in order to produce a given amount of force. Any given level of force can be produced by changing either the *number* of force units recruited or the *duration* in which an individual unit is producing force. Ulrich and Wing (1991) argued that if the level of force is determined *only* by the number of units recruited, then a negatively accelerated increase in force variability would be predicted. However, if different levels of force were created by varying the force duration of each individual unit that was recruited, then an inverted-U function would be predicted. Clearly, more research is necessary in order to determine whether or not this modeling has resolved the controversy.

Modeling the Initial Impulse

The general idea of impulse-variability principles can be understood easily if one considers only the initial impulse for acceleration in a rapid movement. A good example is the ballistic timing task, in which the subject moves a slide along a trackway, past a switch at the end, and attempts to achieve a MT goal defined as the interval from initial movement until arrival at the switch. Here the subject is accelerating for the entire (measured) movement, so the movement is governed by the initial impulse for acceleration. When the experimenter changes the movement amplitude (*A*) or the goal MT, the subject's movement is assumed to be handled by changes in the parameters of the generalized motor program for this rapid action (see chapter 6). Let us examine the effect of variables like movement amplitude and movement time—critical participants in the speed-accuracy trade-off—on the nature of impulse variability in this task.[2]

The Effect of Movement Amplitude.   Consider what happens to the impulse as the person is asked to move twice as far in the same MT. In this case the movement-duration parameter of the generalized motor program must be fixed, so the duration of the impulse will also be constant. However, the overall force parameter must be doubled so that the force produced will be twice as large as for the shorter movement. From the earlier section on force variability (figure 7.10), we know that as the amount of force is doubled, the variability is approximately doubled as well. Therefore, with a doubled force but a constant duration, the entire impulse will have twice the variability, with all of the increase in variability occurring because of the changes in the amplitude of the impulse. The overall result is that the impulse variability is linearly related to the movement amplitude:

$$\text{Impulse Variability} = k_1 \times (A) \qquad (7.4)$$

where k_1 is an empirical constant, and *A* is the movement amplitude (see the section on empirical equations in chapter 2).

The Effect of Movement Time.   Next, consider what happens to the impulse as the MT is halved with a constant movement amplitude. From the notions of generalized motor programs, we know that the overall duration parameter will be halved as well, so that all of the impulses in the action will be half their original duration. We know from figure 7.8 that the variability in the duration of an interval is directly proportional to its duration, so halving the duration of the impulse should reduce its variability *in time* by half as well. Generally, the temporal variability of an impulse is linearly related to MT:

Temporal Variability = $k_2 \times$ (MT)   (7.5)

where k_2 is another proportionality constant. This is interesting (and somewhat counterintuitive) because the variability of one component (temporal) of the impulse becomes *more* consistent as the MT is shortened, while the variability of another component (force) becomes *less* consistent.

But along with this shortening of impulse duration as the MT is halved, the impulse must increase in amplitude (force), so that the increased velocity needed for the shorter MT can be achieved. From physics we know that, for a movement with twice the velocity (i.e., half the MT), the area of the impulse must be twice as large. But the duration is half as long, so the amplitude must be four times as large (i.e., four times the amplitude together with half the duration yields twice the area). Then, because of force-variability principles (figure 7.10), the force variability is increased by a factor of four as well, so that halving the MT produces a fourfold increase in the *force* component of impulse variability. More generally, the force component of impulse variability is inversely related to the squared MT, or

Force Variability = $k_3 \times (1/\text{MT}^2)$ (7.6)

We see that the overall impulse variability is related both (a) directly to the MT in the temporal dimension and (b) directly to $1/\text{MT}^2$ in the force dimension. Combining these two effects of impulse variability (equations 7.5 and 7.6) produces the generalization that

Impulse Variability = $k_4 \times (1/\text{MT})$ (7.7)

where total impulse variability is proportional to $1/\text{MT}$.

Amplitude and Movement Time.   When we combine the effects of A and the effects of MT from equations 7.4 and 7.7, we obtain the relation that

Impulse Variability = $k \times (A/\text{MT})$ (7.8)

where the total variability in an impulse for accelerating a limb is directly related to the amplitude of the movement (A) and inversely related to the duration of the movement (MT). Because the velocity of a movement after an impulse is directly proportional to the size (area) of the impulse, and because the variability in the impulse leads directly to variability in velocity, this rela-

tion implies that the variability in the velocity of a movement when an impulse has stopped acting on it will be directly proportional to A/MT as well. This is a key feature in impulse-variability modeling, and many other interesting predictions emerge from it.

Impulse-Variability Principles in Movement Control

The original impulse-variability theory (Schmidt, Zelaznik, & Frank, 1978; Schmidt et al., 1979), which concerned the effects of various movement variables on initial-impulse variability, seems to account relatively well for the behavior of *single* impulses in a number of rapid movement tasks (see Schmidt et al., 1985 for a review). As a result, the model accounts fairly well for accuracy in tasks in which only a single impulse is acting, such as the ballistic timing tasks described at the beginning of this section.

Errors in Ballistic Timing.   For ballistic timing tasks, we have already mentioned that the variable error in timing (VE$_t$) has been shown to be nearly proportional to the MT (tables 7.1 and 7.2, figure 7.9). The model also accounts for spatial errors—the error in *position* at the moment that the goal MT has elapsed, or W_e. In this case the model predicts that W_e should be independent of MT, and several experiments show this to be essentially so (e.g., Schmidt, 1994; Schmidt et al., 1979, 1985). Therefore, changing the MT affects mainly timing errors, not spatial errors. The principle is just the opposite when variations in A are produced in this task. Here, increasing A causes nearly proportional increases in spatial errors, but causes almost no effect in the timing errors.[3] This seemingly curious set of findings is derivable from the model, and is related to the tight connection between space and time in such situations (see, e.g., Newell, 1980; Newell, Carlton, & Hancock, 1984).

Spatial Errors in Very Rapid Movements.   Some applications of impulse-variability notions can be seen in a task like hitting a baseball, where the limb seems to be driven by a single impulse. Here, in addition to being temporally accurate, the batter must be spatially accurate so that the swing will not miss the ball. We can think of such a movement as shown in figure 7.12, where the limb (or limb plus bat) is moving horizontally toward some ball. Assume that the limb is

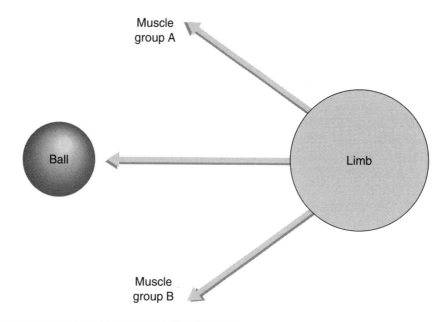

Figure 7.12.   The limb conceptualized as a mass moved by two forces (muscles) operating in different directions.

controlled by two muscle groups A and B, which pull obliquely on it, their combined action being to move the limb toward the ball. What will be the effect on spatial accuracy of increasing the mass of the bat?

If muscle groups A and B are contracting with less than 65% of maximum force, then increasing the mass of the bat will require increased force output in each of them, and the force variability will increase in both muscle groups at the same time (e.g., figure 7.10). This should result in progressively larger variations in the direction of bat travel and in progressively lower probability that the bat will hit the ball. But what if the forces in the two muscle groups are larger, perhaps greater than 65% of maximum? Here, with increased mass of the bat, there would be (from data in figure 7.11) a decrease (or at least a much smaller increase) in the force variability as the forces are increased, resulting in *increased* consistency of bat travel as the mass is increased.

Schmidt and Sherwood (1982) conducted an experiment that seems to show just that. Subjects made horizontal forward arm swings to attempt to hit a target, with a MT that was to be as close to 200 ms as possible. Figure 7.13 shows the spatial accuracy in hitting the target as a function of the mass added to the handle, measured as VE and total variability (E). As mass was added to the unloaded handle, there was first an increase in spatial errors; but the function soon peaked, so

that the errors decreased with further increases in mass. Thus there was an inverted-U relation between spatial accuracy and mass for this task, with the peak at approximately the mass that resulted in about 60–70% of maximum force. This corresponds surprisingly well with the peak in the force/force-variability function found in figure 7.11.

This same experiment was also conducted with variations in MT, this time with the mass held constant. If decreased MT results in increases in force beyond about 65% of maximum, then we should find that making the movement faster results in better accuracy, not less as would be expected from the speed-accuracy trade-off effect. Figure 7.14 shows the results. As the average MT decreased from 158 ms to about 102 ms, there was a progressive increase in the spatial errors, as one would expect. But when the MT was reduced further to 80 ms, requiring approximately 84% of maximum force, there was a decrease in the spatial errors, with the function showing a peak error somewhere near 50% of maximum contraction (102-ms MT). Again, this is compatible with the peak in the force/force-variability function seen in figure 7.11. It is interesting to note that when the movement was very rapid and required 84% of maximum force, the amount of error was nearly the same as that in a very slow movement (130 ms).

Both of these results provide exceptions to the speed-accuracy trade-off ideas presented earlier,

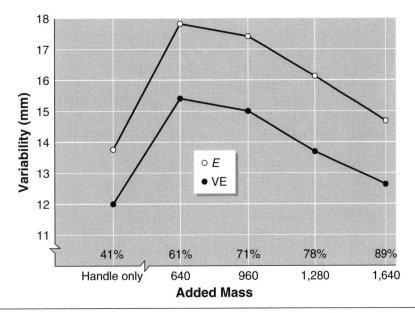

Figure 7.13.   The effect of added mass on the spatial accuracy of a 200-ms arm-swing movement.
Reprinted from Schmidt and Sherwood, 1982.

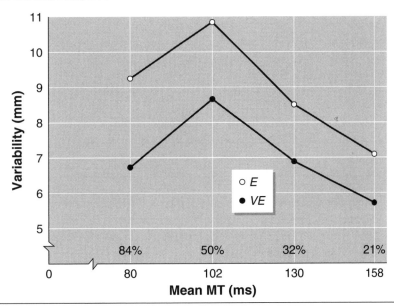

Figure 7.14.   The effect of MT on the spatial accuracy in a horizontal arm-swing movement.
Reprinted from Schmidt and Sherwood, 1982.

as increasing speed (or increasing mass) resulted in *increased* accuracy when the movements were very violent. This supports indirectly the impulse-variability model, in which the variability in forces is expected to be a major determiner of the spatial accuracy in these rapid actions. There are also interesting practical implications. Perhaps telling a baseball player to swing slowly to "make contact" would actually result in less spatial accuracy than giving an instruction to swing "hard." We develop this idea more fully in the next section.

Application to Baseball Batting.   In this section we want to take some of the principles already presented and attempt to use as many as possible in understanding a complex skill like batting a pitched baseball. These principles can be applied to answer questions such as the following: What happens to batting success when the velocity of the bat (or the mass of the bat) is increased? The answer can be considered in terms of the kinds of processes known to be important in such actions. All these processes have been discussed in the last four chapters, but it would seem to be useful to consider them together so they can be more effectively understood and interrelated.

Let us review some basic facts about hitting a baseball. In figure 7.15 are some results collected from a number of studies referred to earlier, as well as from a study by Hubbard and Seng (1954). Essentially, it takes about 460 ms for a ball (moving at 89 mph) to travel from the pitcher to the plate. Hubbard and Seng found that the MT of the bat (the time from the first movement of the bat until it reached the plate) was about 160 ms, so that the bat started moving 160 ms before the ball reached the plate; this is equivalent to about 21 ft (6.4 m) of ball travel.

What would happen if the batter were to speed up the swing 20 ms, from 160 ms to 140 ms? Consider first the effect of this change on the nature of the decision processes prior to swinging. As the person is watching the ball fly toward the plate, it seems reasonable to assume that the most important aspects of the ball's flight are those that are closest to the batter. But notice that by speeding up the swing to 140 ms (see figure 7.15), the batter can view the ball for 20 ms longer. More importantly, that 20 ms is occurring during the time that the ball is as close as possible to the batter before the ultimate decision has to be made. In this way, the batter should be able to make more effective choices regarding the swing, because he is viewing the ball for a longer period of time.

Next, consider the effect of swinging faster on the timing of the bat swing initiation. Remember from the discussions about anticipation in chapter 5 that in order for the bat to arrive at the plate at the proper time (relative to the ball, of course), the batter must be able to anticipate the processes that will intervene between the final (internal) "go" signal and the end of the movement. This is called *effector anticipation*. In the present example, the relevant interval begins at the point marked "Decisions end" and ends when the bat reaches the plate. When the MT is 160 ms, this interval is estimated as 328 ms, and it is 308 ms when the MT is 140 ms. Because this interval must be timed, and because the accuracy in timing an interval is poorer as the interval increases, more accurate effector anticipation should occur when the swing is 140 ms rather than 160 ms long, and less variability in the time of swing initiation should result. Schmidt (1969b), using a laboratory task resembling batting (figure 7.7), found that when the MT was decreased, the variability in *when* the bat swing was initiated was decreased as well. Thus, another advantage of swinging more rapidly relates to timing the onset of the swing so that the end of the swing is coincident with the ball's arrival at the plate.

A third advantage of swinging more rapidly is that the movement itself is more temporally consistent as the MT is shorter. As pointed out earlier, a number of studies (e.g., Newell et al., 1979, 1980;

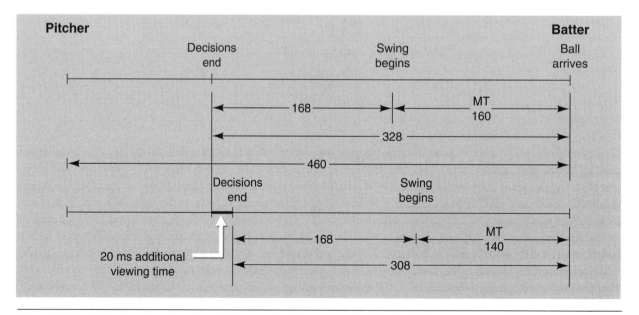

Figure 7.15. A timeline showing the critical events in hitting a pitched baseball. (The top example has a 160-ms MT, and the bottom example has a 140-ms MT.)

Schmidt et al., 1979) report decreased MT variability as the MT is decreased. Newell et al. (1979, 1980) found an effect of movement velocity that is essentially independent of MT, showing that swinging faster (degrees/s) and swinging with less MT (ms) both produce increased consistency in the MT. So when the batter swings harder, the movements become more temporally consistent. Because decreasing the MT increases the temporal consistency of the movement, the swing becomes more predictable and the capability for effector anticipation is increased.

The combination of increased consistency in the time of swing initiation and increased consistency in the duration of the swing itself should lead to increased consistency in the time at which the bat arrives at the plate. For a given level of receptor anticipation (about the ball's flight pattern), increases in the swing speed should therefore result in increased timing accuracy in terms of the arrival of the bat at the plate in relation to the time of the ball's arrival. In the laboratory "batting" task mentioned previously (figure 7.7), Schmidt (1969b) found that the temporal accuracy of meeting the "ball" was greater when the MT was shorter (see table 7.1). Such effects should also occur if the mass of the bat is increased (beyond contraction levels of about 65% of the subject's maximum) with a constant MT, because the increased mass also tends to make the movements more consistent (see figure 7.13; Schmidt & Sherwood, 1982).

If the level of muscle contraction in the bat swing is above about 65% of the batter's maximum, then increased swing speed, or increased bat mass with a constant swing speed, each produces increases in the spatial accuracy of the swing. This is so because with increased levels of contraction there is increased consistency in force production, which results in increased consistency in where the limbs go during the action. In this way, the limbs tend to "do what the program tells them to do" more effectively, and the probability that the bat actually meets the ball at which it is aimed should increase. These kinds of effects have been shown for laboratory tasks (Schmidt & Sherwood, 1982), as well as in sport-related tasks (Zernicke & Roberts, 1978).

Limitations of the Impulse-Variability Theory

The theory cannot account for movement accuracy in aiming tasks (e.g., the linear speed-accuracy

trade-off) in which a *number* of impulses are presumably combined to produce a complete action (e.g., as in figures 7.5 and 7.6), and so the impulse-variability model falls considerably short of the goal of explaining speed-accuracy phenomena in general. A modification of the theory, using similar assumptions about generalized motor programs, force and time variability, and so on, was provided by Meyer, Smith, and Wright (1982). This view does represent an improvement in certain ways, but it suffers from a number of other problems that seem to argue against its adequacy as an account of speed-accuracy effects (see Schmidt et al., 1985; Zelaznik, Schmidt, & Gielen, 1986). At present, it is not clear how rapid movement accuracy should be modeled using these ideas, but we remain confident that the impulse-variability principles described earlier will play a role somehow.

Overall, the impulse-variability theory accounts reasonably well for certain types of ballistic actions that do not require feedback. Thus, the theory provides an important description of some of the centrally generated errors that result in speed-accuracy trade-offs. Later in this chapter we will describe a more recent model of Fitts-type tasks by Meyer and colleagues (1988, 1990) that describes how impulse-variability principles are involved in both the initial and corrective portions of aiming movements.

Equilibrium-Point Theories

As an alternative to theories suggesting that movement distances are controlled on the basis of programmed impulses, there are theories suggesting that the *movement endpoint* is programmed and that the muscle properties determine the trajectory. The relation of these theories to speed-accuracy trade-offs has not been fully investigated (Latash, 1993; Latash & Gutman, 1993). However, these ideas represent a major theoretical advance regarding the way limb-positioning movements are controlled by the central nervous system, so it is important to consider them here.

The Length-Tension Diagram

Muscles, and tendons that connect muscles to bones, have a certain amount of compliance, or *springiness*. In an older view of muscle (e.g., Huxley, 1969), the notion was that the *contractile component* of muscle was responsible for the production of forces and that a *series elastic component* (in the muscular connective tissue and in the tendons) provided elasticity. Although the concept has been known for more than a century (Weber, 1846; see Partridge, 1983), it has been emphasized more recently that the contractile portion of muscle has elasticity as well, such that the entire muscle-tendon unit is analogous to a complicated spring. This concept has influenced thinking about what muscles do when they move bones in skilled actions (see Partridge & Benton, 1981, for a review).

One way to study the properties of muscles is to describe them in terms of a length-tension curve, or the relation between a muscle's length and the tension that it is capable of producing at that length and under a given level of innervation. In an anesthetized animal, the length of the muscle can be predetermined; the nerve is stimulated artificially so that the level of activation to the muscle can be controlled, and the resulting tension is measured. Such a procedure can produce a family of *length-tension diagrams*, with one curve for each of the levels of innervation that the experimenter uses. Some of these curves from Rack and Westbury (1969) are shown in figure 7.16, from a study in which five levels of activation were used (defined in terms of the number of impulses of electrical stimulus per second). Notice that at all levels, a generally increasing relationship was found between the length of the

muscle and the tension it developed. This relationship is roughly what we would expect if the muscle were a spring attached to a lever (the bone). A fundamental mechanical principle about springs—Hooke's law of springs—is that for a given spring, the tension that the spring will produce is directly proportional to the amount that the spring is elongated. Figure 7.17 is a simple hypothetical length-tension diagram that would be produced with the use of springs. The four curves represent four different springs, each with a different *stiffness*—which is the force required to lengthen the spring by one unit (i.e., the change in tension divided by the resulting change in length), represented as the slope of the length-tension curve.

Mass-Spring Mechanisms

The realization by Asatryan and Feldman (1965; Feldman, 1966a, 1966b)[4] that muscles could, in certain gross ways, behave something like complex springs has revealed a possible mechanism for movement control known as *mass-spring* control. Consider a lever, pivoted near one end, with two springs attached on either side. This setup is shown in figure 7.18a. Think of the lever as the bone in the forearm; the pivot is the elbow joint, and the two springs are the groups of muscles that span the joint—the flexors and the extensors. The flexors are really three different muscles in our arms, but consider them collectively as one spring for simplicity.

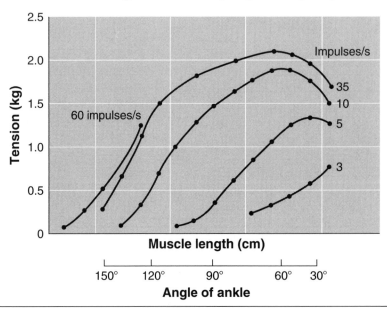

Figure 7.16. Tension produced by muscle as a function of the level of activation (impulses per second) and its length.
Reprinted from Rack and Westbury, 1969.

In figure 7.18b are the hypothetical length-tension curves for these two springs, assuming a constant level of motor activation. First consider the curve labeled "Flexors." Here, as the elbow angle is increased from 30° to 180° (i.e., the elbow is extended), a progressively increased tension is being produced in the flexors because they are being lengthened (stretched). Also, the curve labeled "Extensors" represents the tension

in the extensor muscles when the elbow angle is changed, and as the tension in the flexors increases the tension in the extensors decreases. This is so because as the length of the flexors increases, the length of the extensors decreases, and the tensions they produce are related to their lengths.

For a given amount of stiffness in the springs, the lever would move to an *equilibrium position* (or *equilibrium point*) in its range, representing the point where it would be stabilized by the opposing actions of the two springs. The equilibrium point is represented by the elbow angle in which the tension (or, more properly, torque at the elbow) in the flexor group is just equal to the tension in the extensor group. In the diagram, the two tensions are equal at only one elbow angle: the elbow angle at which the two length-tension diagrams cross each other, at about 95°.

What will happen if we perturb the limb from its equilibrium point to 120° and then release it? At 120° the flexion torque will be higher than the extension torque; this will result in more force being produced in the direction of flexion than in the direction of extension. This imbalance in torques causes the limb to move toward flexion, until the two torques are equal again at the equilibrium point. Notice that the mass-spring system will tend to move back to the equilibrium point after being deflected, regardless of the

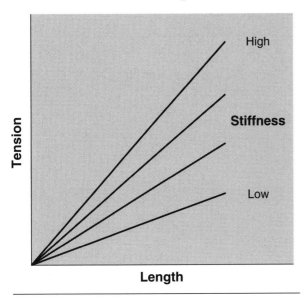

Figure 7.17. Idealized length-tension curves as would be produced from four springs, each with a different stiffness.

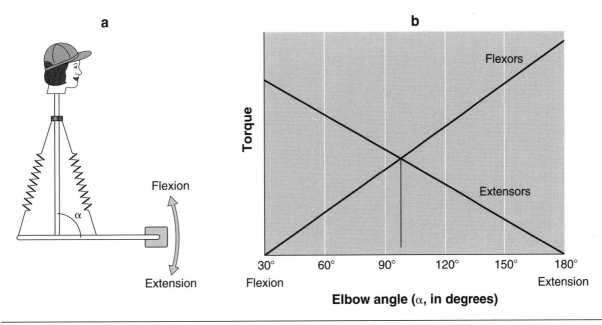

Figure 7.18. The mass-spring, or equilibrium-point model. (a) Muscles seen as springs; (b) the length-tension diagrams for the flexors and extensors plotted for different elbow angles, with the intersection being the equilibrium point where the tensions in the two muscle groups are equal and opposite.

amount or direction of the original deflection. This view helps to explain how limbs can be stabilized in one position, such as in the maintenance of posture (see also figure 5.16).

Equilibrium-Point Principles (α and λ Models)

The mass-spring view perhaps explains some simple things about how we can hold a limb in one place, but how can it explain *movement?* Various closely related models have been proposed by Feldman (1966a, 1966b, 1986) and Polit and Bizzi (1978, 1979) that are slightly different in the ways the processes are thought to work. In the λ model (Feldman), illustrated in figure 7.19, assume that the limb is initially at a particular equilibrium position (110°) defined by the two length-tension functions for flexors and extensors (what Feldman called the *invariant characteristic*). Then, when the flexor group is activated, there is a shift from one length-tension function to another (from Flexors$_1$ to Flexors$_2$ in the figure), which occurs because of two distinctly different changes. First, the function is shifted to the left through a change in the *threshold length* (which Feldman labeled λ). This is the muscle length at which the length-tension curve crosses the zero-tension axis (here shifted leftward from λ_1 to λ_2); it is the muscle length at which the reflex activities just begin to cause the muscle to contract, with tension increasing progressively as the muscle is lengthened further. Second, the *stiffness*

of the muscle is increased as well—seen as the steeper slope of the length-tension function for flexors$_2$ as compared to flexors$_1$.

Notice now that, through these shifts in the length-tension function (or the invariant characteristic), the premovement equilibrium point (i.e., at 110°) has been replaced by the new equilibrium point at 80°. But the limb is still at 110°, and not in equilibrium, because the flexors are exerting *a* units of torque, whereas the extensors are exerting *c* units; the difference in torque *(a − c)* begins to move the limb into flexion. This movement continues until the limb is in equilibrium again, this time at the new equilibrium point of 80°, where the two muscle groups are producing torques that are again equal and opposite (*b* units). The analogous process can also occur in the extensor group, or probably in both groups at the same time in most normal movements. So, through appropriate selection of the activation to the muscle groups spanning a joint, and hence a new equilibrium point, the joint can be moved to any position within its anatomical range. The viewpoint has been referred to as an *equilibrium-point model* because the limb moves to the mechanically defined equilibrium point (Crossman & Goodeve, 1963/1983).

At this point, the Polit-Bizzi and Feldman models become slightly different. According to the α model (Polit & Bizzi, 1978, 1979), the mechanical characteristics of the muscles enable the

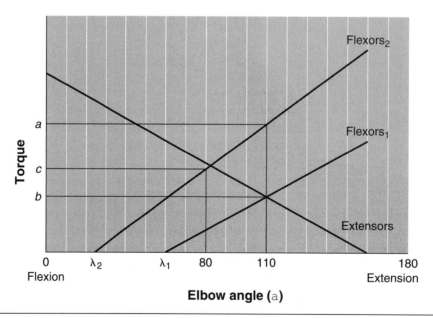

Figure 7.19. Length-tension diagrams for the extensors and flexors for various elbow angles. (The equilibrium point is shifted from 110° to 80° by increased activation in the flexors to produce a new length-tension relation.)

limbs to move to the new equilibrium position without any feedback (see the next section for evidence). On the other hand, the λ model (Feldman, 1966a, 1966b, 1986; Feldman & Levin, 1995; Latash, 1993) holds that the feedback from the spindle activities is an essential part of the process, perhaps to ensure that the muscle maintains approximately constant stiffness as Nichols and Houk (1976) suggested. In any case, no feedback to either higher centers or the stages of information processing was needed to move accurately; errors are not detected and corrected as in a closed-loop system. Another difference concerns what the motor system is thought to control. In the α model, the motor system activates only the alpha motor neurons to change the length-tension function; the muscle spindles and the gamma system are uninvolved. In the λ model, the alpha and gamma systems are controlled together, with the muscle spindles being involved in the control of stiffness.

The controversy surrounding the ability of the λ and the α models to explain certain features of limb control has become rather intense and detailed in recent years. Numerous debates have been published, and these represent a good cross section of the differing opinions that exist on the issue (see Bizzi et al., 1992; Berkinblit, Feldman, & Fukson, 1986; Feldman & Levin, 1995; Gottlieb, Corcos, & Agarwal, 1989; Latash, 1993). However, for present purposes, the equilibrium-point models provide an important contrast with the impulse-timing model of movement control discussed earlier in this chapter. In that model, the critical determiner of the limb's action and trajectory was the amount of force programmed and the *timing* and *duration* of this force. With the equilibrium-point model, the muscle innervation is simply changed to a new level, and the timing of the onsets and offsets of the muscular impulses is presumably not involved.

Finally, an important distinction is that the motor system does not have to "know" where the limb is starting from in order to move it to a new location. As figures 7.18 and 7.19 show, the equilibrium point can be achieved regardless of the starting position. Thus, the equilibrium-point models are somewhat simpler than the impulse-timing view because only two levels of activation are specified to the muscles. With the impulse-timing view, the system must know where the limb is at the beginning of the move-

ment and then must specify the appropriate durations and intensities of the muscular impulses.

Evidence for Equilibrium-Point Control

As indicated earlier, scientists had known for a long time that muscles act like "complicated springs," but it appears to have been the Russian physiologist Feldman (1966a, 1966b; Asatryan & Feldman, 1965) who described relationships between position and torque in human elbow movements (so-called *invariant characteristics*) and proposed how mechanical properties might be used in movement control (see also Crossman & Goodeve, 1963/1983). Feldman's work was not widely known in the West until it was popularized in a very influential paper by Turvey (1977). At about the same time, Polit and Bizzi's work in the United States with deafferented monkeys independently supported similar ideas, and some of this evidence is given next.

Experiments With Deafferented Monkeys. Polit and Bizzi (1978, 1979) used monkeys with deafferented forelimbs; the monkey was rewarded for pointing the hand and an attached lever to a target or for turning the head to a target light. With the hand actions, the monkeys could not, of course, feel the limb move, and they could not see the limb either. The movements were made in the dark, with the target light being turned off as soon as the monkey began to move toward it. The major dependent variable was the terminal location of the movement on particular movement trials. Polit and Bizzi studied these moves when the limb was perturbed in certain ways prior to or during the movement. For example, when the stimulus light was turned on and the animal looked at it, preparing to move, the experimenters would unexpectedly shift the initial position of the limb. Sometimes a mass would be unexpectedly applied to the lever that the animal was to move, or a brief pulse of force was applied that temporarily restrained or aided the movement.

Typical records of these arm movements are shown in figure 7.20. The top three records are from the monkeys prior to deafferentation. An unresisted move is shown in figure 7.20a, and a perturbation is applied (as indicated by the horizontal bar) to aid the movement in figure 7.20b and to resist the movement in figure 7.20c. The same monkeys then performed the movements after recovery from surgical deafferentation. The unresisted move in figure 7.20a appears to be

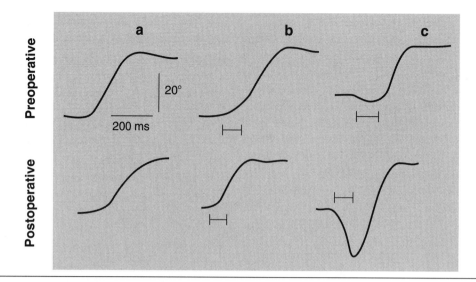

Figure 7.20.   Elbow movements in normal (top) and deafferented (bottom) monkeys. (The endpoint is achieved even if a perturbation, indicated by a horizontal bar, is applied during the movement.)
Reprinted with permission from Polit, A., and Bizzi, E., 1978, "Processes Controlling Arm Movements in Monkeys," *Science, 201,* 1236. Copyright 1978 American Association for the Advancement of Science.

quite like the move before the deafferentation, except that it is slower. When the perturbation was applied to aid the movement (figure 7.20b) or to resist the movement (figure 7.20c), the movement endpoint was achieved regardless of the direction of the perturbation. Sometimes when the target location was close to the starting position, the shift in limb position would take the hand past the target. In these cases the limb moved "backward" toward the target and achieved nearly the same position as when it was unresisted (see also Bizzi, Polit, & Morasso, 1976).

These findings raise some interesting questions. First, the monkeys tended to move directly to the target regardless of the mass that was applied to the limb and regardless of shifts in initial location. All this was accomplished without feedback from limb position, so the hypothesis that the monkey "felt" the change in position or load and altered the motor command to compensate seems to be incapable of explaining these data. It appeared that the motor program determined the endpoint in advance, and that position was achieved regardless of the changes in load or the initial position. The equilibrium-point model argues that when the command is issued to the muscles, the two opposing muscle groups are activated such that the muscles achieve the equilibrium point by mechanical means. The limb "springs to" the target.

The results from Polit and Bizzi's experiments also tend to argue against an impulse-timing hypothesis. According to this hypothesis, the

monkey first determines where the limb is; then the movement is initiated by a contraction of the agonist, and the program turns it off; and finally, a contraction of the antagonist is initiated that brings the limb to a stop at the target. First, if the limb was shifted in its initial position before the movement began, according to the impulse-timing hypothesis the animal would have had to take this into account, because the program (if unaltered) would cause under- or overshooting of the target. Of course, the animal could not detect that the starting position was shifted, yet the limb achieved the correct position anyway. It is difficult to imagine how the impulse-timing hypothesis can explain this finding. Next, recall that even when the monkey's limb was shifted *past* the target position before the movement, the limb moved "backward" toward the target. The impulse-timing hypothesis holds that the limb is moved by a contraction of the agonist first, then of the antagonist, with this order of contraction being specified by the motor program. If so, then the initial movement should have been *away from* the target, not "backward" toward it. The equilibrium-point model of motor programming can explain these findings satisfactorily.

Experiments With Humans.   The studies just discussed warrant skepticism for a number of reasons. First, the experiments were conducted with animals, and it is not certain that these processes also operate in humans. Second, it is never perfectly clear that the deafferentation procedures actually prevented sensory information about the movement from reaching the brain. Bone-conducted vibrations from the movement can be sensed by parts of the body that are not deafferented, for example. Also, the monkey may have "known" where the limb was at the end of the previous move, because a juice reward was given for its being there. Finally, and perhaps most importantly, the monkeys may have adopted an equilibrium-point mode of control purely in response to the fact that Polit and Bizzi had deprived them of all their usual movement mechanisms. Is it possible that these mechanisms do not have any relevance for normal movement control, but have relevance only when other mechanisms cannot be used? Probably not, as a number of experiments with intact humans also support the equilibrium-point view.

Experiments with normal, intact humans also have been conducted to study equilibrium-point control (Schmidt, 1980; Schmidt & McGown, 1980). Subjects produced rapid elbow-flexion movements of a lever to a target in 150 ms. Occasionally, without the subject's being able to predict it, the load on the lever was changed before the movement, and the subject made the limb movement with the changed load conditions. In the first of these experiments, the lever movement was horizontal, and the lever mechanism itself would support the weight. The experimenters were interested in the constant errors in achieving the target on the normal trials (with expected weight) and on the switch trials, for which the weight was either added or subtracted unexpectedly.

Table 7.3 (top) shows the results from this experiment. When the mass was suddenly increased unexpectedly, the movement endpoint (the CE, or constant error) was nearly the same regardless of the load characteristics of the lever. The same was true in the mass-subtracted portion of the experiment. However, the MTs shifted considerably, being far longer when the mass was suddenly added and far shorter when the mass was suddenly subtracted. These results are consistent with the equilibrium-point view, as the movements arrived at the target even when the inertial characteristics of the lever were unexpectedly changed, with only the rate of approach to the target position being affected by the mass conditions.

However, these findings do not rule out the possibility that the limb moved to the target position by some kind of feedback process. After all, feedback channels were intact, and ample time was available to have made a spindle-based, or even RT-based, correction. But the next experiment raises considerable doubt that the subjects used feedback in this way. Here, the same experiment was done but with the lever movements made in the *vertical* plane rather than in the horizontal plane. The equilibrium-point model, in

---

Table 7.3   CE and MT Under "Normal" and "Switch" Conditions for Unidirectional Movements in the Horizontal and Vertical Planes

Horizontal: mass varied		Normal trials	Switch trials
Mass added	CE	+6.36°	+6.81°
	MT	187 ms	278 ms
Mass subtracted	CE	+5.78°	+6.28°
	MT	214 ms	180 ms
Vertical: mass varied		**Normal trials**	**Switch trials**
Mass added	CE	+15.82°	+10.40°
	MT	202 ms	243 ms
Mass subtracted	CE	+7.83°	+15.79°
	MT	196 ms	155 ms

(From Schmidt & McGown 1980.)

this case, predicts that the limb movement endpoint should be affected by the changed weight. Because the target position is achieved by programming an equilibrium point, according to this hypothesis the suddenly added weight will, because of gravity, tend to bias the equilibrium point downward; a suddenly subtracted weight will tend to shift the equilibrium point upward. Thus, the prediction is that the limb will undershoot the target when the weight is added and overshoot it when the weight is subtracted. This is quite different from the predictions for the horizontal-movement case, in which the equilibrium-point model predicts that no shift should occur in the movement endpoints (because gravity is not involved there).

The results of this second experiment are shown at the bottom of table 7.3. When the weight was added unexpectedly, the movement in the switch trials was about 5° shorter than in the normal trials. And when the weight was subtracted unexpectedly, the limb movement was approximately 8° longer than in the normal trials. (Contrast these shifts in endpoint to those shown in the horizontal experiment in the top portion of the table.) Large shifts in MT also occurred, with the added weight slowing the movement and the subtracted weight speeding it. Interestingly, a reflexive closed-loop model would predict that the movement should achieve its desired endpoint, because the limb system would simply move to the position that it "recognizes" as correct, and added weight should have no effect on the terminal location of the limb. Seeing such large shifts in limb endpoint in this experiment casts considerable doubt on the hypothesis that the limb in these rapid movements is positioned by some feedback mechanism. Like the results from the horizontal-movement portion of this experiment, these findings support the equilibrium-point view very well.

Finally, as with the work of Polit and Bizzi, these results fail to support an impulse-timing hypothesis, which predicts that the movement duration should be unaffected by the added or subtracted weight. This is so because the durations of the agonist burst, and the time of offset of this burst and then the onset of the antagonist burst, are determined in advance by the program. The prediction would be that the limb would come to a stop in the correct time but would fall short if the weight were added and overshoot if the weight were subtracted. Both experiments show a shift in MT that is contrary to the impulse-timing hypothesis.

Extensions of the Equilibrium-Point Models

Berkinblit, Feldman, and Fukson (1986) have proposed a very interesting model for sequential actions on the basis of the wiping reflex in the spinal frog (figure 6.7). They argue that this sequential action is really a *series* of approximately seven discrete positions. Each of these positions is achieved by specifying a sequence of equilibrium positions, and each of these positions is achieved exactly as in the equilibrium-point model. The mechanical characteristics of the muscles are responsible for the details of moving to each position from the former one. This model requires something like a central program to control when each of the separate equilibrium points is specified, and so this model tends to be a compromise between the equilibrium-point models and the motor program models (see also Feldman & Levin, 1995).

A recent theory of reaching does not question the validity of the equilibrium-point model, or the important differences between the α and λ versions of it, but rather uses it as a basis for arm trajectory (Rosenbaum et al., 1995, 1997). In this theory, reaching is an action that evolves from recalling a stored *posture* from memory, then specifying a movement trajectory. A posture that is stored in memory is represented as a set of joint positions, each described in terms of an equilibrium point. In this view, information about a remembered posture can be reduced to specifying relatively few degrees of freedom. The solution of arm trajectory planning is thus simplified because the retrieved posture reduces the number of near-optimal alternative trajectories that are available.

The work of Hollerbach (1978, 1981), in which he attempted to simulate handwriting through the use of various dynamical principles, provides another good example of this kind of modeling. Hollerbach conceptualized the muscles that make up the finger movements as springs. Here, muscles or groups of muscles move the finger up (toward the top of the page placed horizontally), down, left, and right, each group capable of being controlled independently, as modeled in figure 7.21. What happens if this system is put in motion? The system

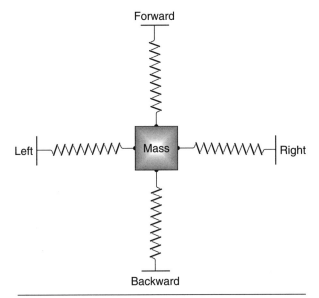

Figure 7.21. A mass-spring model for handwriting. (The forward-backward and right-left spring pairs oscillate to produce writing-like patterns.)

begins to oscillate because of the physical interactions of the springs and the mass that it is to move. If the mass is thrown in a diagonal direction and then released, it will oscillate in a curved path. And if the up-down and right-left springs are of different stiffness, the pattern can be made into an oval (a cycloid). All that is required to keep the mass oscillating is an occasional pulse of force delivered at the proper time in the sequence.

The important point about the Rosenbaum et al. and Hollerbach models is this: considering the well-known property of muscle to behave like a "complicated spring" allows one to explain how a complex trajectory can be achieved with a minimum of complexity in the motor planning (program) stage.

Limitations of the Equilibrium-Point Models

The evidence just presented, both from animals and from intact humans, certainly presents a favorable picture of the equilibrium-point model as one of the fundamental mechanisms in movement control. However, the support for this hypothesis comes from only one kind of movement—simple, unidirectional positioning tasks. To what extent is this kind of mechanism involved in movements that use more than one direction of a limb or in movements that involve more than one limb and that must be coordinated?

Schmidt and McGown (cited in Schmidt, 1980) and Schmidt et al. (1986) have investigated this problem with various kinds of movements. One of these studies used the same kind of apparatus and experimental design as just described for the single-direction moves, but the task involved a reversal in direction. The subject was to move in flexion, reverse the move, and extend the elbow past the starting position so that the time from the beginning of the initial flexion until the time the starting point was again reached was about 300 ms. The mass was unexpectedly added or subtracted from the lever exactly as described before. Of particular interest was where and when the movement reversal occurred under the normal and switch conditions.

The major results are shown in table 7.4. The reversal point was shorter in the movement when the mass was added and longer when the mass was unexpectedly subtracted. The equilibrium-point models would predict that this endpoint would be unaffected by the altered mass, just as it was in the unidirectional moves represented in table 7.3. That this result does not occur is interpreted as evidence against the equilibrium-point model for movements requiring a reversal in direction that must be timed. The impulse-timing model can explain these results by saying that the motor program "told" the agonist when to turn off and that the movement with added weight could not go as far in this fixed amount of time; thus the reversal point with added mass would be short of that in the normal trials.

It is fairly well accepted that the equilibrium-point model is the best account of how a joint achieves its *terminal* position, but there is considerable doubt whether these equilibrium-point models can account for the events that occur at the beginning of the movement. Recall that under the equilibrium model, a movement is created by suddenly shifting the equilibrium point, with the remainder of the movement being handled by mechanical properties of muscle. Other evidence suggests, however, that the trajectories produced in rapid movements are generated by processes somewhat more complicated than this (Atkeson & Hollerbach, 1985; Hollerbach & Flash, 1982). As well, the duration of the agonist electromyogram (EMG) burst is precisely *timed* according to the MT and distance goal of the overall movement (Schmidt et al., 1985; Wadman et al., 1979; Zelaznik, Schmidt, & Gielen, 1986). In particular, the α

Table 7.4   CE and MT for "Normal" and "Switch" Trials for the Reversal Movements in the Horizontal Plane

Horizontal: mass varied		Normal trials	Switch trials
Mass added	CE	28.3°	25.8°
	MT	139 ms	163 ms
Mass subtracted	CE	24.9°	28.6°
	MT	144 ms	123 ms

Note. CEs are in total distance to reversal because no target was used in this experiment. (From Schmidt 1980.)

model has difficulty in explaining the results of Wadman et al. (1979), in whose experiment the unexpected locking of the limb in the initial position nevertheless resulted in the agonist-antagonist-agonist EMG pattern. Since the limb never travels to the point at which the reflexes would shut off the agonist, this finding contradicts the α model's view regarding how EMGs are generated. Also, recall Polit and Bizzi's (1979) deafferentation experiments in which the monkey was rewarded for pointing at an unseen target by moving the elbow joint: if the *shoulder* joint was moved before the action, the overall pointing direction was grossly incorrect. Thus, the equilibrium-point model seemed capable of explaining how a single joint (here, the elbow) achieved a given angle, but it was not capable of accounting for the coordination of the movements among more than a single joint. The equilibrium-point view has several limitations in explaining complex movement behavior, but it seems to be the most effective model to date for explaining how a single joint is positioned accurately.

Correction Models of the Speed-Accuracy Trade-Off

To this point in our discussions about the theoretical basis for rapidly aimed movements, we have ignored the problem of how errors are corrected. However, from previous discussions we know that errors in centrally generated signals are bound to occur. The motor system is inherently "noisy," leading to variability in the generation of impulses or joint positions. Thus, theories describing how these error corrections occur have been important for a more complete understanding of the speed-accuracy trade-off.

The Crossman-Goodeve Model

At the 1963 meeting of the Experimental Psychology Society in England, Crossman and Goodeve presented a feedback-based explanation of Fitts' Law. They suggested that Fitts' Law could be derived mathematically, on the basis of feedback control in movement (with a number of assumptions), without the need to resort to ideas about information theory and motor noise as Fitts (1954) had done. This derivation with its associated argument was described in a more accessible form by Keele (1968) and reprinted in its entirety in 1983.

Crossman and Goodeve (1963/1983) assumed that movement toward a target is made up of two kinds of processes—much as Woodworth (1899) had proposed 50 years earlier—except that the ballistic, distance-covering phase and the feedback-controlled "homing-in" phase were thought to operate in *rapid alternation* during a movement to the target. This mode of control is termed *intermittent* (or *iterative*), and hence their idea has often been termed the iterative-correction model. The model, illustrated in figure 7.22, is based on the premise that a ballistic, distance-covering phase would operate for a *fixed* period of time, moving the limb a certain amplitude toward the target. This initial phase would have a spatial inaccuracy proportional to the distance that had been moved during that time. Then, feedback processes would evaluate the size and direction of the error and issue a second ballistic movement that would serve as a correction. This second movement would also have an error proportional to its (much shorter) distance; its error would be evaluated, another correction would be made, and so on until the movement reached the target. Thus, the model is based on

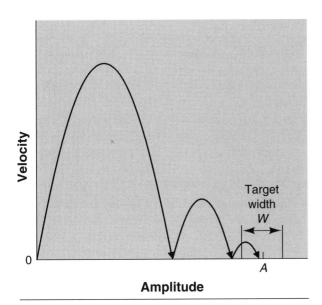

Figure 7.22. Crossman and Goodeve's (1963/1983) iterative-correction model of aiming.
Adapted from Meyer, Abrams, Kornblum, Wright, and Smith, 1988.

rapid alternation between ballistic movement processes and corrective processes during the course of the movement. The MT, which is the critical variable in the Fitts equation, was thought to be based on the *number* of corrective processes that had to be made to achieve the target.

Support for the Model

The number of corrections, and hence the MT, should be related to the amplitude and the target width. For a larger amplitude, the first ballistic movement would be longer and hence would have more error, requiring more subsequent corrections to achieve a target of a given size. For a smaller target width, more corrections would be required in order for the movement to land on the target. Combining these two factors resulted in the same mathematical derivation as Fitts' Law based on processes involving feedback, error detection, and error correction.

Keele (1968) used Crossman and Goodeve's basic idea and added to it the assumptions that the time between corrections was fixed at 190 ms (Keele & Posner, 1968; see chapter 5) and that the error in each movement was about 1/7 of the total distance moved in each correction. Keele argued that each of the corrections was processed in the stages of information processing, requiring attention, and that aimed movements were made up of a series of such corrections leading to the target. With use of these parameters, the Crossman-Goodeve model was found to provide a good

quantitative fit to some of the experimental data (Keele, 1981).

Criticisms of the Model

One major drawback to the Crossman-Goodeve model of rapid aiming movements composed of a series of successive corrections is related to the speed with which humans can process visual feedback. This was a major theme of chapter 5, and it is one of the most fundamental reasons for believing that very rapid movements must be planned in advance through motor programs. Another problem relates to the psychological refractory period: even though one such correction might be able to be made in 190 ms, it is doubtful that the second and third corrections could also be made this quickly (review psychological refractory period effects, chapter 4). These and other criticisms of the Crossman-Goodeve theory have been discussed in more detail in several publications (Schmidt, Zelaznik, & Frank, 1978; Schmidt et al., 1979; Meyer, Smith, & Wright, 1982; Meyer et al., 1988).

Perhaps the most persuasive argument against the Crossman-Goodeve theory was based on kinematic records of subjects' movement trajectories (Langolf, Chaffin, & Foulke, 1976). Transitions between one ballistic segment and the next could be seen as sudden changes in the position or velocity of the limb. Generally, most of the movements studied had one correction (a very few had two), although some had no visible corrections at all, even with MTs of 700 ms. These findings fail to support the hypothesis that a correction occurs every 190 ms in these actions.

Optimized-Submovement Models

One of the major problems with the Crossman-Goodeve model was that, in this formulation, a series of corrective actions *must* occur given the time constraints of the aimed movement. What would happen, for example, if by chance the executed aimed movement occurred exactly as programmed? According to the Crossman-Goodeve model, these (correctly) programmed movements would still undergo corrective processes. From the kinematic records of Langolf, Chaffin, and Foulke (1976) and others, however, it appears that some movements are not corrected at all.

The failure of the Crossman-Goodeve theory to handle these and other data has been addressed by Meyer et al. (1988, 1990) in what they termed the *optimized-submovement* model. Meyer et al. began with the idea that the initial segment of an aiming movement was handled by principles of impulse variability as described earlier in this chapter. But then they went on to describe how corrections can be applied to the trajectory after this initial movement to allow the limb to move accurately to a target. In effect, each correction is a new program that is governed by impulse-variability principles. This concept is similar to the hypothesis that Woodworth proposed in 1899, but it is made more concrete and experimentally testable by a number of additional assumptions concerning how many such corrections should be expected, and where and under what conditions they should be found in a movement as a function of various movement variables.

Dual-Submovement Model

In most aiming tasks, the processes involved in bringing the limb to the target can be described by two situations that are illustrated in figure 7.23. The first situation (middle curve in figure 7.23) occurs when the initial impulse (termed the *primary submovement*); solid lines in figure 7.23 indicate the target and the movement requires no correction. The other situation occurs when the initial impulse either undershoots or overshoots the target, requiring a corrective impulse (or *secondary submovement;* dashed lines in figure 7.23).

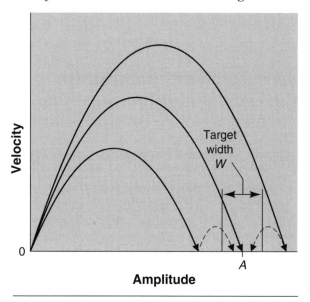

Figure 7.23. The optimized-submovement correction model.
Adapted from Meyer, Abrams, Kornblum, Wright, and Smith, 1988.

Total MT in an aiming task is considered to reflect a strategy whereby a subject attempts to trade off speed for accuracy by *optimizing* the duration of both the initial impulse and, if necessary, the correction. Thus, movement accuracy is achieved in a minimum MT by optimizing the control of the submovement(s)—a nice combination of some of the important open-loop and closed-loop processes that we have discussed in this chapter.

Multiple-Submovement Model

In general, the dual-submovement model fits the experimental data quite well (Meyer et al., 1988). However, Meyer et al. did find that corrections occurred more frequently than predicted under some combinations of target amplitude and width. In a revised version of the model, Meyer et al. (1990) made some additional assumptions to account for the fact that more than one corrective impulse could be made during an aimed movement. This multiple-submovement model was supported by a reanalysis of data from Meyer et al. (1988) using a different kinematic analysis protocol. This reanalysis confirmed that about 80% of all aimed movements were composed of two or three submovements (i.e., one or two corrections; 43% and 37%, respectively).

How Is a Correction Identified and Measured?

Although the Meyer et al. (1988, 1990) models provide a balanced, *hybrid* approach to the issue of open- and closed-loop processes, experimental examination of their theoretical predictions places a critical emphasis on the quantitative analysis of corrective submovements. As we have seen before, motor output processes are rather noisy, and often it is not clear how kinematic data (e.g., position, velocity, acceleration, or jerk) best discriminate between corrections and motor noise. Various techniques have been used to objectify kinematic data, but it is beyond the scope of the present discussion to describe these analytical techniques (cf. Carlton, 1979; Chua & Elliott, 1993; Langolf, Chaffin, & Foulke, 1976; Meyer et al., 1988; Pratt & Abrams, 1996). Regardless of the criteria used, arguments can be raised that the measurement techniques are either too conservative or too liberal, resulting in underestimates or overestimates of the number of corrections made in a trial. Since support for these models depends on the quantitative analysis of submovement processes, the empirical validation of these analytical techniques represents one avenue for further study.

Summary

Three types of speed-accuracy trade-offs were described in this chapter. The earliest formal mathematical statement of this relationship was proposed over 40 years ago by Fitts and is called *Fitts' Law* in his honor. It says that in reciprocal movements, the average MT is linearly related to the Log$_2$ of the ratio of the movement amplitude and the target width. This principle holds for a wide variety of movement situations and types of subjects, and is considered one of the corner-stones of motor control.

Force and force variability are strongly related to each other, with the relationship being essentially linear until forces of about 65% of the subject's maximum are achieved. The force variability levels off or decreases with further increases in force toward the subject's maximum. The laws about MT variability and force variability have been combined into various *impulse-variability* models for rapid limb movement accuracy: the prediction is that the variability of a movement's initial impulse is linearly related to the ratio of the movement amplitude and the MT (A/MT), or average velocity.

An analysis of laws of movement timing shows that as the MT is decreased, an increase occurs in movement-timing consistency. This is in addition to the effect of movement velocity, whereby movement-timing consistency is increased as velocity is increased. These two effects combined imply that more rapid movements in timing tasks lead to increased temporal consistency, contrary to ideas about the spatial speed-accuracy trade-off.

Many aiming movements are influenced by central (programmed) mechanisms and/or closed-loop, corrective actions. Impulse-variability principles describe how programmed impulses affect the trajectory of an aimed limb movement. A different view is suggested by the *equilibrium-point* model, which holds that the limb moves to a position defined by an equilibrium point between the opposing muscles spanning a joint, and that the movement to this position is dependent on the springlike characteristics of the muscles. Such a model is different from an impulse-timing mechanism whereby the amounts of force, as well as the times over which they are applied, are controlled by the motor program.

Early explanations for Fitts' Law were based on *intermittent-control* models, in which the commands for action were produced alternately with the analysis of feedback to determine movement corrections. Several lines of evidence, however, suggest that the intermittent-control model is incorrect. More acceptable views indicate that the timing of an open-loop, distance-covering phase and later correction(s) is *optimized* in some way in order to idealize the inconsistency in the distance-covering phase as the forces applied to the limb are increased.

Notes

[1] Schmidt is very appreciative of this honor. However, given that most laws are "awarded" posthumously, he is reluctant to make that sacrifice.

[2] The analysis of impulses described here is simplified considerably in order to give an overview of impulse-variability modeling. Space here does not permit a discussion of the numerous assumptions underlying the analyses of impulse variability; for a more complete treatment, see Schmidt et al. (1985), Schmidt, Zelaznik, and Frank (1978), or Schmidt et al. (1979).

[3] These effects are not precisely as predicted by the model, however. For example, changing A does change VE$_t$ slightly, and changing MT does change W_e slightly, in both cases because of the effects of velocity discussed earlier (figure 7.9; Newell, Carlton, & Kim, 1994; Newell et al., 1979, 1980). The model needs adjustment in this regard.

[4] It appears that a similar (though generally unacknowledged) view was presented somewhat earlier by Crossman and Goodeve (1963/1983). Their equilibrium-point model has probably been overlooked because it was presented at a conference and not published in more accessible form until 20 years later.

COORDINATION

At one level, we seem to be able to produce coordinated actions easily, almost trivially. We perform countless activities in which the effectors produce different actions at the same time, seemingly without any interference among the limbs at all (e.g., using a knife and fork; playing piano; walking and chewing gum). In tasks like throwing and kicking, the limbs perform very different functions and movements, all without difficulty. Yet at another level, the laboratory data (and a few everyday examples) suggest remarkable interference between the effectors under some conditions. Well-known cases involve the task of patting one's head while rubbing one's stomach, where both hands tend to produce either rubbing or patting actions, but not different actions. Other examples come from Peters (1977), who showed that not one of 100 subjects was able to recite a nursery rhyme with proper rhythm while tapping a 1-3-123 rhythm. Summers, Todd, and Kim (1993) provide further evidence about difficulties in tapping different rhythms with the two hands (producing so-called polyrhythms). These and many other observations suggest the existence of barriers to interlimb coordination that are likely to support genetically defined—and biologically important—activities such as locomotion, but that tend to impede more arbitrary, yet culturally important (piano playing, throwing) or unimportant (rubbing and patting the head and stomach skills that require other patterns of coordination).

It has been recognized for several decades now (e.g., for reviews, see Heuer, 1996; Klapp, 1979, 1981) that a major source of interference in interlimb coordination seems to be related to the temporal structure(s) of the actions being coordinated. Actions with the same temporal organization are easily coordinated, with a tight temporal relationship between the limbs, whereas activities with different temporal organizations are not easily produced, if they can be produced at all. There is clearly more to coordination than this, however, as will be seen in the variety of tasks and means by which researchers have attempted to study the fundamental problems of coordination. One important factor in coordination is the duration of the movements being controlled, and we have organized this chapter by considering the coordination of discrete and continuous tasks in separate sections.

In chapter 2, we distinguished between discrete and continuous tasks in terms of their beginning and end points. Discrete tasks, such as turning on a light switch or swinging a golf club, have definitive start and end points. In contrast, the start and end of continuous tasks, such as running and driving, are rather arbitrary or context dependent. Continuous activities involve different durations each time you do them.

The difference between continuous and discrete tasks in the study of motor control is not trivial. Discrete tasks are often performed quite rapidly (although not necessarily so) and, with these kinds of tasks, considerable theoretical importance is placed on the motor program in preparing the body to move. In contrast, the role of premovement planning is less important for continuous movements, and other factors such as feedback, error detection, and error correction play a more dominant role.

The understanding of coordination represents different challenges for discrete and continuous tasks, and we will describe their study in separate sections of this chapter. However, keep in mind that the problems encountered in coordinating movements in discrete and continuous tasks share similarities. The most prominent of these is the *degrees of freedom* problem (Bernstein, 1967): given that there are more independently moving parts of the body than can be controlled individually, how is the system able to perform actions that so beautifully coordinate these parts? The study of coordination in both discrete and continuous tasks points to some fundamental, yet distinct, principles regarding how the degrees of freedom problem is solved.

Discrete Tasks

The focus of discussion in the previous chapter was the principles by which limb movements, primarily aiming movements, achieved a target with minimum time and maximum accuracy. Although there we referred to principles of "simple" movements, in reality these movements are far from simple. The following sections also describe aimed movements, but here the focus instead is on the kinds of organization that must underlie these apparently "simple" movements.

Eye-Head-Hand Coordination

In chapters 5 and 7 we presented evidence that many tasks involving aiming, including reaching and grasping actions, rely on visual feedback in order to maximize movement endpoint accuracy. Visual feedback information is most precise for this kind of task when the eyes can fixate on the target or object for a significant length of time prior to manual contact (e.g., Abrams, Meyer, & Kornblum, 1990). When a target occurs unpredictably, the localization of the target or object to be contacted must be fixated as rapidly as possible in order to provide sufficient time to *process* the visual information. How is coordination among the eyes, head, and hand achieved in this situation?

Early work with monkeys revealed the existence of a tight relationship between the head and eyes (Bizzi, 1974). Figure 8.1 illustrates five trials in which an unexpected target appears in the periphery of the visual field. From a starting position in which the monkey's eyes and head are pointed straight ahead, the tracings in figure 8.1a reveal that, after a reaction-time latency period, the eyes initially make a rapid *saccade* to fixate the target on the fovea. Movements of the head are initiated at the same time as those of the

eyes, but are much slower, as can be seen in figure 8.1b. As the head moves in the direction of the target, the eyes rotate in a direction opposite to the movement of the head. The timing of the opposing motions of the eyes and head is tightly coordinated, so that the target remains fixated on the fovea. The existence of this coordination between the eyes and head has been known for a long time and is called the *vestibulo-ocular reflex*. In the case of rapid looking, the saccade makes it possible for a quick identification of the unexpected visual signal, and the counterrotation of eyes while the head is turning maintains the fixation.

A similar relationship among the eyes, head, and hand appears to exist when a manual action is required. Biguer, Jeannerod, and Prablanc (1982) found that the onset of eye movements occurs almost simultaneously with initiation activity of electromyogram signals in the arm and neck. This temporal coordination among the eye, head, and limb movements is quite flexible, however, as individual differences are high either when instruc-

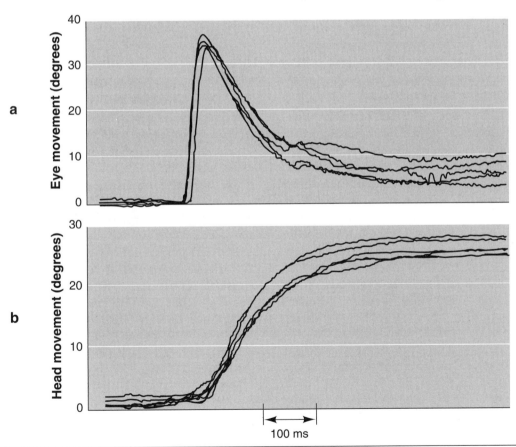

Figure 8.1.   Rotation of the eyes (a) and head (b) during rapid looking at a target.
Reprinted from Bizzi, 1974.

tions do not constrain movement strategies (Abrams, Meyer, & Kornblum, 1990) or when instructions emphasize either movement speed or accuracy (Carnahan, 1992; Carnahan & Marteniuk, 1991). In addition to the temporal relationship among eye, head, and limb movements, there is also a *spatial* facilitation when these degrees of freedom interact. Manual aiming accuracy is better when the head is free to move than when head position is fixed (Biguer, Prablanc, & Jeannerod, 1984; Vercher et al., 1994). It remains unclear, however, whether the advantage is due to a head movement facilitation or an immobilization decrement.

Units of Action

Rapid actions (e.g., with movement times [MTs] of less than a few seconds) seem to be controlled by a pattern of neuromuscular activity that is largely organized in advance. Of course, this is the essential feature of the theory of motor programs described in chapter 6. While many have debated the relative size of the central versus peripheral contributions, it seems incontrovertible that at least some fundamental features of the action are specified in advance.

The principles of simple movements discussed in chapter 7 involved actions in which the primary goal was to move an effector from one location to another. Dialing a telephone number or using a keyboard are examples of this type of action. However, there are other, related actions that have a more complex organization, involving serial and/or parallel coordination of different actions. For example, a computer mouse enables the user to move a cursor on a screen to a target, at which time a click (or double click) of a button on the mouse initiates the icon's function. Here, one action must be completed *before* another action can be performed. If we consider an action that is somewhat longer in duration and greater in complexity, however, such as serving a tennis ball or shifting gears in a car, it is difficult to claim that such longer sequences are completely controlled by single programs. Nevertheless, it is possible that such actions are composed of a string of programs (each lasting 200–300 ms, or more).

Furthermore, each of these programs might be thought of as a *unit of action*—a "piece" of behavior that can be utilized repeatedly in various actions, producing essentially the same movements (but scaled to the environment) each time. For example, we might think of shifting gears in a car as composed of three units: (1) gas up/clutch down; (2) shift lever up-over-up; and (3) gas down/clutch up. (A race car driver might perform this task as one unit.) And a given unit could be observed in other actions; a clutch-down/gas-up unit could be involved in both a gear change from first to second and a gear change from second to third, while another unit (shift-lever movements) would be different in the two actions. In the next section, we present one possible way to identify such units of behavior, based on motor program concepts.

Identification of Units

The underlying idea for the identification of units is based on the notion of generalized motor programs (GMPs), discussed in chapter 6. To review, the GMP is a program with invariant (a) sequencing among muscles, (b) relative timing, and (c) relative forces among the contractions. Superficial features such as overall movement duration and movement size are controlled by parameters that scale (linearly, in this simple view) the surface expression of the GMP's output, yet allow it to retain its invariant structure or pattern.

An invariance in relative timing predicts that the correlations among the times of various temporal events (or "landmarks") in an action should approach 1.0. Now, if we turn the argument around, if an invariance in relative timing happens to be found for a sequence of behavior (i.e., the correlations among landmarks happen to be very close to 1.0), such evidence would be consistent with the hypothesis that a GMP produced that behavior.

Now, consider a longer movement. Suppose that times of the first several landmarks in the movement intercorrelate highly, but that the time of a later landmark does not correlate with any of them. One interpretation would be that the first set of landmarks was governed by a GMP (because relative timing was approximately invariant there) but the latter was not (because the invariance was no longer present). It could be the other way around, with the group of highly related landmarks being located at the end of the movement, perhaps with all these landmarks being unrelated to a landmark at the start.

This provides the essential idea for the identification of units. A unit is a sequence of behavior with essentially invariant relative timing—that is, it has high correlations among the times of component landmarks. When later landmarks of the action no longer share this invariance (i.e., they do not correlate with landmarks in the earlier portions), this indicates that the first unit has ended, or that there is some sort of boundary between it and the next unit.

Methods in Unit Identification

Schneider and Schmidt (1995; also Young & Schmidt, 1990, 1991) asked subjects to learn a coincident-timing task in which a moving object (simulated by a series of lights) had to be "struck" with a handheld lever. After the light illumination began (duration = 1.2 s), the subject made a small preparatory movement to the right, then a backswing to the left, and then a striking movement back to the right (with a follow-through), with the goal of "hitting" the passing target light with the lever.

Various kinematic landmarks (shown as points A, B, C, . . . , H in figure 8.2) were defined as maxima, minima, or zero crossings (except point G, the point at which the lever reached the target) taken from the position-, velocity-, and acceleration-time records (see chapter 2 on kinematic methods). The time at which each of these events occurred was measured

for a series of trials, and the within-subject (over trials) correlations among all of the possible pairs of landmark times were computed. A useful examination involved the correlation of the first landmark with the second, with the third, and so on (A-B, A-C, A-D, . . . , A-H), as well as the correlations between the last landmark (H) and all possible earlier landmarks (A-H, B-H, C-H, etc.).

If the entire action is governed by a single unit, then these correlations should all be relatively high, as all intervals would be scaled proportionally in time. The correlations are shown in figure 8.3. On the left, the correlations are high among the intervals A-B, A-C, and A-D but are low with later intervals. But at the right, the intervals F-H and G-H are highly related, and are not related to earlier intervals. These data suggest that this action has two identifiable units of action, one containing landmarks A-D, and the other containing landmarks F-H, with a boundary between them (from landmark D to F).

The functioning of these units can perhaps be more easily seen in the acceleration-time traces in figure 8.4, where six movements are overlaid.

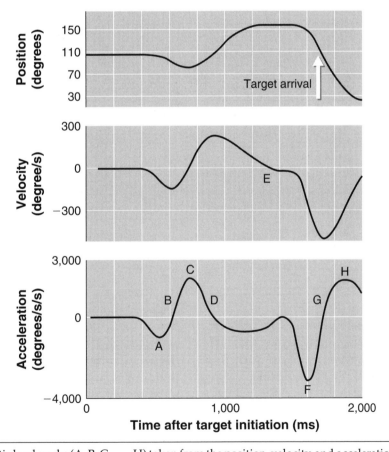

Figure 8.2.   Kinematic landmarks (A, B, C, . . . , H) taken from the position, velocity, and acceleration profiles of an action are used to search for specific units of action.
Reprinted from Schneider and Schmidt, 1995.

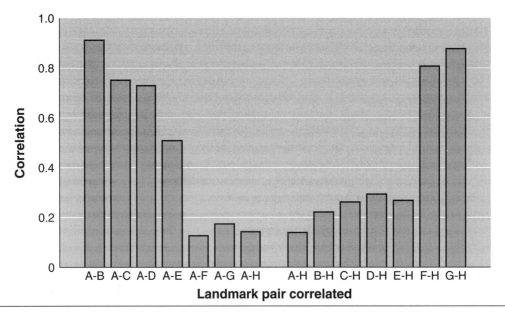

Figure 8.3.   Correlations of the first landmark (A) with later landmarks (left side); correlations of the last landmark (H) with earlier landmarks (right side).
Reprinted from Schneider and Schmidt, 1995.

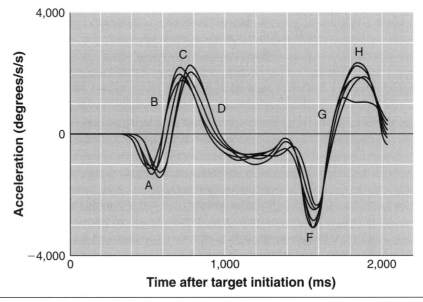

Figure 8.4.   The crossing-over of six acceleration-time traces reveals evidence of a second unit of action after landmark D.
Reprinted from Schneider and Schmidt, 1995.

Notice that the traces are all of the same general form (but adjusted with respect to each other in time) for the first portions of the action (A-D, up to about 1,000 ms); the same is true for those in the last part of the action (F-H). However, the traces lose their common form at about 1,000 to 1,400 ms, with the traces crossing over each other. This period of time is, according to this analysis, the boundary between units. At this time, the subject has completed the first action (the initial backswing) and is preparing to time the initiation

of the forward swing to strike the moving object. Notice also that the first unit (A through D) actually contains two backswing movements (right, then left; see figure 8.4), indicating that this unit is organized across at least two limb movements. These general methods have been used in several real-world tasks; for example, researchers in one study analyzed the unit structure involved in lighting a butane cigarette lighter, identifying three sequential elements (Schmidt et al., 1996).

Reach/Grasp Actions

A different type of unimanual coordination has been studied in the situation in which limb transport ends in *grasping* an object. The composite photograph in figure 8.5 nicely illustrates this action—the functional *aperture* (separation of the thumb and fingers) of the grasping hand opens *during* transport of the hand to the target. The hand does not "wait" and open once it reaches the target, as might be revealed by a units analysis as described in the previous section. Rather, the hand reaches its maximum aperture well before object contact. Thus, the phrase "reach and grasp" seems to be a misnomer—it is actually a well-coordinated "reach/grasp action."

Kinematic details of the reach/grasp components indicate that the attainment of maximum grasp aperture correlates well with the beginning of a low-velocity phase of hand transport during moving toward the object (Jeannerod, 1984). As anticipated by Fitts' Law (chapter 7), MT is related to the width of the object to be picked up (Bootsma et al., 1994; Marteniuk et al., 1990). Of more importance here is that the kinematics of both the reach and grasp components

are related to object width as well. The open squares in figure 8.6 reveal that the time after peak deceleration accounts for all of the increase in MT as the size of the object decreases, suggesting that this part of the transport component was being altered to prepare the grasping component for object capture. As well, the time to attain maximum grasp aperture is achieved sooner for smaller objects (open circles in figure 8.6). This temporal coordination of the transport and grasp components reflects the time needed to achieve the more precise homing-in action in order to grasp the smaller disks (Marteniuk et al., 1990).

As noted by Wing, Turton, and Fraser (1986), research is not necessary to show that arm movements and hand shaping *can be* performed independently, as each action can be done in the absence of the other. When the two are performed together, though, the evidence suggests that reaching and grasping are *not* independently controlled actions. Rather, there is a temporal organization that serves to get the hand in the general vicinity of the target and to prepare it for object capture or manipulation. Researchers have used a number of methods to examine these two cooperative activities. The most com-

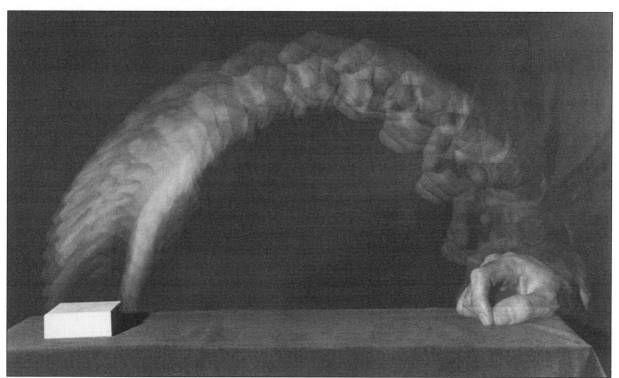

Figure 8.5. Composite photograph of the reach/grasp action.
Reprinted from Goodale and Servos, 1996.

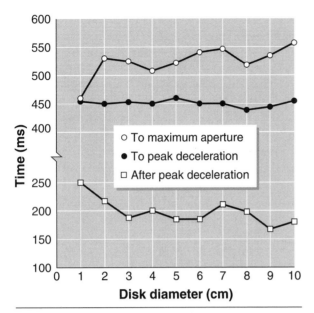

Figure 8.6.   Kinematics of the reach/grasp action during picking up of disks of different diameters.
Reprinted from Marteniuk, Leavitt, MacKenzie, and Athenes, 1990.

mon method involves a *perturbation* during the action, such as an unexpected change in the location of the object (Gentilucci et al., 1992; Paulignan, MacKenzie, Marteniuk, & Jeannerod, 1991), in the size of the object (Castiello, Bennett, & Stelmach, 1993; Paulignan, Jeannerod, MacKenzie, & Marteniuk, 1991), in the spatial orientation of the object (Desmurget et al., 1996), or a mechanical perturbation of the moving limb itself (Haggard & Wing, 1995). In general, these studies demonstrate that any sudden change in either the perceptual or effector attributes of the action will result in a *reorganization* of both the reach and grasp components: the coordinated component parts of the action are not reorganized independently (for further discussion see Goodale & Servos, 1996; Jeannerod & Marteniuk, 1992).

The grasp and manipulation of an object also appear to involve a highly coordinated activity. In the section on triggered reactions in chapter 5, we discussed Johansson and Westling's (1984) "wineglass effect," in which the slight slippage of a grasped object through the fingers triggered (without conscious involvement) an increased grip force, with a latency of only 30 ms or so. However, together with this increase in grip force, the subjects also produced a closely coordinated decrease in the force in the elbow flexor muscles, presumably to slow the rate of lift to decrease slipping and to ensure that the overall goal of the movement (to lift without dropping) was achieved. Also, when

surfaces of different roughness were used (silk, suede, or sandpaper), the subjects readily adopted a pattern of coordination between grip force and lifting force, with the ratio of the two (grip force/lifting force) being systematically larger as the roughness decreased. When the roughness was unexpectedly changed on a trial, the subjects adopted a new pattern of coordination consistent with the new roughness within about 100 ms (see also Cadoret & Smith, 1996).

Bimanual Coordination

Using the two hands together represents a different type of coordination than the type we have just examined. Sometimes the hands perform similar actions (e.g., lifting a baby from the crib; swinging an ax), and sometimes the two actions are different (e.g., holding a bottle with one hand and twisting the cap with the other; using a fork with one hand to stabilize a piece of food while using a knife to cut it with the other hand). How the control of one hand interacts with the control of the other hand while both are moving at the *same time* represents a fundamental problem in movement coordination.

The Fitts Paradigm Revisited

As discussed in chapter 7, the movement distance and the size of the target to which the limb is aimed are strong determiners of MT—a relationship identified most commonly with Fitts' Law. However, this relationship was based on experiments in which only one limb was moving. What happens to MT when two limbs are moved? And more importantly, what happens to MT when the task parameters assigned to the two limbs are different? These questions were addressed in experiments by Robinson and Kavinsky (1976) and more thoroughly by Kelso, Southard, and Goodman (1979). Subjects in the Kelso, Southard, and Goodman study made aiming movements of the two hands whereby each limb moved to a separate target as rapidly as possible. Two target conditions were used. In one condition, the subject moved a short distance to a large target—an "easy" task as defined by Fitts' index of difficulty (ID = 0.8; see chapter 7). In another condition, the task was to move a far distance to a small target, resulting in a much more difficult task (ID = 3.7).

Fitts' Law predicts that the MT for the easy task will be much less than the MT for the difficult task. And this was the result for conditions in which only one limb was moving (i.e., *unimanual* conditions). However, what was the effect on MT when both limbs were assigned an aiming task (i.e., bimanual conditions)? The answer is that it depended on which task was examined. For the more difficult task, the ID was the primary determinant of MT: the target was reached in about the same time (average of 147 ms) regardless of whether the limb moved to the difficult task unimanually, or together with a limb that moved with an "easy" ID or with the same, "difficult" ID. In contrast, the MT for a limb moving to an easy task *changed* depending on the task conditions. The MT was 98 ms in the unimanual conditions. In bimanual conditions, MT for this easy task was slightly slower when the limb moved together with a limb that moved to a target of the same difficulty (105 ms); MT slowed even more (to 130 ms) when the limb movement was paired with that of a limb moving to the difficult task. Also, kinematic analyses indicated that the two hands tended to be "locked" together, in that the time of maximum height of the hand, the time to peak acceleration, the shapes of the trajectories, and so forth were remarkably similar for the two hands.

These findings were replicated by Fowler et al. (1991), who used procedures identical to those of Kelso, Southard, and Goodman (experiment 3) and added another aiming condition in which the task was even more difficult (ID = 5.2). However, in both the Kelso, Southard, and Goodman and the Fowler et al. studies it is important to note that the bimanual MTs for the easy task remained conspicuously *less* than the MTs for the more difficult tasks (see also Corcos, 1984; Marteniuk, MacKenzie, & Baba, 1984). The MTs did not become the same, as might be expected if these limbs were somehow "locked" together in a strict temporal coordination. Thus, it is probably appropriate to conclude that the limb that moved to the more difficult task exerted a *strong determining influence* on the other limb.

This conclusion is supported by the results of a variant of this rapid bimanual task paradigm. Subjects moved both hands the same distance and to the same-sized target, but a cardboard *hurdle* was placed between the start location and the target for one of the limbs only, so that one limb had to move with a higher trajectory than the other to get to the target (Goodman,

Kobayashi, & Kelso, 1983; Kelso, Putnam, & Goodman, 1983). In the Goodman, Kobayashi, and Kelso study, the height of the hurdle was systematically varied from 0 cm (no hurdle) to 40 cm. The MT findings are presented in figure 8.7. As expected, the MT of the limb going over the hurdle increased markedly with increased height of the hurdle. A steady increase in the MT for the limb that had *no hurdle* present was found as well. Once again, however, it is important to note that the increasing MTs of the no-hurdle limb were not synchronized with the increasing MTs of the limb that had to go over a hurdle. The disparity between the MTs of the limbs with and without a hurdle increased with hurdle height, as can be seen by comparing, from left to right, the filled and open circles in figure 8.7.

Spatial Coordination

In both the studies just discussed (Goodman, Kobayashi, & Kelso, 1983; Kelso, Putnam, & Goodman, 1983), the effect of the hurdle on the no-hurdle limb was also seen in the kinematic analyses of the movement trajectories. The trajectory required in order for the limb to clear the hurdle was accompanied by a *similar* tendency in the no-hurdle limb, although the *bias* imposed by the hurdle limb on the no-hurdle limb did not result in a mirror-image mapping of the two limbs.

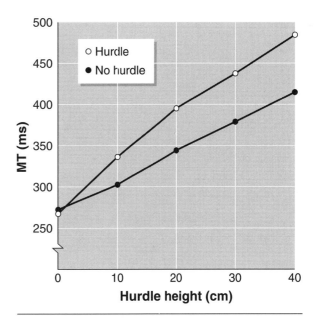

Figure 8.7.   MTs for two limbs. The two limbs are moving simultaneously toward targets of equal difficulty, but only one limb must go over a hurdle that varies in height.

Spatial-coordination effects have also been found in a number of other experimental paradigms. Instead of varying target widths (the Fitts task), Marteniuk, MacKenzie, and Baba (1984) required their subjects to move as rapidly and as closely as possible to a small target point and measured the effective target width (W_e in Schmidt et al., 1979). Of interest here were the between-hand spatial-assimilation effects, indexed by constant error (chapter 2), when the two hands were required to move to targets of different distances. Marteniuk, MacKenzie, and Baba found that a limb tended to overshoot a short target when the other limb moved to a far target; they also observed a small tendency for a limb to undershoot a far target when paired with a limb moving to a short target. Experiments by Sherwood (1991, 1994) suggest that these spatial-assimilation effects are due to the disparity in distances required of the two hands, suggesting that the *force output* of the limb moving the lesser distance was biased by the greater force output required to move the other limb a farther distance.

In all these tasks, the problem was to produce the same action in the two hands, but with different amounts of distance or slightly different trajectories. The timing of the major force-pulses or reversals in direction is nearly identical in the two hands. In terms of motor programming views, the two limbs could have been controlled by the same program, but with different parameters assigned to each of the limbs. These results suggest an interlimb interference in terms of the assigned parameters. One question that arises is whether such assimilation would occur when the tasks require different movement programs.

Swinnen, Walter, and their colleagues have examined these patterns of interference in tasks that required the upper limbs to perform two completely different patterns at the same time (e.g., Swinnen, Walter, & Shapiro, 1988; Walter & Swinnen, 1990)—that is, in tasks for which a given program in the right hand could not have been simply scaled to produce the required action in the left hand. Walter and Swinnen (1990) had

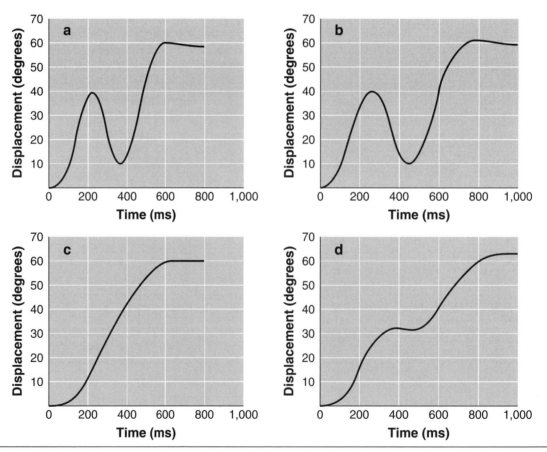

Figure 8.8. Bimanual coordination effects for limbs with different displacement-time goals; two-reversal task (a and b), unidirectional movement (c and d), unimanual performance (a and c), bimanual performance (b and d).
Adapted from Walter and Swinnen, 1990.

subjects produce a movement with two reversals in direction with one hand and a unidirectional movement in the other hand. When these 800-ms actions were done separately, they produced the traces shown in figure 8.8, a and c. But when the subjects were asked to produce the two actions simultaneously, the pattern of the hand performing the complex movement could be detected in the action of the hand doing the simple movement, although the amount of interference was not sufficient to make the hands produce identical movements (figure 8.8, b and d). The patterns of forces in the two hands occurred at essentially the same time, as if the pattern of contractions in the complex-movement hand were somehow overflowing to the simpler hand action. Furthermore, there appeared to be a greater interference when the left hand performed the complex task and the right hand produced the simple task; adding load to the complex-movement hand tended to increase this bias, and practice reduced the interference. Several other intriguing findings have emerged from this paradigm (see Walter, Swinnen, & Franz, 1993, for a review).

These authors have discussed their results in terms of what they call structural and metrical *coupling* between the two hands, with practice serving to uncouple, or *dissociate,* the actions of the hands (e.g., Swinnen, 1992; Walter & Swinnen, 1992). How this uncoupling occurs, though, is not entirely clear. One possibility is that independent control of each hand is acquired through the development of separate motor programs. Another possibility is that some different form of *interdependence* emerges with practice—which now allows the hands to do different things at the same time. Several studies recently have provided hints about the nature of this interdependence, based on the idea that a single motor program is developed that coordinates the interdependence.

Heuer, Schmidt, and Ghodsian (1995; also Schmidt et al., in press) have recently studied movement performances in another situation: here the two hands produce deliberately different patterns, but these patterns are rapid and discrete, and considerable practice is provided. Evidence supports the view that the two hands can be controlled as a single unit (i.e., by a single GMP, as discussed earlier here), even though the two limbs are producing completely different spatial-temporal patterns.

The seated subjects moved two horizontal levers with elbow flexion-extension movements to produce particular space-time patterns that differed for each limb. The right arm produced a flexion-extension-flexion pattern through about 70°, while the left arm simultaneously produced a flexion-extension pattern through about 60°, with MTs ranging from 400 to 600 ms. Subjects had considerable difficulty at first, but after several hundred trials they were able to produce the actions very easily. In fact, subjects became able to speed up or slow down this entire bimanual pattern on command, tending to change the left- and right-hand speed together. But when instructed to produce the hand movements at different speeds (e.g., speed the right hand and slow the left), subjects found this variant nearly impossible to do (Schmidt et al., in press).

From the acceleration-time traces, Schmidt et al. (in press) defined 12 landmarks, essentially as had been done in the analysis of units described earlier. The within-subject (across trials) correlations among all possible pairs of landmarks were then computed. For the hands taken separately, the correlations among the landmarks were generally very high, averaging .91 (right) and .94 (left) when the actions were done as quickly as possible (Schmidt et al., in press). The relatively high correlations among all of the landmarks suggested a one-unit pattern for each hand, as discussed earlier here.

The interesting point for coordination, however, concerns the correlations among the landmarks between the hands. These correlations were also generally very high, especially when the actions were very rapid, and were nearly the same as those for the individual hands (mean = .91). These data imply that the right and left hands were being scaled together in time so that relative timing in the action (both within and between hands) was essentially invariant. Therefore, the right and left hands were part of the same unit of action, on the basis of the logic of units presented earlier. If so, then this pattern of coordination involves control of the hands by the *same* GMP. Apparently, when the two hands do different things at the same time, this does not necessarily mean that they are operating independently.[1]

Continuous Tasks

Try this little experiment, using a blackboard and two pieces of chalk. First, try to write your name with your nondominant hand, at usual speed but moving in the direction opposite to normal (i.e., producing a mirror image of your name). You will probably find that this is very difficult to do and that the pattern is barely legible. Now do the same task again, but this time do it simultaneously with the dominant hand writing normally, so that the hands are writing in opposite directions. You should find that the pattern of the nondominant hand is much smoother and that the two patterns are roughly similar (but mirror images of each other). More importantly, as you perform the two-hand task, notice how the two limbs seem to be "locked" together, as if they were controlled by the same structure. Even though the nondominant handwriting is somewhat more uncontrolled than the dominant, a characteristic pattern still emerges—the same loops, straight parts, and so on. This is an example of a phenomenon that has been known for over a century but has only recently become a topic of renewed research interest.

Early Research

Bimanual coordination of continuous tasks in humans has been an interest of researchers for well over a century (see the boxed text on page 217). For example, right-handed subjects in Langfeld's (1915) experiment tapped one finger as rapidly as possible for 30 s—either the index or middle finger of the right or left hand. Between-finger differences on the same hand were small, but between-hand differences were large: average MTs for the right-hand taps were 181 ms compared with 222 ms for the left hand. This is not too surprising, as many asymmetries in performance are found when one compares the left and right hands of right-handed people (e.g., Elliott & Roy, 1996). However, on some trials, subjects were asked to tap with fingers on both hands such that the taps were made *simultaneously* and as fast as possible. In these bimanual conditions, subjects tapped either with the same finger on both hands (e.g., the right and left index finger) or with different fingers on each hand (e.g., the right index finger and the left middle finger). The average MT for the same-finger condition was 208 ms, which represents a 27-ms *decrement* for the right finger (compared to unimanual tapping) but a 14-ms *facilitation* for the left hand. These facilitation effects were restricted to only the same-finger conditions, however, as

the MT for the bimanual tapping of different fingers was 219 ms. Langfeld (1915) thus showed that in the process of becoming coordinated, the temporal, "independent behavior" of the two hands changed dramatically: the timing of the two hands became much more interdependent.

The struggle between the tendency of one oscillating limb to maintain its independent motor behavior (termed the *maintenance tendency* by von Holst (1937/1973) and the tendency of its behavior to become interdependent with the other oscillating limb (which von Holst called the *magnet effect*) captures the critical feature of temporal coordination of continuous skills. As we will see in the next sections, these strong natural tendencies play an important role in the coordination of actions.

Gait Transitions in Animals

One question that has intrigued researchers regarding coordination concerns the transition between gait patterns in four-legged animals. In chapter 6 we discussed the Shik preparation on cats. Walking could be initiated in spinalized cats by stimulating their limbs on a treadmill. One important finding was that increases in the speed of the treadmill induced changes from a walk to a trot, and occasionally to a gallop. Although the animal could not feel its legs while in locomotion, these specific gait patterns, and more importantly, the qualitative change from one gait to another, still occurred on occasion.

On what basis does an animal select a particular speed within each gait, and what determines *when* the animal will change gaits? One line of thinking is that gait selection and the decision to change gaits are both based on *energy demands*. Consider the analysis of a horse's gaits in figure 8.9 (Hoyt & Taylor, 1981). The histograms in the bottom half of figure 8.9 indicate that the speeds that a horse spontaneously selects when walking, trotting, and galloping represent a rather small subset of the total range of speeds that the horse could select within each of the gaits. Taking this analysis further, Hoyt and Taylor measured the energy cost (defined in terms of oxygen consumption) of horses trained to walk, trot, and gallop at different speeds on a treadmill (sometimes at energy-inefficient speeds). The data in the top half of figure 8.9 suggest that the energy

Woodworth on Coordination

Much of the current work on coordination has its roots in monographs that were not available in English until quite some time after their original publication. Some of these works were eventually translated and published in their entirety (e.g., Bernstein, 1967; von Holst, 1937/1973). In other cases, researchers have made us aware of important, nontranslated works (e.g., Heuer, 1996; Worringham, 1992). Another source for this 19th-century work on coordination, a brief review published in French by Woodworth (1903), has not to our knowledge been previously translated into English. A comparison of the quoted passages to some of the "modern" work on coordination will reveal some remarkable early insights regarding spatial and temporal coordination, which became a dormant issue in research for quite some time. According to Woodworth (1903):

"It is common knowledge that one can execute with ease simultaneous, corresponding movements with the right and left hand. One must, however, make an effort so that they correspond; if one moves the right hand in mid-air, tracing any shape, one must devote attention to the left hand simply for it to move, for it will trace the symmetrical corresponding shape. The connection is more between the innervation of corresponding muscles on both sides of the body.

Munsterberg proved that there was another relationship between movements of both sides. When an arm is balanced in front, the other must naturally balance itself, not in front, but behind; there are also other cases in which symmetrical movements on both sides must naturally alternate with one another. It is not less true that it is easy to execute simultaneous movements that correspond on each side.

Ostermann found that this ease appeared only in bilateral symmetrical movements. If we tried to make simultaneous movement, symmetrical in relation to a horizontal plane, the attempt would result in inexactness and confusion. The attempt had not been 'natural' and was executed without confidence, whereas bilateral symmetrical movements were executed with ease and confidence and some achieved exactness.

Bloch discovered that in order for the symmetrical movements to be executed with ease and precision, both arms have to move at the same time. If one moves an arm toward a certain point, the effort that one will make to place the other arm to the corresponding point will result in inexact movement." (p. 97-98)

costs of walking and trotting were rather high at both extremes of the speed ranges within each gait. More importantly, however, the maximum energy efficiency, defined at the minimum points on the walk and trot curves, corresponded rather well with the speeds that the horses selected when locomoting over ground. Hoyt and Taylor (1981) suggested that energy *efficiency* might represent a basis that is used by an animal both for the selection of specific speeds within a gait and as the *catalyst* to change gaits.

Dynamical Pattern Theory

Another view of gait transitions is theoretically grounded in the *nonlinear dynamics* of physical systems, known as *dynamical pattern theory* (e.g., Haken, Kelso, & Bunz, 1985; Jeka & Kelso, 1989; Kelso, 1995; Turvey & Schmidt, 1994; Wallace, 1996). This theory does not deny that energy demands may be *one* of the reasons for a gait transition. However, it goes further by specifying a number of other conditions that could be associated with the changes that occur in patterns of motion. In all of these conditions, the role of *variability* is critical in bringing about a pattern change.

Gaits can be defined in terms of patterns of *relative phase* (described in chapter 2 in terms of a two-limb system). Measures of average tendency (mean) and variability (standard deviation, SD) can be determined from individual points of

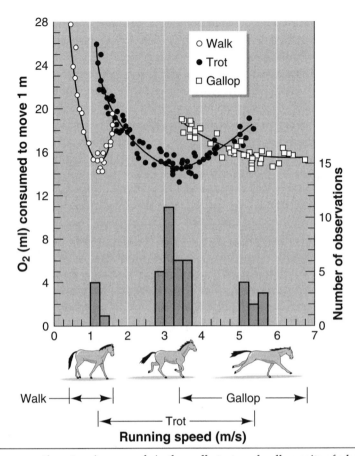

Figure 8.9. Oxygen consumption at various speeds in the walk, trot, and gallop gaits of a horse. The histograms at the bottom represent the preferred speeds that the horse selects in each gait.
Reprinted with permission from Hoyt, D.F., and Taylor, C.R., 1981, "Gait and the Energetics of Locomotion in Horses," *Science, 292,* 240. Copyright 1981 American Association for the Advancement of Science.

relative phase over a time series. A *loss of stability*, indicated by increases in SD, is one of the features of dynamic pattern theory that characterizes a *phase transition*—a change from one movement pattern to another (e.g., a gait transition in the case of locomotion). According to this view, optimal levels of stability occur at certain critical *parameters* of the action (such as speed).[2] When the value of the parameter increases beyond a critical level for a pattern, the relative phase increases in variability (indicating a coordination decrement). For some patterns, (e.g., the walk and trot, but not the gallop), a transition to a new gait is the only way that stability can be regained at the increased speed.

One explanation for the Hoyt and Taylor findings was that the diminished cost efficiency for the walk and trot at higher-than-optimal speeds was associated with a loss of stability in these patterns (Diedrich & Warren, 1995; Holt et al., 1995; Kelso, 1995). But more work is needed in this area of gait transitions, as much of what is known about pattern dynamics is based on re-

search involving human bimanual patterns, which we examine next.

Patterns of Bimanual Coordination

Do this simple experiment (cf. Kelso, 1984). Hold your hands in front of you with the index fingers pointing straight ahead, and make a series of "pinches" by touching the finger to the thumb. Do this with both hands such that you are making one "pinch" about every second with each hand. When we ask students in our classes to do this simple task, with no further instructions, almost everyone does the same thing; the rhythmic pinches done with each hand *naturally* tend to be coordinated such that the fingers and thumbs on both hands are making contact at about the same time. If we measured the relative phase of your coordinated finger actions (chapter 2), we would likely observe that the "pinch" of the one hand occurred at the same time within its cycle as did the pinch of the other hand, relative to its own cycle. Moreover, the timing of the maximum opening between the finger and thumb (about halfway through the cycle) would also likely occur at about the same time for each hand. Since the timing of these (and other) landmarks within each cycle is similar, this coordination pattern is defined as having a relative phase of 0°, commonly known as moving *in-phase*, or in *synchrony* (chapter 2). For this task, the in-phase pattern is considered to be the most natural, or *preferred*, mode of coordination.

Now, holding your hands and moving at about the same speed as before, try performing a different pattern. Make pinching movements with both hands such that the pinches alternate on each hand. You will probably find that this is also quite easy to do. Since the closing of the pinch for one hand occurs while the other pinch is about halfway through its cycle (i.e., when it is at maximum aperture), the relative phase of this pattern is 180°. This pattern is commonly known as moving in *anti-phase*, or in *asynchrony*.

These patterns of continuous bimanual coordination have been studied in experiments using finger-oscillation tasks (e.g., Kelso, 1984), finger-tapping movements (e.g., Tuller & Kelso, 1989; Yamanishi, Kawato, & Suzuki, 1980), wrist rotations (e.g., Cohen, 1971; Lee, Blandin, & Proteau, 1996), and for tasks requiring the swinging of pendulums (Schmidt, Shaw, & Turvey, 1993; Turvey et al., 1986). Results that are typical for all of these tasks are illustrated in figure 8.10 (Yamanishi, Kawato, & Suzuki, 1980). In this

study, the relative-phase accuracy and variability for the in-phase (0°) and anti-phase (180°) patterns, as well as for eight intermediate phase relations, are plotted.[3] The evidence is convincing: the in-phase and anti-phase patterns are performed with much better accuracy (figure 8.10a) and less variability (figure 8.10b) than for any of the other phase relations. In addition, there is a slight tendency for the in-phase pattern to be performed better than the anti-phase pattern. What is clear is that these two movement patterns represent natural and stable coordination modes for the timing of continuous, oscillatory, bimanual movements.

Unintended Phase Transitions

Now try another little experiment. Perform the in-phase pattern as before, but this time gradually speed up the movements until you are going as fast as possible. Do the same with the anti-phase task. If you are like the subjects in experiments by Kelso (1984; Kelso, Scholz, & Schöner, 1986), your performance should look something like the data illustrated in figure 8.11. The open symbols in this figure represent the anti-phase pattern; the filled symbols represent the in-phase pattern. Mean performance is presented in figure 8.11a and variability in figure 8.11b. As expected, both patterns are performed close to their intended goal and with relatively low variability at low oscillation frequencies. And this trend continues for the in-phase pattern. However, the

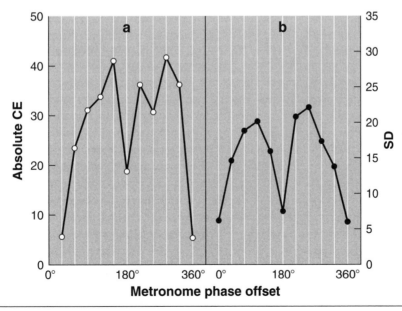

Figure 8.10.   Absolute CE (a) and SD (b) of relative phase for limbs moving at phase offsets between 0° and 360°. Adapted from Yamanishi, Kawato, and Suzuki, 1980.

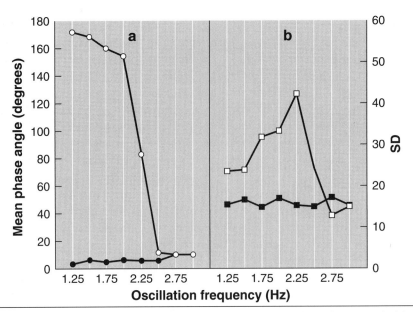

Figure 8.11. Bimanual coordination performance for patterns initiated in anti-phase (open symbols) and in-phase (filled symbols) for mean relative phase (a) and SD (b).
Reprinted from Kelso, Scholz, and Schöner, 1986.

influence of movement speed on the anti-phase pattern is rather startling: at about 2.25 Hz the pattern begins to *switch* from an anti-phase to an in-phase mode of coordination. Notice also that in figure 8.11b, the anti-phase pattern actually begins to become more variable at about 1.75 Hz, suggesting that the loss in stability somehow precipitated the switch. Kelso's subjects were told not to correct for these pattern switches, so once the switch occurred, the performance of the anti-phase pattern was identical to that of the in-phase pattern at the higher speeds. This basic set of findings has been replicated many times, using different effector pairs (see Lee, Blandin, & Proteau, 1996, for a summary).

These transitions between upper-limb coordination patterns are different in many ways from the gait transitions we discussed earlier (e.g., we don't start "hopping" when running speed increases). However, there are some interesting similarities, such as the natural preferences for certain coordination modes and the loss of stability that precedes a phase transition. Unintended phase transitions also illustrate one of the important principles of dynamic pattern theory—the concept of *self-organization*. The natural tendency to perform certain patterns and to switch into patterns that are more efficient under certain parameter conditions seems to manifest itself without the conscious involvement often associated with volitional control. The concept of self-organization suggests that patterns of coordina-

tion emerge *spontaneously* from the interaction of the available degrees of freedom of the system.

Intended Phase Transitions

We have already seen that the in-phase pattern is the stronger and more stable of the two preferred, bimanual timing modes. Now, let's go back to our little experiment one more time. Start by coordinating your pinching movements in the anti-phase pattern at a relatively slow pace (say, one per second). At some point, try to switch to an in-phase pattern as quickly as possible. Then do the opposite—try to switch as rapidly as possible from the in-phase pattern to the anti-phase pattern. Experiments of this kind typically show that it takes longer to completely switch from the in-phase mode to the anti-phase mode than vice versa (e.g., Kelso, Scholz, & Schöner, 1988; Scholz & Kelso, 1990). The switching can be achieved more quickly, however, if pattern stability has been diminished by moving at higher speeds (Carson et al., 1996). Similar differences between the two bimanual coordination modes are seen when a mechanical device is introduced that *perturbs* coordination: the in-phase pattern is easier and faster to reacquire following a perturbation than is the anti-phase pattern (Scholz, Kelso, & Schöner, 1987).

The implications of these findings are consistent with the unintended phase transitions discussed earlier. Since the in-phase pattern is a stronger, more stable mode of coordination, it is easier to voluntarily switch *into,* and the anti-phase pattern is easier to switch *away from,* when one is intentionally trying to make these switches.

Self-Organization and Intention

Self-organization emphasizes the natural dynamics of the pattern-organizing capabilities of the motor system. However, there is no denial that conscious decisions are involved as well. The nature of the relationship between the two appears to represent another "struggle" in the emergence of coordinated behavior, not unlike the struggle between the maintenance tendency and the magnet effect described by von Holst (1937/1973). The nature of this struggle can be demonstrated with one of the examples described earlier. Starting with anti-phase pinches, there will be a strong tendency to switch to an in-phase pattern as movement frequency is increased. If the subject had been instructed to let the hands do what comes naturally, and to not intervene consciously, the switch to the in-phase pattern would be completed and the new (in-phase) pattern would be maintained (e.g., Kelso, 1984; Kelso, Scholz, & Schöner, 1986). However, if the subject had been instructed to maintain the goal pattern at all times, increased oscillation frequencies would result in some in-phase "intrusions" in the time series, but the tendency to perform a less stable, although clearly anti-phase, pattern would be maintained (Lee, Blandin, & Proteau, 1996).

One way to view the process of self-organization is to think of it as an *influence* on coordination that *relieves* the executive of some of the decision-making responsibilities about action, perhaps freeing attentional capacity to be devoted elsewhere. Thus, self-organization allows the system to continue on, essentially automatically, subject to a conscious intervention.

Other Patterns of Coordination

The findings regarding continuous bimanual coordination, discussed in the previous sections, have much in common with some of the research presented earlier regarding discrete tasks. There appears to be something about the constraints on simultaneous motions that makes certain patterns of coordination easy to perform yet generates interference when other patterns are being performed. The biomechanical advantage afforded by symmetry of mirrored actions on the two sides of the body might be one reason the in-phase pattern is more stable than the anti-phase pattern. Another suggestion is that in-phase patterns involve the simultaneous activation of homologous muscle groups whereas anti-phase patterns involve the *alternation* of homologous muscles. One method for probing such questions involves examining the stability of various other modes of interlimb coordination. Do preferred modes of coordination exist when other body segments are paired? And if so, do these pairings have features in common with the bimanual coordination modes?

Upper- and Lower-Limb Coordination

Common activities such as driving, sewing, and playing musical instruments (e.g., the piano and drums) require that we coordinate the timing of our hands and arms with feet and leg movements. These coordinated actions reveal some findings similar to those for bimanual coordination and some that are distinctive to this type of coordination, as exemplified in experiments by Baldissera and Cavallari (Baldissera, Cavallari, & Civaschi, 1982; Baldissera et al., 1991; Baldissera, Cavallari, & Tesio, 1994; also Carson et al., 1995). For example, subjects in the Baldissera, Cavallari, and Civaschi (1982) studies were asked to coordinate ankle movements in the upward direction (dorsal flexion) or downward (plantar flexion) with specific combinations of wrist movements. When the forearm was fixed in the *supine* position, movements that were coordinated in the *same direction* (i.e., plantar flexion with wrist extension and dorsal flexion with wrist flexion) were more stable than actions that were coordinated in the opposite direction. However, with the forearm immobilized in the *prone* position, the stronger coordination mode was observed with the opposite pairing of muscle groups: plantar flexion was now more strongly related to wrist flexion and dorsal flexion to wrist extension. The common finding among these limb pairings was that the stronger coordination modes occurred for movements in the *same direction.* The evidence for the differential strength of these particular preferred coordination modes was similar to that for the bimanual modes discussed previously; the weaker coordination pattern showed higher relative-phase variability and frequent unintended transitions to the stronger (same direction) pattern.

For the bimanual patterns discussed previously, one could argue that the in-phase bimanual pattern was more stable because it involved the timing of similar muscular groups (simultaneous flexion and extension), since movements in the same direction (i.e., anti-phase) were *less* strongly coordinated than were movements in the opposite direction. Such an argument fails to explain the findings of Baldissera and colleagues, however, because the coordination strength of the ankle movements with wrist flexion-extension could be *reversed* by simply changing the forearm orientation (i.e., prone or supine). A similar effect of spatial orientation can be seen in the coordination of the wrist and elbow movements within a single arm (Buchanan & Kelso, 1993; Kelso, Buchanan, & Wallace, 1991). This evidence suggests that the pattern of findings for the stability of the different coordination modes is not dependent on the specific muscle groups used, but rather on the *spatial* orientation of the actions.

The effect of spatial orientation in coordinating two limbs is illustrated quite well in studies by Kelso and Jeka (1992) and Serrien and Swinnen (1997a, 1997b). Consider various pairs of limb movements that could be produced in the sagittal plane, as illustrated in figure 8.12. Three different types of interlimb pairings can be produced: those involving *homologous* (same) limb pairs (left and right arms; left and right legs), *ipsilateral* (same side) limb pairs (left leg and arm; right leg and arm), or *contralateral* (diagonal) limb pairs (left leg and right arm; left arm and right leg). These three types of coordination patterns were examined by Kelso and Jeka (1992) under conditions in which the limbs moved either in the same direction or in the opposite direction, and the results are illustrated in figure 8.13. In general, the limbs moving in the same direction were more stable than the limbs moving in opposite directions. Also, the same limbs (homologous pair) were relatively stable when they moved either in the same direction or in opposite directions. Upper- and lower-limb coordination was better for contralateral pairs than for ipsilateral pairs, especially when the limbs moved in opposite directions (see also Swinnen et al., 1995).

Again, notice that for this coordination task (sagittal plane), moving in the same direction was as stable as moving in the opposite direction. This effect is quite different from that found for bimanual movements in the frontal plane, as we discussed earlier. Thus, these data strongly imply that the *rules* of movement coor-

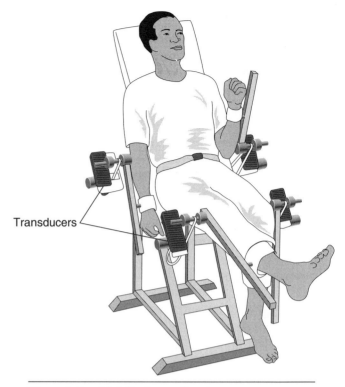

Figure 8.12. Multilimb coordination apparatus.
Reprinted from Jeka, Kelso, and Kiemel, 1993.

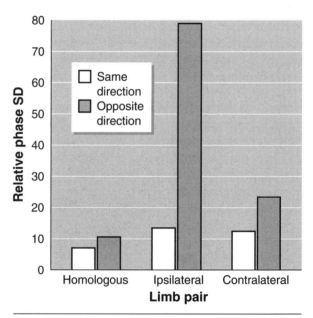

Figure 8.13. SD of relative phase for various interlimb pairings.
Adapted from Kelso and Jeka, 1992.

dination depend on a number of factors, not the least of which are the effectors involved, their orientation and planes of motion, interactions with the physical environment, and intended goals.

Between-Person Coordination

Interlimb coordination is obviously influenced by common neural pathways (cf. chapters in Swinnen et al., 1994). This cannot be the case, however, when coordinated actions occur between two (or more) people. Coordinated activities between people often have a well-defined, *explicit mutual goal* (Schmidt et al., 1994), as in sport (e.g., synchronized swimming) and in the workplace (e.g., when several people combine to move a heavy object). Coordinated actions may also arise from mutual goals that are *implicit*, emerging as subtle social interactions between people (e.g., in conversation; Schmidt et al., 1994).

Studied experimentally, mutual interactions between people share many commonalities with the kinds of behaviors that we have seen in interlimb coordination studies. For instance, Schmidt, Carello, and Turvey (1990) asked subjects to swing one leg in temporal coordination with another person, who was also swinging one leg (see figure 8.14). The mutual goal between the two subjects resembled the (within-subject) bimanual, finger-wiggling task used by Kelso (1984). And the findings were similar; the antiphase pattern was more variable and difficult to maintain at high movement frequencies than the in-phase pattern (Amazeen, Schmidt, & Turvey, 1995; Schmidt, Carello, & Turvey, 1990). The importance of these findings is that a similar set of effects emerged when these movements were coordinated, even though each *individual* movement was controlled by a separate nervous system.

Complex Temporal Coordination Patterns

The existence of preferred, natural coordination patterns might leave one with the impression that all temporal activities of the limbs are relatively easy to coordinate. Try the following easy task. Tap the index fingers of both your hands simultaneously on a flat surface. Now, make two taps of the right hand for every tap of the left hand (i.e., taps of the left hand coincide with every second tap of the right hand—termed a 2:1 rhythm). Then do 3:1 and 4:1 rhythms; all of these should be easy to do when the two hands are performing the same rhythm, that is, when the rhythms are *harmonic*, or integer related (e.g., Farnsworth & Poynter, 1931; Lashley, 1951).

Temporal coordination becomes much more difficult when the rhythms are not harmonic. For instance, it is very difficult to maintain a rhythm with one hand while doing something else as rapidly as possible, such as tapping with the other hand (Klapp, 1979), or speaking a syllable (Klapp, 1981). Even more difficult is the situation in which two concurrent activities have their own rhythms, for example, tapping a rhythm while reciting a nursery rhyme with the proper cadence (Peters, 1977).

Recent studies have focused on nonharmonic rhythms, or *polyrhythms*, to identify what makes

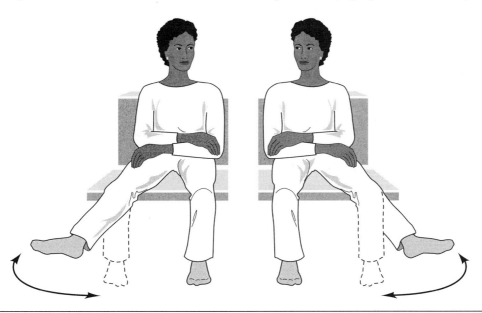

Figure 8.14.   The between-person coordination task.
Reprinted from Schmidt, Carello, and Turvey, 1990.

certain timing patterns so difficult to produce. Consider a situation in which one hand produces three beats during a given interval and the other hand produces two beats during the same time interval (a 3:2 polyrhythm). For example, if the time interval is 1,200 ms, the faster hand produces a beat every 400 ms and the slower hand produces a beat every 600 ms. The two beats occur simultaneously only once every cycle (at 1,200 ms). Although this 3:2 polyrhythm is much harder to perform than any of the harmonic combinations, it is relatively "easy" to perform in comparison to 5:2, 4:3, 5:3, and 5:4 polyrhythms, which are progressively more difficult (Deutsch, 1983; Summers et al., 1993). But what makes these polyrhythms so difficult?[4]

Figure 8.15 presents data from an experiment by Summers et al. (1993), who compared the coefficients of variation (SD divided by mean, expressed as a percentage) for various polyrhythms as a function of hand speed and musical training. What is evident from this figure is that the difficulty the nonmusicians had in performing these polyrhythms was in timing the beats of the hand that was moving *more slowly*. Summers et al. (1993; Summers & Pressing, 1994) explained these findings by considering the faster hand's rhythm as the baseline rhythm (the "clock"). The task of coordinating the slower hand involved interspersing the slower beats at certain intervals in between the beats of the faster hand. The filled squares in figure 8.15 support the conclusion that the difficulty of a polyrhythm is associated with the *number of beats* that the slower hand needs to intersperse between beats of the faster hand (Deutsch, 1983). Moreover, such a strategy is performed much less effectively by nonmusicians because they tend to intersperse the slow beats at approximately 50% of the interval duration between beats of the faster hand (Summers et al., 1993). This unskilled strategy is rudimentary, although it makes sense because it effectively copes with a very difficult situation by drawing upon an *anti-phase* coordination pattern, which as we have seen, is a natural relationship.

Spatial Coordination

Much of the current interest in the continuous, cyclical coordination of limbs has been directed at temporal relationships. Much less frequently investigated, although of considerable importance, is the nature of *spatial* coordination. This is rather

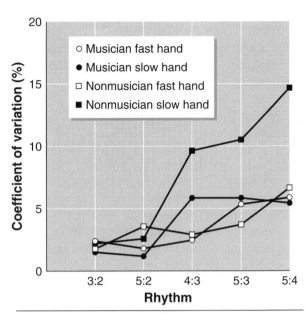

Figure 8.15. Variability in temporal coordination for polyrhythms of increasing difficulty in musicians and nonmusicians.
Reprinted from Summers, Rosenbaum, Burns, and Ford, 1993.

surprising in view of the frequency and functional importance of simultaneous performance of two different actions. For example, the task of driving sometimes involves performing different actions with the four limbs, and some types of automobile accidents seem to be particularly related to spatial biasing effects between the limbs (Schmidt, 1991).

Spatial biasing can be observed quite readily in the "pat the head while rubbing the stomach" example. When one tries to do this task, there is a tendency to bias the spatial trajectories of both limbs: the limbs are drawn toward performing one or the other task, or perhaps some novel combination of the two tasks. An experimental version of this coordination task by Franz, Zelaznik, and McCabe (1991) suggests that a novel combination may be the more natural coordination pattern. The subjects' task was to draw circles and lines. In some conditions, a single hand drew only one pattern; in other conditions, both hands drew the same pattern; and in another set of conditions, one hand drew a line while the other hand drew a circle. The results from these conditions are illustrated in sample trials represented in figure 8.16. Both lines and circles were drawn accurately and consistently under the single-hand and dual-hand "same" conditions. However, when the hands drew different patterns, the variability increased dramatically; the circles became more linear, and (to a lesser degree on the

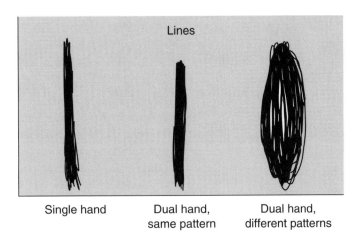

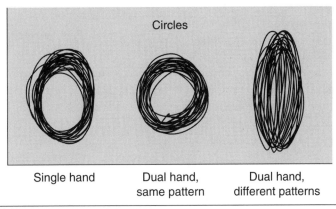

Figure 8.16. Drawing lines and circles under unimanual and bimanual conditions.
Reprinted from Franz, Zelaznik, and McCabe, 1991.

average) the lines became somewhat circular. But much more work is needed on spatial-coordination effects in order to establish firm principles (see Chan & Chan, 1995; Franz, 1997; Franz et al., 1996; Spijkers & Heuer, 1995; Swinnen, Jardin, & Meulenbroek, 1996).

Summary

Even quite simple movements require the organization of various independently moving parts of the motor system. Aiming movements, though simple at one level, involve the coordination of the eyes and head when perception and action are visually guided. One method of analyzing the organization of discrete tasks is to search for separate *units* of action—parts of movements that are temporally independent from other parts of the movement. In contrast, the reach/grasp action represents a type of discrete movement in which the limb-transport component of the movement is quite obviously distinct from the object-manipulation component. Evidence suggests that,

although these components seem to be separable, their actions are highly interdependent.

Discrete *bimanual* actions have also been an important focus of study. Studies using a two-hand version of the Fitts task reveal considerable influences of one limb's movement on the spatial and temporal actions of the other limb. These influences are even more pervasive if the actions of one limb have increased kinematic complexities. Recent evidence suggests that the development of a new motor program may be a way in which the motor system solves these coordination difficulties.

The coordination of continuous, cyclical actions presents a contrast to that of discrete actions, where the motor program plays an important role. Some continuous, interlimb coordination patterns are quite stable, and others are less so. Important insights regarding pattern organization are revealed by *phase transitions*, in which the destabilization of a pattern leads to a change in the basic form of the pattern. These transitions have been shown in animals and in humans, leading some to suggest that these patterns have a strong, *self-organizing* basis. Evidence from a number of bimanual and interlimb coordination paradigms has provided support for this view, although some controversy exists about the cooperative role that occurs between intention and self-organization in the emergence of coordination patterns.

Notes

[1] These analyses were also done with nonoverlapping intervals among the landmarks, which eliminates the bias in the correlations because of overlapping of some of the landmarks. Heuer, Schmidt, and Ghodsian (1995; Schmidt et al., in press) have developed a theory of bimanual coordination based on GMPs that uses a statistic termed a covariance ratio (COVR), which is sensitive to the extent to which the hands are coordinated together in time. The COVR data are consistent with the view that the two hands are controlled by a single GMP, but details of this work are beyond the scope of this presentation.

[2] This is referred to as a *control parameter* in the language of dynamic pattern theory—a parameter that, when varied, causes a nonlinear change in the behavior of the system. We do not use the term here for the sake of clarity, as we have been using the term *control* much more generally throughout the book.

[3] The measure of accuracy presented here is different from that of Yamanishi, Kawato, and Suzuki (1980). They reported constant error, averaged over subjects. However, as noted in chapter 2, the average constant errors for subjects who are biased differently can underestimate the average inaccuracy for a *group*—and these individual differences, in opposite directions of bias, were evident in the Yamanishi et al. data. Thus, we have replotted their data in terms of absolute constant error (chapter 2). The results show much the same pattern as the variability data.

[4] Interestingly, the Heuer, Schmidt, and Ghodsian (1995) task described earlier was a rapid, 3:2 "polyrhythm," which was performed rather easily (after practice). That discrete and continuous versions of a similar task might have remarkably different effects on coordination performance is deserving of more research.

INDIVIDUAL DIFFERENCES AND CAPABILITIES

Why is one person a better gymnast than another, even after the same amount of practice? What are the abilities or aptitudes that contribute to success as a skilled woodworker? How many basic, inherited motor capabilities do humans possess, what are they, and how can they be measured? These are just some of the questions considered in this chapter on individual differences—that is, the factors that make individuals different from one another.

The approach to motor behavior represented by this chapter is a marked departure from the approaches in the earlier chapters. The fundamental distinction is this: with the earlier approach, which is typically termed *experimental*, the concern was for the effect of certain independent variables on certain other, dependent variables. In *experiments*, these effects are revealed by the changes in the average behavior of a group of subjects. With the *differential* approach, however, the concern is for how the individuals *within* a group differ from each other. Because these two scientific traditions are so different in method and goal, they are usually treated as separate points of view. We will examine more closely some of the differences between these two approaches in the next sections.

Experimental Versus Differential Approaches

There are a number of fundamental differences between the ways in which motor behavior is studied and understood in the experimental and differential approaches. In the following discussion, we focus on just two of the major differences—the scientific goals and the scientific methods used by the two approaches.

Different Scientific Goals

The most obvious difference between the experimental and differential approaches lies in the goals of these two traditions. The experimental approach is primarily concerned with understanding the effects of certain independent variables (e.g., amount of lighting in an environment during moving) on some dependent variable (e.g., the accuracy of the movement). In this example, the interest is in how visual processes work in (all) humans to aid movement accuracy. A fundamental belief is that humans are not really very different from one another (especially when human-to-human differences are contrasted with human-to-giraffe differences); so when the subjects in a group are treated alike, the behavior of all humans (or of a "typical" human) can be estimated by considering the effect of the light on average accuracy. By experimenting, the researcher can hope to arrive at statements such as "Removing vision tends to decrease accuracy in movements with long MT," as did Keele and Posner (1968), to cite just one example.

In these kinds of experiments, little concern is shown for any one individual in the group who may have more trouble with reduced vision. Almost no interest is shown in the possibility that one person might use a different strategy than another or have more skill than another. These factors are usually averaged out and never seen in the group data. In fact, if some individual differs "too much" from the mean behavior level of the group, common experimental practice is to remove this *outlier* from consideration. Thus, variations among people are considered "noise," or a nuisance, and many methods are employed to eliminate or control such between-subject variations in experiments.

With the differential, or individual-differences, approach, on the other hand, the primary focus is on the differences between or among individuals. Thus, the things that the experimentalist considers "noise" in experiments are the very things that the differentialist considers interesting and worthy of study! Generally, the differential approach is concerned with two basic issues.

First, concern is shown for the nature of the underlying *abilities* (or *capabilities*), the ways in which these abilities differ in "strength" in different people because of genetic variations or experience, and the ways in which different tasks are interrelated. For example, are tasks involving strength related to other tasks involving accuracy in motion? Does high strength performance imply that the person will have low accuracy performance? A second problem, closely related to the first, entails *prediction*, or the estimation of performance in one situation based on measurements taken in some other situation. For example, how do intelligence test scores relate to success in graduate school? Or, how does height relate to success in gymnastics?

The differential approach deviates from the experimental approach because it concerns attempts to explain and predict differences among people, rather than general phenomena that are seen in the average person. As might be expected, such differences in goals naturally create differences between the points of view of the differentialists and the experimentalists. Indeed, such differences have become so great that the two groups of psychologists are almost totally separated, with separate methods of doing research, statistical designs, goals, textbooks, and scientific journals. These differences were described, and decried, by Cronbach (1957) in his article entitled "The Two Disciplines of Scientific Psychology." There have been attempts to bring these camps closer together (e.g., Underwood, 1975); but resistance to amalgamation is strong, and little progress has been made.

Different Scientific Methodologies

The experimentalists and the differentialists answer their respective questions quite differently. While we have devoted considerable space to the experimental approach, a brief review of its characteristics will help to make clear how it contrasts with the differential approach.

Experimental Methods

Essentially, the "true" experiment involves the manipulation (or artificial variation) of some independent variable while all other (or at least most other) variables are held constant. This can be done by administering one level of the independent variable to one group of people and another level to another group, and noting the differences in some dependent variable (called a between-subjects or between-groups design). Sometimes only one group of people is used (called a within-subjects design). One level of the independent variable is administered to the group at one time and the other level is administered at another time, with differences between the two times (in terms of the dependent variable) being the chief comparison of interest. We have discussed many examples of both of these designs in previous chapters.

In such experiments, the critical comparison is between the means of groups of people (or of a single group tested under two different conditions). Typically, no regard is given to the variations among people within the group, except for the usual reporting of statistics that describe the extent to which people differed. In any case, such dispersion statistics are rarely the primary concern in experiments; rather, they are included to assure that the variations among people were not so large as to obscure or change the conclusions drawn about the differences between means. Finally, the conclusions that come from these experiments are usually stated in cause-and-effect terms; thus, the variations in the independent variable caused the changes in the dependent variable. As such, experimental methods provide relatively powerful ways of coming to an understanding of one's scientific area.

Differential Methods

The differential methods contrast starkly with those just described, relying substantially on correlational (or associational) techniques whereby the *relationships* between or among variables are studied. In its simplest form, the differential approach uses one group of people and at least two tests measured on each individual. (Remember that the experimental method often uses at least two groups of people and one test, or dependent variable.) The primary concern is the extent to which one test (e.g., height) relates to another test (e.g., accuracy) in the same people, with the nature of the relationship being determined by the size and sign of a statistic called the *correlation coefficient* (which we will consider in a subsequent section). With these correlational methods, the relationship between the two tests, or among the groups of tests if more than two are used, is the chief concern. Sometimes the relationship is computed between a group of tests (called a test "battery") and some other single measure. An example is the relationship between a fitness battery (consisting of five subtests) and some other measure, such as probability of becoming a successful firefighter.

A second major method of individual-differences research uses essentially the same logic, but the appearance of the procedures may make it seem that the methods are experimental. Consider a study to determine the relationship between age and capability to throw. Typically the researcher chooses one group of people at one age and another group at another age and compares the group means on some "dependent" variable, such as throwing accuracy. This appears to be an experiment, because there are two groups and one dependent variable and the focus is on the group means. But it is not really an experiment, because the level of the independent variable (age) is not *manipulated* by the experimenter; that is, the ages of the people in the group were already established when the subjects were chosen, and such a procedure is merely a study of the relationship between age and throwing accuracy. Such variables are usually called *individual-difference variables;* examples are race, gender, musical background, and country of birth. Thus, studying which individual-difference variables are related to certain kinds of performances is a primary concern of the differential approach. Indeed, textbooks have been written about age, race, and gender as individual-difference variables (e.g., Osborne, Noble, & Weyl, 1978).

With the differential approach, conclusions about the results tend to be phrased in language quite unlike that for the experimental approach. Whereas in experiments one is often "permitted" to conclude that the independent variable *caused* changes in the dependent variable (because other variables were held constant or "controlled"), in differential studies causation can seldom be inferred logically. The major reason is that in studying the relationship between height and throwing accuracy, for example, many other things may differ. For example, a person's weight is usually associated with height, so one cannot be certain that a relationship between height and accuracy is really not due to the relation between weight and accuracy. Also, taller people are usually older (if one is considering children), and one could easily confuse the height-accuracy dependency with an age-accuracy dependency. The primary limitation in these studies is that the level of the variable of concern is not manipulated (artificially determined by the experimenter). Rather, the variable is allowed to vary naturally, and the scientist measures its value and attempts to understand how it relates to some variable that is also varying naturally. Such procedures are often called *natural experiments,* and a good example is the study of variables associated with the eruption of volcanos. Certainly, variables leading to an eruption cannot be manipulated experimentally, and the differential approach is used.

On Humanism

Many students receive the impression from this kind of discussion that the differential approach, with its apparent "concern for the individual," is more humanistic than the "cold, hard" experimental approach that treats everyone alike and averages people together as though they were simply numbers. In a small sense, this is correct. But in other ways the differential approach is even less humanistic than its experimental counterpart. Suppose that we are interested in the relationship between height and success at basketball and find with differential methods that greater height is related to increased success at basketball. Such knowledge apparently allows us to discriminate among people of various heights. That is, regardless of one's real ability, we can, on the basis of this relationship between height and skill, decide that no person under 5 ft 9 in. (175 cm) shall play on the team. If that does not sound so bad, then consider this analogous situation. We find that, on the average, females have less electrical knowledge than males and thus may conclude that women should never be hired as telephone installers. It works the other way too, as males under the age of 25 (regardless of their real driving ability) are charged higher auto insurance rates than are females, largely because of the relationship between gender and the number of accidents among people between 16 and 25. The point is that both approaches can be antihumanistic, depending on the particular application involved.

Correlational Methods

An important statistical tool used in research on individual differences is the *correlation coefficient.* In fact, the correlation is the "language" of individual-differences research. The correlation is a measure of the degree of *association* between two tests. The usual situation is to have a relatively large group of subjects (e.g., 50), with two different tests administered to each person. These two tests can be motor or verbal, and they can have the same or markedly different scoring systems. In some situations, the test may be simply the level of a dichotomous (i.e., two-state) variable, such as gender (for example, males could be given a score of 0, females a score of 1), or it may be whether or not one had played competitive basketball. The next section describes some of the ways these data are treated.

Scattergrams

One of the ways these data can be described is by a special kind of graph called a *scattergram.* Here, the two axes are the scales of the two tests, respectively, and each of the subjects is represented as a dot, located according to his or her scores on the two tests. Consider the data shown in table 9.1, which have been plotted on the scattergram in figure 9.1. The data are hypothetical scores that might be obtained on a common playground and consist of age (in years) and the time for a 100-m dash (in seconds). In figure 9.1, the scores for these 10 people are plotted, so that each of the 10 dots on the graph represents each person's joint scores on the two tests.

A relationship apparently exists between the score on the age variable and the score on the running test, indicating that, as the age score becomes larger, the number of seconds on the running test tends to become smaller. Note that there are some individual exceptions: Subject 1 (13.1 years) had a longer running time than Subject 2 (11.6 years). Of course, these variables are not related to each other perfectly, and instances arise when a younger child is able to complete the 100-m test in less time than an older child. But, in general, the 10 subjects showed a relationship between these two variables.

Notice also that in figure 9.1, the points suggest that a line could be drawn through them, perhaps representing the "direction" in which the "cloud" of points is oriented. The "line of best fit" in correlations is called a *regression line.* Such a point can be located "by eye," but techniques called *regression analyses* allow one to fit the line to the points according to mathematical criteria. Once

the line is established, its empirical equation can be written (see the section on empirical equations in chapter 2). The equation is of the form

$$Y = a + bX \qquad (9.1)$$

in this example, where the value Y is running time, X is age, a is the intercept, and b is the slope.

Direction of the Relationship

In the example just described, as the value of the age variable increases, the value of the running time variable tends to decrease. This kind of relationship is called an *inverse* relationship, or a *negative* relationship. Accordingly, the equation of the line representing this kind of relationship has a negative slope constant *(b)* (chapter 2). In other situations, we will find that as one of the variables increases, the value of the other variable tends to increase as well; this is a direct, or positive, relationship. In such cases, the slope constant of the regression equation has a positive value, showing that the line of best fit slopes upward to the right.

In many cases, the direction of the relationship shown in such data is dependent on the scoring system used. Consider the data in table 9.1. In the fourth column we have expressed each subject's 100-m dash scores as average running speed (km/hr) rather than as the time required to travel 100 m. This change in scoring system "inverts" the group of scores, so that the person who had the largest time score has the smallest speed score, and the person with the smallest time score has

Table 9.1   Hypothetical Data for Age and 100-m Dash Performance

Subjects	Age (years)	100-m dash Time (s)	Average speed (km/hr)
1	13.1	13.5	26.6
2	11.6	12.8	28.1
3	12.2	12.0	30.0
4	16.1	10.5	34.3
5	9.2	16.1	22.4
6	8.5	15.2	23.7
7	8.1	16.0	22.5
8	11.3	14.1	25.5
9	12.2	13.0	27.7
10	7.3	18.0	20.0

Note. Speed data were computed from the time data.

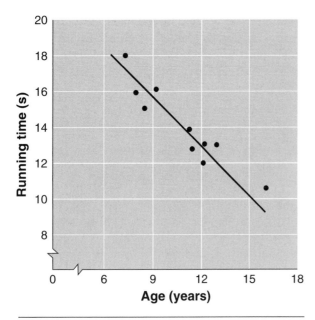

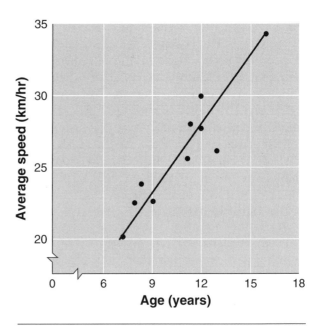

Figure 9.1. A scattergram showing the relationship between age and running time. (Data are from table 9.1, and each dot represents one of the 10 subjects.)

Figure 9.2. A scattergram showing the relationship between age and running speed. (Data are from table 9.1, where speed is computed from running time; each dot represents one of the 10 subjects.)

the largest speed score. When the age data are plotted against the average running speed scores in figure 9.2, the relationship becomes a positive one, with increases in age tending to be associated with greater average running speed. The empirical equation can be fit just as above, but now the slope constant *(b)* has a positive value rather than a negative one. Thus, a positive relationship is not any "better" than a negative one; the sign of the relationship simply indicates the direction in which the line of best fit is sloped, and it can be altered by a simple change in the scoring system. There are, of course, numerous examples of both directions of slope in the motor control literature.

Strength of the Relationship

A second characteristic of these relationships between variables is *strength.* By strength, we mean the extent to which the relationship is perfectly linear, or the extent to which all of the subjects' points fall exactly on the line of best fit. Figure 9.3 shows two scattergrams that represent relationships of different strengths. In the plot in figure 9.3a, the relationship can be considered to be quite strong because nearly all the points seem to fall close to the line of best fit. In the plot in figure 9.3b, however, the relationship is not very strong, because the points tend to fall away from the line of best fit. Alternatively, one could say that the line fits the data well in the

plot in figure 9.3a, but does not fit the data very well in the other plot. An example of two variables that might be strongly related is children's age and weight, as older children tend to be larger, thus heavier. An example of a relationship that is weak might be one between weight and running speed; that is, the weight of a child would not have much relationship to the speed with which he or she could run.

These two aspects are the primary descriptors used to characterize relationships in the literature. They are separate, in that a strong relationship can be either positive or negative and a negative relationship can be either strong or weak.

Predicting From a Relationship

One of the most important reasons scientists want to know the nature of the relationship between two variables is for the purpose of *prediction.* For example, if we know that the relationship between age and running time has been found to be as described in figure 9.1, then on a new group of playground children we can estimate (or predict) the 100-m time given the age of a person not in the original data set, without actually measuring running time. That is, knowing that the next person has an age of 11.6 years, we can predict that his or her running time will be approximately 13.4 s (work this out from the scatterplot). Such pro-

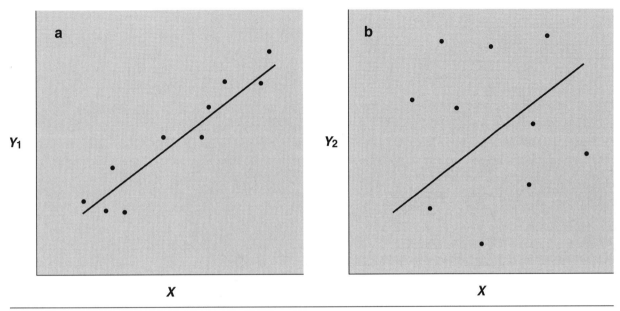

Figure 9.3. Hypothetical scattergrams for a strong (a) and a weak (b) relationship.

cedures are used extensively in everyday situations, such as in predicting the probability of having an automobile accident from one's age, or predicting success in graduate school from achievement test scores.

As the strength of the relationship increases, the predictability of one variable from the other increases as well. When the relationship is perfect and all the individual data points fall exactly on the line of best fit, perfect predictions can be made. That is, no error is made in predicting from a relationship in which all the points fall exactly on the line of best fit. When the data are related less perfectly, such as in the example shown in figure 9.3b, then considerable error is made in predicting the *Y* variable from the *X* variable. Thus, the strength of the relationship—but not the direction—is the primary determinant of the extent to which a relationship can be used to predict.

Correlations

These concepts of strength and direction of relationships taken from data on human subjects can be quantified using a statistic called the *correlation coefficient*. The correlation, abbreviated *r*, can only take on values that range from +1.0 through zero to –1.0. The two aspects of the correlation to be concerned about are the sign of the correlation and its absolute size. The sign of the correlation indicates the direction of the relationship, exactly

as described in the previous sections. That is, if the correlation between height and weight was +.80, then the regression line of these two scores in a scatterplot would be sloped upward and to the right. The absolute size of the correlation indicates the strength of the relationship and hence is critical for evaluating the extent to which one can use the relationship for predictive purposes. In figure 9.4 are five hypothetical examples of correlations and the associated scatterplots. Both a +.90 and a –.90 correlation are near-perfect relationships, as all the data points fall almost exactly on the lines, although the lines are sloped in opposite directions in these two examples. Correlations of +.50 and –.50 are moderate in strength, and the points fall considerably away from the lines of best fit. A correlation of zero is weakest in terms of the strength of the relationship, indicating that no predictive capability is possible between these two variables. Formulas for the calculation of correlations can be found in most statistics textbooks (e.g., chapter 7 in Thomas & Nelson, 1996; chapter 7 in Vincent, 1995).

A convenient method for estimating this strength of relationship is to square the correlation coefficient and multiply by 100 to convert it into a percentage score. Generally, the correlation squared indicates the extent to which the two correlated tests can be considered to measure the same thing, which gives a measure of the usefulness of the relationship for predictive purposes. Notice that this fits nicely with the earlier discussion of the strength and direction of relationships. The percentage in common for two tests that correlate +.90 or two others that correlate −.90 is the same (e.g., $.90^2 \times 100 = -.90^2 \times 100 = 81\%$), indicating that the strength of the relationship does not concern the sign. The strength of the relation is 100% if the correlation is either +1.0 or −1.0 ($1.0^2 \times 100 = 100\%$), and the percentage in common is zero if and only if the correlation is zero ($.00^2 \times 100 = 00.0\%$). Finally, notice that for two tests to have 50% in common with each other, the correlation between them must be approximately ±.707 (i.e., $\pm.707^2 \times 100 = 49.98\%$).

Reliability

People can differ from each other in at least two fundamental ways. First, two people might be fundamentally and consistently different from each other in some stable characteristic such as height. Such differences will be enduring and constant across both time and testing conditions. But the two individuals might also be different in other ways that seem to result from chance effects or variability in our behaviors. If on just a single trial, one person makes a pool shot and another does not, we might not be willing to say with certainty that the two people are different in pool-shooting capability, as on the next shot the performance success may be opposite. Finding differences between two individuals on some measure of performance does not necessarily indicate that these differences are stable and enduring. The stable, enduring differences among people are the subject of this chapter on individual differences. In fact, the definition of individual differences is *the stable, enduring, and underlying differences among people* (Henry, 1959).

The reliability coefficient provides a way to evaluate the extent to which the differences among people on some test are due to individual differences (stable, enduring differences) or to chance or transitory effects. The reliability coefficient is really another use of the correlation, but in this instance the concern is with the correlation of a test "with itself." This is not really nonsense as it might appear, as the following example will demonstrate.

Assume that five subjects each perform six trials on a reaction-time (RT) task. To compute the reliability, the scores for a single test are divided into "halves" according to one of a number of different methods. One common method is called

the "odd-even" method; the sum of (or average of) the odd-numbered trials is computed as a separate score from the sum of the even-numbered trials. The extent to which the odd and even sums tend to deviate from each other is a measure of the amount by which there are random variations in the individual trial data. Indeed, if there were no variation at all, then the sum of the odds and the sum of the evens would be exactly the same for a given subject. Next, the correlation coefficient is computed between the odd and even scores. For each subject there are two scores—the sum of the odds and the sum of the evens, the essential "ingredients" for computing a correlation. In this case, these two "tests" are both RT, but now measured on different trials. In doing the computations, the correlation between the odd and even trials is what is typically called the *reliability coefficient*.

Reliabilities can, theoretically, take on any value between +1.0 and −1.0, because they are computed with the correlation coefficient. But in practical situations, the reliability seldom is negative and usually ranges from .00 to +1.0. The reliability of a test can be interpreted in various ways. One way is to consider the reliability coefficient as a percentage, multiplying it by 100. The observed variation among people is made up of (a) differences among people in their stable, enduring traits (termed *individual differences*) and (b) random (or other) fluctuations that tend to make people appear to be different from each other. If so, the reliability is the percentage of the observed variability (all sources of variability combined) that is accounted for by individual differences. When the reliability is quite low (e.g., .2), then only 20% of the variation is accounted for by individual differences, with about 80% of the variation being due to random (and other) variations.

As mentioned earlier, the primary concern of individual-differences research is in the relationship between pairs of tests. Statistically, the size of the correlation between two tests is limited by the reliability of either (or both) of the tests being correlated.[1] Therefore, in evaluating the size of the correlation between two tests, one must be certain that the reliability of each of the tests being correlated is reasonably high—ideally .80 or higher. Finally, the reliability coefficient represents a measure of the "stability" of the test under different applications. More properly, it represents the stability of the *subjects' performances* on

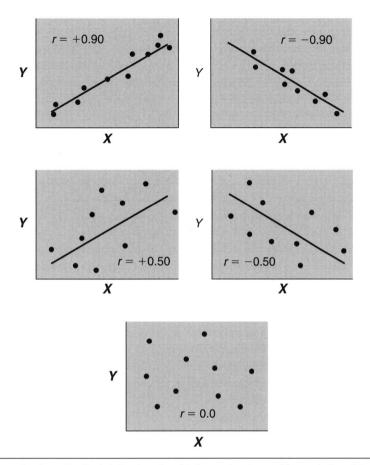

Figure 9.4. Scattergrams for hypothetical data showing high, moderate, and low relationships.

the test, as the test itself usually cannot be considered as being either stable or unstable. One might expect that as the number of trials administered to each subject is increased, the mean performance of the subjects would become more stable and the reliability coefficient would increase. A measure of RT based on 100 trials is far more reliable than one based on only one trial, since with the former measure the nonsystematic variations would have been "averaged out" to some extent, resulting in a better measure of the subject's "true" capability to react. Accordingly, the number of trials that make up a test is a strong determinant of the reliability of the test, to the point that if the number of trials is increased enough, the reliability can actually be brought to 1.0 (e.g., Gullicksen, 1950). As easy as this is to do (usually), there is seldom a good excuse for a test with low reliability.

Abilities

Probably the most important topic in the area of individual differences is *abilities*. In this section,

we will begin by providing a definition of the concept of ability, and then we will turn to some of the research indicating the structure of abilities.

Abilities Defined

The term *ability*, which is often used interchangeably with the terms *capability* and *aptitude*, usually refers to a hypothetical construct that underlies (or supports) performance in a number of tasks or activities. An ability is usually thought to be a relatively stable characteristic or trait. These traits are typically regarded as having been either genetically determined or developed through relatively automatic processes in growth and maturation, and they are not easily modifiable by practice or experience. Abilities represent the collection of "equipment" that a person has at his or her disposal, determining whether or not a given motor task can be performed either poorly or well.

Abilities are usually inferred from patterns of performance on groups of tasks, largely using correlations as the primary method of measurement. For example, suppose we find that for a group of individuals, those people who perform well on task A also perform well on task B. In addition, we find that those people who perform poorly on task A also perform poorly on task B. This pattern of findings is what one would expect if tasks A and B were related, or correlated statistically. If two tasks are related, then it is possible to infer that they are related because of some underlying property or process that is included in both tasks. The differential motor behavior scientist is interested in the possibility that the underlying properties common to these two tasks are abilities—or enduring, stable traits that contribute to the performance of these two tasks. For example, if task A is a sprint start in swimming while task B is a sprint start in running, a correlation between the RTs in these two tasks might mean that both tasks have reaction speed as an underlying ability. The tasks are different, but they have at least one underlying similarity.

Abilities Versus Skill

Another way to understand the concept of abilities is to distinguish it from the notion of skill. While often these two terms are used interchangeably in casual conversation, they should be separated when one is thinking about individual differences. An ability is a relatively stable, underlying trait that is largely unmodifiable by practice on a particular task or activity. Skills, of course, can be modified by practice or experience (the last part of this book deals with these changes with practice—called motor learning). Thus, abilities are underlying capabilities that support certain skills. For example, the capability to react may underlie a number of specific skills such as sprint starts in swimming or a quick reaction in driving a car. Think of a given skill as being composed of a number of different abilities. Thus, the skill of driving a car may be made up of various abilities, such as those involved in vision, an ability to switch attention from one event to another, and an ability to anticipate.

Abilities as Limiting Factors

Abilities can also be conceptualized as representing limitations on performance, or as defining a person's potential for success in a particular activity. Neither of your authors will ever become a professional basketball player regardless of the amount of time and effort we devote to the game,

because we do not possess the requisite abilities for it. Two individuals could have the same skill level at a given time, but one of them could have far greater potential because he or she has greater abilities for the skill in question. The other person is likely to be frustrated by attempts to improve beyond the limitations defined by his or her underlying capabilities.

Varieties of Abilities

Abilities can take many forms. One form common to many sports is body configuration. For example, the ability (or trait, if you prefer) of height is important to basketball; similarly, small people rarely succeed in American football, and large people rarely succeed in gymnastics. Such characteristics are surely genetically defined and are almost impossible to modify by training or practice. Another variety of ability is related to certain emotional or personality characteristics. For example, certain personalities are more amenable to team sports than to individual sports, and some people are more excitable or anxious than others. Finally, the abilities that will most concern us here could be called "motor abilities." They are the underlying characteristics that tend to contribute to success in moving the limbs in particular ways; further on we will discuss reaction time, movement speed, and manual dexterity, among others as abilities. These abilities are often not as easy to measure or isolate for study as are abilities relating to body configuration, but they are no less important for understanding why certain people become more skilled than others.

The Structure of Motor Abilities

How many motor abilities are there? What are they, and how can they be measured? These questions have been asked for many years, and the answers have changed systematically as more effective techniques for studying abilities have been developed. First, consider some of the earlier thinking about motor (and cognitive) abilities that has led to present-day beliefs.

General Motor Ability

An early notion about motor abilities—one that is still widespread among people not familiar with the research—was the idea that all motor responding was based on a single, all-encompassing ability (Adams, 1987). This idea goes by different names, such as "athletic ability," "coordination," "motor ability," or a more formal label of *"general motor ability."* All these terms imply essentially the same thing: we are structured so that a single capability to move can be defined, with this capability having relevance to any motor task in which we choose to engage. That is, if a person had a strong general motor ability, then that person would be expected to succeed in almost any motor task. These ideas, which were generated in the 1930s, were no doubt supported by the common observations (on playgrounds, in athletics, and so on) that certain individuals could (or so it seemed) do anything they tried (so-called all-around athletes), while other individuals could not do well at any motor task they tried. Given these casual observations, it seemed to make sense to postulate an underlying factor that effectively related all the various tasks in athletics to one another: a general athletic (or motor) ability.

This idea of general motor ability was probably led by the analogous research on cognitive abilities that was prevalent in the 1930s. It is beyond the scope of this chapter to present much detail, but one important concept that emerged from this work was that of *intelligence.* It was during this period that the measures of IQ (intelligence quotient) were developed, and educators and parents became strong believers in the predictive power of IQ tests as measures of a child's capacity for "success" in society. The IQ was designed as a measure of the hypothesized general mental ability; the idea was that this single mental ability was important for success in almost any mental activity in which the person engaged. For this reason, IQ tests were heavily used in educational settings to divide children into academic ability groupings, to determine whether or not a child should be held back or "skipped" in grade level, and to make decisions about entrance to college or special programs.

In the 1950s and 1960s, however, the concepts of general intellectual ability and general motor ability both came under serious attack. With respect to motor skills, the threat came from essentially two major sources: (a) the work on individual differences conducted by Henry (see figure 1.3) and his students at Berkeley and (b) the research program related to individual differences in pilotry and similar tasks that was conducted by Fleishman and his associates

through the U.S. Air Force. These two important programs, although quite different in terms of methods and interpretations, had strong impacts on the concept of general motor ability.

Predictions From the General Motor Ability Notion

The general motor ability hypothesis has one important prediction that has been tested frequently, concerning the sizes of the correlations among tests of various skills. The logic goes like this. Take a group of individuals and test them on task A; after a great deal of practice the people tend to order themselves on this task from "best" to "worst." According to the general motor ability hypothesis, the "best" performers are most proficient because of a strong general motor ability; conversely, the "worst" performers have a weak general motor ability. Thus, the performance on this task can be taken as a measure of the strengths of these subjects' general motor ability.

Now, suppose that these same people are tested on task B; task B can be either similar to or vastly different from task A—it does not matter for the theory. How should these people tend to be ordered on task B, given their order on task A? The argument is that because the individuals who are "best" on task A are in this position as a result of a strong general motor ability, and because the general motor ability applies to all motor tasks, then these same individuals should be "best" at task B. Similarly, the individuals "worst" at task A should be "worst" at task B as well.

This kind of prediction can be seen by the hypothetical data in the scatterplot shown in figure 9.5, where each individual is represented by a dot whose position on the scatterplot is determined by scores on each of the two tasks A and B. Notice that the individual with the highest score on A also has the highest score on B, the individual with the third highest score on A also has the third highest score on B, and so on. The subjects tend to be *ordered* similarly on the two tasks. This situation demonstrates a high correlation (toward +1.0 in this case) between tasks A and B. Thus, a major prediction of the general motor ability hypothesis is a high correlation between any two motor tasks selected for study. If the correlation turned out to be low (i.e., near zero), this would not support the general motor ability concept. And should this pattern of low

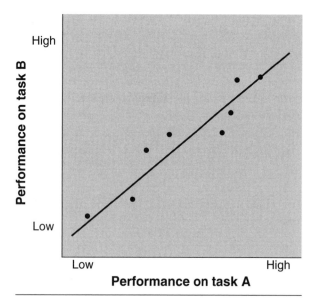

Figure 9.5. Hypothetical data presented in a scatterplot showing a relationship between tasks A and B; each subject is represented as a dot, positioned according to the scores on task A and task B.

correlations happen in a wide variety of separate studies, then considerable doubt would be cast on the general motor ability hypothesis. Let us examine correlations among tasks that have been found in the literature.

Correlations Among Skills

Perhaps 30 to 50 separate investigations in the published literature deal with the correlations among well-practiced skills, but we will discuss only three of these studies in order to give a general idea of how this work is done (for a review see Marteniuk, 1974). One example from Henry's laboratory is a study by Bachman (1961). A group of 320 people practiced two motor tasks that supposedly involved balancing in some way. One of these, the Bachman ladder task (see figure 2.8), involved the subject's climbing a freestanding ladder. The subject stood on a gymnastics mat and began climbing until the ladder toppled over. When it did, the subject quickly picked it up to begin climbing again, and so on. The score was the number of rungs climbed (with skipped rungs subtracted) in a 30-s trial. Subjects had 10 trials, and the average performance on this task was taken as their ability level on the last two trials.

Bachman's second task was the stabilometer (see figure 2.5c). This apparatus was an unstable balancing board on which the subject stood; it was pivoted so that the right foot moved down as

the left foot moved up, similar to what happens when you are standing in a rocking canoe or above the fulcrum of a teeter-totter. By appropriate action, the subject could halt the rocking and keep the board still, but a great deal of practice was required to learn to do this. The task was scored in "movement units," or the amount of movement of the board that occurred in a 30-s trial. The subject performed 10 trials, and ability was estimated as the average of the last two trials—similar to the performance measure for the ladder.

Bachman (1961) found that for various subgroups of subjects (defined by age and gender), the correlations between success on the ladder and success on the stabilometer ranged from +.25 to –.15, with most correlations being very close to zero. Thus, the low relationships between the ladder and stabilometer tasks did not permit predictions of success on one from the score for the other. We can see the meaning of the low correlations more easily if we consider that taking the *largest* correlation (+.25) and squaring it to determine the percentage in common between these two tasks gives $.25^2 \times 100 = 6.25\%$ in common. About 94% of the abilities in these tasks were specific to each task and not shared by the other.

Consider another study. Lotter (1960) had subjects perform striking and kicking movements with the hand and foot, respectively, in a RT setting. The arm movement involved a forward-downward movement to hit a suspended tennis ball as quickly as possible (for the left and right hands separately); the leg movement involved kicking a small plate with a movement resembling a placekick in American football (again, for the right and left legs). Thus there were six possible *pairs* of tasks between which a correlation could be computed. The arm-arm correlation was .58, and the leg-leg correlation was .64. These correlations were considerably higher than those found by Bachman (1961), but they are based on the same task performed with limbs on opposite sides of the body. The correlations between arm and leg, with both on the same side of the body or on opposite sides (i.e., left arm vs. right leg), were lower: .24, .36, .23, and .18. Using the rule for computing the percentage in common, the same tasks on opposite sides of the body had approximately 37% in common, whereas the different tasks (arm vs. leg) had approximately 6% in common, based on the averaged correlations. Even though the two tasks involved rapid striking activity, they were apparently different enough in terms of their underlying abilities that they did not correlate very highly with each other. An interesting question is whether the arm-arm and leg-leg correlations were so much higher than the others because these pairs used the same motor program while the others did not. In any case, Lotter's data do not support the general motor ability hypothesis.

In another example, Parker and Fleishman (1960) had 203 subjects perform a battery of 50 tests in conjunction with an armed services testing program. This produced a 50×50 correlation *matrix*, whereby every test is correlated with every other test and the resulting correlations are placed in a large table, or matrix. The majority of tests performed in the Parker and Fleishman study correlated about .40 or lower with each other; only rarely was there a correlation of .50 or higher, and the highest correlation was .85 between tests that were practically identical (e.g., walking a 2-m balance beam vs. a 4-m balance beam, with the same beam being used in both tests). Thus, from this and other batteries of tests that have been studied, the general pattern is low correlations, with a few high ones when the tasks are practically identical.

Many more studies like these have been done, but the point has been made by now: generally, low correlations are found among different skills. This pattern does not support the notion of a general motor ability or even of general motor subabilities such as general athletic ability. Notice also that there did not appear to be a general balancing ability, since Bachman's (1961) two balancing tasks (the ladder and stabilometer) did not show correlations with each other. Also, there did not appear to be a general hitting ability, as seen by the fact that Lotter's (1960) striking tasks correlated very poorly. The various motor tasks that humans perform, on the basis of this evidence at least, appear to be supported by a collection of relatively independent abilities, with a different combination of abilities being required for each task.

Henry's Specificity Hypothesis

In the late 1950s, Henry (1958/1968, 1961) proposed the idea, in direct contradiction to the general motor ability hypothesis, that motor abilities are *specific* to a particular task. Essentially there were three aspects to this hypothesis. First,

Henry thought that the number of motor abilities was very large—perhaps in the thousands. Second, he believed that these abilities were independent, so that the strength of one particular ability is unrelated to the strength of any other ability; we have a large collection of abilities, some of which are "good," some of which are "weak," and others of which are "average." Third, each task or skill that we perform depends upon a large number of these abilities. When the task is changed, the particular collection of abilities that support the performance must change to meet the new task demands.

Probably the most important prediction of the specificity hypothesis is that two tasks, even if they appear to be quite similar (such as throwing a baseball and throwing a javelin), will tend to correlate nearly zero with each other. This is the case because the groups of abilities that underlie these two tasks are, according to this view, two distinct collections with almost no abilities in common. Also, because these abilities are assumed to be independent of each other, the correlation among skills should be zero, or at least very low. The evidence tends to support such a viewpoint.

In addition, the Henry hypothesis predicts that *transfer* among skills should be quite low (Schmidt & Young, 1987). Transfer is defined as the attainment (or loss) of proficiency in one task as a result of practice or experience at some other task (we will consider this further in chapter 14). If the two tasks have no abilities in common, then no element practiced in one of them will contribute (or transfer) to the other. Generally, the transfer literature supports Henry's hypothesis, showing essentially that motor transfer is generally low and positive. We will deal with this evidence when we discuss some phenomena related to motor learning later in the book.

An Exception to Henry's Specificity Hypothesis

Although Henry's hypothesis about specificity of individual differences has been widely accepted for many years, recent work by Keele, Ivry, and others indicates that *timing* may represent an exception to Henry's view. This new work suggests that there is a general "timekeeping" ability that underlies performance of a number of tasks. The research focuses on how the temporal aspects of movements are organized in the central nervous system, and examines correlations among various tasks requiring central control of timing. In one study (Keele & Hawkins, 1982), correlations between maximum rates of tapping by various body parts (finger, thumb, wrist, arm, and foot) ranged from .60 to .80. In another study, Keele, Ivry, and Pokorny (1987) asked subjects to maintain a regular beat by tapping with the finger or arm at 400-ms intervals. Here the prime measure was the regularity of the intertap intervals, measured by the standard deviation of the produced time intervals. The correlation between the standard deviations produced with finger and arm tapping was .90, suggesting a high degree of commonality between the two tasks. Interestingly, Keele, Ivry, and Pokorny also included a task in which subjects were required to produce certain forces with the finger and arm. The correlation between performance in the force-production task and that in the timing task was about .20. The dissociation of performance abilities within the same subjects—showing specificity of individual differences for the force and timing tasks, but generality across different timing tasks—is strong evidence against a strict view of Henry's hypothesis.

Findings in support of a common timing ability have been extended in a number of ways. Moderate correlations (.36 to .48) between the timing of limb and jaw movements was reported by Franz, Zelaznik, and Smith (1992). In addition, Keele et al. (1985) found that the correlations between perception of timing and the production of timing can be relatively high (with rs of about .60), suggesting a link between perception and production of action.

It has also been proposed that common timing abilities underlie certain movement-related disorders (see Ivry & Corcos, 1993, for a review). Williams, Woollacott, and Ivry (1992) found that children classified as motorically "clumsy" were more variable in both motor and perceptual timing than age-matched controls. However, hypotheses suggesting that timekeeping problems are the locus for stuttering have not been supported by research (Hulstijn et al., 1992; Zelaznik, Smith, & Franz, 1994). Nevertheless, research with groups of individuals who have neurological disorders suggests that the cerebellum may play a particular role in timekeeping ability (Ivry & Keele, 1989; Ivry, Keele, & Diener, 1988). A group of patients with lesions in the cerebellum

was found to have diminished motor and perceptual timing performance (compared to patients with Parkinson's disease and those with cortical or peripheral neuropathologies).

These findings have led Keele and Ivry (1987) to suggest a *modular view* of individual differences (see also Jones, 1993). In this view, the brain is organized to perform certain functions rather than certain tasks. *Modules* represent neural systems that support a particular function. A timing module represents a type of timekeeper that functions to support the performance of both perceptual and motor tasks under a wide range of sensory and effector mechanisms. This work represents an interesting new direction for studying individual differences in skills, and future research may indeed reveal the existence of other modules that represent more general types of performance capabilities than were suggested by Henry.

Factor-Analytic Studies

A second major research thrust that tended to argue against the general motor ability hypothesis was the factor-analytic method, so called because it used a statistical tool termed *factor analysis*. Various investigators have used this general method, but certainly the most active was Fleishman (1964, 1965, 1967; see Fleishman & Bartlett, 1969 for reviews). After a brief discussion of the factor-analytic method, some of the major findings from this body of research will be presented.

Factor Analysis.   Factor analysis is a complex statistical method based on correlations, but an understanding of the technical aspects of this method is not necessary for an appreciation of the kinds of knowledge that it has generated. The essential details are these. Typically, a large number of people (e.g., 100 to 200) perfor each of a number of tests (e.g., 50). Factor analysis groups the tests into *clusters*, or *factors*, so that the number of factors is considerably less than the number of original tests (e.g., 10 or so, depending on a number of other considerations). The tests that make up a particular cluster or factor have the property of showing relatively high correlations with each other, whereas two tests that are members of different factors tend to show low correlations with each other.

This perhaps will be clearer if we consider the diagram in figure 9.6. Say there were 20 tests, and the factor analysis grouped them into five clusters, or factors, each represented by a square. The circled numbers within the squares refer to the test numbers (which are, of course, purely arbitrary), and the numbers on the lines joining two tests represent the correlation between the two indicated tests. For clarity, only some of the 20 tests or five factors are shown.

Notice that for Factor I, the tests that are included tend to show relatively high correlations with each other (.52, .49, and .65), indicating that these tests, to some extent, tend to be measures of some common underlying ability or abilities. Notice also that for Factor II, the tests tend to correlate with each other as well (.60, .48, and .50) and therefore tend to measure some common ability. However, a test in Factor I (e.g., Test 9) does not correlate well (r = .06) with any test in Factor II (e.g., Test 13). Also, Test 6 (in Factor II) and Test 2 (in Factor III) do not correlate well with each other (r = .10). The interpretation is that the tests within a factor tend to measure one or more basic abilities. Each of the factors tends to represent a different set of abilities. In this way the factor-analytic technique seems to allow the division of a large group of tests into a smaller group

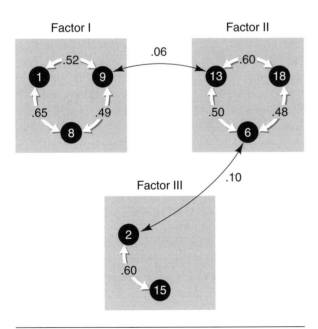

Figure 9.6. Three clusters (represented by boxes) of tests (shown as circles) that would result from a factor analysis. (Correlations between tests within a cluster are higher than correlations between tests in different clusters.)

of factors, each of which is thought to represent a separate ability or abilities.

Identifying the Abilities. The next step in the factor analyst's job is to determine what abilities the factors represent. We can illustrate this process with one of Fleishman's (1957) studies, in which 200 people were each given 18 tests. The result of a factor analysis is a factor *matrix*, shown in table 9.2. Across the top of the table are the nine factors that emerged in the analysis, analogous to the clusters or groupings of tests in figure 9.6. On the left side of the table are the tests that were administered, ordered arbitrarily. The numbers in the body of the table are called the *factor loadings*, which indicate the extent to which the test in question is a "measure of" the ability or factor in that column; the factor loading is often thought of as the correlation between the test and the ability that it represents. For example, consider Test 2 (Reaction Time). This test has a high loading (.60) on Factor I but a relatively small loading on Factor II (.15). On the other hand, Test 4 (Pattern Comprehension) has a high loading on Factor II (.66) but a very small loading on Factor I (.12). Here, we can say that Reaction Time is a measure of Factor I (but not of Factor II), whereas Pattern Comprehension is a measure of Factor II (but not of Factor I). Had we displayed these factors as clusters as in figure 9.6, Reaction Time and Pattern Comprehension would have been represented as members of different clusters.

It is through the values of the factor loadings in these matrices that the scientist comes to understand the structure of the abilities that underlie the various tests studied. Consider Factor IV first, as the point is made clearly in this case. Scan the factor loadings for Factor IV, noting which ones are high. You will find that all the loadings are less than .30 except for two—a .52 for the Mechanical Principles test and a .65 for General Mechanics. On this basis, the scientist would be tempted to believe that Factor IV has something to do with the performer's knowledge of mechanical principles, and to name this factor accordingly. Fleishman named Factor IV "Mechanical Experience." Now look at Factor II. The tests that have high loadings on Factor II are Pattern Comprehension (loading = .66), Mechanical Principles (loading = .53), and perhaps Speed of Identification (loading = .44). On this basis, Fleishman named this factor "Visualization." In some cases

Table 9.2   A Factor Matrix

	Factors									
Variable	I	II	III	IV	V	VI	VII	VIII	IX	h^2
1. Instrument comprehension	18	22	18	13	54	02	15	–01	20	48
2. Reaction time	60	–15	03	–03	08	07	16	–07	–09	43
3. Rate of movement	43	19	–02	–06	09	09	22	–01	14	31
4. Pattern comprehension	12	66	18	07	34	26	11	–07	08	69
5. Mechanical principles	03	53	22	52	09	07	06	12	05	63
6. General mechanics	05	19	12	65	14	02	11	–03	10	52
7. Speed of identification	27	44	14	17	21	27	01	00	00	61
8. Visual pursuit	14	23	38	05	25	23	10	16	17	40
9. Complex coord. trials 1–5	05	35	21	26	35	38	42	22	04	73
10. Complex coord. trials 12–16	23	16	23	21	19	47	46	41	22	86
11. Complex coord. trials 49–53	42	13	–03	22	19	38	47	52	–07	92
12. Complex coord. trials 60–64	43	12	01	20	19	34	40	58	06	89
13. Rotary pursuit	28	15	15	15	13	16	55	01	00	49
14. Plane control	16	07	–06	28	20	33	31	–11	20	41
15. Kinesthetic coordination	–01	–16	45	28	16	35	09	11	00	29
16. Unidimensional matching	14	16	34	14	08	19	45	14	06	45
17. Two-hand matching	16	21	14	15	–01	70	08	02	15	63
18. Discrimination reaction time	28	24	23	20	46	40	04	–16	00	63

Note. Decimals omitted. Factors are identified as follows: I = Speed of Arm Movement; II = Visualization; III = Perceptual Speed; IV = Mechanical Experience; V = Spatial Orientation; VI = Response Orientation, VII = Fine Control Sensitivity; VIII = Complex Coordination "Within Task" Factor; IX = Residual Factor; h^2 is called the communality, and is the sum of the squared factor loadings for that test (e.g., $.18^2 + .22^2 + \ldots + .20^2 = .48$). (From Fleishman 1957.)

(Factor IV), the name of the factor is rather obvious from the nature of the tests that "load on" it. In other cases (such as with Factor II), the name of the factor is not so obvious. A number of different factor analyses, all using some of the same tests, may be required to identify a particular factor.

Notice that a given test can load on two factors at the same time. An example is Test 5 (Mechanical Principles), which loads on both Factor II (loading = .53) and Factor IV (loading = .52). What does this mean? One interpretation is that this test is made up of at least two abilities (Visualization, Mechanical Experience) and that it measures both of these abilities at the same time. This is in keeping with the idea that any given performance or skill (e.g., Test 5) can be thought of as composed of many abilities. Other patterns can be seen across the factor loadings shown in table 9.2.

Finally, notice that the pattern of factor loadings is different for the various factors. That is, the tests that load highly on one factor are typically not the same tests that load highly on the other

factors. Each of the factors seems to have its own "personality" in terms of which tests have high loadings and which tests have low loadings. Compare Factors I and II, for example. Here, the tests with the highest loadings on one have very low loadings on the other. This observation is really the same as that in figure 9.6, where each of the factors appeared to represent a separate ability or group of abilities. Because each of the factors is separate, it is logical that the tests measuring these separate factors will be separate as well.

Through such techniques, Fleishman and his colleagues, together with a few others, have provided a series of hypothesized underlying abilities that seem to be relevant to various aspects of motor behavior. In the next section, some of these abilities are outlined to give the flavor of this work.

Motor Abilities Identified by Factor Analysis

The following list of abilities has been determined in a number of separate studies. The list is not exhaustive; it merely provides an idea of the kinds of abilities that have been inferred from these methods. These abilities all come from Fleishman's work (e.g., Fleishman, 1964, 1965, 1967; Parker & Fleishman, 1960) and bear the names given by him. After each we have provided an example of a "real-world" task in which this ability might be used, based largely on conjecture.

- *Control Precision.* This ability underlies the production of movements for which the outcomes must be rapid and precise, but which are made with relatively large body segments. Example: swinging an ax.

- *Multilimb Coordination.* This ability underlies tasks for which a number of limb segments must be coordinated while moving simultaneously, such as the two hands, the two feet, or the hands and feet. Examples: juggling, playing a piano.

- *Response Orientation.* This ability underlies tasks for which rapid directional discriminations among alternative movement patterns must be made, and it is apparently related to the ability to select a correct movement under choice-RT situations. Examples: actions performed by a defensive lineman in American football or a hockey goalie.

- *Reaction Time.* This ability underlies tasks for which there is one stimulus and one response and which require the subject to react as quickly as possible after a stimulus in simple-RT situations. Example: sprint start.

- *Speed of Arm Movement.* This ability underlies tasks for which the limb must be moved from one place to another very quickly and the measure of performance is movement time (MT). Example: a jab in boxing.

- *Rate Control (Timing).* This ability underlies tasks for which the movement speed of the limbs must be adjusted to the movements of the environment so that the person's limbs are timed correctly. Example: tracking tasks, as in steering a race car.

- *Manual Dexterity.* This ability underlies tasks for which relatively large objects are manipulated, primarily with the hands and arms. Example: hammering a nail.

- *Finger Dexterity.* This ability underlies tasks for which small objects are manipulated, primarily with the fingers. Examples: repairing a wristwatch, sewing.

- *Postural Discrimination.* This ability underlies tasks for which subjects must respond to changes in postural cues in the absence of vision in making precise bodily adjustments. Example: walking in the dark.

- *Response Integration.* This ability underlies tasks for which the person must utilize and apply sensory cues from several sources into a single, integrated response. Example: throwing a pass in a football game.

- *Arm-Hand Steadiness.* This ability underlies tasks in which the person must be quiet and steady. Example: aiming in riflery or archery.

- *Wrist-Finger Speed.* This ability underlies tasks for which alternating movements (e.g., tapping) must be made as quickly as possible; it seems to represent the rapid coordination of the muscles required for up-and-down movements of the fingers and wrist. Example: piano trills.

- *Aiming.* This ability underlies tasks for which the subject must aim or point at a target, attempting to hit it with very quick movements. Example: dart throwing.

- *Physical Proficiency Abilities.* In addition to the abilities listed for the movement-control area, other abilities have to do with physical or structural aspects of the body. Some of these as outlined by Fleishman (1964) are Extent (Static) Flexibility, Dynamic Flexibility, Static Strength, Dynamic Strength, Trunk Strength, Explosive Strength, Gross Body Coordination, Gross Body Equilibrium, and Stamina (Cardiovascular Endurance). These nine abilities can be thought of as underlying dimensions of physical fitness or physical proficiency, and they appear to be separate from the skills-oriented abilities just listed.

Role of the Factors in Skills

Some interesting features of this list of hypothesized factors should be mentioned. First, if some individual has a strong ability with respect to Arm-Hand Steadiness, the strength of any other ability (say Reaction Time) could be high, low, or intermediate. With this observation in mind, it is interesting to consider that a number of factors represent what is often called "quickness." For example, Response Orientation represents a RT situation for which there is more than one stimulus-response alternative (i.e., choice RT). Here, Reaction Time refers to RT tasks for which there is only one stimulus-response alternative (i.e., simple RT), and Movement Time refers to the abilities necessary to move the limb quickly once the action has been started. Interestingly, "quickness" is not really represented as a single ability; rather, it seems to be defined by different abilities depending on the environmental situation or on what part of the action is measured (RT or MT). Henry (1961) and many others have shown essentially zero correlations between RT and MT, suggesting that they are based on separate abilities.

Also, note that Manual Dexterity and Finger Dexterity are separate abilities. Both pertain to the hands, but for different-sized objects. If this is correct, then what does it mean to say that a person "has good hands"? To answer this question adequately, we would have to know about at least two different abilities. Also, most of the abilities defined in the previous section (with the exception of the physical proficiency abilities) are defined with tasks that use the hands for manipulations of various controls in various ways defined by the task. Yet, depending on the ways in which the hands are used (e.g., to react quickly, to move quickly, to move in conjunction with another hand, to move in time to some external object, to move accurately), different abilities are involved. Clearly, the structure of human motor abilities is far more complicated than common sense would lead us to believe. And it seems to be a gross oversimplification to make a statement such as "John is good with his hands." In order for this statement to make any sense, it must be combined with information about *how* the hands are used.

A related point is that the particular collection, or pattern, of these abilities appears to change markedly as only minor changes in the task or situation are imposed on the performer. For example, the employment of a choice-RT ability or a different simple-RT ability depends on the number of stimulus-response alternatives presented to the subject; changing the situation from a simple- to choice-RT situation presumably results in the "abandonment" of one ability in favor of another.

This concept has been shown more formally in some of Fleishman's work in which the nature of the control-display relations was varied experimentally. In this work, the task always remained the same with respect to the movements made, but the way in which the movement was signaled from the display was changed. The situation was somewhat analogous to driving a car in which the seat and controls can be oriented in any direction with respect to the car's direction of travel. As the directional orientation was altered, systematically different abilities were brought into play while others were dropped; still others remained constant. This notion underlines the problem in trying to measure abilities in one situation, hoping to apply these measures for prediction of success in a similar, but not quite identical, situation. If the task has changed much at all, then it is likely that different abilities will be used in the two situations, leading to false estimates of the nature of abilities in one task based on measures in the other. The use of abilities by subjects appears to be highly varied, which makes understanding them very difficult indeed.

Finally, it has been tempting to try to align the understanding of human abilities defined by factor-analytic methods with the experimental research described in the first sections of this book. Fleishman and Bartlett (1969) discuss the hypothesis that the abilities identified by factor analysis are measures of separate ways in which humans process information, with each of these information-processing mechanisms being essentially independent. In some situations, this connection is easy to imagine; for example, the simple- and choice-RT abilities could be differentiated on the basis that the choice situation involves the information processes related to resolving uncertainty (as in Hick's law, chapter 3), while the simple situation involves the prestructuring of a motor program. Similarly, abilities like Rate Control (or anticipation, timing) involve the processes related to analysis of incoming sensory information.

Criticisms of the Abilities Approach

This section would not be complete unless we mentioned that the abilities approach, primarily that using factor-analytic methods, has not been without its critics. One problem is methodological (see Kleine, 1982, 1985). There are many varieties of factor analysis and of other techniques (called "rotations") that are applied to factor-analytic outcomes to aid in interpretation. Arbitrary choices about the way in which the same data are analyzed can change the nature of the factors that emerge from these analyses and thus alter the interpretation in terms of the abilities that the scientist is trying to understand. Fleishman's work has been criticized—unfairly, in our opinion—for being limited in scope, dealing primarily with young men in the armed services. Rarely were women used as subjects; children were never included, nor were older people. Thus, the studies suffer some limitation in generalizability. Remember also that Fleishman's research support came primarily from the armed forces, where a major concern was the understanding of the abilities involved in pilotry. It is natural that these studies used adult men only, as they were done in the 1950s and 1960s when women played less prominent roles in the armed services than they do at present.

Finally, the abilities that have emerged from these studies have been based on skills for which the person is typically seated and using the hands (occasionally the feet as well), and for which the performance is noncompetitive. These kinds of performances are but one kind of action involved in the total spectrum of motor activity, and the abilities that emerged from these studies probably are somewhat limited as a result. After all, if no task requiring Ability A was included in the original battery of tests to be factor analyzed, then Ability A could never emerge. A large number of abilities that are important for other kinds of tasks have undoubtedly been missed as a result. These are problems for future research to resolve.

Ability Structures in Everyday Activities

The conclusions from the previous sections—that abilities are very specific, and that skills do not correlate with each other unless they are virtually identical—are often troublesome to students because they do not, at first glance, appear to agree with a number of common observations. On playgrounds, for example, some children seem to be able to do well at nearly any motor task they try, whereas others are nearly always ineffective. Most of us have known so-called all-around athletes, who seem to perform well at any sport activity they attempt. Such observations, if they were general enough, would be in opposition to the concept of abilities described earlier, because a general factor far more powerful than we have discussed would have to be proposed. How can this apparent contradiction be rationalized?

A number of forces other than ability structures can act to produce success in activities like sports. Some parents encourage their children to participate in many sports, while others emphasize music or literature; such encouragement to excel in numerous motor activities contributes to motor learning, to the acquisition of more skills in various activities, and to the *appearance* of a strong general motor factor. Furthermore, playground activities favor those children who are larger and more physically mature than average, leading mature children to practice many sports and relatively immature children perhaps to avoid sports. Also, children with certain personality or emotional characteristics will be more disposed to sport than others, and this will contribute to more practice in many activities and the appearance of a large general motor factor. A kind of "rich get richer" phenomenon develops, whereby a little experience and encouragement can result in more experience, more encouragement, and so on; and such processes can be completely absent for some children. There are probably many such forces that would lead one segment of society to become effective at many sports, while others remain ineffective at any of them, without necessarily having to assume some powerful general motor ability. Practice and experience can be extremely important influences in shaping one's particular collection of skills.

However, there may be all-around athletes who possess abilities for a wide variety of sport skills, although the number of such people must be very small. The viewpoint presented here is that the abilities that such people have inherited are aligned relatively well with the requirements of many sport tasks, and that their learned skills will be numerous because of practice and various other factors already mentioned. The pattern of abilities that has happened (by chance or as the product of genetics) to align itself so well with sport tasks might be expected to be found once in a while, just as is any rare combination of events. But it is incorrect to generalize from such unusual instances and conclude that some general motor ability exists in various strengths for everyone. The conclusion is simply not supported by scientific evidence.

Taxonomies

A *taxonomy* is a classification scheme used to assign things to various categories. We have already discussed a few of these classification methods in chapter 2, in connection with open versus closed skills and continuous versus discrete skills, for example. More elaborate systems for classification are now being developed on the basis of the underlying structure of the abilities involved in motor tasks.

The basic notion is that one of the ways to classify tasks is in terms of the pattern of abilities that underlie them, rather than more superficial and obvious characteristics such as whether the performance is discrete or continuous. For example, performance on the pommel horse in gymnastics might be made up of Strength, Rate Control, and Multilimb Coordination, with each contributing a certain proportion to the whole. These descriptions of tasks in terms of their abilities are just beginning to be developed. Again, the leader in this area has been Fleishman (e.g., Fleishman & Stephenson, 1970). Two of these general taxonomic methods are described next (for others see Gawron et al., 1989).

Factor-Analytic Classifications

With this method, after a great deal of experience with the various motor tasks in previous factor analyses, the scientist sees that certain tests seem always to result in the emergence of certain factors or abilities. A good example is the various tests of rapid movement that, when included in factor analyses, typically produce a factor that is labeled Movement Speed. Such stable findings lead to the establishment of a particular MT test as the "best" measure of the ability of Movement Speed, with the "best" test being defined in terms of ease of administration, the sizes of the loadings, and so on. These tests are often elevated to the status of *reference tests*, or the generally agreed-upon measures of a particular motor ability.

Now, if this reference test is included in another, subsequent factor analysis, in which tests for an entirely different activity (e.g., pilotry) are included, we can understand the structure of this task somewhat if we note the extent to which it loads on the Movement Speed ability defined by the reference test. If high loadings on the Movement Speed ability are obtained, then we can say that the new activity has a Movement Speed component. By including other reference tests at the same time, each representing a different predetermined ability, we can pinpoint the abilities represented in this new activity.

A good example is provided in the factor matrix shown in table 9.2. Tests 1 through 8 are tests of various kinds of skills, such as Instrument Comprehension, Reaction Time, and so on. These eight tests are the reference tests, items that had been studied extensively so that their underlying abilities were understood. Now notice that Tests 9 through 12 are all based on the same apparatus, once called the complex-coordination task (see figure 2.5d), in which the person manipulates the forward-backward and left-right movements of an aircraft-type "joystick," as well as the left-right movement of foot pedals, to respond to a pattern of lights presented on a display.

What abilities underlie the complex-coordination task? For simplicity's sake, consider only the initial performance measures, trials 1–5 (Test 9). The highest factor loadings for this task were for Factor VII (.42) and Factor VI (.38), with Factors II and V having slightly smaller loadings (.35). We can therefore say that this task (at this stage of practice at any rate) is based on Fine Control Sensitivity (VII) and Response Orientation (VI), and to some extent Visualization (II) and Spatial Orientation (V). By comparison, none of the other factors seem to be involved very much. In this way, such a procedure "defines" this task in terms of its underlying ability structure, just as a recipe defines what a licorice milk shake is.

In theory, this procedure can be applied to any new task, such as the game of golf. We could use a large number (e.g., 50) of well-practiced and skilled golfers and administer to them reference tests, perhaps the eight tests we have mentioned. (We might wish to use somewhat different tests if there is reason to believe that some factor definitely is, or definitely is not, involved in golf.) Then, we administer a golf performance test and examine the reference tests and the golf test with factor analysis. The loadings that emerge should give an indication of the nature of the abilities involved in golf.

This is not as simple as we have perhaps made it sound. A major problem is having "good," well-understood reference tests in the first place. Fleishman's research has provided a start, but there are limitations to the generality of this work, as we have pointed out. And many abilities that might be involved in golf may not be uncovered, as they may not be represented by any of the reference tests. But with progressive additions to knowledge about the underlying abilities, the reference tests will become more numerous and more effective, making the task of discovering new tests easier in the future. This method has a great deal of potential for practical application for new jobs in industry, for which the nature of the abilities needs to be known.

Task Analysis

A considerably easier but less effective way to determine the nature of underlying abilities is through a series of procedures that has been termed *task analysis*. The essential idea is to "analyze" (i.e., "break down") the task to consider what kinds of abilities might be involved in it. The performers themselves are guided to respond, often with paper-and-pencil tests, in or-

der to provide additional insight into the underlying abilities. Look at the flowchart in figure 9.7, taken from Fleishman and Stephenson (1970; Fleishman, 1975). Consider a skill such as the throwing task performed by a shortstop in baseball. Begin at the top of the chart, asking whether or not speed is important to performance of this task. It is, so move to the right and ask whether accuracy is important also. Follow the arrow dictated by that decision. If baseball players or coaches are asked to use such procedures to evaluate throwing, researchers can arrive at a tentative understanding of the kinds of abilities required for this action. We would probably come to the

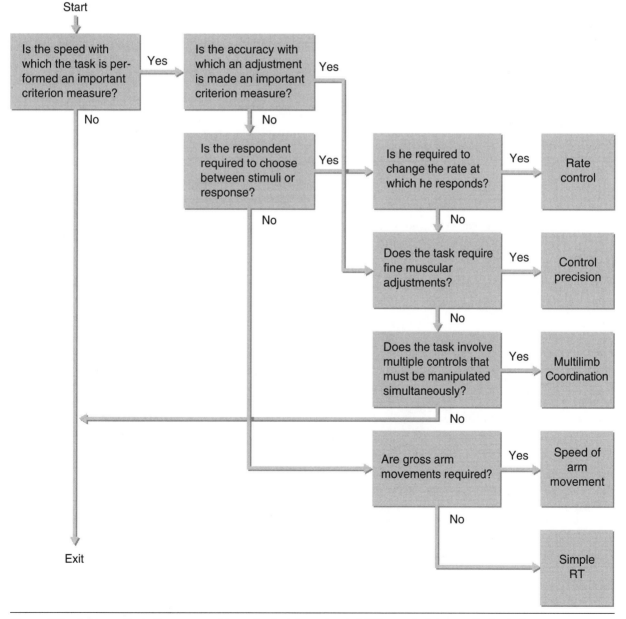

Figure 9.7.   A binary flow diagram used to make decisions about abilities underlying particular tasks.
Adapted from Fleishman and Stephenson, 1970.

decision that this task involves Control Precision, because speed, accuracy, and fine control are all needed for success. These methods are only in the beginning stages of development and problems obviously exist, such as ambiguities that make it difficult to give satisfactory answers to the questions in the boxes.

A related method, used by Farina and Wheaton (1970) and Fleishman (1975), is to devise a scale such as that shown in figure 9.8. In this case, expert performers are again asked about their tasks, but here the subject is given a scale with certain "anchor points" on it. The performer is asked to rate how regular (or predictable) the stimuli involved in a particular job are. The "anchors" are other tasks with which the person is already familiar, such as looking at a picture or receiving Morse code. Each has a relatively well-understood "location" on the rater's own dimension of regularity. Then the person is asked to rate some performance in which he or she is an expert, such as fielding ground balls in baseball, and to mark the scale in terms of this characteristic for the task in question. We would mark this scale at about 4 for baseball, as the balls do vary in speed and direction but in relatively predictable and limited ways. The reader might give it a different value. Through a series of such scales, each describing a particular ability that is suspected to underlie the task, one can estimate which abilities seem to be most involved and which seem to be least involved. While this method is relatively imprecise, it seems to provide an easy way to approximate the abilities that underlie performance on a particular task or job.

Prediction

A companion to the research on abilities, the second major aspect of the work on individual differences is the problem of prediction. The fundamental problem is to be able to say (or predict) with some degree of accuracy what a person's score or level of skill will be on one task as a result of information about that person's skill on some other task.

These problems exist everywhere in the practical world. For example, insurance companies

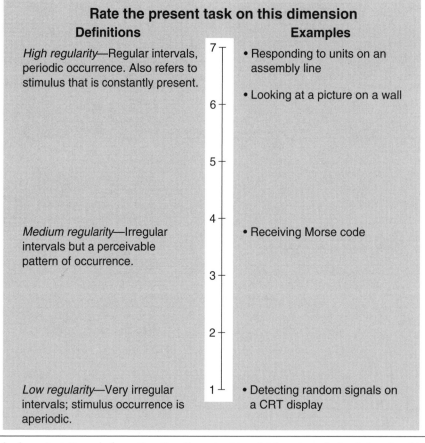

Figure 9.8. A task-characteristic scale for estimating the extent to which a given factor is involved in a particular task. Adapted from Farina and Wheaton, 1970.

attempt to predict the probability that you will have a heart attack on the basis of information that you supply on an application form, such as age, occupation, and gender. Also, universities attempt to predict success in graduate school from tests that supposedly measure certain intellectual abilities (e.g., the Graduate Record Examination). More important to motor skills is the need to predict success in jobs or occupations on the basis of abilities testing, using such predictions as a basis for hiring procedures. Professional football teams attempt to predict success from various measures of body composition and from motor performance measures.

Prediction in this sense implies the concept of *futurity*—forecasting some event or behavior before it happens. While this is the primary kind of application of individual-differences work, it is not the only way the idea of prediction is used. A second way involves the study of which tests best "predict" (or are correlated with) some other score that we already have in hand. Such techniques are intimately involved in the *development* of test batteries, and some of these procedures are described in the next section.

Test Battery Development: An Example

Suppose that you are a personnel director for a large company and that you want to predict success in some particular job in the company. For many jobs, this is easy. If you know the relevant *skills*, you can simply measure whether an applicant has these skills. But a problem arises with a job for which the applicants have had no previous experience. Common examples involve accepting applicants into a flight-training program in the Air Force or hiring a person to perform a particular assembly-line job that exists only in your company. The problem is to determine whether or not the applicant has the necessary abilities to do this job when he or she is eventually trained to do it, as no applicant would be expected to have the particular skill without prior experience.

Posing the Problem

Consider this problem addressed a number of years ago by Schmidt and Pew (1974), who were asked to design a battery of tests to predict success in becoming a dental technician. In this occupation, the primary task is to make appliances for the mouth, such as crowns, bridges, and artificial teeth, according to a dentist's prescription. The job involves use of the fingers and hands in the manipulation of tools and various materials such as gold, plastics, and wax. Employees usually perform their tasks seated at a workbench, and the job is relatively sedentary. The major problem was that the dental-appliance firm had a turnover rate of 80% per year. The employees simply could not, or would not, continue in the job for very long, even though the pay was quite good. The management suspected that they were not hiring people with the proper abilities.

Task Analysis

The first step in developing a test battery was to evaluate just what employees had to do on the job. A description of the job resulted from this analysis. The authors then asked what kinds of abilities might be required in these particular skills. Earlier studies on abilities provided a number of possibilities such as Manual Dexterity, Finger Dexterity, and Steadiness. Thus, the first tests included in our preliminary battery were reference tests of the abilities that we guessed were involved in the job. A second group of tests consisted of *face valid tests*, meaning that the performances involved in the tests were closely related to the actual performance on the job. For example, perceptual tests in which the subjects had to choose which of four model teeth most closely matched a reference tooth in size and color were used; in another test, they were to match two-dimensional pictures of teeth with three-dimensional models.

A third group of tests was thought to relate to fundamental mechanisms in motor control and learning, many of which we have discussed in detail in other chapters. For example, to measure the consistency of muscular impulses, there was a test called Velocity Production, for which rapid, ballistic movements of the fingers and a stylus, with a goal MT of 100 ms, were required. The Fitts tapping task was also used, as various authors have felt that this task measures the rate of information processing involved in making movement corrections. A ballistic aiming task of a stylus to a target, using primarily the hands and fingers, measured the consistency of programmed output. Thus, this part of the project involved a great deal of brainstorming, in which one would think up abilities that might be involved in the job and ways that they might be measured, either through established methods or by a method that could be created.

Predictor Variables

The result of this process was 24 *predictor tests*—tests from which success on the job was to be predicted. Note that in this example, the idea of prediction does not imply futurity, as the concern was to develop ways of combining these predictor tests so that the success on the job of existing employees could be predicted. (Of course, having established this optimum combination, management would use this battery to predict success for future applicants who had not been trained in the skills.) These 24 predictor tests, about equally divided among the three categories previously described (reference tests, face valid tests, and tests of underlying processes), were then administered to 44 of the current employees, all of whom had had at least one successful year on the job.

Criterion Variable

Probably the most critical aspect of the project was the development of a *criterion score*. This score was the best estimate of the employee's level of skill on the job, and it might take many forms. In this instance the supervisors were asked to rank the employees from "most skilled" to "least skilled," and to do this in a group session in which each employee's skill was discussed and a consensus about the final ordering was achieved. It was this rank that was to be predicted with the battery of tests. In other occupations, the criterion score might be one's yearly production level, quality of play in a sport as judged from game films, peer ratings of performance on the job, or any other measure providing a "best" estimate of success.

The criterion score is what one is really trying to predict. Alternatively, if one could have some advance information about the applicant's criterion score before hiring, the task of hiring (or not hiring) people would be trivial. We would simply hire the person with the highest criterion score. The problem is that this criterion score is not available for new applicants because they have had no training on the job, so we must estimate it (or predict it) from tests of the abilities that underlie the activity.

Validation

At this stage, the task was to determine which of the 24 predictor tests were the most valid (or useful) in predicting the criterion. This was done in two ways. First, the correlation between each of the predictor tests and the criterion was computed. The decision was to not use any test that correlated less than .15 with the criterion, as such a test would have so little in common with the criterion ($.15^2 \times 100 = 2.25\%$) that it would probably not be worthwhile to include it in a test battery. This preliminary screening of tests revealed 14 tests that correlated .15 or greater with the criterion. This pattern of low correlations, even after the tests had been chosen because they would probably correlate with success on the job, was not surprising given the evidence about specificity of skills.

The next step was deciding which tests, and in what combination, were most effective in predicting the criterion score. One common problem is that two tests, both of which correlate, say, .40 with the criterion score, might correlate .60 with each other. It is likely that these two tests tend to measure the same ability and are thus redundant in predicting the criterion score, so that including one would be as effective as including both. Decisions like this are based on a statistical procedure called *multiple correlation.*

Multiple Correlation

Multiple-correlation methods are very similar to "regular" correlation measures, except that the multiple correlation (abbreviated R) is the correlation between the criterion score and a weighted *combination* of the predictor scores. Imagine combining the predictor scores (for example, [1.0 × Test 1] plus [2.5 × Test 2] plus [8.0 × Test 9] plus [5.5 × Test 24] to form a single sum for each subject. If we correlated this weighted sum (a single score) with the criterion score (another single score) using traditional correlation as described earlier, we would have a kind of multiple R. The only difference is that inherent in the multiple-correlation procedures is the automatic determination of the weights in the sum, so that the correlation between the weighted sum and the criterion score is maximal. That is, the multiple-correlation technique automatically adjusts the weights so as to achieve a maximum correlation between the predictors and the criterion, and thus it "decides" which of the predictors are most and least effective in predicting the criterion and in what combination. This procedure produces what is called a *regression equation,* which is the specification of the weights and the variables that best predict the criterion score, the employees' rankings. In the present case, this equation had the form

$$\text{RANK} = .589(\text{BA}) + .422(\text{TL}) + \\ .560(\text{SS}) + .297(\text{RL}) \quad (9.2)$$

where the abbreviations (BA, TL, SS, and RL) are the predictor test names: Ballistic Aiming, Tapping (Left Hand), Spatial Scaling, and Rotated Letters, respectively. The final step was determining the test battery that would be used to predict success with new applicants. It should be recognized that the prediction would be best if we were to use all 14 tests, but the time needed to measure 14 test performances on every new applicant would not be worth the effort. Thus, there is a trade-off between the number of tests and the size of the multiple R. Adding tests raises the R, but with each added test the multiple R is raised by a smaller and smaller amount, eventually to the point that adding another test will not be useful. The final battery involved 4 tests. For these 4 tests, the multiple R was .50. Think of this R in the same way as a traditional correlation. The battery had accounted for about .50^2 × 100 = 25% of the variance in the criterion score with the various predictors. Thus, about 75% of the abilities that were important for this job were not included in the battery of tests.

Applicability

This particular example of prediction of success in dental technicians is one of many examples we could have given. Each would have demonstrated the same major methods. The method can be applied to a variety of situations with only slight modification. The techniques are relatively time consuming and expensive (because of testing time), but various ways of cutting costs with minimal reductions in effectiveness can be employed. The area of industrial personnel selection has used these techniques for years, and the armed services have employed them in pilot selection programs. A few professional football teams use batteries of tests that have been developed in ways like those described here, but this is more the exception than the rule.

Some Efforts at Prediction of Skill

With use of the basic methods just described, attempts have been made to develop batteries of tests that would predict success in various situations in the military, in industry, and in professional sports. Clearly the most systematic and large-scale effort in this regard has been the attempt to develop prediction batteries for U.S. Air Force and Navy pilots. The problem is very serious, as the Air Force and the Navy cannot afford to train a large group of unselected recruits to determine who will and who will not "make it." There is a strong possibility of accidents, of the loss of very expensive equipment, and even the loss of life if the "wrong" people are included in the training. For these reasons primarily, a great deal of research has been directed toward the problem, mostly during the post-World War II years, the 1940s and 1950s.

Fleishman has been one of the most active researchers in this area; in fact, most of the knowledge about motor abilities discussed earlier in this chapter comes indirectly from the Air Force and Navy pilot training programs. Some of the important findings are presented in the next section. For more information on these programs of research, see Fleishman (1956) or Adams (1953, 1956, 1987).

Prediction of Pilot Success

In this research, the criterion score—the score that is the "best" measure of the behavior to be predicted—is usually a measure of success in flight school. This in itself is a complex score, consisting of instructors' ratings of flying skills, performances on a wide variety of knowledge tests, evaluations based on "leadership" qualities, and various subjective evaluations of personality. Typically, this research is done using a large group of potential pilot trainees, measuring a variety of motor and perceptual tests (the predictors) as well as assessing the criterion score of success in flight school, and then using multiple-correlation methods to determine which predictors, and in what combination, are the most useful for predicting success in flight school. About 10 tests have been so identified, and they are described next.

Two of the tests closely resemble the task of controlling an airplane. The complex-coordination test (see figure 2.5) involves manipulation of a joystick and foot pedals to control a three-dimensional display. The rudder control test entails controlling the direction of a cockpit-like structure with foot pedals. These tests have validity coefficients—that is, correlations with the criterion score—of $r = .45$ and .40, respectively.

Other tests are used that do not resemble the task of pilotry so obviously. One is the pursuit rotor (figure 2.5), in which the person attempts to follow a rotating target with a handheld stylus; its validity is .30. A pursuit confusion test, in which a target is tracked in a diamond-shaped pattern, correlates .30 with the criterion. A two-hand coordination test (figure 2.5), in which the two hands control perpendicular movements of a pointer to follow a target, correlates .30 with the criterion. And a direction control test, in which the proper movement must be selected quickly in response to a signal, correlates .34 with the criterion.

Notice that none of the predictor tests, by itself, correlates very highly with the criterion measure, the highest of these correlations being .45. Remember, this means that at most about 20% ($.45^2 \times 100 = 20.25\%$) of the abilities are common between the "best" test and the criterion score. However, when these tests were combined to form a *battery*, Fleishman found that four of the tests in combination predicted the criterion score about as well as a much more time-consuming battery of 14 paper-and-pencil tests that had been used previously. When the psychomotor tests were added to the printed tests to form a larger battery, the multiple R increased from the previous value of .47 to .57. In some cases, the total battery of printed and psychomotor tests correlated .70 with the criterion score. This is about the highest level of prediction that can be claimed in the Air Force program.

One has to be impressed that, despite the amounts of money, time, and effort devoted to this program, the predictability of pilot success is quite low. Remember that a multiple R of .70, which is the highest value reported in this research, means that less than half of the relevant abilities in pilotry have been identified by the battery of tests (i.e., $.70^2 \times 100 = 49\%$). There is still a long way to go to predict success effectively. The next half of the problem is the toughest of all, as the obviously involved and easily measured abilities have already been identified.

Reasons for Lack of Predictability

The pilot research is typical of numerous situations in which prediction of success is attempted from batteries of tests (including the one described earlier, Schmidt & Pew, 1974). Why has the prediction of success been so difficult?

Certainly, the most important problem is that human motor abilities are not understood very well. Even with the work of Fleishman and others, research on individual differences has not been extensive. The abilities discovered to date are quite tentative; they are not well understood in terms of their underlying physiological or psychological processes, and they tend to be limited in generality to situations using the hands. With a better understanding of these underlying abilities, we would be in a far stronger position to predict success in various occupations and sports.

A related problem is that even though a person may have a solid hunch about which abilities might be involved in a particular activity, the research necessary to develop effective *tests* of these abilities has not been done. The development of tests is a long, time-consuming process in which the instructions to subjects, the scoring procedures, and the configuration of the apparatus are constantly adjusted, with the hope that each change will produce larger correlations with the criterion score. Test development also has the goal of increasing test-retest *reliability*, for lack of reliability places upper limits on the correlation of the predictors with the criterion. Payne (1983) argued that lack of reliability of predictor and criterion tests was a major contributor to the relatively low multiple correlations found in the Air Force program. Developing effective tests with high reliability and validity requires many subjects and considerable testing time, making the overall task of test battery development a difficult one.

A third problem is that the number of human abilities appears to be quite large. The number of abilities that will underlie a particular job, such as pilotry, will be quite large as well. Thus, in order to predict success in the activity, we must somehow obtain a measure of the majority of these underlying abilities. Of course, when we do not know what these abilities are or how to measure them, the result is only moderate success in prediction.

The problems in prediction are many, yet this kind of research is important for many reasons. Individuals will naturally be happier if they can be directed toward occupations for which they have the requisite abilities and away from occupations for which they are not suited. Also, efficiency of the institution will be increased and accidents will be reduced. The payoff clearly seems worth the price.

Individual-Difference Variables

In this final section we describe some research about certain kinds of individual-difference variables and the ways in which they are related to skilled performance. An individual-difference variable, sometimes called an *organismic variable*, is usually some definable trait that can be measured in people, such as age, height, weight, gender, skin color, or number of brothers and sisters. It has been of some interest to determine what relationships these variables have to the performance of certain kinds of skills. Such questions as "Do men outperform women on tests of pursuit tracking?" or "How much does movement speed decline as age increases beyond 40?" are tied to this general way of studying individual differences.

The studies that are done to examine individual-difference variables can be termed *pseudo-experiments* largely because they appear to be "true" experiments but really are not. That is, subjects are typically classified into one of a number of categories, such as male/female, old/young, or novice/expert. Then, to examine the "effect" of this classification, we find out how one subgrouping differs on the average from the other subgrouping. Of course, there can be more than two subgroupings (e.g., short, medium, and tall people, or each of the 10-year categories from 20 to 80 years of age). What is important to remember about these studies is that the interpretation of any differences between the average performance of the various subgroups is usually stated in a form in which differences between the subgroupings are changes in the dependent variable studied: for example, one might find that age is *related to* skill in the pursuit rotor. However, it is not logically correct to infer that the differential ages of the two groups of subjects were necessarily the cause of the differences in performance. Any number of factors related to (correlated with) a person's age could just as easily be the cause. Age effects could be caused by associated differences in body weight, height, strength, amount of previous movement experience, and a host of other factors.

Space does not permit a discussion of many of these individual-difference variables, so we will concentrate on those that have been studied the most and that have the most interest and relevance for understanding human skilled performances. The discussion will focus on four important variables: age, gender, intelligence, and level of expertise. Others, such as race or country of national origin, sociological variables like number of siblings and birth order, and body configuration variables like height, eye color, weight, percentage of fat, and fitness, have obvious importance but will not be dealt with here. For more on these kinds of variables, see Noble (1978) or Singer (1975).

Effects of Age on Skilled Performance

The study of the effects of age has traditionally been divided according to two separate age spans. There are studies of what is called *motor development*, that is, of children as they mature and gain experience. A second category of studies is related to *aging*, or the processes related to the effects of age on performance of individuals in the upper age categories. The kinds of changes in skills seen during these two age spans are markedly different, even though the variable of interest—age—is the same in both cases.

Motor Development

One major finding that emerges from the motor development research is that as age progresses to about 18 years, large and systematic gains occur in nearly every conceivable aspect of motor performance (see Keogh & Sugden, 1985, for a review). These improvements can be divided into categories related to biomechanical changes (Zernicke & Schneider, 1993), posture (Woollacott & Sveistrup, 1994), strength (Blimkie & Bar-Or, 1996), capacities to anticipate and predict (von Hofsten, 1983), ability to process information from complex displays, speed of decision and movement, accuracy in throwing (Halverson, Roberton, & Langendorfer, 1982), and so on (see also Gabbard, 1992; Payne & Isaacs, 1991). We could probably make the case that in some way, most of the laboratory and real-life tasks studied involve the various abilities discussed in earlier sections of this chapter. And these abilities appear to develop, through maturation or experience or both, with increasing age up to about 18 years. So, it is not surprising at all that, on the average, older children typically outperform younger children.

One of the common hypotheses in the motor development literature today is the idea that as humans become older, they increase in their capacities for processing of information (e.g., Thomas, 1980). Certainly this theme is important for adults and is an important idea in the individual-differences work as well (Fleishman & Bartlett, 1969; Sternberg & Wagner, 1989). Thus, in the performance of skills, children appear to be relatively deficient in the rate and amount of information that they can handle. Children appear to have smaller capacities to hold information in short-term memory, shorter attention spans, and perhaps less effective mechanisms for processing information necessary for movement (e.g., feedback or environmental cues—see Thomas, Thomas, & Gallagher, 1993).

In contrast to the information-processing view, another hypothesis that has attracted increasing attention in recent years considers the development of coordination skills within the context of dynamical pattern theory (see chapter 8). By this view, motor development (and infant development in particular) involves the emergence of coordination skills as a function of the interaction of body parts with each other and with the environment (Thelen & Smith, 1994; Thelen & Ulrich, 1991). This view has introduced new theoretical and methodological strategies to the study of motor development and presents an exciting challenge to future research.

Aging Effects

One of the fastest growing areas in the behavioral and biological sciences is *gerontology*, or the study of aging. The primary concern here is with the upper age levels and the associated changes in the motor system that affect movement abilities. Aging studies, like motor development studies, have been conducted on numerous variables related to motor behavior, such as postural control (Teasdale, Bard, LaRue, & Fleury, 1993; Wade et al., 1995; Woollacott & Manchester, 1993), rapid arm movements (Pohl, Winstein, & Fisher, 1996; Pratt, Chasteen, & Abrams, 1994), tracking (Jagacinski, Liao, & Fayyad, 1995), and learning (Chaput & Proteau, 1996; Swanson & Lee, 1992). A comprehensive review of all these variables and many others related to aging processes can be found in Spirduso (1995).

One of the most widely studied variables is the effect of aging on RT. Recently Fozard et al. (1994) examined the changes in simple and choice RT in males and females ranging in age from a mean of

20 years to 90 years. As can be seen from the data in figure 9.9, there is a marginal slowing in simple RT with age, but a more dramatic slowing in choice RT. The decline in performance of tasks requiring speeded decisions, especially for tasks of increasing complexity, seems to be one of the most general findings in the aging research (Salthouse, 1985; Spirduso, 1995).

Another consistent finding in the aging literature is that people move more slowly as they age. We see such effects on speed not only in tasks for which speed is measured directly, but also in tasks for which speed is evaluated indirectly. For example, in tasks for which accuracy and speed are required, the overall score will often suffer with increasing age because speed decreases. Or there may be a marked shift in the speed-accuracy trade-off, with speed decreasing and accuracy either increasing or being held constant. According to early thinking about these speed deficits with age, this slowing was reflective of slowing in neurological activities in the central nervous system—not only those involved in nerve conduction times but also those involved in decision making and other aspects of information processing. Later studies suggested, however, that this slowing may be related to the fact that older people appear to be more "cautious" than younger people (Welford, 1984). If so, being unwilling to make errors on a task makes a person—

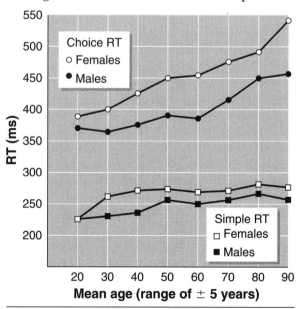

Figure 9.9. Effects of age and gender on simple and choice RT.

Reprinted from Fozard, Vercruyssen, Reynolds, Hancock, and Quilter, 1994.

old or young—appear to be slow. Strategic factors are currently the subject of much continued research in aging and human performance (e.g., Morgan et al., 1994).

Although aging research tends to focus on the factors that *decline* with age, this does not represent the entire picture. There are many aspects of performance that are maintained well into advanced years. Thus, aging research does have a very optimistic side to it as well. The challenge for research in this area will be to identify factors that mediate decline in cognitive and motor behavior variables with a view toward intervention methods.

Gender Effects on Skilled Performance

Investigators have examined the differences between the genders on nearly every motor task imaginable (for reviews see Thomas & French, 1985; Thomas, Nelson, & Church, 1991). Some researchers have been directly concerned with these differences, while others have seen gender differences as incidental findings in studies directed toward other questions.

Certainly one common observation would suggest that males outperform females in many, if not most, motor tasks. Some of these differences are obvious, such as the different levels of Olympic records for swimming, track and field, and so on for women and men. These casual observations are borne out in the literature, which reports that men outperform women in motor behaviors such as various athletic skills, strength, pursuit tracking, ladder climbing, throwing, jumping, and running (e.g., Noble, 1978; Singer, 1975). It is difficult to know whether or not these differences have to do with gender per se, because for many of these tasks, success is correlated with body size and other factors (Thomas, Nelson, & Church, 1991).

It is interesting to consider those tasks in which women outperform men. Various authors have shown that women perform tasks requiring sensory discrimination (e.g., color discrimination) more effectively and that women are better than men at tasks such as rapid manipulation (card sorting, dotting, tapping, aiming), when speed and repetition are important (Noble, 1978). Gender effects that favor women have also been found for the inverted-alphabet task (which involves printing the alphabet upside down and

backward as quickly as possible) and for many small-motor tasks (see Noble, 1978, for a review).

Rather than simply documenting that males are or are not different from females on some task, a more fruitful approach is to ask what the sources of these effects, if present, may be. In one example of this approach, Laszlo et al. (1980) used a task in which subjects had to roll (by hand) pool balls to strike a target a few meters away. When the background, or surrounding environment, was very "quiet" and plain, males and females performed about the same on this task, with males having a slight edge. But when the environment and background were complex, either visually because of distracting lines and shapes or auditorily because of tape-recorded traffic noise, there were strong detrimental effects on performances of females but no such effects on those of males. Is it possible that females found it more difficult than males to ignore the irrelevant information in the environment? If so, these differences in the ways that males and females appear to handle or process information could have important influences in sport and industrial settings; but at this stage we do not know exactly why these effects occurred. And these findings are probably related to Witkin's (1949) well-known observations of gender differences in handling spatial information; women appear to be more tied to external environmental information (i.e., they are more "field dependent") than men (see also Cratty, 1964).

Perhaps we should not take all these gender differences at face value. First, one has to wonder how important they are. A great deal of variability exists among both men and women, and the distributions overlap considerably on most tasks. That is, even though men are statistically better at some tasks than women, usually many women in the sample outperform most of the men in the sample. Second, it is not at all clear what proportion of gender differences are due to gender per se. As we know, many socially imposed standards of behavior are different for males and females; boys have been traditionally praised for playing sports, while girls have been traditionally praised for being "feminine" and passive. Our society is beginning to emerge from a time when these effects were probably very strong. Third, it is possible that many of the differences in performance between males and females are due to the differential movement experiences of the two genders. Finally, as mentioned earlier, well-documented differences exist in body size and strength, which could be major determinants of success in athletic skills. When these factors are not present, the gender differences are considerably less, with women outperforming males at many tasks (see Gill, 1992).

Intelligence and Motor Performance

Intelligence is usually defined as a capacity of the individual to act purposefully, to think rationally, and to deal effectively with the environment. In our society, which stresses activities involving abstract concepts, reasoning, and the acquisition of knowledge and education, the idea of intelligence implies abilities related to cognitive skills, such as might be learned in the classroom. It is therefore difficult to define intelligence (some have defined intelligence as "whatever intelligence tests measure"), and a large variety of different tests are available.

Intelligence (measured as an *intelligence quotient* or *IQ*) has had a rough time of it lately. For one thing, a dominant theme in the ideas about IQ has been that it measures the ability or capacity to learn new facts and concepts. Yet studies that have measured IQ and the "rate" of learning new verbal materials (see DuBois, 1965) have failed rather consistently to show that IQ predicts the "ease" with which new material is learned. In addition, serious social problems have been associated with IQ tests and with the strong possibility that the tests are "culturally biased." The IQ tests, like any test, are measures of *performance.* Such tests, based as they are on word knowledge and verbal proficiency (among other things), are likely to be biased in favor of those people who have had the benefit of these teachings in home and in school. The problem in the United States has been most severe with respect to poor, primarily black and Hispanic, people for whom opportunities have not been equal to those for more affluent whites. As a result, it is not clear that the notion of IQ is very meaningful (but see Jensen, 1970, 1978). Yet it is one of the measures that is still used and widely discussed.

We *might* expect that intelligence—whatever it is—would be related positively to success in skilled activities. One point of view is that we appear to be processors of information when we produce motor skills, so more effective informa-

tion processing as a result of greater IQ would lead to more effective performance. For such reasons, we might expect to see strong differences in motor skills among groups classified according to IQ, or correlations between IQ and performance.

But such relationships have not generally been found. Ryan (1963) reported no relationship between academic achievement (presumably related to IQ) and performance on a balancing task (stabilometer). Start (1964) showed that IQ and learning of a novel gymnastics stunt were correlated only .08, suggesting few common abilities between the two tests. Tests of mental abilities and tests of motor abilities are generally related only minimally in children and adults (e.g., Thomas & Chissom, 1972); but Ismail, Kephart, and Cowell (1963) found moderate relationships between motor tests and academic achievement. Also, there are only minor differences between athletes and nonathletes in terms of academic success in high school or college, with some studies showing advantages for athletes and others showing disadvantages. (These differences are difficult to evaluate, however, as there are also differences in what kinds of courses are taken, how many credits per term are taken, and so on.) The possible reasons for the lack of association of IQ with motor skill performance are probably two: (a) intelligence is not very much involved in the production of movements, and (b) IQ tests are not good measures of intelligence. We suspect that both viewpoints may be correct.

There are intelligence-related differences in skilled performance when the IQ range examined is extended downward, however. While the reasons that deficiencies in IQ are so strongly related to motor behavior have not been well understood, there are various hypotheses. One is the idea that people with very low IQ are generally less active physically so that the decrements are perhaps due more to a lack of movement experiences in childhood than to any deficiency in mental functioning. A second idea is that at severely low IQ levels, there is a general depression of the functioning of the entire central nervous system, including those parts that are primarily involved with motor control and motor learning. Yet in many cases, people with low IQs have been trained to perform very skillfully on production-line tasks in which motor performance is critical but decision making is not. Such issues, however, require far more research (Hoover & Wade, 1985).

Expert-Novice Differences: Expertise

The acquisition of motor skill and the processes that affect the quality and speed of learning are issues that will be dealt with in the next part of the book. However, the examination of differences between people who are already skilled and those who are minimally skilled represents a relatively new and rapidly growing area of individual-differences research (Ericsson, 1996; Starkes & Allard, 1993).

Expert-novice differences research is characterized by various methodological approaches, each contributing unique information about the ways in which distinctions can be made between people of varying levels of skill in certain activities (Abernethy, Burgess-Limerick, & Parks, 1994; Chamberlin & Coelho, 1993). We will briefly summarize some of these approaches.

Remembering Briefly Presented Information

Early work in cognitive psychology (Chase & Simon, 1973; deGroot, 1965) revealed that master chess players had excellent recall of games they had played previously. To examine this apparent superior "memory" under controlled experimental conditions, expert and novice chess players were briefly shown chessboards of games that had been partially completed and then asked to remember the information by reconstructing the game board after it had been removed from view. As expected, the experts were much better than the novices at this recall task. However, when the "game" that was shown was in actuality a series of randomly arranged chess pieces, the experts were no better at reconstructing the board than were the novices. Clearly, the recall advantage was quite specific to the nature of the expertise: the pattern displayed in an actual game had meaning and relevance to the expert, but not so for randomly arranged pieces. Thus, the recall advantage was specific to the domain of the subject's expertise.

These important findings have been replicated in studies of sport expertise, particularly for sports having a prominent perceptual component. For example, Abernethy, Neal, and Koning (1994) compared expert and novice snooker players' recall of ball positions during an actual match. Although the experts were better at the task than

the novices, no differences were found when the balls were scattered randomly on the table. Similar findings have been reported in sports such as basketball, volleyball, field hockey, and football (see reviews in Chamberlin & Coelho, 1993; Ericsson & Lehmann, 1996; Shea & Paull, 1996; Starkes & Deakin, 1984).

Visual Analysis of Displays

Eye movement recording devices allow the experimenter to analyze the parts of a visual display that a subject fixates during visual search. By this technique, researchers have tried to identify whether experts and novices differ in terms of how they gather visual information from the environment, particularly when watching the actions of an opponent. Experts do tend to have greater visual search "economy," as revealed by fewer fixations compared to novices (e.g., Helsen & Pauwels, 1993). However, the eye movement recording techniques have generally been ineffective in distinguishing between *what* experts and novices fixate in a display (Abernethy, 1993).

A more promising approach to analyzing expert-novice visual processing differences has been to record on videotape what a performer may be viewing in a game situation. Experts and novices are then compared on various performance measures given certain temporal and/or spatial alterations that are made to the videotape. For example, hockey goalies might be asked to predict where a shot will go when a videotape is stopped at various times prior to or just after an opponent has contacted the puck with the stick (e.g., Salmela & Fiorito, 1979). Spatial occlusion methods include masking certain relevant and irrelevant parts of a display, such as the various parts of the arm and racket of a badminton opponent (Abernethy & Russell, 1987). In general, studies of this nature have revealed that experts pick up important visual information earlier and from more spatially distinct sources than do novices.

Domain Knowledge Reports

An alternative type of methodology for studying expert-novice differences is the analysis of self-report data. In this method the verbal reports of athletes engaged in certain sport-specific situations are subjected to a protocol analysis (e.g., French & Thomas, 1987). The objective of this analysis is to identify domain-specific differences in knowledge about certain tactics, procedures, rules, nuances, and so on that distinguish the expert from the novice. Obviously, this qualitative type of information is not obtained through the more conventional methods that we have described. Studies of this type are relatively recent and provide a number of interesting hypotheses about knowledge differences between experts and novices (e.g., McPherson, 1993, 1994; Starkes et al., 1996). However, the validity of the method has also been questioned (Abernethy, Thomas, & Thomas, 1993).

Specificity of Expert-Novice Differences

Henry's hypothesis, which states that individual differences are task specific, seems to also extend to the differences seen between novices and experts. Much of the work already discussed here revealed that, where differences do occur, they are almost always specific to the task or knowledge represented by the nature of the expert's expertise. In fact, there is a considerable body of research that has failed to show any differences between experts and nonexperts in general measures of motor ability, such as RT, visual abilities, and general knowledge (Abernethy, Neal, & Koning, 1994; Starkes & Deakin, 1984).

One exception to this principle of specificity of expert-novice differences, as we noted in our earlier discussion, may be related to *timing*. For instance, Yamanishi, Kawato, and Suzuki (1980) found that musicians performed both in-phase and various out-of-phase bimanual tapping tasks with more stability than nonmusicians. Summers and Pressing (1994) also report that musicians are generally more capable of performing difficult polyrhythm patterns than nonmusicians. Thus, certain types of musical experts (but perhaps not all types) have superior timing skills that may generalize to nonmusical tasks. Whether or not "motor experts" possess other skills and abilities that are generalizable awaits further research.

Individual Differences as an "Experimental" Method

To conclude, it is important to mention that the individual-differences approach and the experimental approach are not as separated as they might seem on the basis of the discussion earlier in this chapter. Certainly the tendency exists on the part of differential and experimental scientists to continue to be separated in

method and subject matter, but a few have attempted to bring the fields closer together. One such effort (see Underwood, 1975) has been to provide tests of theories, which have been most closely related to the experimental tradition, by individual-differences methodologies.

Suppose some theory predicts that experimentally (artificially) increasing some independent variable should have a tendency to increase some dependent variable. Ordinarily, a researcher would examine this prediction by taking a group of subjects, manipulating the independent variable, and noting the associated changes in the value of the dependent variable. This is, of course, the classic experimental method.

But a similar thing can be done with an individual-differences approach. Instead of experimentally inducing changes in the independent variable, the researcher could take a large group of subjects and classify them according to their (naturally determined) scores on this independent variable, perhaps into two separate groups. If the theory is correct, then the group classified as highest on the independent variable should outperform (on the dependent variable) the group classified as low on the independent variable. Or, in a method that is essentially the same, a correlation could be computed between the performance on the independent variable and the performance on the dependent variable; if the theory is correct, then the correlation should not be zero, as some association should exist between the independent and dependent variables. However, the method is limited—as the individual-differences approach always is—by the lack of capability to show that some relationship was a casual one. Even so, such studies could be used as companions for experimental work, and could represent important converging evidence for (or against) a particular theoretical viewpoint.

Summary

The study of individual differences concerns the variations among individuals on various tasks or behaviors. This kind of research differs strongly from the experimental approach in which differences among individuals are ignored in order to concentrate on the average performances of larger groups of people affected by certain independent variables. Two major subdivisions of individual-differences research can be identified.

The major focus is on abilities, defined as stable, enduring characteristics or traits, probably genetically defined, that underlie certain movement skills or tasks. Since the 1930s, there have been many points of view about the structure of motor abilities. Some convergence has occurred on the idea that humans possess a relatively large number of separate motor abilities (perhaps 50 to 100), that these abilities are independent, and that a given skill or task may have many of these abilities underlying it. Henry's specificity theory and Fleishman's work on factor-analytically determined abilities tend to point to this kind of conclusion. Both of these approaches indicate that the idea of a general motor ability defining proficiency on all motor tasks is surely not correct, although timing ability appears to be an exception.

A second major division of individual-differences research is related to *prediction*. In studies of prediction, the relationships between scores on various tests (the *predictors*) are used to predict or estimate the scores on some other test (the *criterion*). A common example is the prediction of an applicant's probable success on the job from various measures of abilities involved in that job. The development of predictive batteries of tests is time consuming, and the effectiveness of such batteries of motor tests in predicting some criterion behavior is disappointingly low, even when a great deal of research funding and effort have been directed toward the problem. The major difficulty is that abilities are not well understood, that many abilities need to be understood, and that not enough research effort has been directed at these important problems.

A large number of individual-difference variables has been studied. These variables, such as age, height, gender, and country of birth, provide an easy basis for classifying people, so that the performance on some task can be studied "as a function of" these variables. Four major divisions of research variables have attracted considerable research interest: (a) age effects, both from the point of view of growth and maturation and from the point of view of older age levels (gerontology); (b) gender effects; (c) intelligence effects as they relate to motor performance; and (d) expert-novice differences. While such studies provide information about the "effects" of these variables, the results are often confounded by other variables related to these classification variables (e.g., body size being correlated with gender or age).

Notes

[1] The limiting factor is that the correlation between test X and test Y is theoretically less than the square root of the reliability of either test X or test Y; that is, $r_{xy} \leq \sqrt{r_{xx}}$ or $r_{xy} \leq \sqrt{r_{yy}}$. See Gullicksen (1950).

PART 3

MOTOR LEARNING

This point in the text represents a shift in emphasis with respect to the treatment of motor skills. The concern so far has been with skilled performance—often at high levels of proficiency—and the numerous internal processes that make these performances possible. We now shift to a different, but related problem: the learning of skills as a result of practice or experience. The problem is different from the issue of skilled performance, because we will be focusing on the *changes* in skill, rather than the nature of skill at some particular level. As such, different methods and logic are needed to understand these performance changes; and in chapter 10, we document some of the more important ones. Later in this part, we will use these methods to describe some of the laws and principles that have been discovered about motor learning. Chapters 11 and 12 describe how conditions of practice and augmented feedback influence learning. In chapter 13, we present the various ways in which the learning process has been conceptualized by researchers. This part closes in chapter 14 with a discussion of factors that influence retention (how learning is retained over periods of no practice) and transfer (how learned behavior can be applied in novel situations).

MOTOR LEARNING CONCEPTS AND RESEARCH METHODS

Learning is a truly critical part of our existence. Think where we humans would be if we could not profit by the experiences and practices in which we all engage. You would not be able to read the words on this page, we would not be able to type the words that appear here, and no one would be able to speak. In short, we would be simple beings indeed if we were forced to behave in the world equipped only with the skills we inherited. The fact that we can acquire new knowledge and skills has led to a robust interest in the ways in which people learn, in the critical variables that determine how people will profit from experience or practice, and in the design of instructional programs.

We do not have the space here to do justice to the entire topic of learning. There are examples of learning in all organisms (even the simplest of single-celled organisms), and the learning that humans enjoy is the most complex of all. Thus, many forms of human learning will not be discussed here, such as the learning of verbal materials, the learning of concepts, and the learning of interpersonal skills. We will concentrate on the acquisition of motor skills, as defined in chapter 2. Essentially, the concern will be with the effects of practice and experience on performance, in an attempt to understand the relevant variables that determine gains in proficiency.

Motor Learning Defined

Learning in general, and motor learning as the learning of skilled behaviors in particular, have been defined in a variety of ways. Four distinct characteristics are included in the definition. First, learning is a *process* of acquiring the *capability* for producing skilled actions. That is, learning is the set of underlying events, occurrences, or changes that happen when practice enables people to become skilled at some task. Second, learning occurs as a direct result of practice or experience. Third, learning cannot (at our current level of knowledge) be observed directly, as the processes leading to changes in behavior are internal and are usually not available for direct examination; rather, one must *infer* that learning processes occurred on the basis of the changes in behavior that can be observed. Fourth, learning is assumed to produce relatively permanent changes in the *capability* for skilled behavior; changes in behavior caused by easily reversible alterations in mood,

motivation, or internal states (e.g., fatigue) will not be thought of as due to learning.

A synthesis of these four aspects produces the following definition: *Motor learning is a set of processes associated with practice or experience leading to relatively permanent changes in the capability for movement.* We discuss these aspects in more detail next.

Motor Learning Is a Set of Processes

A *process* is a set of events or occurrences that, taken together, lead to some particular product, state, or change. For example, in reading we are interested in processes that transform visual information to provide meaning; in motor control we focus on processes of retrieving a motor program from memory; and in physiology we can discuss processes in maintaining blood pressure. Similarly, practice and learning can be seen as a set of analogous processes that, taken together, lead to the acquisition of the capability for moving. These processes are assumed; in other words, we assume that some set of processes must have taken place in order for learning to have occurred with practice. However, what these processes are (exactly) is not specified, and in fact the nature of these processes is what learning theorists try to understand. Thus, an important focus is on what happens—in terms of the underlying processes—when people practice and acquire new skills.

Learning Produces an Acquired Capability for Movement (Habit)

The processes of learning—like all processes—generate or result in a product or state. In the case of motor learning, this state is an increased *capability* for moving skillfully in the particular situation. Notice that we have not defined learning as a change in *behavior* per se, as many have done (e.g., Morgan & King, 1971). In this sense, the goal of practice for the learner is to increase the "strength" or the "amount of" this internal state, so that the capability for skill will be maximized in future attempts. The researcher's goal is to understand the *nature* of the internal processes that have led to the increases in the state; thus, hypothetical processes are proposed by theorists to account for learning in experimental settings. Also, the researcher wants to understand the nature of the state itself, perhaps in terms of the codes involved or the kinds of control it exerts on behavior; such knowledge will tend to provide an answer to the question of *what* was learned.

James (1890) termed this internal capability for movement "habit" (with only minor reference to the usual use of the word), but it has been named in other ways by other theorists. Regardless of its label, the notion of some internal state that is the product of learning represents a critically important distinction. Defining learning as producing a capability for movement directs our focus to the internal state and the processes that have led to it, rather than simply to the behavior. More importantly, the concept of a capability for movement implies that if the capability is present and "strong," then the skilled behavior may occur if the external conditions, motivation, and other surrounding factors are present; if the conditions are not favorable, then the skilled behavior might not occur—for example, if fatigue were present or motivation were low. That is, behavior may vary for a number of reasons, only some of which are a result of change in the internal capability for movement produced by practice. This concept provides a basis for the *learning versus performance distinction* that is a major theme of this chapter.

Numerous changes in humans can contribute to their capability for movement in skilled situations, but many of these have little to do with learning as defined here. For example, we know that increased maturation or growth can lead to improvements in skill, as older children generally outperform younger ones. Similarly, changes in strength or endurance from physiological training could contribute to certain kinds of skills, such as those used in weight lifting or soccer. However, we would not want to include such improvements in a definition of learning because, in the examples just mentioned, practice or experience is not the basis for the changes in capability. We will be searching for situations in which changes in capability are primarily related to changes acquired through experience.

Motor Learning Is Not Directly Observable

It should be clear that motor learning is not directly observable. The processes that underlie changes in capability—and the nature of the capability itself—are probably highly complex phenomena in the central nervous system, such as changes in the ways sensory information is orga-

nized or changes in the patterning of muscular action. As such, they are rarely directly observable, and one must infer their existence from changes in motor behavior. This feature of motor learning makes it particularly difficult to study, as experiments must be designed so that the observed changes in behavior allow the logical conclusion that there were associated changes in some internal state.

Motor Learning Is Relatively Permanent

Another feature of motor learning is that it is relatively permanent. When one engages in practice and learns some activity, something lasting occurs, something that does not simply pass away in the next few minutes or hours. More dramatically, we could say that when you practice and learn, you will never be the same as you were before. Learning has the effect of changing the learner (if only slightly) in a relatively permanent way.

With respect to skill learning, this distinction is important because it rules out the changes in skills that can come from a variety of temporary performance factors. For example, skills can appear to improve if the person is in the "right" mood, if motivation is temporarily high, or if certain drugs are administered. Yet each of these changes in behavior will probably vanish when the temporary effect of the mood, for example, "wears off." Thus we should not attribute these changes in behavior to motor learning, because they are not sufficiently permanent.

An analogy may help to clarify this point. If you cool water sufficiently, you will find that it becomes solid (ice); you can reverse the effect completely to produce water again simply by warming the ice. Not so with boiling an egg. Boiling an egg for 10 min will produce changes that are not reversible when the egg is cooled. Some relatively permanent change has been made in the egg, but this is not the case with the water.

This analogy applies well to the concept of motor learning and performance. The nature of the water or of the egg can be observed directly, and they both behave in predictable ways when the independent variable (temperature) is applied. But beneath the surface is some unobservable change in the nature of the substance; in one case (the water), this change is completely reversible and not relatively permanent, while in the other (the egg), the change is not reversible. With human learning, many analogous variables can be applied in order to change the observed behavior (skill), but these may or may not change the internal structure of the person in a relatively permanent way. If the effect of some independent variable can appear and disappear as the value of the variable is changed, then this change in behavior cannot be associated with anything relatively permanent, and hence is not thought to be due to learning. How permanent is "relatively permanent?" This is a vague term, and scientists studying learning are rarely clear about it. But the intention of this discussion should be clear; learning should have some lasting effect.

Measuring Motor Learning

Given that motor learning is a set of processes that underlie the changes in a capability for movement, how can such a capability be measured in order to understand what variables affect it? It will be helpful to consider a typical motor learning experiment to explain some of the major points in the measurement process.

Performance Curves

In a simple experiment on learning, a large group of individuals is asked to practice on some motor task, and the experimenter charts their performances as a function of "trials" (a *performance curve*). For example, figure 10.1 is a graph from Fleishman and Rich (1963) showing performance on the two-hand coordination task. Subjects had to follow a moving target by movements of two crank handles, one controlling forward-backward direction of a pointer and one controlling right-left movements (see figure 2.5). The average time on target (in minutes) for a group of 20 subjects is plotted as a function of successive blocks of four 1-min trials. A clear trend can be seen for the scores to increase with practice, with the increases being somewhat more rapid at first and then leveling off later.

When the measure of performance is some error score, it is common for scores to decrease, as shown by the performance curve in figure 10.2. These data, from Quesada and Schmidt (1970), are from subjects' performances on a timing task. Here, the subject had to operate a switch when a moving pointer became aligned with a stationary

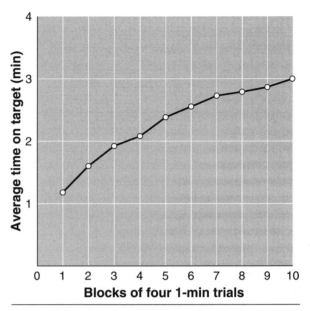

Figure 10.1. A performance curve showing increases in the score with practice.
Reprinted from Fleishman and Rich, 1963.

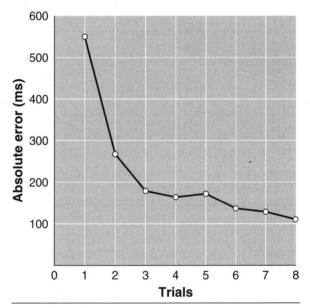

Figure 10.2. A performance curve showing decreases in the score with practice.
Adapted from Quesada and Schmidt, 1970.

one, and error was the interval between the switch movement and the actual moment of coincidence. Average absolute error decreased rapidly at first, and more gradual decreases occurred later in practice.

Even though the two performance curves (figures 10.1 and 10.2) change in opposite ways with practice, they both represent gains in skill, and almost certainly can be interpreted as caused by motor learning. Such effects are usually some of the most powerful in the study of motor behavior.

In fact, if scientists wish to prevent subjects from learning, they must take very strong precautions. But what is usually of more interest than whether or not learning occurred is whether learning was greater in one condition than in some other condition. Thus, the question of interest is related to the role of variables that influence learning of the motor task. In order to make meaningful inferences about whether or not condition A produced more learning than condition B, special procedures are needed to analyze these performance scores in motor learning experiments.

Motor-Learning Experiments

Graphs such as those shown in figures 10.1 and 10.2 are often thought to represent the acquired capability for movement (i.e., habit) in the subjects during practice from trial to trial, and to some extent they probably do. For this reason, such curves are often loosely termed *learning curves*, as it is tempting to regard the changes in performance as reflecting the product of the internal capability for movement generated by learning. The notion that these curves exactly "mirror" the internal state (the amount of habit) is oversimplified, however, and scientists are very cautious about interpreting the changes in curves like those in figures 10.1 and 10.2 as a reflection of motor learning. Some of these considerations are outlined next.

Performance Measures

The first reason that performance curves perhaps should not be thought of as a reflection of learning is that *performance*—not the *capability* for moving—is measured as a function of trials. Because the capability (habit) cannot be measured directly, any change in habit that has occurred must be inferred from the changes in performance. Thus, it seems more logical to term such curves *performance curves* rather than learning curves.

Between-Subject Variability

A second problem in making inferences about learning from these performance curves is that they are insensitive to the differences between individuals that arise as a function of practice. Consider how a performance curve is produced. A large number of people (the larger the better, usually) is used. All subjects' first-trial scores are averaged to obtain the data point for trial 1, all

subjects' trial 2 scores are averaged to obtain the data point for trial 2, and so on. This averaging procedure has a number of advantages, such as "canceling out" any random (perhaps essentially meaningless) variations in persons' scores due to inattention, errors in measurement, and other factors not directly related to the internal habit changes. But at the same time, this averaging procedure tends to hide any differences that may have existed between people on a particular trial, or it may hide important trends in improvement with practice.

These effects can be particularly important in the study of learning. Consider two hypothetical people whose performances over a number of trials are shown in figure 10.3. Person 1 has a difficult time improving in the task until late in performance, when finally performance improves markedly. But Person 2 seemed to improve in performance early in the sequence, with little change occurring later.

Now consider what happens if these two subjects' scores are averaged in ways that are typical for studies of larger groups. In figure 10.3, the center line is the average of the performances for the two subjects for each of the trials. The pattern of improvement with practice is considerably different now. It might be tempting to say that the average capability for responding accumulated gradually and consistently. This, of course,

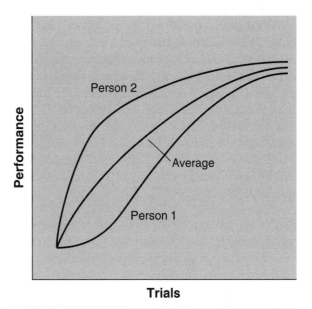

Figure 10.3. Hypothetical performance curves for two individuals, together with the curve representing the average of their performances.

would be misleading, as neither of the subjects who produced the average performance curve showed this trend. Thus, it could certainly be that learning does not occur gradually at all, as is evidenced by the individual performance curves. Rather, learning might sometimes occur as more of an abrupt "revolution" than as a gradual "evolution" in the ways in which the subjects perform the task.

Within-Subject Variability

As mentioned previously, one of the important aspects of the averaging procedure is the elimination of errors in measurement and of factors that seem to obscure the "true" capabilities of the people on a particular trial. As seen in chapter 7, a typical finding is that people inherently vary from trial to trial, even if they are attempting to do the "same" thing for each. But is trial-to-trial variation for a particular person due to some meaningless random fluctuation in the motor system, or is it due to some meaningful change in the way the person attempted the task on a particular trial?

The problem can be better illustrated with an example. Consider the task of free-throw shooting in basketball when the subjects are relatively inexperienced. Certainly a great deal of variability exists in this task from trial to trial, and much of this variability does not seem to represent fundamental changes in the ways the people attempt the task. If a large group of people is examined on this task, with performance scored as "correct" or "incorrect," each person will have a pattern of scores that shows a large number of apparently randomly ordered hits or misses, with somewhat more hits as practice continues. And different people will have the hits and misses scattered across the trials differently.

A performance curve can be plotted with these data, with the measure for a particular trial being the *probability of success* on that trial (figure 10.4). With this measure, the data point for trial 1 will be the total number of hits divided by the total number of attempts (i.e., the number of subjects), or the proportion of subjects that shot successfully on trial 1; the method is similar for trial 2. When plotted, the average performance curve usually rises gradually, perhaps moving from .10 to .40 in 100 trials. From such a curve it is tempting to conclude that the capability for accurate shooting grew slowly as a result of practice. But notice that not a single subject showed this pattern of performance! Indeed, there is no way that a given

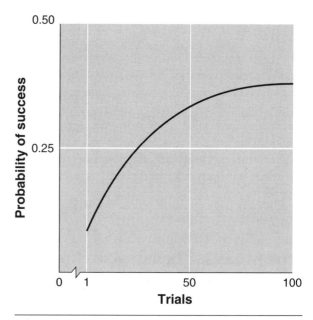

Figure 10.4. An average performance curve for which probability of success is the dependent measure. (On a particular trial, any given subject can receive only 0 or 1.)

person could ever achieve a score of .20 on a particular trial, as a single subject can only achieve 1.0 (hit) or 0 (miss) on a single trial. Thus, the average performance curve in figure 10.4 obscures all the variations that occurred within people across trials and encourages us to make conclusions about the learning process that may be incorrect.

Ceiling and Floor Effects

Ceiling and floor effects are a third kind of problem that lead to erroneous conclusions about learning processes from group performance curves; these are present in many of the tasks used in motor learning experiments. In most tasks, absolute scores exist that no one will exceed. For example, there can be no fewer than zero errors, no less than 0 s for some timed task, or no more than 30 s for a time-on-target score in a 30-s performance trial. Thus, as people approach these ceilings (the limitation in score at the top of the scale) or floors (the limitation at the bottom of the scale), the changes in the performance levels of the people doing the task become increasingly *insensitive* to the changes in habit that may be occurring in the people as they practice. As a person approaches some ceiling or floor, it becomes increasingly "difficult" to improve performance; in gymnastics, for example, it is far "easier" to improve one's score from 6.0 to 6.5 than it is to improve from 9.0 to 9.5, when "perfect" is 10.0.

In addition to these absolute scoring ceilings and floors, psychological or physiological floors and ceilings can be present as well. For example, the 4-min mile was at one time a barrier that we thought would remain unbroken. Now the barrier is considerably lower, but it could very well be that no human will ever break a 3-min mile. Will anyone ever long jump more than 30 ft? As performers approach these physiological limits, it becomes increasingly more difficult to improve.

Scoring Sensitivity and the Shape of Performance Curves

The primary problem is that the "rate" of progress (the slope of the performance curve) toward some ceiling is usually quite arbitrary and dependent on the ways in which the task is measured. The rate does not seem directly linked to the rate of change in the capability for movement that underlies this change in behavior. A powerful example of this principle comes from a study by Bahrick, Fitts, and Briggs (1957, "simple task"). The authors studied 25 male subjects on a continuous tracking task for 10 90-s practice trials. The pattern of the track that the subjects had to follow, and the movements of the lever that the subjects made when following it, were recorded for later analysis.

The authors analyzed the single set of performances in three different ways. First, they assumed that the width of the target the subject had to follow was small, 5% of the total width of the screen. (There was, in fact, no target width as far as the subjects were concerned, as all they saw in the performance trials was a thin line that moved on the screen.) By going over the tracking records and examining the number of seconds in a trial during which the subject was in this imaginary 5% target band, the authors obtained a separate measure of the "time on target" for every subject and trial. Then, the data from trial 1 were averaged for all the subjects to form the trial 1 data point in figure 10.5 for the curve marked "5%." The data for other trials for this target size were handled in a similar way.

The authors then performed this procedure a second time, scoring the subjects using a different tolerance for error (again, there was no target width as far as the subjects knew). Here, the target width was 15% of the width of the screen, and the subjects were evaluated in terms of the number of seconds during a trial that the pointer was in this target zone. As the criterion of success was much

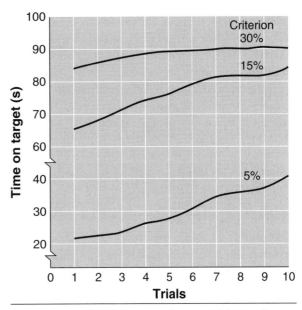

Figure 10.5. Time on target for a tracking task as a function of trials for three different scoring criteria. (The 5% criterion indicates that the target used for scoring was 5% of the screen width, and so on.)
Reprinted from Bahrick, Fitts, and Briggs, 1957.

more lenient (the "target" was wider, therefore easier to hit), the time-on-target scores were naturally larger, forming a second performance curve marked "15%" in figure 10.5. Finally, the procedure was done again, this time with a very wide target that was 30% of the width of the screen. In figure 10.5 the performance curve for these data is labeled "30%."

The important point about these data is that all three curves are based on the *same* performances, but the differences between them are produced by the ways in which the experimenter has chosen to evaluate those performances. We might conclude (if we did not know that all the data came from the same performances on the same subjects) on the basis of the 5% curve that habit gains are a positively accelerated (concave upward) function of trials, and on the basis of the 30% curve that habit gains are a negatively accelerated (concave downward) function of trials. This is, of course, nonsense; one pattern of habit gain emerged (whatever it was), but evidence about this one pattern was obtained in three different ways that gave three different answers about how the capability for responding progressed with practice.

The differences are apparently caused by the fact that making the criterion "easier" (moving from 5% to 30% target widths) moves the person through the range from floor to ceiling, over which the *sensitivity* of the scores to the level of skill is different. Thus, the same learning has occurred in all three curves from trial 1 to trial 3, but very different amounts of *performance improvements* are displayed depending on which target zone one chooses to use. So, what is the pattern of habit change that occurred with practice? We have no idea, on the basis of these data, and we can conclude (erroneously) anything we choose just by selecting the "right" target width to study (see also Wilberg, 1990).

Implications for Experiments on Learning

These considerations present strong constraints on what can be understood from experiments on learning, often making it impossible to provide clear interpretations about what happened to habit in the study. Consider this hypothetical example. We want to study whether children learn more than adults as a result of a given amount of practice at some new task. (We could as easily ask about males versus females, older

versus younger adults, and so on.) We choose a task such as the rotary pursuit test that is foreign to both the children and the adults and allow both groups to practice.

One of the findings that emerges consistently from the work on children's motor behavior is that adults nearly always perform better than children (although video game performance may be an exception). If we were to use a pursuit rotor with a very small target and a fast speed of rotation (a so-called difficult task), allowing the children and adults to practice for 50 30-s trials, we might expect curves such as those that appear in figure 10.6a. Here, both hypothetical groups begin with nearly no time on target, but the adults improve more than the children, because they are relatively closer to hitting the target than are the children. With a little practice, their initial advantage in motor control begins to show up in terms of increased time on target, whereas the children show no such effects even though they may be moving slightly closer to the target. We may (erroneously) con-

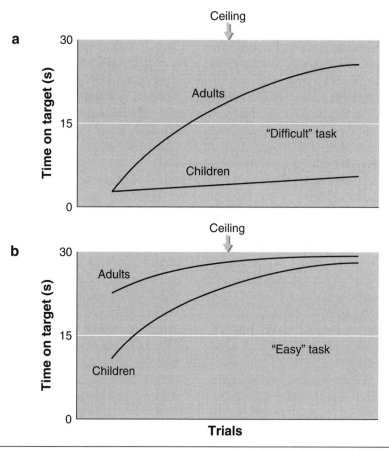

Figure 10.6. Hypothetical performance curves for adults' and children's performances on a "difficult" or an "easy" task. (Depending on the scoring criterion, one can [erroneously] conclude that adults learn more than children [a] or that children learn more than adults [b].)

clude that the adults learned more than the children because their performance gains were larger.

Now consider what happens if we do the "same" experiment, but with an "easy" version of the rotor task in which the target is large and the speed of rotation is slow (figure 10.6b). Now the adults begin very near ceiling, and the children are somewhere in the middle range. The adults have little capability to demonstrate continued improvement, whereas the children start in a sensitive area of the scoring range where a little practice produces maximum score gains. In this case, the gains in score are much larger for the children than for the adults. We might (again, erroneously) conclude that the children learned more than the adults.

This nonsense is caused by the marked differences in the sensitivity of the scoring system to changes in the subjects' behaviors and movement patterns—that is, in the sensitivity to changes in the level of habit of the subjects. The central region of the scoring system (15 s time on target) is very sensitive to changes in the subjects' habit, whereas the regions near the ceiling and floor tend to be relatively insensitive to such changes in habit. In fact, if we wanted to show that children and adults learned the same amount, we could easily choose a scoring criterion intermediate in "difficulty." So, given the choice of the sensitivity of the scoring system, we can produce any conclusion we desire about the relative amounts of learning in children and adults.

But games like this are not science, and it does not make sense to play them. Even so, scientists do not know how to resolve this particular problem, and thus we have no idea whether children learn more than adults or vice versa. The lesson is that such effects are always present in learning studies, and scientists have to be aware of the potential artifacts that they may produce in coming to their conclusions about learning (see also Estes, 1956; Sidman, 1952). Fortunately, experimental designs that minimize this kind of problem are available. Some of these designs are described in the next section.

Designing Experiments on Learning

One of the major goals in the study of motor learning is to understand which independent variables are involved in maximizing learning, which are involved in impairing learning, and which have no effect whatsoever. Clearly, such knowledge is important for both the development of useful theories of learning and for practical application in teaching and other learning situations.

Given the definition of learning and the limitations on the kinds of behavioral changes that scientists are willing to classify as learning changes, how do we go about deciding whether a certain variable influences learning or not? One obvious way is to ask two large groups of people to perform and learn a novel motor task. Then we administer one level of the independent variable to one group of people and another level of the independent variable to the other group, and measure the performance levels achieved after considerable practice. The group that has performed "best" at the end of the practice sequence presumably has learned the most. While this approach sounds reasonable, the assessment of learning is not so easily made, as shown in the following example.

Example: Blocked Versus Random Practice

There are a large number of independent variables that could be used as examples, but we have selected one that has received a great deal of research attention in recent years. Also, as it concerns the scheduling of practice, the variable has many practical applications to teaching situations. Suppose you are given three tasks to practice and a limited number of trials in which to practice each task. How would you structure the practice sequence such that learning is maximized from this limited amount of practice? Many sequences are possible, but two represent the most extreme. *Blocked practice* is a sequence in which all the trials on one task are done together, uninterrupted by practice on any of the other sequences. *Random practice,* on the other hand, occurs when the same task is not repeated on consecutive trials. Notice that in both sequences the same number of trials is performed on each task. The only difference is that in blocked practice, all the trials on one task occur consecutively, whereas in random practice, practice on each task is interspersed with practice on the other tasks. This issue of practice sequence is important in a wide range of learning situations, as trainers, employers, and teachers need to know how to structure practice in order to maximize the effectiveness of the practice time available.

For now, assume we want to know what the effects of blocked practice (as compared to random practice) are on the learning of these novel motor tasks. The pioneering study in this research area was conducted by Shea and Morgan (1979). They asked subjects to learn to respond to different-colored stimulus lights by making movements with one arm to four specific target locations, as fast as possible. Three movement patterns were learned, each paired with a light of a different color. On each pattern, 18 practice trials were provided, for a total of 54 practice trials. Subjects in the blocked group completed all 18 trials of one pattern before practicing a different pattern (different subgroups were formed to counterbalance the practice orders so that not every blocked subject performed the same task first, and so on). Subjects in the random group switched patterns on each trial (actually, the restriction used by Shea and Morgan was that no more than two trials on any particular task could be performed in a row).

The results of this experiment are shown in figure 10.7. The dependent variable was the average time to perform the task, defined as the duration of the reaction to the stimulus light (RT) plus the time taken to complete the arm movement pattern (MT). Performance over blocks of

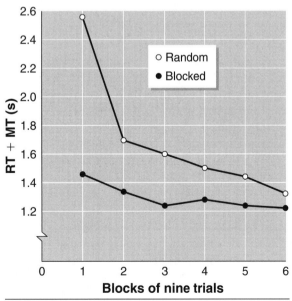

Figure 10.7. Blocked and random effects during practice.
Adapted from Shea and Morgan, 1979.

practice trials are plotted along the x-axis.[1] The findings are very clear. Blocked practice resulted in an immediate performance advantage compared to random practice. And, though the performance difference was reduced over blocks of trials, there was still a slight advantage favoring the blocked group at the end of practice.

Which group learned more? Asking this question is essentially the same as asking "What is the effect of practice order on learning?"—because being able to define which group learned more allows one to answer the question involving the effect of practice order on learning. At first glance, the answer seems very clear: blocked practice facilitates learning because performance was enhanced immediately and throughout the entire practice sequence as compared to performance in random practice.

But maybe the answer is not so clear as we may have thought at first. Consider the following competing hypotheses:

Hypothesis 1: The blocked group learned more than the random group. This hypothesis suggests that the differences in learning are manifested in the differences in performance, with the blocked group performing more effectively because of a greater acquired capability for responding. Or, we might say that switching between practice patterns has interfered with the acquisition of the capability for responding in the random group.

Hypothesis 2: The random group has learned as much as (or more than) the blocked group, but performs more poorly during the practice trials because of the temporary performance effects of continuously switching between task patterns. In other words, it is possible that the true capability for responding by these two groups cannot be compared meaningfully by their acquisition performance results because of the temporary influence of the frequent task switches in the random group.

Hypotheses 1 and 2 clearly concern two distinctly different effects of independent variables in practice—one that is relatively permanent, and another that is temporary. This is a very old idea, as such learning theorists as Tolman (1932), Guthrie (1952), and Hull (1943) recognized long ago that not all the changes in performance curves during practice may be caused by relatively permanent effects of an independent variable. This general notion has been formalized somewhat over the years to provide what is known today as the *learning versus performance* distinction—a critical concept in the study of learning in general and motor learning in particular.

Upon viewing figure 10.7, you may intuitively feel that Hypothesis 1 is correct. But with the evidence at hand here, there is no way to discriminate between the two hypotheses, and they have to be seen as equally likely to be correct until more evidence can be brought to bear on the question. One method used in these situations involves obtaining an estimate of the "relatively permanent" effects of the practice order variable as distinct from the temporary effects. In these situations, a technique called a transfer design is used to great advantage.

Transfer Designs

The problem with the results that we have so far is that we cannot tell whether the differences between the groups in figure 10.7 are due to the "relatively permanent" effects, as Hypothesis 1 would have it, or whether they are due to temporary interference effects (Hypothesis 2). It is clear from the findings that the frequent

switches cause the subjects in the random group to perform the task patterns more slowly, and even 54 trials of practice are not enough to overcome the performance advantage of the blocked-practice sequence. But do these performance differences reflect a true difference in what was *learned* during practice?

One way to resolve this uncertainty is to provide a test of learning that is independent of the practice data. This is essentially the logic behind the methods of assessing learning in various practical skills; the effects of driving-range practice are viewed in the context of how well you score in your next round of golf, the skills practiced by surgeons and dentists have their ultimate test on the patient's health, and the value of a driving lesson in a vacant parking lot is put to the test on the road. These are examples of *transfer designs.*

The transfer design used by Shea and Morgan included a test, 10 min after the practice period had ended, in which subjects performed three trials on each of the patterns in a random order. This could be considered analogous to the golf example. Regardless of the order in which you practiced various club selections on the driving range, the order in which you select clubs on an actual course has the appearance of being more random than blocked, as the outcome of the previous shot determines the club selection for the next shot. If the independent test for learning conducted by Shea and Morgan supported Hypothesis 1, we would expect to see the transfer

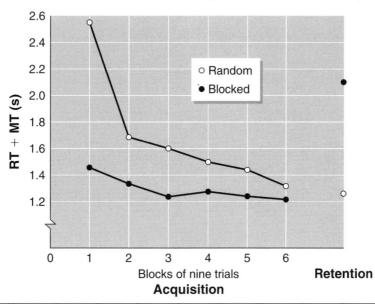

Figure 10.8.   Blocked and random effects during practice and in retention tests 10 min after practice.
Adapted from Shea and Morgan, 1979.

test performed better by the blocked group than by the random group. However, if the random group actually learned more than would be inferred from the practice data, as suggested by Hypothesis 2, then we might expect to see the differences disappear between the blocked and random groups on the transfer test.

The effects of blocked and random practice in the Shea and Morgan study, as seen on the right side of figure 10.8, provide overwhelming support for Hypothesis 2. In fact, the performance advantage that had been seen during practice was *reversed* when performance was assessed on the transfer test. These data suggest that blocked practice, instead of being better for learning than random practice, is actually *worse* for learning! In chapter 11 we will have much more to say about these effects and the hypotheses that have been suggested to explain why they occur. For now it is important to understand, as shown in this example, that a practice variable can have opposite effects on temporary performance levels versus the relatively permanent levels that must be assessed in order to make statements about learning.

Structure of Transfer Designs

Transfer designs are critical to the study of motor learning, as they provide a way of studying various independent variables with respect to their effects on the learning of motor tasks. These designs have several important features.

Temporary Effects Allowed to Dissipate. Before a transfer test can be conducted, it is important that the temporary effects of the independent variable be allowed to dissipate. This may be less essential for experiments on random and blocked practice than it is, say, for studies on the effects of fatigue on motor learning (e.g., Godwin & Schmidt, 1971). In studies of fatigue it is common to measure performance under conditions in which a group of subjects has induced muscular fatigue while practicing a novel task, and to compare their performances with those of another group that has practiced the task without the fatiguing conditions. The effects of fatigue severely disrupt performance during the practice trials. But, before the learning effects of fatigue can be evaluated in a transfer test, these temporary effects of fatigue on performance must be allowed to dissipate. A delay is provided that is of sufficient duration to permit an assessment of learning not confounded by any temporary effects that are still lingering as a result of the independent variable.

Have a look now at figure 10.9. In their work, Shea and Morgan (1979) were unsure what length of delay would be sufficient to allow the temporary effects to dissipate. So they made a wise decision and asked half of the subjects in each group to perform the transfer test after a 10-min delay, and asked the other half to return after a delay of 10 days to perform the transfer test. Notice that had they asked all subjects to perform

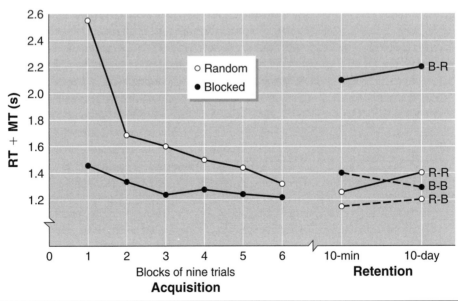

Figure 10.9. Blocked and random effects during practice and in various conditions of immediate and delayed retention. Adapted from Shea and Morgan, 1979.

both transfer tests, it is possible that the results in the 10-day test could have been influenced by the performance in the 10-min test. Using a split-groups procedure eliminated the possibility that the delayed transfer test may have been *contaminated*. The results of the randomly ordered transfer tests are shown in the circles joined by the solid line in figure 10.9 (right-hand side). The performance times after a 10-day delay are slightly longer than after a 10-min delay. However, the *relative difference* remains virtually the same between the random- and blocked-practice groups (R-R and B-R, respectively, in figure 10.9).[2]

Common Level of Independent Variable.   There are various types of transfer designs. In one type, all groups are transferred to a common level of one of the independent variables. That is, both groups of subjects in the transfer phase practice the task with the same value of the independent variable. For the Shea and Morgan (1979) data presented in figure 10.8, both groups were shifted to a random-practice sequence for the transfer phase. There are reasons a researcher might pick one particular level of an independent variable for the transfer test, such as its similarity to real-world conditions. If one wanted to assess "gamelike" conditions, then a random order might be more appropriate than a blocked transfer test. If one wanted to assess transfer performance when individuals are tired (such as at the end of a work shift or game), then a transfer test under fatigued conditions might be more appropriate than under nonfatigued conditions. However, other transfer options are available.

Double-Transfer Designs.   There is a potential problem with using one level of the independent variable for the transfer test. For example, with reference to figure 10.8 the argument could be made that by the use of a random transfer test, there was an advantage in favor of the group that had practiced with the random order. This is so because the blocked group was required to switch the order in which they performed the movement patterns, and the effect of *switching conditions in itself* could have influenced the transfer results. This design-issue concern has been around for many years, and is most adequately dealt with by using a *double-transfer design* (e.g., Denny, Frisbey, & Weaver, 1955).

Fortunately, Shea and Morgan (1979) also anticipated this potential effect of switching conditions and used a double-transfer design. In addi-

tion to going through the randomly ordered transfer trials illustrated in figure 10.8, all subjects performed a set of blocked trials as well. The results of the complete double-transfer design are presented in figure 10.9. We have already discussed the effects of the practice groups when subjects were switched to the random transfer test (groups R-R and B-R). There are three important things to note regarding the findings for the blocked transfer test (groups R-B and B-B). First, performance of all the groups in the blocked transfer test (i.e., the circles joined by dashed lines) is generally better than the performance of the groups in the random transfer test. This simply means that the transfer test itself was having an influence on performance that was similar to the influence it had during practice. Second, the differences between the random and blocked groups on the blocked transfer trials were still evident, although they were smaller than those in the random transfer test. Third, and perhaps of most importance here, is that switching the random-practice group to the blocked transfer trials did not eliminate the transfer performance advantage they had over the blocked group. Even though the blocked transfer test *may* have favored the blocked-practice group (because no switch was required), the random-practice group still maintained an advantage. The double transfer design does not eliminate the possibility that switching conditions between practice and transfer will affect performance. However, the completeness of the design gives us a better overall picture of the temporary, permanent, and extraneous effects that certain variables have and the ways in which these influence our assessment of learning effects.

Possible Experimental Outcomes

Next, consider some hypothetical independent variables and some of the possible experimental outcomes, shown in figure 10.10. Assume a task in which the score increases with practice, and an independent variable that tends to exert its effects in the direction of making the task scores larger. An example might be motivational instructions on the Bachman ladder. To the left in figures 10.10a and 10.10b are the original-practice curves, showing that the groups with the two levels of the independent variable performed differently on the task. To the right in these figures are three possible outcomes when the two groups are

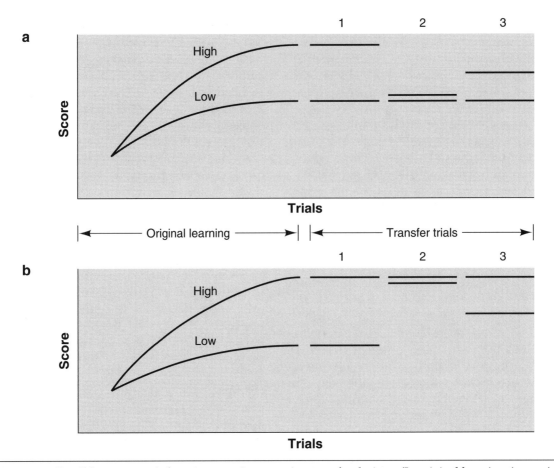

Figure 10.10.   Possible outcomes in learning experiments using transfer designs. (In original learning, increasing the independent variable increases the task scores [a] or decreases them [b]; cases 1, 2, and 3 in the transfer trials are some possible outcomes of transferring to the "low" {a} or "high" {b} value of the independent variable.)

shifted to a common level of the independent variable (i.e., low {a} or high {b} motivational instructions) after sufficient rest from the task to dissipate any temporary effects of the independent variable.

In the first situation (case 1), the original separation of the two groups is maintained exactly, suggesting that all of the effect of the independent variable was "relatively permanent," so that the variable can be considered as affecting learning of the task. In the second situation (case 2), the original separation of the two groups has vanished completely, suggesting that all of the effect of the independent variable was temporary, with none of it due to learning effects. Finally, in the third situation (case 3), some of the original separation has disappeared upon transfer, but not all of it. Thus, the conclusion would be that the variable in question has a component affecting performance temporarily, but also has a component affecting learning of the task. The argument is similar with variables that seem to have de-

pressing effects on performance (e.g., fatigue, massing, distraction).

Learning Variables and Performance Variables

With the use of these experimental designs, it has been possible to classify experimental variables into essentially two categories. One of the categories is that of the *performance variable*. According to its definition, this kind of variable has immediate effects on performance while it is present, but when the level is altered in transfer, the effect is altered as well. A performance variable is thus one that affects performance but not in a "relatively permanent" way. Using the analogy presented earlier, cooling water to make ice is a "performance variable," because the effect of the variable vanishes when it is taken away.

A *learning variable*, on the other hand, affects performance after the variable has been removed. That is, the variable influences performance in a "relatively permanent" way, affecting the learning of the task. Examples can be seen in the first hypothetical outcome in figure 10.10, where the effect of the independent variable remains even when the level of the variable is changed. To extend our analogy, boiling an egg for 10 min is a "learning variable."

Finally, variables may be both learning *and* performance variables. That is, many of the variables that will be examined in later chapters influence performance when they are present, as some part of the effect dissipates when the variable is taken away. Yet some other part of the effect remains when the level of the variable is changed, suggesting that the variable also has affected learning in the task. Examples like this can be seen in the third hypothetical situation in figure 10.10, where not all of the effect of the independent variable has dissipated upon transfer.

Some Alternative Methods for Measuring Learning

Many situations exist in which the measurement of performance, and thus the measurement of learning, does not give a good estimate of the "amount" that someone has learned in practice. The problem is often that the performance scores have approached a ceiling or floor during the course of practice, so that all the subjects appear to be the same on the task because all the scores hover close to the ceiling or floor. In such situations, attempts to show that a given independent variable has effects on learning will be thwarted because continued practice on the task can result in no changes, as the scores are already maximized or minimized.

These problems can arise in at least two different settings. One of these involves simple tasks, for which all subjects perform nearly maximally in only a few practice trials. Here, continued practice can result in no effects on the performance score. A second situation relates to a particular type of complex task—those that people have had a great deal of experience with in the past, such as driving a car. Because subjects are so well practiced, little improvement in skills will be evidenced as they continue to practice. The problem again is that subjects are so close to a performance ceiling that no additional improvements can be shown. Other examples are the performance of high-level sport skills and the perfor-

mance of various highly skilled jobs in industry.

In chapter 2, we discussed secondary-task methods for the measurement of skills. The problem there is similar to the present one, as the measures of the subject's behaviors in a particular task may not give a good indication of the level of skill this person possesses. The example we used was driving under the influence of fatigue. The accumulations of fatigue from long, uninterrupted stretches of driving were not observed in vehicle-control movements at all. However, when subjects were asked to perform a simultaneous secondary task, decrements in this task were observed as a function of the duration of the previous driving, suggesting that there was a decrement in "spare capacity" with increasing levels of fatigue (e.g., Brown, 1962, 1967).

Secondary Tasks and Alternative Learning Measures

The measurement of performance on a task often does not tell us much about the person's level of learning. Additional practice (e.g., driving a car) will probably result in some additional learning of the skill even at advanced levels of proficiency, but the experimenter may not be able to see these effects because the subjects are so close to the performance ceiling or floor, as the case may be. By using secondary-task methods, one can often see these changes more clearly.

Assume that two groups of subjects practice a task and that they have reached a performance ceiling. The performance could be at ceiling because the task is relatively simple and easy to learn, or it could be that there has been an extensive amount of practice on a relatively complex task like driving; it does not matter for the ideas presented here. Figure 10.11 shows some hypothetical curves that could result. Now, suppose that one of the groups (A) is told to discontinue practice, whereas the other group (B) continues to practice. Group B's curve is shown as a continuation of the earlier performance curve along the ceiling, as there can be no further improvements in the score after the ceiling has been reached. This procedure, in which a person practices further after having reached some criterion of success, is often called *overlearning*.

Did any learning of the task go on during the overlearning trials? Which of the two groups had learned more after all the practice had been

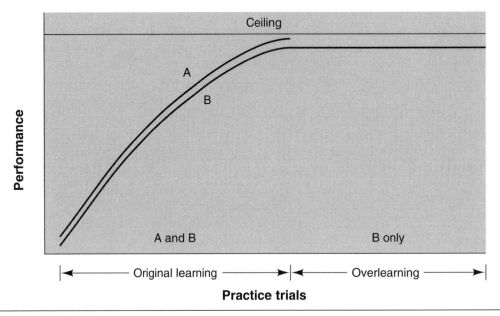

Figure 10.11. Hypothetical performance curves from original learning to a ceiling (groups A and B) and "overlearning" trials at the ceiling (group B only).

completed? We might suspect that the continued practice at the ceiling did something to the subjects, but we have no way to make this conclusion from the performance curves in the task, as both groups have the same final score—essentially at the ceiling. We will address these questions using this basic experimental design in the next three sections, so keep the situation indicated in figure 10.11 in mind. In each case, various methods with secondary tasks can be used to answer these questions.

Automaticity and Learning

One hypothesis that has received considerable empirical support is that skills become more *automatic* (see chapter 4) in the sense that systematically less interference with certain simultaneous secondary tasks will be shown. What would be the effect of imposing a simultaneous secondary task in the example shown in figure 10.11? We could (as Brown [1962] did) have the subjects do a mental task requiring the detection of a duplicated letter in a stream of auditorily presented letters. The measure of importance would be the extent to which the subjects could improve on this task as they were practicing the main task. Some hypothetical results are presented in figure 10.12. We would probably see continued improvement in the accuracy of the secondary task, even during the overlearning trials for which the score was essentially fixed at the ceiling on the main task. The improvement in the secondary task

would suggest that learning was going on during the overlearning, with practice reducing the attentional load and allowing more accurate task performance. This technique has not been used a great deal, but it is useful in situations like this.

Effort and Learning

Closely related to the notion of automaticity is the notion of *effort* (Kahneman, 1973). As people learn a motor skill, they appear to be able to do the task with less and less physical and mental effort, possibly because they learn to perform with more efficient movements or because they process information more efficiently. If so, then simultaneous physiological measures could be used to show that, during the overlearning trials in which the subjects are practicing the task at the ceiling, the effort in the task continues to be further reduced with learning. Measures like oxygen consumption (assessed by techniques associated with physiology of exercise) or heart rate (also a measure of effort) could be used. If during these overlearning trials we find less effortful performances, we would interpret such data as showing that the continued practice trials produced some additional learning, and that it was manifested as a decrease in the effort extended.

Speed of Decision and Learning

Another method is effective in situations in which the main task involves decision making, such as

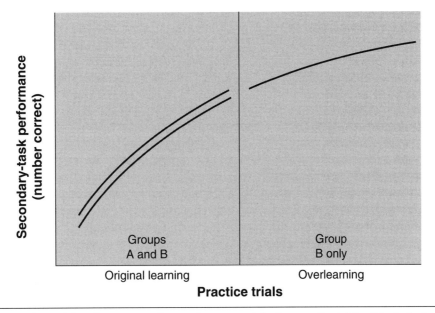

Figure 10.12.   Hypothetical data from a secondary task measured during practice trials of the task shown in figure 10.11. (The secondary-task score continues to increase even though the main task score is at a ceiling.)

in learning to make the correct movement when one of several different stimuli is presented. Early in the overlearning trials, subjects are perhaps barely able to choose the correct movement when the stimulus is provided. But later in overlearning, they can choose it easily and far more quickly. What if, in addition to measuring whether or not the subject could make the correct response, we measured the *latency* with which the subject did so (Adams, 1976a)? We would probably see that the latency of the response (which is not yet at a floor) would decrease markedly even though the accuracy of the response did not change at all (since accuracy performance was at the ceiling). This procedure will not work with all motor tasks, but it seems ideally suited to those situations in which accurate decisions have to be made. If such outcomes occurred, we would conclude that the decreased response latencies indicated a continuation of learning even though the subjects were at the ceiling, the learning being manifested as increases in *speed* with constant accuracy.

Memory and Learning

Inherent in the notion of learning is the concept of memory (chapters 3 and 14). In fact, most experimental psychologists define learning in terms of memory, saying that something has been learned when a person has a memory of it. In this sense, memory and habit are very similar constructs. The evidence that one has learned a skill is that he

or she can do it again at some time after the original-practice session.

With respect to the problem of overlearning, if the group with overlearning learned while practicing at the ceiling, the two groups should differ on a *retention* test given some weeks later, perhaps producing a pattern of results something like that shown in figure 10.13. Here, the group with overlearning trials should outperform the group without these trials on the first retention-test trial. Both groups would have lost, in this instance, some of what they had learned in the original session, but the group without the overlearning would be further below the ceiling than the group with the overlearning, leading to the conclusion that a stronger memory (habit) for the task existed after the overlearning condition. Evidence for a stronger habit after a retention interval could indicate that more was learned in the first place. We conclude that learning occurred even when the performance scores did not change in overlearning trials when scores were limited by the ceiling.

In addition to data on the initial performance on the retention test, useful information can be found in the patterns of improvement during retention-test performance. Typically, group B would be expected to improve at a faster rate than group A, reaching the ceiling somewhat more quickly as a result (and also because they had less loss in the first place). But another

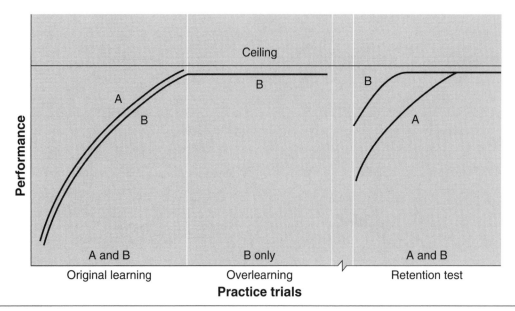

Figure 10.13.   Retention as a measure of original learning. (Original learning and overlearning trials are shown at left, with hypothetical scores from a retention test shown at right; the finding that B outperforms A on the retention test indicates that B learned during the "overlearning" trials even though no change in task performance could be seen.)

measure, first discussed long ago by Ebbinghaus (1913) and more recently by Nelson (1985), is the savings score (see also chapter 14). Here, the amount of additional practice "saved" in reaching some criterion score (in this case, the ceiling) on the retention test is measured. From figure 10.13, if group A required, for example, 25 trials to reach the ceiling again, and group B reached the ceiling in about 10 additional trials, overlearning would have produced an average savings of 15 trials. Savings scores are also of considerable practical interest in industry and the military because they indicate the amount of additional (time consuming and costly) practice that will be needed to return people to various criteria of "readiness" for a particular job.

Generalizability as a Learning Criterion

We normally think of learning as having the goal of improving our behavior on a *particular* movement (e.g., to serve more effectively in tennis), but broader benefits of practice should also be recognized. One of these is generalizability—the extent to which practice on one task contributes to the performance of other, related skills. As highlighted in chapter 6 in the section on generalized motor programs, our capability to perform a task like throwing is not based on one particular throwing movement. Rather, we appear to be able to

use a generalized throwing program for a variety of throwing tasks, but with the selection of appropriate parameters for the kind of object to be thrown as well as the distance and trajectory. We could regard throwing practice as having the goal of contributing to one's *overall* throwing capability as well as to the actual skills practiced. In this sense, we can measure the effectiveness of a practice session not only by how well the particular skills practiced are acquired, but also by how well other similar skills (that are not practiced directly) are acquired. This would involve measuring performance on other similar skills in a transfer test—analogous to the measurement of the retention characteristics of some main task as in figure 10.13. Then the acquisition condition producing the most effective performance on this transfer test would be judged as having the highest generalizability. We can therefore think of the measurement of generalizability as another in a group of alternative measures of learning. The details of these evaluations are related to the measurement of *transfer*, which we will consider in chapter 14.

Summary of Alternative Learning Assessments

All these methods are consistent with the fundamental notion (presented earlier) that learning is the set of internal, unobservable processes that occur with practice or experience, resulting in a changed underlying capability for moving. Therefore, it is not surprising that even when obvious changes do not occur in the main task, these learning processes can be demonstrated by a variety of other means, such as decreases in the interference created for other simultaneous activities, reduction in effort, increases in the speed with which a main task demanding accuracy is completed, changes in retention capabilities, or alterations in generalizability to other similar skills. These techniques highlight the idea that learning is internal and complex, having many forms in many different situations. Above all, we stress here the deficiency in the oversimplified idea that learning is merely a change in behavior on the task in question. It is clearly a much more complex process than that.

Issues About the "Amount" of Learning

On the basis of experiments on learning, researchers are often tempted to make statements phrased in terms of the amount of learning that has occurred as a result of practice. For example, we might wish to say that a group of subjects practicing with one condition learned 20% less than a group with another condition. Or you may wish to say that Jim learned twice as much as Jack on this task. Do such statements really have any meaning?

The problem is that habit is a construct that cannot be observed directly. Usually little basis exists for making quantitative statements about it, because it can only be estimated from performance scores. Recall the experiment by Bahrick, Fitts, and Briggs (1957) discussed earlier. By a simple change in the way the task was scored (the change in the strictness of the criterion of success), the authors obtained almost any scores they wanted, and they could easily change the shapes of the performance curves. For example, looking back at the data from their experiment in figure 10.5, we computed that the subjects with the 5% scoring criterion improved 86% as a result of practice, that the same subjects improved 29% with the 15% criterion, and that they improved 8% with the 30% criterion. How can we assess the "amount" of habit gain that occurred here? Will we say that it was 8% or 86%? That decision is purely arbitrary, and we would be equally incorrect in saying either.

The best one can do is to make statements about the *relative* amounts that two groups have learned, or about the relative amounts that two people have learned, essentially with statements like "group A learned more than group B." The issues are somewhat different for the case in which groups are compared to each other versus the case in which individuals are compared against each other, so these two situations will be discussed in turn.

Group Differences

Consider again the transfer paradigm discussed earlier in this chapter. Figure 10.14a is a typical example, showing that a change in the independent variable tends to increase the scores on the task. Here, the experimenter does not really have any idea about how much learning occurred, but can make statements about two things: the fact that both groups learned, and the fact that for however much learning there was, group A learned more than group B did. Because the two groups began practice on trial 1 with the same level of performance, and because during the course of practice they progressed to different levels of performance, the conclusion that group B learned less than group A in this case seems unavoidable. Remember that the test of the relative amount learned should always be on the transfer trials, as it is only there in the sequence that the temporary effects of the independent variable are equated for the two different levels of initial capability. Now consider figure 10.14b, where the two groups began practice at different levels of performance and, hence, different levels of initial capability. This initial difference could be attributable to some systematic difference in the nature of the subjects (e.g., males vs. females or children vs. adults), or it could be attributable to simple random sampling effects, whereby the groups simply differ by chance. In either case, both groups learned, but we are in a difficult position with respect to saying which group learned more. You can see that both groups gained about the same amount in terms of the score on the task, but you have no way of knowing whether the amount of change in the capability was larger or smaller for group A or group B.

The problem is that the differences in the initial level of performance on the task have confounded interpretation about which of the groups learned more. Thus, in designing these kinds of

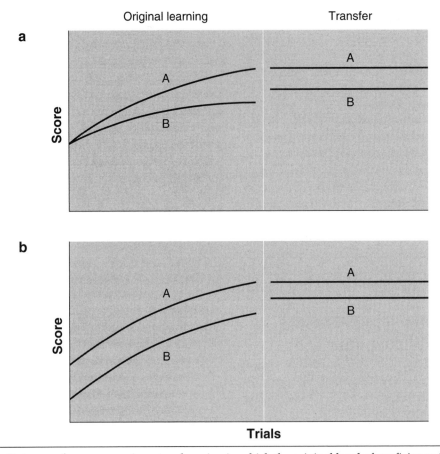

Figure 10.14. Outcomes from an experiment on learning in which the original level of proficiency for the two groups was controlled (a) or was not controlled (b).

ex-periments it is essential, if this question is to be asked about the data, to be certain that the two groups of subjects are equated at the beginning of practice so that differences in the performance at the end of practice (on the transfer test) can be attributed to changes in the amount learned. This can be accomplished by administering a pretest on the learning task, ranking subjects from highest to lowest on this test, and then assigning the subjects with odd-numbered ranks to one group and those with even-numbered ranks to the other group. In this way the groups are almost exactly equal on the first trial, and the problem is eliminated (other matching techniques are available as well).

There are some drawbacks to using a pretest. One is that the pretest provides some practice on the experimental task, which then reduces the size of the changes to be observed under the different levels of the independent variable. As another drawback, this procedure has the additional limitation that the first trials on a motor task are usually not strongly correlated with the last trials in the sequence—that is, with the final trials on which the relative amount of learning is assessed. Such cor-

relations are frequently as low as .20. If so, then the variable that is matched (initial performance) is not going to influence the "equality" of the groups on the transfer trials to a very strong degree.

A second method is to use large groups that are randomly formed from some larger group. In this way the groups will be expected to differ due to chance effects; but if the groups are large (e.g., 25 people per group), then the chance differences in the group means on the motor task should be relatively small. This procedure has the advantage that it does not provide subjects the experience on the task before the independent variable is administered, but it has the disadvantage that chance differences can occasionally occur. More on this issue can be found in Schmidt (1971a, 1972a).

Could you "correct for" the initial differences in performance (as seen, e.g., in figure 10.14b) by subtracting the initial difference from the differences that occurred in the transfer trials? While arithmetically this can be done, such procedures produce nearly meaningless interpretations of the relative amount learned. The problem is that the sensitivity of the scoring system to changes in the internal capability is different at various places on the performance scale. Thus, subtracting the initial differences in performance from the differences in performance at the end of practice will probably lead to an adjustment that is far too large. Because we have no idea how much too large this adjustment will be and we have no way to find out, such adjustments probably should not be used.

Of course, these adjustments are exactly equivalent to computing "learning scores," or the differences between the initial and final performance for one group, and comparing these differences to the difference between the initial and final performance scores for the other group (Schmidt, 1971b). The use of "learning scores" or "gain scores" is not as prevalent as it was some years ago, largely for the reasons mentioned.

Individual Differences in Learning

The problem just raised is similar in many respects to that of comparing the amount learned by one person to the amount learned by another person. This is a common problem in the study of individual differences in learning, as sometimes it is of interest to determine whether or not some measure of an ability correlates with the amount that someone will learn (e.g., Bachman, 1961 and many others). Naturally, in order to compute the correlation, one must achieve a measure of the "amount learned" by each person. But we have just argued that such measures are not meaningful if they are based on the differences between the initial and the final performance.

A second situation in which these kinds of measures are usually taken is in determining grades. Often, a measure of the student's initial level of proficiency is taken at the beginning of instruction, and another measure of proficiency is taken after the instruction has been completed; grades are then assigned on the basis of the difference between the initial and final performance levels, presumably in terms of "amount learned."

The fundamental problem with this technique is that the difference between initial and final performance is not a good measure of the "amount learned," for the reasons already discussed. Also, in philosophical and educational terms, in most aspects of life we are judged on the basis of what we can *do*, not on the basis of how much we have *improved*. If someone received an A in physics because she could pass the examinations at the end of the course, no one cares that she could have

passed the examinations on the first day of class because her mom had taught her physics earlier. Evaluating improvement scores in teaching or research settings is generally laced with difficulty, and should be avoided.

"Rate" of Learning

We have argued that using scores from acquisition data to calculate measures of "amount" of learning leads to many problems in interpretation. A problem similar to those already noted arises in the measure of "rate" of learning. The idea of a learning rate has been common in sport folklore ("so-and-so is a fast learner"). Attempts to measure the speed of acquisition are often based on the steepness or "slope" of the performance curve. For instance, look back at the plot of the two hypothetical subjects in figure 10.3. It might be tempting to say that Person 2 is a "faster" learner than Person 1 because the slope of the curve is much steeper in the early stages of practice. However, such conclusions fall prey to exactly the same problems as with trying to measure the amount of learning.

Importance of Understanding Learning and Performance Variables

The problem of identifying which of the many independent variables are critical for learning, and which are relevant only for performance, is important not only for development and testing of theories of motor learning, but also for application to a variety of practical situations. We treat these two issues briefly here but discuss them again throughout the remainder of the text.

Importance for Theory

Theories make predictions about how certain independent variables will affect learning. For example, in the past a dominant view was that errors are harmful to learning. A goal of practice was to eliminate errors as rapidly as possible, according to this idea. The error was in thinking that practice performance reflected learning and that errors in performance could be taken as evidence of errorful learning. Findings like the Shea and Morgan results presented earlier show quite clearly that levels of performance during practice can be quite misleading if used to make conclusions about learning. These data cast considerable doubt on theories that place a primary emphasis on the level of performance in practice as an indication about learning. Experiments that use transfer designs are more appropriate to provide critical tests of theories that predict effects of certain independent variables on learning. Many examples of this kind of theory testing are presented in the following chapters.

Importance for Teaching Applications

A second practical outcome is that knowledge about which variables affect performance temporarily, and which affect learning, allows the production of more effective settings for instruction in various motor tasks in sport, industry, therapy, and so on. For example, techniques like physically restricted guidance and errorless practice became popular for a while because of the theoretical view that errorful performance is fundamentally harmful to motor learning. This theoretical view was used as a basis for treatment and practice regimes in physical therapy, education, and other fields. Although physical restriction may have a positive value (for safety and confidence), this seems to be important only for performance reasons—not for assessment of the more permanent capability for movement that we associate with learning. The topic of this relation between theory and practice, as it pertains specifically to issues of learning, will arise numerous times throughout the remainder of the book.

Summary

The study of motor learning is considerably different from the study of performance in that the focus is on the *changes* in performance that occur as a direct result of practice. Motor learning is defined as a set of internal processes associated with practice or experience leading to a relatively permanent change in the capability for skilled behavior, a state sometimes termed *habit*. Such a definition must be carefully worded to rule out changes in behavior that are due to maturation or growth, or to momentary fluctuations in performance attributable to temporary factors.

In the typical motor learning experiment, two or more groups of subjects are used, each of which practices a task under a different level of an independent variable. A common method of data analysis involves *performance curves*, or plots of average performance on each trial for a large number of subjects. These curves can hide a great deal of important information about learning, however, such as individual differences in learning or changes in strategies. They tend to characterize motor learning as a slow, constantly evolving process requiring continued practice, whereas other evidence suggests that learning is often sudden, insightful, or even "revolutionary." As a result, interpretations about the nature of learning from performance curves must be made carefully.

Learning experiments usually involve what is called a *transfer design*, in which the groups of subjects practicing at different levels of the independent variable are transferred to a common level of that variable. These designs provide for the separation of the relatively permanent effects (due to learning) and the temporary effects of the independent variable. Those independent variables affecting performance "relatively permanently" are called *learning variables*, and those affecting performance only temporarily are called *performance variables*.

In many situations, the performance scores are near a ceiling or floor, at which no changes can occur because of task-imposed or biologically imposed limitations on performance. In such situations, a number of secondary-task methods can be used, such as measures of latency, measures of attention or effort, measures of retention, or measures of generalizability. With all the methods, it is seldom possible to speak meaningfully about the actual *amount* that a person or a group has learned.

Note

[1] Note, however, that a block of nine trials represented three trials on each of the three patterns. For the random group, the first data point represented the average of the first nine trials of the experiment. For the blocked group, the first data point represented the average of trials 1, 2, 3 (the first three trials on the initial pattern that was practiced) and trials 19, 20, 21 and 37, 38, and 39 (as these are the first three trials on the other two patterns). Performance could have been plotted chronologically across practice for this blocked group as well, although it really does not matter for our present discussion.

[2] In transfer, the first letter denotes the condition in acquisition, while the second letter denotes the condition in transfer.

CHAPTER 11

CONDITIONS OF PRACTICE

In chapter 10, we considered the research methods and logic used to gain knowledge about the many variables affecting motor learning. In this chapter we discuss the various conditions under which a learner can practice motor skills. This chapter is about experiments that use these techniques, the focus being on the major independent variables that are important for motor learning. There are many such variables, of course, and space limitations prevent a complete discussion of all of them. We have confined the discussion to those variables having the largest effects (i.e., those that make the biggest difference) and those that are usually under the direct control of the experimenter. With this focus, the material will relate rather closely to the design of instructional settings such as would be seen in schools, to training for jobs in industry or the military, and to rehabilitation. Also, we emphasize here those variables in which there is the greatest theoretical interest. This also indirectly provides a strong contribution to practical application, because well-established theories have many real-world implications that can be inferred from them (Kerlinger, 1973). Generally, the chapter is about attempts to understand the many variables that determine the effectiveness of the conditions of practice.

The Most Important Condition: Amount of Practice

One practice variable dwarfs all the others in terms of importance, and is so obvious that it need hardly be mentioned at all—practice. Clearly, more learning will occur if there are more practice trials, all other things being equal. Perhaps we do not need to say any more about the amount of practice than this: in structuring the practice session, the number of practice attempts should be maximized.

But does this generalization always apply? Ericsson, Krampe, and Tesch-Römer (1993) note that the term "practice" can take on various meanings. They further suggest the term *deliberate practice* to denote the kinds of activities that instructors, teachers, and therapists commonly use on a daily basis. Specifically, Ericsson, Krampe, and Tesch-Römer define deliberate practice in terms of "activities that have been specially designed to improve the current level of performance. . . . Deliberate practice requires effort and is not inherently enjoyable. Individuals are motivated to

practice because practice improves performance" (p. 368).

In the remainder of this chapter we will be talking about ways in which methods of deliberate practice can be modified, structured, improved, and otherwise changed so as to influence performance. However, always keep in the back of your mind the distinction between factors that influence temporary improvements in performance and those that have relatively permanent effects.

Prepractice Considerations

In this section we will concentrate on the various ways in which learning can be enhanced when the learner is not directly engaged in practice. Much of this discussion concerns those factors that have been shown to operate before the practice session begins—involving the preparation of the learner for the upcoming practice sequence.

Motivation for Learning

It is important that people be motivated to learn a motor task in order for maximally effective learning to occur. If the learner perceives the task as meaningless or undesirable, then learning of the task will probably be minimal. If the level of motivation is too low, people might not be sufficiently motivated to practice at all; *no* learning would be the result. Aside from this rather obvious conclusion, a number of reasonably complex determinants of learning exist as a function of motivational level.

Making the Task Seem Important

Before beginning the practice session, it is important that the learner see the task as one that is desirable to learn. Much of this kind of motivation appears already to be established in people because of culturally derived emphasis on certain activities. But in many cases it is important to show why it would be useful to have a certain skill. A teacher once pointed out that the usual all-male games (e.g., tackle football) were fine for playing among young males, but that a time would come in life when less violent recreational skills might be preferred. Such a comment emphasized the importance of learning other activities. Similarly, some might consider badminton a rather leisurely game that is played in the backyard on warm summer days—that is, until they see a game involving skilled players. A person might be much more interested in learning these skills after seeing them performed by role models in world-class competition; interest in golf has risen tremendously since Tiger Woods joined the Professional Golfers' Association tour, for example. These motivating methods are easy to use, and they probably make large differences in the ways learners approach a new skill and in how well they will learn it. Unfortunately, there is very little experimental evidence on these points.

Goal Setting

Another frequently used motivational technique is goal setting, whereby performers try to attain goals that are set before they begin practicing. This technique has been studied extensively in research related to industrial and organizational psychology (for reviews see Locke & Latham, 1985; Tubbs, 1986), and more recently in sport and exercise (for reviews see Burton, 1993; Locke, 1991; Weinberg, 1994), and suggests some interesting principles for performance and learning.

Probably the most intuitively appealing and most often used goal in all types of daily activities is do your best. Encouragements such as "Try to get as many done as possible," "Do the best job you can," and "Give it 100% out there" are typical of "do your best" types of goals. However, research suggests that "do your best" goals are not as effective as other types of goals. Locke and Latham (1985) nicely summarized the psychological research and suggested that specific, difficult goals produce better performance than either no goals or vague, ambiguous goals such as "do your best." Locke and Latham proposed four advantages of setting specific, difficult goals; these can be considered analogous to the advantages of setting an agenda for an important meeting. These kinds of goals (1) focus one's activities, (2) help to regulate the effort that is directed toward these activities, (3) help maintain vigilance in attempting to reach the goals, and (4) serve as a referent against which achievement can be compared.

Goal-setting studies in sport and exercise research, however, have not consistently supported Locke and Latham's conclusion that specific, difficult goals are the best ones for performance. Problems in conducting research in sport and exercise in relation to goal setting may account for these inconsistent effects (see also Locke, 1991). Since sport and exercise tasks are often intrinsically motivating and competitive, subjects may have a vested interest in their outcome as participants in a study. People who are told not to set a specific goal or are told to use a vague goal may, in fact, secretively set specific, perhaps difficult goals, thereby masking the potential impact of goal-setting variables. Thus, the rather disappointing effects of goal setting in sport and exercise studies do not necessarily mean that goal setting is not an important factor in the performance of motor skills (cf. Burton, 1993; Weinberg, 1994). Rather, the fact that the tasks in these studies lend themselves to intrinsic goal setting may overshadow the experimenter's manipulations, making it difficult to detect the true effects of goal setting in sport and exercise.

Kyllo and Landers's (1995) meta-analysis (quantitative review) of the literature suggests that one small, but consistent finding does appear in the sport and exercise research. The authors found that specific, absolute goals of moderate difficulty were beneficial to the performance of sport and exercise tasks. In addition, there was evidence that both short-term goals and a combination of short-term and long-term goals facilitated performance as compared to long-term goals only.

One limitation of the research literature is that performance and learning effects have not often been distinguished. Much of the goal-setting literature is dominated by studies on performance, since goal setting seems to have a large impact on factors such as motivation. However, there have been some studies that do address goal-setting effects on learning. For example, Boyce (1992) examined three groups of subjects who set different goals while they were learning to shoot a rifle. One group of subjects was told to "do your best." Another group was encouraged to set their own specific goals. A third group was assigned specific goals by the experimenter that were made progressively higher on each practice day. The goal-setting procedures were established following a pretest and were applied on 5 days of practice sessions over a 3-week period. A retention test assessed learning 1 week after the last practice session. The results are shown in figure 11.1. The group of subjects told to "do your best" performed slightly better than the other groups on the first practice day, but not on the other days. These differences were also maintained on a retention test, suggesting that the specific goal-setting procedures had beneficial effects on both performance and learning.

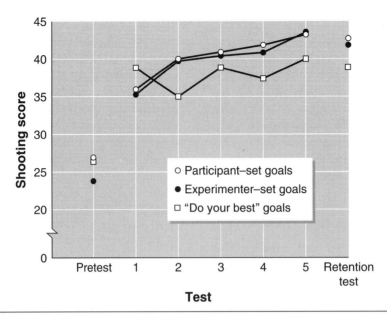

Figure 11.1. Effects of goal setting on learning a shooting task.
Adapted from Boyce, 1992.

Verbal Information

After the learner has become motivated to learn the task, it is important to give the person some sort of "idea" or image of the task to be learned. There are many ways to do this, of course—with videotapes, verbal instructions, and demonstrations, among others. Some of these are discussed next.

Instructions

One of the most common ways of giving students an initial orientation to the new skill is through verbal instructions, usually presented by the teacher or instructor. An early study by Solley (1952) demonstrated the long-lasting effects of initial orientation. In this study, three groups of subjects practiced a two-step lunge toward a target and then stabbed it with a forward arm swing. Over 6 days of practice the respective groups were encouraged to perform the action with an emphasis on speed, with an emphasis on accuracy, or with an equal emphasis on speed and accuracy. The results were quite dramatic. The group instructed to emphasize accuracy was the most accurate over practice; the group instructed to emphasize speed was the fastest; and the group giving equal emphasis to speed and accuracy performed at intermediate levels on both measures. A strong feature of the study was that it included transfer tests over 6 additional days of practice, in which all groups were encouraged to

give equal emphasis to speed and accuracy. The effects seen during practice were maintained in transfer, especially for performance speed, indicating that the instructional "set" had an impact on both performance and learning.

Instructions can also provide useful and important information about the movement itself, such as the initial positions of the limbs in relation to apparatus or implements used, the stance, what to watch and listen for, and what to do. Perhaps more importantly, an overall "idea" or image of the movement can be conveyed that can serve as a guide for the first attempt. Also, instructions can emphasize the ways in which one can recognize one's own errors—for example, "After the movement, check to see that your arm is straight." These kinds of instructions can serve to stimulate the development of error-detection capabilities (see chapter 13).

It certainly seems that instructions are a critical aspect of learning. Consider the following situation. A learner comes into a room where a complex piece of laboratory equipment is located, one that is totally foreign to the subject. The only instruction the teacher has given is "Go!" Imagine the subject's bewilderment at trying to figure out what to do. He or she would not know whether to sit on the apparatus, push it around the room, or try to take it apart. Clearly, instructions about what task to perform, how to perform it, and what to attempt to achieve as a score will be critical at this stage in the learning process.

Another feature of this kind of instruction is that it tells the learner what *not* to do—for example, "Don't sit on it; rather, hold it like this." Without instructions, subjects might require a great deal of practice, effort, and time to discover these things on their own.

But as important as instructions are, it is generally believed that instructions are often overused in learning situations. Words alone are relatively crude descriptions of the complex kinds of movements that a learner is attempting to achieve; just try to describe the actions in pole-vaulting, for example. Only the most global, general aspects of the intended movement are going to be transmitted through verbal instructions. Also, a learner can remember only so many instructions, and few of these important points will be assimilated on the first trials of practice. This problem seems even more critical when one is dealing with children, whose attention spans are probably much shorter than those of adults. One solution is to describe in words those aspects of the skills that are absolutely essential for the first trial or two, making sure that learners achieve them in early practice. Then, as the first important elements are achieved, learners can be instructed verbally (or with other techniques) as to the next most important aspect(s) to attend to, and so on. One problem is that few investigations have been carried out on the nature of instructions, and much work remains to be done in assessing their value in learning (Green & Flowers, 1991; Wulf & Weigelt, 1997).

Learning and Awareness (Implicit Learning)

One of the supposed benefits of verbal instructions is to make the learner aware of certain components of the task before practice begins. There is some research, however, suggesting that learning of some tasks can occur even though the subject is oblivious to the perceptual regularities of the task. In a classic study in this area, conducted by Wickens and Pew (see Pew, 1974b), subjects practiced a pursuit tracking task by moving a lever in order to try to match a perceptual input signal on a computer monitor. A trial comprised three 20-s segments. During the first and last of these segments the perceptual signal was generated randomly by the computer, and the random sequence was different on each of the 24 trials completed during each session on 16 days of practice. The perceptual signal during the

middle segment was always the same. The results of the study revealed that improvements on the repeated, middle segment occurred much faster than on the random segment. More importantly, however, interviews with the subjects after Day 11 revealed that *none* had any idea that the middle portion of the trial was always repeating! It seems that the augmented learning of the middle segment had occurred even though the subjects were unaware that any part of the task had been different from the others. These results have been replicated by Magill, Schoenfelder-Zohdi, and Hall (reported in Magill, in press) in experiments in which the *first* segment was repeated—again with *none* of the subjects being aware of any regularities in the perceptual stimuli. As well, recent studies have shown that these effects persist in transfer tests, again without the subjects' awareness (Wulf & Schmidt, 1997). These findings suggest tantalizing and counterintuitive insights into the effects that implicit knowledge about task features has on learning. This area of implicit learning needs much more work before practical implications about instruction and training can be suggested, although applied studies of this kind are being initiated (Masters, 1992).

Knowledge of Mechanical Principles

How much should learners know about mechanical properties underlying a particular movement task? Will such knowledge, if provided before the learning of the task begins, be an aid to future performance and learning? Early work by Judd (1908) on dart throwing to targets submerged under water gave some initial indications that such information was useful. Judd taught his learners the principles of refraction, whereby the light rays from the submerged target were bent so that the target was not really where it appeared, and this provided initial advantages when the targets were moved to different depths of submersion. Similar results were obtained by Hendrickson and Schroeder (1941) in a task that required shooting an air gun at underwater targets.

Mechanical principles are also a part of instruction in sport skills, such as swimming (propulsion) and billiards (ball spin, geometry). However, explicit knowledge of mechanical principles may not always be necessary to the performance of certain tasks. Polanyi (1958) cites an example of a champion cyclist who did not know the mechanical principles involved in the maintenance of balance on the machine, implying that such principles may not be critical for learning the task. The implication here is consistent with the point made in the preceding section—that at least some learning can occur in the absence of explicit knowledge (Krist, Fieberg, & Wilkening, 1993).

Perceptual Pretraining

Another prepractice technique is to give the learner exposure to the stimuli that will be experienced in the task. In this way, the temporal and spatial regularities can be learned, and the performance of the task with the actual stimuli may be more effective when the entire task is put together. As examples, a baseball batter can watch the flight of a curve ball a number of times before swinging at one; a race car driver can walk through a road-racing course before driving it. A typical experiment would involve the presentation of stimulus information separately before practice, requiring the subject to make verbal (or other) responses not used in the actual performance of the task. For example, while traversing the course the race car driver could be asked to make verbal responses having to do with the direction of a turn and its "tightness."

Adams and Creamer (1962) used a technique like this in a laboratory situation. Subjects were to learn a tracking task that involved moving a lever to follow a stimulus dot in a regular sine-wave pattern. Before practice on the task began, some subjects were asked to watch these stimuli and to respond by pressing a button every time the stimulus reversed direction, attempting to anticipate its movement. After considerable experience with this task, subjects were transferred to the task in which the same stimuli were used; but now, instead of pressing the button, they were required to make lever movements with the hand to follow the dot. Subjects who had experienced the perceptual pretraining were more accurate in tracking than were subjects who had not had this experience. Similar findings were produced by Trumbo, Ulrich, and Noble (1965) when they had subjects learn to name each stimulus position in a regular series. When subjects had learned to anticipate the order of stimulus positions through this naming activity, they were more effective in responding to those stimuli in a tracking task (see also Schmidt, 1968, for a review). In practical

settings, such stimulus presentations should be structured so that the learner attends and responds to them in some way rather than merely watching passively. However, the findings of these studies indicate that there is potential for learning from perceptual inputs; this represents an underlying concept in the research to be discussed in the next section.

Modeling

It seems clear that instructions alone are relatively ineffective as aids to learning motor skills and that other techniques can be used along with instructions to greatly facilitate initial performance. One important way to do this is to demonstrate the skill so that learners can directly observe the elements of the action. The learner can then model the action during initial practice. Another variant, of course, is to use videotapes or photos of skilled performers. At a superficial level, these procedures seem to be the same, with the demonstrator or model providing information about the task to be learned and perhaps some essential details about technique. Shrewd entrepreneurs have seized upon the simplicity of this idea in marketing videotapes of expert athletes demonstrating their talents. But, while these specific techniques are widely used, there is reason to doubt the learning benefit they provide (Druckman & Bjork, 1991). Nevertheless, there is mounting evidence that under certain circumstances, modeling techniques are important for the acquisition of motor skills (for reviews see Ferrari, 1996; McCullagh, 1993; McCullagh, Weiss, & Ross, 1989; Scully & Newell, 1985). In the following sections we will discuss some of the important issues regarding the effects of modeling on learning motor skills.

What Is Learned?

People observe for different reasons. While one person may go to a concert solely to be entertained, another may be there to keenly observe the musicians play, wishing to pick up things to remember and try later. An aspect of this latter situation—how and what information is learned from observation—is our interest in this section. Much of the work done in the area of modeling credits Bandura with the theoretical framework for the development of this research (see Adams, 1987). Unfortunately, research in motor learning has been slow to develop theoretical constructs to account for modeling processes. This situation will likely change in the near future, as research activity in modeling has increased rapidly in recent years (Adams, 1990).

Strategies. One of the earliest studies on modeling effects showed quite nicely that *movement strategies* can be learned by observation. The task used by Martens, Burwitz, and Zuckerman (1976) was called "shoot the moon" and involved trying to move a ball atop two rods by varying the distance between the rods. Two strategies for success were modeled. The "creeping" strategy was a conservative approach to the task whereby the distance between the rods was adjusted slowly in order to move the ball along the top of the rods. This strategy typically produces consistent, but only moderately successful results. In contrast, the "ballistic" strategy involved a rapid and more violent adjustment of the rods. This strategy typically produces quite variable levels of achievement; yet when they are high, they can be very high. The data from this study showed that observers of these two different modeling strategies, when given the opportunity to perform the task, tended to mimic the strategies they had observed. The role of movement strategies in the modeling literature has not been widely investigated, and much more work could be done in this area.

Spatial Information. Information that can be represented spatially can be modeled quite readily, especially if the spatial attributes are presented in a static, discrete manner. A series of experiments by Carroll and Bandura (1982, 1985, 1987, 1990) has shown quite convincingly that spatial information can be learned and represented through modeling (see also Weeks, Hall, & Anderson, 1996). Modeling of dynamic skills is also effective. For example, a study of females with no prior dance training revealed more benefit after subjects watched videotaped ballet sequences than after they had looked at a series of still photographs of the dance (Gray et al., 1991). The investigators concluded that the modeled information contributed to learning the qualitative features of the ballet routine. These conclusions are supported by experiments that modeled skiing actions (Whiting, Bijlard, & den Brinker, 1987) and gymnastic rope skills (Magill & Schoenfelder-Zohdi, 1996).

Temporal Information. A more subtle type of information to be modeled is information about *time,* and various methods for presenting temporal information have been used (Adams, 1986; Doody, Bird, & Ross, 1985; McCullagh & Little, 1989; Zelaznik, Shapiro, & Newell, 1978; Zelaznik & Spring, 1976). For example, Zelaznik and colleagues provided one group of subjects with the recorded sounds of another subject making a correct timing movement prior to any practice. After the presentation of the modeled information, this group was able to perform the movement more accurately than another group who had not listened to the sounds. The "listening group" could even improve slightly in the task without any knowledge of results (KR). The interpretation of these findings is that the listening experience provided the subjects with a reference of correctness, and the reference allowed an evaluation of the auditory feedback produced by the movement and subsequent adjustments on the upcoming trials (see also Wrisberg & Schmidt, 1975). Similar techniques have been tried with auditory feedback in fly casting (Lionvale, cited in Keele & Summers, 1976) and other tasks (Keele, 1986), but without much success in improving learning. More research must be done on this issue before a successful practical application can be made to other motor learning situations.

Expert Versus Learning Models

One of the key assumptions of the videotapes that provide sport instructions is that highly skilled performers make the best models. Although this assumption seems to be intuitively appealing, there is little evidence to support it. For instance, Pollock and Lee (1992) studied the effectiveness of demonstrations of a computer video game to groups of individuals who had had no prior practice on the task. Subjects either watched an expert perform the task or watched a novice who was learning the task for the first time. After three modeling trials, the observers in both groups showed a substantial benefit of having watched their respective models (as compared to a control, no-model group), but did not differ as a result of having viewed the expert or the learning model. A further 12 observation trials followed by practice substantiated both the modeling benefit and the absence of any effect due to the model skill level. Similar effects have been found by McCullagh and Meyer (1997) using a weight-lifting task.

A more surprising finding in this research is that under some circumstances, the provision of a learning model can result in *better* observational learning than the use of an expert model. This research area was initiated by Adams (1986), who used learning models to demonstrate the performance of a manual timing task. Adams found that observation alone was insufficient for learning this task. However, considerable learning was seen if the model's KR was also presented to the observer. This is so because the observer can gain information from the model about the movement performed (both visual and auditory), from the augmented feedback presented to the model (as KR), and from seeing the success of the model's attempt to use that feedback on the next performance of the task. In this way, the observer benefits not only from "observing" the performance, but also from observing the processing operations of the model in the attempt to improve performance.

The research method used by Adams (1986) was extended by McCullagh and Caird (1990), who directly compared the effectiveness of learning models and expert models on Adams's task. Three observation groups were compared. One group had repeated exposures to a tape of a perfect execution of the timing goal. Two other groups watched a tape of a model who was learning the task; one group also received the model's KR and one did not. As illustrated in figure 11.2, the largest effects were found for those who observed the

learning model and also received the model's KR (open squares). These subjects improved their performance consistently over the acquisition period, in the absence of any KR about their own performance, and both retained their performance levels and transferred to a novel timing goal better than either of the other observation groups.

These findings suggest an important application to modeling real-world tasks. Novice athletes are likely to get little insight from watching experts, other than perhaps gaining some basic information about how to perform a task. While viewing professional golf on television, for example, we get the greatest *learning* benefit from seeing these experts make mistakes. The mistakes occur so infrequently that the commentators usually replay the action and point out exactly what went wrong—what movement error resulted in the flubbed shot. In other words, the model demonstrated an incorrect action, which was accompanied by KR that identified the error. Thus, the real issue in this research may not be about the skill level of the model, but rather about what type of information is being demonstrated—errors or perfect templates of an action. It is likely that we learn more from mistakes than we do from correct performances.

Distribution of Practice

One of the variables that instructors and therapists have under their control is the scheduling of

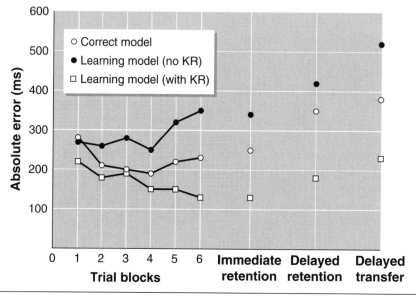

Figure 11.2.   Effects of model skill level and availability of model's KR on learning.
Adapted, by permission, from McCullagh, P., and Caird, J.K., 1990, "A Comparison of Exemplary and Learning Sequence Models and the Use of Model Knowledge of Results to Increase Learning and Performance," *Journal of Human Movement Studies, 18,* 227.

periods of *work* (i.e., time spent in actual practice) and *rest* (i.e., time not practicing the task). This scheduling can be considered within a short time frame, as when one selects the amount of work and rest within a 45-min therapy session. Or the scheduling may be considered in terms of a longer scale, as when one chooses the length and frequency of sessions per week. The important question is whether or not the frequency and length of rest periods have an effect on learning the skill being practiced in the work periods. In other words, what is the best way to distribute the time spent in work versus the time spent resting—or simply, what is the best *practice distribution*?

Defining "Massed" and "Distributed" Practice

Research on practice-distribution effects has often used the terms *massed practice* and *distributed practice*. In one sense, "massing" means to put things together—in this case, running work periods very close together with either no rest at all or very brief rest intervals in between. By default, distributing practice means spacing these intervals of work apart with longer periods of rest. However, these labels are not truly satisfactory, because researchers often use these terms to describe the two extremes of practice distributions. Many experiments used more than two distribution conditions (e.g., Ammons, 1950; Bourne & Archer, 1956). Thus, these terms must be considered within the context of other conditions within any particular experiment. Different experiments, however, often established distribution conditions that were quite different from one study to another. Experiments are frequently designed such that "massed practice" involves periods of work that are substantially longer than the amount of rest between trials, eventually leading to fatigue in many tasks. For "distributed" practice, on the other hand, the amount of rest between trials often is equal to or greater than the amount of work within the trial, leading to a somewhat more "restful" practice sequence.

Virtually all the research on distribution-of-practice effects has been conducted using continuous tasks, for which the work period might be 20 or 30 s in duration. The most common apparatus for this research was the pursuit rotor tracking task. However, tasks such as mirror tracing, the Bachman ladder, and inverted-alphabet printing tasks were also popular. The effects of practice distribution using continuous tasks will be discussed first. Only a few studies have been done using discrete tasks. However, the findings are quite different from those of studies using continuous tasks, and will be presented later.

Distribution-of-Practice Effects on Performance

Many experiments were done in the 1940s and 1950s on practice-distribution effects (for a review, see Lee & Genovese, 1988). Even though these experiments involved wide differences in methods (such as the length of work and rest periods, number of trials, etc.), the results are remarkably similar. Put simply: *Given constant periods of work, short rest periods depress performance relative to longer rest periods.*

Findings from a study by Bourne and Archer (1956) are typical of the performance effects seen in experiments on practice distribution. The task was pursuit rotor tracking (see figure 2.5). Five different groups of subjects were compared; all groups had work periods of 30 s. In one group (the 0-s rest group), subjects practiced continuously for 21 trials, with no rest at all. For the other four groups, each of the work periods was interspersed with periods of rest. One group had rest periods of 15 s, and the other three groups had rest periods of 30, 45, or 60 s.

Bourne and Archer's findings were quite clear: the longer the rest period, the better the performance. Looking closely at figure 11.3, one can see that a systematic separation of the various distribution-of-practice groups had emerged quite clearly by about trial 7, and that these differences became larger with further practice. Many other examples of effects like these could be provided. Reviews by McGeoch and Irion (1952), Bilodeau and Bilodeau (1961), and Lee and Genovese (1988) describe more findings of this type.

Distribution-of-Practice Effects on Learning

For tasks such as the pursuit rotor, continuous practice would likely cause muscular fatigue to develop, and this fatigue could be expected to depress performance. In fact, looking at figure 11.3, one might argue that fatigue may have depressed performance even with some rest

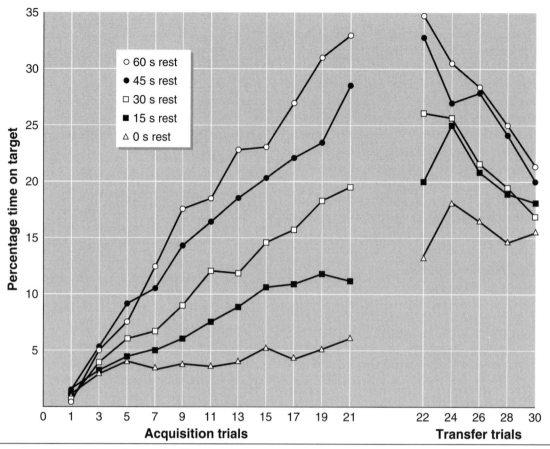

Figure 11.3.   Distribution-of-practice effects on a pursuit rotor task in acquisition and retention. Trials were 30 s in duration, and separate groups received either 0, 15, 30, 45, or 60 s between practice trials. Retention trials were done with 0 s rest between trials.

Reprinted from Bourne and Archer, 1956.

between trials. Thus, because at least part of the decrement in performance displayed by these groups was due to temporary fatigue, not all of the performance depression could be attributed to differences in the relatively permanent development of skill. So, how much was due to learning?

To assess this issue, Bourne and Archer gave all of their subjects a 5-min rest period following the last acquisition trial. After this rest period, subjects performed a common transfer test in which all groups were shifted to a massed schedule—all trials were performed with 0-s rest between periods of 30 s of work. The rationale here was that if muscular fatigue was entirely responsible for the differences between groups during the acquisition trials, then the groups should be similar in performance after the dissipation of the fatigue. This was not the case, as can be seen in figure 11.3 (right-hand side).

Several items in these transfer data are noteworthy. The most important is that substantial differences were maintained between the groups

after the rest period—transfer performance being increasingly better for groups that had longer periods of rest between work periods during the acquisition trials. This finding suggests that the practice distribution had a relatively permanent effect, which is supported quite well by the literature (Lee & Genovese, 1988).

Another item worth noting in these data is that the differences between the groups on the first transfer trial (trial 22) are smaller than the differences between groups on the last acquisition trial (trial 21). Thus, some of the practice-distribution effect was due to the temporary, detrimental influence of fatigue. Still, the differences due to changes brought about by learning remained large on the transfer trials. The last item to notice is that massing the transfer trials also had a depressing effect on performance. However, even after 9 transfer trials with no rest (i.e., on trial 30), the groups that had initially practiced with some rest between trials still performed better than the group that had practiced with no rest.

We have used the Bourne and Archer (1956) study to illustrate the effects of practice distribution on performance and learning. It is a particularly good example of this effect because more than two distribution groups were used and because a transfer design was used to separate the temporary from the permanent effects of the practice variable. However, several conclusions drawn from this study require further discussion (see also Lee & Genovese, 1989b).

Length of the Retention Interval

One complicating factor about the Bourne and Archer experiment is that a 5-min rest period following continuous practice may not have been long enough to allow the temporary influence of muscular fatigue on performance to dissipate (Ammons, 1988; Lintern, 1988). Thus, the transfer trials still may have been influenced by the same temporary effects that influenced acquisition performance (e.g., fatigue). A number of studies using longer rest intervals following practice, however, do not support this argument. For example, a few studies had subjects leave the lab and return later for the transfer trials (e.g., 1 day in Adams, 1952; 10 weeks in Reynolds & Bilodeau, 1952). The maintenance of distribution-of-practice effects after a period of time when these temporary effects had surely dissipated offers support for the learning difference concluded from the Bourne and Archer study.

Do the Learning Effects "Wash Out"?

The Bourne and Archer data show that performance differences in transfer begin to converge by trial 30. The convergence of effects following some transfer trials has been argued by some to cast doubt on the "relative permanency" of the learning effect. An important study by Adams and Reynolds (1954) further calls this issue into question. In this study, distributed practice was defined as 30 s of work with 30-s rest. Massed practice involved the same trial duration but with only 5-s rest. One group received 40 trials under distributed conditions. Four more groups received initial practice for 5, 10, 15, or 20 trials, respectively, under massed conditions; they then rested for 10 min, and finally transferred to the distributed-practice condition for the remainder of the 40 practice trials. Adams and Reynolds found that when the various massed-practice groups were shifted to distributed practice, they caught up (though not entirely) within a few trials to the level of performance of the group that had practiced entirely under distributed-practice conditions. A small flaw in the design, however, makes these effects difficult to interpret. The problem is that the groups that transferred to distributed-practice conditions received the benefit of a 10-min rest. The distributed group, which may have experienced some temporary fatigue effects, did not benefit from such a rest. Thus, it is difficult to know whether or not the differences that were almost "washed out" were temporary or more permanent differences.

A clever design by Ammons (1950) helps to clarify this issue. Groups received rest periods that ranged from 0 s and 20 s, up to 12 min and 24 hr between each 20-s trial on the pursuit rotor task. A 20-min rest period followed the 36th practice trial, after which subjects performed an additional 36 transfer trials with no rest between trials (many more transfer trials than had been used by Bourne and Archer, 1956). By the end of this transfer period, only small differences remained between the groups. However, Ammons (1950) asked subjects to return to the lab for *another* set of transfer trials, 1 day later. The differences that had been seen on the first transfer test—and apparently washed out by the transfer trials—were "restored" after this additional rest period. These data are a strong indicator that practice distribution has large effects on temporary performance levels and relatively permanent influences on learning.

Distributing Practice Over a Longer Time Scale

Perhaps of more direct significance to instructors and therapists are the effects of practice distribution when conducted on a much longer time scale than the single-session experiments often carried out. A few such studies have been conducted, and the results are generally similar to those of the studies done in a single session. In a very early investigation of this type, right-handed subjects were asked to throw javelins with their left hand (Murphy, 1916). All subjects practiced on 34 separate days. Massed-practice subjects performed on consecutive days (Monday to Friday) for 7 weeks. The distributed group practiced three times per week for 12 weeks. Results at the end of the 34th day of practice and on a retention test performed 3 months later showed both performance and learning benefits for the distributed group. Similar findings were reported by Baddeley and

Longman (1978) for postal workers who were training to use a keyboard. In this study, separate groups of postal workers trained for 60–80 hr using one of four schedules: work periods were conducted either once or twice per day, with the duration of each work period being 1 or 2 hr. The data for the practice period and for retention tests performed 1, 3, and 9 months later showed that the condition that massed the practice the most (2 × 2) resulted in the poorest performance and learning (see figure 11.4). Although the other three groups did not differ in these retention tests, the effects of the "most distributed" group (1 × 1) are likely diminished because practice for this group was stopped after a total accumulation of 60 hr, as compared to the 80 hr of practice for the other three groups. These data appear to suggest that there is some generalizability of the results obtained in experiments of relatively short duration to studies involving practice and retention over much longer periods of time.

Total Practice Time

From the previous sections, it would appear that it is not beneficial for learning to mass trials in the practice session. But there is another important variable that interacts with massing—the *time* involved in practice. Recall that in the experiments presented so far that used massing, the number of practice trials was held constant; and because the amount of time between practice trials was different for the massed and distributed conditions, the overall practice time was allowed to vary. That is, a group receiving massed practice will have a shorter total practice period than will an equivalent group with distributed practice.

Consider the Baddeley and Longman (1978) study just described. Although the group that practiced for 2 hr per session twice per day (2 × 2) showed the poorest acquisition and retention performance, their practice period was completed in one-half to one-quarter of the time used by the other groups to complete the training. Additional

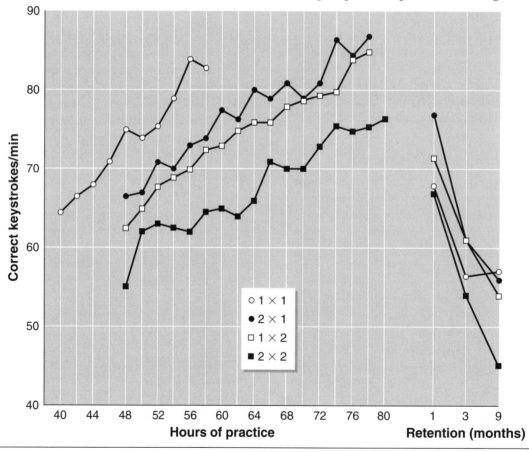

Figure 11.4.   Training postal workers to use a keyboard under different practice-distribution schedules (1 × 1 refers to sessions conducted once per day of 1 hr duration each; 2 × 2 refers to two sessions per day of 2 hr duration each, etc.). Adapted from Baddeley and Longman, 1978.

training for this group would likely have resulted in improved performance and learning.

The issue of practice distribution and total practice time involves a *trade-off*. Distributed practice results in the most learning per time in training but requires the most total time to complete. Massed practice results in reduced benefits per time in training but requires the least total time.

Safety Issues

Finally, it should be clear that massing has strong effects on performance of many tasks and that the risks of injury in dangerous tasks are going to increase with massed practice. The laboratory tasks described here are not particularly dangerous, but many tasks used in sport (e.g., giant swings on the horizontal bar) and industry (e.g., work with a hydraulic paper cutter) entail considerably more opportunity for serious injury if errors are made. And most certainly for people in rehabilitation, whose motor coordination has already been affected, the risk of injury is of vital concern to the therapist. Thus, caution should be used in designing training regimes in situations in which factors such as fatigue could put the learner at risk.

Discrete Tasks

The evidence about discrete tasks is far less complete than for continuous tasks. Carron (1967, 1969) used a peg-turn task in which the subject moved 44 cm from a switch to grasp a peg in a hole, turned the peg end-for-end to reinsert it into the hole, and then returned to the key again as quickly as possible. This movement was discrete and required a movement time (MT) of from 1,300 to 1,700 ms, depending on the level of skill of the performers. Carron had subjects learn this task under two conditions: distributed (the amount of rest between trials was 5 s) and massed (the amount of rest between trials was only 300 ms, with a 5-s rest every 10 trials). Carron found no effect of the massing conditions on performance of the task on the first day while the massing was present. When he tested the subjects 48 hr later as a measure of learning, he found that the subjects in the massed condition actually performed slightly faster than the subjects in the distributed condition (1,430 vs. 1,510 ms), but it is probably more reasonable to say there were no real differences. For this discrete task, massing appeared to be neither a performance variable

nor a learning variable, contrary to the rather strong effects of massing found for continuous tasks.

More recently, Lee and Genovese (1989a) investigated this apparent continuous-discrete difference directly, in parallel experiments employing very similar timing tasks. For the continuous task, there was a tendency for subjects in the distributed conditions in acquisition to perform more effectively than those in the massed conditions. This effect carried over into the delayed (7 days) transfer test, so that practice under distributed conditions in acquisition resulted in more learning, regardless of whether the transfer-test conditions were distributed or massed. This was essentially the same as had been found with the other continuous tasks (see previous section). However, for the discrete task, there was a slight tendency for the massed condition to be more effective in acquisition. Also, the learning effects on delayed transfer depended on the conditions in transfer. Even though massed practice was more effective during the acquisition phase, the distributed practice in acquisition was clearly superior for delayed transfer tests under distributed conditions. On the other hand, when the delayed transfer test was performed under massed conditions, massed practice in acquisition was clearly superior for learning. This provides at least one example indicating that massed practice can be more effective for learning than distributed practice.

It is probably premature to generalize very strongly from these two studies. But they do raise serious questions whether the effects of massed practice for discrete tasks will be simple generalizations from the wide body of findings from continuous tasks. In the first place, massing did not impair performance during acquisition in Carron's (1967, 1969) studies, and massed practice actually improved performance during acquisition in Lee and Genovese's (1989a) study. And those acquisition practice conditions that were most effective depended in a complicated way on the massing conditions in transfer. Certainly we do not understand these phenomena very well, and more studies should be concentrated on the role of these practice conditions for discrete motor learning tasks that are so highly represented in many everyday activities (e.g., kicking, throwing).

Future Research on Practice-Distribution Effects

You may have noticed that since the 1940s and 1950s when much of the research on distribution-of-practice effects was conducted, with only a few exceptions, work on this issue has stopped. Why is this the case? One possibility is that everything we could know about the topic is now known. However, this is unlikely to be true; for example, the different effects for continuous versus discrete tasks have never been satisfactorily explained. Two reasons for this lack of work relate specifically to theory testing. One reason for the decline in research in this area is that topics in learning with more exciting theoretical appeal have attracted the researchers' attention. The other reason relates to the downfall of Hull's theory (Ammons, 1947; Hull, 1943), which stimulated much of the early work in this area: Hull's theory was never replaced by another formulation that would serve as an impetus for further research (Adams, 1987; Ammons, 1988; Magill, 1988b; Newell, Antoniou, & Carlton, 1988).

It is clear that practice-distribution effects have important implications for the design of training sessions for learning motor skills. However, the applied nature of this work seems to be insufficient to drive sustained research in this area. Only when (and if) theory development resumes on this issue, it seems, will new experiments be designed and carried out.

Variability of Practice

Another factor that has been shown to affect learning is the amount of variability in a practice sequence. In one sense, this is obvious. Many tasks have variability inherent to them (*open skills*), such as fielding ground balls in baseball or steering a car down an unfamiliar road. An important part of learning such tasks is acquiring the capability to cope with novel situations; practicing under constant (unvarying) situations would probably not be appropriate. But in another sense, this effect is not so obvious, especially when the task involves *closed skills,* for which the environmental conditions are always quite similar (e.g., archery, bowling). Here, because the criterion task to be learned is always the same, it would seem that practice under these exact conditions would be most effective for learning. Yet

the evidence suggests that varied practice may be important in closed tasks as well.

Much of the research on variability of practice has been conducted to test certain predictions of *schema theory* (Schmidt, 1975b). One prediction was that transfer to novel tasks would be enhanced after practice in variable, as compared to constant, practice conditions (see chapter 13 for more on schema theory). We discuss only a few of these studies; reviews of many more of these experiments are available (Lee, Magill, & Weeks, 1985; Shapiro & Schmidt, 1982; Van Rossum, 1990).

Variability-of-Practice Effects in Retention

One way to obtain an indication of the effect of practice variability is to assess retention performance, after a period of time following the acquisition session, for one of the tasks that has been practiced. A few studies have done this by comparing the relative impacts of constant and varied practice on retention of the tasks that were practiced. There is a design complication with this type of study, however, as subjects in the different groups practice different tasks; thus what has been practiced and what is assessed in retention cannot be equated. This does not pose a problem, however, for results such as those we will see in studies conducted by Shea and Kohl (1990, 1991).

Subjects in the Shea and Kohl experiments were asked to learn to generate a goal force by squeezing a hand grip that was connected to a force transducer. In one experiment (Shea & Kohl, 1991, experiment 1), subjects performed 100 trials on the criterion task, which was to produce a force of 150 N. One group (criterion) received only these acquisition conditions. Another group (criterion + variable) received the same number of acquisition trials on the criterion task but, in addition, practiced goal forces that were ±25 or ±50 N relative to that of the criterion task (i.e., 100, 125, 175 and 200 N). Notice, however, that this variable-practice group not only had the same amount of specific practice as the criterion group, but also practiced at tasks that surrounded the criterion task—which confounds the role of the variable practice with additional practice. So, Shea and Kohl also included a third group of subjects (criterion + criterion) that practiced the criterion task, as well as performing additional practice trials on the criterion task, so that the total number of practice trials was equal to the total practiced by the variable group.

Performance on the criterion task for these groups in acquisition and in a retention test 1 day later is presented in figure 11.5. The criterion + variable practice group performed more poorly on the criterion task almost all the way through the acquisition period in comparison to the other two groups. This detrimental effect on performance is similar to the effects of random practice that we saw in the Shea and Morgan (1979) study discussed in chapter 10. However, after the retention interval, subjects in the criterion + variable practice group performed better on the retention test than both the criterion-only group and the criterion + criterion group. These findings indicate that practice at tasks that were similar to (and "surrounded") the criterion task, actually *facilitated* the retention of the criterion task.

Variability-of-Practice Effects in Transfer

In one of the first studies investigating transfer, McCracken and Stelmach (1977) had subjects move their right arms from a starting key to knock over a barrier, with a 200-ms goal MT from initiation to barrier contact. The distances to the barrier could be changed in different conditions (15, 35, 60, and 65 cm), with a constant 200-ms goal in the practice phase. Table 11.1 shows the

two-group design. A Constant group was actually made up of four subgroups, each of which had practice at only one of the barrier distances for 300 trials. The Variable group, on the other hand, had the same number of trials as the Constant group (i.e., 300), but these trials were varied in that all four barrier distances were practiced in a random order (75 trials of each).

In a transfer-test phase, the two groups performed a *novel* (50-cm) distance, both immediately after training and after a 2-day interval. Thus, with this basic design the authors evaluated the effect of variable versus constant practice on the performance of a novel variation that had never been performed previously. This design addresses an effect of learning quite different from that studied in the retention design by Shea and Kohl (1991) discussed in the preceding section. In that study, Shea and Kohl assessed how well one *common* task, practiced by all the groups, was *retained* as a function of the other tasks that had also been practiced. In the McCracken and Stelmach study, the primary research interest was the effect of varied versus constant practice on the capability to perform a *new task*.

The results are shown in figure 11.6, where the absolute errors are plotted for the trials at the end of the acquisition phase, as well as for the trials on the two transfer-test phases. In the original-practice phase, the Constant group had less absolute error than the Variable group. This finding is

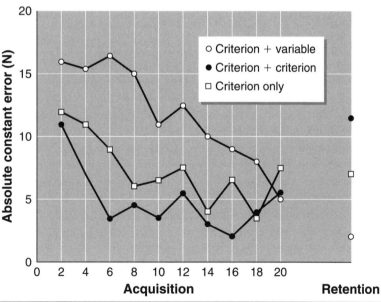

Figure 11.5. Comparison between variable-practice conditions and practice at the criterion task during acquisition and retention performance on the criterion task.
Adapted from Shea and Kohl, 1991.

Table 11.1   Experimental Design for an Experiment on Variability in Practice

Group	Original practice 300 trials Day 1	Transfer-test phase	
		Immediate Day 1	Delayed Day 2
Constant			
Subgroup a	15 cm only	50 cm	50 cm
Subgroup b	35 cm only	50 cm	50 cm
Subgroup c	60 cm only	50 cm	50 cm
Subgroup d	65 cm only	50 cm	50 cm
Variable	15, 35, 60, 65 cm	50 cm	50 cm

(Adapted from McCracken and Stelmach 1977.)

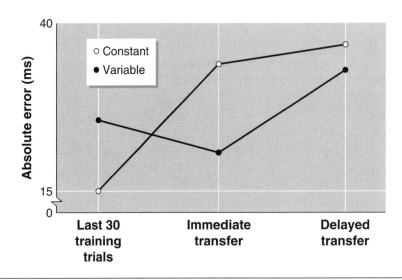

Figure 11.6.   Performance in a ballistic timing task as a function of variability in practice conditions.
Adapted from McCracken and Stelmach, 1977.

similar to the results shown by Shea and Kohl (see figure 11.5). The critical contrast, however, is on the immediate transfer-test phase, when the movement was novel for both groups. Here, the order of the groups was reversed, with the Variable group now having less absolute error than the Constant group. This trend persisted into the test phase 48 hr later, but with the difference between groups being considerably smaller. Thus, it appeared that variability in practice (during the original-practice phase) allowed the subjects to learn the task more effectively, permitting them to perform a new version of it on the transfer phase with less error than the Constant group (see also Wrisberg & Ragsdale, 1979). Variable

practice seemed to be important in generating a capacity to perform a novel version of this task. But this novel task (50 cm) was clearly within the original range of experience of the Variable group (i.e., from 15 to 65 cm), and one could argue that the Variable group had more practice than the Constant group at tasks closer to the transfer task. Would such effects also be seen if the novel transfer task was *outside* the range of previous experience?

Catalano and Kleiner (1984) used a timing task in which the subject was to press a button when a moving pattern of lights arrived at a coincidence point. Using a design much like that of McCracken and Stelmach (1977), they had a mph; a Constant group (with four subgroups) practiced at only one of these speeds. Then, on a subsequent transfer test, all subjects transferred to four *novel* light speeds that were outside the range of previous experience (i.e., 1, 3, 13, and 15 mph). The performance of the two groups on these transfer tests is shown in figure 11.7. The absolute errors were smaller for the Variable group than for the Constant group, and the differences were present even when the "distance" from the range of previous experience was quite large. Variable practice appeared to increase the "applicability" of the learning that occurred in acquisition, contributing to the performance of novel variations of the task that were well outside the range of the stimuli experienced in the acquisition phase. In other words, variable practice seemed to increase *generalizability*, an important criterion for motor learning as discussed in chapter 10. Also, one cannot argue that the Variable group was more effective simply because it had experienced the range of speeds involved in the transfer test, as neither group had experienced them.

Other Factors Influencing Effects of Practice Variability

When adults are used as subjects, there is reasonably strong evidence that increased variability is

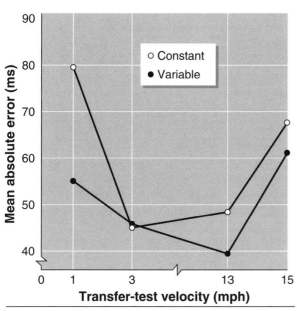

Figure 11.7.   Mean absolute timing error for novel transfer of light speeds as a function of the variability in practice conditions in acquisition.

Adapted and reproduced with permission of authors and publisher from: Catalano, J.F., & Kleiner, B.M. Distant transfer in coincident timing as a function of variability of practice. *Perceptual and Motor Skills*, 1984, 58, 851-857. © Perceptual and Motor Skills 1984.

beneficial for learning (as measured on novel transfer tests), and basically no evidence that variable practice is detrimental to learning (Shapiro & Schmidt, 1982). However, a number of studies show very small effects, and others show essentially no effects, casting some doubt on the "strength" or generality of these effects (Van Rossum, 1990). Overall, in practical settings it is reasonably safe to say that attempts to make the practice more variable for learners will result in greater learning and generalizability. However, some of the issues that complicate this general statement are presented in the following paragraphs.

Age of Learner

The effects of practice variability seem to depend on the nature of the learners. Certainly the most obvious classification is that of children versus adults. In their review of the literature on practice variability, Shapiro and Schmidt (1982) noted that the advantage for variable versus constant practice for children was strong in nearly every study conducted. For example, using a strictly closed throwing skill with young children, Kerr and Booth (1977, 1978) found in two experiments that variable practice was more effective than constant practice when subjects were transferred to a novel version of the task. Even more surprising was the finding that for learning this novel variation of the task, practice at variations of the task approximating the novel task was more effective than was practicing the *novel task itself!* Practice variability appears to be a powerful variable in children's motor learning (see also Green, Whitehead, & Sugden, 1995; Wulf, 1991).

Gender of Learner

Another individual-difference variable of interest is gender. Wrisberg and Ragsdale (1979), with basically the same task as that used by Catalano and Kleiner (1984; see figure 11.7), found that college women profited from practice variability much more than college men did. In fact, it appeared that male subjects may not have profited at all, as all of the group differences were attributable to the women subjects. With children, as well, more gain was made by first-grade girls as a result of variability in practice than by first-grade boys (Allen, 1978). Thus, variability in practice tended to be more effective for females than for males, at least in these two studies.

Scheduling Variable Practice

We mentioned earlier that the effects of variable practice in adults have not always been consistent—some studies showing positive effects and others showing no effects (although none that we know of has shown negative effects). A review of those studies showing no effects by Lee, Magill, and Weeks (1985) revealed an interesting pattern of findings. Many of these experiments had structured the variable-practice sessions such that most or all of the practice on any single variant of the task was conducted together, in a *blocked-practice sequence*. Although we will have much more to say about the effects of random and blocked practice in the next section, the conclusion drawn by Lee, Magill, and Weeks (1985) was that for variable practice to be most effectively utilized (relative to constant practice) it should be randomized in order, rather than blocked.

Interpreting Variability-of-Practice Effects

Most of the studies on variability have been done in the context of schema theory (chapter 13). The basic premise is that, with practice, people develop rules (called *schemas*) about their own motor behavior. Think back to the ideas about the generalized motor program (chapter 6), indicating that a set of parameters must be applied to the program in order for it to be performed. Schema theory proposes that subjects learn a rule in the practice sequence. The rule is a relationship between all the past environmental outcomes that the person produced and the values of the parameters that were used to produce those outcomes. This rule is maintained in memory and can be used to select a new set of parameters for the next movement situation—even a novel variation—that involves the same motor program. Knowing the rule and what environmental outcome is to be produced, the person can select the parameters for the program that will produce it. The schema theory is related to variability in practice because the theory predicts that learning of the rule will be more effective if the experience is varied rather than constant. We will refer to these experiments on variability in practice in chapter 13 when we discuss schema theory in more detail.

Another important finding from the literature on variability in practice is that the occurrence of learning during the acquisition phase was revealed by performance on a *novel* version of the task in transfer. This was true regardless of whether the novel version was inside (McCracken & Stelmach, 1977) or outside (Catalano & Kleiner, 1984) the range of variation experienced in the acquisition phase. As we will point out in chapter 13, such evidence suggests that what was learned was *not* some particular movement, but rather the (generalizable) capability to produce any of a variety of movements of this type. These results are explained well by schema theory, in that the variable practice produces a rule (or schema) for selecting parameters of the generalized motor program (e.g., for throwing), and this rule can be used for any novel movement using the same motor program.

Why should variable practice be more effective for children and females? One idea is that children are less experienced at motor skills than are older (adult) subjects, so the rules (schemas) that the children acquire in laboratory settings have already been achieved by the adults in their earlier experiences with motor tasks. Also, the laboratory tasks are very simple, and it is possible that the adults already have at their disposal the rules (schemas) necessary to perform the novel tasks whereas the children must learn some of them in the experimental setting. Here, then, variable practice is more effective for children than for the adults because the children have considerably "more to learn" than the adults. Similarly, if females at a given age are, on the average, less experienced in movement than males, then it may be that females behave as though they are "younger," in a movement sense, than males. Perhaps as a result of some lack of movement experiences, the rules that relate the movement parameters to the movement outcomes (the schemas) are less well developed than they are in males, so that the females profit by practice variability in these experiments more than the males do.

But why might schema learning be better under random-practice as compared to blocked-practice schedules? It is this issue to which we now turn our attention.

Contextual Interference: Blocked Versus Random Practice

The focus of the preceding section was the effectiveness of practice on a variety of tasks relative to practice on only one task variation, as measured in retention and transfer tests (i.e., tests of learning). The issue here is related: assuming that variable practice is probably better for retention and transfer, the question we will address is whether or not it makes a difference how the variable practice is *scheduled*.

Contextual interference was used in chapter 10 as an example of how different interpretations of learning could be derived from studies involving periods of practice, retention, and transfer. Given that one has *X* tasks to practice (or *X* variations of a task) and *N* trials to conduct on each task, the issue of scheduling is how to order the *N* trials on each task.

Two extreme types of practice schedules have frequently been compared in contextual interference studies. *Blocked* practice involves practicing all *N* trials on one task before any practice is begun on another task. All *N* trials are then completed on the next task before practice begins on a third task, and so on, until all tasks have been practiced. *Random* practice involves the same number of tasks and the same number of trials on each task as in blocked practice. The difference is that in random practice a trial on one task (call it *task A*) may be followed by a trial on *task B*, then a trial on *task C*, and so on, until all *N* trials on all *X* tasks have been completed.

Consider golf practice at a driving range as an analogy. Suppose you plan your practice by dividing the bucket of 60 balls into, say, 20 shots each with a driver, a 5-iron, and a pitching wedge. Blocked practice would involve hitting all 20 balls with one club before switching to another club. Random practice would involve switching clubs after each shot. We could use many similar examples of blocked and random practice related to training sessions in industrial and rehabilitation settings.

We presented the results of the Shea and Morgan (1979) study in detail earlier (see Example: Blocked Versus Random Practice in chapter 10, and also figures 10.7, 10.8, and 10.9). To summarize briefly, blocked practice resulted in better performance during acquisition in comparison to random practice (figure 10.7). However, immediate and delayed tests of retention were performed much more rapidly after practice in a random acquisition schedule (figure 10.8). This difference between groups was larger when the retention trials were performed in a random sequence,

although there was a difference even in a blocked retention order (figure 10.9). Thus, regardless of whether the retention test was to be performed under random or blocked conditions, it was always more effective to *practice* these tasks under random conditions. This is a curious finding, especially when we realize that the random condition in acquisition resulted in slower performance than the blocked condition. The finding certainly runs counter to the general idea that, in practice, we should always attempt to organize the conditions so that performance is maximized.

Research on contextual interference for learning motor skills was initiated with the study of Shea and Morgan, although a few isolated studies of practice-scheduling effects had been published earlier (see Chamberlin & Lee, 1993, for references). The Shea and Morgan study was influenced considerably by the theoretical insights of William Battig (see boxed text on page 304). Together, the work of these authors has made a substantial impact on research in motor learning during the past two decades. This research can be loosely divided into two categories: (1) studies that have attempted to address the generalizability of the random-blocked differences and (2) work that has tested hypotheses regarding why contextual interference effects occur in learning motor skills. We examine each of these issues next.

Generalizability of Contextual Interference

Issues about the *generalizability* of contextual interference effects might be rephrased to ask the question, "How much faith should I put in the implications arising from the Shea and Morgan study?" Should random and blocked differences be expected to emerge under a variety of different conditions, using different tasks, for different subjects, and so on? Overall, there is a rather wide generalizability to the contextual interference effect.

Task Influences

The original Shea and Morgan (1979) demonstration of the contextual interference effect used a task in which subjects were required to make patterns of arm movements by knocking over small wooden barriers. The goal was to complete the pattern accurately, and as fast as possible, in

W.F. Battig and Contextual Interference

Research in the area of contextual interference owes a debt of gratitude to William F. Battig. Throughout a distinguished career, this cognitive psychologist maintained an interest in memory and learning, frequently conducting studies using both verbal and motor tasks. Early in his research, Battig showed that factors that make a task more "difficult" for the subject enhanced remembering and transfer. For example, requiring (vs. not requiring) learners to pronounce nonsense "words" (e.g., XENF), whose letters corresponded to individual finger movements, made performance on *another* version of the finger task more effective (Battig, 1956).

Battig interpreted these and related findings in terms of the following statement: *intertask facilitation is produced by intratask interference* (Battig, 1966, 227). *Intra*task interference referred to the hinderance caused by attempting to keep multiple items in immediate memory at one time (e.g., the interference between the "word" pronunciations and the finger movements). By *inter*task transfer, Battig was referring to the transfer of learning to other, similar motor tasks. These findings ran counter to intuition, as we would expect that transfer to other tasks would be most effective if the first task had been learned under the most optimal conditions for performance.

But the field of psychology was not prepared to consider such radical ideas, perhaps because the concepts ran so counter to existing theories of memory and learning. Little attention was paid to these notions, even though Battig and his colleagues continued to publish more demonstrations of these counterintuitive findings (e.g., Battig, 1972; Hiew, 1977). A responsive chord was finally struck with the publication of his expanded ideas on *contextual interference;* in this paper, Battig (1979) presented a rather wide framework conceptualizing the findings that had been accumulated. These ideas were expanded shortly thereafter (Battig & Shea, 1980) within the realm of motor skill learning, in which Battig's influence has made a very important mark.

Battig identified two important sources of interference that could arise during practice. One factor related to the *order* in which multiple items were studied or practiced. If the same task was practiced repeatedly, then only this one task needed to be held in working memory, and interference should be *low*. However, if practice involved many switches between multiple tasks, then interference should be *high*. This source of interference has been the object of considerable study and is the focus of the present discussion on contextual interference. The other source of interference was the nature of the material to be practiced. If the items (or motor tasks) were quite similar, then the interference arising during practice would be *high* because of the increased confusion. Items or tasks that were quite different or distinct would cause low interference.

Above all, the most important element of the contextual interference arising from a set of tasks or items to practice was *how the learner responded to the interference.* Battig suggested that subjects respond to situations of high or low interference with correspondingly high or low levels of elaborative and distinctive processing. These ideas have been expanded by the work of John Shea and his colleagues and represent one of the primary explanations of the contextual interference effect.

response to a stimulus light. These findings have been replicated a number of times using similar task requirements (e.g., Del Rey, Liu, & Simpson, 1994; Lee & Magill, 1983b; Shea & Wright, 1991; Wright, 1991). Other laboratory studies have revealed similar random-blocked differences using tasks that emphasize the timing of actions (e.g., Lee & Magill, 1983b; Proteau et al., 1994; Wulf & Lee, 1993), perceptual anticipation (e.g., Del Rey, 1989; Del Rey, Wughalter, & Whitehurst, 1982), the regulation of force (Shea, Kohl, & Indermill, 1990; Shea et al., 1991), and error-detection capabilities (Sherwood, 1996), to list just a few.

In all of these laboratory tasks, the actions to be performed were relatively simple, leading some to question the potential value of this research for practical situations involving much more complicated, "real" tasks (e.g., Newell & McDonald, 1992). However, these reservations may be unfounded. A recent study by Tsutsui, Lee, and Hodges (1998) showed that random practice facilitated the learning of new patterns of coordinating bimanual limb movements. Kinematic analyses of the movements that were produced showed superior coordination skill for the newly learned patterns after random practice versus after blocked practice. The similarity of these findings to the results in studies using much simpler tasks suggests that contextual interference effects may indeed be generalizable to learning tasks involving daily activities.

Contextual interference effects have also been found in a number of applied studies, such as investigations on learning badminton serves (Goode & Magill, 1986; Wrisberg, 1991; Wrisberg & Liu, 1991), rifle shooting (Boyce & Del Rey, 1990), volleyball skills (Bortoli et al., 1992; but also see French, Rink, & Werner, 1990), and kayaking skills (Smith & Davies, 1995), as well as in a study of baseball batting (Hall, Domingues, & Cavazos, 1994). Subjects in most of these applied studies were novices in the skills to be learned, with the exception of those in the study by Hall, Domingues, and Cavazos (1994), who were college-level baseball players and thus already quite skilled at the task. All subjects in this study performed two extra batting-practice sessions per week for 6 weeks. The batting sessions involved practice in which the pitcher threw 15 fastballs, 15 curves, and 15 change-ups. Groups of batters received these pitches in either a blocked or a random order over the entire 6-week period. They also performed two transfer tests in which pitches were delivered in both random and blocked orders.

The results of the Hall, Domingues, and Cavazos (1994) experiment are presented in figure 11.8, including the results for a control group that did not receive the extra batting practice. This control group performed more poorly on the transfer tests than did either practice group, suggesting that the extra batting practice was

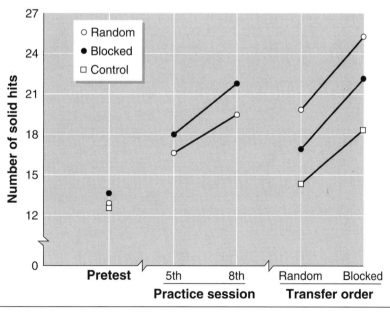

Figure 11.8.   Contextual-interference effects in baseball batting.
Adapted and reproduced with permission of authors and publisher from: Hall, K.G., Domigues, D.A., & Cavazos, R. Contextual interference effects with skilled baseball players. *Perceptual and Motor Skills,* 1994, 78, 835-841. © Perceptual and Motor Skills 1994.

beneficial regardless of the order in which the pitches were thrown. However, the most interesting finding was the observed contextual interference effect in practice and transfer. Notice in figure 11.8 that the performances of the blocked group on the blocked transfer test and of the random group on the random transfer test were nearly identical to their respective performances in the eighth practice session. It was when performance was assessed on the *common* transfer tests that the true value of the practice sequences in learning came through, as random practice facilitated transfer under both orderings of pitches. Thus, it would appear from this study that even experienced athletes can benefit from random practice.

Subject Influences

In the preceding section we presented evidence that variability-of-practice differences were larger in children than in adults. The evidence relating to contextual interference effects is not quite as clear, however, as some studies have shown typical retention and transfer effects (e.g., Pollock & Lee, 1997; Wulf, 1991) whereas others have not (e.g., Del Rey, Whitehurst, & Wood, 1983; Pigott & Shapiro, 1984). There is some evidence that the magnitude of contextual interference effects may also depend on experience. Del Rey and her colleagues have shown, for example, that transfer in an anticipation task after random practice is facilitated more for subjects with experience in

open skills than for novices (Del Rey, 1989; Del Rey, Wughalter, & Whitehurst, 1982).

Other Practice Schedules

Given *X* tasks and *N* trials per task, there is a wide variety of ways in which practice could be scheduled. Having *all* of the trials for one task performed in drill-type sequence represents an extreme scheduling manipulation. *Never* performing two consecutive trials on the same task might be considered the opposite extreme. A condition that might be considered "moderate," relative to these extremes, was examined by Lee and Magill (1983b). In their *serial* condition, practice was rotated among three tasks that were to be practiced, but always in the same order (e.g., B-C-A-B-C-A-B-C-A, etc.). Thus, practice was nonrepetitive, as in random practice, but the next task to practice was always predictable, as in blocked practice. As can be seen in figure 11.9, the performance of the serial group was nearly identical to that of the random group, leading to the suggestion that the repetitiveness of blocked practice may be the key factor that both facilitates acquisition and degrades learning.

An important question that arises is whether or not a practice schedule that represents some "middle ground" in terms of repetitiveness of practice might be beneficial to *both* performance and learning. Studies by Pigott and Shapiro (1984) and Al-Ameer and Toole (1993) support this

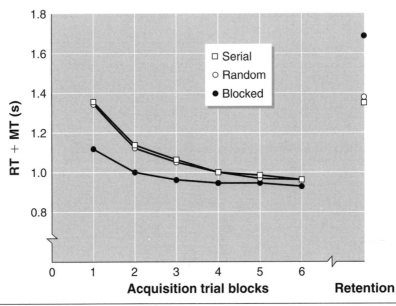

Figure 11.9.   Comparison of blocked and random practice with a serial practice schedule.
Adapted from Lee and Magill, 1983.

possibility. In the Al-Ameer and Toole study, subjects practiced a task similar to that in the Shea and Morgan (1979) study under either random or blocked sequences. Results for both acquisition and retention replicated the Shea and Morgan findings. But Al-Ameer and Toole also added two groups that performed small *randomized blocks of trials,* in which a subject would practice one task for two or three trials, then randomly switch to another task and practice that for two or three trials. The results showed that randomized blocks of three trials facilitated acquisition performance (relative to random practice), and that randomized blocks of either two or three trials were just as beneficial to learning as random practice.

These findings are important, as they suggest that it may be possible to reduce the acquisition performance decrement normally seen with random practice without sacrificing the long-term learning benefit as a consequence. The results are also important for applying the findings from contextual interference experiments to tasks involving daily activities. One major drawback with a completely random schedule is that constantly switching from one task to another may be rather difficult. For example, consider tasks that involve training a new worker on specific job-related skills. If these tasks are located in separate rooms in a plant, it is logical to do at least *some* blocked practice before switching to a new task. The initial findings for the randomized-blocks schedule suggest that this condition combines many of the positive features from both the blocked- and random-practice schedules.

Hypotheses About the Contextual Interference Effect

Before the first contextual interference studies were published, learning researchers seemed to be quite comfortable with the general understanding that any practice variable that promoted acquisition performance would also promote learning. The findings of Shea and Morgan (1979) caused many motor learning researchers to become much less comfortable with this general understanding. How could a variable that slows improvement and retards the overall level of performance in practice be so potent in facilitating retention? This *paradox* generated new thinking and debate, not only about why contextual interference effects occur, but also with regard to the motor learning process in general. Several

hypotheses have been advanced to explain the differences observed between random- and blocked-practice effects. And, though the hypotheses that follow may seem to present competing views, they really have much in common to say about the learning process.

Elaborative and Distinctive Processing Hypothesis

One of these hypotheses, proposed by Shea and colleagues, holds that random practice forces the learner into more *elaborative and distinctive* conceptual processing of the tasks to be learned (Shea & Morgan, 1979; Shea & Titzer, 1993; Shea & Zimny, 1983, 1988). During a random schedule, practice on one task is usually followed by practice on a completely different task. Thus, the preparation for action before movement and the evaluation of performance afterward may be quite different from the preparatory and evaluative processing that was completed on the previous trial. According to the elaborative and distinctive processing view, the differences in task requirements during random practice promote more *comparative and contrastive* analyses of the actions required to complete these tasks. As a result, the representation of each task following random practice is more *memorable* than in blocked practice, in which the opportunity for contrasting the different tasks is minimized because of the repetitive nature of the schedule. The advantages shown by random schedules in retention and transfer result from more *meaningful* representations of a given movement task and more elaborate distinctions between the various task versions.

Verbal reports from subjects involved in these experiments provide one line of evidence in support of the elaboration and distinctiveness hypothesis. Postexperiment interviews indicated that subjects in the random condition understood the tasks in a qualitatively different way than did subjects who performed blocked practice (Shea & Zimny, 1983). Compared to subjects in the blocked-practice group, subjects in the random group reported a much larger number of elaborate mental representations for distinguishing the shapes of the various movement patterns (e.g., noting that one pattern was essentially a mirror image of another, or that a given pattern was the only one with a reversal in direction; Shea & Zimny, 1983). In contrast, the blocked subjects reported that they tended to run the movements off without much thought, more or less "automatically."

Using a concurrent verbal report protocol, Zimny (reported in Shea & Zimny, 1988) found that subjects who were engaged in random practice made comments about specific tasks, as well as between-task comparisons, about twice as often during random practice as in blocked practice (see also Del Rey & Shewokis, 1993). These verbal report data support the superior contrastive value of random practice as predicted by the elaborative and distinctive processing hypothesis.

A different type of support for the elaborative and distinctive view was provided in a study in which random and blocked physical practice trials were alternated with three imagery practice trials (Gabriele, Hall, & Lee, 1989, experiment 1). For two groups, all three of the imagery trials were conducted on the task that had just been practiced physically (blocked imagery). In the other two groups, random mental practice involved imaging the three tasks that *had not* been performed on the preceding physical practice trial. Regardless of how the physical trials were practiced, random imagery facilitated retention more than blocked imagery, supporting the view that this contrastive processing during practice was beneficial for learning.

A more direct experimental manipulation was examined in studies by Wright (1991; Wright, Li, & Whitacre, 1992). Using an arm movement task similar to that employed by Shea and Morgan (1979), four groups of subjects all engaged in blocked practice. One group performed no additional processing, while subjects in the other groups performed certain cognitive activities between practice trials. After each practice trial, subjects in two of the groups were asked to describe verbally the order of movements of one of the tasks—either the task just completed or one of the other tasks. In the fourth group, subjects were asked to make specific comparisons between the task just performed and one of the other tasks. The prediction was that processing in this last condition would be most like the processing engaged in by subjects in random practice. The prediction was supported, as subjects in the intertask processing condition were better in retention than the other three groups. Interestingly, the additional processing in the other two groups with intervening cognitive descriptions did not improve retention at all, suggesting that the qualitative nature of the processing was more important than the quantity.

Forgetting and Reconstruction Hypothesis

A different explanation of the contextual interference effect was proposed by Lee and Magill (1983b, 1985), and is based on the ideas about the spacing effect presented by Jacoby (see boxed text on page 309). According to the *forgetting and reconstruction* view, the action planning that occurs just prior to a practice trial is influenced by what has been done in the previous trial. In blocked practice, a previously constructed action plan is available in working memory because the same task has just been performed. However, since tasks are ordered intermittently in random practice, the previously constructed action plan must be abandoned for the next trial(s) (in order to perform the other tasks) and must be *reconstructed* when that task is practiced once again. Thus, the value of a practice trial depends on the reconstructive processing undertaken. Remembering the "solution" from a previous trial (as in blocked practice) promotes good performance in acquisition, but does not promote the kind of processing that facilitates learning as measured in retention and transfer. In contrast, random practice causes forgetting, which is detrimental to acquisition performance but beneficial to retention and transfer.

Notice that this view of contextual interference follows the same logic as the spacing effect in memory (boxed text on page 309). In fact, there is evidence that memory for motor skills also shows a spacing effect (Lee & Weeks, 1987; Marshall, Jones, & Sheehan, 1977; Weeks et al., 1991). An important difference, however, is that the paradigm used to study the spacing effect is quite different from the learning paradigm that produces the contextual interference effect.

One prediction of the forgetting and reconstruction view that has been empirically tested in a learning paradigm relates to the cause of forgetting. The idea here is that on a given task, *any* activity between practice trials that causes short-term forgetting should promote learning. Note that this prediction is different from the elaborative and distinctive processing view, which suggests that distinctiveness arises from the similarity of different tasks in working memory during random practice. Several studies have examined this prediction; the evidence, though not strong, has been generally positive in support of the hypothesis (Lee & Magill, 1983a, 1987; Magill, 1988a; Young, Cohen, & Husak, 1993).

Larry Jacoby and the Spacing Effect

One of the puzzles about working memory is the curious statement that *"forgetting helps remembering"* (Cuddy & Jacoby, 1982). This statement sounds strange because forgetting (which we will discuss in chapter 14) is usually thought of as a *reduction* in the capability to remember; saying that "forgetting helps remembering" sounds like nonsense. However, the evidence from experiments on the *spacing effect* in verbal memory suggest that this statement is not as bizarre as it seems. In these experiments, subjects are typically given a long list of words that they are asked to study and to recall some time later on a test of memory. The list often comprises words presented only once as well as words that are presented more than once. For the words presented more than once, they may be repeated either immediately (a zero "lag" condition) or with a small or large number of intervening words. The spacing effect is the finding that recall of words that have been repeated with long lags is better than recall of words repeated with no lag or short lags.

Larry Jacoby (Cuddy & Jacoby, 1982; Jacoby, 1978; Jacoby & Dallas, 1981) proposed the idea that forgetting helps memory because the *processing* undertaken during study is determined by what is remembered about the material from the last processing of it. If the information is remembered well, then the material to be studied will not be fully processed on its second presentation. If the information has been forgotten, then the material will be more fully processed once again.

The critical issue for Jacoby is that the value of a repetition lies in the degree to which it promotes full processing of the information on *each* presentation. Processing information is similar to solving a problem. The results of the processing constitute a solution, much like the solution obtained by multiplying two numbers together. If the same problem arises soon after the solution has been determined, then the mental arithmetic need not be undertaken to solve the problem again because the solution is readily available in working memory. However, if the solution has been forgotten, then full processing must be undertaken in order to solve the problem again. Memory, according to Jacoby, is a product of the processing activities. "The means by which a solution is obtained influences subsequent retention performance: subsequent retention suffers when the solution is remembered" (Jacoby, 1978, p. 666).

A different approach to examining the forgetting and reconstruction hypothesis was tested in a study by Lee, Wishart, Cunningham, and Carnahan (1997). An important component of the prediction relates to the information in working memory when a trial is practiced. Instead of trying to induce forgetting, Lee et al. attempted to introduce into working memory the information necessary for the upcoming trial by means of a model. The rationale was that if the "solution" was present, then the problem-solving activity normally undertaken during random practice would be avoided. The experimenters used a timing task, with subjects making patterns of key presses on a computer keyboard. The random- and blocked-practice groups performed in acquisition and retention as expected. A third, *random plus model* group also practiced in a random order; however, the computer generated a visual map of the task along with an auditory template of the timing requirements three times before each pattern was practiced. The idea was that if the model *guided* the learner through the action-planning process, then the reconstruction benefits normally encouraged by random practice would be diminished.

The absolute constant error (|CE|) results are presented in figure 11.10. Two points of interest can be readily seen. First, even though practice was conducted in a random order, the performance of the group provided with modeled information was excellent. In fact, this random + model group outperformed the blocked group on the very first block of practice trials. And, as

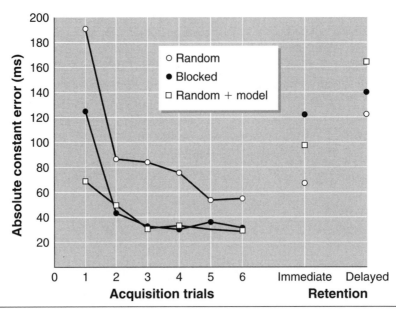

Figure 11.10.   Elimination of the random-practice decrement in practice and the random-practice benefit in retention with a guiding model.
Reprinted from Lee, Wishart, Cunningham, and Carnahan, 1997.

expected, there was a strong negative influence of the model in immediate and delayed retention tests: the learning advantage normally seen following random practice was eliminated by the presence of the modeled information during practice.

One final research area that has surfaced with regard to the forgetting and reconstruction view deals with the nature of the planning activity. The hypothesis is that for random practice, the action prepared for one task is inappropriate for a completely different task and thus a new preparation is required. However, what happens if the "new task" has the same invariant characteristics as the previous task and requires only a different parameterization? According to the ideas presented in chapter 6, the same generalized motor program could be used with just a new scaling of movement parameters, thereby reducing much of the repreparation normally required by random practice. The prediction for tasks of this type would be a reduced contextual interference effect (Magill & Hall, 1990). Research on this specific prediction of the forgetting and reconstruction hypothesis has just begun, although the evidence at this point does offer support for the view (Hall & Magill, 1995; Lee, Wulf, & Schmidt, 1992; Wulf & Lee, 1993; but see also Sekiya et al., 1994).

Evaluating the Hypotheses

On balance, there appears to be considerable support for both the elaborative and distinctive processing account and the forgetting and reconstruction view of contextual interference. One of the problems in comparing these hypotheses is that there are few situations in which different predictions can be contrasted. Thus, the hypotheses should not be seen as *competing* predictors of the contextual interference effect, but rather as complementary theoretical views about the ways in which learners comply with the processing operations encouraged under different practice and task conditions.

Other Hypotheses

Of course, it is possible that future research will show that both the elaboration and distinctiveness and the forgetting and reconstruction views are wrong. Research on contextual interference effects is still rather new, and other hypotheses have been developed to account for these effects. For example, Wulf and Schmidt (1994a) argued that random practice is beneficial for learning because it makes KR *less useful* during practice—which, as we will discuss in chapter 12, is often a good strategy for learning. Others have suggested that the detrimental effect in retention occurs because of greater *retroactive inhibition:* the early tasks practiced by the blocked group are more difficult to recall because of the interference caused by practicing the other tasks in the interim (Del Rey, Liu, & Simpson, 1994; Shea & Titzer, 1993). Views that rely less on cognitive factors include suggestions that contextual interference effects arise as a *dynamic interaction* between the learner and the environment (Newell & McDonald, 1992) or within the constraints of *connectionist modeling* (Horak, 1992; Masson, 1990; Shea & Graf, 1994).

Practical Implications

Whatever the theoretical explanation for these curious effects, it is clear that they are present in both laboratory and practical situations, that they lead to relatively large differences in learning, and that they seem to represent stable principles of motor learning. As a result, they should have important practical implications for the design of learning environments in sport, industry, and therapy. The "traditional" methods of continuous drill on a particular action (i.e., practicing one skill repeatedly until it is correct) are probably not the most effective way to learn. Rather, the evidence suggests that practicing a number of tasks in some nearly randomized order will be the most successful means of achieving the goal of stable learning and retention. Of course, these findings highlight the learning-performance distinction discussed earlier in this and the preceding chapter; here we have a situation for which the conditions in acquisition that make performance most effective (blocked practice) are *not* the most effective for learning—an important general consideration for those designing workable practice sessions. Although the application of these ideas is strongly implicated (Dempster, 1988; Goettl, 1996), much work remains to be done on these issues with different kinds of tasks and various training settings before we can be confident about how to effectively apply these principles.

Mental Practice

Hypotheses regarding the contextual interference effect relied heavily on concepts regarding mental operations to explain the rather paradoxical relation between acquisition and retention effects. In fact, in a number of the experiments described in the previous section, the effects on physically practicing the task in a random or blocked order were influenced considerably by the way in which the subject was directed to think about certain tasks or activities. For example, Wright (1991) showed that blocked practice was enhanced by asking subjects to mentally compare

the set of tasks to be practiced. Similarly, Gabriele, Hall, and Lee (1989) found that mental imagery added a boost to retention performance when combined with physical practice. These are examples of a broader phenomenon in the motor skills literature known as *mental practice effects*. In general, mentally practicing a skill (i.e., imagining performing it, without any associated overt actions) can be shown to produce large positive transfer to skill in the actual task. These techniques, sometimes referred to as *covert rehearsal*, have been studied extensively throughout this century.

Is Mental Practice as Effective as Physical Practice?

Experimental assessment of mental practice effects usually requires several different groups of subjects, at a minimum. All subjects are given a pretest on a task to be learned, followed by the experimental manipulation, then a posttest on the learning task. The mental practice manipulation often entails a covert rehearsal of the task, sometimes involving certain strategies (such as imagery techniques). In this case, however, learning due to only mental practice effects cannot be inferred from only a retention test. Rather, in order to show that mental practice was effective, one must demonstrate that performance on the posttest exceeded performance in a control group that did not perform intervening practice or that performed practice on an unrelated task. In addition, mental practice is usually compared to a third condition in which a group of individuals *physically* practice the task for the same amount of time as the mental practice group. Some experiments also include *combination* conditions; here a group of subjects alternates between trials of mental and physical practice. Of course, many experiments use other variations of these mental practice manipulations, reviewed most recently by Feltz and Landers (1983; Feltz, Landers, & Becker, 1988).

A very nice demonstration of all these various practice conditions is provided in a complex study by Hird et al. (1991). Twelve groups of subjects participated in the experiment. Six groups were asked to learn a pegboard task, inserting pegs of different colors and shapes as rapidly as possible into squares cut in a board. The other six groups performed the pursuit rotor task. For each task, subjects performed a pretest, seven sessions of training (on separate days), and a posttest. During the training sessions the 100% physical practice group performed eight trials on the task while the 100% mental practice group covertly practiced the task for the same amount of time. Three other groups performed combinations of practice, consisting of two, four, or six trials of physical practice combined with six, four, or two trials of mental practice (i.e., 75% physical practice [P]:25% mental practice [M]; 50P:50M; and 25P:75M groups). The control group performed on an unrelated task (the stabilometer) for the same amount of time during these training sessions.

The difference in performance between the pretest and posttest for each group in the Hird et al. study is presented in figure 11.11. The sets of findings for the two tasks are remarkably similar. The groups given mental practice (100%M) were more effective than the no-practice (control) groups, but not nearly as effective as the groups given the same amount of physical practice (100%P). In addition, the results for the combination groups showed that learning was enhanced with higher proportions of the training trials spent in physical, compared to mental, practice (e.g., compare the 75P:25M groups with the 25P:75M groups in figure 11.11).

The Hird et al. (1991) findings are in complete agreement with the reviews of the mental practice literature conducted by Feltz and Landers (1983; Feltz, Landers, & Becker, 1988). The findings suggest that *whenever possible,* physical practice is preferable to mental practice for learning. However, when physically practicing a task is not possible, mental rehearsal is an effective method for augmenting a subject's learning.

Hypotheses About Mental Practice Effects

Why then, is mental practice effective for learning a motor skill? Certainly, one of the components of mental practice involves learning the *cognitive elements* in the task; that is, learning what to do (Heuer, 1985). Given the requirement of rehearsing mentally, the learner can think about what kinds of things he or she might try, can predict the consequences of each action to some extent on the basis of previous experiences with similar skills, and can perhaps rule out inappropriate courses of action. This view suggests that not very much motor learning is happening in mental practice, the majority being the rapid learning associated with the cognitive elements of the task. Such a view fits well with data from Minas (1978, 1980), who used a serial throwing task in which subjects had to throw balls of different weights and textures into the proper bins. The main finding was that mental practice contributed to the learning of the sequence (the cognitive element) but did not contribute very much to the learning of the particular throwing actions (motor elements).

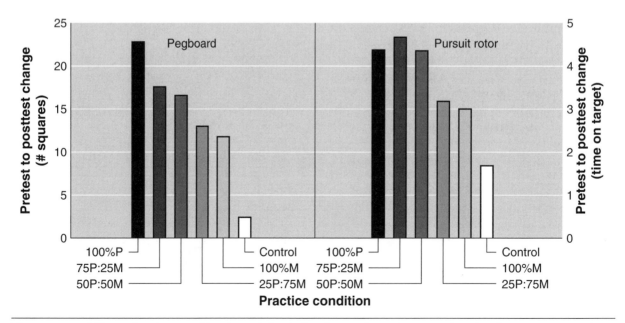

Figure 11.11.   Effects of various combinations of physical and mental practice on pegboard and pursuit rotor tasks. Adapted from Hird, Landers, Thomas, and Horan, 1991.

But others think that there is more to mental practice than this simple view about learning the cognitive elements in a task. One view is that the motor programs for the movements are actually being run off during mental practice but that the learner simply turns down the "gain" of the program so that the contractions are hardly visible. Research on so-called *implicit speech*, in which subjects are told to imagine speaking a given sentence, shows patterns of electromyogram activity from the vocal musculature that resemble the patterns evoked during actual speech. One possibility is that very small forces (not sufficient to cause movements) are produced and the performer receives Golgi tendon organ feedback about them (chapter 5), as the Golgi tendon organs are extremely sensitive to small forces. Another possibility is that the "movements" are sensed via feedforward and corollary discharge (i.e., "internal feedback"), generated when the motor programs are run off (chapter 5). Yet another possibility discussed earlier in this chapter is that *planning* a movement (which should be part of mental practice) is itself beneficial to learning. Unfortunately, there is little evidence available to distinguish among these hypotheses (see Heuer, 1985, for a detailed discussion).

Part Versus Whole Practice

A very common technique for teaching motor skills is to break them down into smaller parts, to eliminate the burden of repeating the simpler parts of the entire task. Also, this would seem to be an effective procedure when the task is very complex and cannot be grasped as a whole. Examples are numerous, such as practicing separately the arm and leg strokes in Red Cross swimming methods and practicing specific stunts in gymnastics that later become part of a larger routine.

The ultimate test of whether or not these methods are effective is the amount of transfer that can be shown from the practice of the part to the performance of the whole task. It seems obvious that if practice is given on the part, it would certainly transfer highly to the whole task, as the part would seem to be identical to one element of the whole. The problem with this idea is that practice on the part in isolation may so change the motor programming of the part that for all practical purposes it is no longer the same as it is in the context of the total skill. It turns out that whether or not part-whole practice is effective depends on the nature of the task (Wightman & Lintern, 1985).

Serial Tasks

Seymour (1954) conducted extensive research on industrial tasks that are serial in nature. One task consisted of a series of elements to be performed on a lathe. Some of the elements were difficult, requiring a great deal of practice to master; some were easy and could be accomplished on the first try. Seymour found that if the difficult parts were practiced separately, without any corresponding practice on the less difficult parts, there was considerable transfer of the part to the whole task. Similar findings were produced by Adams and Hufford (1962), who studied part-practice of various discrete actions involved in aircraft flying. More recent examples involve learning special multicomponent video games designed especially for research purposes (Mané et al., 1989). In these cases, transfer from part-practice can be *greater than* 100%, in that the benefits afforded by some amount of practice on the parts in isolation can be greater than those obtained with an equal amount of time devoted to the whole task (see also Newell et al., 1989; Wightman & Sistrunk, 1987).

According to one way of viewing these effects, in part-task practice the learner does not have to spend time on the parts of the task that have been already mastered, and the practice is more efficient. The task can be reassembled in many ways, of course, but an efficient method is *backward chaining*, in which the last element in the sequence is systematically preceded by earlier and earlier parts until the whole chain is completed (Wightman & Lintern, 1985; Wightman & Sistrunk, 1987). Mere practice on a part isolated from the sequence does not appear to be as useful for transfer (Sheppard, 1984).

Continuous Tasks

For continuous tasks, in which the behavior continues more or less uninterrupted (as in walking or steering a car), the parts that can be isolated frequently occur at the same time as other parts. This is, of course, in sharp contrast to the situation for serial tasks, in which discrete parts are sequentially organized. Also, in continuous tasks the parts must frequently be *coordinated* with each other; and it might seem that breaking into this pattern of coordination to practice a part might not be highly effective, as it is the coordination between these parts that must be learned. Swimming strokes have this characteristic, as the arm strokes, breathing, and kicking actions must be coordinated to form an effective whole.

Briggs and Brogden (1954) and Briggs and Waters (1958) used a lever-positioning task that required positioning in two dimensions (forward-backward, left-right) simultaneously and continuously, much like the positioning of the "joystick" that is done in an airplane to control the motions of the plane. They found that practice on the separate dimensions alone transferred to the whole task, but that this practice was less effective than practicing the whole task for the same period of time. It is possible that the most effective way to learn such tasks is to practice the whole, unless the task is highly complex or contains rather trivial elements.

Another situation that produces slightly different findings involves those tasks in which the parts *interact* while they are being performed simultaneously. One complex example involves the operations necessary to take a helicopter from the ground into flight. According to Zavala et al. (1965), the operator must handle four separate controls. The first is a *cyclic pitch-control stick*, which is really a stick control for two dimensions in one (roll and pitch). When moved in a particular direction, it causes the helicopter to tilt in that direction. Thus, it can be used to control roll (side to side) and pitch (nose up or down) simultaneously. Second, a *collective pitch lever* is mounted to the left of the pilot, and up-and-down movements of this lever control the vertical component of the flight. Third, a *throttle* is located as a twist grip on the pitch control just mentioned; it controls the engine speed in the same way the accelerator in an automobile does. Fourth, *antitorque pedals* under the pilot's feet control the pitch of the small propeller at the tail of the helicopter, thus controlling the direction of the plane and compensating for the torque produced by the overhead rotors.

The problem for the person learning this task is that these components interact strongly. That is, when the throttle control is used to speed up the rotor or the pitch control is adjusted, there is a tendency for the helicopter to turn in the direction opposite the rotation of the rotor. This must be counteracted by an appropriately graded foot-pedal movement to maintain the proper heading. But also, the helicopter will increase its tendency to roll and attempt to dive; both of these motions must be counteracted by the adjustment of the cyclic-control stick. Thus, when the lift of the rotors is increased in the attempt to get the plane into the air, three other adjustments must be made simultaneously to prevent it from turning upside down. The amount of control change in these three dimensions depends on the amount of lift that is imparted to the helicopter via the other pitch control. It is said that these control dimensions interact because the setting of one of them will depend on the setting applied to the others.

It would be tempting to take this highly complex task and break it down into separate parts. But this breakdown seems to sidestep the most important problem for the learner: how to coordinate these actions. Any one of the dimensions can easily be performed separately, but this practice would not be very effective for learning the total task. In general, the limitations of part-to-whole transfer methods will probably depend on the extent to which the parts of the task interact within the whole task. As for the helicopter, it would seem that an effective way to learn the task would be to practice in a ground-based simulator, where all dimensions would be learned together without the fear of an accident (see more on *simulators* in chapter 14).

Discrete Tasks

Can we apply this evidence about part versus whole practice to discrete tasks whose MTs are very short (e.g., less than 1 s)? Probably not, as the evidence gives a different picture in these situations.

For example, Lersten (1968) had subjects learn a hand movement task (the rho task) that required a rapid movement with two components. The subject grasped a handle and rotated it in the horizontal plane through 270° until it hit a stop, whereupon the subject was to release the handle and move forward to knock over a barrier. This was to be done as quickly as possible (MTs were about 600 ms). Thus a circular component was followed by a linear component, both of which could be practiced separately by various groups. Another group of subjects practiced only the whole task. Lersten found that practice on the circular component alone transferred only about

7% to the performance of the circular phase in the context of the whole task. Other conditions produced no transfer to the whole task. Even more important, Lersten found that the practice on the linear component alone transferred *negatively* (about –8%) to the whole task. That is, practicing this linear component in isolation produced less learning on the whole task than not practicing at all! Overall, the findings suggest that practicing these isolated components of the whole task produced essentially negligible transfer to the performance of the whole task.

Sequential Parts

How can these findings be explained? First, even though the task Lersten used was "serial" in nature, it must be seen as quite different from the serial tasks used by Seymour (1954). One clear difference is in terms of the overall MT, with Seymour's tasks having durations in the order of minutes and Lersten's task lasting for only about 600 ms. It seems reasonable to assume that Lersten's task was governed by a single motor program containing the instructions for both the circular and the linear components, as well as the instructions for the transition between the two (timing the release of the handle, for example). If so, then practicing the circular part in isolation would result in the subject's practicing a program different from that involved in the circular part within the context of the whole skill, because the circular part did not entail a handle release. In contrast, the serial tasks that Seymour (1954) used can be thought of as a series of programs strung together. Practicing one of them in isolation is the same as practicing that program in the context of the total skill, so part-to-whole transfer is high.

These ideas suggest that the major determinant of whether or not part-to-whole transfer will "work" is the extent to which the movement is governed by a single program. If the movement is very fast, it will almost certainly be governed by one motor program, and it should be practiced as a whole. Second, if the movement is slower but there is a "break" in the action that is easily adjusted, it is possible that the movement is governed by more than one program. An example is the break between the toss action and the hit action in a tennis serve; the toss seems programmed, but then there is a feedback-based break so that the hit program can be adjusted to the exact location and timing of the ball toss. In a springboard dive, the takeoff and tuck are probably programmed, but the timing of the "untuck" movements must be feedback based, determined by visual or vestibular information. These tasks could probably be split into their component parts for separate practice, and part-to-whole transfer would probably be higher.

Simultaneous Parts

A second situation is that in which the parts of the task are simultaneous, rather than serial as in Lersten's example. Many examples exist, such as playing the piano (left and right hands) or any other task for which one part of the body has to be coordinated with another. Transfer research on these questions is nearly nonexistent, though, and the decisions about part-whole transfer are mostly speculative.

First, it seems from the data presented in chapter 8 that rapid, discrete two-handed simultaneous movements must be controlled by a single program, with the program containing instructions for both hands. Practicing the movements of one hand in isolation probably results in the development of a different program than practicing that "same" movement in the context of a total two-handed skill. Konzem's (1987) data suggested that the program to make a "V" with the right hand was probably different from the program required to make a "V" with the right hand and a "γ" with the left hand simultaneously. The principles underlying coordination of the separate limbs in an action are not well understood, and more work on this is needed; but it seems clear that breaking down a task into its components will not always result in large part-to-whole transfer.

Lead-Up Activities

A closely related question for the teaching of skills concerns the use of so-called lead-up activities. In these situations, certain simpler tasks are thought to be in some way fundamental to the learning of more complex tasks, so the simpler tasks are formally taught as a part of the procedure for learning the more complex task. These procedures are often used in gymnastics as the instructors talk of a progression of subtasks leading eventually to the complex goal response. The question, again, can be thought of as one of transfer from the lead-up task to the goal movement. Such activities might have the disadvantage of being, by necessity, different from the goal action, and the motor transfer from them could be very small. Certainly this conclusion is in keeping with the evidence on transfer. But, unfortunately, no effective experiments on lead-up activities can be found, so this conclusion has to be seen as speculative.

On the other hand, lead-ups may have many positive aspects. First, in many tasks (e.g., stunts in gymnastics) there is a strong element of fear. Lead-ups, being simpler and less dangerous, may serve a useful role in reducing fear responses that can be detrimental to a more complex movement. This fear-reduction aspect is borne out in studies using "desensitization techniques," whereby people are taught to eliminate phobic responses (e.g., fear of snakes, or heights) by performing lead-up activities that bring them progressively closer to the target fear (e.g., progressively more "realistic" snakes, eventually leading to an actual snake; see Bandura, 1969, or Bandura, Blanchard, & Ritter, 1969). Also, many lead-ups are designed with a particular action in mind. In gymnastics, again, the "kipping" action (a forceful, timed extension of the hip) is thought to be involved in a large number of skills. Learning to kip in one simple lead-up activity possibly will transfer to the "same" action in a more complex and dangerous activity.

Guidance

A technique frequently used in teaching and in rehabilitation involves *guidance,* whereby the learner is in some way guided through the task to be learned. Actually, guidance refers to a variety of separate procedures, ranging from physically pushing and pulling the learner through a sequence, to preventing incorrect movements by physical limitations on the apparatus, or even to the simple act of verbally "talking someone through" a new situation. These guidance procedures tend to prevent the learner from making errors in the task.

What does the evidence on guidance suggest? Much of the research on guidance by Holding (1970; Holding & Macrae, 1964; Macrae & Holding, 1965, 1966), Singer (1980; Singer & Pease, 1976; Singer & Gaines 1975), and others (reviewed by Armstrong, 1970a), using various

tasks and guidance procedures, shows considerable positive effects of guidance procedures on performance during acquisition. We should remember, however, that guidance will usually have, by definition, strong effects on *performance* during the trials in which it is administered. Of course, as we have discussed previously, performance gains during acquisition may not represent relatively permanent changes attributable to learning, and the important question is whether such performance gains will survive a transfer test in which the guidance is removed.

One of the definitive studies in this area was performed by Armstrong (1970b). He compared various forms of physical guidance in a task for which the learner had to make an elbow movement having a complex spatial-temporal pattern (see figure 6.17), with MTs of 3 or 4 s. Three of his groups are of specific interest here. One group practiced the task and received terminal, kinematic feedback (knowledge of performance [KP]) after each trial. In addition, after the last in a block of 15 trials, subjects in this group were shown a plot of their last trial in combination with a template of the goal pattern. Another group was given concurrent visual feedback of both the movement being made by the subject and the movement of the template as it was traced on the monitor. In a third group, the movement device moved by the subject was mechanically controlled such that any deviations from the target path were physically corrected. Practice was conducted over 3 days, which also included a transfer test on the third day during which all subjects performed the task with no augmented information. The results, presented in figure 11.12, were very dramatic. As can be seen, the guidance device restricted errors so that performance was nearly perfect throughout the entire practice period. The concurrent feedback was also quite effective in reducing performance error during practice—clearly not as effective as the guidance device but much better than the terminal feedback. But Armstrong's results showed that the guidance effects provided only temporary boosts to performance. As can be seen on the right side of figure 11.12, the transfer trials were performed best by the terminal-feedback group, and very poorly by both the guidance and concurrent-feedback groups. In fact, the latter two groups

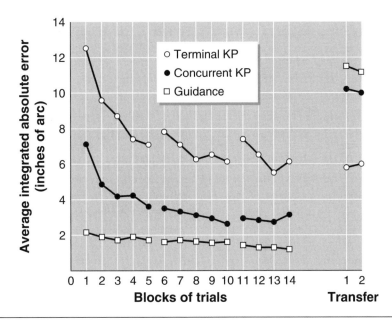

Figure 11.12.   Comparison of physical guidance with terminal- and concurrent-feedback effects on acquisition and transfer.
Reprinted from Armstrong, 1970.

performed the transfer trials at almost the same level as had the terminal KP group early in practice.

Together with other results (e.g., Schmidt & Wulf, 1997; Singer & Pease, 1976), Armstrong's findings raise considerable doubt about the benefits of guidance techniques as learning aids. More recent research shows that some guidance can be beneficial when interspersed with active practice trials (Hagman, 1983; Winstein, Pohl, & Lewthwaite, 1994). These various findings permit a number of tentative generalizations about learning. First, guidance may be most effective in early practice when the task is unfamiliar to the learners. Much of the apparent contribution of guidance procedures is involved in getting the movement "into the ballpark" so that later refinements can be made. Also, guidance may make the stimulus information simpler to handle by giving a preview of what is to happen in the task. Second, guidance may be most effective for tasks that are very slow in time (e.g., matching some perceived state such as a force or a position). Presumably guidance gives the learner a good indication of the nature of the state that is to be matched, so that movements may be adjusted to match this state later. Direct and indirect lines of evidence, however, suggest that guidance will be less effective for tasks that are rapid and ballistic and/or for tasks that involve

the learning of motor programs (e.g., Armstrong's spatial-temporal pattern).

A final aspect of guidance that is rarely studied is the prevention of injury and reduction of fear. In many guidance procedures, the guidance is relatively "loose" unless the individual produces an error that could result in a serious injury. Gymnasts use manual assistance and spotting belts regularly to ensure that a mistake will not result in a serious fall (see figure 11.13). Similar "techniques" are used by parents when their children begin to ride a bicycle without the training wheels. An adult running down the street beside the child, either with a guiding hand or without, is an easily recognizable image of guidance. Such procedures provide a great deal of confidence for learners and are highly effective in reducing the fear and potential disruptions in skill learning. The key feature is that guidance is minimal, while fear of injury is nearly eliminated. Even so, there remains the problem of the guidance serving as a "crutch," so that when it is removed there will be a marked reduction in the skill level. Gymnasts say that it is difficult to perform a risky new skill "out of the [spotting] belt" for the first time, as the performer knows that now a mistake could cause a serious injury. It would seem that there is no substitute for practicing the skill on your own as soon as it is safe to do so.

Principles of Practice Specificity

Many of the issues addressed in this chapter reveal a common dilemma for those designing practice settings—deciding how to establish performance conditions in the acquisition phase that will best prepare the learner for the criterion conditions under which the learning will be applied. The general hypothesis, that we should attempt to match those conditions in acquisition practice with those expected in the criterion "test" performance, is an old one based on common sense. It has been called the *specificity of learning hypothesis* in motor behavior (e.g., Barnett et al., 1973), stemming from Henry's (1958/1968) work on individual differences (see chapter 9). The view holds that because skills are very specific (i.e., generally uncorrelated with each other), changing the conditions under which a task is performed will require a substantial shift in the underlying abilities. Therefore, because practicing a task under one set of conditions and then performing it as a criterion task under different conditions would require a shift in abilities, the conditions in practice and "test" should be equated whenever possible. In other areas, this view has been called the hypothesis of *state-dependent learning*. A number of researchers have examined whether learning (usually verbal) materials in one state (under the influence of drugs or tobacco, or in a particular mood, or even in a particular room) would be more effective if the test conditions used that same state and less effective if the state were changed at the time of criterion test (see chapters in Davies & Thomson, 1988).

However, the astute reader will recall some evidence presented earlier in the chapter that seems to violate this specificity effect. For example, distributed-practice conditions were better for retention than massed practice when the retention trials were conducted in a distributed fashion (which is consistent with specificity predictions), but also when the retention trials were *massed* (Bourne & Archer, 1956)—a finding that is opposite to a strict specificity prediction. A similar finding is obtained in relation to the contextual interference effect; random practice produces better retention performance than blocked practice under conditions in which retention trials are either blocked or randomly ordered.

What is happening here? We suggest that these different practice effects are related to different

types of specificity phenomena that emerge as a function of the interaction between certain conditions of practice and the conditions of retention (or transfer). These different types of specificity are discussed next.

Sensory and Motor Specificity

Although the topic is not often discussed in relation to *motor learning*, evidence from exercise physiology studies shows that performance assessment following muscular adaptations to training reveals the largest strength gain in the specific exercises that were done during training. For example, findings in this literature generally show large specificity effects when training and performance comparisons involve the same types of exercise (e.g., isometric and concentric exercise), the same ranges of motion, and to a lesser degree, the same movement velocity (Morrissey, Harman, & Johnson, 1995; Sale & MacDougall, 1981). The similarity of these specificity effects to those seen in motor learning experiments is quite remarkable. However, the degree to which these divergent fields of study address common processes (e.g., neural adaptations to practice) is a topic that awaits further research.

Motor learning studies suggest a different type of neural specificity of practice. These effects are illustrated nicely in a series of studies by Proteau and his colleagues in which subjects aimed a stylus at a target. Subjects in different conditions practiced this task with KR for varying numbers of trials (ranging from very few trials to several days of practice); they were then asked to perform retention trials without KR. The various practice conditions manipulated the amount of inherent visual feedback the subject was able to gather before, during, and after the movement. These conditions included full vision of the subject's arm, the stylus, and the target, at one extreme, to a condition with absolutely no visual feedback at the other extreme. Various other visual conditions have been included in other experiments (e.g., Elliott, Lyons, & Dyson, 1997; Proteau, 1992, 1995). In general, these studies show that after practice, if the transfer test has required subjects to perform without visual feedback, then the groups that do the best are the ones that learned the task with the least amount of vision during practice; typically, the worst performance is by the group that had the most vision available.

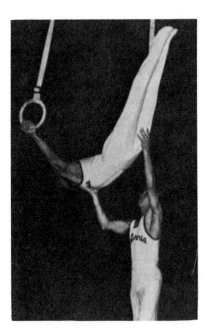

Figure 11.13.   Guidance in learning a gymnastics stunt.

These findings are not surprising, as we know that vision tends to dominate all other sensory modalities when it is available. Thus, when practicing with vision the subject may come to rely on its availability to support performance, and then will suffer when performing in the absence of vision. However, Proteau and his colleagues took their research one step further, showing that when vision was *added* in transfer, performance deteriorated considerably for the groups that had performed in the absence of vision during practice (Proteau, Marteniuk, & Lévesque, 1992). Findings such as these have led Proteau and colleagues to suggest that learning involves a *sensorimotor representation* that integrates the motor components with the sensory information available during practice. This sensorimotor representation results in specificity during transfer such that performance is optimized to the degree that the conditions available during transfer match those conditions available during practice.

Context Specificity

A logic similar to Proteau's is used to look at the nature of specificity of practice conditions in a more general way. This research has been done often in psychology and reveals a kind of "mixed bag" of effects. For example, various environmental factors that compose a study *context* (heat, color, room conditions, etc.) seem to have an influence on remembering the information that has been learned. When a person attempts to recall the information later (e.g., in an exam), the same contextual information, if present, can serve as cues to help retrieve the information (Davies & Thomson, 1988).

The evidence for context specificity in motor learning is not abundant, although it does appear to be consistent with the general set of findings in cognitive psychology. For example, subjects in a study by Wright and Shea (1991) learned sequences of key press patterns, with the computer monitor providing stimulus cues specific to each pattern (i.e., the information about which keys to press was presented in different colors, shapes, and positions on the screen and was accompanied by auditory cues that were specific for each pattern). Performance in retention was maximized when the cues were matched with the same patterns as had been practiced, leading to the conclusion that the stimulus information provided a *context* that was learned as part of the representation for the movement sequence (see also Wright & Shea, 1994).

One possible relation of this research to practical experience is the so-called *home advantage* in sport. The typical finding in most professional team sports is that a team achieves a higher proportion of its wins (or points) when playing at home than when playing on the road. This finding has been well documented in the literature: it has been remarkably consistent for many years, across the various major team sports, and is found at both the college and professional levels (Courneya & Carron, 1992). Several potential hypotheses for the home advantage seem to be ruled out, such as effects of travel, crowd size, and aggressiveness. But one factor that could not be ruled out is related to the idea of context specificity—that certain factors related to the court or field on which the game is played (and on which the home team practices) provide a home advantage (Courneya & Carron, 1992). Perhaps the contextual information provided by the surroundings of the practice area constitutes an advantage when games are played in the same venue. This hypothesis must be viewed quite cautiously, however, as the evidence that lends support to it is weak (e.g., Pollard, 1986).

Processing Specificity

The specificity effects presented in the preceding sections seem to provide some guidelines for establishing certain constraints on the effectiveness of practice, when considered in light of the conditions under which retention or transfer conditions will be conducted. However, trying to anticipate the conditions of retention or transfer, and then matching practice conditions to them, is often difficult if not impossible in the real world. A rather different kind of specificity in *learning* has to do with the *processing* that a learner undertakes during practice.

The idea of processing specificity is similar to a concept that has been labeled "transfer-appropriate processing" by Morris, Bransford, and Franks (1977; Bransford et al., 1979; Lee, 1988). The idea is that the effectiveness of the practice activities can be evaluated only in relation to the goals and purposes of the transfer test. We can evaluate "relative amount learned" only with respect to some particular transfer task or transfer conditions; acquisition conditions that might be "good" for one transfer test might be "bad" for another.

We have seen processing specificity in a number of instances in this chapter. Distributed practice is better than massed practice for retention under both distributed and massed retention trials. Variable practice can be better for retention of a specific task than specific practice on that task alone. Random practice is usually better than blocked practice for both random and blocked retention orders. And we also saw that observational learning can be enhanced by watching a learning model as compared to an expert model (e.g., McCullagh & Caird, 1990; figure 11.2). A processing-specificity view explains this latter finding as follows: the observer can view how the learning model attempts to perform the task, can receive information about the results of the model's performance, and can see how the model uses that information to make adjustments on the next attempt. In other words, the observer is drawn into the *same problem-solving process* that he or she will encounter when actually performing the task (Adams, 1986). In contrast, observing an expert engages the observer in a kind of processing that will be very different from the processing involved in the trial-and-error, problem-solving activities one performs when attempting to learn the motor skill.

The notion of processing specificity addresses more than just the obvious, contextual, or incidental similarities between practice and retention/transfer situations. Processing specificity suggests that it is the similarity of the underlying *processes* (not simply the superficial *conditions*) between acquisition and criterion transfer performance that will be the critical determinant of the "goodness" of practice. In these cases, the "best" practice conditions are those that require subjects to practice and learn the same underlying *processes* that will be ultimately used in the retention or transfer test. That is, practice will be best if it fosters the processes most *appropriate* to performance on the transfer test. Sometimes, of course, when the superficial environmental conditions described by the specificity of learning hypothesis are the same in practice and transfer, the underlying processes are the same as well. But often this is not the case.

In relation to all the practice variables noted previously, though the superficial conditions in acquisition versus transfer may differ, the gain provided by learning some new appropriate processing capability overshadows any switch in conditions, so that the overall result is improved performance on the transfer test. This hypothesis of processing specificity does not identify the nature of the appropriate processes learned in acquisition, however, and these still must be discovered by research. But it is a step forward from other specificity hypotheses that are stated only in terms of matched environmental or internal conditions. It appears that designers of training settings must understand the *processes* underlying the criterion transfer performances and attempt to generate activities for practice that will use the same (hence appropriate) processes.

Summary

This chapter deals with the major independent variables that affect the learning of motor skills and thus those variables that have an influence on the design of instructional programs. Of most importance is the amount of practice itself. One can do a considerable amount of learning before actually physically practicing a motor skill. Much of this learning involves the performer's trying to *figure out what to do.* Perceptual presentations of information prior to practice seem to be generally more effective than verbal descriptions. However, methods engaging the learner in information-processing activities that encourage problem solving will likely help to benefit the use of prepractice augmented information.

The structure of practice also has very important influences on learning. Distributed practice facilitates performance and learning more than massed practice does, although these effects seem to be specific to the learning of continuous tasks. Practice sequences in which the task conditions are deliberately varied from trial to trial are slightly more effective than constant-practice conditions for adults and far more effective for children. Randomly ordered practice is detrimental to performance as compared to blocked practice, but facilitates retention and transfer. Mental practice, though not as effective as physically practicing a task, does facilitate learning when physical practice is not possible. Decisions about whether to break a task down into its component parts for practice or whether to practice the task as a whole depend entirely on the nature of the task. If practicing the parts means changing the task itself, then whole practice will probably be more effective. And guidance can be a useful aid in some situations, but overuse of guidance techniques can also be detrimental to learning.

We have emphasized often that the value of practice sessions must be assessed mainly in tests of retention and transfer. Complicating this evaluation of learning is the fact that the relation between the nature of practice and the nature of the retention and transfer conditions also influences performance. Specificity in learning suggests that the sensory-motor, contextual, and processing activities of the retention and transfer tests influence to a considerable extent the "value" that we attribute to certain practice conditions.

AUGMENTED FEEDBACK

As we saw in the preceding chapter, information about what to do can be provided to an individual prior to any overt practice. The present chapter should be considered an extension of that discussion. Rather than looking at the effects of prepractice augmented information about *what to do,* here we will discuss the effects of providing augmented information about *what was done.* The distinction between the two types of augmented information, however, is far deeper than just the temporal distinction concerning when the information is presented to the learner. In being provided augmented *feedback* information, the learner has knowledge about what was being attempted before the movement started and perhaps some inherent knowledge about the outcome of the movement. These kinds of information can be compared to the augmented information about what was done to form a basis for making changes in future movements. The form of this information, the amount of it, and the time at which it is presented can all affect performance and learning. Not many of the variables studied so far have that kind of powerful influence, and most writers agree that such information is the single most important variable (except, of course, for practice itself) for motor learning (e.g., Bilodeau, 1966). Understanding the principles of how such information "works" will provide additional bases for decisions about the design of teaching or training environments.

The study of feedback information is important for theoretical reasons as well. Any variable that critically affects motor learning must be understood if the learning process is to be revealed. Many theories of learning are strongly based on the evidence that indicates how such information is used by the motor system, and a small part of this chapter is devoted to these theoretical ideas.

Classifications and Definitions

Consider as the broadest class all the various kinds of sensory information that individuals can receive, including all those sources that have to do with the many diverse aspects of our lives. Of course, not all such information is related to our movements: the sound of wind in the trees as we walk through a forest is not relevant in this respect. Of those sources of information that are related to our movements, we can speak of (a) those that are available before the action and (b) those that are available during or after the action. Before the action, such information signals the position of your limbs, the sight of a ball flying toward you, the nature of the environmental setting, and so on. During or after the action, you receive information produced by the movement, such as the way it felt, sounded, and looked, as well as the result the movement produced in the environment (e.g., the actions of a ball that has been struck). This latter class is usually termed *movement-produced feedback,* or simply, *feedback.* The term "feedback" can be further subdivided into two broad classes: *inherent* feedback (sometimes called "intrinsic" feedback) and *augmented* feedback.

Inherent Feedback

People can gain information about many aspects of their own movements through various sensory channels. These forms of information are inherent to the normal execution of a particular movement. For example, you know that an error was made in a basketball shot because you see that the ball did not go into the basket. Also, the stinging sensations as you land on your back in a pool after a faulty dive inform you that something probably went wrong. Just about every movement we can make has associated with it certain sources of inherent feedback that provide a basis for evaluating those movements. Such feedback is usually rich and varied, containing substantial information regarding performance. Depending on the nature of the movement and the source of inherent feedback, sometimes the performer knows that something has gone wrong before the movement is even completed. The information provided as the movement is executed is sufficiently useful that the movement outcome can be predicted before it occurs. At other times the nature of the movement and the source of feedback are such that the evaluation of the movement must occur after it is completed.

In many situations this inherent feedback requires almost no evaluation at all; one sees that the bat missed the ball or one can feel the fall while skating on ice or pavement. Thus, some errors seem to be signaled immediately and clearly. But other aspects of inherent feedback are not so easily recognizable, and perhaps the performer must *learn* to evaluate them. Examples might be the gymnast learning to sense whether or not the knees are bent during a movement, or a patient with a recent hip replacement who is learning to put partial weight through the leg while walking with canes. It is thought that inherent feedback is compared to a learned reference of correctness, with this reference acting in conjunction with the feedback in an error-detection process. Such self-detected errors have been referred to as *subjective reinforcement* (Adams, 1971; Adams & Bray, 1970). Without such a reference of correctness, many forms of inherent feedback probably cannot be used to detect errors.

Augmented Feedback

In contrast to inherent feedback, *augmented feedback* is information provided about the task that is supplemental to, or that augments, inherent feedback. For example, you can receive information from a buzzer when your car exceeds a certain speed—information that is not normally available when one drives a car. The augmented information could be provided verbally, for example, in the presentation of one's time after a 100-m dash or the set of scores after a gymnastics or ice skating routine. This information is not strictly verbal in gymnastics and ice skating, but it is in a form that is capable of being verbalized.

A number of useful dimensions for augmented feedback are summarized in table 12.1. First, one can distinguish between *concurrent* and *terminal* feedback. Concurrent feedback is delivered during the movement (e.g., the information about engine speed that the racing driver receives from the tachometer), while terminal feedback is postponed until after the movement has been completed (e.g., the gymnast's score). Another dimension of augmented feedback is the time at which it is delivered; it can be either *immediate* or *delayed* by some amount of time. The feedback can be verbal (or capable of being verbalized) or nonverbal (e.g., a buzzer indicating that a car is going too fast). Also, the performance can be sampled for a period of time, with the *accumulated* feedback indicating the average performance for the past few seconds; or the feedback can be *distinct*, representing each moment of the performance (e.g., feedback from a speedometer). (See Holding, 1965, and Singer, 1980, for additional dimensions.)

These various dimensions of augmented feedback can be thought of as independent of one another. For example, if the augmented feedback is terminal, it could be either verbal or nonverbal, and it might be delayed or immediate. These dimensions, then, should be thought of as separate descriptors of augmented feedback that are necessary to define most kinds of feedback commonly used.

Knowledge of Results

One of the important categories of augmented feedback is termed *knowledge of results (KR)*. Essentially, KR is verbal (or verbalizable), terminal (i.e., postmovement) feedback about the *outcome* of the movement in terms of the environmental goal. It forms one combination of the various possible dimensions of augmented feedback

---

Table 12.1   Dimensions of Augmented Feedback

Concurrent: Presented during the movement

Terminal: Presented after the movement

Immediate: Presented immediately after the relevant action

Delayed: Delayed in time after the relevant action

Verbal: Presented in a form that is spoken or capable of being spoken

Nonverbal: Presented in a form that is not capable of being spoken

Accumulated: Feedback that represents an accumulation of past performance

Distinct: Feedback that represents each performance separately

Knowledge of Results (KR): Verbalized (or verbalizable) postmovement information about the outcome of the movement in the environment

Knowledge of Performance (KP): Verbalized (or verbalizable) postmovement information about the nature of the movement pattern (verbal-terminal) seen in table 12.1. Examples are seen when the instructor says "You were off target that time" or a computer screen presents the symbolic information "long 12" (meaning that the movement was 12 units too long). Knowledge of results can be highly specific, or it can be very general. Knowledge of results can also contain a rewarding component, such as "very good."

Unfortunately, confusion abounds in the motor skills literature concerning the use of the term KR. First, note that KR is about movement *outcome* in terms of an environmental goal ("You missed the ball") and that it is *not* feedback about the movement itself ("Your elbow was bent"). Usually this distinction is easily made; in shooting a basketball, for example, the goal and the movement to produce it are clearly separable. But often these two aspects of feedback are difficult to distinguish—for example, in a situation in which the goal of a movement is the movement itself, as in a gymnastics move. Knowledge of results is also augmented, and it sometimes duplicates inherent information (e.g., "You missed the shot"). Some authors (e.g., Holding, 1965) use KR to mean inherent plus augmented information about goal achievement, but this is not in keeping with the usual schemes of classification. Occasionally, other terms are used for KR as defined here, such as *information feedback* (Bilodeau, 1966) or *reinforcement* (which implies a reward). Despite these inconsistencies, the tendency is to use the term KR as we have defined it here: verbal, terminal, augmented feedback about goal achievement. (See the review by Salmoni, Schmidt, & Walter, 1984 for additional distinctions.)

Knowledge of Performance

An additional kind of feedback information concerns the *movement pattern* that the learner has made (e.g., "Your elbow was bent"). Gentile (1972) called this type of feedback information *knowledge of performance (KP)* to distinguish it from KR as defined previously (see table 12.1). Knowledge of performance is probably more related to the kinds of feedback instructors give to their students, being directed toward the correction of improper movement patterns rather than just the outcome of the movement in the environment. Also, KP can refer to aspects of the movement of which the subject is only vaguely aware, such as the behavior of a particular limb in a complex movement. And it can refer to processes in the body about which the subject normally *cannot* be aware, such as blood pressure or the activity of a particular motor unit—often referred to as *biofeedback* (Basmajian, 1989).

Research on Augmented Feedback

How do scientists conduct research to understand feedback and learning? What forms of feedback are useful in motor learning, and how are these forms of feedback most effectively presented to the learner? A major problem for such research is that, in most natural situations, it is difficult to *control* the information received by a performer. For example, there are many sources of feedback in the task of shooting a basketball, and it is difficult to know which sources are being used at any one time and how they are being used. Many researchers in motor behavior alter the environment so that minimal feedback information is provided to the subject, and then add back feedback information artificially (in the form of augmented feedback or KR) so that these effects can be studied directly. This technique usually involves experiments with tasks that are highly artificial, but a basic understanding of the functioning of error information can result.

Paradigms for Augmented Feedback Research

Although many definitions exist (Kuhn, 1962), a *paradigm* often refers to a standardized way of gaining knowledge through research.[1] The study of KR variables in motor learning research was directly influenced by research in experimental psychology, and these traditions remain today. Seldom stated explicitly is the assumption that the (augmented) KR provided in these artificial learning situations is fundamentally like the (inherent) error information a person would normally receive in a more natural setting. Is it correct to say that the information "You moved 2 cm too far" in a blindfolded linear-positioning movement works fundamentally in the same way as the vision of a shot missing the basket in basketball? Certainly different processes are involved, but it is entirely possible that the use of the error information is the same in both situations, in that the information provides a basis for changing the movement on the next attempt in order to make it more accurate. If this assumption is correct, then this is a method for coming to an understanding of the way in which inherent feedback works to produce learning in natural environments where no KR is present.

The other side of the argument is that such research, using tasks that are so simple and artificial, may have little to tell us about the ways in which the rich and varied sources of inherent feedback work in more natural settings. Not enough is known about feedback and learning to allow resolution of this question at present. For now, our assumption will be that the study of KR is a means to the understanding of the operation of inherent feedback in natural environments. However, you should remember that the principles may not be quite the same in these two situations.

The dominant paradigm for understanding the functions of feedback information in learning is a legacy from the historical influences of experimental psychology (see boxed text on page 328). The *KR paradigm* typically uses a movement task that is very simple; the most common has been the linear-positioning task, for which the person must learn to move a slide or a lever to a given position, usually while blindfolded. In such tasks, the person cannot effectively evaluate his or her performance outcome without some supplemental information. If the instruction is to move 20 cm, the subject cannot know whether a given attempt to move that distance was correct or not. True, the feedback from the limb is present to signal the movement details, but the individual likely does not have the reference of correct-

ness against which to evaluate the inherent feedback, and has no information about the "success" of the movement. In some sense, the feedback has not been "calibrated" to the environment.

With this kind of task, one can study the use of feedback or KR by adding it back in a systematic way. The most elementary of these experiments might involve the contrast between providing KR and providing no KR at all. A more refined experiment might manipulate the time of presentation of the KR, the way in which the KR is presented (e.g., on a television screen or by an experimenter), or the nature of the KR (e.g., general or precise). In this way, experiments that vary the nature of the feedback given to the learner can be done in the same ways as experiments about any other independent variable. The only difference is that the task used must allow control over highly effective inherent feedback.

Temporal Events of Knowledge of Results

Most of the experiments on KR and motor learning are structured so that the temporal relation among the events in a trial are closely controlled. These events are shown in figure 12.1. The subject performs Movement 1 (M_1); then after a delay called the KR-delay interval, the KR for that trial (KR_1) is delivered by the experimenter. The delay from the presentation of KR until the next movement is termed the *post-KR delay*, during which it is presumed that the person is processing the KR and deciding on the next movement. The sum of the KR-delay and post-KR-delay intervals is termed the *intertrial interval* (or intermovement interval). Usually the intertrial interval is on the order of 10 to 20 s, but of course these intervals can

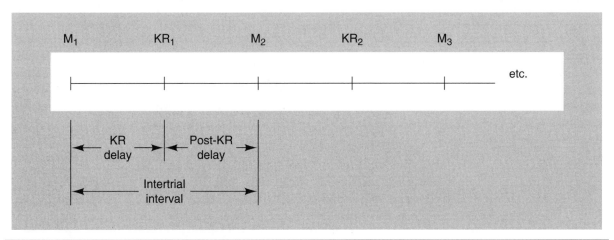

Figure 12.1.   Temporal placement of events in the KR paradigm.

Knowledge-of-Results Paradigm Influences in Psychology

The classic learning theories of Pavlov, Watson, Thorndike, Guthrie, Tolman, Hull, and others during the first half of this century established a framework for research that is more or less firmly entrenched in our laboratories today. The two dominant empirical approaches were the classical and the instrumental conditioning paradigms. The classical conditioning research of Pavlov (e.g., Pavlov, 1927) was typified by the pairing of a stimulus that elicited a reflexive action with a stimulus that did not elicit that reflexive action. In one of his simplest experiments, Pavlov paired the presentation of meat powder to a hungry dog, along with an auditory stimulus. The meat powder brought about a salivatory response and, over repeated paired presentations, so did the auditory stimulus.

Development of the instrumental learning paradigm was probably influenced most by Thorndike. The main feature of this approach was the idea that if an animal's behavior in a learning situation was followed quite soon by reward, the behavior was elicited more frequently. In theory, an association was formed between the situation and the behavior. If this behavior was repeatedly reinforced, the association was strengthened. Thus, the reward was considered instrumental to the occurrence of learning.

The classical and instrumental conditioning paradigms differ in some important respects. In classical conditioning, the unconditioned stimulus is presented on every trial and is not dependent on the response of the subject, and the learned actions are usually involuntary. For instrumental learning, the conditioning stimulus is not always present for each trial and is dependent on the response of the subject, and the learned actions are usually voluntary. A feature common to both, though, is the manner in which the strength of the learned association is assessed. This assessment is done by means of experimental extinction—a phrase coined by Pavlov to refer to the *apparent* elimination of the learned response.

Extinction is observed in the classical conditioning paradigm when the conditioned stimulus is repeatedly presented in the absence of the unconditioned stimulus. Repeated presentations usually result in the apparent elimination of the conditioned response. That is, the earlier conditioning has become extinguished. The time (or number of trials, responses, etc.) required to extinguish the conditioning, which operationally define the *resistance to extinction,* is considered to be directly related to the strength of the conditioning: stronger conditioning results in more persistent elicitation of the conditioned response.

A very similar logic operates in the instrumental learning paradigm. Experimental extinction is observed when the previously rewarded behavior is no longer reinforced. Strength of the conditioned response is measured by the resistance to extinction, defined as the continuance of the behavior in the absence of the reward.

The instrumental conditioning paradigm was well suited for the study of motor behavior and was begun with a study by Thorndike (1927). Over a period of nine practice sessions, Thorndike's subjects drew lines of 3, 4, 5, and 6 in. The first session was without KR. The next seven sessions saw performance improve steadily with KR. The last session, without KR, resulted in a marked deterioration in performance. In Thorndike's view, learning occurred through a strengthening of the connection between a stimulus (the movement goal) and a response to that stimulus (the movement). The importance of KR was that it increased the likelihood of a correct execution of the movement. In turn, each correct execution strengthened the appropriate underlying habit strength. The connection between the stimulus and response was unconscious, and the role played by KR was automatic. The purpose of the no-KR trials was to extinguish the connection between the goal and the response.

The rationale underlying Thorndike's line-drawing experiment was not to study the laws of motor learning, but rather to investigate the generality of his Law of Effect using a motor task. For our present purposes, however, Thorndike's experiment is remembered for introducing the KR/no-KR paradigm to a later generation of researchers who were interested specifically in human motor learning. This influence may also be considered one of Thorndike's legacies (cf. Adams, 1978).

The withdrawal of KR as a form of experimental extinction was theoretically motivated by the Law of Effect and was addressed using motor responses in two studies that followed Thorndike's 1927 publication (Lorge & Thorndike, 1935; Trowbridge & Cason, 1932). In retrospect, the removal of KR as a type of experimental extinction had quite a different purpose than later no-KR trials in the explicit study of motor learning (Adams, 1971). The result of experimental extinction is the eventual *absence* of the behavior. In motor learning experiments, the purpose for withdrawing KR was to assess some measure of the *quality* of behavior (although there were exceptions, e.g., Black & Black, 1970).

be practically any length to serve the purposes of a particular experimental situation.

Learning Versus Performance Effects

In the typical KR paradigm, the variables (such as amount of KR; absolute and relative frequency; precision; length of, and activity during, the KR-delay, post-KR-delay, and intertrial intervals) are typically manipulated over a series of *acquisition* trials. After these trials, all the conditions of the particular KR manipulation (usually separate groups) are transferred to a common condition of KR. By far the most common *transfer* test is a series of no-KR (or "KR withdrawal") trials. Although other paradigms have been used, this KR/no-KR method is rooted in tradition, both in terms of the distinction between performance and learning that its use affords, and in terms of its heritage in animal and human experimental psychology research (see boxed text on page 328).

A strong argument in support of the typical KR paradigm was made by Salmoni, Schmidt, and Walter (1984). The authors argued that the two phases of the typical KR paradigm permitted a direct comparison of the effects of a KR variable on performance and learning. Making a distinction similar to other distinctions between learning and performance (chapters 10 and 11), they argued that a KR variable that exerted an influence *only* while being manipulated was a performance variable. A KR variable that exerted an influence after the manipulation was withdrawn

(and after the temporary influences had dissipated) was a learning variable.

Several arguments support the preference for the no-KR transfer test over other transfer tests in the assessment of KR effects on performance and learning. One argument places the onus squarely on tradition, holding that the KR/no-KR paradigm was the first type of paradigm used in examining KR effects in motor learning, and that its use provided a comparative analysis with the conditioning literature. Another argument is that learning can be addressed in a more steady state under no-KR than under KR trials, since continued improvements in performance are unlikely to occur in the absence of KR (Salmoni, Schmidt, & Walter, 1984). A further contention is that a series of no-KR trials provides a more consistent estimate of performance capabilities and thus a more reliable account of learning effects, since performance is stabilized more in the absence than in the presence of KR (Rubin, 1978). Last, the use of a no-KR test of learning is consistent with many practical applications: augmented information supplied during training or rehabilitation is often unavailable when "real" performance is required (e.g., in a game or when away from the clinic).

Potential Applications of Augmented Feedback Research

Virtually all the research done on feedback and motor learning has involved information about movement outcome (KR). For a person who has had extensive practice at a sport or occupational activity, it would seem far more effective to provide information about the *patterns* of movement the person made—defined earlier as *KP*. Why is there a focus on KR (movement outcome) when KP (movement pattern) is what will probably be most useful for application? Probably the most important reason is that in experiments on KR, the movement outcome can usually be measured easily and corrections on the next trial can be easily charted. But when the experimenter wants to give KP, there is great difficulty in measuring the pattern of movement and then noting how the pattern changed on the subsequent trial. Until recently, these procedures were tedious (using film analysis, strip-chart records, and so on), and motor behavior workers chose not to use them. However, with the use of computing technology and increased emphasis on biomechanical techniques, researchers are beginning to examine KP as a source of error information.

For now, we will assume that the mechanisms of all types of augmented feedback are essentially the same. That is, we assume that what the learner does with these various kinds of information is identical, the major distinction being that these different kinds of information refer to different aspects of the movement. Thus, for example, the principles that have been discovered for KR would be applicable to situations when KP would be given. This could be incorrect, of course, but until evidence appears to the contrary, we think this assumption is reasonable.

Evaluating the Effects of Augmented Feedback

In this section, some of the fundamental principles of augmented feedback for motor learning situations are presented. A number of conclusions can be drawn from the literature, probably because this area has received a great deal of study in motor skills research (for reviews see Adams, 1987; Magill, 1993; Salmoni, Schmidt, & Walter, 1984; Swinnen, 1996), and also because the effects found are so robust and large relative to those of other variables considered. First, we discuss a basic question: whether or not augmented feedback is a variable affecting performance and/or learning. Then we discuss the research variables related to KP. Last we present

the rather large and complex effects of KR variables on performance and learning.

Learning Versus Performance Effects

Most of us probably suspect that KR has important effects on both performance and learning, so it is perhaps not crucial that we document these effects. But we have been fooled by our intuitions before, so we will briefly review some of the critical evidence on this issue.

Augmented Feedback Is a Learning Variable

Using the paradigm described in the previous section, Bilodeau, Bilodeau, and Schumsky (1959) employed a linear-positioning task with four groups of subjects. One group had KR after the first 19 of the 20 acquisition trials, and a second group received no KR at all in the 20 trials. Two other groups received KR for 2 and 6 trials, respectively, before having KR withdrawn for the remainder of the 20 practice trials. The main findings are shown in figure 12.2, where absolute error is plotted as a function of trials for these four groups. Group 19 (with 19 KRs) showed an initial sharp decrease in error, followed by a more gradual decrease. On the other hand, group 0, which had no KR at all, showed essentially no change in performance over the 20 practice trials. For the remaining two groups, improvement occurred on trials that followed the administration of KR, but the improvement ceased when KR was withdrawn, with slight decrements in performance afterward.

Did KR affect the learning in this task? As with any other variable that could affect learning and/or performance, these data can be interpreted in at least two ways. First, we could conclude that group 19 learned more than group 0, as evidenced by the fact that they performed more effectively. But another possibility is that KR had affected performance only temporarily, perhaps through some kind of motivational or "energizing" process. Thus, it could be that when these temporary effects of KR are allowed to dissipate with rest (as with fatigue effects), the temporary effects of KR will vanish and performance will regress to the original level (see chapter 10).

A partial answer to this question was provided by Bilodeau, Bilodeau, and Schumsky when they transferred their group 0 subjects to the KR conditions for an additional 5 trials. In the right portion of figure 12.2, the absolute errors on these

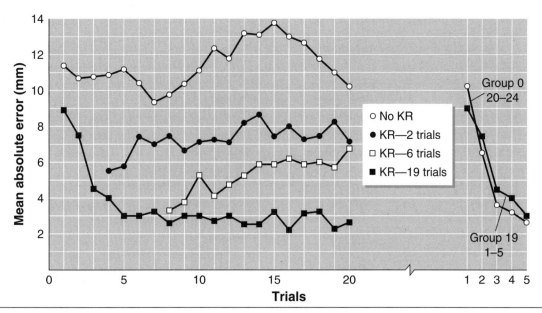

Figure 12.2. Absolute errors in a linear-positioning task as a function of KR. (The group numbers indicate the number of KRs received before KR withdrawal; group 0 switched to a KR condition at the right, where its performance is compared to group 19's first five trials replotted from left.)
Reprinted from Bilodeau, Bilodeau, and Schumsky, 1959.

5 trials are plotted together with those for the first 5 trials of group 19. The size of the errors, as well as the pattern of change with trials, was practically identical for these two sets of trials. That is, group 0 in this transfer condition performed nearly the same as group 19 at the beginning of their practice trials. Thus, we can say the 20-trial no-KR practice sequence for group 0 did not produce any learning at all, and consequently that KR is a learning variable. And KR is not just a variable that *affects* learning; rather, when KR is not present in such situations, learning is *eliminated*. While the Bilodeau, Bilodeau, and Schumsky study uses a kind of transfer design, it does not use the typical transfer procedures recommended as described earlier. Similar conclusions, however, have come from a number of other studies in which relative amount learned was evaluated on no-KR transfer tests (Bennett & Simmons, 1984; Newell, 1974; Trowbridge & Cason, 1932).

Knowledge of results does not always have such dramatic effects on learning motor skills, though. For example, with the use of a tracking task for which KR was or was not provided after each trial, KR had only minimal effects on performance and learning (Archer, Kent, & Mote, 1956; Bilodeau, 1966). Similar effects have been found for learning an anticipation-timing task (Magill, Chamberlin, & Hall, 1991). Is the answer that the information about errors is somehow not important for learning these tasks? We do not think so.

While practicing the task, subjects are able to detect their own errors through the inherent feedback (visual in these cases) provided during the normal course of the trial. This visual information probably serves the same function as the verbal KR did in the linear-positioning experiment described earlier. This observation is in accord with the idea that the presentation of information about errors to the learner is more effectively studied in situations in which learners cannot evaluate their own errors.

Augmented Feedback Is a Performance Variable

The evidence clearly points to (temporary) performance effects of KR in addition to the learning effects we have just described. For example, KR can be motivating, or "energizing," for the learners. Some early research shows that in comparison to practicing with no KR, when KR is provided, subjects report that they are more interested in the task, they seem to put more effort into practice, and they persist longer after the KR is removed (Arps, 1920; Crawley, 1926; Elwell & Grindley, 1938). In relatively boring situations such as *vigilance* tasks, in which subjects are asked to spend hours monitoring a display for the appearance of a particular target stimulus, KR about the subject's performance has an "alerting" (or energizing) effect, and it can act to counteract sleep loss (Poulton, 1973). All these phenomena exert strong influences on behavior, but these effects will probably disappear as soon as the subject rests or shifts conditions in a transfer test. In addition, KR about errors can *acquire* a motivation-like role if it is paired with noxious stimuli (Payne, 1970; Payne & Dunman, 1974), or with goal-setting procedures (see chapter 11).

Another temporary effect of KR is related to its informational properties, whereby KR informs the subject of the errors that have been made and indicates what to do next. Thus KR provides something like *guidance* for the learner. In chapter 11 we presented evidence that guidance is very effective for performance when it is present but that all or part of the beneficial effect can disappear when the guidance is removed (e.g., Armstrong, 1970a; see figure 11.12). In an analogous way, then, KR (acting as guidance) might provide a strong informational support for performance when it is being administered, with the benefits disappearing as soon as the KR is removed or the task conditions are changed (Salmoni, Schmidt, & Walter, 1984).

Untangling the Learning Versus Performance Effects

From the previous sections we have seen that variations in KR can have powerful effects on performance when KR is present, but there is good reason to question whether such effects are always "relatively permanent" to the extent that they can be thought of as learning effects. The scientific problem is to distinguish the variables that produce transient performance changes from those that produce relatively permanent changes. Transfer designs used in the ways discussed in chapters 10 and 11 provide a good way to make this distinction in experiments on KR. However, except for a few (e.g., Annett, 1959; Griffith, 1931; McGuigan, 1959), early feedback researchers did not take this learning-performance distinction seriously, apparently assuming that any variation of feedback was automatically a learning variable. As we will see, there are many situations in which this assumption is simply incorrect.

Knowledge of Performance

We begin our analysis of augmented feedback variables by looking at studies of information that is provided to learners about the patterns of actions they make. It was Gentile (1972) who termed these kinds of feedback "knowledge of performance." Many forms of KP are possible; they may range from rather casual comments about performance, made by a teacher or coach, to complex feedback generated by computer in a simulator and delivered to the learner on-line in computer-aided instruction (Phillips & Berkhout, 1976). Some of these kinds of KP are discussed in the following sections.

Videotape Replays

It would certainly seem reasonable to think of videotape replays as a powerful mode in which to present KP. From a motor skills viewpoint, replays will contain a record of many of the errors made, and the individual can detect these directly and attempt to correct them on the next trial. However, for all the logic leading to the use of videotape replays, as well as their use in many sport situations, little research evidence exists that this method of presenting KP, *by itself*, is very effective. Rothstein and Arnold (1976) and Newell (1981) have reviewed this work, finding that numerous experiments fail to show positive effects of these techniques for motor learning. Some evidence even suggests that videotape replays might actually hinder learning (Ross et al., 1985). One suggestion is that videotape replays might provide *too much* information, especially if the skill is complex and the viewer does not know which of the many details are important. In support of this notion, Rothstein and Arnold pointed out that studies using *cuing*, in which subjects were directed or taught to examine certain aspects of the display during replay, showed more positive effects of video replays than did studies using undirected viewing.

The benefits of cued or directed viewing of videotape replays were shown clearly in a study by Kernodle and Carlton (1992). Subjects practiced throwing a sponge ball with their nondominant arm. After each throw, they were provided with KR regarding the distance thrown (subjects closed their eyes on ball release, making the augmented feedback more important for learning) or were shown a videotape replay of the trial just completed. One group of subjects was provided only the videotape, with no additional augmented information. Previous research, however, had shown that combining verbal KP with other forms of augmented feedback can be quite beneficial to learning (Wallace & Hagler, 1979). So, another group received a verbal cue to specifically watch one particular aspect of the movement during the videotape replay (e.g., "Focus on the hips during the throwing phase"). A final group, before watching the videotape, was given additional augmented feedback in the form of specific error-correction information (e.g., "Rotate the hips from left to right during the throwing phase"). Subjective ratings of throwing performance were assessed during no-feedback trials on five transfer tests over a 4-week period and are illustrated in figure 12.3. The results were clear: the strongest learning effects were seen with the videotape replays accompanied by error-correcting cues, although considerable gains were achieved with the attention-focusing cues as well. The videotape replay alone was no better than simply providing KR. Similar results were obtained when measures of distance thrown were analyzed.

It is important to remember that video replays need not be of the learner; they can also present the performance of a model (chapter 11). However, in both uses of videos as forms of augmented information, research has shown that they are most effective when supplemented with additional, attention-directing augmented information. Practically speaking, video replays should probably be augmented by an instructor who can pick out the important details and can instruct the learner to ignore the irrelevant aspects.

Kinematic Feedback

Recall that *kinematics* refers to measures of "pure motion" without regard to the forces that pro-

duced them (chapter 2). Feedback about kinematics involves various measures derived from movement such as position, time, velocity, and patterns of coordination. When coaches or teachers give information about movement patterning (e.g., "You bent your elbow that time"), they are really providing a (loosely measured) form of kinematic information, a form of KP. Expert music or dance instructors and sport coaches seem to be able to sense "what went wrong" and to provide verbal descriptors that can serve as suggestions for change. Of course, many different features of the movement can be described and used for feedback, and a major issue has been the discovery of what kinds of kinematic information would be most useful for learning and performance (e.g., Swinnen, 1996; Newell, 1991; Newell & Walter, 1981).

Early studies of kinematic information feedback were done by Lindahl (1945; see also Tiffin & Rogers, 1943), who analyzed patterns of foot-pedal actions in skilled industrial workers operating a cutting machine. Lindahl determined the most effective pattern of foot motion from measurements of highly skilled workers and then used this pattern both as a standard and as a basis for providing feedback to new employees about their foot patterning. Such kinematic feedback greatly facilitated training; in as few as 10 weeks of practice, new trainees could be brought to the level of employees who had 9 months of experience. Knowledge of performance about the most

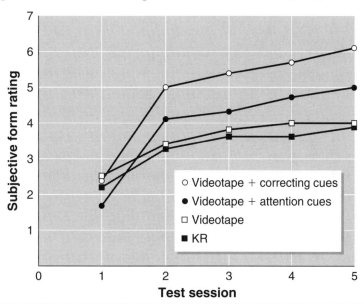

Figure 12.3. Improvements in throwing performance under various conditions of videotape replays. Adapted from Kernodle and Carlton, 1992.

effective patterns of actions—not easily observable without additional measurements of the fine details of foot movements—was apparently critical to the establishment of proper actions in the new performers.

A key feature of kinematic feedback is that it informs the subjects about some aspect of the movement pattern that is otherwise not perceivable. In some cases, a whole pattern of multijoint coordination is presented (e.g., by videotape or computer graphics), showing important information about the movement of a particular joint in relation to another (e.g., Hatze, 1976). It is possible that the subject could gain this information on his or her own, but it is unlikely that a learner would focus on the particular aspects that the instructor considers to be critical. Other kinds of information cannot be sensed at all, however, such as relative timing differences in two joints or subtle changes in velocity, and the kinematic feedback can allow the learner to become aware of these features. Also, feedback information about subtle aspects of the movement's goal has been shown to be useful; Phillips and Berkhout (1976) had subjects learn gear shifting and acceleration in a simulation of a heavy truck, and showed that computer-aided feedback about smoothness of acceleration produced marked gains measured later on a no-feedback transfer test.

But how effective is kinematic KP when compared with other types of augmented feedback? Several studies have been conducted on this issue, and the findings reveal some interesting principles. Most of this research suggests quite clearly that the effectiveness of kinematic feedback depends on the nature of the task goal. For example, subjects in two experiments reported by Newell, Carlton, and Antoniou (1990) were asked to draw geometric shapes on a tabletop. The task goal (a circle) was known in the first experiment, but in a subsequent experiment the task goal was unknown (an irregularly enclosed geometric shape). The subjects were given one of three types of feedback: (1) KR about the error between their movement and the goal; (2) a computer-generated replay of the pattern plus the KR; or (3) a computer-generated display of the feedback of the produced movement superimposed on a template of the task goal, plus KR. Learning (as measured in a retention test without any augmented feedback) was not affected by the nature of the feedback when the task goal was

well known to the subjects (the circle in experiment 1). However, when the task goal was unknown, there was a clear advantage for the group that received the KR plus the augmented feedback superimposed on the task goal. The benefit of augmented kinematic feedback may be optimized when its content specifies information that *cannot* otherwise be generated from other sources such as inherent feedback or from other less detailed sources of augmented feedback.

The role of task goal information and available sources of feedback may also be related to the findings reported by Swinnen et al. (1993). Subjects in this study practiced a discrete, bimanual coordination task in which the goals of the two limbs were not the same. The goal of the left limb was a unidirectional elbow flexion movement. At the same time, a flexion-extension-flexion movement of the right elbow was to be performed. Without practice this task is very difficult to accomplish, as there is a tendency to perform the same actions in each arm (see chapter 8). Swinnen et al. (1993) found that the ability to perform the separate limb goals showed little improvement with practice in the absence of augmented feedback. Surprisingly, however, learning was facilitated equally well by KR (a simple outcome measure of coordination performance) and by the precise augmented kinematic feedback profiles of the two limbs. According to Swinnen et al., the findings supported the idea that the limb coordination information provided by the KR was sufficient to enable subjects to try new strategies to learn the task. Thus it was practice, and strategies brought about by information sources that affected practice, that determined the true effectiveness of kinematic feedback.

In this research the effectiveness of kinematic feedback was assessed in tasks in which the feedback was identical to the goal of the movement. For example, augmented feedback about a dive or an ice skating jump would be related directly to the movement, as the quality of the movement is in fact the task goal. However, in other skills, the outcome of an action may be quite distinct from the motions that produced it. For example, the same trajectory of a batted ball can be produced by infinitely different movements. How does kinematic feedback about movements affect the acquisition of skills in which the movements are not isomorphic with the task goal? A computer-controlled analogue of a baseball batting task was developed by Schmidt and Young (1991) to examine these issues. The task required subjects to "strike" a moving-light "object" by passing a movement lever through it as it went by. The goal was to maximize distance, as defined by a combination of the velocity and timing accuracy at the contact point. On the basis of research suggesting that a particular movement pattern produced the best outcome scores (Schmidt & Young, 1991), Young and Schmidt (1992) conducted a study to assess what kinematic feedback variables facilitated learning when presented in relation to the optimal movement pattern. Their findings revealed that each kinematic variable that was manipulated (mean or variability of the reversal point; mean or variability of the time of the reversal) tended to facilitate the acquisition of that kinematic variable in the production of the movement. However, only the mean reversal-point kinematic feedback was better than outcome KR in maximizing performance outcome. The effects of KP appear to be enhanced, however, when an optimal movement pattern is not used as a reference criterion, again suggesting that the kinematic information may be most useful when it promotes active, problem-solving activities in the learner (Brisson & Alain, 1996a, 1996b).

It appears that the benefits of kinematic feedback depend on a number of factors. The relevance of the information to the success of the movement and/or task goal, and the uniqueness of the kinematic feedback compared to inherent feedback sources or less precise augmented feedback sources (such as KR), have important influences on the impact of kinematic feedback.

Biofeedback

Going a step further, feedback can be given about features of the movement that cannot ever be perceived directly—a key feature of *biofeedback training*. If a particular biological process (e.g., blood pressure) is measured electronically and used as feedback, then subjects can learn to voluntarily control these (normally unconscious) processes (see Richter-Heinrich & Miller, 1982, for a review). Years ago, Basmajian (1963) gave subjects visual and auditory feedback of their own electromyograms (EMGs) and showed how such information could allow the subject to learn to control a single motor unit that is not normally under voluntary control. This general idea has

been tried (with only moderate success) in teaching subjects who are deaf to speak, with the subjects' sounds being transformed into visual information presented on a television screen (Nickerson, Kalikow, & Stevens, 1976). On the other hand, Mulder and Hulstijn (1985) showed that feedback information about the EMG from the muscles controlling the big toe contributed to learning toe movements, and that the gains remained even after the feedback was removed. Brenner (1974) and Lang (1974) argued that there is a close relationship between these biofeedback procedures for training unconscious processes on the one hand and kinematic feedback for training motor learning on the other (see also Roberts, 1986). However, there has been little research to develop these issues further.

Kinetic Feedback

Whereas kinematic measures are variables describing pure motion, kinetic measures are descriptors of the *forces* that produce the kinematic variables. We have long recognized that muscular forces and the durations over which they act are fundamental outputs of the central structures thought to organize movements; the impulse-timing hypothesis discussed in chapters 6 and 7 is one statement of that basic view. As a result, researchers have often thought that feedback in terms of kinetics would be a "natural" kind of information for the motor system to use for learning.

Some early work supports this viewpoint. English (1942) utilized force feedback from a trigger-squeeze to facilitate riflery training. Howell (1956) had subjects learn a runner's sprint start and recorded forces applied against a strain gauge (a force sensor) that was attached to the foot plate in the starting blocks. The forces recorded over the time of the action provided a *force-time curve*, which was shown to subjects after each trial as a form of kinetic feedback. Subjects could use this information to optimize the form of the force-time curve (i.e., to produce a maximum impulse). Newell and Walter (1981) and Newell, Sparrow, and Quinn (1985) have provided similar examples with other tasks. Unfortunately, only recently have transfer tests been used in this kind of research to determine the learning versus performance effects of kinetic feedback. It appears that the effects of this extra information are relatively permanent, as they persist in a short-term no-feedback retention test (Newell, Sparrow, & Quinn, 1985) as well as in tests that occur after a long delay interval (Broker, Gregor, & Schmidt, 1993). The use of this type of feedback about forces has the potential to be very effective for skills learning, and much more research effort could profitably be directed to this problem.

Knowledge of Results

The literature on KP tells us that augmented feedback about the movement pattern is most effective for learning when that *specific* information cannot be derived from other sources. We now turn our attention to the vast amount of research on KR—augmented information about the movement outcome. Experiments in this research area have frequently used very simple tasks, such as blindfolded limb-positioning tasks and timing tasks. The reason is that with these kinds of tasks, very little if any learning at all can occur in the absence of KR. In this way, the relative effectiveness of various manipulations of KR can be examined in terms of their impact on the learning *process*.

Precision of Knowledge of Results

The *precision* of KR refers to the amount of accuracy contained in the information. For example, if the subject is attempting to make a 10-cm movement and the actual movement was 10.13 cm, KR could be provided in a variety of ways. First, KR could be presented in a qualitative way—"correct" or "wrong." In the case of "wrong," KR could then be given more precisely by saying "long" or "short," meaning that the person moved beyond or short of the target. More precision in the KR could be provided by saying "wrong by 1," meaning 1 mm off. Or, one could say "long .1," meaning that the movement was .1 cm too long, or "long 13, "meaning that it was 13 mm too long. The KR could be even more accurate than this, measuring movement accuracy to a very fine degree (e.g., in nanometers). Various combinations of qualitative and quantitative forms of KR have been examined, and these manipulations have rather large effects on performance and learning.

Qualitative Versus Quantitative Knowledge of Results

One issue related to the precision of KR is the kind of information that is presented. Information can

be presented about the *direction* of the error in some, but not all, forms of KR. Information can also be provided about the *magnitude* of the error, irrespective of direction. Some of these forms of KR have information about both factors (e.g., "long 13"). Generally, the evidence suggests that there is some benefit to providing information about magnitude of error, but this information is far more useful if the direction is also specified. Knowing that an error was made in a particular direction gives a strong indication of the ways in which the movement must be modified next time, but information only about magnitude does not.

Another issue related to the precision of the KR report is the amount of accuracy. A classic study in this area was conducted by Trowbridge and Cason (1932). Four groups practiced drawing 3-in. lines for 100 trials. One group never received KR. Another group received nonsense syllables after drawing each line (a control condition). A third group received qualitative KR in the form of "right" (if the line was within ±1/8 in. of the goal) or "wrong" from the experimenter. The last group was given precise, directional KR in terms of the exact deviation, in eighths of an inch (longer or shorter), from the goal length.

During both acquisition and a no-KR retention test that followed immediately after practice, accuracy was better for the precise and the right/wrong KR groups than for either the nonsense KR or the no-KR group (figure 12.4). Furthermore, precise KR was better than the right/wrong type of KR. These effects have been replicated often (Bennett & Simmons, 1984; Magill & Wood, 1986; Reeve, Dornier, & Weeks, 1990; Salmoni et al., 1983), supporting the conclusion that precise, quantitative KR is generally more effective for learning than qualitative KR.

These techniques do not permit the separation of information about precision of KR from information about the direction of reported error. Studies conducted since the Trowbridge and Cason study have separated these effects and have generally shown that the more precise the KR, the more accurate the performance, up to a point, beyond which no further increases in accuracy are found as KR is made more precise (for reviews, see Newell, 1981, or Salmoni, Schmidt, & Walter, 1984). Subjects presumably know that they cannot be responsible for errors smaller than a certain size (e.g., 1 mm), as the movement-control mechanisms themselves are more vari-

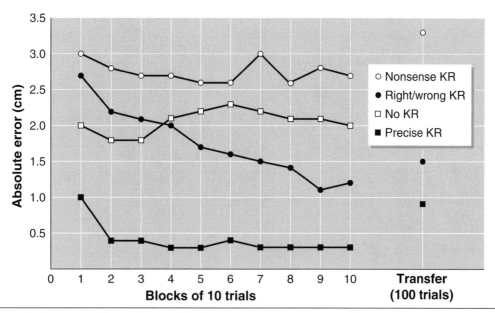

Figure 12.4.   Qualitative- and quantitative-KR effects in acquisition and transfer.
Reprinted from Trowbridge and Cason, 1932.

able than this. It is likely that subjects "round off" very precise KR to a more meaningful level of precision.

Bandwidth Knowledge of Results

An alternative to giving either qualitative or quantitative KR is provided by the *bandwidth-KR* method (Sherwood, 1988). With this method, similar in some ways to the qualitative-KR methods first used by Trowbridge and Cason (1932), the nature of augmented feedback is determined by a bandwidth or tolerance for error about the movement goal. In most studies using this method, qualitative KR in the form of "correct" or "right" is provided to the subject when the performance outcome lies *within* the boundaries of the bandwidth. In contrast, specific KR that gives both the magnitude and the direction of error is provided when performance *exceeds* the bandwidth. Depending on the actual dimensions of the bandwidth, subjects are told that they were correct when close to the target and are given precise corrective feedback when substantial error has occurred. This method is probably what many teachers and therapists do naturally—correcting relatively poor performance and praising relatively good performance!

Bandwidth KR has rather substantial effects on performance and learning. In fact, the research suggests that learning is facilitated as the bandwidth gets *larger*. There is probably an optimal bandwidth size, although more research needs to

be done to establish what this might be. One of the first studies in this area was conducted by Sherwood (1988; see also Annett, 1959). Subjects were to learn to make a rapid elbow flexion movement in as close to 200 ms as possible. Subjects in a control group (0% BW) were told their exact movement time after each trial. In two other conditions, subjects were given movement-time KR only if their outcomes exceeded a tolerance limit around the movement time goal (±5% or ±10%). Performance inside the bandwidth received no *explicit* KR—which subjects had been instructed to interpret as meaning "correct." Although these bandwidth conditions had no differential effects on acquisition performance, as can be seen in figure 12.5, learning (as measured on a no-KR retention test) was positively related to the size of the bandwidth.

Sherwood's results raise a number of important questions. One obvious question concerns how often the different types of KR were presented. Every subject in the experiment received one type of KR on every trial—either explicit movement-time KR or implicit KR that performance had been correct. The properties of movement-time KR, or specific KR about movement error in general, are well known and will become clear as we proceed through this chapter. However, the learning properties of information about "correct" performance are not well understood. One consequence of the bandwidth-KR procedure is that as the tolerance limits are increased,

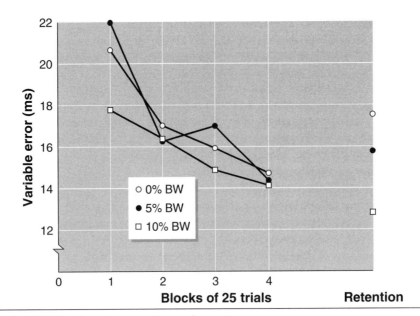

Figure 12.5. Bandwidth-KR effects in acquisition and retention.
Adapted and reproduced with permission of author and publisher from: Sherwood, D.E. Effect of bandwidth knowledge of results on movement consistency. *Perceptual and Motor Skills*, 1988, 66, 535-542. © Perceptual and Motor Skills 1988.

the proportion of trials followed by error KR diminishes. As will be seen later in this chapter, less frequent error KR in acquisition has also been associated with increased levels of learning. So, the question is whether or not the bandwidth effect is anything more than just a reduced KR-frequency effect. To examine this question, Lee and Carnahan (1990a) used bandwidth groups of 5% and 10% together with control groups; the control groups received KR on the same trials as yoked counterparts in the bandwidth groups had, but no KR on those trials in which their bandwidth counterparts received information that performance was correct. The bandwidth groups performed better in retention than did their respective control groups, suggesting that the provision of the "correct" KR gave an additional boost to learning beyond that normally associated with less frequent KR. Similar results have also been reported by Butler, Reeve, and Fischman (1996).

One of the potentially strong learning effects of the bandwidth procedure is that the frequencies of error KR and correct KR are altered as skill improves—error KR is reduced and correct KR increases. This seems to be important, as methods of reducing the size of the bandwidth over the course of practice, keeping the proportions of error and correct KR relatively constant, have been ineffective (Goodwin & Meeuwsen, 1995; Lee, Maraj, & Wishart, 1995). These findings should be interpreted cautiously, however, as it could be that some attempts to shrink the bandwidth size may be effective to a degree, depend-

ing on the nature of task, the stage in learning, and the size to which the bandwidth is reduced.

As we said earlier, these effects make considerable sense. When helping people learn, you might provide assistance when they are doing something wrong, but not when they are correct (in other words, "If it ain't broke, don't fix it"). The key seems to be in deciding when is the best time to intervene with augmented feedback. If an optimal bandwidth existed for each person, it would likely depend on a number of factors that would change with practice (Lee & Maraj, 1994).

Learner-Determined Presentation of Knowledge of Results

A different experimental approach to optimizing the presentation of KR has just recently been investigated (Chen & Hendrick, 1994; Hendrick & Chen, 1995; Janelle, et al. 1997; Janelle, Kim, & Singer, 1995). In this particular paradigm, subjects are asked to perform a movement task and receive augmented feedback only when they *wish* to receive it. Some preliminary findings using this subject-determined presentation paradigm are quite interesting: retention is facilitated for subjects who choose when to receive KR, even in comparison to control groups who receive the same amount of KR (but experimenter determined)! Although more research using this paradigm is clearly needed, we suspect that these findings may reflect some processes in common with the results of the bandwidth-KR effects—such that when the presentation of KR is determined by a subjective bandwidth or actually by the subject, it is more meaningful to the learner than when presented too often or when otherwise unnecessary. The subject-determined KR paradigm seems to be a potentially fruitful avenue for future research, both for theory and for application.

Erroneous Knowledge of Results

Imagine a situation in which the provider of augmented feedback is *inaccurate* in giving the feedback. For example, in some bowling alleys an illuminated indicator at the end of the alley provides KR in terms of how many pins have been left standing after the first ball has been bowled. Since there are times when one pin is hidden from the bowler's view by another pin, the augmented feedback can be important. If one or more of the lights happen to be burned out, a bowler can get an incorrect impression of the number of pins that are still standing. What is the impact of the KR if it is not accurate?

Buekers and Magill (1995) have conducted studies on the effects of erroneous KR on an anticipation-timing task—a task for which inherent (visual) feedback is normally sufficient for learning to occur (Magill, Chamberlin, & Hall, 1991). Subjects in these studies are sometimes provided with augmented feedback indicating that performance took place 100 ms later than it actually had. For example, someone who had been 65 ms *early* in anticipating the arrival of the stimulus was told that he or she had been 35 ms *late*. The consequence of this erroneous feedback is a motor behavior whereby the subjects perform the task with a constant error (CE) of up to −100 ms. These effects are relatively long lasting, with large negative CEs occurring after 1 week with no practice in no-KR retention tests (Buekers, Magill, & Hall, 1992) and in transfer tests to novel stimulus speeds (McNevin, Magill, & Buekers, 1994).

These erroneous KR effects seem to indicate that the accuracy of augmented feedback can have very powerful effects on performance and learning, whereby subjects negate or discount the accuracy of their own error-detection capabilities in favor of believing the (erroneous) augmented feedback. The impact of erroneous KR appears to be the strongest when it is presented on every practice trial during acquisition. Studies in which trials with erroneous KR are alternated with trials providing correct KR (Buekers, Magill, & Sneyers, 1994), and those in which trials with erroneous KR follow a practice period with correct KR (Buekers & Magill, 1995), show quite diminished performance effects and no learning effect of erroneous KR. Thus, *periodic* KR that is counterintuitive to inherent feedback may not be as disruptive to learning as the situation in which the learner is consistently faced with conflicting augmented information.

Schedules of Knowledge of Results

We have seen in two previous sections (on bandwidth KR and subject-determined KR) that determining when to give KR and what type to give can have a large impact on performance and learning. These effects relate closely to a class of KR-*scheduling* variables over which the experimenter has specific control. As we will see, these variables also have profound learning and performance effects.

Relative and Absolute Frequency Effects

If error information is required for learning, we might next ask whether more KR will result in more learning. People who study KR distinguish between two measures of the "amount" of KR that is provided: *absolute frequency* and *relative frequency* of KR.

Absolute frequency of KR is simply the number of KR presentations received over the course of practice. If 80 practice trials are given, and the person receives KR after every other trial for a total of 40 presentations, then the absolute frequency of KR is 40. On the other hand, relative frequency of KR refers to the *percentage* of trials on which KR is provided. It is the number of times KR is provided divided by the total number of trials, multiplied by 100 for conversion to a percentage. In this example, the relative frequency of KR is $(40/80) \times 100 = 50\%$.

Which of these two KR-scheduling measures is the more critical for learning? Bilodeau and Bilodeau (1958) were the first to investigate this question, using a task in which subjects without vision turned a knob to a target position. For the four different groups, KR was provided after (a) every trial, (b) every third trial, (c) every fourth trial, or (d) every 10th trial, producing relative frequencies of KR of 100%, 33%, 25%, and 10%, respectively. The number of trials performed by these groups, however, was adjusted so that all groups received 10 KR presentations; for example, the group with 100% relative frequency received 10 trials, and the group with 33% relative frequency received 30 trials. Thus, the experiment involved groups that had different relative frequencies, but constant absolute frequencies (10) of KR.

In figure 12.6, the results of 10 trials for each of the four groups are presented. Only the trials *immediately following* the presentation of KR are plotted. This is, of course, every trial for the group with 100% relative frequency of KR, only one-third of the trials for the group with 33% relative frequency, and so on. The amount of error on each trial, as well as the pattern of change of the errors as trials progressed, was nearly the same for the four groups. Even though the groups differed greatly in terms of the relative frequency of KR, when the absolute frequency was equated, no difference in performance was found between groups. For performance, the critical feature of KR in this experiment was the number of times that KR was given; the relative proportion of trials followed by KR appeared not to be an important variable. Another way to think of this is that the no-KR trials were meaningless, neither contributing to nor detracting from performance of the task. Motor learning researchers initially took the equal performances of the various groups in figure 12.6 to mean that absolute frequency is important for learning and that relative frequency is irrelevant.

But notice that the Bilodeau and Bilodeau study did not use a transfer design to separate the transient effects of relative frequency from the learning effects. Hence, we have no way of knowing whether varying relative frequency affected learning. More recently, experimenters have included these transfer tests, although the effects on learning have been rather ambiguous. Some studies showed that reduced relative frequencies of KR produced learning effects that were *as large as* those in 100% KR conditions (e.g., Lee, White, & Carnahan, 1990, experiment 2; Sparrow & Summers, 1992, experiment 1; Winstein & Schmidt, 1990, experiment 1). Yet, using similar tasks and slightly modified methods, other studies showed that reduced relative-frequency conditions produced *more* learning than 100% KR conditions (e.g., Lee, White, & Carnahan, 1990, experiment 3; Sparrow & Summers, 1992, experiment 2; Vander Linden, Cauraugh, & Greene, 1993; Weeks, Zelaznik, & Beyak, 1993). Thus, it seems that instead of being irrelevant for learning, reduced relative-frequency effects may be beneficial to learning!

This general result has surprised many because it says that the no-KR trials, instead of being meaningless for learning as they appeared to be in the Bilodeau and Bilodeau (1958) study, contributed to the learning in some way. Further, this contribution was not manifested during practice when the KR was present, but was seen in a delayed retention test. Decreasing relative frequency certainly does not diminish learning and may actually facilitate it.

But there is one additional concern with these studies. When the relative proportion of trials that

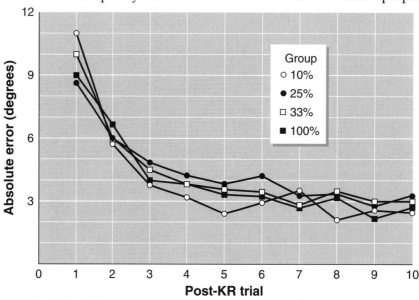

Figure 12.6. Absolute errors in positioning for trials immediately following KR. (Group numbers indicate the percentage relative frequency of KR.)
Reprinted from Bilodeau and Bilodeau 1958.

are followed by KR is reduced, a confounded variable arises. Compared to a 100% KR condition, if the total number of trials during practice is held constant, then reduced relative frequency of KR also results in reduced *absolute* frequency of KR. If the researcher decides to make the absolute frequency the same as in the 100% condition, then the total number of trials must be increased for the reduced relative-frequency group. In all the studies cited here, the total number of trials was kept constant. Thus, the effects of reduced relative frequency must be considered in light of the fact that fewer absolute numbers of KR presentations were given. When we recall that learning increases with the absolute number of KR presentations, perhaps it is not surprising that the effects of relative frequency are rather mixed. It may very well be that the positive effect of reducing the relative frequency has been offset by the negative effect of fewer KR presentations. This certainly contradicts the earlier conclusions that providing more feedback is all-critical for motor learning. And, note that delayed no-KR transfer tests were required in order to show these effects—further supporting the use of such transfer designs in motor learning research.

The effects of relative frequency appear to be clearer if the method used for reducing the presentations of KR is a "fading" procedure. Here, giving *fewer* KRs (trials constant) seems to greatly improve learning (Winstein & Schmidt, 1990; Wulf & Schmidt, 1989). The method usually involves providing KR relatively often during the initial stages of practice and then gradually withholding the presentation of KR more and more toward the end of practice. This method actually has an effect very similar to what naturally happens using the bandwidth-KR procedure, because skill improvements increase the likelihood that performance will lie within the bandwidth and that the provision of error KR will be withheld.

The effects of reduced relative frequency are complicated still further if one considers the nature of the task that is learned. Recently, experimenters have shown that when subjects practice several versions of a generalized motor program, reduced relative frequency of KR facilitates the learning of invariances common to the movement pattern, but not the parameterization characteristics (Wulf, Lee, & Schmidt, 1994; Wulf & Schmidt, 1989; Wulf, Schmidt, & Deubel, 1993).

How should we interpret all these effects? It is tempting to draw a parallel between these relative-frequency findings and the work on animal (and human) instrumental learning with *partial reinforcement*. In this latter work, it is widely known that if one rewards the organism for only a portion of responses, performance during training is degraded somewhat as compared to performance when every response is rewarded. However, if the animals are given an *extinction test*, in which all reinforcement is withdrawn, the animals with lower percentages of reinforcement in acquisition show more resistance to extinction (see Fantino & Logan, 1979). This partial-reinforcement effect is not an explanation of the motor effects, however, and we should be careful not to assume from this work that the processes underlying human motor learning are necessarily the same as those underlying reward and reinforcement in animals. There are many differences between the findings from the two paradigms as well, as we will see later.

An interesting explanation for the relative-frequency effect in motor learning was suggested by Salmoni, Schmidt, and Walter (1984; see also Schmidt, 1991; Schmidt & Bjork, 1992; Schmidt & Shapiro, 1986; Winstein & Schmidt, 1990). When KR is given on every trial (relative frequency of 100%), this condition is very effective for performance when KR is present because of a number of temporary factors already discussed (e.g., guidance, motivational, and energizing properties). However, the subject comes to rely too heavily on this information and actually fails to process information necessary for learning the task in a relatively permanent way; subjects use KR as a "crutch." Subjects in conditions of lower relative frequency, however, do not have such a strong performance enhancement from KR and so are "forced" to engage in other processes during the acquisition phase. These processes result in the subjects' learning something fundamentally *different*, such as the capability to detect one's own errors or to be consistent. Perhaps reducing the relative frequency also encourages one to make between-task comparisons, which might facilitate the abstraction of common movement attributes (Wulf, Lee, & Schmidt, 1994). This learning is not revealed during the acquisition phase, but it does contribute to performance on delayed no-KR transfer tests. According to this hypothesis, "too much" KR in acquisition is detrimental if the goal is to be able to produce the movement without KR later, as it usually is. As we will see, this hypothesis can explain a number of seemingly contradictory findings in the KR literature.

A few practical implications are possible. First, KR is certainly important for learning, as the results generally say that increasing the amount of feedback, other things being equal, is beneficial to performance and learning. But KR can be given too often; in these cases learners come to rely too heavily on its motivating or guiding properties. This enhances performance during practice in which KR is present, but it is probably detrimental to learning as measured on a delayed test in which the learner must perform without KR. Also, relative frequency of KR should be large in initial practice, when guidance and motivation are critical; but then the instructor should systematically decrease relative frequency of KR as the performer becomes more proficient.

Trials Delay and Summary Knowledge of Results

The literature discussed so far has involved situations in which KR for a given trial is presented before the next trial (i.e., KR_n occurs before trial$_{n+1}$ in figure 12.1). However, what happens if the KR from a given trial occurs *after* the performance of the next few trials? Such a procedure, at first glance, would appear to be extremely disrupting for performance; it would be difficult for the learner to know which KR to associate with which movement, particularly when KR is increasingly separated from the trial to which it refers. We can probably think of practical situations in which

this effect might occur—for example, when a learner performs a number of trials in a series, *after which* the instructor or therapist gives information about each trial or maybe about just one of the trials in the series. In such situations, the first trial in the sequence is separated from its KR by the intervening trials.

This method of giving KR has been formalized by Bilodeau (1956, 1966, 1969) under the heading of *trials delay*. In contrast to what occurs in the usual KR paradigm, we see in figure 12.7 that one or more trials is interpolated between a given movement and its KR. In figure 12.7a, M_1 and KR_1 are separated by M_2—there is a one-trial delay between a given movement and its KR. In figure 12.7b is a two-trial delay, with two trials separating a given movement and its KR.

Bilodeau (1956) investigated the effects of trials delay using a lever-positioning task with blindfolded subjects. In two experiments, she varied the number of trials by which KR was delayed: in experiment 1 she used 0-, 1-, 2-, and 3-trials delay, and in experiment 2 she used 0-, 2-, and 5-trials delay. Subjects were fully informed about this technique and were questioned to make certain that they understood how KR was being administered.

The data from the two experiments are shown in figure 12.8, where absolute error in positioning (for trials following KR) is plotted against trials for the various trials-delay conditions. For both experiments, as the trials delay was increased, performance accuracy systematically decreased. This can be seen both in the "rate" of approach to the final performance level and in the level of

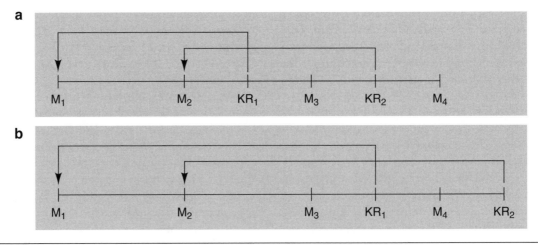

Figure 12.7. The trials-delay technique, showing a trials delay of one (a) and two (b). (A given movement and its KR are separated by other trials of the same task.)

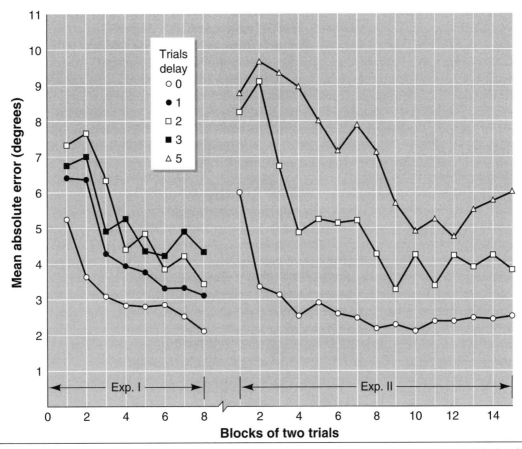

Figure 12.8. Absolute error in positioning as a function of the amount of trials delay. (The group label indicates the number of trials separating a movement and its KR.)
Reprinted from Bilodeau, 1956.

final performance. These findings differed somewhat from earlier ones by Lorge and Thorndike (1935), who had found that improvement in performance did not occur at all under the trials-delay method. But there can be little argument that trials delay is a variable that has drastic negative effects on performance. In the earlier literature (e.g., Bilodeau, 1966), the interpretation of these trials-delay effects was in terms of learning, but these experiments did not use transfer designs to separate the temporary and relatively permanent effects. However, Lavery (1962; Lavery & Suddon, 1962) and others (e.g., Anderson, Magill, & Sekiya, 1994) have used transfer designs in the study of this variable (and modifications of it), and their surprising results have had important influences on our thinking about how KR operates.

Lavery (1962) used several tasks in which a ball was propelled up a track to a target. Three methods were used to give KR. One was the usual condition in which KR is given after every trial, called "Immediate." A second method was "Sum-

mary," in which the performance on every trial in a 20-trial sequence was shown, but only after the 20th trial had been completed; no KR was given after each trial as in Immediate. This summary technique was more or less the same as the trials-delay technique, as the KR for trial 1 was separated from its trial by the other 19 movements in the block, trial 2 by the other 18, and so on. Finally, the third condition involved *both* the immediate postmovement KR and the summary, labeled "Both." After an initial no-KR practice day, 5 days of practice were given under these conditions.

Performance on all the tasks averaged together is shown in figure 12.9. In acquisition, the number of correct trials was far less for the Summary group than for the two groups with KR after each trial (i.e., Immediate and Both). The addition of the summary information to Immediate to create Both did not improve performance very much relative to providing the usual postmovement KR (Immediate), and so it is clear that the major determinant of performance was the immediate KR. But we knew this before, as this pattern of

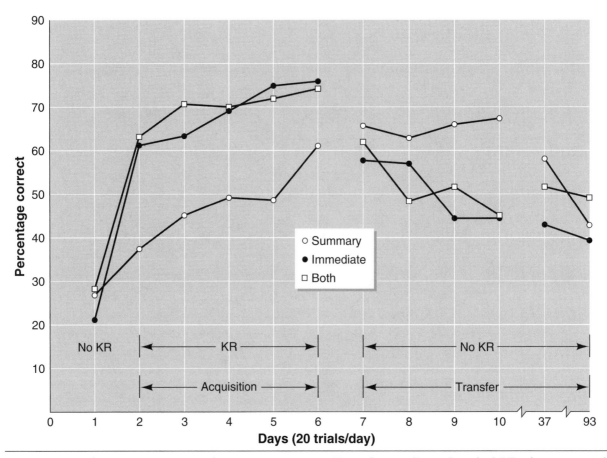

Figure 12.9. Percentage correct trials for various summary-KR conditions. (Immediate had KR after every trial; Summary had KR about every trial presented after each block of 20 trials; and Both had both forms of KR.)
Reprinted from Lavery, 1962.

results is similar to the pattern in the study by Bilodeau (1956) in that performance in acquisition (while KR was present) was hindered by the trials-delay technique.

Now consider the measure of relative amount learned in this experiment—the performance on the transfer trials on Days 7, 8, 9, 10, 37, and 93 for which no KR was provided at any time. The group that was formerly least accurate (i.e., Summary) was now the most accurate, and the other two groups, which had been the most accurate (i.e., Immediate and Both), were now the least accurate. Furthermore, the latter two groups appeared to have lost accuracy with each successive no-KR day, while the Summary group did not. The effects persisted to Day 37 but were essentially gone by Day 93.

Which group learned the most? Using the performance on the transfer test as the measure of relative amount learned, as described earlier, we are forced to conclude that the Summary (trials-delay) condition was more effective for learning than either the Immediate or the Both condition.

Notice that this is yet another example showing that the most effective condition for performance in acquisition was the least effective for learning! The basic experiment was repeated by Lavery and Suddon (1962), but with the same trials-delay methods as used by Bilodeau (1956), and the results were nearly the same as those shown in figure 12.9.

At first glance, we might be drawn to the interpretation that the summary KR per se was in some way effective for learning, providing a benefit over and above the normally useful Immediate-KR condition. But look again. If summary KR was "good" for learning, then we should expect the Both group (which also had summary KR) to have benefited in a similar way. To the contrary, though, we see that the Both group performed almost identically to the Immediate group, both in the acquisition phase and in the no-KR transfer phase. One view is that, when KR was added to the normally effective summary-KR procedure to form the Both group, it *lowered* the level of learning to that of the Immediate group. In our interpretation (see Salmoni, Schmidt, & Walter, 1984; Schmidt, 1991; Schmidt et al., 1989), it was not that summary KR was beneficial for learning, but that immediate KR was *detrimental* to learning! This is in keeping with the guidance hypothesis that immediate KR provides "too much" information for learners, causing them to rely on it too heavily; thus the subject is not forced to learn the information-processing activities critical for performance when KR is removed in the transfer test. Summary KR provides much less effective guidance, and presumably forces the subject to learn the task in a somewhat different way, independent of the guiding properties of KR.

Optimizing Summary Length

It would seem that summary KR could easily be overdone, with summaries of so many trials that the guidance properties of KR would be minimal. Such thinking leads to the idea that there would be an *optimal* number of trials to be summarized, and that this optimum might also vary with task complexity in some way. In an experiment by Schmidt et al. (1989), summary KR was provided as a graph of performance against trials and was given after either 1 trial (an immediate-KR procedure) or after 5, 10, or 15 trials. In a relatively simple movement-timing task, increased summary length systematically degraded performance in the acquisition phase when KR was present, as Lavery had found earlier. But surprisingly, in a delayed no-KR transfer test, the most

accurate performance was achieved by the group that had (in acquisition) received the 15-trial summaries, with systematically increasing error as the acquisition summary length decreased. The effect appeared to be related to long-term retention, with systematically poorer retention as the summary length decreased. The longest summaries produce the most learning—no clear optimal summary length was evident. Similar findings were also reported by Gable, Shea, and Wright (1991), with subjects in a 16-trial condition performing best and no evidence for an optimal summary size.

In another investigation using a more complex, anticipation-timing task with KP provided rather than KR, summaries given after either 1, 5, 10, or 15 trials (Schmidt, Lange, & Young, 1990) were used as in the study just described. Figure 12.10 shows the performance in acquisition and on a delayed no-KP transfer test. Again, increasing the summary length degraded the performance in the acquisition phase, with systematically lower scores as the summary length increased. But on the delayed no-KP transfer test, the most effective summary length for learning was 5 trials; shorter (1-trial) and longer (10- and 15-trial) summaries showed less effective learning. A similar set of results was also reported by Yao, Fischman, and Wang (1994); acquisition performance was poorest for conditions with the longest summary lengths (using summaries of 1, 5, and 15 trials). In the no-KR retention test,

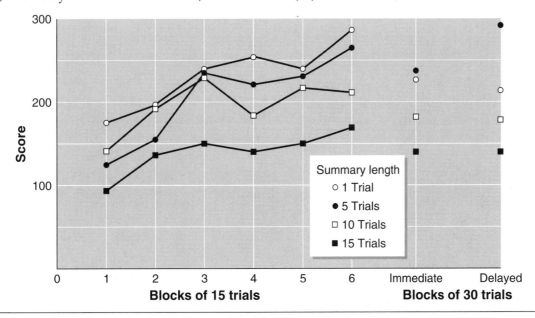

Figure 12.10. Performance score for various numbers of trials included in a summary. Reprinted from Schmidt, Lange, and Young, 1990.

however, the 5-trial summary condition was superior to both the every-trial and 15-trial summary conditions. It seems clear from these studies that if optimal summary lengths do exist, these are likely to be task specific—perhaps in relation to the task's complexity (see also Guadignoli, Dornier, & Tandy, 1996).

Average Knowledge of Results

In the typical summary-KR condition, performance on a series of trials is presented to the subject in the form of a graph that organizes the augmented feedback about *all* of the trials in summary fashion. When multiple KRs need to be presented, the information is more readily utilized when given graphically than when given numerically (Cauraugh, Chen, & Singer, 1993). It is likely that this is so because the numeric information overloads the processing capabilities of the learner. However, there is an interesting variant of the summary procedure that has been called *average KR*. Here, instead of showing KR about a block of trials in the summary, the average performance of the block is determined and is provided as KR. In this way, the average represents a *statistical summary* (represented as the mean) of the block of trials rather than a *graphical summary*. Two conditions in the Yao, Fischman, and Wang (1994) study, in which conditions where the mean CE in performance (averaged over 5 or 15 trials), were included along with every-trial, 5-trial, and 15-trial summary conditions. The results for a temporal measure of performance are

presented in figure 12.11 (results for a spatial measure were similar). As described earlier, acquisition performance was related directly to the summary size, and no-KR retention performance was best for the 5-trial summary group and poorest for the every-trial group. Of particular interest, however, was that the groups receiving average summaries performed similarly to the groups that received graphical summaries. This was consistent for both acquisition and retention and for both the 5-trial and 15-trial summary conditions. These data might suggest that the learning and performance effects of summary KR may be similar regardless of whether the summary is presented graphically or statistically (see also Weeks & Sherwood, 1994; Young & Schmidt, 1992). The similarity of effects of graphical and statistical forms of summary KR is also explained well by the guidance properties of KR, as the two work in similar ways to reduce the informational guiding properties of augmented feedback. But attempts to further tease apart the specific impact of KR summaries have had mixed success (Guay, Salmoni, & McIlwain, 1992; Sidaway, Moore, & Schoenfelder-Zohdi, 1991; Wright, Snowden, & Willoughby, 1990).

Blocked Versus Random Knowledge of Results

Up to this point, most of the research that we have reviewed has involved augmented feedback about one information source. But consider the scheduling implications if there were many sources for which feedback could be provided. Suppose, for

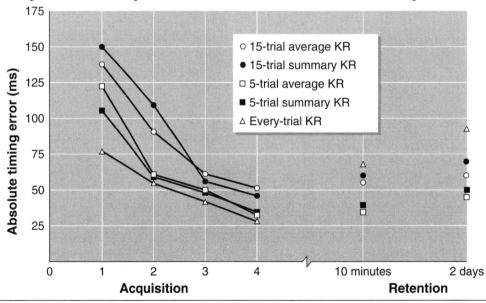

Figure 12.11. Absolute timing errors for various summary- and average-KR conditions.
Reprinted from Yao, Fischman, and Wang, 1994.

example, one were to provide KP about the gait of a post-stroke patient. Many potential sources of feedback could be used, but the amount of feedback would likely be overwhelming if all the feedback sources of information were used at once. So, therapists intuitively withhold much of this feedback. Suppose only one source of feedback were to be provided. On what basis should this one source be chosen? Should it be the one most affecting the gait? The one that is most important for a safe gait? Or should it be chosen according to some other criterion? Moreover, if augmented feedback is provided relatively often, should it be about the same information source or different sources? To our knowledge, such issues have not been addressed in the KP literature, although the scheduling issue has been studied using KR as augmented feedback (Lee & Carnahan, 1990b; Swanson & Lee, 1992).

Subjects performed a three-segment timing task in the Lee and Carnahan study, with a specific timing goal for each segment. All subjects were provided with KR about one segment after each trial. The question was whether KR should be repeatedly given on the *same* segment on consecutive trials (blocked-KR schedule) or whether KR should be given about a *different* segment after each trial (random-KR schedule).[2] The results were rather surprising: random KR was better for both performance *and* learning of the task. In acquisition, KR was beneficial when provided for a given segment, but performance deteriorated once KR was withdrawn from that segment (see also Swanson & Lee, 1992). Blocked KR focused learners only on the segment about which they were currently receiving KR, whereas random KR encouraged subjects to process information about all three segments on each trial.

These results suggest another way in which KR can have an overly directive or guiding function. In terms of the guidance hypothesis, blocked KR may have been directing the subject's attention to the one segment on which he or she was receiving KR, and treating that segment as just one part of the whole task. When KR was shifted elsewhere, it guided the subject to a different part of the task, again decomposing the task into parts. This research seems more directly applicable to the functioning of KP, with different aspects of the movement quality potentially becoming the source of feedback. However, the implications of the work await further study using these more

appropriate types of augmented feedback.

Temporal Locus of Knowledge of Results

The next two sections deal with the question of *when* in the learning sequence KR should be presented. The question really concerns the three intervals defined in figure 12.1—the KR delay, the post-KR delay, and the intertrial interval—and the ways in which experimentally altering them affects learning and performance. The problem is complicated by the fact that when one of the intervals is lengthened experimentally (e.g., KR delay) and another is held constant (e.g., post-KR delay), then the third interval (in this example, the intertrial interval) must also increase. The effects of the KR delay and the intertrial interval are *confounded*, so that any resulting change in learning cannot logically be attributed exclusively to either one of them. This fact sometimes makes it difficult to be certain about the particular roles these intervals have in the learning process, as we see in the following sections.

Knowledge-of-Results Delay Interval

The KR-delay interval is the amount of time that KR is delayed after a movement. Beginning with Lorge and Thorndike (1935) and continuing through the present, many experimenters have examined feedback delays and motor learning. For a variety of reasons, scientists have always expected to find that increasing the KR delay degrades learning. One reason is that analogous effects in instrumental learning in animals are particularly strong. Delaying the reward (e.g., a pellet of food) slightly in time from the animal's bar-press movement has large effects on animal learning, and delaying the reward too much eliminates learning completely (Fantino & Logan, 1979; Tarpy & Sawabini, 1974). Scientists expected something like this for human motor learning and KR as well. A second reason is that with humans, as the feedback delay from the associated movement is increased, the poorer should be the learner's memory of the movement that was made. This would seem to weaken the possibility for the learner to *associate* commands for the movement with its actual outcome—a concept critical to many early theoretical ideas about learning.

However, as reviewed by Salmoni, Schmidt, and Walter (1984), the experiments in human motor learning examining the delay of KR have almost uniformly failed to show that increasing the KR delay has any effect at all. For example, Lorge and Thorndike (1935) used delays of either 1, 2, 4, or 6 s and found no effect in an acquisition phase; but no transfer design was used here to evaluate effects on learning. Perhaps the delay was not sufficiently long. Other studies have used much longer delays ranging from a few seconds to a few minutes, and one even used a delay of 1 week! Whereas a few studies have found small, somewhat inconsistent effects on performance, the majority of research has not (e.g., Schmidt & Shea, 1976). Recent work has used various transfer designs to assess the temporary versus relatively permanent effects of KR delay. There are numerous studies showing no effects, or at best very small effects, and we must doubt that delaying KR has a *detrimental* effect on motor learning.

In contrast, there is some evidence to suggest that detriments to learning can occur if the KR delay is *too short*. Swinnen, Schmidt, Nicholson, and Shapiro (1990) compared groups of subjects who received KR after each trial—either at a short delay after performance was completed (3.2 s) or *instantaneously* upon completion of the trial. As illustrated in figure 12.12, acquisition performance was not affected on the first day of practice by the KR conditions. Performance improvements increased steadily for the delayed-KR group on a second day of practice, but not for the instantaneous-KR group. Learning, as measured in no-KR retention tests after various time intervals, was also facilitated by having KR delayed for a short time. Or was it? A closer look at figure 12.12 suggests a more appropriate interpretation: that the instantaneous KP enhanced performance to a point, but retarded both continued improvement and retention without KP after that. These results also fit well with an interpretation suggesting that the augmented feedback was determining the processing operations of the learner when present during the practice period.

Post-Knowledge-of-Results Delay Interval

Next, consider the other portion of the intermovement interval—the post-KR-delay interval, or the time between the presentation of KR and the production of the next movement. In contrast to the hypothesis that the subject is trying to remember the aspects of the movement during the KR-delay interval, during the post-KR-delay interval it appears that other processes are occurring. In particular, KR has now been delivered, indicating that the movement was incorrect in some way. Now the learner must generate a movement that is *different* from the previous one, hopefully one that is more correct. So, in contrast to the hypothesis that during the KR-delay interval the learner is a holder of information, in the post-KR-delay interval the learner is thought to be an active and creative movement modifier.

If the subject is actively processing KR to change the movement during post-KR delay, then short-

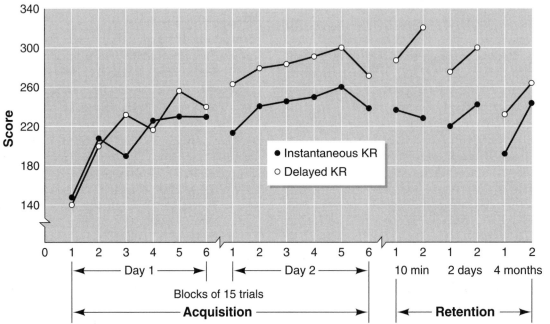

Figure 12.12. Performance scores of instantaneous- and delayed-KR conditions in acquisition and retention.
Reprinted from Swinnen, Schmidt, Nicholson, and Shapiro, 1990.

ening the post-KR-delay interval past a certain point should decrease learning in the task, as the person would not have the opportunity to develop an effective new movement. Some support for this view exists in the verbal learning literature using *concept-formation tasks*. For example, the subject might be presented with a picture containing a number of objects (e.g., squares, triangles, circles) that vary along dimensions such as color, size, and location in the space. The subject's task is to view this picture on trial 1 and to state a concept (i.e., a generalization) that accounts for the information in the picture, such as "Square things are red and round things are blue." After this choice, the experimenter gives KR (e.g., "wrong"), and the subject is shown another picture with the same underlying concept and asked to respond to it. The problem for the learner is to generate an effective, new concept that will hopefully be the one that the experimenter has identified. This is, of course, analogous to developing a new movement pattern that the motor skills experimenter has in mind. With these tasks, decreasing the post-KR-delay interval increases the number of trials needed to arrive at the correct concept in both adults (e.g., Bourne & Bunderson, 1963; Bourne et al., 1965; White & Schmidt, 1972) and children (Croll, 1970), probably because of the limitations in the opportunity to generate new hypotheses.

The literature on motor learning and performance, however, does not show close parallels to these findings for concept formation. In the acquisition phase, decreasing the post-KR-delay interval does have slight detrimental effects on performance accuracy in both adults (Weinberg, Guy, & Tupper, 1964) and children (Gallagher & Thomas, 1980), but no transfer designs were used in these studies to assess learning effects. When transfer designs are used, however, decreasing post-KR delay also degrades learning, but only when KR delay is held constant, and not when the intertrial interval is held constant. Salmoni, Schmidt, and Walter (1984) argued, therefore, that it was the intertrial interval that seemed to be the important one for learning. But there is still some evidence that learning might be reduced when the post-KR delay is very short. Taken together, the evidence does not suggest that the length of this interval, per se, is very important for learning. But this is not to deny the role of processes that occur here, as they could occur

quite rapidly for these very simple motor tasks, and varying the length of the interval might not severely limit processing.

Intertrial Interval

The intertrial interval, or the sum of KR delay and post-KR delay (figure 12.1), has been the object of considerable *indirect* study—mainly because it varies when either one of the intervals composing it varies, and not because of much interest in the intertrial interval per se. According to a review by Salmoni, Schmidt, and Walter (1984), there are many conflicting results on intertrial-interval effects for performance during the acquisition phase, obtained from a variety of experimental procedures: little generalization seems possible. McGuigan (1959) and Dees and Grindley (1951) have shown, however, that increasing the intertrial-interval length increases learning as measured on no-KR transfer tests. Perhaps longer intertrial intervals result in increased forgetting of the *solution* to the motor problem generated on the previous trial and thus require an active generation of the motor program again on the next trial. These forced generations could be very important for the learning process, as has been inferred from the contextual-interference literature discussed in the previous chapter. To the extent that this literature can be generalized to practical situations, it appears that the intertrial intervals should not be shortened excessively. But more study of these various intervals is needed, using tasks of varying complexity, before we can claim to understand the processes at work.

Interpolated Activities During Knowledge-of-Results Intervals

What is the effect of requiring the learner to perform various activities during otherwise "empty" KR intervals? This question is motivated by an information-processing viewpoint about KR, according to which certain other activities should interfere with various processes that occur during these KR intervals and thus the effects should be seen in learning of the task. As we will see, however, various interpolated activities have either no influence, a positive effect, or a negative impact on learning, depending on the nature of the interpolated activity and the delay interval during which it is interpolated.

Interference During the Knowledge-of-Results Delay Interval

The influence of various activities during the KR-delay interval may be referred to as "interfering" if they distract the learner from processing the inherent feedback from the performance just completed. For example, Shea and Upton (1976) had subjects perform linear-positioning movements, but *two* positions were to be practiced and learned on each trial rather than one. On a given trial, the subject would produce Movement 1, then Movement 2, then would engage in the performance of other movements (or would rest if in the other condition), then after 30 s would receive KR about Movement 1 and Movement 2, then engage in the next trial, and so on. Figure 12.13 shows the average absolute errors (errors on the two positions are averaged together) for these two groups on the original-practice trials and on the no-KR transfer trials. Filling the KR-delay interval increased absolute error on the acquisition trials, indicating that the extraneous movements had a negative effect on performance. And, from the transfer trials shown in the right-hand portion of the figure, it seemed clear that the decrements in performance caused by the extraneous movements did, in fact, interfere with the learning of the tasks. Marteniuk (1986) and Swinnen (1990) have provided similar results using more complex motor tasks.

What is happening here? One interpretation of these findings is that the subjects usually engaged in various information-processing activities during the KR-delay interval and that the requirement of the extraneous movements in some way interfered with this processing, degrading learning as it did. What kinds of processing might these be? Marteniuk (1986) argued that the interference is from relatively high-level planning processes. But it is also possible that the subject must retain in short-term memory the sensory consequences (the "feel") of the movement until the KR is presented, so that the two can be integrated. The retention of information is important in order to develop an error-detection capacity (knowledge to detect errors based on inherent feedback sources). If other movements are required, then there will be either a blocked capacity to hold the information in short-term memory or a reduced precision of the inherent feedback, resulting in less effective use of KR when it is presented.

Subjective Estimations During the Knowledge-of-Results Delay Interval

Support for the interpretation just outlined is provided in situations in which subjects are *encouraged* to undertake error estimation during the KR-delay interval. Hogan and Yanowitz (1978) required (or did not require) subjects to estimate their own errors in a ballistic timing task prior to receiving KR on each trial. In an acquisition session with KR present, there were essentially no differences between the two groups. But in a

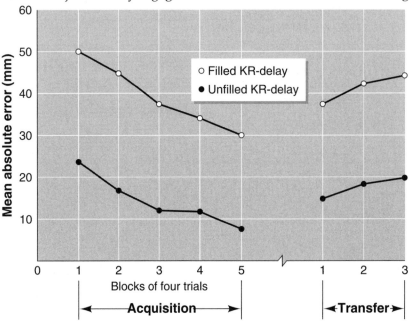

Figure 12.13. Absolute errors in positioning as a function of the processing demands imposed during the KR-delay interval. Reprinted from Shea and Upton, 1976.

transfer test without KR, the subjects who were estimating maintained performance nearly perfectly, whereas those subjects who did not estimate regressed systematically over trials. One interpretation is that the estimation conditions in acquisition forced the subjects to attend to their own movement-produced (inherent) feedback to a greater extent than the no-estimation conditions did, thus enabling them to acquire an error-detection capability. This capability was not particularly useful in acquisition because of the powerful guiding properties of KR. But in no-KR transfer, subjects who had gained this error-detection capability through estimation in acquisition were able to maintain performance, whereas the no-estimation subjects were relatively unaware of their own errors and drifted off target. More recently, Swinnen (1990; Swinnen, Schmidt, Nicholson, & Shapiro, 1990) has extended and refined the Hogan-Yanowitz paradigm in various ways, using different tasks and transfer tests, in an attempt to understand these phenomena more completely. Overall, there continues to be support for the notion that forced error estimation in acquisition is effective for learning as measured on no-KR transfer tests, especially when the test is delayed by 2 days. But some of these experiments do not show this effect, causing some doubt about how general these phenomena might be. One problem is that in the "no-estimation" condition, subjects on some trials engage in this estimation spontaneously, thus diluting the difference between the no-estimation and estimation conditions (reminiscent of problems in the goal-setting experiments discussed in chapter 11).

The issues about error detection are important for theoretical reasons, but there is a strong practical application to them as well. We can think of the self-detected error as a kind of substitute for KR, as it informs the subject about the size and direction of the error that was just made. It is unfortunate that nearly all the focus in learning environments is on performance and that there is almost no concern for the development of the learner's error-detection capacity. If procedures could be developed for increasing the strength of error detection, then learners could provide KR to themselves, even if the teacher or coach were not present; they would thus be able to learn without KR. In addition to providing the bases for effective movement performance, good teachers and coaches attempt to establish such error-detection capabilities that can substitute for removed KR later.

Interference During the Post-Knowledge-of-Results Delay Interval

The focus of processing activities during the KR-delay interval is on movement-produced inherent feedback. During the post-KR delay, however, the processing activities are likely focused on using augmented feedback to alter movement behavior on the next attempt. A number of early studies in which interpolated activities were inserted in the post-KR interval found that performance was degraded (e.g., Boucher, 1974; Rogers, 1974; but see Magill, 1973), but these studies did not use transfer procedures to assess learning (see Schendel & Newell, 1976, for a discussion). Later studies that used transfer tests produced mixed results: Swinnen (1990) and Benedetti and McCullagh (1987) found that interference during the post-KR delay was detrimental to learning in a no-KR retention test; Lee and Magill (1983a, 1987) found no detrimental effects of interpolated activities in a transfer test; and Magill (1988a) found that such activities were actually beneficial. The rather unsettled nature of this research makes it difficult to infer practice applications. However, given the comparative strength of these effects, it would appear that instructors should be more concerned about extraneous activities in the KR-delay interval than in the post-KR-delay interval.

Theoretical Issues: How Does Augmented Feedback "Work"?

In the previous sections, various separate facts have been presented in connection with the functioning of augmented feedback in motor learning situations. Some of these have had obvious relevance for practical situations, whereas others have distinct implications for how we believe feedback operates in humans to facilitate learning. In this section, we consider some of these implications.

How Augmented Feedback Can Enhance Learning

The research presented in this chapter suggests three possible ways that KR and KP operate to affect learning in a positive way, and theories of learning have generally adopted one or more of these positions. Both KR and KP are considered to have *informational, motivational,* and *associational* functions. These concepts are considered next.

Informational Functions

In previous sections we have drawn attention to a number of features that are common to KR in human motor learning situations and reward in animal learning situations. Both KR and reward are presented contingent on the nature of the movement, and both are given after the movement. What is the evidence that KR and reward are really different?

That KR and reward might be similar is not a new idea at all, and it is the foundation of the empirical Law of Effect, from Thorndike (1927; see Adams, 1978, 1987). This law states that the organism tends to repeat rewarded movements and tends to extinguish (or avoid) movements followed either by no reward or by punishment. For motor learning, according to this concept, KR indicating small errors or no error was thought of as a reward, and KR indicating large errors was thought of as "punishment." In this way, the movements followed by nonreward were eliminated, and those followed by reward (i.e., zero or small error) tended to be repeated, leading to decreasing errors with practice.

Numerous lines of evidence suggest that humans do not use KR as proposed by this interpretation of the Law of Effect. First, when KR is not presented (on no-KR trials), subjects tend to *repeat* those movements rather than to eliminate them. Only when KR is presented do subjects change their movements, and then quite clearly in the direction of the target. It would seem that subjects are not using the KR as a reward, but rather as *information* about what to do next. In addition, even a short delay of reward in animal learning severely retards acquisition, and delaying reward by 30 s or so can eliminate learning. Of course, we do not find these effects at all in humans, as the delay of KR seems to have no effect on motor learning. Thus, reward in laboratory rats and KR in humans seem to involve fundamentally different principles of operation (see boxed text on page 353).

For these major reasons, the current belief about augmented feedback is that it produces learning more by the provision of *information* about what was wrong with the previous trials, and by *prescriptive* means to improve performance (Newell,

1991), than through the rewarding of correct movements and the "punishment" of incorrect ones. This interpretation would seem to contradict the findings from manipulations of bandwidth KR; in these experiments, information conveying to the subject that performance was correct gave an additional boost to learning in comparison to the learning in no-KR trials (Lee & Carnahan, 1990a). We suggest that the boost to learning came from the information content provided by this "no error" type of feedback. That subjects resist making changes to performance on the basis of what might be "noise" might be a way of avoiding the negative influences of too frequent augmented feedback (see Inducing Maladaptive Corrections later on in the chapter).

One further suggestion is that KR serves its *optimum* informational role when the learner is *uncertain* about the reliability of his or her inherent sources of information. A dictionary provides a useful analogy here. The dictionary is like KR in that it is an externally available, objective, and reliable source of knowledge, such as of the spelling or the meaning of a word. The decision to consult a dictionary arises because we have questioned the reliability of our intrinsic knowledge, and we do not consult the dictionary otherwise. Thus, the dictionary provides the means for assessing and improving the reliability of our intrinsic knowledge. One hypothesis arising from this analogy is that augmented feedback should be optimally useful when the subject asks for it—a concept that has received support from recent experiments (see the earlier section on learner-determined presentation of KR).

Motivational Functions

As mentioned earlier, receiving information like KR and KP can play a strong motivating, or "energizing," role. KR and KP make the task seem more interesting, keep the learner alert, cause the learner to set higher performance goals, and generally make boring tasks more enjoyable. Most of these effects are probably performance phenomena, which can be expected to subside when the feedback is withdrawn after training. But there is an indirect learning effect that should not be ignored. When learners are highly motivated, they are inclined to practice more often, longer, and with more intensity and seriousness. Of course, deliberate practice per se is a critical variable for learning, and any factor that increases it will almost surely enhance learning (Ericsson,

Elwell and Grindley on the Directive Role of Knowledge of Results

The first major challenge to Thorndike's ideas regarding the role of KR in the context of motor learning was provided by Elwell and Grindley (1938). The argument was that KR could serve as more than just a rewarding function. They stated:

> In the acquisition of a muscular skill, such as that described in the present paper, the learning cannot be regarded merely as the strengthening of the tendency to repeat movements which have been "rewarded" (by a high score). If a subject missed the bull's-eye he tried, next time, to correct for his error by altering his response in the appropriate direction. . . . Knowledge of results, when the movement was not completely successful (i.e., when it did not result in a bull's-eye) introduces also *a tendency towards a specific kind of variation of the response which has just been made.* We may call this the "directive effect" of knowledge of results. (p. 51)

The directive role of KR was conscious and not automatic. Elwell and Grindley's ideas, which were developed more completely in three subsequent papers (Dees & Grindley, 1951; MacPherson, Dees, & Grindley, 1948, 1949), formed the basis for what was later called the *informational* role of KR.

1996; Ericsson, Krampe, & Tesch-Römer, 1993). So these motivational properties of feedback, even though we class them as performance variables, may *indirectly* be strong learning variables.

Associational Functions

A different view is that KR is associational—providing associations between stimuli and movements. One version of this concept is provided within schema theory (Schmidt, 1975b), according to which KR is thought to operate associationally as well as in the ways that Adams (1971) has suggested. In schema theory, with respect to rapid movements that are presumably controlled by motor programs, the person associates the KR received on a trial (a measure of what happened in the environment) with the parameters of the motor program that were issued to produce that outcome in the environment. With practice, the person comes to develop a rule (or schema) about the relationship between what the limbs were "told to do" and "what they did when told to do it." On this basis, knowing what kinds of internal commands tend to produce certain kinds of movements, the learner has a basis for selecting the parameters of the movement on future trials. Thus, in this view, KR serves more than a guidance function toward the target; it also

provides a rule about the relationship between internal commands and the outcomes that were produced in the environment.

How Augmented Feedback Can Degrade Learning

Another view of how KR works is that it guides the learner to the proper movement. Thus, when the learner makes a movement, KR informs the person about how the movement was inadequate, and the learner then changes the movement to one that (hopefully) will be more adequate. Knowledge of results thus carries inherent "instructions" about which aspects of the movement should be changed as well as about the directions those changes should take. According to this position, KR does not provide any direct strengthening of the movement but creates it indirectly by guiding the person to the proper action. Once the proper actions are being produced, other processes take over to help the person learn the task.

This view is fundamental to Adams's (1971) learning theory, which says that KR presented after each trial of a slow positioning movement guides the person toward the correct location. Then, as the learner achieves positions close to the target, he or she also receives kinesthetic feedback associated with the proper position, and this feedback forms an internal representation of being at the target (a reference of correctness). This internal representation becomes stronger with each successive trial near the target and thus provides an increasingly effective means for detecting errors. Thus, according to Adams, KR has a guidance role in driving the subject closer and closer to the target so that a reference of correctness can be formed.

Considered in this way (as envisaged by Adams, 1971), the guiding influences of augmented feedback on learning should always be positive. As we have seen, however, in some experiments the KR effects showed that increased guidance degraded learning (leading to doubts about Adams's theory; see chapter 13). We consider reasons why feedback can degrade learning in the next sections (see also Salmoni, Schmidt, & Walter, 1984; Schmidt, 1991; Schmidt & Bjork, 1992).

Blocking Other Processing Activities

When augmented feedback is provided frequently, immediately, or otherwise in such a way that various processing activities are not undertaken, then there will likely be a decrement in learning. This may occur for two reasons. The first is based on the rationale that the error-detection process uses a specific type of knowledge that must be learned. Movement-produced feedback can be a rich source of information that can be used to support performance in the absence of augmented feedback. However, detecting errors through inherent feedback sources is a learned process. One of the negative influences of augmented feedback is to *block* the processing of inherent sources of feedback. Augmented feedback is often a very salient source of information, and one that will be attended to even when doing so may not be in the learner's best interest (Buekers, Magill, & Hall, 1992). The presentation of instantaneous KP (Swinnen, Schmidt, Nicholson, & Shapiro, 1990), which was discussed earlier, is an example of a case in which the saliency of the augmented feedback is maximized. We interpret results of this type to suggest that the augmented feedback blocked the processing of alternative sources of information and reduced the learning effectiveness of the practice session as measured in retention.

Inducing Maladaptive Corrections

One of the fundamental views about the directive function of augmented feedback is that it tells the learner what went wrong and how to fix it. As we found in our discussion of precision of KR, more precise KR can be beneficial, but only up to a point. The idea is similar here. Augmented feedback can be useful as long as it does not prescribe corrections that are more precise than the learner's motor system is capable of producing. Consider two basketball free throws, for example. If the first shot was short of the front rim (an "air ball"), the player would likely adjust for the next shot with a force-parameter rescaling. However, if the first shot went through with a "swish" there would be no reason to make any alterations on the next shot. But, because the circumference of the rim is quite a bit larger than that of the ball, augmented feedback could be provided to the player about the precise amount that the "swish" was off center. Although the player might use this augmented feedback to try to "correct" the shot, the correction might be *maladaptive*, in that the next shot might not go in at all. The point is that sometimes augmented feedback can have maladaptive corrective properties (R.A. Bjork, personal communication). Presenting information that encourages a subject to correct for actions that were essentially accurate may have a detrimental impact on learning (Schmidt, 1991).

Bandwidth-KR effects illustrate how maladaptive corrections may be avoided. Under bandwidth-KR conditions, there exists a zone of acceptable error within which movement is considered correct. Defining the actual width of the band of correctness, as well as what would be considered maladaptively corrective and what would be considered too imprecise, is a challenge for future research. However, we suspect that an *optimal KR bandwidth* may be closely related to an individual's movement precision, although even within an individual this is likely to change (e.g., with learning and aging).

Summary

Feedback is that class of sensory information that is movement related, and it can be classified into two basic categories—*inherent* (intrinsic to the task) and *augmented* (supplementary to the task). Two major classes of augmented feedback are KP, which is information about the form of the movement, and KR, which is verbal postmovement information about performance outcome. Much research suggests that information about performance is the single most important variable for motor learning (except for practice itself, of course).

Information about the learner's movements (KP) can be given through videotape replays, recordings of the force-time characteristics of the movement (kinetics), or representations of the movement trajectories (kinematics); and all these appear to have positive effects on performance and perhaps on learning. The impact of KP on learning appears to be best when it precisely specifies information which is critical for movement efficiency and that cannot be obtained from other sources of feedback.

Knowledge-of-results precision refers to the accuracy with which the KR is given. Performance improves with increases in precision up to a point, with no further increases in performance thereafter. Presenting combinations of qualitative and quantitative KR, based upon a goal-related bandwidth of correctness, has both strong applied and theoretical merits.

Early research indicated that the *relative frequency* of KR (the percentage of trials on which KR was given) was irrelevant for learning, whereas the absolute frequency (the number of KR presentations given) was the critical determinant. More recent data using transfer designs contradicts this position, indicating that both are clearly important. Trials on which no KR is given appear to contribute to learning in the task, but not as much as the KR trials do. The trials-delay and summary-KR procedures, in which the KR for a given movement is separated from the movement by other trials, were shown to produce detrimental effects on motor performance, but positive effects on learning.

The effect of delaying KR, that is, the effect of the interval from the movement until KR is presented, has been found to be negligible for learning most motor tasks, as long as KR is not presented too soon after performance. Filling this interval with activities not related to the task degrades learning. However, filling this interval with activities related to the task enhances learning. If the post-KR-delay interval—the interval from the KR until the time the next movement is called for—is too short, subjects appear to have difficulty generating a new and different movement on the next trial. However, filling this interval has uncertain effects on learning.

Augmented feedback appears to have several possible mechanisms for enhancing learning. It acts as *information*. It acts to form *associations* between movement parameters and resulting action. And it acts in a *motivational* role. Augmented feedback also has a guidance property that can degrade learning. Much more research is needed to understand which of these roles are most important, depending on the learner, the task, and the movement situation.

Notes

[1] Although we have distinguished between various types of augmented feedback, of which KR is one, we will generally refer to many aspects of this work in relation to the term KR. However, exceptions will be made when a clear distinction is necessary.

[2] Note, however, that these random- and blocked-KR conditions are quite different from the random- and blocked-practice schedules discussed in the contextual-interference section in chapter 11. In the present discussion, the same task is performed on each trial—the difference being the order by which KR about one of the three potential augmented feedback segments is provided.

CHAPTER

13

THE LEARNING PROCESS

So far in the discussion of motor learning, our major concern has been the most important empirical findings about the acquisition of skills. It is time now to consider the underlying reasons these findings seem to hold and to ask about the nature of the motor learning processes that cause the motor system to behave in the ways identified in previous chapters.

In this chapter, we consider the many ways in which the motor learning process has been conceptualized by various people at different times in the history of the field. All these theoretical perspectives have as their basic goal an understanding of the changes in skill that we all know occur with practice. However, we will see that a phenomenon as broad and common as this can be explained in various ways and at a number of levels of analysis (biomechanical, cognitive, and so on). At the same time, we will see that the concepts basic to these various theoretical ideas are already familiar from previous chapters, having to do with such notions as the building of new motor programs, changes in attentional requirements, the development of error-detection processes, and the like.

The chapter is divided into three major sections. The first section presents some fundamental ideas about the learning process. With this information in mind, together with information from the previous two chapters, we then present various theoretical views about motor learning. Two of these, considered major theoretical advances in the history of motor learning research, are presented in the second section of the chapter. The third section presents different perspectives on the learning process—perspectives that in one form or another, can be considered major hypotheses about learning.

Characteristics of the Learning Process

Without a doubt, the most notable thing that happens when people practice is that they demonstrate increased proficiency in the task. Sometimes this is so obvious that it hardly needs to be mentioned, while in other cases the changes are more subtle and require special methods for observation and measurement. In this section we describe a number of ways in which the learning process has been characterized, in terms of the various descriptions of the ways individuals change in their capability to perform a motor skill with practice.

The Law of Practice

One of the most frequently observed characteristics about the change in performance that accompanies practice is that the improvements in (average) performance are generally large and rapid at first and then become systematically smaller as practice continues. Thus, whether the measure of performance increases or decreases (see figures 10.1 and 10.2) with practice, performance curves are usually *negatively accelerated* functions of practice—the "rate" of improvement changes toward zero as practice continues. Although a few particular tasks might not show this kind of relationship, or certain performance phenomena might distort it considerably (e.g., random practice), as a general rule the majority of the behaviors studied in motor learning seem to show practice curves with this overall form.

Defining the Law of Practice

A negatively accelerated relation between performance and practice trials has many of the general features of a very common equation that is termed a *power function*, in which the time, T, to complete an action can be expressed as

$$T = a\,P^{-b} = a/P^b \qquad (13.1)$$

where a and b are constants, and P is some measure of the amount of practice (e.g., number of trials). Here, as practice increases and P becomes larger, the ratio a/P decreases, resulting in smaller time to complete the action, T; the larger the constant b, the more "rapid" are the decreases with practice. Analogous power functions can also be defined for tasks with scores that increase with practice, such as the pursuit rotor or Bachman ladder task (Bachman, 1966). For these the sign of b is reversed.

One important feature of power functions such as that in equation 13.1 is that the plot of the *logarithm* of performance (T) against the *logarithm* of the number of practice trials (P) will yield a *linear* function. For example, taking the logarithm of both sides of equation 13.1 yields:

$$\text{Log } (T) = \text{Log } (a) - b\,(\text{Log } P) \qquad (13.2)$$

Notice that, from the discussions of empirical equations earlier in the book, equation 13.2 is simply a special case of the standard equation for a linear function, $Y = a + b X$, where here Y is Log (T), a is the constant Log (a), and X is Log (P). Therefore we can summarize equation 13.2 easily by saying that the relationship between Log (T) and Log (P) is linear, with an intercept of Log (a) and a slope of $–b$.

Generality of the Law of Practice

Fitts (1964), and later Newell and Rosenbloom (1981), pointed out that practice on numerous tasks with widely differing movement measurements, goals, and measures of performance—motor tasks and verbal tasks alike—tended to follow this logarithmic *law of practice*. The first analysis of this kind was presented by Snoddy (1926). Subjects learned to draw figures while viewing only the mirror image of their drawing hand, with practice continuing over 100 days (one trial per day). The data, plotted in figure 13.1 using a log-log scale as suggested by the law of practice, shows a generally linear relationship, except perhaps for the first few data points. This is an example in which the score increases with practice. Another example comes from Crossman (1959) in a study of factory workers who made cigars using a small hand-operated jig. In figure 13.2 is a plot of the average time for cigar production against practice time (a decreasing function), also in log-log scales. This plot is also generally linear, only flattening out near the region of high practice where the minimum cycle time of the

machine itself became a factor in performance. See Fitts (1964) and Newell and Rosenbloom (1981) for many more examples and a fuller discussion.

An important interpretation of these logarithmic relationships is that the rate of improvement at any point in practice tends to be linearly related to the "amount left to improve" in the task. So, early in practice, when there is much learning left to accomplish, the speed of improvement is very rapid as compared to that at the end of practice when there is not so much "room for improvement" remaining. Furthermore, many of the experiments in support of the law of practice show that improvements continue to occur for years, even though these later gains may be very small. Consider, for example, the situation in Crossman's (1959, figure 13.2) data, where improvements can be seen even after seven years of practice, and after 10 million cigars! Learning is never really completed, even in the simplest of tasks. Finally, remember that the law of practice is just a *description* of the relationship between practice trials and performance; it does not provide any *explanation* of the underlying processes in learning.

Stages of Motor Learning

Many have noticed that learners appear to pass through relatively distinct stages or phases as they practice a skill. Bryan and Harter (1897, 1899) were among the first to study the

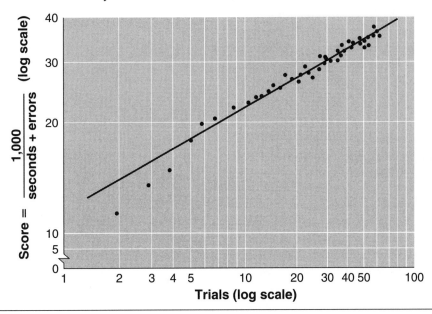

Figure 13.1. Scores in a mirror-tracing task as a function of extended practice. Reprinted from Snoddy, 1926.

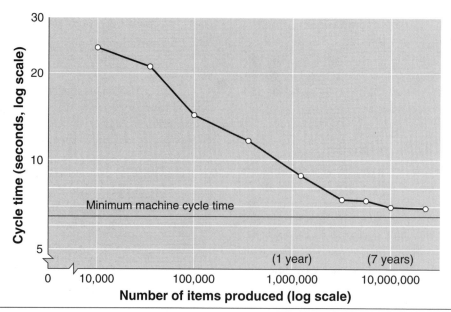

Figure 13.2.   Completion time in making cigars as a function of extended practice. Reprinted from Crossman, 1959.

acquisition of skill in considerable detail (see the boxed on page 361). Learning as a two-stage process was proposed early on by Snoddy (1926). As we noted earlier, subjects in Snoddy's research learned to make hand movements using only a mirror—a task that requires abilities needed by a dentist, for example. According to Snoddy (1926), the *adaptation* stage involved acquisition of the neuromuscular pattern required to perform the task. Once the pattern was learned, the *facilitation* stage had to do with improving the efficiency of the pattern. Other two-stage views were later suggested by Adams (1971) and Gentile (1972). Fitts (1964; Fitts & Posner, 1967), and later Anderson (1982, 1995), discussed learning in terms of three phases of practice. These are called the *cognitive phase*, the *associative phase*, and the *autonomous phase*.

Cognitive Phase

When the learner is new to a task, the primary concern is to understand what is to be done, how the performance is to be scored, and how best to attempt the first few trials. Naturally, considerable cognitive activity is required so that the learner can determine appropriate strategies. Good strategies are retained, and inappropriate ones are discarded. As a result, the performance gains during this phase are dramatic and generally larger than at any other single period in the learning process. Performance is usually very inconsistent, perhaps because the learner is trying many different ways of solving the problem.

As you might imagine, the use of instructions, models, augmented feedback, and various other training techniques (discussed in chapters 11 and 12) is most effective during this phase. Probably most of the improvements in the cognitive stage can be thought of as verbal-cognitive in nature, the major gains being in terms of what to do rather than in the motor patterns themselves. Adams (1971) termed this stage the *verbal-motor stage*.

Associative Phase

The second phase of motor learning begins when the individual has determined the most effective way of doing the task and starts to make more subtle adjustments in how the skill is performed. Performance improvements are more gradual, and movements become more consistent. This phase can persist for many days or weeks, with the performer gradually producing small changes in the motor patterns that will allow more effective performance. Many writers (e.g., Adams, 1971; Fitts, 1964) think that the verbal aspects of the task have largely dropped out by this stage, with the performer concentrating on how to do the particular pattern rather than on which pattern of action should be produced. This stage is the one most often studied in experiments on motor learning, and it is called the *motor stage* by Adams (1971).

Autonomous Phase

After many months, perhaps years, of practice, the learner enters the autonomous phase, so named because the skill has become largely *auto-*

Bryan and Harter's Hierarchy of Habits

A fascinating early set of studies regarding the perceptual and motor changes that occur with learning was conducted by William Lowe Bryan (a psychologist) and Noble Harter (a telegrapher and student of Bryan's). The result of their shared interests was two landmark papers regarding the acquisition of telegraphic skills (Bryan & Harter, 1897, 1899). In these papers, Bryan and Harter presented the results of some experiments in which they compared novice and expert telegraphers, as well as some data they obtained by charting the acquisition of telegraphy skill over many months of practice. Many interesting findings can be found in these papers (Lee & Swinnen, 1993), but we will focus on one in particular.

Skill, in Bryan and Harter's view, was a process of achieving a *hierarchy of habits*. At the most basic level, telegraphy involves the ability to discriminate (perceptually and motorically) between *units* of time. A dot is one unit of continuous auditory signal. A dash is three units of continuous time. One unit of no signal occurs between dots and dashes within a letter (e.g., the letter *G* is a dash-dash-dot). Three continuous units of no signal denotes that a new letter is beginning, and six units marks a new word. This "language" of telegraphy lent itself well to Bryan and Harter's view of learning as a hierarchy of habits. The most fundamental skill was learning to discriminate units of time—a skill that is learned quickly. The alphabet became the next challenge, although this too is usually learned quickly and performance in sending and receiving code improves rapidly. However, Bryan and Harter then noticed something peculiar about the practice curves of some of their subjects: periods of time would go by during which little or no improvement occurred at all, followed later by rapid improvements. They called these periods *plateaus* in performance that occur prior to the formation of a new, advanced capability. They proposed that, rather than hearing dots and dashes, the telegraphers "hear" letters, and with practice, words, and for the most skilled, even larger units of a sentence. The plateaus in performance occur because the maximum performance capability of one habit places a constraint on performance, which is then lifted when a higher order habit is formed. Although some of Bryan and Harter's views have been challenged at times (e.g., Keller, 1958), many of the basic concepts of progression through stages and to higher orders of skill have been retained in a number of conceptualizations of skill acquisition that remain popular today.

matic in the sense discussed in chapter 4. That is, the task can now be performed with less interference from other simultaneous activities. It is easy to find examples of high-level performers engaging in secondary tasks without interference—for example, the concert pianist who can shadow digits or do mental arithmetic without interference while sight-reading and playing piano music (e.g., Allport, Antonis, & Reynolds, 1972; Shaffer, 1971, 1980). As we have seen, this automaticity is usually evidenced with respect to only particular kinds of simultaneous tasks, primarily those that we could class as verbal-cognitive; some other motor task could in fact interfere with

a performance in the autonomous phase, as discussed in chapter 4 in detail. Even so, the performer gives the impression that he or she is performing without having to "pay attention" to the actions. This stage has the benefit of allowing the person to process information from other aspects of the task, such as the strategy in a game of tennis or the form or style of movement in ice skating or dance.

A major problem for motor behavior research is that this stage, which is of immense importance for understanding high-level skills, is rarely studied in experiments on motor learning. The reasons are obvious. In paradigms in which subjects practice on laboratory tasks, such practice should continue for months before even beginning to approximate the levels of skill shown by high-level musicians, athletes, and industrial workers. It is very difficult to convince subjects to devote this kind of effort in experiments. Alternatively, we could use other, more natural tasks that learners are practicing anyway; but it is difficult to manipulate and control the many variables that would need to be used for a scientific understanding of the learning processes.

Some efforts at understanding the principles of automaticity have been made in this direction by Schneider and colleagues (Schneider & Fisk, 1983; Schneider & Shiffrin, 1977) in reaction-time tasks, and by Logan (1985, 1988) using speeded-decision tasks. Unfortunately the work in motor behavior has tended to avoid this problem. Certainly, much more could be done in this area.

Individual Differences and Motor Learning

Some important hypotheses for motor learning are framed in the language and methods of individual-differences research (see chapter 9). Beginning with the concept that a given motor performance is based upon some small set of underlying motor abilities, one hypothesis simply states that this set of abilities changes in its makeup as practice continues. The abilities themselves do not change; this would violate the assumption (discussed in chapter 9) that abilities are to a large extent genetically defined and unmodifiable by practice. But what does change, according to this view, are the particular abilities within the collection that underlies the skill being learned.

Studies Using Individual-Difference Variables

Fleishman and Hempel (1955) and Fleishman and Rich (1963) contributed important investigations in this area. In the Fleishman-Rich study, subjects practiced the two-hand coordination task, in which two crank handles had to be manipulated to cause a pointer to follow a moving target on a target board (figure 2.5). One handle controlled the right-left movements of the pointer, and the other controlled the forward-backward movements, so that diagonal movements could be made with suitable combinations of the two.

Separate from the practice on the two-hand coordination test, the subjects were given two additional tests. In one of these, they were asked to lift small weights and to judge whether a given weight was heavier than, lighter than, or the same as a standard weight. This test was called *kinesthetic sensitivity* by Fleishman and Rich, because it seemed to be based on abilities related to how sensitive the motor system was to applied tensions. A second test called *spatial orientation* was a paper-and-pencil test designed to assess the abilities related to a subject's perception of his orientation in space.

First, Fleishman and Rich divided their group of people into two, on the basis of their performance on the kinesthetic sensitivity test; then they plotted the performances of these two groups of people separately for the two-hand coordination test. Remember, these two groups of people were not treated differently on the two-hand coordination test, but their performances were plotted separately based on their proficiency in the kinesthetic sensitivity test. As seen in figure 13.3a, the subjects classed as high and low on the kinesthetic sensitivity measure were not different on the two-hand coordination test in early trials; but later in practice the subjects high in kinesthetic sensitivity began to outperform those low in kinesthetic sensitivity. Was kinesthetic sensitivity an important ability for the two-hand coordination test? The answer depends on the level of practice. For early practice, kinesthetic sensitivity was not important, but it became important as practice increased. Thus, kinesthetic sensitivity is an ability increasing in importance with practice, at least for this task.

Next, consider the spatial orientation measure. The situation was the same as before, with the groups classified as high and low on this test being plotted separately on the two-hand coordination test (figure 13.3b). Now, though, the subjects classed as high on this test were better performers on the two-hand coordination test than subjects classed as low, but only for initial performance. At the end of practice, the advantage for those classed as high in spatial orientation had disappeared. Is spatial orientation important for performance of this task? Again, the answer depends on the stage of practice. This, then, is an ability that is important for early proficiency in this task but appears to have nothing to do with performance in later practice.

Another way to view these results is this. For the two-hand coordination test, there is some

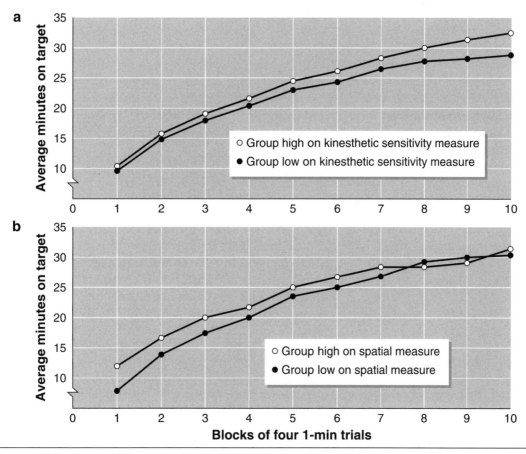

Figure 13.3. Performance on the two-hand coordination test as a function of practice trials. (a) Groups classed as high and low on a kinesthetic sensitivity test are plotted separately; (b) groups classed as high and low on spatial orientation are plotted separately.
Reprinted from Fleishman and Rich, 1963.

collection of abilities that underlies it on trial 1. This collection of abilities may be quite large, but it includes some abilities related to the spatial orientation measure, and it does not include any abilities related to the kinesthetic sensitivity measure. As practice continues, the collection of abilities (not the abilities themselves) changes, so that at the end of practice the task is made up of a somewhat different set of abilities. This collection could include some of the same abilities as in early practice, but it now has abilities related to kinesthetic sensitivity and does not have any abilities related to spatial orientation. When performers are skilled, they apparently use different abilities to produce an action than when they are unskilled. Practice results in a shift in the abilities underlying a task (see also Bartram et al., 1985).

Practice and the Predictability of Skilled Performance

If this changing component abilities hypothesis— that the collection of abilities underlying a par-

ticular skilled performance becomes rearranged systematically with practice—is correct, then we should also find that the *prediction* of success in the skill will be based on different ability measures in early versus late practice. In a way, this is what Fleishman and Rich (1963, figure 13.3) showed. Early in learning (but *not* later in learning), performance on the two-hand coordination test could be predicted (to some extent) from knowledge of the subject's scores on the spatial relations test; that is, the subjects classified as *high* on this measure outperformed (on the average) those subjects classified as *low.* However, late in practice (but *not* early in practice), the two-hand coordination test performance could be predicted from the kinesthetic sensitivity measure. In keeping with our earlier discussion of individual differences in chapter 9, this notion of prediction implies that the *correlation* computed between the two-hand coordination test and, for example, the kinesthetic sensitivity test would be zero in initial practice and larger in later practice. More generally, the hypothesis that the collection of abilities underlying some skill will change with practice says essentially that the correlations between measures of various abilities and the criterion task performance will change with practice.

Intertrial Correlation Analyses

Take any motor task you like, and measure each of a large number of subjects on each of a series of trials. Then correlate every trial with every other trial and place these values in a matrix called an *intertrial correlation matrix*. Such a matrix is shown in table 13.1, reproduced from Jones's (1962, 1966) work on the two-hand coordination test. The bottom half of the matrix is omitted for simplicity (it is the mirror image of the top half—e.g., trial 1 can be correlated with trial 2, and trial 2 can be correlated with trial 1, producing the same result). There are a number of interesting features of tables like this, as has been pointed out by Jones (1966).

Remoteness Effects. First, notice that across any row of the table, the correlations become systematically smaller; they drop from .79 to .70 in the first row, from .87 to .82 in the second row, and so on. But this top row represents the correlations of trial 1 with trial 2, trial 1 with trial 3, trial 1 with trial 4, and so on up to trial 1 with trial 8. Thus, there are an increasing number of trials between the two trials being correlated as we move to the right along any row. As a general rule, as the number of intervening trials increases, the

Table 13.1   An Intertrial Correlation Matrix

Trial	1	2	3	4	5	6	7	8
1		.79	.77	.74	.73	.71	.71	.70
2			.87	.87	.84	.82	.82	.82
3				.91	.89	.87	.85	.86
4					.91	.88	.86	.88
5						.89	.90	.90
6							.93	.93
7								.94
8								

Note. The boxed-in section forms the diagonal of the matrix, and the shaded portion is the "superdiagonal." (Adapted from Jones 1966).

correlation between any two trials decreases. This effect is often called the *remoteness effect*, because the correlations between the trials depend on how remote (how far apart) the trials are from each other.

What is the meaning of this well-established remoteness effect? First, remember that the correlation between two tests (in this case, two trials of the "same" test) is related to the number of common abilities shared by them. As two tests become more separated in the practice sequence, and their correlations systematically drop, it is possible to say that the performance mechanisms on these trials are becoming more and more different, being dependent on fewer and fewer of the same abilities. In this sense, the remoteness effect is just another way to say that the motor task changes with practice—the changes being in the makeup of the set of underlying abilities. Also, the lowered correlations mean that the ordering (from best to worst) of individuals in the group is changing, with the order of the subjects becoming systematically more different (relative to that for trial 1) as practice continues (see also Adams, 1957).

Adjacent-Trial Effects. Examine the data in table 13.1 again, this time concentrating on the correlations between adjacent trials—that is, between trials 1 and 2, between trials 2 and 3, and so on. These correlations can be found on what is called the *superdiagonal* (the shaded area), or the line of correlations that lies just above the diagonal of the matrix (denoted by the diagonal line of unfilled squares in table 13.1). Notice that as the adjacent trials are chosen later and later in the sequence, the correlations steadily increase. The correlation between trials 1 and 2 is .79, whereas the correlation between trials 7 and 8 is .94, the highest in the matrix. This is also a well-known finding, and it can be interpreted in terms of the changing component abilities hypothesis already discussed. Notice that as the correlation between any two tests (here, trials of a given test) increases, the tests can be said to contain more and more abilities in common. In this way, we can think of the performances as becoming systematically more stable in terms of their underlying ability structure. Alternatively, it can be said that later in practice, learners do not reorder themselves from trial to trial to the same extent that they did earlier in practice.

Practice as a Process of Simplification. As pointed out by Jones (1966), almost every task studied so far has these two characteristics in the intertrial correlation matrices—decreasing correlations with remoteness and increasing correlations for later and later adjacent trials. However, an even more restrictive descriptor of the correlation matrix is what is called the *superdiagonal form*. For a matrix to have this particular form, any four arbitrarily chosen correlations within the matrix must possess a particular mathematical relationship with each other. (A discussion of the nature of this relationship is beyond the scope of this text, but see Jones, 1966 for a discussion.) For Jones, the important point is that this restrictive relationship among correlations is predictable (i.e., can be derived) from the hypothesis that the number of abilities systematically decreases with practice, so that the task comes to depend on just a few abilities at the end of practice.

Integrating Individual Differences and Stages of Learning

A different view from that presented by Jones suggests that early in practice, performing the task should be based on abilities having to do with thinking, reasoning, mechanical knowledge, and so on. Later in practice, these abilities should not be involved, and perhaps abilities such as movement speed, reaction time, strength, steadiness, and the like become the most important. A theory of individual differences that formalizes this view has been developed by Ackerman (1988, 1989, 1990, 1992). In his theory, Ackerman integrates the concept of stages of learning (Anderson, 1982, 1995; Fitts, 1964) with a hierarchical view of abilities.

Ackerman's theory proposes that general intellectual abilities (information-processing skills) are the most important determiners of individual differences in performance during the first phase (the cognitive phase) of skill acquisition. Once the idea of the task has been acquired, the role of general intelligence as a determiner of individual differences drops off; it is replaced by perceptual speed abilities during the associative phase in performance. Individual differences in psychomotor abilities play their most prominent role during the autonomous phase in learning.

Predicting Individual Differences During Different Stages. According to Ackerman's theory, the correlation between tests of intellectual, perceptual speed, and psychomotor abilities will differ during different stages in learning. These predictions are illustrated in the three graphs in figure 13.4. Figure 13.4a suggests that the correlation between individual differences in general intellectual ability and task performance will be highest during the cognitive phase (phase 1) and will drop off quickly thereafter. The correlation between individual differences in perceptual speed tests and task performance is predicted to be low during the cognitive and autonomous stages (phases 1 and 3) but much higher during the associative stage (phase 2), as presented in figure 13.4b. Figure 13.4c depicts very little contribution of individual differences in psychomotor abilities until the autonomous stage (phase 3), at which point increasingly higher correlations are predicted.

Evidence for Ackerman's Integrated Model. In one of a series of experiments, Ackerman asked subjects to perform a simple reaction-time (RT) task for six sessions, during which subjects pressed a key on a numeric keypad in response to the number shown on a screen (e.g., press the "1" key in response to the number "1"). As would be expected, subjects had little difficulty in figuring out what to do in this task, and therefore would be expected to perform as if starting in the phase 2 of practice rather than in phase 1. The correlations of task performance (RT) with measures of general and perceptual speed abilities are presented in figure 13.5. As can be seen, the correlations are higher for perceptual speed ability than for general ability in the training phase, as is predicted for phase 2 performance. Moreover, the general shape of the trend that these correlations take over the six sessions is similar to the predictions illustrated in figure 13.4 for phase 2 of practice.

However, beginning in session 7, Ackerman transferred his subjects from the simple, compatible stimulus-response (S-R) mappings to less compatible mappings in which subjects pressed the key designated by a two-letter abbreviation system; the first letter referred to the numeric keypad *row* (e.g., L = lower row), and the second letter referred to the numeric keypad *column* (e.g., M = middle column). Thus, the stimulus "LM" (lower middle) would indicate that the "2" key should be pressed; a "UR" stimulus (upper right) would denote the "9" key. The rationale here was that this incompatible mapping system would require considerable cognitive activity initially in

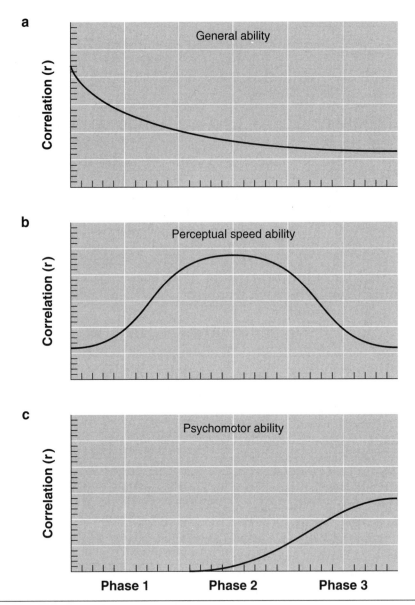

Figure 13.4.   Predicted correlation of individual differences in general intellectual, speed, and psychomotor abilities at different stages of learning.
Reprinted from Ackerman, 1990.

practice, forcing the learner back into phase 1 of practice. As can be seen on the right side of figure 13.5, the correlations between RT performance and the abilities tests were much higher early in transfer for the general ability, but were similar to those for perceptual speed ability later in practice. Again, the shape of these functions over practice in the transfer phase appears rather similar to the predictions seen in figure 13.4 for phase 1 of practice.

These findings provide support for Ackerman's theory. In addition, Ackerman (1988) found support for the psychomotor abilities predictions when reanalyzing some data sets from Fleishman (1956; Fleishman & Hempel, 1955, 1956). These data showed that the correlations between the rate of arm movement (a psychomotor ability) and performance on three different performance tasks *increased* with practice, as predicted by the theory (see also Adams, 1957).

At this point, Ackerman's theory requires more testing using complex motor and perceptual-motor tasks. However, the initial findings appear to be quite promising in terms of identifying how the nature of abilities relates to task performance, and how these abilities change as a function of practice and the conditions under which the tasks are performed.

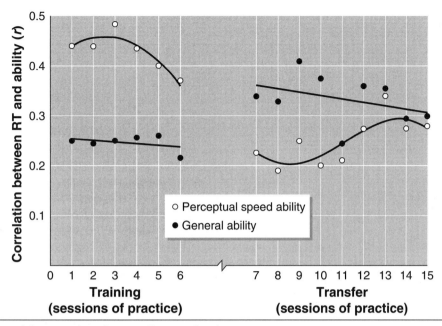

Figure 13.5. Test of theoretical predictions illustrated in figure 13.4.
Adapted from Ackerman, 1988.

Error-Detection Capabilities

It is well known that a major outcome of practice is the capability to produce more effective movement behaviors, but an additional outcome of practice is that learners become more capable of *evaluating* their own movement behaviors. That is, it seems that a learner develops a kind of *error-detection* capability with practice that can then be substituted for augmented feedback to inform the individual about errors.

For example, *juggling* is often considered a difficult motor skill to acquire, and we marvel at the ability of experts to juggle a number of objects over long periods of time without making errors. One of the distinguishing features of expert jugglers seems to be their ability to detect errors in the way that the hand releases the object. If the force is too large or too small (affecting the amplitude of the object thrown), or if the angle of release is slightly off line (affecting the location where it will be caught by the other hand), then adjustments will have to be made in order to maintain the juggling pattern. Beek and Lewbel (1995) have argued that novices and experts differ in what type of information they use and how quickly they detect an error; novices tend to use visual feedback of the object in flight, while experts can tell when an error occurs by monitoring the sensory feedback as the object leaves the hand. Thus, some of the skill differences between novices and experts can be accounted for by the

"advance" information an expert receives indicating that an error has occurred.

Studying the acquisition of error-detection mechanisms in skills is complicated, however, because different types of skills produce different results. A major distinction is between rapid and slow movements, examined next.

Evidence Involving Rapid Movements

Schmidt and White (1972) used a ballistic-timing task in which the subjects were to move a slide 23 cm, with a follow-through, so that the movement time (MT) was as close to 150 ms as possible. The procedure was to have the subject make a movement, then to have the subject guess the MT outcome score in milliseconds, and then to present knowledge of results (KR) in milliseconds. The subject's guess was subtracted from the goal MT and termed *subjective error*. The actual score was subtracted from the goal score and termed *objective error*. The reasoning was that if people acquire an increased capability to detect their own errors with practice, the agreement between the subject's subjective and objective scores should increase. That is, the subjective score should be an increasingly more accurate estimator of the subject's actual performance.

The statistic used to estimate this agreement was based on correlations. For a block of 10 trials, each subject would have 10 objective scores and 10 subjective scores. These pairs of scores were correlated for each subject separately for each of

17 blocks of 10 trials in the experiment. The idea was that, if the error-detection capability was weak, almost no agreement would exist between the objective and subjective errors, and the correlation should be near zero. But if error detection increased in accuracy with practice, then the objective and subjective scores should agree to a greater extent, and the correlation should increase.[1]

The average within-subject correlations are presented in figure 13.6. On the first block, the average correlation was about .28, indicating a relatively weak association between objective and subjective errors. But as practice continued, the average correlation increased to the point that on Day 2 the values approached 1.0. This evidence suggests that the learners became more and more sensitive to their own errors through the development of error-detection processes (see also Rubin, 1978).

How does the performer use the error detection? It is reasonable to assume, based on the information about closed-loop processes presented in chapter 5, that if the movement was rapid (as was the case in Schmidt and White's study), the subject would compare the feedback from the movement to the reference of correctness to define an error after the movement was completed. The error-detection process is not responsible for producing the action, and it evaluates the correctness of the action only *after* the

movement has been completed. For reasons discussed before, there is insufficient time for the performer to take in the feedback, evaluate it, and make corrections before the movement is completed. So the motor program is thought to produce the movements, and the comparison of movement-produced feedback with the learned reference of correctness is responsible for evaluating the movement afterward.

Evidence Involving Slow Movements

This is not so with slow movements. It appears that, for some slow movements at least, the error-detection processes may be responsible for actually producing the action. Because there is ample time to use feedback, it is thought that the subject in a positioning movement evaluates intrinsic feedback against the learned reference of correctness and moves to the position recognized as correct (Adams, 1971). If so, the error-detection capacity, being used to position the limb at the target, cannot then be used again as a basis for telling the experimenter about the error in positioning after the movement. With slow movements, if the subject is asked to report the error in positioning, he or she will have no idea whether or not the movement was on target.

Schmidt and Russell (1974) performed an experiment analogous to that of Schmidt and White but using a slow, linear-positioning task. In contrast to the findings from Schmidt and White

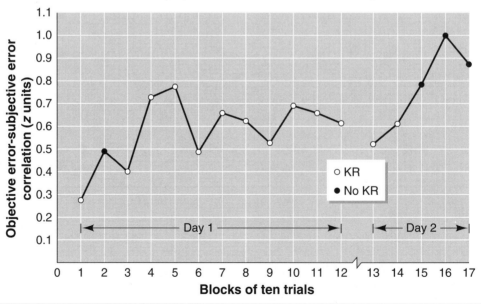

Figure 13.6. Average within-subject correlation between objective and subjective error as a function of practice trials. (Increased correlation is interpreted as gains in capability to detect errors; correlations are transformed to Z′ units.) Reprinted from Schmidt and White, 1972.

(figure 13.6), Schmidt and Russell found consistently low within-subject correlations between objective and subjective errors, with most of the correlations being only about .20, even after 100 trials of practice. These findings suggest that the error-detection processes were used to position the limb in the slow task and that further estimates of error after completion of movement were based largely on guesswork by the subjects (see also Nicholson & Schmidt, 1991). These ideas figure heavily in the concepts of schema theory, presented in the next section of this chapter.

Two Theories of Motor Learning

In the 1970s, two important papers were published on the motor learning process: on *closed-loop theory* (Adams, 1971) and *schema theory* (Schmidt, 1975b). Because of the impact that these theories had on subsequent motor learning research, we describe them in some detail next.

Closed-Loop Theory

Adams (1971) developed his closed-loop theory of motor learning using a well-established set of empirical laws of motor learning, most of which were based on slow, linear-positioning movements. He believed that the principles of performance and learning that applied to these movements were the same as for any other kind of movement and that using a well-established set of empirical laws from positioning movements would produce a solid basis for theorizing.

A Feedback Emphasis

Adams believed that all movements are made by comparing the ongoing feedback from the limbs to a reference of correctness that is learned during practice, termed the *perceptual trace*. When the individual makes a positioning movement, inherent feedback is produced that represents the particular locations of the limb in space. These stimuli "leave a trace" in the central nervous system (hence the name perceptual trace). With repeated movements, the individual comes closer and closer to the target over trials; and on each of the trials another trace is laid down, so that eventually a kind of "collection" of traces develops. Because with KR the learner is responding close to the target after only a few trials, each trial provides feedback that tends to represent the *correct* movement. In turn, the collection of traces

(perceptual trace) comes to represent the feedback qualities of the correct movement. Then, on subsequent trials, the learner moves to that position in space for which the difference between the ongoing feedback produced and the perceptual trace is minimal. Because the perceptual trace is stronger with each KR trial, the errors in performance decrease with practice.

Adams provided a guidance role for KR, although his writings do not use this term. Learners, according to Adams, are not passive recipients of reward, but rather are actively engaged in verbalization and hypothesis formation about the task to be learned. To Adams, KR provides information to solve the motor problem. After a trial, KR is given that provides information about how the next movement should be made to better achieve the task goal. In early learning, the learner uses KR in relation to the perceptual trace to make the movement more precise, so that KR guides the movement to the target on successive trials. In such a view, KR does not produce learning directly. Rather, it creates the appropriate situation (i.e., being on target) so that the actual learning mechanisms can operate (i.e., the movement's feedback producing an increment in "strength" for the perceptual trace).

Adams also sought to explain how learners develop error-detection capabilities. He argued that after the movement was completed, the individual could compare the feedback received against the perceptual trace, the difference representing the error in responding that the person could self-evaluate or report to the experimenter as subjective reinforcement. Presumably, this subjective reinforcement could be used to keep the movement on target without KR; and, according to the theory, keeping the movement on target can provide gains in learning because the feedback continues to add to the perceptual trace, again without KR in later learning.

Contrary to earlier closed-loop theorists, Adams realized that in order for the system to have the capacity to detect its own errors, two memory states must be present—one to produce the action and one to evaluate the outcome. What if the same state that produced the movement also evaluated it? If the movement were chosen incorrectly, the feedback from the movement and the reference of correctness would always match, producing a report of no error on every attempt. In Adams's theory, though, the perceptual trace represents the correct movement, and the movement is selected and initiated by another memory state that Adams called the *memory trace*—a "modest motor program" responsible for choosing the direction of the action, initiating it, and giving it a "shove" toward the target. Then, the perceptual trace takes over the control of the movement to cause it to come to a stop at the final target location.

One of the interesting implications of Adams's theory is that any errors produced during the course of training are harmful to learning. This is the case because when an error is made, the feedback from it is necessarily different from the feedback associated with a correct movement, and the perceptual trace will be degraded a little bit as a result. One prediction, then, is that guidance should be particularly useful as a training method, as it prevents errors.

Limitations and Contradictory Evidence

One characteristic of "good" theories is that there should be no contradictions among the logically derived predictions. Contradiction does appear to exist in Adams's theory, though, regarding subjective reinforcement for *slow* positioning movements. Adams has the perceptual trace providing (a) the basis for placing the limb at the correct target location and (b) a basis for knowing how far that movement was away from the target location after the movement has been completed. Schmidt (1975b) argued that, if the perceptual trace is used to position the limb, then no additional information can be available about the amount of actual error produced. As discussed previously, Schmidt and Russell (1974; Nicholson & Schmidt, 1991) provided evidence that no error-detection mechanism exists after the completion of slow positioning movements, even after 100 trials of practice, contrary to Adams's predictions. However, Schmidt and White (1972; Nicholson & Schmidt, 1991) found strong error-detection mechanisms after *rapid* movements, for which the perceptual trace presumably cannot be used during the movement to guide the limb. Adams does not make a distinction between these fast and slow movements, yet the evidence shows that they develop and use error-detection mechanisms very differently (e.g., Newell, 1976b).

Certainly one of the most damaging lines of evidence with respect to Adams's theory is the work on deafferentation in animals (Taub, 1976)

and humans (Lashley, 1917), reviewed in chapter 6. Organisms deprived of all sensory feedback from the limbs can respond skillfully, and they can even learn new actions (e.g., Taub & Berman, 1968). If the only mechanism for controlling skilled actions involved feedback in relationship to a perceptual trace, then these animals should not have been able to produce the actions they did. Adams (1976b) has countered this argument by saying that the animals may have shifted to some other source of feedback, such as vision, to substitute for the lost sensations from the responding limbs. This may be the case for some of these studies, but it does not apply to all of them (e.g., Polit & Bizzi, 1978, 1979; Taub & Berman, 1968). Also, Adams's theory ignores the data from various species showing the existence of central (spinal) pattern generators—structures apparently capable of causing complex actions without feedback from the responding limbs (for reviews, see Gallistel, 1980; Grillner et al., 1991; Marder & Calabrese, 1996). The failure to recognize the role of open-loop processes in movement control is a serious drawback for Adams's theory.

A second line of evidence against Adams's theory was provided by the literature on variability of practice. Because the perceptual trace is the feedback representation of the correct action, making movements *different* from the correct action (in variable practice) should not increase perceptual-trace strength. Thus, Adams's theory predicts that variability of practice should be less effective for learning the criterion target than is practice at the target itself. In chapter 11 we reviewed this literature and found no clear evidence that variable practice was less effective than practice at the transfer target; and sometimes the evidence said that variability in practice was superior to practicing on the transfer target itself! Because Adams's theory explicitly claims that experience at the target location is critical for the development of the perceptual trace, this evidence is quite damaging to his position.

Summary

At the time Adams's theory was proposed, it represented a major step forward for motor learning, as it presented a plausible, empirically based theory for researchers to evaluate. We believe that such evaluations have shown it to have a number of limitations, as outlined here, and that it no longer accounts for the currently available evidence on motor learning. But the theory served its intended purpose. It generated substantial research and thinking, and it paved the way for newer theories that account for the older data together with newer data.

Schema Theory

Largely because of a dissatisfaction with Adams's theory, Schmidt (1975b) formulated a theory that was considered as a rival to Adams's. The primary concern with Adams's position was the lack of emphasis on open-loop control processes, and the schema theory has a strong open-loop dependency. Yet, at the same time, many aspects of Adams's theory are very appealing, such as the emphasis on subjective reinforcement, the concern for slow movements, and the need to have one memory state that is responsible for producing the movement and another that is responsible for evaluating it. Thus, schema theory borrowed heavily from Adams and others in the hope of keeping the most effective parts and replacing or eliminating defective ones. Also, the theory is based heavily on our knowledge about motor control such as that presented in chapters 5 and 6, and it uses these concepts in conjunction with ideas about learning processes to attempt to explain the learning of both rapid and slower movements (see also Schmidt, 1980).

Two States of Memory: Recall and Recognition

Schema theory holds that there are two states of memory, a *recall memory* responsible for the production of movement and a *recognition memory* responsible for movement evaluation. For rapid, ballistic movements, recall memory is involved with the motor programs and parameters, structured in advance to carry out the movement with minimal involvement from peripheral feedback. Recognition memory, on the other hand, is a sensory system capable of evaluating the movement-produced feedback after the movement is completed, thereby informing the subject about the amount and direction of errors. Such structures satisfy the goal of having the agent that produces the action be different from the agent that evaluates its correctness, one of Adams's main ideas.

In slow positioning movements, recall memory is not thought to have an important role. The major problem for the learner is the comparison between movement-produced feedback and the reference of correctness. In these movements, the recall state merely pushes the limb along in small bursts, with the individual stopping when the movement-produced feedback and the reference of correctness match. Here, the agent that produces the action is the same as the agent that evaluates it; hence no postmovement subjective reinforcement can exist as is the case for rapid movements. We have already presented evidence that rapid movements do, and slow movements do not, provide postmovement subjective reinforcement (Nicholson & Schmidt, 1991; Schmidt, Christenson, & Rogers, 1975).

Schema Learning

The schema concept is an old one in psychology, having been introduced by Head (1926) and later popularized by Bartlett (1932). For these researchers, the schema was an abstract memory representation for events or skilled actions, thought of as a rule, concept, or generalization. Schmidt (1975b) attempted to use the basic idea of the schema (or rule) to form a theory of how skills are learned.

At the heart of Schmidt's view of schema learning is the idea of the generalized motor program, structured with invariant features (such as phasing), with parameters being required in order to specify the particular way that the program is to be executed (see chapter 6 for details). After a movement is made with a generalized motor program, the individual briefly stores four types of information. The first of these is information about the initial conditions (bodily positions, weight of thrown objects, and so on) that existed before the movement. Next, the learner stores the parameters assigned to the generalized motor program. Third, the outcome of the movement in the environment in terms of KR is stored. And, finally, the learner stores the sensory consequences of the movement—how the movement felt, looked, sounded, and so on. These four sources of information are stored only long enough that the performer can abstract some relationships among them. Two such relationships, or schemas, are thought to be formed.

Recall Schema.   The first of these relationships is termed the *recall schema* because it is concerned with movement production. Figure 13.7 represents the kind of process that could be occurring. On the horizontal axis are the outcomes in the

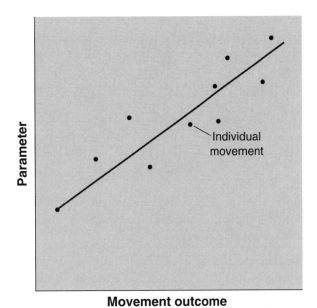

Figure 13.7. The hypothetical relationship between movement outcomes in the environment and the parameters used to produce them.
Adapted from Schmidt, 1982.

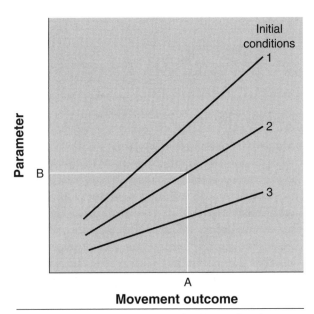

Figure 13.8. The hypothetical relationship between movement outcomes in the environment and the parameters that were used to produce them for various initial conditions: the recall schema.
Adapted from Schmidt, 1982.

environment, such as the distance a softball traveled when it was thrown. On the vertical axis are the parameters that an individual assigned to the motor program. The co-occurrence of the parameter and the movement outcome produces a data point on the graph. With repeated movements using different parameters and producing different outcomes, other data points are established, and the individual begins to define a *relationship* between the size of the parameter and the nature of the movement outcome; this relationship is represented by the *regression line* drawn through the points. With each successive movement using the program, a new data point is produced and the relationship is refined slightly. After each of these adjustments, the stored data are "thrown away," so all that remains of the movement is the rule, called the recall schema.

But this is not the entire story. The relationship also includes information about the initial conditions of the movement, shown in figure 13.8. Here, the relationship between the parameters used and the outcome produced will depend on the nature of the initial conditions, such as different objects to be thrown. These different initial conditions are represented as different regression lines in figure 13.8.

How does the individual use the recall schema? On a future trial using this generalized motor program, the person notes the desired environ-

mental outcome, labeled point A on figure 13.8. Also, the particular initial conditions are noted (e.g., the weight of the object to be thrown), which might fit into the category represented by the second line. Then, with use of the relationship established by past experience, the rule is employed to select the parameter that will come closest to accomplishing the particular environmental outcome, labeled point B. The value of this parameter is then applied to the program to produce the action.

Recognition Schema. The recognition schema, for movement evaluation, is thought to be formed and used in a similar way (figure 13.9). Here the schema is composed of the relationship between the initial conditions, the environmental outcomes, and the *sensory consequences*. This relationship is represented as the three lines shown in the figure.

The recognition schema is thought to be used in a way analogous to that for the recall schema. Before the movement, the individual selects a movement outcome and determines the nature of the initial conditions. Then, with the recognition schema, the person can estimate the sensory consequences that will occur if that movement outcome is produced. These, called the *expected sensory consequences* (labeled point C), serve as the basis for movement evaluation. The expected sensory consequences are analogous to Adams's perceptual trace.

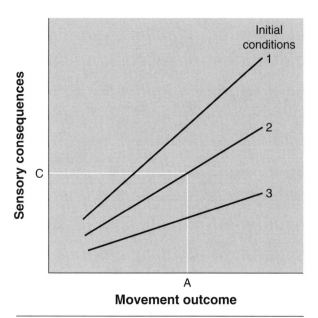

Figure 13.9. The hypothetical relationship between movement outcomes in the environment and the sensory consequences produced for various initial conditions: the recognition schema.
Adapted from Schmidt 1982.

Some Predictions About Schema Learning

The theory says that we learn skills by learning *rules* about the functioning of our bodies—forming relationships between how our muscles are activated, what they actually do, and how those actions feel. Thus, movements for which any of the four stored elements are missing will result in degraded learning of the rules. One of the most critical is movement outcome information (or KR); if the person does not receive information about the movement outcome (from KR or other sources), then even if the other features are present, no strengthening of the schema can occur because the location on the horizontal axis will not be known. Similarly, if sensory consequences are missing (e.g., as in temporary deafferentation), then no recognition schema development can occur. In passive movements, no parameters are issued to the program (indeed, no program is to be run off), so no recall schema updating can occur. Also, according to schema theory, there are positive benefits from the production of movements whether they are correct or not. This is so because the schema is the rule based on the relationship among all stored elements, and this relationship is present just as much for incorrect movements as for correct ones. Adams's theory, you may remember, views errors as disruptive, as they degrade the perceptual trace.

Variability of Practice.   The theory predicts that practicing a variety of movement outcomes with the same program (i.e., by using a variety of parameters) will provide a widely based set of experiences upon which a rule or schema can be built. When the range of movement outcomes and parameters is small, all the data points such as those shown in figure 13.7 are clustered in one place, and less certainty exists about the placement of the line. When a *new* movement is required, greater error will occur in estimating the proper parameters, expected sensory consequences, or both. Shapiro and Schmidt (1982) found considerable evidence that practice variability is a positive factor in motor learning, especially for children's motor learning (see Variability of Practice, chapter 11).

Novel Movements.   A particular movement outcome (specified by a particular value of the parameter) need not have been produced previously in order to be produced in the future. This is so because the basis for producing a new movement is a *rule* about parameter selection based on the performance of earlier similar movements. Research has shown that, after varied practice, novel movements can be produced about as accurately as they can be if the novel movement had been practiced repeatedly, and sometimes *more* accurately. This evidence suggests that motor learning may be primarily rule-learning and not the learning of specific movements. These kinds of effects seem particularly strong in open skills, for which the movements are never repeated exactly on two consecutive trials. Such ideas have been used for a long time in movement education situations with children, where the pupils are presumably developing a set of rules or schemas about their motor behaviors, and consequently being helped to be more proficient performers in novel situations in the future (Nicholson & Schmidt, 1991; Schmidt, 1976b, 1977).

Error Detection.   Schema theory predicts that there should be no capability for error detection after a slow movement, whereas such capability should exist after a rapid movement. This is the case because the error-detection capability is actually used to produce the slow movement, leaving behind no capability with which to detect errors. As mentioned during the discussion of Adams's theory, empirical evidence supports this kind of prediction (Schmidt & Russell, 1974; Schmidt & White, 1972).

Knowledge-of-Results Frequency. Strengthening of the schema depends on the subject's knowledge of the movement outcome, so higher levels of KR relative frequency would be expected to enhance schema learning as compared to lower levels. At first glance, however, when relative KR frequency effects on overall learning were evaluated in chapter 12, the results appeared to contradict the schema theory prediction because reduced frequencies either had no effect on learning or in some cases enhanced it, rather than degrading it. However, when the effects of parameter versus program learning have been separated, experimenters have found that the main prediction does hold: increased relative frequency of KR does appear to enhance parameter learning (Wulf & Schmidt, 1996; Wulf, Schmidt, & Deubel, 1993).

Limitations and Logical Problems

One major strength (and limitation) of the theory relates to the emphasis on the generalized motor program. While we believe that the evidence strongly supports such a motor-program view (see chapter 6), the entire structure is vague in terms of how the program is formed in the first place, how the rules about parameters and sensory consequences are developed and used, how the individual makes the first movement before any schema can exist, why reduced KR frequencies degrade parameter learning but enhance program learning, and so on. Also, if in the future the generalized motor program idea were shown to be incorrect, so too would schema theory be, as the theory depends strongly on it.

The theory seems well suited to the explanation of novel movements, particularly in situations involving those skills classified as open. But what about the learning that goes on within motor learning experiments? This is one of the most important experimental outcomes that must be explained by a theory of learning. Here, the theory says that the schema changes radically with each practice trial so that the parameters come to be chosen more effectively with practice. This is inconsistent with the idea that the schema is a stable rule established over the course of many years, however.

Summary

Schema theory has provided an alternative to Adams's closed-loop theory of motor learning. Compared to Adams's theory, it has the advantage that it accounts for more kinds of movements, it seems to account for error-detection capabilities more effectively, and it seems to explain the production of novel movements in open-skills situations. Some logical problems need to be solved, and it is not clear that this can be done without discarding the entire theoretical structure. There are some apparent failures of the evidence to agree with the theoretical predictions as well (e.g., Klein, Levy, & McCabe, 1984). While the theory was a step forward, it should be clear that it does not provide a complete understanding of the data on motor learning. Even so, the theory provides a useful framework for thinking about skill learning, because it is consistent with the literature on the generalized motor program.

Differing Theoretical Perspectives of Motor Learning

The ideas presented next are probably best described as hypotheses about the learning of motor skills. They really do not satisfy the basic criteria for consideration as *theories* for a number of reasons. First, many of them are directed at only certain kinds of tasks, such as continuous tasks, positioning tasks, and tracking; and more generality is usually required for a theory. As well, many of these ideas concern only a few experimental variables, and theories (such as closed-loop theory and schema theory) are usually thought to have more complete structures that are capable of explaining the effects of a variety of independent variables. Nevertheless, the theoretical perspectives that we consider next represent important advances in furthering our understanding of the complex interaction of processes involved in motor learning.

Hierarchical Control Perspectives

As people learn, at least with some tasks, a shift occurs in the method of motor control to progressively "lower" levels in the nervous system. The idea that motor behavior is hierarchical means that some higher level in the system is responsible for decision making and some lower level is responsible for carrying out the decisions. With respect to the information-processing analysis, the decision-making processes of the system are considered to be "higher" in the hierarchy than the motor programming apparatus. The hierarchical control model goes on to say that with practice, control is systematically *shifted* from the "higher" to the "lower" levels in the system.

Pew (1966) used a task in which the subject watched a screen and controlled the movement of a dot on it by pressing one or the other of two buttons. Pressing the right button caused the dot to accelerate to the right, and the acceleration could be halted and reversed by pressing the left button, which caused acceleration to the left. Without pressing any buttons, the dot accelerated off the screen in one direction or another. The subject's task was to keep the dot in the center.

In figure 13.10 is a record from one of the subjects, with the velocity and position of the dot shown for early and late practice. In early practice (figure 13.10a), the subject was making about three button presses per second, and the dot was never positioned near the center of the screen for very long. The mode of control seems to be that the subject pressed the button, waited for the feedback from the screen, decided that the dot was accelerating off the screen, then planned a movement to reverse it, pressed the button, and so on. Here, the subject is using the executive (e.g., the information-processing stages) level predominantly, so that the highest level in the system is consistently involved in the production of every movement.

Compare figure 13.10a to figure 13.10b, which is from the same subject but later in practice. Here the motor behavior is quite different. First, the rate of responding is much faster, about eight movements per second. Next, the dot is much closer to the target, because the button was pressed

to reverse the direction of the dot before the dot got very far away from the target. Although we cannot be absolutely certain, the mode of control appears to have changed. It appears that now a long string of movements is prestructured as a unit, perhaps governed by a motor program. Thus, each of the button presses is not controlled by a separate decision from the executive level. Pew viewed this finding as evidence for the hypothesis that with practice, the subject shifted the control from an executive-based level to the lower level control of the motor program, freeing the decision mechanism for other activities and making the movement more effective.

It is easy to see the advantages of shifting the control from the decision-making level to the motor program level. Foremost is the freeing of the attentional mechanisms for use on higher order aspects of the task (e.g., strategy), for doing other simultaneous tasks, or for simply resting so that the organism does not become fatigued. This freeing of attention is one of the major events that occur when people learn, and it is discussed further in the next sections.

Making Movements Automatic

Since a century ago (e.g., James, 1890), the idea of automaticity has been that, as a by-product of learning, skilled performers become able to perform with minimal attention cost and minimal interference from other cognitive information-processing activities. In chapter 4, we qualified this basic idea considerably, saying that "automatic" responding appears to involve a lack of

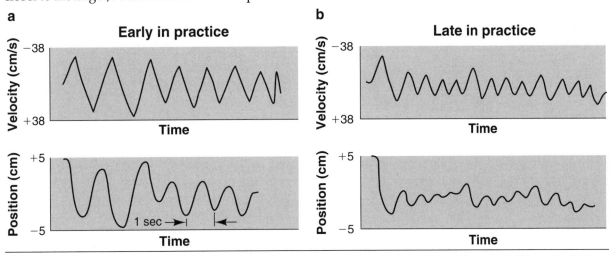

Figure 13.10. Performance records from a button-press tracking task in early (a) and late (b) practice. (Top records show instantaneous velocity, and bottom records show position with target represented as zero; responding is more rapid and more accurate in later practice.)
Reprinted from Pew, 1966.

interference with respect to particular secondary tasks; the notion that a given task is interference free for all secondary tasks is not supported by the evidence (Neumann, 1987). However, it does seem likely that the interference from many simultaneous cognitive information-processing activities is decreased, or even eliminated, with practice, thus freeing the individual to engage in other higher order aspects of the task, such as planning strategies in tennis, or form and style in music and dance.

Automaticity can be considered in essentially two ways. First, and most common, is the idea that specialized information-processing structures are learned with practice and that they handle portions of the processing requirements of the overall task, such as feature detection and movement selection (e.g., Logan, 1988; Neumann, 1987; Schneider & Fisk, 1983; Schneider & Shiffrin, 1977; Shiffrin & Schneider, 1977). Each of these processes can occur when the appropriate stimulus conditions are presented, and is essentially triggered into action without awareness; indeed, sometimes the process cannot even be prevented (Schneider, 1985). By handling information processing in this way, the performer decreases the interference with other cognitive activities that compete for the common resources. If in a given task all these processes can be so acquired, then the task can be thought of as "automatic," in that the entire movement can occur without interference from particular groups of secondary tasks. In this view, the organism does not decrease the amount of environmental information processing that must be accomplished; rather, it processes this information via specialized structures more quickly and with less interference from other simultaneous tasks.

However, another view is possible (see Schmidt, 1987). In at least some kinds of tasks that are predictable and stereotyped, a major process of learning appears to be a shift from high-level conscious control to a lower level programming control, as discussed in the previous section. With predictable tasks, the regularities of the environmental information can be learned and therefore can be anticipated during performance. If so, then the person does not have to process this information directly, but rather preprograms long sequences of movement based on the prediction of the environmental information. Musicians "memorize" sheet music so that they are not

dependent on it, and experienced drivers no longer have to watch their feet as they move from accelerator to brake in the car. Thus, being able to avoid processing environmental information frees those (conscious) information-processing activities for other tasks and makes the task appear "automatic," at least with respect to particular kinds of activities. In this view, the individual does not necessarily process information any more effectively or faster, but rather learns to avoid having to process information by shifting to motor programming modes of control.

Of course, it could be that both of these viewpoints are correct but that each is relevant for a different class of movement tasks (e.g., those that have predictable, and those that have unpredictable, environmental information). Even within a particular skill, one can imagine specialized structures for detecting environmental information; then long sequences of preprogrammed output could be generated that reduce the reliance on such information for the next few hundred milliseconds. Both viewpoints provide ways of conceptualizing the acquisition of "automaticity" in high-level motor learning, and they present interesting issues for research in skills.

Creating Motor Programs

Of course, we know that many changes occur in our programmed movements when they are subjected to practice, with actions tending to become more consistent, smoother, less effortful, and more routine or automatic with experience. These are all powerful changes, and in the next sections we consider some of the experimental evidence for them.

The Acquisition of Movement Pattern Consistency. One important change in movement behavior with practice is that the movement outcomes tend to become more consistent, predictable, and certain with experience. Recall that the measure of variable error (chapter 2) was designed to capture this aspect of motor behavior. But in addition, the movement behavior that produces these outcomes tends to become more smooth, stereotyped, stable, and consistent. In the study of these phenomena, the patterns of movement are measured by various kinematic procedures (e.g., video analysis, position-time records, computer simulation). Changes in the trial-to-trial consistency of these measures has been noted in an impressive variety of tasks such as driving (Lewis, 1956), throwing (Stimpel, 1933), handwheel cranking (Glencross, 1973), table tennis (Tyldesley & Whiting, 1975), tracking (Darling & Cooke, 1987; Franks & Wilberg, 1984), keyboarding (Salthouse, 1986), bimanual coordination (Lee, Swinnen, & Verschueren, 1995), and many others. Such generalizations perhaps seem fairly obvious in closed skills, which have as a major goal the production of a consistent action in a stable environment. However, Tyldesley and Whiting (1975) showed that world-class table tennis players have highly consistent movement patterns even when the location and velocity of the ball are changed from trial to trial. These changes in movement pattern consistency probably represent some of the most persistent phenomena in the motor learning area.

Exploiting the Mechanical-Inertial Properties of the Limbs. Another important change that occurs with practice is the alteration of movement control so that the motor system can *take advantage of* (or exploit) the built-in mechanical-inertial properties of the limbs. This notion is tied strongly to mass-spring control, discussed in chapter 7, in which certain springlike properties of the limb system can be used to the performer's advantage to reduce the need for complex computations and information processing, to reduce energy costs, or to make the movement faster and more forceful. This is an old idea, expressed by Bernstein in 1947 (translated in 1967).

Recently, Schneider et al. (1989) have studied this question using film analysis of rapid three-joint arm movements together with a biomechanical analysis that allowed the estimation of torques in each of the participating joints. Near the middle of this maximum-speed movement, the subject was required to reverse his hand movement at a target, at which the arm was briefly extended upward at about 45°. Early in practice, the subjects tended to use a shoulder flexion torque at the target (reversal point), as if they were holding their arm up against gravity. But later in practice, the shoulder flexion torque tended to drop out, to be replaced by an *extension* torque. Now the limb appeared to be "thrown" at the target, to be "caught" by the shoulder *extensors* in order to reverse its direction and bring it back down quickly. Certainly, the structure of the motor program had changed markedly across practice, employing systematically different muscle groups for essentially the same set of positions

early and late in practice. There were many other changes in movement trajectories and in the forces produced as well. The interpretation was that the motor system learned to use various passive inertial properties of the system, and that the benefit could be realized not only in terms of increased speed but also in terms of decreased energy costs. These studies clearly support Bernstein's hypothesis and reveal many interesting changes that occur in the movement-control processes over the course of learning.

The Acquisition of Sequencing: The Gearshift Analogy. Another hierarchical change in movement control with practice involves the ways in which movements are sequenced. Keele (1976) suggested that motor programs might be generated by stringing together smaller programmed units of behavior so that eventually this string of behavior is controllable as a single unit—such as in learning to shift gears in a car. As you probably remember, the act of shifting gears when you were first learning was a slow, jerky, step-by-step process; you lifted your foot from the accelerator, then depressed the clutch, and then moved the shift lever (probably in three distinct movements as well), until the entire act was completed (or until the car rolled to a stop going up a hill). Contrast this behavior to that of a race car driver, who shifts gears in a single, rapid action. Not only does the movement occur much more quickly, but also the elements of the action are performed with precise timing, and the actions of the hands and both feet are coordinated in relatively complex ways. In relation to the behavior of the early learner, the action seems to be controlled in a very different way, perhaps as a single programmed unit.

Keele suggested that the various elements are learned in a progressive way to form the entire action. Figure 13.11 is a diagram of how this might work. Assume there are seven elements in the entire sequence and that these are at first controlled one at a time, each by a separate motor program. With some practice, the first two elements might come to be controlled as a single unit, the next three elements could compose another unit, and the last two could compose a third. Finally, with considerable experience, the entire sequence might be controlled as a single unit. This view is of a type of hierarchical control in that it specifies how the program is structured from the beginning, progressively growing in

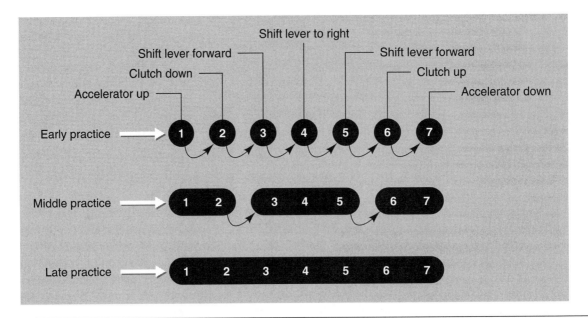

Figure 13.11.   The gearshift analogy. (Initially, seven elements are each controlled by separate programs; later, they become grouped so that they are organized into a few units or even into a single unit.) (Adapted from Keele, 1976, personal communication.)

length by adding parts. Other possibilities exist as well (Marteniuk & Romanow, 1983).

We should be able to see evidence of the changes in these structures by using a fundamental principle of variability: the variability (inconsistency) of the elements *within* a unit should be considerably smaller than the variability between units. In figure 13.11 (middle practice), if we were to measure the interval from the end of element 2 to the beginning of element 3, the variability of this interval from trial to trial would be greater than the variability from the end of element 3 to the beginning of element 4. This is the case because the first two elements (2 and 3) are in different units (controlled by different programs), while the latter two (3 and 4) are supposedly in the same program. Turning this logic around, if we found intervals in the sequence in which variability was very high, this could be taken as evidence that the behaviors occurring at the opposite ends of this interval of time are members of different motor programs. This is essentially the method used by Young and Schmidt (1990, 1991) and Schmidt et al. (in press) to investigate the acquisition of new bimanual coordination programs (see also chapter 8).

Combinations of Reflexes.   Another way that motor programs are thought to be formed in practice is through the combination of funda-

mental reflexes (Easton, 1972, 1978). According to this viewpoint, higher levels in the motor system are capable of tuning or adjusting lower spinal levels so that the existing reflexes (e.g., the stretch reflex) can be controlled in ways that result in skilled actions. Thus, rather than hypothesizing that the motor system builds a set of commands that come to exist as a stored motor program, Easton held that the "commands" are really ways of controlling the preexisting reflexes. Such emphases on reflexes are also seen in the views of Fukuda (1961) and Hellebrandt et al. (1956), as discussed in chapter 5; but here, while the reflexes are thought to be of assistance to the overall programmed action when increased force or speed is required, they are not the fundamental basis of it. But Easton's viewpoint also has a great deal in common with the ideas of Greene (1972), Turvey (1977), and others, all of whom argue that rapid movements consist of controlling structures that are constrained to act as a single unit, perhaps by tuning of spinal systems or by utilization of reflexes.

Progression-Regression Hypothesis

Of particular relevance to tracking tasks is a hypothesis presented by Fitts et al. (1959) about how changes in motor behavior occur with practice. In many tracking movements, both in the laboratory and in the outside world, the movements of the track to be followed are made up of a number of components that can be described according to the physical principles of motion. At the simplest level is the position of the track at any moment. The next most complex aspect of the track is its velocity at any moment. A third and yet more complex aspect of the track is its acceleration at any moment. In designing servo systems to regulate some mechanical system, engineers can devise a simple system that responds only to the position of the track, a system that responds to the position and velocity, or a highly complex system that responds to the position, velocity, and acceleration. With each increase in number of components being tracked, progressive increases are required in the complexity and expense of the mechanical or electronic devices that are to track them.

The *progression-regression hypothesis* for humans presented by Fitts et al. (1959) holds that when the learner practices a tracking task, a progression develops in the learner's behavior in the direction of acting more and more like a complex tracking system. Early in practice, the person responds only to the simplest elements of the display (position). With increased practice, the learner becomes able to use velocity information, and even later comes to use information about acceleration as well. The regression portion of the hypothesis refers to what happens to the learner under stressful conditions or when forgetting of the movement has occurred (perhaps as a result of a long layoff). According to the hypothesis, the person regresses to a simpler level of control (from acceleration to velocity, or from velocity to position), with systematically reduced accuracy as a consequence. Thus, the hierarchical nature of learning involves moving between levels of more or less complex information.

A number of experimenters have studied learning in tracking tasks with respect to the progression-regression hypothesis. Fuchs (1962) found that the role of position cues in tracking decreased with practice, while the role of acceleration cues increased; and these effects were reversed when a secondary task was added to induce stress (see also Garvey, 1960). More recently, researchers have improved on the methods used in the earlier work and have provided additional evidence for a shift in movement control consistent with the hypothesis (Hah & Jagacinski, 1994; Jagacinski & Hah, 1988; Marteniuk & Romanow, 1983). At least for track-

ing tasks, learners appear to respond to systematically different aspects of the track with practice and to reverse these trends with stress. We should be careful not to go too far with these conclusions, because we have no independent way of knowing exactly which stimuli were being used here. But the evidence is certainly consistent with the progression-regression hypothesis, and it contributes to an understanding of the hierarchical nature of the underlying changes in motor control when skill is achieved with practice or reduced under stress or with forgetting. Much more could be done on this topic.

Dynamical Pattern Perspectives

In contrast to the hierarchical control perspective, which is based largely on concepts such as *representations* (e.g., motor programs), the dynamical control perspective uses concepts that are rooted in biological and physical systems research (see chapter 8). Recall that the term "dynamics," as used by proponents of this perspective, refers to patterns of motion that may change over time. In this section on learning, dynamics takes on two meanings: it implies a system that can change both *temporarily* and *permanently.* The dynamical approach is not just one perspective, as there are several variants, representing many different levels of analysis of the moving system. Some of these, such as neural network modeling (Jordan, 1990; Kawato & Gomi, 1992) and evidence from brain imaging techniques (reviewed by Worringham, Smiley-Oyen, & Cross, 1996), are beyond the scope of this discussion.

The fundamental similarity among the dynamical conceptualizations of learning is in the idea that control *emerges* as the result of an interaction between the component parts of the body and the environment, and that it *changes* as a result of that interaction as well. The concept of a central executive, which was important for the hierarchical control perspective, plays virtually no role in the dynamical pattern perspective. As presented in chapter 8, the key concept of this perspective relates to the ways in which it solves the *degrees of freedom problem*. In this chapter we focus on hypotheses about the *process* by which the problem is solved.

Solving the Degrees of Freedom Problem

Suppose you were asked to make an overhand ball throw such that the ball landed as far away as possible, but as close as possible to a straight line that ran in the direction of the throw. Although you could probably perform the task well with the dominant arm, such a performance would be characterized as very unskilled when performed with the nondominant limb. In all likelihood, your performance would be characterized by a body motion that severely restricted the range of motion of each of the limb's joint angles. The body motion would probably be described as much more fixed and restricted than the fluid action of the body's motion when the throw was performed with the dominant arm. This example characterizes an important concept of learning initiated by the work of Bernstein (1967; see chapter 1). The concept is that learning involves a process of *solving the degrees of freedom problem*—figuring out ways in which the independent parts of the moving body can be organized in order to achieve a task goal.

Releasing Degrees of Freedom.   Bernstein suggested that early in practice the learner attempts to "freeze" as many of the degrees of freedom as possible, allowing as few as possible of the body parts to move independently. With practice, more and more of the degrees of freedom are "thawed out"—individual body parts appear to move either with more independence or with a different dependency. In the throwing example, one possible strategy for the nondominant limb would be to *fix* or limit the degrees of freedom, thus achieving a crude, low level of success at the task. Bernstein suggested that with learning, the biomechanical constraints on the degrees of freedom are replaced with flexible mechanisms of neural constraints that allow both for greater independent motion and for a higher level of success.

Bernstein's introspections about the learning process have received support from a number of investigators, who have addressed the releasing of degrees of freedom in different ways. In one study (Vereijken et al., 1992), subjects practiced a ski simulator task in which they were required to use whole-body movements in order to move a platform from side to side over curved metal rails

Figure 13.12.   The ski simulator apparatus.
Reprinted from Vereijken, Whiting, and Beek, 1992.

(see figure 13.12). The sides of the platform were anchored to a frame by rubber springs; when the springs were subjected to force from the "skier," the platform would oscillate from one side of the frame to the other. Subjects practiced this task over 7 days, attempting to produce large-amplitude displacements of the platform.

Changes in the movement of the platform and some of the kinematic measures of performance are presented in figure 13.13. Pretest amplitude measures showed that subjects had difficulty in moving the platform (figure 13.13a, top), although these small amplitudes were made with relatively high frequency (figure 13.13a, bottom). In figure 13.13b we can see that these pretest platform movements had been made with quite *restricted* angular movements of the hip, knee, and ankle. Subjects seemed to be "freezing" the range of motion of the lower limb and trunk in order to get some movement of the platform. By the end of the first day of practice, the range of motion of each of the joints had been extended considerably, resulting in much larger amplitudes of the platform but at a cost of a reduced frequency. By the end of the seventh day of practice, oscillation frequency had increased dramatically, and there were further increases in amplitudes and joint ranges of motion. Thus, greater success in displacement and frequency of platform oscillations were achieved with much more fluid motion of the lower limbs and trunk—supporting Bernstein's suggestion that practice results in a release of the degrees of freedom

(Vereijken, Whiting, & Beek, 1992; see also Arutyunyan, Gurfinkel, & Mirskii, 1968, 1969; Newell, van Emmerik, & Sprague, 1993).

Reorganizing Degrees of Freedom. Another key concept suggested by Bernstein was that independent degrees of freedom are assembled into functional units that are constrained to act together. When two or more independently moving degrees of freedom "combine" to perform as one functional movement, we can say that the independent parts are coupled—they act as *coordinative structures* (or *functional synergies*) to influence the independent parts to work as if they were a single unit. You see an example of coupling independent degrees of freedom when you try the task of rubbing your stomach while patting your head. In this task you are asking the two limbs to perform two different actions. How does your motor system deal with this task? Most likely, if you have never practiced the task before, you will find it difficult because of the strong tendency to perform two similar actions—either patting both the head and the stomach or rubbing both (chapter 8). However, research suggests that with practice, you can overcome the tendency to move these parts together.

A series of studies that demonstrated the effects of practice has been conducted by Walter and Swinnen (1992, 1994; Swinnen et al., 1993; Swinnen et al., 1990b). Subjects were asked to simultaneously initiate rapid, discrete actions of the left

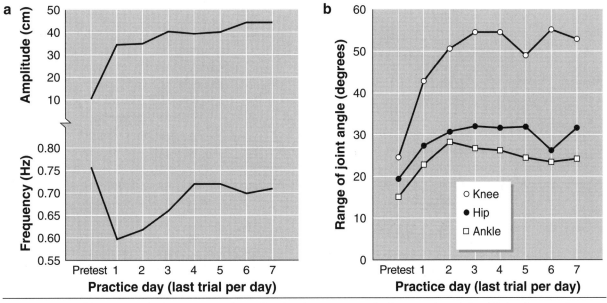

Figure 13.13. Changes in the frequency and amplitude of movements during practice of the ski simulator task. Adapted from Vereijken, Van Emmerik, Whiting, and Newell, 1992.

and right limbs. The left arm moved a lever toward the body with a single, rapid elbow flexion movement. The right arm also moved a lever toward the body. However, midway through the movement the right arm was required to reverse the direction of movement twice. Thus, the subject's task was to simultaneously produce a unidirectional, flexion movement of the left arm and a flexion-extension-flexion movement of the right arm (figure 8.8).

As with the task of rubbing your stomach while patting your head, Walter and Swinnen found that subjects tended to perform similar actions with the two limbs: there was a *less* pronounced reversal for the limb that the subject intended to reverse, and there was evidence of a reversal in the limb that the subject did *not* intend to reverse (Swinnen, Walter, & Shapiro, 1988). Thus, neither of the limb movements was performed as intended. Rather the functional unit was of two limbs performing similar, albeit hybrid actions of the individual goals, as indexed by high correlation of the kinematics of the two limbs.

Learning was viewed in terms of the success with which each limb performed its own goal. Experiments showed that learning occurred with practice, and that it was enhanced if supplemented with augmented feedback (Swinnen et al., 1990b; Swinnen et al., 1993). Learning was also enhanced under *adapted* conditions, whereby the actions were performed slowly at first and then gradually with increased speed (Walter & Swinnen, 1992). Related findings have been provided in experiments involving the acquisition of handwriting skills (Newell & van Emmerik, 1989) and dart throwing (McDonald, van Emmerik, & Newell, 1989), as well as in bimanual aiming tasks involving asymmetric amplitudes (Sherwood, 1990; Sherwood & Canabal, 1988).

One interpretation of these findings is that by overcoming the existing coupling of degrees of freedom, the limbs are somehow *uncoupled* in a way that allows them to move more or less independently. However, this represents the source of some controversy, as others have shown that learning a new bimanual pattern actually results in an *increased* dependence between the hands: that learning results in the development of new bimanual generalized motor programs involving tight, complex linkages between the limbs (Schmidt et al., in press). This controversy is complicated by the evidence that the rapidity of the movement task has a large role in the control

and learning of coordinated actions (chapter 8). More research is needed to address these issues.

Learning New Bimanual Relative-Phasing Patterns

In chapter 8 we presented evidence that there are two preferred coordination patterns by which continuous oscillations of two limbs or fingers can be reliably produced—*in-phase* and *anti-phase* coordination (the observed coordination pattern is measured in terms of the phase lag between the individual cycles; 0° or 180° in these two instances). Of course, theoretically, there are an infinite number of bimanual coordination patterns that could be produced. Without practice, none of these are as stable as the in-phase and anti-phase patterns (Yaminishi, Kawato, & Suzuki, 1980). But research suggests that new patterns can be learned, leading to a number of important issues about the learning process as a consequence (Kelso, 1995; Lee, Swinnen, & Verschueren, 1995; Schöner, Zanone, & Kelso, 1992; Zanone & Kelso, 1992, 1994).

One important advantage of this research is that it provides a means to examine changes in the acquisition of a new pattern relative to the performance (and any changes in performance) of the existing coordination patterns. As we have argued many times already, new skills are built upon previously acquired capabilities. However, discovering the nature of existing capabilities has been difficult, and many experimenters therefore have attempted to avoid the issue by developing novel motor tasks that were as *dissimilar* as possible to any existing skills that a subject might possess. However, the bimanual coordination experiments by Zanone and Kelso introduced a means of exploiting both the existing and acquired capabilities in their experimental design.

In one experiment (Zanone & Kelso, 1992), subjects attempted to coordinate the relative phasing (see chapters 2 and 8) of the index fingers on both hands by rhythmically oscillating them in time to two blinking lights, which alternated in 90° relative phase. Before, during, and after each of five days of practice, Zanone and Kelso had subjects perform a type of transfer test in which the visual metronomes started by blinking simultaneously (in 0° relative phase) and then increased in phase offset by 15° after every 20 s until 180° relative phase had been reached.

The main finding was that the 90° pattern was learned and became relatively stable with practice. An unexpected finding, though, was that some subjects showed a *reduced* stability for the anti-phase (180°) pattern as practice accumulated on the 90° pattern. This finding provided support for Zanone and Kelso's argument that learning does not involve simply adding a new element, capability, or skill to a subject's repertoire. Rather, learning occurs against the background of an individual's *intrinsic dynamics*, resulting not only in the acquisition of new patterns but also in a change in the stable patterns themselves.

The Zanone and Kelso finding is a controversial one, as one implication could be that new learning may result in unlearning of previously acquired skills. Other studies using the research strategy introduced by Zanone and Kelso suggest that the destabilization of the anti-phase pattern is only a performance bias, not a permanent destabilization in performance (Fontaine, Lee, & Swinnen, 1997; Lee, Swinnen, & Verschueren, 1995). However, much more research needs to be done to investigate these and related learning predictions based on the dynamical pattern perspective (see Kelso, 1995; Zanone & Kelso, 1994).

Summary

The empirical laws of motor learning presented in previous chapters are the focus of hypotheses or theories that are directed at explaining them, and this chapter presents some of the more important of these formulations. A preliminary analysis of skill learning shows learning to be an ongoing process that is probably not ever completed, with performance improvements following a logarithmic "law of practice." Learners appear to pass through various phases when acquiring a skill: a *cognitive phase* in which emphasis is on discovering what to do, an *associative phase* in which the concern is with perfecting the movement patterns, and an *autonomous phase* in which the attentional requirements of the movement appear to be reduced or even eliminated.

A major direction for understanding skill learning has been provided by the individual-differences tradition. A significant finding is that the set of abilities underlying a skill appears to change with practice, so that the abilities underlying a skill are systematically different in practiced and unpracticed subjects. The change is in the direction of less involvement of cognitive abilities and greater involvement of motor abilities with practice. These characteristics of abilities and learning provide insight into why the accurate prediction of high-level motor behavior is so difficult to achieve.

Two major theories of motor learning are *closed-loop theory* and *schema theory*. Closed-loop theory holds that the learner acquires a reference of correctness (called the *perceptual trace*) through practice and that the improvements in skill result from the increased capability of the performer to use the reference in closed-loop control. Schema theory is based on the idea that slow movements are feedback-based, with rapid movements being program-based; with learning, the subject develops rules (or schemas) that allow for the generation of novel movements. Both theories can claim a number of lines of experimental support, but neither is capable of explaining all the variable evidence on motor learning.

Two other theoretical perspectives have spawned a number of hypotheses about the learning process. The *hierarchical control perspective* holds that the control of the skill is systematically shifted from higher level control processes to lower level processes involving motor programming. Motor programs are assumed to be constructed through practice, but it is not known how much structuring occurs. As well, there is an increase in the capability of learners to detect their own errors, leading to subjective reinforcement that can be a substitute for KR. The *dynamical control perspective* rejects the concept of an executive that controls movement. Performance and learning emerge as the result of an interaction among the degrees of freedom involved in moving. Releasing and reorganizing degrees of freedom are two processes that accompany practice. The examination of humans who are learning new patterns of relative phasing is a method that offers many new possibilities for future research in this area.

Note

[1] Other statistics have been used to estimate error-detection capabilities as well, such as the absolute error between objective and subjective scores (Newell, 1974) and signal detection analyses (Rubin, 1978).

RETENTION AND TRANSFER

To this point the major concern has been with the variables, principles, and processes related to the acquisition of motor skills. To be able to perform a skill well enough to call it "learned" is only one part of the problem, however, as usually a strong need exists to perform the skill at some time in the future—hopefully without having to relearn it from the original levels of performance. Such concerns about how well skills are retained over time are of both theoretical and practical importance—theoretical because of the need to understand how the motor system is structured so that skills can be produced "on demand," and practical because usually much time and effort have gone into the learning of the skills, and we need to know how such investments can be protected from loss. So this chapter is about the empirical relationships and principles concerned with *retention* and *transfer*.

Fundamental Distinctions and Definitions

You may have the impression that motor learning and motor memory are two different aspects of the problem, one having to do with gains in skills, the other with maintenance. This is so because memory is often thought of by psychologists and others as a place where information is stored. Statements like "I have a good memory for names and dates," or "The subject placed the phone number in long-term memory," are representative of this use of the term. The implication is that some set of processes has led to the acquisition of the materials, and now some other set of processes is responsible for keeping them "in" memory.

Memory

The more common meaning of the term *motor memory* is "the persistence of the acquired capability for performance." In this sense, habit and memory are conceptually similar. Remember, the usual test for learning of a task related to how well the individual could perform the skill on a transfer test (or retention test). That is, a skill has been learned if and only if it can be retained "relatively permanently" (see chapter 10). If you can still perform a skill after not having practiced it for a year, then you have a memory of the skill. Thus, the memory is the *capability* for performance, not a place where that capability is stored. Depending on one's theoretical orientation about motor learning, memory could be a motor program, a reference of correctness, a schema, or an intrinsic coordination pattern. From this viewpoint, as you can see, learning and memory are just "different sides of the same behavioral coin," as Adams (1976a, p. 223) has put it (see also Adams, 1967).

Forgetting

Another term used in this context is *forgetting*. The term is used to indicate the opposite of learning, in that learning refers to the acquisition of the capability for movement whereas forgetting refers to the loss of such capability. It is likely that the processes and principles having to do with gains and losses in the capability for moving will be different, but the terms refer to the different directions of the change in this capability. "Forgetting" is a term that has to do with theoretical constructs, just as "learning" does. Memory is a construct, and forgetting is the loss of memory; so forgetting is a concept at a theoretical, rather than a behavioral, level of thinking.

As shown in table 14.1, the analogy to the study of learning is a close one. At the theoretical level, learning is a gain in the capability to move, while forgetting is the loss of same. And, on the behavioral level, learning is evidenced by relatively permanent gains in performance, while forgetting is evidenced by relatively permanent

---

Table 14.1   The Analogous States of Motor Learning and Motor Forgetting

	Theoretical level	Behavioral level
Motor learning	Acquiring the capability for moving, gains in memory	Relatively permanent gains in performance with practice
Motor forgetting	Losing the capability for moving, or forgetting, loss of memory	Relatively permanent losses in performance, or retention losses

losses in performance, or losses in retention. So, if you understand what measures of behavior suggest about learning, then you also understand the same about forgetting.

Retention and Transfer

Retention refers to the persistence or lack of persistence of the *performance,* and is considered at the behavioral level rather than at the theoretical level (table 14.1). It might tell us whether or not memory has been lost. The test on which decisions about retention are based is called the *retention test,* performed after some *retention interval;* and the data from such a test are all the behaviorists have to find out about memory or forgetting. If performance on the retention test is as proficient as it was immediately after the end of the original learning, then we might say that no memory loss (no forgetting) has occurred. If performance on the retention test is poor, then we may decide that a memory loss has occurred. However, because the test for memory (the retention test) is a performance test, it is subject to all the variations that cause performances to change in temporary ways. Thus, it could be that performance is poor on the retention test for some temporary reason (fatigue, anxiety), and thus it could be falsely concluded that a memory loss has occurred.

For all practical purposes, a retention test and a *transfer test* are very similar. In both cases, the interest is in the persistence of the acquired capability for performance (habit). The two types of tests differ in that the transfer test has subjects switching to different tasks or conditions, whereas the retention test usually involves retesting subjects on the same task or conditions.

Measuring Retention and Transfer

Tests of retention and transfer provide indicators about the persistence of an acquired habit during an absence from practice, or about the way in which previous practice influences performance on a new task. Unfortunately, straightforward conclusions from such tests are not always possible. Next, we present the most common and important of the various methods and measures of retention and transfer that have been devised by researchers, will suggest which ones provide the most useful information.

Retention of Learning

In motor memory research, a number of different measures of retention have been used, and these different methods provide somewhat different interpretations about the underlying forgetting processes. Chief among these methods are *absolute retention* and various forms of *relative retention.*

Absolute Retention

By far the most simple and scientifically justifiable measure of retention is absolute retention, defined simply as the level of performance on the initial trial(s) of the retention test. Figure 14.1

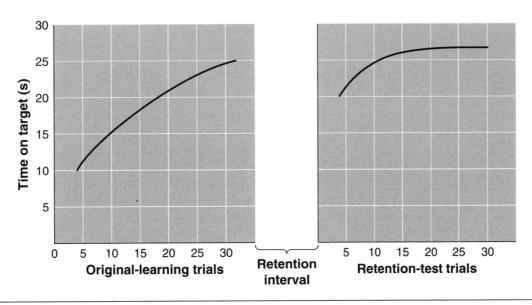

Figure 14.1. Hypothetical performance curves on the pursuit rotor for original-learning and retention-test trials.

shows the hypothetical scores of a group of subjects who practiced the pursuit rotor for 30 trials and then, after a retention interval, performed a retention test involving 30 additional trials. The absolute retention is approximately 20 s of time on target (TOT). Notice that the absolute-retention score is not based in any way on the level of performance from which the retention losses began in original learning.

Relative Retention

Various measures of relative retention are possible, such as those using a *difference score* and those using *percentage scores*. These measures express the absolute-retention score *relative to* scores obtained during practice.

Difference Score. Probably the most common relative-retention score is a difference score that represents the "amount" of loss in skill over the retention interval. It is computed by taking the difference between the performance levels at the end of the original-learning session and the beginning of the retention test. In the example given in figure 14.1, the difference is 5-s TOT, as the group had 25-s TOT before the retention interval and 20 s afterward. Such measures are aesthetically pleasing to many investigators because they seem (erroneously) to represent the forgetting processes more or less directly.

Percentage Score. A second kind of relative-retention score is a percentage score, which represents the "amount" of loss in retention over the retention interval relative to the amount of improvement that occurred on the task in the original-learning session. That is, the percentage score is the difference score (as just defined) divided by the amount of change in performance during the original-learning trials (another difference score), then multiplied by 100 for conversion into a percentage. In the example in figure 14.1, the percentage score is the difference score (5 s) divided by the amount of performance change in original learning ($25 - 10 = 15$ s) and multiplied by 100, or $5/15 \times 100 = 33.3\%$. The meaning of this score is that one-third of the amount of original improvement was lost over the retention interval. Be careful, though, because such estimates will be sensitive to temporary factors that alter performance in the acquisition phase (e.g., random practice) and thus alter the size of the denominator. However, these scores are sometimes useful when one wishes to compare (usually informally) the retention on two different skills, perhaps with different scoring systems.

Savings Score. A third measure of retention, used long ago by Ebbinghaus (1913) and to some extent today (e.g., Nelson, 1985), involves the "savings" in relearning. That is, after a retention interval, one measures the number of trials required for the subjects to reach the level of proficiency achieved in original practice. In the example in figure 14.1, the savings score would be approximately 12 trials, the amount of practice in the retention test required to reach 25-s TOT again. Notice that the number of trials to relearn is generally less than for original learning; therefore, the more complete the retention, the faster should be this "rate" of relearning, even if the first trial or so shows poor performance.

Contrasting the Various Retention Measures

While it may seem that these various methods merely provide subtle differences in the measurement of a single process (forgetting), this is not the case. According to an analysis of the problem some years ago (Schmidt, 1971a, 1972a), the relative-retention scores are flawed by a variety of factors. The basis of the problem is that all these scores come from *performance* measures, with changes in performance being used to infer something about the changes in the internal state (memory) that underlies performance. Therefore, all the problems with performance curves that we mentioned with respect to the measurement of learning (ceiling and floor effects, for example, in chapter 10) also apply to the measurement of forgetting. In particular, difference scores are subject to a variety of influences that cloud interpretations about forgetting, casting doubt on the usefulness of the difference-score method described earlier. Moreover, the percentage score is based on two difference scores, one divided by the other to gain the percentage, clouding the issue even further.

The problem is not just a technical or academic one (Schmidt, 1971a). Some of the most fundamental variables in forgetting have empirical effects that seem to depend completely on the ways in which retention is measured. For example, consider the variable of amount of original learning, or the number of practice trials on the original-learning session shown in figure 14.1. If forgetting is measured by the absolute-retention method, then numerous studies show that absolute retention increases as the amount of original practice increases, just as we might suspect. But if retention is measured by the relative-retention methods, then relative retention (computed from the same set of data) *decreases* as the amount of original practice increases (see Schmidt, 1972a). Thus, the statement of the law relating retention of skills to the amount of original practice is completely different depending on how retention is measured. Obviously, this has caused, and will continue to cause, many confusing situations for students who are attempting to understand the principles of motor forgetting. The absolute-retention score minimizes these problems, and it is the most simple and straightforward one to use.

Transfer of Learning

Transfer is usually defined as the gain (or loss) in the capability for performance in one task as a result of practice or experience on some other task. Thus, we might ask whether practicing a task like badminton would produce benefits or losses (or neither) for another task such as tennis. If it turns out that the performance of tennis is more effective after badminton experience than it would have been under no previous badminton experience, then we would say that the skills acquired in badminton have "transferred to" the skills involved in tennis. It is as if something that is learned in the badminton situation can be carried over to (or applied to) the task of playing tennis (Schmidt & Young, 1987).

Transfer Experiments

Experiments on the transfer of learning can use a variety of experimental designs, but we will not consider them all here (see Ellis, 1965, for a complete description). In the simplest of all designs, assume that there are two groups of subjects (groups I and II). In table 14.2, group I practices task A for some arbitrary number of practice trials, after which group I transfers to practice on task B. Group II does *not* receive task A at all, but merely begins practicing task B.

You can think of tasks A and B as any two activities; they could be different tasks such as badminton and tennis or they could be two slightly different variations of the *same* task, such as the pursuit rotor at different speeds. Thus, when the two groups begin practicing task B, the only

Table 14.2 A Simple Design for an Experiment on Proactive Transfer of Learning

Group	Transfer task	Test
I	Task A	Task B
II	—	Task B
III	Task Z	Task B

systematic difference between them is whether or not they have had experience on task A beforehand.

Positive and Negative Transfer.   Consider the possible results of such an experiment as shown in figure 14.2. Here, the task of interest is task B, and the task A performance is not graphed. In figure 14.2a, group I, which had task A prior to task B, performs task B more effectively than does group II, which did not have the experience with task A. We conclude that experience on task A has provided increased capability for task B, about 30 score units on the first task B trial. When the practice on task A improves subsequent performance on task B, we say that positive transfer occurred.

Now consider that, for group III, practice on some other task Z might have a detrimental effect on task B (see table 14.2). An example is shown in figure 14.2b. Here, group II performs task B exactly as in figure 14.2a, but task B performance for group III is markedly inferior to that of group II. For the reasons just mentioned, we conclude that experience on task Z has interfered with group III's capability for task B. In this case, *negative transfer* occurred from task Z to task B.

Proactive and Retroactive Transfer.   In the examples given so far, the transfer is termed *proactive* because the transfer seemed to work "forward" in time from task A or Z to task B. However, we can also consider *retroactive transfer,* that is, transfer that seems to work "backward" in time. Consider the design shown in table 14.3. Here, two different treatment groups (groups IV and V) both perform task B. Then, group IV performs task Q while group V performs nothing. Later, both groups return to task B for a retention test. If the retention performance on task B is more effective for group IV than for group V, we say that

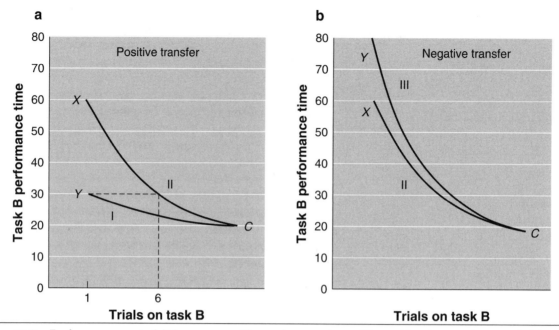

Figure 14.2. Performances on task B for a group with no prior experience (II) or with prior practice on task A (group I) or task Z (group III). (a) If group I outperforms group II, then positive transfer has occurred; (b) If group III performs more poorly than group II, negative transfer has occurred.

Table 14.3   A Retroactive Transfer Design

Group	Initial practice	Transfer task	Retention test
IV	Task B	Task Q	Task B
V	Task B	—	Task B

positive retroactive transfer occurred from task Q to task B; practicing task Q seemed to "enhance" the capability already learned on task B. Alternately, if the performance of task B on the retention test is less effective for group IV than for group V, we say that negative retroactive transfer (or interference) occurred; here, practicing task Q seemed to "erode" the capability for the previously learned task B.

The retroactive and proactive transfer designs are similar in that they both consider the performance on the *initial* trials of task B in the retention test (or test phase in table 14.2) to be the critical data indicating transfer. Some measures of these different performances are described in the next sections.

Measurement of Transfer

The "amount" of transfer from one task to another can be assessed in a number of ways, all of which suffer from the basic problems raised

many times before about the measurement of performance and learning; thus none of these methods will be very satisfactory in actually measuring transfer. Rather they are used to describe the relationships among curves such as those in figure 14.2 and are occasionally helpful in discussion of the results of different transfer experiments.

Percentage Transfer. One method of measuring transfer (see figure 14.2a) is to consider the gain in performance as a result of experience on task A (i.e., the numerical difference between points Y and X in the figure, or 30 score units) as a percentage of the "total amount learned" by group II in the experiment (i.e., the numerical difference between points X and C, or about 40 score units). Thus, the amount of improvement in task B by group II is seen as the total improvement possible in task B, and thus group I's experience with task A has provided 30 out of the possible 40 units of improvement, or 75%. In terms of a more general formula,

$$\text{Percent Transfer} = \frac{X - Y}{X - C} \times 100 \quad (14.1)$$

in which $X = 60$, $Y = 30$, and $C = 20$ score units. The formula can also be used for negative transfer as shown in figure 14.2b. Here, the values X and C remain the same, but Y (the initial performance level on task B by group III) is larger than it was for group I (i.e., 80). Being careful to keep the signs of the numbers straight, and noting that the numerator of the equation is a negative number (i.e., $X - Y$, or $60 - 80$, or -20), we calculate transfer as $-20/40 \times 100 = -50\%$.

One can crudely interpret the percentage transfer as the percentage of improvement on task B as a result of prior practice on task A. Positive transfer of 100% would imply that the performance on the first trial of task B for group I would be at the final level of performance (i.e., C) demonstrated by group II. Transfer of 0% would mean that the two groups are the same in initial performance on task B (i.e., both at level X). The reason this measure is inadequate, of course, is that the amount of improvement on task B (i.e., $X - C$) will depend on the amount of practice provided, on the scoring system used for task B, on the nature of the subjects, and on countless other arbitrary factors that affect the shapes of performance curves. But percentage transfer does serve a useful purpose in describing the relationships among the curves; just be careful not to take the finding of, say, 75% transfer too literally. It describes only the outward manifestations (i.e., performance) that result from the habit transfer.

Savings Score. Another, far less frequently used method for describing the amount of transfer is a savings score, as already discussed. Here, the savings score represents the amount of practice time "saved" (i.e., reduced) on task B by having first practiced task A. In figure 14.2a, group I (which had practiced task A previously) begins its performance of task B at a level of performance equivalent to that shown by group II after six trials. It is possible to say that group I "saved" six trials in the learning of task B by having first learned task A. But this is not the whole story; the "savings" on task B are almost certainly compensated for by a "loss," because task A had to be practiced, and the practice time on task A is usually going to be longer than the amount "saved" on task B. That is, for learning task B, usually nothing is as efficient as practicing task B (but see chapter 11 for a few exceptions).

Such "savings" begin to have importance when the financial cost of practice is considered. A common example is in learning to fly an airplane, such as the McDonnell Douglas MD-11. To actually practice in the MD-11 would be very costly, so computer-based simulators that closely resemble the airplane cockpit are frequently used (see figure 14.12). Here, the time "spent" in the simulator (task A) is inexpensive relative to the time "saved"

in learning to fly the MD-11 (task B), and it is safer as well. In such situations, the effectiveness of a simulator-based training program is often evaluated in terms of financial savings, such savings being the amount of hours saved on task B (the MD-11) times the number of dollars per hour of practice on task B. In the case of the MD-11, dollar amounts of savings can be very large.

Retention and Motor Memory

One of the most frequently studied theoretical issues in psychology—an issue that people often disagree about—concerns memory. Is memory a result of some processing of an event, or does memory refer to the processing *itself*? Are there different types of memory, such as memories for movements, for sensations, for smells, and the like, or is there just one memory, whose *retention characteristics* are a product of the nature and type of processing that is conducted? Questions such as these are hotly debated topics in psychology and beyond our purpose here (e.g., see Anderson, 1995; Richardson-Klavehn & Bjork, 1988). Rather, we will present some of the evidence that is known about the retention (this section) and retention loss (next section) of motor skills.

Retention of Skill for Continuous Tasks

That many motor skills are nearly never forgotten is almost a cliché. Examples such as swimming and riding a bicycle, in which performance after many years is nearly as proficient as it was originally, are frequently cited. Ideas about such examples, though, are seldom based on acceptable experimental methods; on the other hand, many laboratory examples of these situations have been studied and seem to say the same thing.

Although many studies could be cited to illustrate the point, we will consider a representative study with long retention intervals by Fleishman and Parker (1962). They used a three-dimensional compensatory tracking task (Mashburn task, figure 2.5), with movements of the hands in forward-backward and left-right dimensions and movement of the feet in a left-right dimension. They gave subjects 17 daily sessions, and then separate groups performed retests after either 9, 14, or 24 months. The scores for original-learning and retention tests are shown in figure 14.3, where all three retention groups have been averaged together in original practice. After the retention intervals, the various groups were nearly equivalent, and none had shown any appreciable losses in proficiency, even after 2 years of layoff. Some tendency was seen for the 2-year group to have slightly less proficiency than the groups with shorter retention intervals, but the differences were small and the losses were regained completely in three sessions. These small differences are not very meaningful when one compares the retention-test performance to the level of performance at the start of practice. Certainly this continuous task was retained nearly perfectly for 2 years.

Other studies, using different tasks, have shown very similar effects. Meyers (1967), using the Bachman ladder-climb task, demonstrated nearly no loss in performance for retention intervals of up to 12 weeks. Ryan (1962), using the pursuit rotor and stabilometer tasks, found nearly no retention losses after retention intervals of 21 days; later, Ryan (1965) found only small losses in performance on the stabilometer task with retention intervals of up to 1 year. There are many other examples, and the generalization continues to hold. Continuous motor tasks are extremely well retrained over very long retention intervals, just as the cliché about the bicycle would have us believe.

Retention of Skill for Discrete Tasks

While there is ample evidence of nearly complete retention of continuous skills, the picture appears

to be quite different for discrete skills. Consider an example by Neumann and Ammons (1957). The subject sat in front of a large display with eight pairs of switches located in a circular pattern. The subject was to turn the inner switch "on" and then discover which switch in the outer circle was paired with it; a buzzer sounded when the correct match was made. Subjects learned the task to a criterion of two consecutive errorless trials, and then retention intervals of 1 min, 20 min, 2 days, 7 weeks, and 1 year were imposed for different groups of subjects.

The main findings are presented in figure 14.4. Some losses in performance appeared after only 20 min, and the losses became progressively greater as the length of the retention interval increased. In fact, after 1 year, the performance was actually poorer than the initial performance in original learning had been, suggesting that the forgetting was nearly complete. However, notice that in all cases the relearning of the task was more rapid than the original learning (as indicated by the slopes of the relearning and original-learning curves), indicating that some memory for the skill was retained.

Continuous Versus Discrete Tasks

Why is there such a large difference in the retention characteristics of continuous and discrete skills, with continuous tasks having nearly perfect retention and discrete tasks having such poor

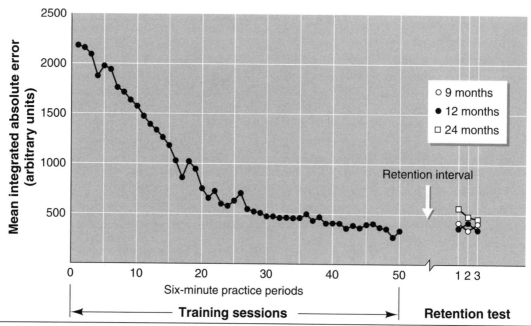

Figure 14.3. Mean performance on a three-dimensional tracking task in original learning and after three retention intervals. Reprinted from Fleishman and Parker, 1962.

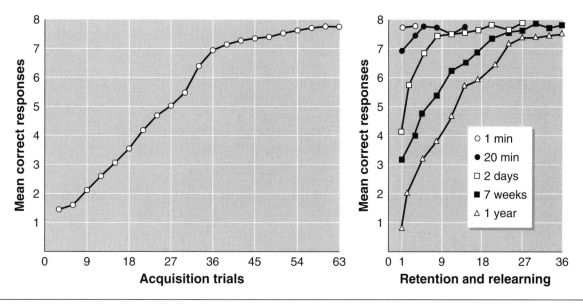

Figure 14.4.   Mean performance of a discrete task in original learning and after various retention intervals. Reprinted from Neumann and Ammons, 1957.

retention? A number of hypotheses have been proposed to explain these differences, and they are discussed next.

Verbal-Cognitive Components

One hypothesis is that verbal-cognitive components are somehow more quickly forgotten than motor components; because discrete tasks seem to have a heavier emphasis on verbal-cognitive elements (learning which switch goes with which light in the Neumann-Ammons study, for example), there is more loss for the discrete tasks over time. While it is true that most of the discrete tasks that have been studied in retention situations seem highly verbal-cognitive in nature (e.g., Schendel & Hagman, 1982), there is no reason that discrete tasks must be. Certainly, one can think of many discrete tasks that have relatively little reliance on verbal-cognitive abilities (e.g., throwing, striking, pole-vaulting). What would be the retention characteristics of a discrete task that was highly "motor" in nature?

Lersten (1969) used an arm movement (rho task) in which a circular and a linear movement component had to be performed as quickly as possible. He found approximately 80% loss (of the original amount of improvement) in the circular phase, and a 30% loss for the linear component, with retention intervals of 1 year. Similarly, Martin (1970) used a task in which the subjects moved the hand over two barriers and then returned to a starting switch as quickly as possible,

finding approximately 50% retention loss over a 4-month retention interval. The amount of loss in retention for discrete skills that can be considered "mostly motor" in nature is similar to the loss experienced by Neumann and Ammons's subjects (figure 14.4), suggesting that there is more to these effects in retention than just the "motorness" of the tasks.

Amount of Original Learning

One of the major factors determining absolute retention is the amount of original learning, with retention increasing as the amount of original practice increases. In the typical continuous task, there might be trials of 30 s in duration, each trial consisting of many separate "discrete" actions. In tracking, for example, there are many instances in which the pointer and track become separated, with each instance requiring a separate adjustment. Contrast this situation to that for discrete tasks, for which a trial typically consists of but a single adjustment or action. It stands to reason, therefore, that with the same number of learning trials, the continuous task is far more highly practiced than the discrete task. This extra level of original learning, according to this hypothesis, leads to increased retention, since it is well known that absolute retention is directly related to the amount of original practice.

What Is a "Trial"?

Another notion, related to the one just presented, is that the definition of *trial* is quite arbitrary; a trial can refer to anything from a 200-ms reaction-time performance to a 2-min bout of performance on a tracking task. This poses a problem for defining the amount of original practice for the task, and it is also a problem in connection with the retention test. Remember, the level of absolute retention is measured in terms of the performance on the first few "trials" of retention-test performance. Now if a "trial" is a 2-min performance, there could be a great deal of relearning occurring within a trial for the continuous task, with no relearning within a trial for a rapid discrete performance. So the initial movements within the first trial for the continuous task could show considerable retention loss, but the experimenter might not detect it because the poor initial performance would be "averaged" with the later portions of the trial on which performance was more proficient. Because this could not occur for the discrete task, it is possible that the amount of forgetting is typically underestimated for the continuous task and not for the discrete task, making the two kinds of tasks appear to be different in their retention characteristics when they might otherwise not be. Fleishman and Parker (1962) have found a great deal of relearning within a continuous-task trial, as might be suspected.

Retention Loss

In this section we present three examples of ways in which retention loss has been studied in motor performance, followed by a discussion of some related theoretical and experimental issues about the processes through which retention loss occurs. Each example highlights some important differences about performance loss that are revealed under different task constraints.

Example #1: Iconic Memory and Motor Performance

As we discussed in chapter 5, motor performance benefits considerably from the availability of visual information, especially for tasks such as manual aiming that require precise movements. However, there is considerable evidence to suggest that *continuous* visual information is not necessary to support good performance. This is so because our memory for the visual information can "fill in" the gaps if the continuous supply of vision is cut off. For example, suppose you took aim at the bull's-eye in dart throwing and the room

lights went out just before you released the dart. How would performance be affected? Research using experiments that closely resemble this and other, similar scenarios suggests that performance would depend on the length of time you were in the dark before performing the movement.

A number of studies by Elliott and his colleagues suggest that motor performance deteriorates quickly because the persistence of the visual information (the icon) fades rapidly from memory (Sperling, 1960). For example, subjects in a study by Elliott and Madalena (1987) moved a stylus to a target under various conditions of available room light. A control condition provided subjects with continuous visual feedback of the target and stylus. In another condition, the room lights were extinguished as the subjects initiated their movements; thus the movements (which had durations of 200–500 ms) were made in the absence of direct visual information. The other three conditions also involved movements without visual information available; however, these movements were made after the room lights had been extinguished for 2, 5, or 10 s.

As can be seen in figure 14.5, subjects could perform the aiming movements well without visual feedback if the movement was *completed* within half a second after the room lights were turned off. After a wait in the dark of at least 2 s, however, performance was markedly disrupted. Elliott and Madalena (1987) interpreted these

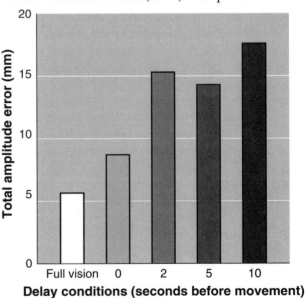

Figure 14.5.   Total amplitude error in aiming under conditions of vision and without vision under various delay conditions.

Adapted from Elliott and Madalena, 1987.

findings to suggest that a very short-lived memory for visual information is able to support performance rather accurately (see chapter 3; and see reviews by Elliott, 1990, 1992). However, the information is prone to forgetting due to a *decay* of the icon—a process whereby information loss is attributable to the passage of time.

The findings of Elliott and Madalena (1987) and others indicate that motor performance can be supported for a brief time by a short-term sensory store, which loses information quite rapidly. These findings suggest a process similar to that proposed in the oldest theory of forgetting, a theory with much intuitive appeal: the *trace-decay* theory. It is a passive theory of disuse, according to which the reason information is forgotten is that it is not practiced, and it therefore "decays" with time. The memory of an item, event, or skill is thought to be represented as a neurological trace, and this trace becomes weaker with time, in much the same way that iron rusts. Then, when the information or skill is demanded at some future time, the trace is too weak or ill defined to be able to support performance effectively, if at all. This idea accounts well for the common effects of disuse and, of course, for the fact that time seems to be a strong factor in forgetting.

Considerable research on trace-decay effects in slow, linear-positioning tasks has been conducted using what is called the *short-term motor memory paradigm* (chapter 3). This involves the presentation and recall of movement over very

brief time intervals, often only seconds in duration. These studies used methods that paralleled those of experiments in memory for verbal materials, early investigations having been conducted by Brown (1958) and Peterson and Peterson (1959). In one of the first of the motor studies, Adams and Dijkstra (1966) required the subject to move to a stop that defined a target position, then return to a starting location for a retention interval, and then attempt to move to the target position again (but with the stop removed). Subjects were blindfolded and were never given knowledge of results (KR) about their movement accuracy. In addition, subjects were given various numbers of "reinforcements," whereby the position was presented 1, 6, or 15 times before the retention interval. So the procedures were analogous to those in the verbal short-term memory paradigm: short retention intervals, no KR, prevention of rehearsal, and once-presented items (except for the conditions with multiple "reinforcements").

The major findings are presented in figure 14.6. The absolute errors on the recall trials are presented as a function of the number of "reinforcements" and the length of the retention interval. As the length of the retention interval increased, the error in recall also increased, with the increases being nearly maximized by the time the retention interval was 80 s in length and with no further increases thereafter. Similar to memory for verbal items, memory for these linear-positioning movements appears to have a

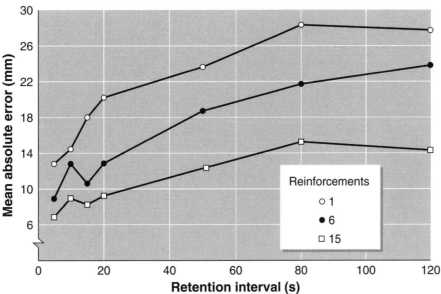

Figure 14.6. Mean absolute error in positioning as a function of the retention-interval length and the number of "reinforcements."
Reprinted from Adams and Dijkstra, 1966.

forgetting process that is nearly complete in about 1 min. Also, this forgetting can apparently be slowed by practice; the errors were systematically smaller as the number of times the subject moved to the stop increased.

One interpretation is that the movement to the stop created a short-term memory representation of the feedback qualities of the correct position, and this representation was weakened over the course of the empty retention interval. Therefore, the individual had a progressively more "faint" reference of correctness to which to compare the feedback from the limb during the retention test. However, it is also possible that forgetting can occur by means other than trace decay. This idea is presented in the next example.

Example #2: Memory for Parameterized Motor Programs

Now consider a very different memory-related paradigm, developed by Rosenbaum and his colleagues (Rosenbaum et al., 1986; see also Rosenbaum, 1991). The subject's task is easy to simulate: the basic requirement is to speak aloud as many letters as possible in 10 s, alternating between a loud voice and a soft voice with each letter spoken. The key factor in the Rosenbaum et al. experiment was the *memory set* that was repeatedly cycled. For example, if we use upper case to denote the loudly spoken letters and lower case to denote the softly spoken letters, then a

four-letter memory set would be represented as *AbCdAbCdAbCdAb* and so on, with the four-letter sequence being continuously recycled until 10 s had elapsed. Notice that a loud presentation was always required for the letters *A* and *C*, and a soft presentation was always required for *b* and *d*.

The repetitive nature of this recycling task is the same for any *even*-numbered memory set, making such a set relatively easy to perform. Now compare this to the sequence *AbCaBcAbCaBcA*. Notice now that the stress on a specific letter *changes* on each repeated cycle. This feature is consistent for all *odd*-numbered memory sets and makes them much more difficult to perform. The speed and error data from the Rosenbaum et al. experiment are presented in figure 14.7. As you would expect, more letters in the even-numbered memory sets (2, 4, 6, 8) were produced in 10 s than in the odd-numbered sets (3, 5, 7, 9) (figure 14.7a). Conversely, trials on which errors occurred were more frequent for the odd-numbered than the even-numbered sets (figure 14.7b).

How can we relate these findings to memory? One view is that speaking a letter involves *parameterizing* a generalized motor program for that letter—the specific parameter of interest being whether the letter is spoken loudly or softly. Once the letter is produced, a memory of that parameterization will *facilitate* performance on the next pronunciation, but only if the *same* parameterization is required. If the opposite stress is required,

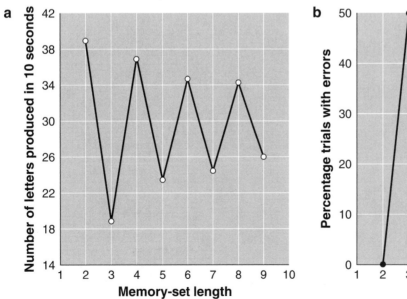

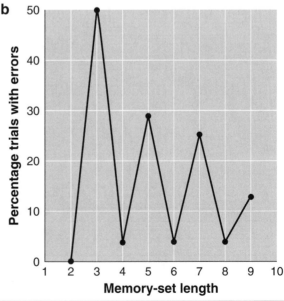

Figure 14.7.   Total number of letters spoken (a) and percentage of trials with errors (b) as a function of memory-set length. Adapted from Rosenbaum, Weber, Hazelett, and Hindorff, 1986.

the memory for the previous parameterization will *interfere* with performance, as the remembered parameterization must be abandoned and a new one produced.

But notice one other important finding in both the speed and error data in figure 14.7. As the length of the memory set increases, the performances of the even- and odd-numbered strings begin to converge. This finding suggests a *weakening* of the influence of the previous parameterization on a subsequent parameterization: the memory effect, which previously had either facilitated or degraded performance, was *reduced* when more letters intervened between the next performance of any one letter. If the memory sets had been extended even further (e.g., to 19 and 20 letters), the performance differences between the odd- and even-numbered letter strings might have been eliminated completely.

Two possible influences seem to be going on in the Rosenbaum et al. (1986) study. As the length of the memory set increased, the *time* between any two pronunciations of the same letter increased, resulting in a trace decay of the previous parameterization. The mere passage of time is not all that happens, though, because as the memory set increased, more intervening letters were prepared and executed, which caused more *interference* with the memory of the parameters applied to any specific letter on the last performance of it. Thus, it is possible that the cause of forgetting had something to do with these events, rather than mere passage of time as trace-decay theory would have it. Interference theory is an active theory of forgetting, in which memory is actively degraded by other events. Such events, according to the theory, can be of two basic kinds: *proactive interference* and *retroactive interference* (Underwood, 1957).

Proactive and Retroactive Interference

According to one way of thinking of an event as interfering with some learned information or skill, the interference occurs between the original occurrence of the memory and the time when the memory recall is attempted. The term *retroactive* implies that the interference "works backward" on the memory; of course, it does not work backward at all, but it does nevertheless serve to disrupt the recall of something that occurred before the interference. Interference can occur in a less obvious way when something that enters memory before the criterion memory task causes

interference with the recall of that criterion information. The term *proactive* implies that the information already in memory interferes with more recently acquired information.

Using the short-term motor memory paradigm described previously, a number of experimenters have attempted to assess the mechanisms causing forgetting in relation to interference theory. With respect to *proactive interference*, neither Adams and Dijkstra (1966) nor Posner and Konick (1966) found evidence that later positions to be remembered in a sequence were less accurate than earlier ones— a finding that would be expected if the proactive interference from the earlier movements were disrupting the memory of the later positions; such findings had been shown in verbal behavior. One reason these proactive effects may not have occurred in the motor studies was that the intertrial intervals were very long (3 min in Adams and Dijkstra's study), possibly providing an opportunity for forgetting of an earlier movement before a later movement could be presented.

Ascoli and Schmidt (1969) studied proactive effects by concentrating the prior movements into a short period of time. They presented either zero, two, or four positions just prior to a criterion movement. A retention interval was provided (either 10 or 120 s); then recall of the criterion movement was followed by the recall of the preliminary movements (if any). In figure 14.8,

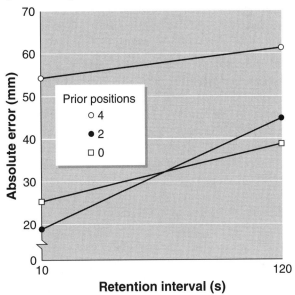

Figure 14.8. Mean absolute error in positioning as a function of the retention-interval length and the number of previous positions.
Adapted from Ascoli and Schmidt, 1969.

absolute errors in recall are presented for the two retention intervals and for the various numbers of prior movements. Errors increased as the length of the retention interval increased. But of more interest was the finding that the four-prior-position condition showed more error than either the zero- or two-prior-position conditions. A major effect was seen for constant error, with increased prior positions making the movements systematically too short. The data can be interpreted to mean that proactive interference is a factor in the retention of these positioning movements, supporting the interference theory (see Stelmach, 1969).

With respect to *retroactive interference,* some earlier researchers had failed to find effects of activities placed between the presentation and the recall of the test movements, casting serious doubt on the interference theory. But none of these studies reported constant errors, and the finding that proactive interference had its major effects on constant error raised the possibility that retroactive effects would be seen in the same way. In a reanalysis of earlier data, Pepper and Herman (1970) found that movements produced during the retention interval tended to have negative effects on the movement accuracy when measured in terms of constant error. Subsequently, Patrick (1971) and Milone (1971) also provided evidence for retroactive interference. The research using the short-term motor memory paradigm also examined a number of issues that influenced retention. These are reviewed briefly next.

Cue-Separation Techniques. What does the performer remember and recall in these positioning tasks? One possibility is that the person remembers the sensory qualities of the target position and attempts to match these sensations through a closed-loop process during the recall movement. That is, the person might be attempting to move to that position that is *recognized* as correct (see Schema Theory, chapter 13). Another possibility, however, is that the person remembers the distance moved, rather than the location of the target, and remembers a motor program that will move the limb a certain distance. These two possible cues (location vs. distance cues) were confounded in the earlier experiments on motor short-term memory. However, Keele and Ells (1972), Marteniuk (1973), and Laabs (1973) used an ingenious but simple method for unraveling these two potential cues.

For example, Laabs (1973) had subjects move to a stop (just as in the Adams-Dijkstra study) for the presentation of the stimulus materials. Then he formed two different conditions for recall. In both of these conditions, subjects began at a *different* starting position for the recall movement. In one condition, subjects were asked to recall the same location on the track as before, so the distance of the recall movement was different from that of the presentation movement, rendering information about distance less effective. In the other condition, the subject was asked to move the same distance as in the presentation movement, so the location of the presentation movement was less useful to the subject for recall.

Laabs's major findings were that accuracy was far greater in the condition in which the location cue had to be recalled than in the one in which the distance cue had to be recalled. Subsequent research has suggested that subjects have a difficult time remembering the cues about movement distance and that positioning movements are probably based on some memory of location, although retroactive interference effects for location and distance information may occur in complex ways in some instances (Imanaka & Abernethy, 1991, 1992; Walsh et al., 1979).

The Preselection Effect. In the usual paradigm for motor short-term memory studies, the subject is asked to move to a stop that is defined by the experimenter, and thus the subject does not have any advance knowledge about where the movement endpoint will be until he or she contacts the stop. Marteniuk (1973) and Stelmach, Kelso, and Wallace (1975) broke tradition with this method when they asked subjects to choose their own movement endpoints. In effect, the instruction was to move to a position of the subject's choice (a stop was not provided); then the subject returned to the starting position and was asked to reproduce the position after a retention interval. This so-called *preselection* method led to much more accurate recall than the experimenter-selected method. An analogous finding in memory for verbal items, termed the "generation effect," was found after these motor memory investigations were conducted (e.g., Slamecka & Graf, 1978).

When the subject is faced with these reproduction situations, it is likely that the nature of the paradigm will influence the way in which the person stores the information. For example, if the person does not know where the target will be (standard paradigm), this could force the individual to process sensory cues about the target location, perhaps leading to a strategy wherein the recall of the movement is through closed-loop processes. In the preselection method, however, the performer can generate a movement plan in advance, perhaps programming it, and thus ignore the sensory consequences of the movement—simply rerunning the program at the retention test. This may also suggest that memory for programs or parameterizations may be more stable than memory about the feedback for correct locations.

Spacing of Repetitions. Earlier we presented the findings of the Adams and Dijkstra (1966) study, in which many repetitions of the movement reduced the loss of information during the retention interval. These findings have been replicated often (reviewed in Lee & Weeks, 1987), suggesting that a memory representation is stronger or more resistant to forgetting with "practice." One of the more curious findings, however, is that the repetition effect is enhanced if the repetitions themselves are not immediately repeated, but instead are spaced apart—especially so if interference occurs between these repetitions (e.g., Lee & Weeks, 1987; Weeks et al., 1991). One explanation for this *spacing effect* is that the forgetting that occurs between repetitions actually serves to *improve* memory on the retention test (see the boxed text on page 309). This finding

is similar to the contextual-interference effect discussed in chapter 11 and suggests that common underlying factors may be involved.

Example #3: Warm-Up Decrement

To this point in the chapter, the focus has been on memory losses. But as mentioned earlier, not all retention losses are due to memory losses, as evidenced by such temporary factors as loss of motivation, day-to-day fluctuations in performance, effects of drugs, and illness. Many of these have been discussed with respect to the measurement of performance (chapter 2) and learning (chapter 10), and they are all involved in motor retention as well. But a special kind of decrement in motor performance has a small literature of its own, and it deserves mention. This effect is called *warm-up decrement*.

The phenomenon can be easily introduced with an example. Adams (1952, 1961) studied a large group of subjects on the pursuit rotor task, providing thirty-six 30-s trials per day for 5 days; the performance data are shown in figure 14.9. The typical improvement with practice during a session of trials is seen, but a relatively large decrement in performance is produced after each of the long rest periods. This decrement appears to be quite severe, and it is equivalent in size to the gains experienced in 5 to 10 trials; it is rather short-lived, being eliminated in only a few practice trials. The phenomenon has been known for

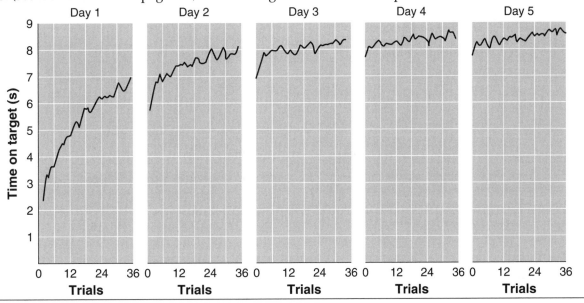

Figure 14.9. Mean performance on the pursuit rotor task for 5 days. (The decrements in performance from the end of one day until the beginning of the next are termed "warm-up decrement.")
Reprinted from Adams, 1961.

a long time and has been found in nearly every motor task that has been studied (see Adams, 1961, for a review). This decrement was thought to be related in some way to the need to "warm up" for the task again after the rest, and the phenomenon came to be called *warm-up decrement*. It can be of potential importance when individuals are asked to perform after a rest period, as occurs with the worker operating a dangerous machine after a coffee break or the athlete going into the game from the bench.

Two major classes of explanation for warm-up decrement can be described. A *forgetting hypothesis* holds that the loss in skill is due to forgetting of the type mentioned in the previous sections, while various versions of the *set hypothesis* argue that the loss in skill is due to a relatively temporary loss of bodily adjustments or states. These views and the evidence for them are contrasted in the following sections.

Warm-Up Decrement as Forgetting

One major hypothesis, and probably the earliest and simplest explanation to be considered, is that warm-up decrement is simply another form of forgetting, or the loss of memory for the skill. In this view, the rest period allows certain forgetting processes to occur, with the initial phases of these processes being relatively rapid. These account for the rather large performance decrements seen with only a few minutes of rest. The improvements in performance with resumed practice are, in this view, due to relearning of the task whose memory was lost over the rest period.

Warm-Up Decrement as a Loss of Set

In another view, the loss of skill is related to the loss of *set*—one or more temporary internal states that underlie and support the skill in question. Warm-up decrement is caused by the loss (or disruption) of this set over the rest period. This hypothesis says that memory of the skill is not lost over the rest period; or perhaps very small memory losses do occur, but they are far too small to account for the large decrements seen. With practice resumed on the task after the rest, the individual regains the lost set and performance is improved.

Early Evidence on the Set Hypothesis. The set hypothesis seemed reasonable for many years, as it is easy to imagine how such a process might disrupt skills with rest, especially in the face of the nearly perfect retention of skills like the pur-

suit rotor task. Yet no evidence existed for these set-loss phenomena until Irion's (1948) data with verbal skills suggested a way to study the problem. Irion's idea was a lost set should be able to be reinstated by certain activities that are related to the action in question but that cannot be thought of as contributing to the memory for it. Irion used verbal learning as the main task, with two groups; both practiced the verbal task, then had a rest, then resumed practice again. One of the groups remained inactive in the rest period. The other group engaged in color-naming during the end of the rest period—an activity presented on the same apparatus and having the same rhythms as the verbal-learning task, but using none of the learned items from the main task. If the set hypothesis is correct, color-naming should reinstate the lost set produced by the rest, and the initial performance on the verbal-learning task should be more accurate than for the group that simply rested. It was. Because color-naming cannot increase memory strength for the paired associated task, the implication is that color-naming reinstated the lost set, in some way *preparing* the subjects for the upcoming verbal task.

Numerous studies were done to evaluate the set hypothesis with motor skills, but with few successes. In one such investigation, Ammons (1951) used the pursuit rotor; during the rest he had subjects watch another active subject or follow the target area with the finger, for example, in an attempt to eliminate warm-up decrement. No procedures were found that would eliminate it (see Adams, 1955). These data seemed to say that either (a) the set hypothesis was wrong for motor behavior or (b) the appropriate nonmemory set-reinstating activities had not been discovered. In either case, the set hypothesis was not well supported. This evidence is reviewed more completely by Adams (1961, 1964) and by Nacson and Schmidt (1971).

Recent Evidence on the Set Hypothesis. Nacson and Schmidt (1971) tested a slightly different version of the set hypothesis and provided considerable support for it. In this view, performance is supported by a number of adjustments (or "sets"), such as adjustment of *arousal* to the most effective level for the particular task and subject, directing of *attention* to the proper source of input, and so on. During practice, various supportive mechanisms are constantly adjusted so that performance is maximized; during rest, these functions are adjusted to levels most compatible with rest, leading to an ineffective pattern of adjustment when the task is resumed. Practicing a task requiring the same adjustments (set) as the main task just before returning to it should reinstate those adjustments, leading to a reduction in warm-up decrement.

The task used by Nacson and Schmidt (1971) involved a right-hand force production; the subject had to learn to squeeze a handle with a 21-kg force, with KR given after each trial and 10-s rest between trials. After trial 20, a 10 min rest was given, and then practice resumed for another 10 trials. The independent variable was the nature of the activities presented in the 10-min rest period. One group (Rest) was allowed to rest for 10 min. Another group (Exp) had 5 min of rest, followed by 5 min of another force-estimation task; this task, though, involved the left arm rather than the right arm, elbow flexors rather than the gripping action, and a different level of force (9 kg). So it could not be argued that this task would contribute to the memory of the right-hand grip task. After 18 trials of this task with the same intertrial interval and KR, subjects were shifted immediately to the right-hand grip task for the retention test.

The absolute errors in the main (right-hand gripping) task are shown in figure 14.10 for the two groups before and after the rest period. The group that simply rested (Rest) for 10 min showed

the typical warm-up decrement after the rest, but the group with the left-hand activities (Exp) showed almost no warm-up effect, suggesting that the activities in the rest period reinstated the lost set. Similar findings have been shown for a linear-positioning task (with a positioning task as the warm-up task) by Nacson and Schmidt (1971; Schmidt & Nacson, 1971), and by Schmidt and Wrisberg (1971) using a movement speed task (with another movement speed task as the warm-up task). These data also argue against the hypothesis that warm-up decrement is simply forgetting; this hypothesis cannot explain why a different warm-up task (which seems to have no memory elements in common with the main task) should produce improvements in main task performance.

Other data (Schmidt & Nacson, 1971) show that the reinstated set is rather transient in nature. If as few as 25 s of rest are inserted between the reinstatement of the set and the resumption of practice on the main task, the set is completely lost again. Also, activities can be designed that will *increase* warm-up decrement even more than resting does. For example, Schmidt and Nacson (1971) showed that a grip-strength task (with maximum force) performed just before the resumption of practice on a linear-positioning task caused a very large increase in error on the first post-rest trial, suggesting that the maximum grip task required a different set that was

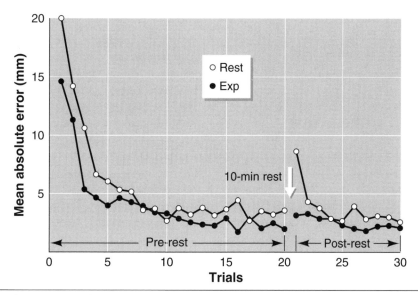

Figure 14.10.   Absolute error in a force-estimation task for original learning and after a 10-min rest. Group Rest rested during the interval, and Group Exp performed a left-hand force-estimation task; error is measured as a polygraph pen displacement.
Adapted from Nacson and Schmidt, 1971.

incompatible with careful linear positioning. Other experiments indicate that *imagery* practice of the task just prior to the resumption of performance can reduce the warm-up decrement, although the nature of the reduction seems to be task specific (Ainscoe & Hardy, 1987; Anshel & Wrisberg, 1988, 1993; Wrisberg & Anshel, 1993).

All these experiments are rather consistent in saying that the warm-up effect is caused by some loss of internal adjustments (or set) over the rest period. These adjustments are critical to effective performance in the task, but they are not a part of the memory for it. Just as the race car has to be brought to the proper temperature before maximal performance can be achieved, so too, it appears, must the human be brought into the proper state of adjustment for high-level skilled performance. It is not clear exactly what is being adjusted in these experiments, but probable candidates are the level of arousal, the rhythm and timing for the trial cycle, the attention to the proper sources of feedback, and so on.

These findings have considerable relevance for high-level performances, especially after performance is interrupted by rest or when major changes in tasks are required. For example, in golf, there are probably different sets for driving and putting, each of which must be reestablished before the shot (which may partially explain why golfers often take practice swings before attempting to hit the ball). In basketball, players must shift quickly from an offensive set when their own team has the ball to a defensive set when a pass is intercepted. Failure to adopt the proper set could result in ineffective performance for a few seconds, long enough for the opponent to score an easy goal.

Transfer of Learning

A number of decisions about the design of practice sessions are based heavily on an understanding of transfer of learning—the gain (or loss) in proficiency in one skill as a result of practice on some other skill. Often, the task actually practiced in a session is not the activity of primary interest, the real concern being for some other task believed to be related to this activity. One example is the use of drills. The instructor usually does not really care whether the student can perform these drills well per se; rather, the instructor assumes that by practicing them, the

student will learn something that will transfer to some other task (e.g., performance in a basketball game) that is of major interest. To use drills successfully, one must be certain that experience on the drill transfers to the desired *criterion task*.

Another example is the common method whereby the task is broken down into its components for practice. The assumption is that practice on the parts will transfer to the whole task (chapter 11). Still another example is the use of simulators of various kinds, such as a pitching machine to simulate a "real" pitcher or a simulator to duplicate an aircraft cockpit. Does practice on these simulators transfer to the criterion behavior? The choices about whether or not to use these methods, and about how they should be structured if used, depend heavily on an understanding of transfer of learning. Some of the principles of motor transfer are considered next.

Basic Principles of Transfer

Many studies using different techniques and tasks have produced a vast array of different and sometimes contradictory findings on transfer (see Cormier & Hagman, 1987, for a review). Two major points emerge from the work on motor skills. First, the amount of transfer seems to be quite small and positive unless the tasks are practically identical. Second, the amount of transfer depends on the "similarity" between the two tasks (Schmidt & Young, 1987).

Motor Transfer Is Small

When the transfer from one task to a completely different task—sometimes called *intertask transfer*—is studied, we typically find that the transfer is small or negligible. Such evidence comes from studies concerned with attempts to train some behavior or trait in one situation by providing presumably related experiences in different situations. For example, investigations by Lindeburg (1949) and Blankenship (1952) showed that "quickening exercises" (various laboratory tasks that require rapid decision and action) provide no transfer to other tasks that require quickness. This is certainly not surprising in light of what is known about the specificity of motor abilities, as the activities in the quickening exercises probably used different motor abilities than the task to which the exercises were supposed to have contributed. Evidence suggests that general traits such as quickness, balance, and coordination cannot be improved by the use of different activities supposedly involving that trait; and we would not expect that an *ability* would be improved by practice anyway.

What if the tasks are more similar? Here, the transfer among tasks tends to be higher than for the previous situation, but still the amount of transfer is typically small. For example, Lordahl and Archer (1958) used the pursuit rotor task, with different groups of subjects practicing at 40, 60, or 80 rpm for 30 trials. All groups then switched to the 60-rpm version of the task for the evaluation of the transfer effects. The group that had 60 rpm in both the training trials and the transfer trials was used as the standard against which the transfer in the other two groups was assessed; that is, it served the role of group II in figure 14.2. Using the calculation for the percentage transfer introduced earlier in this chapter, the transfer from the 40- and 80-rpm versions of the task to the 60-rpm version was 12% and 31%, respectively. Namikas and Archer (1960), using the same procedures, found somewhat higher transfer, ranging from 42% to 64%. Remember that in these experiments the transfer is between the pursuit rotor and *itself*, with only the speed of rotation changed to define the different "tasks." It is somewhat surprising that the transfer is so small, but numerous other experiments find essentially the same thing.

These generally small transfer effects seem to fit with a number of other phenomena that we have discussed already. First, the transfer findings coincide with the ideas about individual differences. In chapter 9, a conclusion was that motor abilities are both numerous and specific and that even similar tasks appear to correlate very weakly with each other (with the possible exception of timing ability). If so, then in transfer experiments when the task is changed in even a small way (e.g., changing the turntable speed of the pursuit rotor), it is likely that different and unrelated abilities are called into play. Thus, there might be low transfer among even very similar tasks because the abilities are almost completely different.

These findings also fit well with the motor program notion. In chapter 6, a major idea was that two tasks with different phasing (within-task timing) characteristics were assumed to be governed by different programs. If a shift in conditions requires subjects to abandon one program in favor of another, then they will be practicing two different programs in the two different variations of the "same" motor task. This is analogous to speeding up a treadmill so that jogging is substituted for walking, each activity having its own program (e.g., Shapiro et al., 1981). It is difficult to say how wide the range of conditions produced by a given motor program might be, but we suspect that many programs exist and that they are shifted rather freely when the conditions change. Viewed in this way, it is not surprising that the tasks do not transfer to each other.

Transfer Depends on Similarity

A second and related generalization about transfer of motor learning is that transfer depends on the similarity of the two tasks being considered. The idea of similarity is certainly not new, as Thorndike and Woodworth (1901) proposed that transfer depends on the number of "identical elements" that exist in common between two tasks. If one task had elements that were totally different from the elements in another task, then no transfer would be expected. Transfer would be 100% if the two tasks had all their elements in common. The problem with this theory was that it never specified what an "element" was and how it could be measured, so the theory cannot be tested experimentally. In the previous paragraphs, the implication is that the "elements" could be (a) abilities in common between the two tasks, (b) motor programs that are used for the two tasks, or (c) both. And other possibilities exist.

The theories of transfer have been improved considerably since the publication of this early idea. A major contribution was Osgood's (1949) *transfer surface*, which provided a description of the amount of transfer of *verbal* learning as a joint function of the similarity of the stimulus elements and the response elements. Holding (1976) presented a related idea for motor skills. In all these cases, the notion of similarity is a dominant theme, as it always has been. But these recent theories are not completely satisfactory, as a large number of transfer phenomena do not appear to be explained by them. The problem seems to be related to our lack of understanding about what "similarity" is, and what the "elements" are that are supposedly similar in various tasks. Perhaps research with abilities and motor programs will contribute to this area, but it is too early to tell. The conclusion from viewing this literature is that motor transfer is not well understood at all (Schmidt & Young, 1987).

Negative Transfer

We have mentioned that transfer is not always positive and that losses can occur in one skill as a result of experience on another. This is called *negative transfer*. Many people believe that negative transfer is relatively common and that the skill losses produced by it can be quite large. Almost cliché is the story that tennis in the summer ruined the person's badminton game in the winter, presumably because the two tasks are quite similar yet somewhat incompatible (e.g., the wrist action in the two strokes). But the research on transfer nearly always shows low but positive transfer; negative transfer is seldom the outcome. However, negative transfer can be produced if the proper conditions are presented, such as those provided by Lewis, McAllister, and Adams (1951).

Lewis, McAllister, and Adams used the Mashburn task, in which a two-dimensional arm control and a foot control are operated simultaneously to control the positions of lights on a display. After the subject practiced for a varying number of trials (either 10, 30, or 50) with the usual configuration of the task, subjects were switched to a condition in which the control-display relationships were reversed. For example, in order to move the light on the screen to the left, the lever had to be moved to the right rather than to the left, as had been the case before. All three dimensions of the task (right-left, backward-

forward, right foot-left foot) were reversed. This is analogous to driving a car in which the "normal" movements of the controls are suddenly backward (e.g., steering wheel turned clockwise to go left, brake pedal released to stop). After either 10, 20, 30, or 50 trials on this reversed task, subjects were switched back to the original configuration of the task to see whether skill had been lost or gained. This is a retroactive transfer design (as shown in table 14.3).

In figure 14.11, the differences on the main task between the number of matches before and after reversed-task practice are plotted. A decrement score of zero means that the standard task was performed just as well after the reversed task as before, meaning that no negative retroactive transfer occurred; larger decrement scores imply more negative transfer. Transfer was generally negative, and negative transfer increased as the number of reversed-task trials increased. This is what you might expect, as the amount of interference from this reversed task should be larger if it is more completely learned. (There was also an effect of the number of original-practice trials of the task with standard controls, but it is far from clear what this means; see Schmidt, 1971a, for a more complete discussion of this effect.) This is an example of clear and unmistakable negative retroactive transfer, and similar findings have been produced in other studies using similar procedures (see Lewis, 1953; Schmidt, 1971a; Schmidt & Young, 1987).

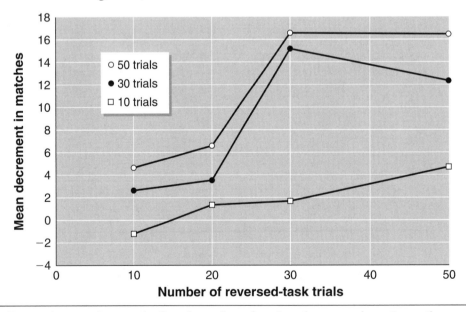

Figure 14.11. Retroactive negative transfer (interference) as a function of amount of practice on the reversed task and the amount of original practice on the standard task.
Reprinted from Lewis, McAllister, and Adams, 1951.

However, the negative transfer produced in these studies seemed mainly cognitive and may not have had much to do with *motor* negative transfer. The reversed conditions probably left the subjects confused about what to do and may not have disrupted the motor control processes in the task at all. This argument is not strong, though, as it is difficult to know what the relevant motor and cognitive processes are in such tasks. Yet it seems logical to assume that a major portion of the problem for the subjects on returning to the standard task was confusion about what the limbs controlling each of the three dimensions of the task were supposed to do.

Ross (1974) attempted to produce negative transfer in a situation in which it could not be argued that confusion prevailed about what to do, so that any remaining negative transfer would be attributable to the loss of skill in controlling the limbs. She produced a laboratory analog of the tennis-badminton situation, in which the limb movements in the two tasks were identical except for one critical part of the action near the end. Subjects learned one version of the task that required a forceful ending; they then learned the alternative task, which was the same except that a light touch was required at the end. Then Ross transferred subjects back to the original task with the forceful ending (a retroactive transfer design). Little negative transfer occurred, and what did occur was eliminated in 10 practice trials at the original task. These data supported the idea that the major problem for subjects in the Lewis, McAllister, and Adams experiment was confusion about the cognitive elements and not a loss of limb control.

However, other studies suggest that negative transfer of limb control can be quite large. For example, Shapiro (1977, 1978) had subjects learn complex patterns of movements with a particular experimenter-imposed timing. Later, subjects were instructed to speed up the movement, which they had no trouble doing. But when they were also told to *ignore* the temporal pattern they had learned earlier, subjects had a great deal of difficulty producing a new temporal structure. Instead, they sped up the original temporal structure, more or less as one would speed up a phonograph record. (These studies are discussed in more detail in chapter 6; see figure 6.18). This can be seen as a kind of negative transfer, where producing the "new" pattern at maximal speed

was interfered with by the prior experience with the "old" temporal structure. This might turn out to be an important finding for understanding transfer. Schmidt and Young (1987) suggest that tasks whose phasing and sequencing are the same will tend to transfer to each other positively; two tasks whose sequencing is the same, but whose timing is different, will tend to transfer to each other negatively; most tasks, with neither sequencing nor timing in common, transfer to each other hardly at all.

Similar effects for learning new coordination-timing patterns were described in chapter 13. Strong negative transfer effects are exerted by the intrinsic patterns (in-phase and anti-phase patterns) when one attempts to learn a new pattern, such as a 90° relative-phase coordination (Zanone & Kelso, 1992; Lee, Swinnen, & Verschueren, 1995); this suggests that some negative transfer can result from the experiences that subjects bring into the laboratory (i.e., before learning any specific task). Certainly much more can be discovered about negative transfer effects from this kind of research.

Another example involves second-language learners; here we consider the production of a particular language's speech sounds (but not its grammar or vocabulary) as a motor skill. Common experience tells us that the difficulty in producing a particular speech sound in English, for example, is critically related to the speaker's first language. The same acoustic goal is often produced differently by speakers whose native language is French versus German; these difficulties represent negative transfer from French (or German) to English. If negative transfer were *not* occurring, these pronunciation difficulties would not be common to a particular language group. We would not expect to find, for example, French accents in English. Yet such accents are clearly differentiated from German accents, and these phenomena seem to represent some of our strongest evidence for negative transfer.

Finally, it seems reasonable to think that two tasks, each containing a number of "elements," may have some similar elements leading to positive transfer and have other, dissimilar elements contributing to negative transfer. In Shapiro's (1977, 1978) studies, at the same time negative transfer of phasing occurred, positive transfer of sequencing might also have been occurring. Other aspects of the task might not transfer at all—positively or negatively. This idea can be seen in many tasks in sports, for example, handball and racquetball. There appear to be many common elements between these two games, such as the angles that the ball bounces off the walls of the court and the strategies of the game, all of which might lead to positive transfer. Yet at the same time, other elements of the game would appear to lead to negative transfer, such as the exact positioning of the body just before the shot, or the actions in the shot itself. The point is that whether or not two tasks transfer positively or negatively might depend on a kind of "balance sheet" on which the elements that transfer positively are "weighed" against those that transfer negatively. This is not an adequate theory of transfer, but it may help to conceptualize some of the things that happen when two tasks interact.

Simulation and Transfer

An important and commonly used method for training people in motor (and cognitive) tasks is simulation. The main feature of simulations is that they provide a practice task that is related to some *criterion task* (the overall goal of the learning process) in some way. For example, pilots may practice procedural skills on ground-based devices that mimic the cockpit of the airplane, as seen in figure 14.12. The hope is that the practice of these skills in the simulator will transfer to the actual skills in the airplane (the criterion task).

Simulators

Many examples of simulators in learning situations may be mentioned. At one end of the scale are expensive and highly sophisticated devices that simulate large and complex systems. For example, the simulators for learning to fly are often elaborate, with exact mock-ups of the cockpit area, instrumentation, and so on. The pilot/learner is often given televised displays from the windshield showing airport runways approaching; the instrumentation is complete and functioning; and the "feel" of the controls is as similar to that in the real airplane as possible. In some simulators, even movements of the cockpit as a whole simulate the flight of an airplane in a storm. In these situations, the information displayed on the gauges and dials is produced by a computer, and the learner's responses are monitored by computers as well. Comparable devices are used to simulate the behavior of a weapons system, and recently simulators for controlling the behavior of nuclear power plants have been developed. As you might imagine, these devices are expensive to produce and operate.

On the other hand, many simulation devices are relatively simple and inexpensive. Many of us learned to drive by practicing on driver simulators that had not-so-realistic configurations of an automobile's controls, so that the proper motions could be learned before we tried them in a real car.

Figure 14.12. The MD-11 flight simulator.
Courtesy of Dr. Diane Shapiro, Douglas Products Division of the Boeing Company.

Dentists in training practice their skills on plaster-of-paris models of the jaw, sometimes with the "jaw" on a workbench or even in the position it would be in if it were the upper jaw of a patient. A simulator can require almost no apparatus; for example, you can practice putting on a living room rug.

Simulators provide a number of advantages, such as cost and/or time effectiveness, increased safety, and the increased convenience of having the simulator available for use at any time in any weather. And yet simulators have a number of serious drawbacks. First, the "worth" of any simulation device has to be measured in terms of the amount of transfer that it provides to the criterion task. If the simulator does not provide transfer to the criterion task, the device is essentially useless in terms of the purpose for which it was originally intended. Thus, the evaluation of simulation devices usually places heavy emphasis on analysis of the transfer of learning from the device to the criterion task (Alessi, 1988; Lintern et al., 1989; Schendel et al., 1985).

From the earlier discussion of transfer, one point that consistently emerged is that motor transfer is generally quite low unless the two tasks are so similar as to be practically identical. From these basic research findings, as well as from the literature on the specificity of skills (chapter 9), it appears that many simulators will not transfer well to the criterion tasks for which they were designed. Certainly a critical part of simulator evaluation is the conduct of a transfer experiment, perhaps with various versions of the simulator, to evaluate the amount of transfer that is actually produced.

To the extent that the simulator and the criterion task are similar, transfer should increase from one to the other. Recognition of this fact has led the designers of simulation devices to make them very realistic—for example, the simulated airplane cockpit that moves as if in a storm. Much effort is devoted to making the controls feel as they do in the airplane, with proper resistances, feedback, and so on to maximize the similarity. This makes good sense. If differences between simulator and criterion task are too great, it is possible that separate motor control mechanisms might be used, producing no transfer.

Simulation devices are usually excellent for teaching procedural details, the proper order of a sequence of activities, and the like. These aspects of the overall task are important, and considerable time can be "saved" by using simulators at early stages of practice, as sequence knowledge appears to be transferable between different effector systems (Fendrich, Healy, & Bourne, 1991; Keele et al., 1995). There is less certainty that the motor elements of the task are so easily simulated, however. It would appear that when complex movements are simulated, even with very complex and expensive simulators, there is a big difference between the behaviors produced on the simulator and those produced on the criterion task. Thus, while simulators clearly have their place in the training of procedures, their utility in terms of the training of movement patterns might not be very great.

Simulations are often applied rather blindly without regard for the kinds of transfer that are to be produced. Many examples are seen in athletics, in which certain kinds of behaviors are simulated in various drill procedures. The use of blocking dummies in American football may be helpful in the early stages of learning a play when the athletes have questions about where to go and whom to block, but there would seem to be little utility in using them beyond this point. Players would seem to require practice in blocking other players who do not wish to be blocked; this is, of course, very difficult to simulate. It is difficult to evaluate the effectiveness of these various procedures because we have no research about the transfer of these drills to game situations. But we would guess that the faith placed in many of these procedures is probably overdone. Certainly it would make sense to examine any such drills or simulations very carefully.

Virtual Reality

A different type of simulation has been developed in recent years that uses computer-aided technology to mimic the perceptual-motor attributes of certain tasks. *Virtual reality* devices often simulate the perceptual (usually visual and auditory) demands of a task, together with a simulated effector system, and display these on a computer monitor. The actions of a subject can be mapped in terms of the actions of the simulated effector system, with the expected (computer-generated) consequences displayed. One advantage of such devices is that they are much less costly to produce than many of the simulators already discussed. And, once developed, these computer programs should be modifiable so that newer versions need not be built again from scratch.

Although virtual reality devices hold promise as training devices or simulators for real tasks, their usefulness has only just begun to be examined (Wickens & Baker, 1995). Given what is known already about simulators and transfer, we suspect that the greatest usefulness of virtual reality devices in transfer-of-training situations may be for learning procedural aspects of a skill and may be limited in terms of actual perceptual and motor skill transfer. Such a prediction is supported by the findings of Kozak et al. (1993), who examined the transfer of training of a virtual reality training device in a speeded, grasp-and-move task. Subjects who were trained on the transfer task (grasping and moving a series of cans) performed much better during the transfer trials than subjects who had trained on a virtual reality simulation of the transfer task. In fact, these virtual reality-trained subjects performed no better on the transfer task than did a control group that had no training of any kind prior to the transfer trials. But other research, in which table tennis skills were simulated, has produced much more positive results (Todorov, Shadmehr, & Bizzi, 1997). Clearly, this is an exciting area for future research.

Summary

Learning, memory, retention, and transfer are very closely related concepts. Motor memory is the persistence of the acquired capability for responding, and losses in memory are called forgetting. Forgetting is usually measured by performance losses on a retention test, administered after a retention interval. Different measures of retention can be computed, although the absolute-retention measure is the best.

A variant of the learning experiment is the transfer experiment, in which the effect of practicing one task on the performance of some other task is evaluated. Transfer is often measured as a percentage, indicating the proportion of possible improvement in one task that was achieved by practice on the other task. Studies of transfer are important for evaluating training and other instructional programs.

Continuous skills are retained nearly perfectly over long retention intervals. Discrete skills, on the other hand, can show marked performance losses during the same retention intervals. The reasons for this difference in retention are not clear, but they are probably not based on the tendency for continuous tasks to be more "motor" than discrete tasks are. Perhaps the difference has its basis in the idea that continuous tasks, with more practice time in a typical experiment, are more resistant to forgetting because they are learned more completely.

The loss of information related to motor performance can occur in various ways. Information can decay from memory due to a passive process, or can be lost due to retroactive or proactive interference. Warm-up decrement is a retention loss caused by the imposition of a short rest in a series of practice trials. Research supports the set hypothesis, which holds that warm-up decrement is a loss, during rest, of a pattern of nonmemory adjustments critical to performance.

Transfer of learning is involved in the study of conditions of practice. Two basic principles of transfer are (a) that it depends on the similarity between tasks and (b) that motor transfer is usually small but positive. Negative transfer can be produced under certain conditions, but it is probably mostly cognitive in nature. Devices such as simulators, as well as virtual reality environments, provide promise for positive transfer, although their value seems to be highly specific to the similarity between the training and transfer tasks.

APPENDIX

LOGARITHMS TO THE BASE 2

Number	.0	.1	.2	.3	.4	.5	.6	.7	.8	.9
0.		−3.32	−2.32	−1.74	−1.32	−1.00	−0.74	−0.51	−0.32	−0.15
1.	0.00	0.14	0.26	0.38	0.49	0.58	0.68	0.77	0.85	0.93
2.	1.00	1.07	1.14	1.20	1.26	1.32	1.38	1.43	1.49	1.54
3.	1.58	1.63	1.68	1.72	1.77	1.81	1.85	1.89	1.93	1.96
4.	2.00	2.04	2.07	2.10	2.14	2.17	2.20	2.23	2.26	2.29
5.	2.32	2.35	2.38	2.41	2.43	2.46	2.49	2.51	2.54	2.56
6.	2.58	2.61	2.63	2.66	2.68	2.70	2.72	2.74	2.77	2.79
7.	2.81	2.83	2.85	2.87	2.89	2.91	2.93	2.94	2.96	2.98
8.	3.00	3.02	3.04	3.05	3.07	3.09	3.10	3.12	3.14	3.15
9.	3.17	3.19	3.20	3.22	3.23	3.25	3.26	3.28	3.29	3.31
10.	3.32	3.34	3.35	3.36	3.38	3.39	3.41	3.42	3.43	3.45
11.	3.46	3.47	3.49	3.50	3.51	3.52	3.54	3.55	3.56	3.57
12.	3.58	3.60	3.61	3.62	3.63	3.64	3.66	3.67	3.68	3.69
13.	3.70	3.71	3.72	3.73	3.74	3.75	3.77	3.78	3.79	3.80
14.	3.81	3.82	3.83	3.84	3.85	3.86	3.87	3.88	3.89	3.90
15.	3.91	3.92	3.93	3.94	3.94	3.95	3.96	3.97	3.98	3.99
16.	4.00	4.01	4.02	4.03	4.04	4.04	4.05	4.06	4.07	4.08
17.	4.09	4.10	4.10	4.11	4.12	4.13	4.14	4.15	4.15	4.16
18.	4.17	4.18	4.19	4.19	4.20	4.21	4.22	4.22	4.23	4.24
19.	4.25	4.26	4.26	4.27	4.28	4.29	4.29	4.30	4.31	4.31
20.	4.32	4.33	4.34	4.34	4.35	4.36	4.36	4.37	4.38	4.39
21.	4.39	4.40	4.41	4.41	4.42	4.43	4.43	4.44	4.45	4.45
22.	4.46	4.47	4.47	4.48	4.49	4.49	4.50	4.50	4.51	4.52
23.	4.52	4.53	5.54	4.54	4.55	4.55	4.56	4.57	4.57	4.58
24.	4.58	4.59	4.60	4.60	4.61	4.61	4.62	4.63	4.63	4.64
25.	4.64	4.65	4.66	4.66	4.67	4.67	4.68	4.68	4.69	4.69
26.	4.70	4.71	4.71	4.72	4.72	4.73	4.73	4.74	4.74	4.75
27.	4.75	4.76	4.77	4.77	4.78	4.78	4.79	4.79	4.80	4.80
28.	4.81	4.81	4.82	4.82	4.83	4.83	4.84	4.84	4.85	4.85
29.	4.86	4.86	4.87	4.87	4.88	4.88	4.89	4.89	4.90	4.90
30.	4.91	4.91	4.92	4.92	4.93	4.93	4.94	4.94	4.94	4.95
31.	4.95	4.96	4.96	4.97	4.97	4.98	4.98	4.99	4.99	5.00
32.	5.00	5.00	5.01	5.01	5.02	5.02	5.03	5.03	5.04	5.04
33.	5.04	5.05	5.05	5.06	5.06	5.07	5.07	5.07	5.08	5.08
34.	5.09	5.09	5.10	5.10	5.10	5.11	5.11	5.12	5.12	5.13
35.	5.13	5.13	5.14	5.14	5.15	5.15	5.15	5.16	5.16	5.17
36.	5.17	5.17	5.18	5.18	5.19	5.19	5.19	5.20	5.20	5.21
37.	5.21	5.21	5.22	5.22	5.22	5.23	5.23	5.24	5.24	5.24
38.	5.25	5.25	5.26	5.26	5.26	5.27	5.27	5.27	5.28	5.28
39.	5.29	5.29	5.29	5.30	5.30	5.30	5.31	5.31	5.31	5.32
40.	5.32	5.33	5.33	5.33	5.34	5.34	5.34	5.35	5.35	5.35

Note. To find the Log_2 (23.5), for example, enter the row labeled 23, then move to the right under the column headed .5; the result is 4.55.

GLOSSARY

Abilities—Stable characteristics or traits, genetically defined and unmodifiable by practice or experience, that underlie certain skilled performances.

Absolute constant error (|CE|)—The absolute value of CE for each subject; a measure of amount of bias without respect to its direction.

Absolute error (AE)—The average absolute deviation of a set of scores from a target value; a measure of overall error.

Absolute frequency of knowledge of results—The absolute number of KRs given in a sequence of trials.

Absolute retention—A measure of retention based on the level of performance on the retention test.

Accumulated feedback—Information presented after a series of movements that represents a summary of those performances.

Action-centered interference—A view of attention that localizes interference effects at the response-selection stage.

Adams's theory—A closed-loop theory of motor learning proposed by Adams (1971), focusing heavily on the learning of slow positioning movements.

Adjacent-trial effect—With intertrial correlation matrices, the tendency for the correlations between adjacent trials to increase with practice.

Alpha motorneuron—Large efferent neurons responsible for innervation of the extrafusal fibers of the skeletal musculature.

Anti-phase—A coordination pattern in which two movement components oscillate in 180° relative phase.

Arousal—An internal state of alertness or excitement.

Associative phase—The second of three phases of learning proposed by Fitts, in which learners establish motor patterns.

Attention—A concept that describes limitations in the processing of information.

Augmented feedback—Feedback that is added to that typically received in the task (also called extrinsic feedback).

Automatic processing—Information processing that is relatively fast, that is done in parallel with other processes, and that requires minimal effort (compare with controlled processing).

Autonomous phase—The third of three phases of learning proposed by Fitts, in which learners have greatly reduced the attention demands of the task.

Average knowledge of results—A type of summary-KR method that presents the results of two or more trials as a statistical average.

Average velocity—The speed of a movement, or the movement distance divided by the movement time.

Bandwidth knowledge of results—Tolerance limits on errors that define when to provide qualitative or quantitative KR.

Bit—The amount of information required to reduce the original amount of uncertainty by half.

Blocked practice—A practice sequence in which all of the trials on one task are done together, uninterrupted by practice on any of the other tasks; low contextual interference.

Capacity interference—Interference between tasks caused by limitations in attention.

Catastrophe hypothesis—A nonlinear description of the nonlinear relationship between arousal and performance.

Ceiling effect—A limitation, imposed either by the scoring system or by physiological-psychological sources, that places a *maximum* on the score that a performer can achieve in a task.

Central pattern generators—Mechanisms in the spinal cord capable of providing oscillatory behavior thought to be involved in the control of locomotion and other tasks.

Changing component abilities hypothesis—The hypothesis that the set of abilities underlying a skill shifts systematically as practice continues.

Choice reaction time—RT for a task in which each response to be made is associated with a different stimulus.

Chunking—The combining of individual elements in memory into larger units.

Closed-loop system—A control system employing feedback, a reference of correctness, a computation of error, and subsequent correction in order to maintain a desired state; sometimes called a servomechanism or servo.

Closed skills—Skills that are performed in stable or predictable environmental settings.

Cocktail party problem—The phenomenon, described by Cherry, whereby humans can attend to a single conversation at a noisy gathering, neglecting other inputs.

Cognitive phase—The first of three phases of learning proposed by Fitts, in which learners' performances are heavily based on cognitive or verbal processes.

Cognitive psychology—A psychological tradition in which the nature of unobservable mental processes in human behavior is studied by indirect methods.

Component interaction—A characteristic of some tasks in which the adjustment on one component of the task requires an adjustment of some other component.

Concurrent feedback—Feedback that is presented simultaneously with the action.

Consciousness—The mechanism or process by which humans are aware of sensations, elements in memory, or internal events.

Constant error (CE)—With respect to sign, the average error of a set of scores from a target value.

Contextual interference—The interference effects in performance and learning that arise from practicing one task in the context of other tasks.

Continuous skills—Skills that appear to have no recognizable beginning or end.

Control dynamics—The mechanical characteristics of the levers, handwheels, and the like in control systems; affected by variables such as spring tension and inertia that change the "feel" of the control.

Controlled processing—Information processing that is relatively slow, that is done serially with other processes, and that requires effort (compare with automatic processing).

Coordination—Behavior of two or more degrees of freedom in relation to each other to produce skilled activity.

Correlation coefficient (r)—A statistical measure of the degree of linear association between two variables.

Cost-benefit analysis—A method by which the benefits from anticipating correctly can be weighed against the "cost" of anticipating incorrectly.

Criterion variable—In studies of prediction, the variable or score that is predicted from the predictor variables; the "best" obtainable measure of the construct that is to be predicted.

Crossman-Goodeve theory—A theory of the Fitts relationship that assumed a series of constant-duration movements, each interspersed with feedback-based corrections; an intermittent-control theory of rapid movement.

Cuff technique—A method of temporary deafferentation in which blood flow to the limb is eliminated by a blood pressure cuff, rendering the afferent neurons anoxic so that they cannot deliver sensory information.

Current or contemporary control—Woodworth's idea that the latter portions of a movement were controlled by a feedback-based "homing in" process that allowed a target to be achieved.

Deafferentation—Eliminating, usually by surgery (dorsal rhizotomy), the sensory input to the spinal cord while leaving efferent output intact.

Degrees of freedom—The number of separate independent dimensions of movement in a system that must be controlled.

Degrees of freedom problem—The difficulty in explaining the simultaneous control of multiple, independently moving body parts.

Deliberate practice—Identified by Ericsson as practice that is not inherently enjoyable and is undertaken for the sole purpose of improving performance.

Differential approach—That approach to the study of behavior that focuses on individual differences, abilities, and prediction.

Difficulty—Depending on the particular paradigm, either the ratio of the amplitude to the target widths (Fitts, 1954) or the ratio of the movement amplitude to MT (Schmidt, Zelaznik, and Frank, 1978; Schmidt et al., 1979).

Discrete skills—Skills that have a definite beginning and end.

Discrimination reaction time—RT for a task in which a number of stimuli can be presented, with a response being made only if a given stimulus occurs.

Distributed practice—A sequence of practice and rest periods in which the practice time is relatively restful, often equal to or less than the rest time.

Dorsal rhizotomy—The cutting of the dorsal roots at various segmental levels of the spinal cord, resulting in deafferentation from the associated areas of the body.

Dorsal root—The collection of nerve fibers from the periphery into a bundle near the posterior side of the spinal cord at each spinal level; the major sensory input to the cord.

Dynamic pattern theory—A view that describes coordination as a self-organizing process of pattern formation.

Early responding—Processing all of the aspects of a movement in advance so that the movement can occur at or before the stimulus.

Ecological viewpoint—A point of view emphasizing the study of movement in natural environments.

Effective target width (W$_e$)—The size of the target area that the performer actually uses in a series of aiming movements, calculated as the standard deviation of the movement endpoints.

Effector anticipation—Predicting the duration of internal processes for a planned movement so that it can be made coincident with some anticipated external event.

Elaboration and distinctiveness hypothesis—A view of contextual interference that emphasizes the comparative and contrastive value of tasks in short-term memory.

Electromyography (EMG)—a recording of the electrical activity from muscles.

Empirical equation—An equation describing the outcome of an experiment in which the functional mathematical relationship is estimated from the empirical observations.

Ensemble—The combination of the various sources of sensory information that enable accurate perception of movement and position.

Equilibrium point—For a given level of muscle activation, the hypothetical joint angle at which the torques from the two opposing muscle groups are equal and opposite.

Equilibrium-point models (α and λ)—Limb control models in which a movement endpoint is produced through the specification of an equilibrium point between the agonist and the antagonist muscle groups.

Ergonomics—The study of human beings in work environments (also called human factors).

Error in execution—An error in which the planned spatial-temporal goal of a movement is appropriate, but the movement deviates from the desired path because of factors occurring during execution.

Error in selection—An error in which the planned spatial-temporal goal is inappropriate given the nature of the environment.

Expected sensory consequences—A construct in schema theory; the anticipated feedback sensations that should be received if the movement is correct.

Extrafusal fibers—The muscle fibers of the major skeletal muscles, exclusive of the fibers in the muscle spindles.

Factor analysis—A complex statistical procedure wherein a large number of separate tests are grouped into a smaller number of factors, each of which is thought to represent an underlying ability.

Factor loading—In factor analysis, the statistical values indicating the extent to which the tests measure the various factors.

Feedback—Sensory information that results from movement.

Feedforward control—The sending of information ahead in time to ready a part of the system for incoming sensory feedback or for a future motor command.

Fitts' Law—Mathematical description of the speed-accuracy trade-off in which the average MT is linearly related to $\text{Log}_2 (2A/W)$.

Floor effect—A limitation, imposed either by the scoring system or by physiological-psychological limits, that places a *minimum* on the score that a performer can achieve in a task.

Force variability—The within-subject variability in a series of forces produced either in static or in dynamic contractions.

Foreperiod—The interval between a warning signal and the stimulus to respond.

Forgetting—The loss of memory, or the loss of the acquired capability for responding.

Forgetting and reconstruction hypothesis—A view of contextual interference that emphasizes the role of the construction of previously forgotten action plans as a basis of learning.

Gain—The relationship between the amount of input to a system and the output produced by it; usually expressed as a ratio.

Gamma motorneurons—Small efferent neurons that innervate the intrafusal muscle fibers of the muscle spindle.

Gearshift analogy—An idea presented by Keele about the learning of motor programs, analogous to learning to shift gears in an automobile.

General motor ability—An early concept in which a single ability was thought to account for

major portions of the individual differences in motor behavior.

Generalized motor program—A motor program whose expression can be varied depending on the choice of certain parameters.

Goal setting—A motivational technique in which subjects are encouraged to set performance goals.

Golgi tendon organs—Small stretch receptors located at the musculotendinous junction, providing precise information about muscle tension.

Guidance—A series of techniques in which the behavior of the learner is limited or controlled by various means to prevent errors.

Habit—The acquired capability for moving; an unobservable internal state that underlies skilled performance.

Hick's law—A mathematical statement that choice RT is linearly related to the Log_2 of the number of stimulus-response alternatives, or to the amount of information that must be processed in order to choose a response.

Hierarchical control model—The idea that with practice, the control of the response shifts systematically from attention-demanding higher levels to less attention-demanding motor program levels.

Impulse—From physics, the aggregate of forces applied over time; the area under a force-time curve, or the integral of force over time.

Impulse-timing model—A model of motor programming in which movement trajectory is controlled by impulses that determine the amount and timing of applied forces.

Impulse-variability theory—A theory of rapid actions in which the variability in the muscular impulses leads directly to the variations or errors in movement control.

Index of difficulty (ID)—In Fitts' Law, the $\text{Log}_2 (2A/W)$, or the theoretical "difficulty" of a movement.

Individual differences—Stable differences among individuals on some variable or task.

Individual differences in learning—Differences between or among individuals in the amount or rate of acquisition of skills.

Information—The content of a message that serves to reduce uncertainty.

Information-processing viewpoint—The study of movement in which the human is viewed as a processor of information, focusing on storage, coding, retrieval, and transformation of information.

Inherent feedback—That feedback normally received in the conduct of a particular task (also called intrinsic feedback).

Initial adjustment—Woodworth's term for the initial open-loop portion of an aiming movement.

Initial conditions—A construct in schema theory; the nature of the task and environment prior to the production of a movement.

In-phase—A coordination pattern in which two movement components oscillate in 0° relative phase.

Intercept (*a*)—One of the constants for linear empirical equations; the value on the *Y*-axis when *X* is zero.

Interference theory—A theory that forgetting is caused by interference from other learned materials.

Interneuron—Neurons originating and terminating wholly within the spinal cord that connect various segments of it; some are thought to be involved in the spinal generators.

Intertrial correlation matrix—A table or matrix of correlations between performances on all pairs of trials in a practice sequence.

Intertrial interval—The interval of time between one movement and the next in the KR paradigm.

Intrafusal fibers—The small muscle fibers lying at the polar ends of the muscle spindle.

Invariant characteristic—The relationship between joint position and joint torque established by the central nervous system.

Inverted-U principle—A description of the relationship between arousal and performance that resembles an inverted U when graphed.

Joint receptors—Common term for a number of different receptors that are located in the joint capsules, presumably providing information about joint position.

Kinematic feedback—Feedback about the movement characteristics or movement pattern produced.

Kinetic feedback—Feedback about the force characteristics of a movement.

Knowledge of performance (KP)—Augmented feedback related to the nature of the movement produced.

Knowledge of results (KR)—Augmented feedback related to the nature of the result produced in terms of the environmental goal.

KR delay—The interval between the production of a movement and the presentation of KR.

Law of practice—The common finding that the log of the performance measure tends to change linearly with the log of the amount of practice.

Lead-up tasks—Certain tasks or activities that are typically presented to prepare learners for a more important or more complex task or activity.

Learning—A set of internal processes associated with practice or experience leading to relatively permanent changes in the capability for skill.

Learning curve—A label sometimes applied to the performance curve, in the belief that the changes in performance mirror changes in learning.

Learning score—A difference score, computed as the difference between the initial and final levels of performance; sometimes used in computing the changes in performance as a result of practice.

Learning variable—An independent variable that affects learning.

Length-tension diagram—A graph of the tension produced by a contracting muscle as a function of its length.

Log$_2$ (*N*)—The power to which the base 2 must be raised to achieve *N*.

Long-loop reflex—A stretch reflex with a latency of from 50 to 80 ms, modified by instruction, and mediated in higher brain centers.

Long-term memory—A functionally limitless memory store for abstractly coded information, facts, concepts, and relationships; presumably storage for movement programs.

Magnet effect—Identified by von Holst as the tendency of one effector's rhythmic oscillation to become interdependent with another oscillating limb.

Maintenance tendency—Identified by von Holst as the tendency of one effector to maintain an independent rhythmic oscillation while another effector is oscillating.

Massed practice—A sequence of practice and rest periods in which the rest time is much less than the practice time.

Memory—The persistence of habit; the acquired capability for moving.

Memory trace—A construct in Adams's closed-loop theory; a modest motor program for determining and initiating the movement.

Mental practice—A practice method in which performance on the task is imagined or visualized without overt physical practice.

Mesencephalic preparation—A surgical preparation in which the spinal cord is cut at the midbrain, essentially separating higher centers from the spinal cord.

Modeling—A technique for demonstrating the learning task.

Modular—A view of individual differences that organizes brain activities in terms of functions (such as timekeeping) rather than tasks.

Moment of inertia—A physical quantity defining a body's resistance to rotational forces; the mass of the body multiplied by the square of the distance of the center of the mass from the point of rotation.

Monosynaptic stretch reflex—A segmental reflex produced by stretch of a muscle and its spindles connecting monosynaptically with the alpha motorneurons of the same muscle; it has a latency of about 30–50 ms in humans.

Motivation—An internal state that tends to direct or energize the system toward a goal.

Motor behavior—An area of study stressing primarily the principles of human skilled movement generated at a behavioral level of analysis.

Motor control—An area of study dealing with the understanding of the neural, physical, and behavioral aspects of movement.

Motor development—A field of study concerning the changes in motor behavior occurring as a result of growth, maturation, and experience.

Motor learning—A set of internal processes associated with practice or experience leading to rela-

tively permanent changes in the capability for motor skill.

Motor memory—The memory for movement or motor information.

Motorneuron pools—Collections of alpha motorneuron cell bodies in the gray matter of the cord that serve motor units in the same, or anatomically related, muscles.

Motor program—An abstract representation that, when initiated, results in the production of a coordinated movement sequence.

Motor reaction time—The interval between the first change in EMG and the movement's initiation.

Movement—Changes in joint angles, the position of the entire body, or both.

Movement outcome—A construct in schema theory; the result of the movement in the environment, usually signaled by intrinsic feedback or KR.

Movement time (MT)—The interval between the initiation of a movement and its termination.

Multiple correlation—A statistical procedure in which the weightings of predictor variables are adjusted so that their sum correlates maximally with some criterion variable.

Muscle spindle—Small spindle-shaped structures, located in parallel with the extrafusal fibers, that provide information about muscle length.

Negative transfer—The loss in capability for one task as a result of practice or experience in some other task.

Objectivity—The aspect of measurement related to the extent to which two observers achieve the same score.

Open-loop system—A control system with preprogrammed instructions to an effector that does not use feedback information and error-detection processes.

Operant techniques—Methods for learning in which certain behaviors are reinforced or rewarded, leading to an increase in the probability that they will occur again.

Optimized-submovement model—A view of the speed-accuracy trade-off that optimizes the duration of an initial impulse and, if necessary, one or more corrective impulses.

Parallel processing—A type of information processing in which at least two processes can occur simultaneously.

Parameter—A value specified to the generalized motor program that defines the particular expression of the pattern of activity.

Part-whole methods—The learning technique in which the task is broken down into its parts for separate practice.

Perceptual anticipation—Anticipation of the arrival of a signal through internal mechanisms or processes.

Perceptual narrowing—The focusing of attention so that specific sources of information are more likely to be received but rare events are more likely to be missed.

Perceptual trace—A construct in Adams's closed-loop theory; a reference of correctness in memory that has been learned from feedback at the correct target position.

Performance curve—A plot of the average performance of a group of subjects for each of a number of practice trials or blocks of trials.

Performance variable—An independent variable that affects performance temporarily.

Perturbation—An unexpected physical event that changes the movement or the movement goal.

Phase transition—An abrupt shift from one coordination pattern to another.

Phasing—The temporal structure of a sequence, usually measured by the ratios of element durations and the overall movement duration.

Point-to-point computation—Models of limb control in which the coordinates of each point in a limb's trajectory are achieved sequentially by the motor system at the time of response execution.

Polyrhythm—The rhythm produced when two effectors simultaneously produce their own, nonharmonic rhythms (e.g., three beats with one finger combined with two beats of another finger).

Positive transfer—The gain in capability on one task as a result of practice or experience on some other task.

Post-KR delay—The interval of time between the presentation of KR and the next movement.

Precision of KR—The level of accuracy with which KR describes the movement outcome produced.

Prediction—The process in which the score on a criterion variable is estimated from one or more predictor variables based on the association between them.

Predictor variable—The variable(s) from which a criterion variable is predicted.

Premotor reaction time—The interval from the stimulus presentation to the initial change in EMG.

Preparation—Reorganization of attention and information processing so that a signal can be received and responded to quickly.

Preprogramming—The process of preparing the motor program for initiation.

Preselection effect—In short-term motor memory work, the phenomenon that the memory for subject-selected movements is stronger than for experimenter-selected movements.

Proactive interference—In the interference theory, a source of forgetting caused by learning imposed before the original learning of some to-be-remembered task.

Probe technique—A secondary-task method that uses RT to assess the attention demands of a primary task.

Progression-regression hypothesis—The idea that learning produces a progression to more complex control strategies and that stress or forgetting produces a regression to more simple levels.

Psychological refractoriness—The delay in the response to the second of two closely spaced stimuli.

Random practice—A practice sequence in which the tasks being practiced are ordered (quasi-) randomly across trials; high contextual interference.

Reach/grasp action—An action that coordinates the limb-transport component with the opening and closing of the grasp component.

Reaction time (RT)—The interval between the presentation of an unexpected stimulus and the initiation of a response.

Recall schema—A construct in schema theory; the relationship between past parameters, past initial conditions, and the movement outcomes produced by these combinations.

Receptor anticipation—Anticipation of the arrival of a stimulus due to sensory information about its time of arrival.

Recognition schema—A construct in schema theory; the relationship between past initial conditions, past movement outcomes, and the sensory consequences produced by these combinations.

Reflex-reversal phenomenon—The phenomenon by which a given stimulus can produce two different reflexive responses depending on the function of the limb in a movement.

Regression line—The line of best fit between two variables, whose slope and intercept are determined by regression analysis.

Relative force—An invariant feature of the motor program that defines the relationships between the forces produced in the various actions in a movement.

Relative frequency of knowledge of results—The percentage of trials for which KR is provided; the absolute frequency divided by the number of trials.

Relative phase—A measure of temporal coordination that expresses the position of one limb within its cycle relative to the other limb within its cycle.

Relative retention—Measures of retention in which the performance on the retention test is evaluated in relation to the level of performance reached in original learning.

Reliability—The aspect of measurement related to the repeatability of a score.

Remoteness effect—In intertrial correlation matrices, the tendency for trials that are progressively more separated in the practice sequence to correlate systematically lower with each other.

Response-chaining hypothesis—A movement-control theory whereby each element in a sequence is triggered by movement feedback from the previous element.

Response-programming stage—A stage of information processing in which the previously chosen response is transformed into overt muscular action.

Response-selection stage—A stage of information processing in which the response associated with the presented stimulus is selected.

Response time—The interval from the presentation of a stimulus to the completion of a movement; the sum of reaction time and movement time.

Retention interval—The interval between the end of original learning and the retention test.

Retention test—A performance test administered after a retention interval for the purpose of assessing learning.

Retroactive interference—In the interference theory, a source of forgetting caused by practice imposed between the original learning and the retention test for a to-be-remembered task.

Reversal hypothesis—A view of the relationship between arousal and performance that is based on individual differences in the interpretation of one's arousal level.

Root-mean-square error (RMSE)—The square root of the average squared deviations of a set of values from a target value; typically used as a measure of tracking proficiency.

Savings score—A statistic used in transfer experiments, representing the "savings" in practice time resulting from experience on some other task.

Scattergram—A graph on which subjects' scores on two tests are jointly represented as data points.

Schema—The basis for schema theory; a rule, concept, or relationship formed on the basis of experience.

Secondary-task method—A collection of experimental methods whereby learning on a main task can be estimated by use of simultaneous secondary measures of performance.

Selective attention—A mechanism for directing attention or capacity to a given stimulus input.

Self-organization—From dynamic pattern theory; a view that describes motor control as emerging from the interaction of the components of the movement system.

Sensitivity—That aspect of measurement dealing with the possibility of detecting changes in a dependent measure in relation to varying experimental conditions.

Sequencing—An invariant feature of motor programs in which the order of elements is fixed.

Serial processing—A style of information processing in which stages of processing are arranged sequentially in time.

Serial tasks—Movements in which a series of discrete elements are combined, with the order of elements being important.

Set—A non-memory pattern of adjustments that supports performance.

Set hypothesis—A hypothesis holding that warm-up decrement is caused by loss of set.

Short-term memory—A memory store with a capacity of about seven elements, capable of holding moderately abstract information for up to 30 s; analogous to consciousness; a "work space" for processing.

Short-term sensory store—A functionally limitless memory store for holding literal information for only about 1 s.

Similarity—A construct in most theories of transfer, indicating the extent to which certain aspects of two tasks are the same.

Simon effect—A type of stimulus-response compatibility effect in which irrelevant directional or locational information interferes with the action.

Simple reaction time—Reaction time from a task in which a single known response is produced when a single stimulus is presented.

Simplification hypothesis—The idea that the factor structure of a skill becomes progressively simpler with practice.

Simulator—A training device in which certain features of a task are duplicated, allowing for practice that resembles the transfer task.

Single-channel hypothesis—A theory of attention suggesting that the system can process only a single stimulus leading to a response at any given time.

Skills—Movements that are dependent on practice and experience for their execution, as opposed to being genetically defined.

Slope (b)—One of the constants of a linear equation; the inclination of the line.

Spacing effect—In memory experiments, repetitions of the criterion task that are increasingly separated in time are remembered more effectively.

Spatial anticipation—The anticipation of which stimulus (or the response to it) will occur; also called event anticipation.

Spatial-temporal goal—A subgoal for the performer in which a pattern of limb movement defined in terms of both space and time is selected; the major product of running a motor program.

Specificity of individual differences—Henry's theory of the structure of motor abilities, according to which motor tasks are thought to be composed of many independent abilities.

Specificity of learning—The concept that the similarity of the environmental conditions and processing in practice, compared to those in transfer, has a strong influence on transfer performance.

Speed-accuracy trade-off—The general principle describing a person's tendency to decrease the accuracy of a movement when the speed of it is increased.

State anxiety—A temporary state of worry or concern about a particular situation or activity.

Static contraction—Contractions in which the muscle is not changing length as it is producing force; sometimes called *isometric* contractions.

Stiffness—A characteristic of muscles and springs defined as the change in tension divided by the change in length.

Stimulus-identification stage—A stage of information processing in which the stimulus is identified, and features or patterns are abstracted; often divided into separate encoding and identification stages.

Stimulus onset asynchrony (SOA)—The interval of time between the onsets of two stimuli, as in the double-stimulation paradigm.

Stimulus-response compatibility—The degree to which the set of stimuli and associated responses are "naturally" related to each other.

Stimulus-response viewpoint—A tradition in psychology and motor behavior stressing the responses produced as a function of stimuli presented, without regard to the intervening mental events or processes.

Storage problem—A problem with early notions of motor programming in which the number of necessary programs was so large that their storage in the central nervous system seemed impossible.

Stress—A negative motivational state that tends to direct the individual away from some particular situation.

Structural interference—Interference among tasks caused by the simultaneous use of the same receptors, effectors, or processing systems.

Subjective reinforcement—A construct in Adams's closed-loop theory; term used to describe the subject's self-generated error signal, based on comparing feedback against a reference of correctness.

Summary knowledge of results—Augmented information about a set of performance trials presented after the set is completed.

Task analysis—A process of determining the underlying abilities and structure of a task or occupation.

Tau (τ)—A view of time-to-contact information based on the rate of expansion of the approaching object on the retina of the eye.

Taxonomy—A system of classification.

Temporal anticipation—The anticipation of when a given stimulus will arrive or when a movement is to be made.

Temporal variability—The inconsistency of some event with respect to time.

Terminal feedback—Feedback given after the movement's completion.

Time-to-contact (T_c)—Information about the time remaining until a moving object arrives at the eye.

Total variability (E)—The standard deviation of a set of scores about a target value; a measure of overall accuracy.

Trace-decay theory—A theory holding that forgetting is caused by the spontaneous "decay" or weakening of memory over time.

Trait anxiety—A general tendency to be anxious or stressed that is characteristic of a particular individual.

Transfer-appropriate processing—The concept that practice should be arranged so that the processing capability learned is appropriate for some goal criterion task or conditions.

Transfer design—An experimental design for measuring learning effects, in which all treatment groups are transferred to a common level of the independent variable.

Trials-delay technique—A procedure in which the presentation of KR for a movement is delayed, during which the learner practices one or more other movements.

Triggered reaction—A coordinated response to an environmental stimulus whose latency is shorter than RT yet longer than the long-loop reflex.

Unit of action—A "piece" of behavior that can be utilized repeatedly in various actions, producing essentially the same movements (but scaled to the environment) each time.

Validity—That aspect of measurement related to the extent to which a test measures what the experimenter wanted it to measure.

Variability in practice—A prediction of schema theory; transfer is predicted to be facilitated when goals are systematically varied from trial to trial during practice.

Variable error (VE)—The standard deviation of a set of scores about the subject's own average score; a measure of movement consistency.

Variable error in timing (VE_t)—The within-subject standard deviation of the duration of some process or event.

Verbal pretraining—The presentation of stimulus or display elements of the task in isolation so that they can be more easily responded to later in whole-task performance.

Vestibular apparatus—The receptors in the inner ear that are sensitive to the orientation of the head with respect to gravity, to rotation of the head, and to balance.

Visual proprioception—Gibson's concept that vision can serve as a strong basis for perception of the movements and positions of the body in space.

Warm-up decrement—The decrement in performance occurring after a rest period.

Wineglass effect—A slip of an object through the fingertips that triggers an increased grip force within 30 ms or so.

Zones of optimal functioning—A modification of the inverted-U principle to include individual, task, and environmental differences.

References

Abbs, J.H., & Gracco, V.L. (1983). Sensorimotor actions in the control of multi-movement speech gestures. *Trends in Neuroscience, 6,* 391-395.

Abbs, J.H., Gracco, V.L., & Cole, K.J. (1984). Control of multi-movement coordination: Sensorimotor mechanisms in speech motor programming. *Journal of Motor Behavior, 16,* 195-232.

Abbs, J.H., & Winstein, C.J. (1990). Functional contributions of rapid and automatic sensory-based adjustments to motor output. In M. Jeannerod (Ed.), *Attention and performance XIII* (pp. 627-652). Hillsdale, NJ: Erlbaum.

Abernethy, B. (1988). Dual-task methodology and motor skills research: Some applications and methodological constraints. *Journal of Human Movement Studies, 14,* 101-132.

Abernethy, B. (1993). Searching for the minimum essential information for skilled perception and action. *Psychological Research, 55,* 131-138.

Abernethy, B., Burgess-Limerick, R. (1992). Visual information for the timing of skilled movements: A review. In J.J. Summers (Ed.), *Approaches to the study of motor control and learning* (pp. 343-384). Amsterdam: Elsevier.

Abernethy, B., Burgess-Limerick, R., & Parks, S. (1994). Contrasting approaches to the study of motor expertise. *Quest, 46,* 186-198.

Abernethy, B., Neal, R.J., & Koning, P. (1994). Visual-perceptual and cognitive differences between expert, intermediate, and novice snooker players. *Applied Cognitive Psychology, 8,* 185-211.

Abernethy, B., & Russell, D.G. (1987). Expert-novice differences in an applied selective attention task. *Journal of Sport Psychology, 9,* 326-345.

Abernethy, B., Thomas, K.T., & Thomas, J.R. (1993). Strategies for improving understanding of

motor expertise [or mistakes we have made and things we have learned!!]. In J.L. Starkes & F. Allard (Eds.), *Cognitive issues in motor expertise* (pp. 317-356). Amsterdam: Elsevier.

Abrams, R.A., Meyer, D.E., & Kornblum, S. (1989). Speed and accuracy of saccadic eye movements: Characteristics of impulse variability in the oculomotor system. *Journal of Experimental Psychology: Human Perception and Performance, 15,* 529-543.

Abrams, R.A., Meyer, D.E., & Kornblum, S. (1990). Eye-hand coordination: Oculomotor control in rapid aimed limb movements. *Journal of Experimental Psychology: Human Perception and Performance, 16,* 248-267.

Ackerman, P.L. (1988). Determinants of individual differences during skill acquisition: Cognitive abilities and information processing. *Journal of Experimental Psychology: General, 117,* 288-318.

Ackerman, P.L. (1989). Individual differences and skill acquisition. In P.L. Ackerman, R.J. Sternberg, & R. Glaser (Eds.), *Learning and individual differences: Advances in theory and research* (pp. 165-217). New York: Freeman.

Ackerman, P.L. (1990). A correlational analysis of skill specificity: Learning, abilities, and individual differences. *Journal of Experimental Psychology: Learning, Memory, and Cognition, 16,* 883-901.

Ackerman, P.L. (1992). Predicting individual differences in complex skill acquisition: Dynamics of ability determinants. *Journal of Applied Psychology, 77,* 598-614.

Adamovich, S.V., & Feldman, A.G. (1984). Model of the central regulation of the parameters of motor trajectories. *Biophysics, 29,* 338-342.

Adams, J.A. (1952). Warm-up decrement in performance on the pursuit-rotor. *American Journal of Psychology, 65,* 404-414.

Adams, J.A. (1953). *The prediction of performance at advanced stages of training on a complex psychomotor task* (Research Bulletin 53-49). Lackland Air Force Base, TX: Human Resources Research Center.

Adams, J.A. (1955). A source of decrement in psychomotor performance. *Journal of Experimental Psychology, 49,* 390-394.

Adams, J.A. (1956). *An evaluation of test items measuring motor abilities.* (Research Rep. AFPTRC-TN-56-55). Lackland Air Force Base, TX: Human Resources Research Center.

Adams, J.A. (1957). The relationship between certain measures of ability and the acquisition of a psychomotor criterion response. *The Journal of General Psychology, 56,* 121-134.

Adams, J.A. (1961). The second facet of forgetting: A review of warm-up decrement. *Psychological Bulletin, 58,* 257-273.

Adams, J.A. (1964). Motor skills. *Annual Review of Psychology, 15,* 181-202.

Adams, J.A. (1967). *Human memory.* New York: McGraw-Hill.

Adams, J.A. (1968). Response feedback and learning. *Psychological Bulletin, 70,* 486-504.

Adams, J.A. (1971). A closed-loop theory of motor learning. *Journal of Motor Behavior, 3,* 111-150.

Adams, J.A. (1976a). Issues for a closed-loop theory of motor learning. In G.E. Stelmach (Ed.), *Motor control: Issues and trends* (pp. 87-107). New York: Academic Press.

Adams, J.A. (1976b). *Learning and memory: An introduction.* Homewood, IL: Dorsey.

Adams, J.A. (1977). Feedback theory of how joint receptors regulate the timing and positioning of a limb. *Psychological Review, 84,* 504-523.

Adams, J.A. (1978). Theoretical issues for knowledge of results. In G.E. Stelmach (Ed.), *Information processing in motor control and learning* (pp. 229-240). New York: Academic Press.

Adams, J.A. (1986). Use of the model's knowledge of results to increase the observer's performance. *Journal of Human Movement Studies, 12,* 89-98.

Adams, J.A. (1987). Historical review and appraisal of research on the learning, retention, and transfer of human motor skills. *Psychological Bulletin, 101,* 41-74.

Adams, J.A. (1990). The changing face of motor learning. *Human Movement Science, 9,* 209-220.

Adams, J.A., & Bray, N.W. (1970). A closed-loop theory of paired-associate verbal learning. *Psychological Review, 77,* 385-405.

Adams, J.A., & Creamer, L.R. (1962). Anticipatory timing of continuous and discrete responses. *Journal of Experimental Psychology, 63,* 84-90.

Adams, J.A., & Dijkstra, S. (1966). Short-term memory for motor responses. *Journal of Experimental Psychology, 71,* 314-318.

Adams, J.A., & Hufford, L.E. (1962). Contributions of a part-task trainer to the learning and relearning of a time-shared flight maneuver. *Human Factors, 4,* 159-170.

Adams, J.A., & Reynolds, B. (1954). Effect of shift in distribution of practice conditions following interpolated rest. *Journal of Experimental Psychology, 47,* 32-36.

Adrian, E.D., & Buytendijk, F.J.J. (1931). Potential changes in the isolated brain stem of the goldfish. *Journal of Physiology, 71,* 121-135.

Aiken, L.R. Jr. (1964). Reaction time and the expectancy hypothesis. *Perceptual and Motor Skills, 19,* 655-661.

Ainscoe, M., & Hardy, L. (1987). Cognitive warm-up in a cyclical gymnastics skill. *International Journal of Sport Psychology, 18,* 269-275.

Al-Ameer, H., & Toole, T. (1993). Combinations of blocked and random practice orders: Benefits to acquisition and retention. *Journal of Human Movement Studies, 25,* 177-191.

Alessi, S.M. (1988). Fidelity in the design of instructional simulators. *Journal of Computer-Based Instruction, 15,* 40-47.

Allen, L. (1978). Variability in practice and schema development in children. Unpublished master's thesis, University of Southern California, Los Angeles.

Allport, A. (1987). Selection for action: Some behavioral and neurophysiological considerations of attention and action. In H. Heuer & A.F. Sanders (Eds.), *Perspectives on perception and action* (pp. 395-419). Hillsdale, NJ: Erlbaum.

Allport, A. (1993). Attention and control: Have we been asking the wrong questions? In D.E. Meyer & S. Kornblum (Eds.), *Attention and performance XIV.* Cambridge, MA: MIT Press.

Allport, D.A., Antonis, B., & Reynolds, P. (1972). On the division of attention: A disproof of the single channel hypothesis. *The Quarterly Journal of Experimental Psychology, 24,* 225-235.

Amazeen, P.G., Schmidt, R.C., & Turvey, M.T. (1995). Frequency detuning of the phase entrainment dynamics of visually coupled rhythmic movements. *Biological Cybernetics, 72,* 511-518.

Ammons, R.B. (1947). Acquisition of motor skill: I. Quantitative analysis and theoretical formulation. *Psychological Review, 54,* 263-281.

Ammons, R.B. (1950). Acquisition of motor skill: III. Effects of initially distributed practice on rotary pursuit performance. *Journal of Experimental Psychology, 40,* 777-787.

Ammons, R.B. (1951). Effects of pre-practice activities on rotary pursuit performance. *Journal of Experimental Psychology, 41,* 187-191.

Ammons, R.B. (1988). Distribution of practice in motor skill acquisition: A few questions and comments. *Research Quarterly for Exercise and Sport, 59,* 288-290.

Anderson, D.I., Magill, R.A., & Sekiya, H. (1994). A reconsideration of the trials-delay of knowledge of results paradigm in motor skill learning. *Research Quarterly for Exercise and Sport, 65,* 286-290.

Anderson, J.R. (1982). Acquisition of cognitive skill. *Psychological Review, 89,* 369-406.

Anderson, J.R. (1995). *Learning and memory: An integrated approach.* New York: Wiley.

Andres, R.O., & Hartung, K.J. (1989). Prediction of head movement time using Fitts' Law. *Human Factors, 31,* 703-713.

Angel, R.W. (1977). Antagonist muscle activity during rapid arm movements: Central versus proprioceptive influences. *Journal of Neurology, Neurosurgery, and Psychiatry, 40,* 683-686.

Angel, R.W., & Higgins, J.R. (1969). Correction of false moves in pursuit tracking. *Journal of Experimental Psychology, 82,* 185-187.

Annett, J. (1959). Learning a pressure under conditions of immediate and delayed knowledge of results. *The Quarterly Journal of Experimental Psychology, 11,* 3-15.

Annett, J. (1969). *Feedback and human behavior.* Middlesex, England: Penguin.

Anshel, M.H., & Wrisberg, C.A. (1988). The effect of arousal and focused attention on warm-up decrement. *Journal of Sport Behavior, 11,* 18-31.

Anshel, M.H., & Wrisberg, C.A. (1993). Reducing warm-up decrement in the performance of the tennis serve. *Journal of Sport & Exercise Psychology, 15,* 290-303.

Anzola, G.P., Bertolini, G., Buchtel, H.A., & Rizzolatti, G. (1977). Spatial compatibility and anatomical factors in simple and choice reaction times. *Neuropsychologica, 15,* 295-302.

Apter, M.J. (1984). Reversal theory and personality: A review. *Journal of Research in Personality, 18,* 265-288.

Apter, M.J. (1989). *Reversal theory: Motivation, emotion, and personality.* London: Routledge.

Archer, E.J., Kent, G.W., & Mote, F.A. (1956). Effect of long-term practice and time-on-target information feedback on a complex tracking task. *Journal of Experimental Psychology, 51,* 103-112.

Armstrong, T.R. (1970a). *Feedback and perceptual-motor skill learning: A review of information feedback and manual guidance training techniques* (Tech. Rep. No. 25). Ann Arbor: University of Michigan, Dept. of Psychology.

Armstrong, T.R. (1970b). *Training for the production of memorized movement patterns* (Tech. Rep. No. 26). Ann Arbor: University of Michigan, Dept. of Psychology.

Arps, G.F. (1920). Work with knowledge of results versus work without knowledge of results. *Psychological Monographs, 28,* 1-41.

Arutyunyan, G.A., Gurfinkel, V.S., & Mirskii, M.L. (1968). Investigation of aiming at a target. *Biophysics, 13,* 536-538.

Arutyunyan, G.A., Gurfinkel, V.S., & Mirskii, M.L. (1969). Organization of movements on execution by man of an exact postural task. *Biophysics, 13,* 536-538.

Asatryan, D.G., & Feldman, A.G. (1965). Biophysics of complex systems and mathematical models. Functional tuning of nervous system with control of movement or maintenance of a steady posture—I. Mechanographic analysis of the work of the joint on execution of a postural task. *Biophysics, 10,* 925-935.

Ascoli, K.M., & Schmidt, R.A. (1969). Proactive interference in short-term motor retention. *Journal of Motor Behavior, 1,* 29-35.

Assaiante, C., Marchand, A.R., & Amblard, B. (1989). Discrete visual samples may control locomotor equilibrium and foot positioning in man. *Journal of Motor Behavior, 21,* 72-91.

Atkeson, C.G., & Hollerbach, J.M. (1985). Kinematic features of unrestrained vertical arm movements. *Journal of Neuroscience, 5,* 2318-2330.

Atkinson, R.C., & Shiffrin, R.M. (1971). The control of short-term memory. *Scientific American, 225,* 82-90.

Bachman, J.C. (1961). Specificity vs. generality in learning and performing two large muscle motor tasks. *Research Quarterly, 32,* 3-11.

Bachman, J.C. (1966). Influence of age and sex on the amount and rate of learning two motor tasks. *Research Quarterly, 37,* 176-186.

Bachrach, A.J. (1970). *Diving behavior*. In Scripps Institute of Oceanography, Human performance and scuba diving. Proceedings of the Symposium on Underwater Physiology, LaJolla, CA. Chicago: The Athletic Institute.

Baddeley, A.D., & Longman, D.J.A. (1978). The influence of length and frequency of training session on the rate of learning to type. *Ergonomics, 21,* 627-635.

Bahrick, H.P., Fitts, P.M., & Briggs, G.E. (1957). Learning curves—facts or artifacts? *Psychological Bulletin, 54,* 256-268.

Baldissera, F., Cavallari, P., & Civaschi, P. (1982). Preferential coupling between voluntary movements of ipsilateral limbs. *Neuroscience Letters, 34,* 95-100.

Baldissera, F., Cavallari, P., Marini, G., & Tassone, G. (1991). Differential control of in-phase and anti-phase coupling of rhythmic movements of ipsilateral hand and foot. *Experimental Brain Research, 83,* 375-380.

Baldissera, F., Cavallari, P., & Tesio, L. (1994). Coordination of cyclic coupled movements of hand and foot in normal subjects and on the healthy side of hemiplegic patients. In S.P. Swinnen, H. Heuer, J. Massion, & P. Casaer (Eds.), *Interlimb coordination: Neural, dynamical, and cognitive constraints* (pp. 229-242). San Diego: Academic Press.

Bandura, A. (1969). *Principles of behavior modification*. New York: Holt, Rinehart, and Winston.

Bandura, A., Blanchard, E.B., & Ritter, B. (1969). Relative efficacy of desensitization and modeling approaches for inducing behavioral, affective, and attitudinal changes. *Journal of Personality and Social Psychology, 13,* 173-199.

Barnett, M.L., Ross, D., Schmidt, R.A., & Todd, B. (1973). Motor skills learning and the specificity of training principle. *Research Quarterly, 44,* 440-447.

Barrett, N.C., & Glencross, D.J. (1989). Response amendments during manual aiming movements to double-step targets. *Acta Psychologica, 70,* 205-217.

Bartlett, F.C. (1932). *Remembering: A study in experimental and social psychology*. Cambridge: Cambridge University Press.

Bartlett, F.C. (1958). *Thinking: An experimental and social study*. New York: Basic Books.

Bartram, D., Banerji, N., Rothwell, D., & Smith, P. (1985). Task parameters affecting individual differences in pursuit and compensatory tracking performance. *Ergonomics, 28,* 1633-1652.

Basmajian, J.V. (1963). Control and training of individual motor units. *Science, 141,* 440-441.

Basmajian, J.V. (1989). *Biofeedback: Principles and practice for clinicians* (3rd ed.). Baltimore: Williams & Wilkins.

Battig, W.F. (1956). Transfer from verbal pretraining to motor performance as a function of motor task complexity. *Journal of Experimental Psychology, 51,* 371-378.

Battig, W.F. (1966). Facilitation and interference. In E.A. Bilodeau (Ed.), *Acquisition of skill*. New York: Academic Press.

Battig, W.F. (1972). Intratask interference as a source of facilitation in transfer and retention. In R.F. Thompson & J.F. Voss (Eds.), *Topics in learning and performance* (pp. 131-159). New York: Academic Press.

Battig, W.F. (1979). The flexibility of human memory. In L.S. Cermak & F.I.M. Craik (Eds.), *Levels of processing in human memory* (pp. 23-44). Hillsdale, NJ: Erlbaum.

Battig, W.F., & Shea, J.B. (1980). Levels of processing of verbal materials: An overview. In P. Klavora & J. Flowers (Ed.), *Motor learning and biomechanical factors in sport* (pp. 24-33). Toronto: University of Toronto.

Bayley, N. (1935). The development of motor abilities during the first three years. *Monograph of the Society for Research in Child Development, 1,* 1-26.

Bean, C.H. (1912). The curve of forgetting. *Archives of Psychology, 3,* 1-45.

Beatty, J., & Wagoner, B.L. (1978). Pupillometric signs of brain activation vary with level of cognitive processing. *Science, 199,* 1216-1218.

Beek, P.J., & Lewbel, A. (1995, November). The science of juggling. *Scientific American, 273,* 92-97.

Beevor, C.E., & Horsely, V. (1887). A minute analysis (experimental) of the various movements produced by stimulating in the monkey different regions of the cortical centre for the upper limb as defined by Professor Ferrier. *Philosophical Transactions, 178,* 153.

Beevor, C.E., & Horsely, V. (1890). A record of the results obtained by electrical excitation of the so-called motor cortex and internal capsule in the orangutang. *Philosophical Transactions, 181,* 129.

Belen'kii, V.Y., Gurfinkel, V.S., & Pal'tsev, Y.I. (1967). Elements of control of voluntary movements. *Biofizika, 12,* 135-141.

Benedetti, C., & McCullagh, P. (1987). Post-knowledge of results delay: Effects of interpolated activity on learning and performance. *Research Quarterly for Exercise and Sport, 58,* 375-381.

Bennett, D.M., & Simmons, R.W. (1984). Effects of precision of knowledge of results on acquisition and retention of a simple motor skill. *Perceptual and Motor Skills, 58,* 785-786.

Berkinblit, M.B., & Feldman, A.G. (1988). Some problems of motor control. *Journal of Motor Behavior, 20,* 369-373.

Berkinblit, M.B., Feldman, A.G., & Fukson, O.I. (1986). Adaptability of innate motor patterns and motor control mechanisms. *Behavioral and Brain Sciences, 9,* 585-638.

Bernstein, N.A. (1947). *On the structure of movements.* Moscow: State Medical Publishing House.

Bernstein, N.A. (1967). *The co-ordination and regulation of movements.* Oxford: Pergamon Press.

Bernstein, N.A. (1996). On dexterity and its development. In M.L. Latash & M.T. Turvey (Eds.), *Dexterity and its development.* Mahwah, NJ: Erlbaum.

Biguer, B., Jeannerod, M., & Prablanc, C. (1982). The coordination of eye, head, and arm movements during reaching at a single visual target. *Experimental Brain Research, 46,* 301-304.

Biguer, B., Prablanc, C., & Jeannerod, M. (1984). The contribution of coordinated eye and head movements in hand pointing accuracy. *Experimental Brain Research, 55,* 462-469.

Bilodeau, E.A. (Ed.) (1966). *Acquisition of skill.* New York: Academic Press.

Bilodeau, E.A., & Bilodeau, I.M. (1958). Variable frequency of knowledge of results and the learning of a simple skill. *Journal of Experimental Psychology, 55,* 379-383.

Bilodeau, E.A., & Bilodeau, I.M. (1961). Motor-skills learning. *Annual Review of Psychology, 12,* 243-280.

Bilodeau, E.A., Bilodeau, I.M., & Schumsky, D.A. (1959). Some effects of introducing and withdrawing knowledge of results early and late in practice. *Journal of Experimental Psychology, 58,* 142-144.

Bilodeau, I.M. (1956). Accuracy of a simple positioning response with variation in the number of trials by which knowledge of results is delayed. *American Journal of Psychology, 69,* 434-437.

Bilodeau, I.M. (1966). Information feedback. In E.A. Bilodeau (Ed.), *Acquisition of skill* (pp. 255-296). New York: Academic Press.

Bilodeau, I.M. (1969). Information feedback. In E.A. Bilodeau (Ed.), *Principles of skill acquisition* (pp. 255-285). New York: Academic Press.

Bizzi, E. (1974). The coordination of eye-head movements. *Scientific American, 231(4),* 100-106.

Bizzi, E., Accornero, N., Chapple, W., & Hogan, N. (1982). Arm trajectory formation in monkeys. *Experimental Brain Research, 46,* 139-143.

Bizzi, E., Giszter, S.F., Loeb, E., Mussa-Ivaldi, F.A., & Saltiel, P. (1995). Modular organization of motor behavior in the frog's spinal cord. *Trends in Neurosciences, 18,* 442-446.

Bizzi, E., Hogan, N., Mussa-Ivaldi, F.A., & Giszter, S. (1992). Does the nervous system use equilibrium-point control to guide single and multiple joint movements? *Behavioral and Brain Sciences, 15,* 603-613.

Bizzi, E., Polit, A., & Morasso, P. (1976). Mechanisms underlying achievement of final head position. *Journal of Neurophysiology, 39,* 435-444.

Black, P.E., & Black, R.W. (1970). A "Partial reinforcement-extinction effect" in a perceptual-motor task. *Psychonomic Science, 18,* 125-127.

Blankenship, W.C. (1952). Transfer effects in neuro-muscular responses involving choice. Unpublished master's thesis, University of California, Berkeley.

Blimkie, C.J.R., & Bar-Or, O. (1996). Trainability of muscle strength, power, and endurance during childhood. In O. Bar-Or (Ed.), *The child and adolescent athlete* (pp. 113-129). Champaign, IL: Human Kinetics.

Blix, M. (1892-1895). Die Länge und Spannung des Muskels. *Skandinavische Archiv Physiologie, 3,* 295-318; *4,* 399-409; *5,* 150-206.

Book, W.F. (1908). *The psychology of skill.* University of Montana Studies in Psychology (Vol. 1). (Reprinted, New York: Gregg, 1925.)

Bootsma, R.J., Marteniuk, R.G., MacKenzie, C.L., & Zaal, F.T.J.M. (1994). The speed-accuracy trade-off in manual prehension: Effects of movement amplitude, object size and object width on kinematic characteristics. *Experimental Brain Research, 98,* 535-541.

Bootsma, R.J., & van Wieringen, P.C.W. (1990). Timing an attacking forehand drive in table tennis. *Journal of Experimental Psychology: Human Perception and Performance, 16,* 21-29.

Boring, E.G. (1950). *A history of experimental psychology.* New York: Appleton-Century-Crofts.

Bortoli, L., Robazza, C., Durigon, V., & Carra, C. (1992). Effects of contextual interference on learning technical sports skills. *Perceptual and Motor Skills, 75,* 555-562.

Boucher, J.L. (1974). Higher processes in motor learning. *Journal of Motor Behavior, 6,* 131-137.

Bourne, L.E. Jr., & Archer, E.J. (1956). Time continuously on target as a function of distribution of practice. *Journal of Experimental Psychology, 51,* 25-33.

Bourne, L.E. Jr., & Bunderson, C.V. (1963). Effects of delay of informative feedback and length of postfeedback interval on concept identification. *Journal of Experimental Psychology, 65,* 1-5.

Bourne, L.E. Jr., Guy, D.E., Dodd, D.H., & Justesen, D.R. (1965). Concept identification: The effects of varying length and informational components of the intertrial interval. *Journal of Experimental Psychology, 69,* 624-629.

Bowditch, H.P., & Southard, W.F. (1882). A comparison of sight and touch. *Journal of Physiology, 3,* 232-244.

Boyce, B.A. (1992). Effects of assigned versus participant-set goals on skill acquisition and retention of a selected shooting task. *Journal of Teaching in Physical Education, 11,* 220-234.

Boyce, B.A., & Del Rey, P. (1990). Designing applied research in a naturalistic setting using a contextual interference paradigm. *Journal of Human Movement Studies, 18,* 189-200.

Boyd, I.A., & Roberts, T.D.M. (1953). Proprioceptive discharges from stretch-receptors in the knee-joint of the cat. *Journal of Physiology, 122,* 38-59.

Bransford, J.D., Franks, J.J., Morris, C.D., & Stein, B.S. (1979). Some general constraints on learning and memory research. In L.S. Cermak & F.I.M. Craik (Eds.), *Levels of processing in human memory* (pp. 331-354). Hillsdale, NJ: Erlbaum.

Brenner, J. (1974). A general model of voluntary control applied to the phenomenon of learned cardiovascular change. In P.A. Obrist, A.H. Black, J. Brenner, & L.V. DiCara (Eds.), *Cardiovascular psychophysiology: Current issues in response mechanisms, biofeedback, and methodology* (pp. 365-391). Chicago: Aldine.

Bridgeman, B. (1996). Extraretinal signals in visual orientation. In W. Prinz & B. Bridgeman (Eds.), *Handbook of perception and action. Volume 1: Perception* (pp. 191-223). San Diego, CA: Academic Press.

Bridgeman, B., Kirch, M., & Sperling, A. (1981). Segregation of cognitive and motor aspects of visual information using induced motion. *Perception & Psychophysics, 29,* 336-342.

Briem, V., & Hedman, L.R. (1995). Behavioural effects of mobile telephone use during simulated driving. *Ergonomics, 38,* 2536-2562.

Briggs, G.E., & Brogden, W.J. (1954). The effect of component practice on performance of a lever-positioning skill. *Journal of Experimental Psychology, 48,* 375-380.

Briggs, G.E., & Waters, L.K. (1958). Training and transfer as a function of component interaction. *Journal of Experimental Psychology, 56,* 492-500.

Brisson, T.A., & Alain, C. (1996a). Should common optimal movement patterns be identified as the criterion to be achieved? *Journal of Motor Behavior, 28,* 211-223.

Brisson, T.A., & Alain, C. (1996b). Optimal movement pattern characteristics are not required as a reference for knowledge of performance. *Research Quarterly for Exercise and Sport, 67,* 458-464.

Broadbent, D.E. (1958). *Perception and communication.* London: Pergamon Press.

Brodie, E.E., & Ross, H.E. (1985). Jiggling a lifted weight does aid discrimination. *American Journal of Psychology, 98,* 469-471.

Broker, J.P., Gregor, R.J., & Schmidt, R.A. (1993). Extrinsic feedback and the learning of kinetic patterns in cycling. *Journal of Applied Biomechanics, 9,* 111-123.

Brooks, V.B. (1975). Roles of cerebellum and basal ganglia and control of movements. *Le Journal Canadien Des Sciences Neurologiques, 2,* 265-277.

Brooks, V.B. (1979). Motor programs revisited. In R.E. Talbott & D.R. Humphrey (Eds.), *Posture and movement* (pp. 13-49). New York: Raven Press.

Brooks, V.B. (1986). *The neural basis of motor control.* New York: Oxford University Press.

Brown, I.D. (1962). Measuring the "spare mental capacity" of car drivers by a subsidiary auditory task. *Ergonomics, 5,* 247-250.

Brown, I.D. (1967). Measurement of control skills, vigilance, and performance on a subsidiary task during 12 hours of car driving. *Ergonomics, 10,* 665-673.

Brown, J. (1958). Some tests of the decay theory of immediate memory. *The Quarterly Journal of Experimental Psychology, 10,* 12-21.

Bruce, D. (1994). Lashley and the problem of serial order. *American Psychologist, 49,* 93-103.

Bryan, W.L., & Harter, N. (1897). Studies in the physiology and psychology of the telegraphic language. *Psychological Review, 4,* 27-53.

Bryan, W.L., & Harter, N. (1899). Studies on the telegraphic language: The acquisition of a hierarchy of habits. *Psychological Review, 6,* 345-375.

Buchanan, J.J., & Kelso, J.A.S. (1993). Posturally induced transitions in rhythmic multijoint limb movements. *Experimental Brain Research, 94,* 131-142.

Buekers, M.J., & Magill, R.A. (1995). The role of task experience and prior knowledge for detecting invalid augmented feedback while learning a motor skill. *The Quarterly Journal of Experimental Psychology, 48A,* 84-97.

Buekers, M.J., Magill, R.A., & Hall, K.G. (1992). The effect of erroneous knowledge of results on skill acquisition when augmented information is redundant. *The Quarterly Journal of Experimental Psychology, 44A,* 105-117.

Buekers, M.J., Magill, R.A., & Sneyers, K.M. (1994). Resolving a conflict between sensory feedback and knowledge of results, while learning a motor skill. *Journal of Motor Behavior, 26,* 27-35.

Burgess, P.R., & Clark, F.J. (1969). Characteristics of knee joint receptors in the cat. *Journal of Physiology, 203,* 317-335.

Burgess-Limerick, R., Abernethy, B. & Neal, R.J. (1991). Note: A statistical problem in testing invariance of movement using the phase plane model. *Journal of Motor Behavior, 23,* 301-303.

Burgess-Limerick, R., Neal, R.J., & Abernethy, B. (1992). Against relative timing invariance in movement kinematics. *The Quarterly Journal of Experimental Psychology, 44A,* 705-722.

Burton, D. (1993). Goal setting in sport. In R.N. Singer, M. Murphey, & L.K. Tennant (Eds.), *Handbook of research on sport psychology* (pp. 467-491). New York: Macmillan.

Butler, M.S., Reeve, T.G., & Fischman, M.G. (1996). Effects of the instructional set in the bandwidth feedback paradigm on motor skill acquisition. *Research Quarterly for Exercise and Sport, 67,* 335-359.

Cadoret, G., & Smith, A.M. (1996). Friction, not texture, dictates grip forces used during object manipulation. *Journal of Neurophysiology, 75,* 1963-1969.

Canic, M.J., & Franks, I.M. (1989). Response preparation and latency in patterns of tapping movements. *Human Movement Science, 8,* 123-139.

Card, S.K., English, W.K., & Burr, B.J. (1978). Evaluation of mouse, rate-controlled isometric joystick, step keys, and text keys for text selection on a CRT. *Ergonomics, 21,* 601-613.

Carlton, L.G. (1979). Control processes in the production of discrete aiming responses. *Journal of Human Movement Studies, 5,* 115-124.

Carlton, L.G. (1981a). Processing visual feedback information for movement control. *Journal of Experimental Psychology: Human Perception and Performance, 7,* 1019-1030.

Carlton, L.G. (1981b). Visual information: The control of aiming movements. *The Quarterly Journal of Experimental Psychology, 33A,* 87-93.

Carlton, L.G. (1992). Visual processing time and the control of movement. In L. Proteau & D. Elliott (Eds.), *Vision and motor control* (pp. 3-31). Amsterdam: Elsevier.

Carlton, L.G. (1994). The effects of temporal-precision and time-minimization constraints on the spatial and temporal accuracy of aimed hand movements. *Journal of Motor Behavior, 26,* 43-50.

Carlton, L.G., & Newell, K.M. (1988). Force variability and movement accuracy in space-time. *Journal of Experimental Psychology: Human Perception and Performance, 14,* 24-36.

Carlton, L.G., Carlton, M.J., & Kim, K.H. (1997). Visuo-motor delays with changing environmental conditions. Unpublished manuscript.

Carnahan, H. (1992). Eye, head and hand coordination during manual aiming. In L. Proteau & D. Elliott (Eds.), *Vision and motor control* (pp. 179-196). Amsterdam: Elsevier.

Carnahan, H. (1993). The role of three dimensional analysis in the assessment of motor expertise. In J.L. Starkes & F. Allard (Eds.), *Cognitive issues in motor expertise* (pp. 35-53). Amsterdam: Elsevier.

Carnahan, H., & Marteniuk, R.G. (1991). The temporal organization of hand, eye, and head movements during reaching and pointing. *Journal of Motor Behavior, 23,* 109-119.

Carroll, W.R., & Bandura, A. (1982). The role of visual monitoring in observational learning of action patterns: Making the unobservable observable. *Journal of Motor Behavior, 14,* 153-167.

Carroll, W.R., & Bandura, A. (1985). Role of timing of visual monitoring and motor rehearsal in observational learning of action patterns. *Journal of Motor Behavior, 17,* 269-281.

Carroll, W.R., & Bandura, A. (1987). Translating cognition into action: The role of visual guidance in observational learning. *Journal of Motor Behavior, 19,* 385-398.

Carroll, W.R., & Bandura, A. (1990). Representational guidance of action production in observational learning: A causal analysis. *Journal of Motor Behavior, 22,* 85-97.

Carron, A.V. (1967). Performance and learning in a discrete motor task under massed versus distributed conditions. Unpublished doctoral dissertation, University of California, Berkeley.

Carron, A.V. (1969). Performance and learning in a discrete motor task under massed vs. distributed practice. *Research Quarterly, 40,* 481-489.

Carson, R.G., Byblow, W.D., Abernethy, B., & Summers, J.J. (1996). The contribution of inherent and incidental constraints to intentional switching between patterns of bimanual coordination. *Human Movement Science, 15,* 565-589.

Carson, R.G., Goodman, D., Kelso, J.A.S., & Elliott, D. (1995). Phase transitions and critical fluctuations in rhythmic coordination of ipsilateral hand and foot. *Journal of Motor Behavior, 27,* 211-224.

Carter, M.C., & Shapiro, D.C. (1984). Control of sequential movements: Evidence for generalized motor programs. *Journal of Neurophysiology, 52,* 787-796.

Carter, M.C., & Smith, J.L. (1986). Simultaneous control of two rhythmical behaviors. I. Locomotion and paw-shake response in normal cat. *Journal of Neurophysiology, 56,* 171-183.

Castiello, U. (1996). Grasping a fruit: Selection for action. *Journal of Experimental Psychology: Human Perception and Performance, 22,* 582-603.

Castiello, U., Bennett, K.M.B., & Stelmach, G.E. (1993). Reach to grasp: The natural response to perturbation of object size. *Experimental Brain Research, 94,* 163-178.

Castiello, U., & Umiltà, C. (1988). Temporal dimensions of mental effort in different sports. *International Journal of Sport Psychology, 19,* 199-210.

Catalano, J.F., & Kleiner, B.M. (1984). Distant transfer in coincident timing as a function of practice variability. *Perceptual and Motor Skills, 58,* 851-856.

Cauraugh, J.H., Chen, D., & Singer, R.N. (1993). Graphic versus numeric knowledge of results: Which mode? *Research Quarterly for Exercise and Sport, 64,* 213-216.

Cavallo, V., & Laurent, M. (1988). Visual information and skill level in time-to-collision estimation. *Perception, 17,* 623-632.

Chalmers, D.J. (1995, December). The puzzle of conscious experience. *Scientific American, 273(6),* 80-86.

Chamberlin, C.J., & Coelho, A.J. (1993). The perceptual side of action: Decision-making in sport. In J.L. Starkes & F. Allard (Eds.), *Cognitive issues in motor expertise* (pp. 135-157). Amsterdam: Elsevier.

Chamberlin, C.J., & Lee, T.D. (1993). Arranging practice conditions and designing instruction. In R.N. Singer, M. Murphey, & L.K. Tennant (Eds.), *Handbook on research in sport psychology* (pp. 213-241). New York: Macmillan.

Chambers, J.W. Jr., & Schumsky, D.A. (1978). The compression block technique: Use and misuse in the study of motor skills. *Journal of Motor Behavior, 10,* 301-311.

Chan, T., & Chan, K. (1995). Effect of frequency ratio and environmental information on spatial coupling: A study of attention. *Ecological Psychology, 7,* 125-144.

Chapanis, A. (1951). Theory and methods for analyzing errors in man-machine systems. *Annals of the New York Academy of Sciences, 51,* 1179-1203.

Chapanis, A. (1965). *Man-machine engineering.* Belmont, CA: Wadsworth.

Chapman, S. (1968). Catching a baseball. *American Journal of Physics, 36,* 868-870.

Chaput, S., & Proteau, L. (1996). Modifications with aging in the role played by vision and proprioception for movement control. *Experimental Aging Research, 22,* 1-21.

Chase, W.G., & Simon, H.A. (1973). Perception in chess. *Cognitive Psychology, 4,* 55-81.

Chen, D., & Hendrick, J.L. (1994, June). Interactive knowledge of results and the timing of sequential movements. Paper presented at the meeting of the North American Society for the Psychology of Sport and Physical Activity, Clearwater Beach, FL.

Cherry, E.C. (1953). Some experiments on the recognition of speech, with one and two ears. *Journal of the Acoustical Society of America, 25,* 975-979.

Christina, R.W. (1992). The 1991 C.H. McCloy research lecture: Unraveling the mystery of the response complexity effect in skilled movements. *Research Quarterly for Exercise and Sport, 63,* 218-230.

Chua, R., & Elliott, D. (1993). Visual regulation of manual aiming. *Human Movement Science, 12,* 365-401.

Cohen, J., & Schooler, J.W. (Eds.) (1996). *Scientific approaches to consciousness.* Mahwah, NJ: Erlbaum.

Cohen, J.D., Dunbar, K., & McClelland, J.L. (1990). On the control of automatic processes: A parallel distributed processing account of the Stroop effect. *Psychological Review, 97*, 332-361.

Cohen, L. (1971). Synchronous bimanual movements performed by homologous and nonhomologous muscles. *Perceptual and Motor Skills, 32*, 639-644.

Cole, K.J., & Abbs, J.H. (1988). Grip force adjustments evoked by load force perturbations of a grasped object. *Journal of Neurophysiology, 60*, 1513-1522.

Cooke, J.D. (1980). The organization of simple, skilled movements. In G.E. Stelmach & J. Requin (Eds.), *Tutorials in motor behavior* (pp. 199-212). Amsterdam: Elsevier.

Corcos, D.M. (1984). Two-handed movement control. *Research Quarterly for Exercise and Sport, 55*, 117-122.

Corcos, D.M., Jaric, S., & Gottlieb, G.L. (1996). Electromyographic analysis of performance enhancement. In H.N. Zelaznik (Ed.), *Advances in motor learning and control* (pp. 123-153). Champaign, IL: Human Kinetics.

Cordo, P.J., & Nashner, L.M. (1982). Properties of postural adjustments associated with rapid arm movements. *Journal of Neurophysiology, 47*, 287-302.

Cormier, S.M., & Hagman, J.D. (Eds.) (1987). *Transfer of learning: Contemporary research applications*. New York: Academic Press.

Courneya, K.S., & Carron, A.V. (1992). The home advantage in sport competitions: A literature review. *Journal of Sport & Exercise Psychology, 14*, 13-27.

Crago, P.E., Houk, J.C., & Hasan, Z. (1976). Regulatory actions of human stretch reflex. *Journal of Neurophysiology, 39*, 925-935.

Craik, K.J.W. (1948). The theory of the human operator in control systems: II. Man as an element in a control system. *British Journal of Psychology, 38*, 142-148.

Cratty, B.J. (1964). *Movement behavior and motor learning*. Philadelphia: Lea & Febiger.

Crawley, S.L. (1926). An experimental investigation of recovery from work. *Archives of Psychology, 13*, 26.

Creamer, L.R. (1963). Event uncertainty, psychological refractory period, and human data processing. *Journal of Experimental Psychology, 66*, 187-194.

Croll, W.L. (1970). Children's discrimination learning as a function of intertrial interval duration. *Psychonomic Science, 18*, 321-322.

Cronbach, L.J. (1957). The two disciplines of scientific psychology. *American Psychologist, 12*, 671-684.

Crossman, E.R.F.W. (1959). A theory of the acquisition of speed skill. *Ergonomics, 2*, 153-166.

Crossman, E.R.F.W., & Goodeve, P.J. (1963/1983). Feedback control of hand-movements and Fitts' law. Paper presented at the meeting of the Experimental Psychology Society, Oxford, July, 1963. Published in *The Quarterly Journal of Experimental Psychology, 1983, 35A*, 251-278.

Cruse, H., Dean, J., Heuer, H., & Schmidt, R.A. (1990). Utilization of sensory information for motor control. In O. Neumann & W. Prinz (Eds.), *Relationships between perception and action: Current approaches* (pp. 43-79). Berlin: Springer-Verlag.

Cuddy, L.J., & Jacoby, L.L. (1982). When forgetting helps memory. An analysis of repetition effects. *Journal of Verbal Learning and Verbal Behavior, 21*, 451-467.

Darling, W.G., & Cooke, J.D. (1987). Changes in the variability of movement trajectories with practice. *Journal of Motor Behavior, 19*, 291-309.

Davies, G.M., & Thomson, D.M. (1988). *Memory in context: Context in memory*. New York: Wiley.

Davis, R. (1959). The role of "attention" in the psychological refractory period. *The Quarterly Journal of Experimental Psychology, 11*, 211-220.

Decety, J., & Jeannerod, M. (1996). Mentally simulated movements in virtual reality: Does Fitts's law hold in motor imagery? *Behavioural Brain Research, 72*, 127-134.

Dees, V., & Grindley, G.C. (1951). The effect of knowledge of results on learning and performance: IV. The direction of the error in very simple skills. *The Quarterly Journal of Experimental Psychology, 3*, 36-42.

DeGroot, A.D. (1965). *Thought and choice in chess*. The Hague: Mouton.

De Jong, R., Coles, M.G.H., Logan, G.D., & Gratton, G. (1990). In search of the point of no return: The control of response processes. *Journal of Experimental Psychology: Human Perception and Performance, 16*, 164-182.

Del Rey, P. (1989). Training and contextual interference effects on memory and transfer. *Research Quarterly for Exercise and Sport, 60*, 342-347.

Del Rey, P., Liu, X., & Simpson, K.J. (1994). Does retroactive inhibition influence contextual interference effects? *Research Quarterly for Exercise and Sport, 65*, 120-126.

Del Rey, P., & Shewokis, P. (1993). Appropriate summary KR for learning timing tasks under conditions of high and low contextual interference. *Acta Psychologica, 83*, 1-12.

Del Rey, P., Whitehurst, M., & Wood, J.M. (1983). Effects of experience and contextual interference on learning and transfer by boys and girls. *Perceptual and Motor Skills, 56*, 581-582.

Del Rey, P., Wughalter, E.H., & Whitehurst, M. (1982). The effects of contextual interference on females with varied experience in open sport skills. *Research Quarterly for Exercise and Sport, 53*, 108-115.

Dempster, F.N. (1988). The spacing effect: A case in the failure to apply the results of psychological research. *American Psychologist, 43*, 627-634.

Denier van der Gon, J.J., & Thuring, J.P. (1965). The guiding of human writing movements. *Kybernetik, 2*, 145-148.

Denny, M.R., Allard, M., Hall, E., & Rokeach, M. (1960). Supplementary report: Delay of knowledge of results, knowledge of task, and intertrial interval. *Journal of Experimental Psychology, 60*, 327.

Denny, M.R., Frisbey, N., & Weaver, J. Jr. (1955). Rotary pursuit performance under alternate conditions of distributed and massed practice. *Journal of Experimental Psychology, 49*, 48-54.

Desmedt, J.E., & Godeaux, E. (1979). Voluntary commands in human ballistic movements. *Annals of Neurology, 5*, 415-421.

Desmurget, M., Prablanc, C., Arzi, M., Rossetti, Y., Paulignan, Y., & Urquizar, C. (1996). Integrated control of hand transport and orientation during prehension movements. *Experimental Brain Research, 110*, 265-278.

Deutsch, D. (1983). The generation of two isochronous sequences in parallel. *Perception & Psychophysics, 34*, 331-337.

Deutsch, J.A., & Deutsch, D. (1963). Attention: Some theoretical considerations. *Psychological Review, 70*, 80-90.

Dewhurst, D.J. (1967). Neuromuscular control system. *IEEE Transactions on Biomedical Engineering, 14*, 167-171.

Diedrich, F.J., & Warren, W.H. Jr. (1995). Why change gaits? Dynamics of the walk-run transition. *Journal of Experimental Psychology: Human Perception and Performance, 21*, 183-202.

Donders, F.C. (1969). On the speed of mental processes. In W.G. Koster (Ed. & Trans.), *Attention and performance II*. Amsterdam: North-Holland. (Original work published 1868)

Doody, S.G., Bird, A.M., & Ross, D. (1985). The effect of auditory and visual models on acquisition of a timing task. *Human Movement Science, 4*, 271-281.

Drazin, D.H. (1961). Effects of foreperiod, foreperiod variability, and probability of stimulus occurrence on simple reaction time. *Journal of Experimental Psychology, 62*, 43-50.

Druckman, D., & Bjork, R.A. (1991). *In the mind's eye: Enhancing human performance*. Washington, DC: National Academy Press.

Drury, C.G., & Hoffmann, E.R. (1992). A model for movement time on data-entry keyboards. *Ergonomics, 35*, 129-147.

Drury, C.G., & Woolley, S.M. (1995). Visually-controlled leg movements embedded in a walking task. *Ergonomics, 38*, 714-722.

DuBois, P.H. (1965). The design of correlational studies in training. In R. Glaser (Ed.), *Training research and education* (pp. 63-86). New York: Wiley.

Duffy, E. (1962). *Activation and behavior*. New York: Wiley.

Duncan-Johnson, C.C., & Donchin, E. (1982). The P300 component of the event-related brain potential as an index of information processing. *Biological Psychology, 14*, 1-52.

Easterbrook, J.A. (1959). The effect of emotion on cue utilization and the organization of behavior. *Psychological Review, 66*, 183-201.

Easton, T.A. (1972). On the normal use of reflexes. *American Scientist, 60*, 591-599.

Easton, T.A. (1978). Coordinative structures—The basis for a motor program. In D.M. Landers & R.W. Christina (Eds.), *Psychology of motor behavior and sport* (pp. 63-81). Champaign, IL: Human Kinetics.

Ebbinghaus, H.D. (1913). *Memory: A contribution to experimental psychology* (H.A. Ruger & C.E. Bussenius, Trans.). New York: Teachers Colleges. (Original work published 1885)

Eimer, M., Nattkemper, D., Schröger, E., & Prinz, W. (1996). Involuntary attention. In O. Neumann & A.F. Sanders (Eds.), *Handbook of perception and action. Volume 3: Attention* (pp. 155-184). San Diego: Academic Press.

Elliott, D. (1990). Intermittent visual pickup and goal directed movement: A review. *Human Movement Science, 9*, 531-548.

Elliott, D. (1992). Intermittent versus continuous control of manual aiming movements. In L. Proteau & D. Elliott (Eds.), *Vision and motor control* (pp. 33-48). Amsterdam: Elsevier.

Elliott, D., & Allard, F. (1985). The utilization of visual feedback information during rapid pointing movements. *The Quarterly Journal of Experimental Psychology, 37A*, 407-425.

Elliott, D., Chua, R., & Pollock, B.J. (1994). The influence of intermittent vision on manual aiming. *Acta Psychologica, 85*, 1-13.

Elliott, D., Lyons, J., & Dyson, K. (1997). Rescaling an acquired discrete aiming movement: Specific or general motor learning? *Human Movement Science, 16*, 81-96.

Elliott, D., & Madalena, J. (1987). The influence of premovement visual information on manual aiming. *The Quarterly Journal of Experimental Psychology, 39A*, 541-559.

Elliott, D., & Roy, E.A. (Eds.) (1996). *Manual asymmetries in motor performance.* Boca Raton, FL: CRC Press.

Elliott, D., Zuberec, S., & Milgram, P. (1994). The effects of periodic visual occlusion on ball catching. *Journal of Motor Behavior, 26*, 113-122.

Ellis, H.C. (1965). *The transfer of learning.* New York: Macmillan.

Ells, J.G. (1973). Analysis of temporal and attentional aspects of movement control. *Journal of Experimental Psychology, 99*, 10-21.

Elwell, J.L., & Grindley, G.C. (1938). The effect of knowledge of results on learning and performance. *British Journal of Psychology, 29*, 39-54.

English, H.B. (1942). How psychology can facilitate military training—A concrete example. *Journal of Applied Psychology, 26*, 3-7.

Ericsson, K.A. (Ed.) (1996). *The road to excellence: The acquisition of expert performance in the arts and sciences, sports, and games.* Mahwah, NJ: Erlbaum.

Ericsson, K.A., Chase, W.G., & Faloon, S. (1980). Acquisition of a memory skill. *Science, 208*, 1181-1182.

Ericsson, K.A., Krampe, R.Th., & Tesch-Römer, C. (1993). The role of deliberate practice in the acquisition of expert performance. *Psychological Review, 100*, 363-406.

Ericsson, K.A., & Lehmann, A.C. (1996). Expert and exceptional performance: Evidence of maximal adaptation to task constraints. *Annual Review of Psychology, 47*, 273-305.

Espenschade, A. (1940). Motor performance in adolescence including the study of relationships with measures of physical growth and maturity. *Monographs of the Society for Research in Child Development, 5*, 1-126.

Estes, W.K. (1956). The problem of inference from curves based on group data. *Psychological Bulletin, 53*, 134-140.

Evarts, E.V. (1972). Contrasts between activity of precentral and postcentral neurons of cerebral cortex during movement in the monkey. *Brain Research, 40*, 25-31.

Evarts, E.V. (1973). Motor cortex reflexes associated with learned movement. *Science, 179*, 501-503.

Fantino, E., & Logan, C.A. (1979). *The experimental analysis of behavior: A biological perspective.* San Francisco: Freeman.

Farina, A.J., & Wheaton, G.R. (1970). *Development of a taxonomy of human performance: The task characteristics approach to performance prediction* (Technical Report). Silver Springs, MD: American Institutes for Research.

Farnsworth, P.R., & Poynter, W.F. (1931). A case of unusual ability in simultaneous tapping in two different times. *American Journal of Psychology, 43*, 633.

Farrell, J.E. (1975). The classification of physical education skills. *Quest, 24*, 63-68.

Fazey, L., & Hardy, L. (1988). The inverted-U hypothesis: Catastrophe for sport psychology. *British Association of Sports Sciences Monograph No. 1.* Leeds: National Coaching Foundation.

Feldman, A.G. (1966a). Functional tuning of the nervous system with control of movement or maintenance of a steady posture—II. Controllable parameters of the muscles. *Biophysics, 11*, 565-578.

Feldman, A.G. (1966b). Functional tuning of the nervous system during control of movement or maintenance of a steady posture—III. Mechanographic analysis of the execution by man of the simplest motor tasks. *Biophysics, 11*, 667-675.

Feldman, A.G. (1986). Once more on the equilibrium-point hypothesis (λ model) for motor control. *Journal of Motor Behavior, 18*, 17-54.

Feldman, A.G., & Levin, M.F. (1995). The origin and use of positional frames of reference in motor control. *Behavioral and Brain Sciences, 18*, 723-806.

Feltz, D.L., & Landers, D.M. (1983). The effects of mental practice on motor skill learning and performance: A meta-analysis. *Journal of Sport Psychology, 5*, 25-57.

Feltz, D.L., Landers, D.M., & Becker, B.J. (1988). A revised meta-analysis of the mental practice literature on motor skill learning. In D.

Druckman & J.A. Swets (Eds.), *Enhancing human performance: Issues, theories, and techniques. Background papers*. (Part III. Chapter 5, pp. 1-65). Washington, DC: National Academy Press.

Fendrich, D.W., Healy, A.F., & Bourne, L.E. Jr. (1991). Long-term repetition effects for motoric and perceptual procedures. *Journal of Experimental Psychology: Learning, Memory, and Cognition, 17*, 137-151.

Ferrari, M. (1996). Observing the observer: Self-regulation in the observational learning of motor skills. *Developmental Review, 16*, 203-240.

Ferrier, D. (1888). Discussions on cerebral localization. *Transactions of the Congress of American Physicians and Surgeons, 1*, 337-340.

Fischman, M.G. (1984). Programming time as a function of number of movement parts and changes in movement direction. *Journal of Motor Behavior, 16*, 405-423.

Fitch, H.L., Tuller, B., & Turvey, M.T. (1982). The Bernstein perspective: III. Tuning of coordinative structures with special reference to perception. In J.A.S. Kelso (Ed.), *Human motor behavior: An introduction* (pp. 271-281). Hillsdale, NJ: Erlbaum.

Fitts, P.M. (1954). The information capacity of the human motor system in controlling the amplitude of movement. *Journal of Experimental Psychology, 47*, 381-391.

Fitts, P.M. (1964). Perceptual-motor skills learning. In A.W. Melton (Ed.), *Categories of human learning* (pp. 243-285). New York: Academic Press.

Fitts, P.M., Bahrick, H.P., Noble, M.E., & Briggs, G.E. (1959). *Skilled performance* (Contract No. AF 41 [657]-70). Columbus: Ohio State University, Wright Air Development Center.

Fitts, P.M., & Deininger, R.L. (1954). S-R compatibility: Correspondence among paired elements within stimulus and response codes. *Journal of Experimental Psychology, 48*, 483-492.

Fitts, P.M., & Jones, R.E. (1947). *Analysis of factors contributing to 460 "pilot error" experiences in operating aircraft controls* (Memorandum Report TSEA4-694-12, Aero Medical Laboratory). Drayton, OH: Wright Patterson Air Force Base.

Fitts, P.M., & Peterson, J.R. (1964). Information capacity of discrete motor responses. *Journal of Experimental Psychology, 67*, 103-112.

Fitts, P.M., & Posner, M.I. (1967). *Human performance*. Belmont, CA: Brooks/Cole.

Fitts, P.M., & Seeger, C.M. (1953). S-R compatibility: Spatial characteristics of stimulus and response codes. *Journal of Experimental Psychology, 46*, 199-210.

Flach, J.M., Guisinger, M.A., & Robison, A.B. (1996). Fitts's law: Nonlinear dynamics and positive entropy. *Ecological Psychology, 8*, 281-325.

Fleishman, E.A. (1956). Psychomotor selection tests: Research and application in the United States Air Force. *Personnel Psychology, 9*, 449-467.

Fleishman, E.A. (1957). A comparative study of aptitude patterns in unskilled and skilled psychomotor performances. *Journal of Applied Psychology, 41*, 263-272.

Fleishman, E.A. (1964). *The structure and measurement of physical fitness*. Englewood Cliffs, NJ: Prentice-Hall.

Fleishman, E.A. (1965). The description and prediction of perceptual-motor skill learning. In R. Glaser (Ed.), *Training research and education* (pp. 137-175). New York: Wiley.

Fleishman, E.A. (1967). Individual differences and motor learning. In R.M. Gagne (Ed.), *Learning and individual differences* (pp. 165-191). Columbus, OH: Merrill.

Fleishman, E.A. (1975). Toward a taxonomy of human performance. *American Psychologist, 30*, 1127-1149.

Fleishman, E.A., & Bartlett, C.J. (1969). Human abilities. *Annual Review of Psychology, 20*, 349-380.

Fleishman, E.A., & Hempel, W.E. Jr. (1955). The relation between abilities and improvement with practice in a visual discrimination reaction task. *Journal of Experimental Psychology, 49*, 301-312.

Fleishman, E.A., & Hempel, W.E. Jr. (1956). Factorial analysis of complex psychomotor performance and related skills. *Journal of Applied Psychology, 40*, 96-104.

Fleishman, E.A., & Parker, J.F. (1962). Factors in the retention and relearning of perceptual motor skill. *Journal of Experimental Psychology, 64*, 215-226.

Fleishman, E.A., & Rich, S. (1963). Role of kinesthetic and spatial-visual abilities in perceptual-motor learning. *Journal of Experimental Psychology, 66*, 6-11.

Fleishman, E.A., & Stephenson, R.W. (1970). *Development of a taxonomy of human performance: A review of the third year's progress* (Tech. Rep. No.

726-TPR3). Silver Springs, MD: American Institutes for Research.

Fontaine, R.J., Lee, T.D., & Swinnen, S.P. (1997). Learning a new bimanual coordination pattern: Reciprocal influences of intrinsic and to-be-learned patterns. *Canadian Journal of Experimental Psychology, 51*, 1-9.

Forssberg, H., Grillner, S., & Rossignol, S. (1975). Phase dependent reflex reversal during walking in the chronic spinal cats. *Brain Research, 85*, 103-107.

Fowler, B., Duck, T., Mosher, M., & Mathieson, B. (1991). The coordination of bimanual aiming movements: Evidence for progressive desynchronization. *The Quarterly Journal of Experimental Psychology, 43A*, 205-221.

Fozard, J.L., Vercruyssen, M., Reynolds, S.L., Hancock, P.A., & Quilter, R.E. (1994). Age differences and changes in reaction time: The Baltimore longitudinal study of aging. *Journal of Gerontology: Psychological Sciences, 49*, P179-P189.

Frank, J.S., Williams, I.D., & Hayes, K.C. (1977). The ischemic nerve block and skilled movement. *Journal of Motor Behavior, 9*, 217-224.

Franks, I.M., & Stanley, M.L. (1991). Learning the invariants of a perceptual motor skill. *Canadian Journal of Psychology, 45*, 303-320.

Franks, I.M., & Wilberg, R.B. (1984). Consistent reproduction of movement sequences during acquisition of a pursuit tracking task. *Perceptual and Motor Skills, 58*, 699-709.

Franz, E.A. (1997). Spatial coupling in the coordination of complex actions. *The Quarterly Journal of Experimental Psychology, 50A*, 684-704.

Franz, E.A., Eliassen, J.C., Ivry, R.B., & Gazzaniga, M.S. (1996). Dissociation of spatial and temporal coupling in the bimanual movements of callosotomy patients. *Psychological Science, 7*, 306-310.

Franz, E.A., Zelaznik, H.N., & McCabe, G. (1991). Spatial topological constraints in a bimanual task. *Acta Psychologica, 77*, 137-151.

Franz, E.A., Zelaznik, H.N., & Smith, A. (1992). Evidence of common timing processes in the control of manual, orofacial, and speech movements. *Journal of Motor Behavior, 24*, 281-287.

French, K.E., Rink, J.E., & Werner, P.H. (1990). Effects of contextual interference on retention of three volleyball skills. *Perceptual and Motor Skills, 71*, 179-186.

French, K.E., & Thomas, J.R. (1987). The relation of knowledge development to children's bas-ketball performance. *Journal of Sport Psychology, 9*, 15-32.

Frey, H.J., & Keeney, C.J. (1964). *Elementary gymnastics apparatus skills.* New York: Ronald Press.

Fritsch, G., & Hitzig, E. (1870). Über die elektrische Erregbarkeit des Grosshirns. *Archiv Anatomie Physiologie, 37*, 300-332.

Fuchs, A.H. (1962). The progression-regression hypothesis in perceptual-motor skill learning. *Journal of Experimental Psychology, 63*, 177-182.

Fukson, O.I., Berkinblit, M.B., & Feldman, A.G. (1980). The spinal frog takes into account the scheme of its body during the wiping reflex. *Science, 209*, 1261-1263.

Fukuda, T. (1961). Studies on human dynamic postures from the viewpoint of postural reflexes. *Acta Oto-Laryngologica, 161*, 1-52.

Fullerton, G.S., & Cattell, J. (1892). On the perception of small differences. *University of Pennsylvania Philosophical Series, No. 2*.

Gabbard, C.P. (1992). *Lifelong motor development* (2nd ed.). Madison, WI: Brown & Benchmark.

Gable, C.D., Shea, C.H., & Wright, D.L. (1991). Summary knowledge of results. *Research Quarterly for Exercise and Sport, 62*, 285-292.

Gabriele, T.E., Hall, C.R., & Lee, T.D. (1989). Cognition in motor learning: Imagery effects on contextual interference. *Human Movement Science, 8*, 227-245.

Gallagher, J.D., & Thomas, J.R. (1980). Effects of varying post-KR intervals upon children's motor performance. *Journal of Motor Behavior, 12*, 41-46.

Gallistel, C.R. (1980). *The organization of action: A new synthesis.* Hillsdale, NJ: Erlbaum.

Gandevia, S.C., & Burke, D. (1992). Does the nervous system depend on kinesthetic information to control natural limb movements? *Behavioral and Brain Sciences, 15*, 614-632.

Gao, L., & Zelaznik, H.N. (1991). The modification of an already-programmed response: A new interpretation of Henry and Harrison (1961). *Journal of Motor Behavior, 23*, 221-223.

Garvey, W.D. (1960). A comparison of the effects of training and secondary tasks on tracking behavior. *Journal of Applied Psychology, 44*, 370-375.

Gawron, V.J., Drury, C.G., Czaja, S.J., & Wilkins, D.M. (1989). A taxonomy of independent variables affecting human performance. *International Journal of Man-Machine Studies, 31*, 643-672.

Gelfan, S., & Carter, S. (1967). Muscle sense in man. *Experimental Neurology, 18*, 469-473.

Gelfand, I.M., Gurfinkel, V.S., Tomin, S.V., & Tsetlin, M.L. (1971). *Models of the structural-functional organization of certain biological systems.* Cambridge, MA: MIT Press.

Gentile, A.M. (1972). A working model of skill acquisition with application to teaching. *Quest, 17*, 3-23.

Gentilucci, M., Chieffi, S., Scarpa, M., & Castiello, U. (1992). Temporal coupling between transport and grasp components during prehension movements: Effects of visual perturbation. *Behavioural Brain Research, 47*, 71-82.

Gentner, D.R. (1987). Timing of skilled motor performance: Tests of the proportional duration model. *Psychological Review, 94*, 255-276.

Georgopoulos, A.P. (1995). Current issues in directional motor control. *Trends in Neurosciences, 18*, 506-510.

Georgopoulos, A.P., Kalaska, J.F., & Massey, J.T. (1981). Spatial trajectories and reaction times of aimed movements: Effects of practice, uncertainty, and change in target location. *Journal of Neurophysiology, 46*, 725-743.

Gevins, A., Leong, H., Smith, M.E., Le, J., & Du, R. (1995). Mapping cognitive brain function with modern high-resolution electroencephalography. *Trends in Neuroscience, 18*, 429-436.

Gibson, J.J. (1966). *The senses considered as perceptual systems.* Boston: Houghton Mifflin.

Gibson, J.J. (1979). *The ecological approach to visual perception.* Boston: Houghton Mifflin.

Gielen, C.C.A.M., van den Oosten, K., & ter Gunne, F.P. (1985). Relation between EMG activation and kinematic properties of aimed arm movements. *Journal of Motor Behavior, 17*, 421-442.

Gilbreth, F.B. (1909). *Bricklaying system.* New York: Myron C. Clark.

Gill, D.L. (1992). Gender and sport behavior. In T.S. Horn (Ed.), *Advances in sport psychology* (pp. 143-160). Champaign, IL: Human Kinetics.

Glencross, D., & Barrett, N. (1992). The processing of visual feedback in rapid movements: Revisited. In J.J. Summers (Ed.), *Approaches to the study of motor control and learning* (pp. 289-311). Amsterdam: Elsevier.

Glencross, D.J. (1973). Temporal organization in a repetitive speed skill. *Ergonomics, 16*, 765-776.

Godwin, M.A., & Schmidt, R.A. (1971). Muscular fatigue and learning a discrete motor skill. *Research Quarterly, 42*, 374-382.

Goettl, B.P. (1996). The spacing effect in aircraft recognition. *Human Factors, 38*, 34-49.

Goggin, N.L., & Meeuwsen, H.J. (1992). Age-related differences in the control of spatial aiming movements. *Research Quarterly for Exercise and Sport, 63*, 366-372.

Goodale, M.A., & Milner, A.D. (1992). Separate visual pathways for perception and action. *Trends in Neurosciences, 15*, 20-25.

Goodale, M.A., Milner, A.D., Jakobson, L.S., & Carey, D.P. (1991). A neurological dissociation between perceiving objects and grasping them. *Nature, 349*, 154-156.

Goodale, M.A., & Servos, P. (1996). Visual control of prehension. In H.N. Zelaznik (Ed.), *Advances in motor control and learning* (pp. 87-121). Champaign, IL: Human Kinetics.

Goode, S., & Magill, R.A. (1986). Contextual interference effects in learning three badminton serves. *Research Quarterly for Exercise and Sport, 57*, 308-314.

Goodman, D., & Kelso, J.A.S. (1980). Are movements prepared in parts? Not under compatible (naturalized) conditions. *Journal of Experimental Psychology: General, 109*, 475-495.

Goodman, D., Kobayashi, R.B., & Kelso, J.A.S. (1983). Maintenance of symmetry as a constraint in motor control. *Canadian Journal of Applied Sport Science, 8*, 238.

Goodwin, G.M., McCloskey, D.I., & Matthews, P.B.C. (1972). The contribution of muscle afferents to kinaesthesia shown by vibration induced illusions of movement and by the effects of paralyzing joint afferents. *Brain, 95*, 705-748.

Goodwin, J.E., & Meeuwsen, H.J. (1995). Using bandwidth knowledge of results to alter relative frequencies during motor skill acquisition. *Research Quarterly for Exercise and Sport, 66*, 99-104.

Gordon, A.M., & Soechting, J.F. (1995). Use of tactile afferent information in sequential finger movements. *Experimental Brain Research, 107*, 281-292.

Gordon, J., & Ghez, C. (1991). Muscle receptors and spinal reflexes: The stretch reflex. In E.R. Kandel, J.H. Schwartz, T.M. Jessell (Eds.), *Principles of neural science* (3rd ed.) (pp. 564-580). Amsterdam: Elsevier.

Gordon, J., Ghilardi, M.F., & Ghez, C. (1995). Impairments of reaching movements in patients without proprioception. I. Spatial errors. *Journal of Neurophysiology, 73*, 347-360.

Gottlieb, G.L., Corcos, D.M., & Agarwal, G.C. (1989). Strategies for the control of voluntary movements with one mechanical degree of freedom. *Behavioral and Brain Sciences, 12*, 189-250.

Gottsdanker, R. (1970). Uncertainty, timekeeping, and simple reaction time. *Journal of Motor Behavior, 2*, 245-260.

Gottsdanker, R. (1973). Psychological refractoriness and the organization of step-tracking responses. *Perception & Psychophysics, 14*, 60-70.

Gottsdanker, R., & Stelmach, G.E. (1971). The persistence of psychological refractoriness. *Journal of Motor Behavior, 3*, 301-312.

Gould, D., & Krane, V. (1992). The arousal-athletic performance relationship: Current status and future directions. In T.S. Horn (Ed.), *Advances in sport psychology* (pp. 119-141). Champaign, IL: Human Kinetics.

Granit, R. (1970). *The basis of motor control.* New York: Academic Press.

Gray, J.T., Neisser, U., Shapiro, B.A., & Kouns, S. (1991). Observational learning of ballet sequences: The role of kinematic information. *Ecological Psychology, 3*, 121-134.

Green, D.P., Whitehead, J., & Sugden, D.A. (1995). Practice variability and transfer of a racket skill. *Perceptual and Motor Skills, 81*, 1275-1281.

Green, T.D., & Flowers, J.H. (1991). Implicit versus explicit learning processes in a probabilistic, continuous fine-motor catching task. *Journal of Motor Behavior, 23*, 293-300.

Greene, P.H. (1972). Problems of organization of motor systems. In R. Rosen & F.M. Snell (Eds.), *Progress in theoretical biology* (Vol. 2). New York: Academic Press.

Greenwald, A.G., & Schulman, H.G. (1973). On doing two things at once: Elimination of the psychological refractory period effect. *Journal of Experimental Psychology, 101*, 70-76.

Griffith, C.R. (1931). An experiment on learning to drive a golf ball. *The Athletic Journal, 11*, 11-13.

Grillner, S. (1972). The role of muscle stiffness in meeting the changing postural and locomotor requirements for force development by the ankle extensors. *Acta Physiologica Scandinavica, 86*, 92-108.

Grillner, S. (1975). Locomotion in vertebrates: Central mechanisms and reflex interaction. *Physiological Reviews, 55*, 247-304.

Grillner, S., & Wallén, P. (1985). Central pattern generators for locomotion, with special reference to vertebrates. *Annual Review of Neuroscience, 8*, 233-261.

Grillner, S., Wallén, P., Brodin, L., & Lansner, A. (1991). Neuronal network generating locomotor behavior in lamprey: Circuitry, transmitters, membrane properties, and simulation. *Annual Review of Neuroscience, 14*, 169-199.

Guadignoli, M.A. Dornier, L.A., & Tandy, R.D. (1996). Optimal length for summary knowledge of results: The influence of task-related experience and complexity. *Research Quarterly for Exercise and Sport, 67*, 239-248.

Guay, M., Salmoni, A., & McIlwain, J. (1992). Summary knowledge of results for skill acquisition: Beyond Lavery and Schmidt. *Human Movement Science, 11*, 653-673.

Guiard, Y. (1993). On Fitts's and Hooke's laws: Simple harmonic movement in upper-limb cyclical aiming. *Acta Psychologica, 82*, 139-159.

Guiard, Y. (1997). Fitts' law in the discrete vs. cyclical paradigm. *Human Movement Science, 16*, 97-131.

Gullicksen, H. (1950). *Theory of mental tests.* New York: Wiley.

Guthrie, E.R. (1952). *The psychology of learning.* New York: Harper & Row.

Hackfort, D., & Schwenkmezger, P. (1993). Anxiety. In R.N. Singer, M. Murphey, & L.K. Tennant (Eds.), *Handbook on research in sport psychology* (pp. 328-364). New York: Macmillan.

Haggard, P., & Wing, A. (1995). Coordinated responses following mechanical perturbation of the arm during prehension. *Experimental Brain Research, 102*, 483-494.

Hagman, J.D. (1983). Presentation- and test-trial effects on acquisition and retention of distance and location. *Journal of Experimental Psychology: Learning, Memory, and Cognition, 9*, 334-345.

Hah, S., & Jagacinski, R.J. (1994). The relative dominance of schemata in a manual tracking task: Input patterns, system dynamics, and movement patterns. *Journal of Motor Behavior, 26*, 204-214.

Haken, H., Kelso, J.A.S., & Bunz, H. (1985). A theoretical model of phase transitions in human hand movements. *Biological Cybernetics, 51*, 347-356.

Hall, K.G., Domingues, D.A., & Cavazos, R. (1994). Contextual interference effects with skilled baseball players. *Perceptual and Motor Skills, 78,* 835-841.

Hall, K.G., & Magill, R.A. (1995). Variability of practice and contextual interference in motor skill learning. *Journal of Motor Behavior, 27,* 299-309.

Halverson, L.E., Roberton, M.A., & Langendorfer, S. (1982). Development of the overarm throw: Movement and ball velocity changes by seventh grade. *Research Quarterly for Exercise and Sport, 53,* 198-205.

Hammerton, M. (1989). Tracking. In D.H. Holding (Ed.), *Human skills* (2nd ed.) (pp. 171-195). Chichester: Wiley.

Hancock, G.R., Butler, M.S., & Fischman, M.G. (1995). On the problem of two-dimensional error scores: Measures and analyses of accuracy, bias, and consistency. *Journal of Motor Behavior, 27,* 241-250.

Hanin, Y.L. (1980). A study of anxiety in sports. In W.F. Straub (Ed.), *Sport psychology: An analysis of athletic behavior* (pp. 236-249). Ithaca, NY: Mouvement.

Hanin, Y.L. (1989). Interpersonal and intragroup anxiety in sports. In D. Hackfort & C.D. Spielberger (Eds.), *Anxiety in sports: An international perspective* (pp. 19-28). New York: Hemisphere.

Hardy, L. (1990). A catastrophe model of performance in sport. In J.G. Jones & L. Hardy (Eds.), *Stress and performance in sport* (pp. 81-131). Chichester: Wiley.

Hasan, Z., & Enoka, R.M. (1985). Isometric torque-angle relationship and movement-related activity of human elbow flexors: Implications for the equilibrium-point hypothesis. *Experimental Brain Research, 59,* 441-450.

Hatze, H. (1976). Biomechanical aspects of a successful motion optimization. In P.V. Komi (Ed.), *Biomechanics V-B* (pp. 5-12). Baltimore: University Park Press.

Hay, J.F., & Jacoby, L.L. (1996). Separating habit and recollection: Memory slips, process dissociations, and probability matching. *Journal of Experimental Psychology: Learning, Memory, and Cognition, 22,* 1323-1335.

Hay, L. (1981). The effect of amplitude and accuracy requirements on movement time in children. *Journal of Motor Behavior, 13,* 177-186.

Head, H. (1926). *Aphasia and kindred disorders of speech.* Cambridge: Cambridge University Press.

Hellebrandt, F.A., Houtz, S.J., Partridge, M.J., & Walters, C.E. (1956). Tonic reflexes in exercises of stress in man. *American Journal of Physical Medicine, 35,* 144-159.

Hellyer, S. (1963). Stimulus-response coding and amount of information as determinants of reaction time. *Journal of Experimental Psychology, 65,* 521-522.

Helsen, W., & Pauwels, J.M. (1993). The relationship between expertise and visual information processing in sport. In J.L. Starkes & F. Allard (Eds.), *Cognitive issues in motor expertise* (pp. 109-134). Amsterdam: Elsevier.

Hendrick, J.L., & Chen, D. (1995, March). Interactive knowledge of results coupled: KR-delay interval and frequency effects. Paper presented at the meeting of the American Alliance for Health, Physical Education, Recreation and Dance, Portland, OR.

Hendrickson, G., & Schroeder, W.H. (1941). Transfer of training in learning to hit a submerged target. *Journal of Educational Psychology, 32,* 205-213.

Henry, F.M. (1953). Dynamic kinesthetic perception and adjustment. *Research Quarterly, 24,* 176-187.

Henry, F.M. (1959). Reliability, measurement error, and intra-individual difference. *Research Quarterly, 30,* 21-24.

Henry, F.M. (1961). Reaction time—movement time correlations. *Perceptual and Motor Skills, 12,* 63-66.

Henry, F.M. (1968). Specificity vs. generality in learning motor skill. In R.C. Brown & G.S. Kenyon (Eds.), *Classical studies on physical activity* (pp. 331-340). Englewood Cliffs, NJ: Prentice-Hall. (Original work published 1958)

Henry, F.M. (1975). Absolute error vs "E" in target accuracy. *Journal of Motor Behavior, 7,* 227-228.

Henry, F.M. (1980). Use of simple reaction time in motor programming studies: A reply to Klapp, Wyatt, and Lingo. *Journal of Motor Behavior, 12,* 163-168.

Henry, F.M., & Harrison, J.S. (1961). Refractoriness of a fast movement. *Perceptual and Motor Skills, 13,* 351-354.

Henry, F.M., & Rogers, D.E. (1960). Increased response latency for complicated movements and a "memory drum" theory of neuromotor reaction. *Research Quarterly, 31,* 448-458.

Herrick, C.J. (1924). Origin and evolution of the cerebellum. *Archives of Neurology and Psychiatry, 11,* 621-652.

Heuer, H. (1985). Wie wirkt mentale Übung? [How does mental practice operate?] *Psychologische Rundschau, 36,* 191-200.

Heuer, H. (1988). Testing the invariance of relative timing: Comment on Gentner (1987). *Psychological Review, 95,* 552-557.

Heuer, H. (1991). Invariant relative timing in motor-program theory. In J. Fagard & P.H. Wolff (Eds.), *The development of timing control and temporal organization in coordinated action* (pp. 37-68). Amsterdam: Elsevier.

Heuer, H. (1996). Coordination. In H. Heuer & S.W. Keele (Eds.), *Handbook of perception and action. Volume 2: Motor skills* (pp. 121-180). San Diego: Academic Press.

Heuer, H., & Schmidt, R.A. (1988). Transfer of learning among motor patterns with different relative timing. *Journal of Experimental Psychology: Human Perception and Performance, 14,* 241-252.

Heuer, H., Schmidt, R.A., & Ghodsian, D. (1995). Generalized motor programs for rapid bimanual tasks: A two-level multiplicative-rate model. *Biological Cybernetics, 73,* 343-356.

Hick, W.E. (1952). On the rate of gain of information. *The Quarterly Journal of Experimental Psychology, 4,* 11-26.

Hiew, C.C. (1977). Sequence effects in rule learning and conceptual generalization. *American Journal of Psychology, 90,* 207-218.

Hill, L.B. (1934). A quarter century of delayed recall. *Pedagogical Seminary and Journal of Genetic Psychology, 44,* 231-238.

Hill, L.B. (1957). A second quarter century of delayed recall or relearning at 80. *Journal of Educational Psychology, 48,* 65-68.

Hill, L.B., Rejall, A.E., & Thorndike, E.L. (1913). Practice in the case of typewriting. *Pedagogical Seminary, 20,* 516-529.

Hird, J.S., Landers, D.M., Thomas, J.R., & Horan, J.J. (1991). Physical practice is superior to mental practice in enhancing cognitive and motor task performance. *Journal of Sport & Exercise Psychology, 13,* 281-293.

Hoffmann, E.R., & Sheikh, I.H. (1991). Finger width corrections in Fitts' Law: Implications for speed-accuracy research. *Journal of Motor Behavior, 23,* 259-262.

Hoffmann, E.R., Tsang, K.K., & Mu, A. (1995). Data-entry keyboard geometry and keying movement times. *Ergonomics, 38,* 940-950.

Hogan, J.C., & Yanowitz, B.A. (1978). The role of verbal estimates of movement error in ballistic skill acquisition. *Journal of Motor Behavior, 10,* 133-138.

Holding, D.H. (1965). *Principles of training.* Oxford: Pergamon.

Holding, D.H. (1970). Learning without errors. In L.E. Smith (Ed.), *Psychology of motor learning* (pp. 59-74). Chicago: Athletic Institute.

Holding, D.H. (1976). An approximate transfer surface. *Journal of Motor Behavior, 8,* 1-9.

Holding, D.H., & Macrae, A.W. (1964). Guidance, restriction, and knowledge of results. *Ergonomics, 7,* 289-295.

Hollands, M.A., Marple-Horvat, D.E., Henkes, S., & Rowan, A.K. (1995). Human eye movements during visually guided stepping. *Journal of Motor Behavior, 27,* 155-163.

Hollerbach, J.M. (1978). A study of human motor control through analysis and synthesis of handwriting. Unpublished doctoral dissertation, Massachusetts Institute of Technology, Cambridge.

Hollerbach, J.M. (1981). An oscillation theory of handwriting. *Biological Cybernetics, 39,* 139-156.

Hollerbach, J.M., & Flash, T. (1982). Dynamic interactions between limb segments during planar arm movement. *Biological Cybernetics, 44,* 67-77.

Hollingworth, H.L. (1909). The inaccuracy of movement. *Archives of Psychology, 13,* 1-87.

Holmes, G. (1939). The cerebellum of man. *Brain, 62,* 1-30.

Holt, K.G., Jeng, S.F., Ratcliffe, R., & Hamill, J. (1995). Energetic cost and stability during human walking at the preferred stride frequency. *Journal of Motor Behavior, 27,* 164-178.

Hommel, B., & Prinz, W. (Eds.) (1997). *Theoretical issues in stimulus-response compatibility.* Amsterdam: Elsevier.

Hoover, J.H., & Wade. M.G. (1985). Motor learning theory and mentally retarded individuals: A historical review. *Adapted Physical Activity Quarterly, 2,* 228-252.

Horak, M. (1992). The utility of connectionism for motor learning: A reinterpretation of contextual interference in movement schemas. *Journal of Motor Behavior, 24,* 58-66.

Houk, J.C. (1979). Regulation of stiffness by skeletomotor reflexes. *Annual Review of Physiology, 41,* 99-114.

Houk, J.C., & Henneman, E. (1967). Responses of Golgi tendon organs to active contractions of the soleus muscle of the cat. *Journal of Neurophysiology, 30,* 466-481.

Houk, J.C., & Rymer, W.Z. (1981). Neural control of muscle length and tension. In V.B. Brooks (Ed.), *Handbook of physiology: Section 1: The nervous system. Vol. 2. Motor control* (pp. 257-323). Bethesda, MD: American Physiological Society.

Howard, L.A., & Tipper, S.P. (1997). Hand deviations away from visual cues: Indirect evidence for inhibition. *Experimental Brain Research, 113,* 144-152.

Howell, M.L. (1956). Use of force-time graphs for performance analysis in facilitating motor learning. *Research Quarterly, 27,* 12-22.

Hoyt, D.F., & Taylor, C.R. (1981). Gait and the energetics of locomotion in horses. *Science, 292,* 239-240.

Hubbard, A.W., & Seng, C.N. (1954). Visual movements of batters. *Research Quarterly, 25,* 42-57.

Hull, C.L. (1943). *Principles of behavior.* New York: Appleton-Century-Crofts.

Hulstijn, W., Summers, J.J., van Lieshout, P.H.M., & Peters, H.F.M. (1992). Timing in finger tapping and speech: A comparison between stutterers and fluent speakers. *Human Movement Science, 11,* 113-124.

Huxley, H.E. (1969). Structural organization and the contraction mechanism in striated muscle. In S. Devons (Ed.), *Biology and the physical sciences* (pp. 114-138). New York: Columbia University Press.

Hyman, R. (1953). Stimulus information as a determinant of reaction time. *Journal of Experimental Psychology, 45,* 188-196.

Imanaka, K., & Abernethy, B. (1991). The mediating effect of learning on the interference between location and distance recall from motor short-term memory. *Acta Psychologica, 77,* 153-165.

Imanaka, K., & Abernethy, B. (1992). Interference between location and distance information in motor short-term memory: The respective roles of direct kinesthetic signals and abstract codes. *Journal of Motor Behavior, 24,* 274-280.

Irion, A.L. (1948). The relation of 'set' to retention. *Psychological Review, 55,* 336-341.

Irion, A.L. (1966). A brief history of research on the acquisition of skill. In E.A. Bilodeau (Ed.), *Acquisition of skill* (pp. 1-46). New York: Academic Press.

Ismail, A., Kephart, N., & Cowell, C.C. (1963). *Utilization of motor aptitude tests in predicting academic achievement* (Tech. Rep. No. 1). West Lafayette, IN: Purdue University Research Foundation.

Ivry, R., & Corcos, D.M. (1993). Slicing the variability pie: Component analysis of coordination and motor dysfunction. In K.M. Newell & D.M. Corcos (Eds.), *Variability and motor control* (pp. 415-447). Champaign, IL: Human Kinetics.

Ivry, R.B., & Keele, S.W. (1989). Timing functions of the cerebellum. *Journal of Cognitive Neuroscience, 1,* 136-152.

Ivry, R.B., Keele, S.W., & Diener, H.C. (1988). Dissociation of the lateral and medial cerebellum in movement timing and movement execution. *Experimental Brain Research, 73,* 167-180.

Jacoby, L.L. (1978). On interpreting the effects of repetition: Solving a problem versus remembering a solution. *Journal of Verbal Learning and Verbal Behavior, 17,* 649-667.

Jacoby, L.L., & Dallas, M. (1981). On the relationship between autobiographical memory and perceptual learning. *Journal of Experimental Psychology: General, 110,* 306-340.

Jacoby, L.L., Yonelinas, A.P., & Jennings, J.M. (1996). The relation between conscious and unconscious (automatic) influences: A declaration of independence. In J. Cohen & J.W. Schooler (Eds.), *Scientific approaches to the question of consciousness.* Hillsdale, NJ: Erlbaum.

Jagacinski, R.J., & Hah, S. (1988). Progression-regression effects in tracking repeated patterns. *Journal of Experimental Psychology: Human Perception and Performance, 14,* 77-88.

Jagacinski, R.J., Liao, M-J., Fayyad, E.A. (1995). Generalized slowing in sinusoidal tracking by older adults. *Psychology and Aging, 10,* 8-19.

Jagacinski, R.J., & Monk, D.L. (1985). Fitts' law in two dimensions with hand and head movements. *Journal of Motor Behavior, 17,* 77-95.

James, W. (1890). *The principles of psychology* (Vol. 1). New York: Holt.

Jami, L. (1992). Golgi tendon organs in mammalian skeletal muscle: Functional properties and central actions. *Physiological Reviews, 72,* 623-666.

Janelle, C.M., Barba, D.A., Frehlich, S.G., Tennant, L.K., & Cauraugh, J.H. (1997). Maximizing performance feedback effectiveness through videotape replay and a self-controlled learning environment. *Research Quarterly for Exercise and Sport, 68,* 269-279.

Janelle, C.M., Kim, J., & Singer, R.N. (1995). Subject-controlled performance feedback and learning of a closed motor skill. *Perceptual and Motor Skills, 81,* 627-634.

Janis, I., Defares, P., & Grossman, P. (1981). Hypervigilant reactions to threat. In H. Selye (Ed.), *Selye's guide to stress research* (pp. 1-43). New York: Van Nostrand Reinhold.

Jasiewicz, J., & Simmons, R.W. (1996). Response timing accuracy as a function of movement velocity and distance. *Journal of Motor Behavior, 28,* 224-232.

Jeannerod, M. (1984). The timing of natural prehension movements. *Journal of Motor Behavior, 16,* 235-254.

Jeannerod, M., Arbib, M.A., Rizzolati, G., & Sakata, H. (1995). Grasping objects: The cortical mechanisms of visuomotor transformation. *Trends in Neurosciences, 18,* 314-320.

Jeannerod, M., & Marteniuk, R.G. (1992). Functional characteristics of prehension: From data to artificial neural networks. In L.Proteau & D. Elliott (Eds.), *Vision and motor control* (pp. 197-232). Amsterdam: Elsevier.

Jeeves, M.A. (1961). Changes in performance at a serial reaction task under conditions of advance and delay of information. *Ergonomics, 4,* 329-338.

Jeka, J.J., & Kelso, J.A.S. (1989). The dynamic pattern approach to coordinated behavior: A tutorial review. In S.A. Wallace (Ed.), *Perspectives on the coordination of movement* (pp. 3-45). Amsterdam: Elsevier.

Jeka, J.J., Kelso, J.A.S., & Kiemel, T. (1993). Spontaneous transitions and symmetry: Pattern dynamics in human four-limb coordination. *Human Movement Science, 12,* 627-651.

Jenison, R.L. (1997). On acoustic information for motion. *Ecological Psychology, 9,* 131-151.

Jensen, A.R. (1970). The heritability of intelligence. *Engineering and Science, 33,* 1-4.

Jensen, A.R. (1978). The current status of the IQ controversy. *Australian Psychologist, 13,* 7-27.

Johansson, R.S., & Westling, G. (1984). Roles of glabrous skin receptors and sensorimotor memory in automatic control of precision grip when lifting rougher or more slippery objects. *Experimental Brain Research, 56,* 550-564.

Johansson, R.S., & Westling, G. (1988). Programmed and triggered actions to rapid load changes during precision grip. *Experimental Brain Research, 71,* 72-86.

Johansson, R.S., & Westling, G. (1990). Tactile afferent signals in the control of precision grip.

In M. Jeannerod (Ed.), *Attention and performance XIII* (pp. 677-713). Hillsdale, NJ: Erlbaum.

Jones, J.G. (1990). A cognitive perspective on the processes underlying the relationship between stress and performance in sport. In J.G. Jones & L. Hardy (Eds.), *Stress and performance in sport* (pp. 17-42). Chichester: Wiley.

Jones, M.B. (1962). Practice as a process of simplification. *Psychological Review, 69,* 274-294.

Jones, M.B. (1966). Individual differences. In E.A. Bilodeau (Ed.), *Acquisition of skill* (pp. 109-146). New York: Academic Press.

Jones, S.K. (1993). A modular approach to individual differences in skill and coordination. In J.L. Starkes & F. Allard (Eds.), *Cognitive issues in motor expertise* (pp. 273-293). Amsterdam: Elsevier.

Jonides, J., Naveh-Benjamin, M., & Palmer, J. (1985). Assessing automaticity. *Acta Psychologica, 60,* 157-171.

Jordan, M.I. (1990). Motor learning and the degrees of freedom problem. In M. Jeannerod (Ed.), *Attention and performance XIII* (pp. 796-836). Hillsdale, NJ: Erlbaum.

Jordan, M.I. (1995). The organization of action sequences: Evidence from a relearning task. *Journal of Motor Behavior, 27,* 179-192.

Judd, C.H. (1908). The relation of special training to general intelligence. *Educational Review, 36,* 28-42.

Kahneman, D. (1973). *Attention and effort.* Englewood Cliffs, NJ: Prentice-Hall.

Karlin, L., & Kestenbaum, R. (1968). Effects of number of alternatives on the psychological refractory period. *The Quarterly Journal of Experimental Psychology, 20,* 167-178.

Kawato, M., & Gomi, H. (1992). The cerebellum and VOR/OKR learning models. *Trends in Neurosciences, 15,* 445-453.

Keele, S.W. (1968). Movement control in skilled motor performance. *Psychological Bulletin, 70,* 387-403.

Keele, S.W. (1972). Attention demands of memory retrieval. *Journal of Experimental Psychology, 93,* 245-248.

Keele, S.W. (1973). *Attention and human performance.* Pacific Palisades, CA: Goodyear.

Keele, S.W. (1976). Unpublished observations, University of Oregon.

Keele, S.W. (1981). Behavioral analysis of movement. In V. Brooks (Ed.), *Handbook of physiology: Section 1: The Nervous System. Vol. II. Motor control, Part 2.* (pp. 1391-1414). Baltimore, MD: American Physiological Society.

Keele, S.W. (1986). Motor control. In K.R. Boff, L. Kaufman, & J.P. Thomas (Eds.), *Handbook of perception and performance* (pp. 30.1-30.60). New York: Wiley.

Keele, S.W., Cohen, A., & Ivry, R. (1990). Motor programs: Concepts and issues. In M. Jeannerod (Ed.), *Attention and performance XIII* (pp. 77-110). Hillsdale, NJ: Erlbaum.

Keele, S.W., & Ells, J.G. (1972). Memory characteristics of kinesthetic information. *Journal of Motor Behavior, 4,* 127-134.

Keele, S.W., & Hawkins, H.L. (1982). Explorations of individual differences relevant to high level skill. *Journal of Motor Behavior, 14,* 3-23.

Keele, S.W., Ivry, R., & Pokorny, R.A. (1987). Force control and its relation to timing. *Journal of Motor Behavior, 19,* 96-114.

Keele, S.W., & Ivry, R.B. (1987). Modular analysis of timing in motor skill. in G.H. Bower (Ed.), *The psychology of learning and motivation* (vol. 21) (pp. 183-228). New York: Academic Press.

Keele, S.W., Jennings, P., Jones, S., Caulton, D., & Cohen, A. (1995). On the modularity of sequence representation. *Journal of Motor Behavior, 27,* 17-30.

Keele, S.W., Pokorny, R.A., Corcos, D.M., & Ivry, R. (1985). Do perception and motor production share common timing mechanisms: A correlational analysis. *Acta Psychologica, 60,* 173-191.

Keele, S.W., & Posner, M.I. (1968). Processing of visual feedback in rapid movements. *Journal of Experimental Psychology, 77,* 155-158.

Keele, S.W., & Summers, J.J. (1976). The structure of motor programs. In G.E. Stelmach (Ed.), *Motor control: Issues and trends* (pp. 109-142). New York: Academic Press.

Keller, F.S. (1958). The phantom plateau. *Journal of the Experimental Analysis of Behavior, 1,* 1-13.

Kelly, J.P. (1991). The sense of balance. In E.R. Kandel, J.H. Schwartz, T.M. Jessell (Eds.), *Principles of neural science* (3rd ed.) (pp. 500-511). Amsterdam: Elsevier.

Kelso, B.A. (1984). The effects of extended practice on aiming movements in terms of Fitts' Law. Unpublished masters' thesis, York University.

Kelso, J.A.S. (1977). Motor control mechanisms underlying human movement reproduction. *Journal of Experimental Psychology: Human Perception and Performance, 3,* 529-543.

Kelso, J.A.S. (1982). Concepts and issues in human motor behavior: Coming to grips with the jargon. In J.A.S. Kelso (Ed.), *Human motor behavior: An introduction* (pp. 21-58). Hillsdale, NJ: Erlbaum.

Kelso, J.A.S. (1984). Phase transitions and critical behavior in human bimanual coordination. *American Journal of Physiology: Regulatory, Integrative and Comparative Physiology, 15,* R1000-R1004.

Kelso, J.A.S. (1992). Theoretical concepts and strategies for understanding perceptual-motor skill: From information capacity in closed systems to self-organization in open, nonequilibrium systems. *Journal of Experimental Psychology: General, 121,* 260-261.

Kelso, J.A.S. (1995). *Dynamic patterns: The self-organization of brain and behavior.* Cambridge, MA: MIT Press.

Kelso, J.A.S., Buchanan, J.J., & Wallace, S.A. (1991). Order parameters for the neural organization of single, multijoint limb movement patterns. *Experimental Brain Research, 85,* 432-444.

Kelso, J.A.S., Holt, K.G., & Flatt, A.E. (1980). The role of proprioception in the perception and control of human movement: Toward a theoretical reassessment. *Perception & Psychophysics, 28,* 45-52.

Kelso, J.A.S., & Jeka, J.J. (1992). Symmetry breaking dynamics of human multilimb coordination. *Journal of Experimental Psychology: Human Perception and Performance, 18,* 645-668.

Kelso, J.A.S., Putnam, C.A., & Goodman, D. (1983). On the space-time structure of human interlimb co-ordination. *The Quarterly Journal of Experimental Psychology, 35A,* 347-375.

Kelso, J.A.S., Scholz, J.P., & Schöner, G. (1986). Nonequilibrium phase transitions in coordinated biological motion: Critical fluctuations. *Physics Letters A, 118,* 279-284.

Kelso, J.A.S., Scholz, J.P., & Schöner, G. (1988). Dynamics governs switching among patterns of coordination in biological movement. *Physics Letters A, 134,* 8-12.

Kelso, J.A.S., Southard, D.L., & Goodman, D. (1979). On the coordination of two-handed movements. *Journal of Experimental Psychology: Human Perception and Performance, 5,* 229-238.

Kelso, J.A.S., & Stelmach, G.E. (1976). Central and peripheral mechanisms in motor control. In G.E. Stelmach (Ed.), *Motor control: Issues and trends* (pp. 1-40). New York: Academic Press.

Kelso, J.A.S., Stelmach, G.E., & Wannamaker, W.M. (1976). The continuing saga of the nerve compression block technique. *Journal of Motor Behavior, 8,* 155-160.

Kelso, J.A.S., Tuller, B., Vatikiotis-Bateson, E., & Fowler, C.A. (1984). Functionally specific articulatory cooperation following jaw perturbations during speech: Evidence for coordinative structures. *Journal of Experimental Psychology: Human Perception and Performance, 10,* 812-832.

Keogh, J., & Sugden, D. (1985). *Movement skill development.* New York: Macmillan.

Kerlinger, F.N. (1973). *Foundations of behavioral research* (2nd ed.). New York: Holt, Rinehart, and Winston.

Kernodle, M.W., & Carlton, L.G. (1992). Information feedback and the learning of multiple-degree-of-freedom activities. *Journal of Motor Behavior, 24,* 187-196.

Kerr, B. (1973). Processing demands during mental operations. *Memory & Cognition, 1,* 401-412.

Kerr, B. (1975). Processing demands during movement. *Journal of Motor Behavior, 7,* 15-27.

Kerr, B. (1978). Task factors that influence selection and preparation for voluntary movements. In G.E. Stelmach (Ed.), *Information processing in motor control and learning* (pp. 55-69). New York: Academic Press.

Kerr, J.H. (1990). Stress and sport: Reversal theory. In J.G. Jones & L. Hardy (Eds.), *Stress and performance in sport* (pp. 107-131). Chichester: Wiley.

Kerr, R. (1973). Movement time in an underwater environment. *Journal of Motor Behavior, 5,* 175-178.

Kerr, R. (1978). Diving, adaptation, and Fitts Law. *Journal of Motor Behavior, 10,* 255-260.

Kerr, R., & Booth, B. (1977). Skill acquisition in elementary school children and schema theory. In D.M. Landers & R.W. Christina (Eds.), *Psychology of motor behavior and sport—1976.* (Vol. 2). Champaign, IL: Human Kinetics.

Kerr, R., & Booth, B. (1978). Specific and varied practice of motor skill. *Perceptual and Motor Skills, 46,* 395-401.

Klapp, S.T. (1977a). Reaction time analysis of programmed control. *Exercise and Sport Sciences Reviews, 5,* 231-253.

Klapp, S.T. (1977b). Response programming, as assessed by reaction time, does not establish commands for particular muscles. *Journal of Motor Behavior, 9,* 301-312.

Klapp, S.T. (1979). Doing two things at once: The role of temporal compatibility. *Memory & Cognition, 7,* 375-381.

Klapp, S.T. (1981). Temporal compatibility in dual motor tasks II: Simultaneous articulation and hand movements. *Memory & Cognition, 9,* 398-401.

Klapp, S.T. (1995). Motor response programming during simple and choice reaction time: The role of practice. *Journal of Experimental Psychology: Human Perception and Performance, 21,* 1015-1027.

Klapp, S.T. (1996). Reaction time analysis of central motor control. In H.N. Zelaznik (Ed.), *Advances in motor learning and control* (pp. 13-35). Champaign, IL: Human Kinetics.

Klapp, S.T., & Erwin, C.I. (1976). Relation between programming time and duration of the response being programmed. *Journal of Experimental Psychology: Human Perception and Performance, 2,* 591-598.

Klapp, S.T., Hill, M.D., Tyler, J.G., Martin, Z.E., Jagacinski, R.J., & Jones, M.R. (1985). On marching to two different drummers: Perceptual aspects of the difficulties. *Journal of Experimental Psychology: Human Perception and Performance, 11,* 814-827.

Klavora, P. (1977). An attempt to derive inverted-U curves based on the relationship between anxiety and athletic performance. In D.M. Landers & R.W. Christina (Eds.), *Psychology of motor behavior and sport—1976* (pp. 369-377). Champaign, IL: Human Kinetics.

Klein, R., Levy, S., & McCabe, J. (1984). The parameter preferences of acquired motor programs for rapid, discrete movements: I. Transfer of training. *Memory & Cognition, 12,* 374-379.

Kleine, D. (1982). Psychomotorik und Intelligenz. Theoretische und empirische Untersuchungen unter *Berücksichtigung von Übungseffekten im Psychomotorikberich* [Psychomotor skills and intelligence. Theoretical and empirical studies with consideration of training effects in psychomotor information]. Unpublished doctoral dissertation, Free University of Berlin.

Kleine, D. (1985). Psychomotor performance and intellectual abilities. An analysis of the changes in the relationship during practice. Paper presented at the VIth International Congress for Sport Psychology, Copenhagen.

Klemmer, E.T. (1956). Time uncertainty in simple reaction time. *Journal of Experimental Psychology, 51,* 179-184.

Knapp, B. (1963). *Skill in sport: The attainment of proficiency.* London: Routledge & Kegan Paul.

Konzem, P.B. (1987). Extended practice and patterns of bimanual interference. Unpublished doctoral dissertation, University of Southern California.

Kots, Y.M. (1977). *The organization of voluntary movement: Neurophysiological mechanisms.* New York: Plenum.

Kozak, J.J., Hancock, P.A., Arthur, E.J., & Chrysler, S.T. (1993). Transfer of training from virtual reality. *Ergonomics, 36,* 777-784.

Krist, H., Fieberg, E.L., & Wilkening, F. (1993). Intuitive physics in action and judgment: The development of knowledge about projectile motion. *Journal of Experimental Psychology: Learning, Memory, and Cognition, 19,* 952-966.

Kucera, H., & Francis, W.N. (1967). *Computational analysis of present-day American English.* Providence, RI: Brown University Press.

Kugler, P.N., Kelso, J.A.S., & Turvey, M.T. (1980). On the concept of coordinative structures as dissipative structures: I. Theoretical lines of convergence. In G.E. Stelmach & J. Requin (Eds.), *Tutorials in motor behavior* (pp. 3-47). Amsterdam: Elsevier.

Kugler, P.N., & Turvey, M.T. (1987). *Information, natural law, and the self-assembly of rhythmic movement.* Hillsdale, NJ: Erlbaum.

Kuhn, T.S. (1962). *The structure of scientific revolutions.* Chicago: University of Chicago Press.

Kupfermann, I., & Weiss, K.R. (1978). The command neuron concept. *The Behavioral and Brain Sciences, 1,* 3-39.

Kvålseth, T.O. (1980). An alternative to Fitts' law. *Bulletin of the Psychonomic Society, 16,* 371-373.

Kyllo, L.B., & Landers, D.M. (1995). Goal setting in sport and exercise: A research synthesis to resolve the controversy. *Journal of Sport & Exercise Psychology, 17,* 117-137.

Laabs, G.J. (1973). Retention characteristics of different reproduction cues in motor short-term memory. *Journal of Experimental Psychology, 100,* 168-177.

Laban, R. (1956). *Principles of dance and movement notation.* London: MacDonald and Evans.

LaBerge, D. (1973). Identification of two components of the time to switch attention: A test of a serial and a parallel model of attention. In S. Kornblum (Ed.), *Attention and performance IV* (pp. 71-85). New York: Academic Press.

Lang, P.J. (1974). Learned control of human heart rate in a computer directed environment. In P.A. Obrist, A.H. Black, J. Brenner, & L.V. DiCara (Eds.), *Cardiovascular psychophysiology: Current issues in response mechanisms, biofeedback, and methodology* (pp. 392-405). Chicago: Aldine.

Langfeld, H.S. (1915). Facilitation and inhibition of motor impulses: A study in simultaneous and alternating finger movements. *Psychological Review, 22,* 453-478.

Langolf, G.D., Chaffin, D.B., & Foulke, J.A. (1976). An investigation of Fitts' law using a wide range of movement amplitudes. *Journal of Motor Behavior, 8,* 113-128.

Lashley, K.S. (1917). The accuracy of movement in the absence of excitation from the moving organ. *The American Journal of Physiology, 43,* 169-194.

Lashley, K.S. (1942). The problem of cerebral organization in vision. In J. Cattell (Ed.), *Biological symposia. Vol. VII. Visual mechanisms* (pp. 301-322). Lancaster, PA: Jaques Cattell Press.

Lashley, K.S. (1951). The problem of serial order in behavior. In L.A. Jeffress (Ed.), *Cerebral mechanisms in behavior: The Hixon symposium* (pp. 112-136). New York: Wiley.

Laszlo, J.I. (1967). Training of fast tapping with reduction of kinaesthetic, tactile, visual and auditory sensations. *The Quarterly Journal of Experimental Psychology, 19,* 344-349.

Laszlo, J.I., & Bairstow, P.J. (1979). The compression-block technique: A reply to Chambers and Schumsky (1978). *Journal of Motor Behavior, 11,* 283-284.

Laszlo, J.I., Bairstow, P.J., Ward, G.R., & Bancroft, H. (1980). Distracting information, motor performance and sex differences. *Nature, 283,* 377-378.

Latash, M.L. (1993). *Control of human movement.* Champaign, IL: Human Kinetics.

Latash, M.L., & Gutman, S.R. (1993). Variability of fast single-joint movements and the equilibrium-point hypothesis. In K.M. Newell & D.M. Corcos (Eds.), *Variability and motor control* (pp. 157-182). Champaign, IL: Human Kinetics.

Lavery, J.J. (1962). Retention of simple motor skills as a function of type of knowledge of results. *Canadian Journal of Psychology, 16,* 300-311.

Lavery, J.J., & Suddon, F.H. (1962). Retention of simple motor skills as a function of the number of trials by which KR is delayed. *Perceptual and Motor Skills, 15,* 231-237.

Lederman, S.J., & Klatzky, R.L. (1997). Haptic aspects of motor control. In M. Jeannerod (Ed.),

Handbook of neuropsychology (Vol. 11) (pp. 131-148). Amsterdam: Elsevier.

Lee, D.N. (1976). A theory of visual control of braking based on information about time-to-collision. *Perception, 5*, 437-459.

Lee, D.N. (1980). Visuo-motor coordination in space-time. In G.E. Stelmach & J. Requin (Eds.), *Tutorials in motor behavior* (pp. 281-295). Amsterdam: North-Holland.

Lee, D.N. (1990). Getting around with light or sound. In R. Warren & A.H. Wertheim (Eds), *Perception and control of self-motion* (pp. 487-505). Hillsdale, NJ: Erlbaum.

Lee, D.N., & Aronson, E. (1974). Visual proprioceptive control of standing in human infants. *Perception & Psychophysics, 15*, 529-532.

Lee, D.N., Lishman, J.R., & Thomson, J.A. (1982). Regulation of gait in long jumping. *Journal of Experimental Psychology: Human Perception and Performance, 8*, 448-459.

Lee, D.N., & Reddish, P.E. (1981). Plummeting gannets: A paradigm of ecological optics. *Nature, 293*, 293-294.

Lee, D.N., & Young, D.S. (1985). Visual timing of interceptive action. In D. Ingle, M. Jeannerod, & D.N. Lee (Eds.), *Brain mechanisms and spatial vision* (pp. 1-30). Dordrecht: Martinus Nijhoff.

Lee, D.N., Young, D.S., Reddish, P.E., Lough, S., & Clayton, T.M.H. (1983). Visual timing in hitting an accelerating ball. *The Quarterly Journal of Experimental Psychology, 35A*, 333-346.

Lee, R.G., Murphy, J.T., & Tatton, W.G. (1983). Long latency myotatic reflexes in man: Mechanisms, functional significance, and changes in patients with Parkinson's disease or hemiplegia. In J. Desmedt (Ed.), *Advances in neurology* (pp. 489-508). Basel: Karger.

Lee, T.D. (1988). Transfer-appropriate processing: A framework for conceptualizing practice effects in motor learning. In O.G. Meijer & K. Roth (Eds.), *Complex movement behaviour: 'The' motor-action controversy* (pp. 201-215). Amsterdam: Elsevier.

Lee, T.D., Blandin, Y., & Proteau, L. (1996). Effects of task instructions and oscillation frequency on bimanual coordination. *Psychological Research, 59*, 100-106.

Lee, T.D., & Carnahan, H. (1990a). Bandwidth knowledge of results and motor learning: More than just a relative frequency effect. *The Quarterly Journal of Experimental Psychology, 42A*, 777-789.

Lee, T.D., & Carnahan, H. (1990b). When to provide knowledge of results during motor learning: Scheduling effects. *Human Performance, 3*, 87-105.

Lee, T.D., & Genovese, E.D. (1988). Distribution of practice in motor skill acquisition: Learning and performance effects reconsidered. *Research Quarterly for Exercise and Sport, 59*, 277-287.

Lee, T.D., & Genovese, E.D. (1989a). Distribution of practice in motor skill acquisition: Different effects for discrete and continuous tasks. *Research Quarterly for Exercise and Sport, 60*, 59-65.

Lee, T.D., & Genovese, E.D. (1989b). Some reminiscences on distribution of practice effects. *Research Quarterly for Exercise and Sport, 60*, 297-299.

Lee, T.D., & Magill, R.A. (1983a). Activity during the post-KR interval: Effects upon performance or learning? *Research Quarterly for Exercise and Sport, 54*, 340-345.

Lee, T.D., & Magill, R.A. (1983b). The locus of contextual interference in motor-skill acquisition. *Journal of Experimental Psychology: Learning, Memory, and Cognition, 9*, 730-746.

Lee, T.D., & Magill, R.A. (1985). Can forgetting facilitate skill acquisition? In D. Goodman, R.B. Wilberg, & I.M. Franks (Eds.) *Differing perspectives in motor learning, memory, and control* (pp. 3-22). Amsterdam: Elsevier.

Lee, T.D., & Magill, R.A. (1987). Effects of duration and activity during the post-KR interval on motor learning. *Psychological Research, 49*, 237-242.

Lee, T.D., Magill, R.A., & Weeks, D.J. (1985). Influence of practice schedule on testing schema theory predictions in adults. *Journal of Motor Behavior, 17*, 283-299.

Lee, T.D., & Maraj, B.K.V. (1994). Effects of bandwidth goals and bandwidth knowledge of results on motor learning. *Research Quarterly for Exercise and Sport, 65*, 244-249.

Lee, T.D., Maraj, B.K.V., & Wishart, L.R. (1995). Unpublished data, McMaster University, Hamilton, Ontario.

Lee, T.D., & Swinnen, S.P. (1993). Three legacies of Bryan and Harter: Automaticity, variability and change in skilled performance. In J.L. Starkes & F. Allard (Eds.), *Cognitive issues in motor expertise* (pp. 295-315). Amsterdam: Elsevier.

Lee, T.D., Swinnen, S.P., & Verschueren, S. (1995). Relative phase alterations during bimanual skill acquisition. *Journal of Motor Behavior, 27*, 263-274.

Lee, T.D., & Weeks, D.J. (1987). The beneficial influence of forgetting on short-term retention of movement information. *Human Movement Science, 6,* 233-245.

Lee, T.D., & White, M.A. (1990). Influence of an unskilled model's practice schedule on observational motor learning. *Human Movement Science, 9,* 349-367.

Lee, T.D., White, M.A., & Carnahan, H. (1990). On the role of knowledge of results in motor learning: Exploring the guidance hypothesis. *Journal of Motor Behavior, 22,* 191-208.

Lee, T.D., Wishart, L.R., Cunningham, S., & Carnahan, H. (1997). Modeled timing information during random practice eliminates the contextual interference effect. *Research Quarterly for Exercise and Sport, 68,* 100-105.

Lee, T.D., Wulf, G., & Schmidt, R.A. (1992). Contextual interference in motor learning: Dissociated effects due to the nature of task variations. *The Quarterly Journal of Experimental Psychology, 44A,* 627-644.

Lee, W.A. (1980). Anticipatory control of postural and task muscles during rapid arm flexion. *Journal of Motor Behavior, 12,* 185-196.

Leonard, J.A. (1953). Advance information in sensori-motor skills. *The Quarterly Journal of Experimental Psychology, 5,* 141-149.

Leonard, J.A. (1954). An experiment with occasional false information. *The Quarterly Journal of Experimental Psychology, 6,* 79-85.

Leonard, J.A. (1959). Tactual choice reactions: I. *The Quarterly Journal of Experimental Psychology, 11,* 76-83.

Lersten, K.C. (1968). Transfer of movement components in a motor learning task. *Research Quarterly, 39,* 575-581.

Lersten, K.C. (1969). Retention of skill on the Rho apparatus after one year. *Research Quarterly, 40,* 418-419.

Leuba, J.H., & Chamberlain, E. (1909). The influence of the duration and of the rate of arm movements upon the judgment of their length. *American Journal of Psychology, 20,* 374-385.

Lewis, D. (1947). Positive and negative transfer in motor learning. *American Psychologist, 2,* 423.

Lewis, D. (1953). Motor skills learning. In A.B. Nadel (Ed.), *Symposium on psychology of learning basic to military training problems* (HR-HTD 201/1, pp. 45-84). Washington, DC: Department of Defense.

Lewis, D., McAllister, D.E., & Adams, J.A. (1951). Facilitation and interference in performance on the modified Mashburn apparatus: I. The effects of varying the amount of original learning. *Journal of Experimental Psychology, 41,* 247-260.

Lewis, R.E.F. (1956). Consistency and car driving skill. *British Journal of Industrial Medicine, 13,* 131-141.

Lindahl, L.G. (1945). Movement analysis as an industrial training method. *Journal of Applied Psychology, 29,* 420-436.

Lindeburg, F.A. (1949). A study of the degree of transfer between quickening exercises and other coordinated movements. *Research Quarterly, 20,* 180-195.

Lintern, G. (1988). Distributed practice: Are there useful insights for application or theory? *Research Quarterly for Exercise and Sport, 59,* 298-302.

Lintern, G., Sheppard, D.J., Parker, D.L., Yates, K.E., & Nolan, M.D. (1989). Simulator design and instructional features for air-to-ground attack: A transfer study. *Human Factors, 31,* 87-99.

Locke, E.A. (1991). Problems with goal-setting research in sports—and their solution. *Journal of Sport & Exercise Psychology, 13,* 311-316.

Locke, E.A., & Latham, G.P. (1985). The application of goal setting to sports. *Sport Psychology Today, 7,* 205-222.

Locke, E.A., Shaw, K.N., Saari, L.M., & Latham, G.P. (1981). Goal setting and task performance: 1969-1980. *Psychological Bulletin, 90,* 125-152.

Logan, G.D. (1982). On the ability to inhibit complex movements: A stop-signal study of typewriting. *Journal of Experimental Psychology: Human Perception and Performance, 8,* 778-792.

Logan, G.D. (1985). Skill and automaticity: Relations, implications, and future directions. *Canadian Journal of Psychology, 39,* 367-386.

Logan, G.D. (1988). Toward an instance theory of automatization. *Psychological Review, 95,* 492-527.

Logan, G.D. (1994). On the ability to inhibit thought and action: A user's guide to the stop signal paradigm. In D. Dagenbach & T.H. Carr (Eds.), *Inhibitory processes in attention, memory, and language* (pp. 189-239). San Diego: Academic Press.

Lordahl, D.S., & Archer, E.J. (1958). Transfer effects on a rotary pursuit task as a function of first-task difficulty. *Journal of Experimental Psychology, 56,* 421-426.

Lorge, I., & Thorndike, E.L. (1935). The influence of delay in the after-effect of a connection. *Journal of Experimental Psychology, 18,* 186-194.

Lotter, W.S. (1960). Interrelationships among reaction times and speeds of movement in different limbs. *Research Quarterly, 31,* 147-155.

MacKenzie, C.L. (1995). *Virtual hand lab system.* Paper presented at the annual meeting of the Canadian Society for Psychomotor Learning and Sport Psychology, Vancouver, BC.

MacLeod, C.M. (1991). Half a century of research on the Stroop effect: An integrative review. *Psychological Bulletin, 109,* 163-203.

MacLeod, C.M., & Dunbar, K. (1988). Training and Stroop-like interference: Evidence for a continuum of automaticity. *Journal of Experimental Psychology: Learning, Memory, and Cognition, 14,* 126-135.

MacNeilage, P.F. (1970). Motor control of serial ordering of speech. *Psychological Review, 77,* 182-196.

MacPherson, S.J., Dees, V., & Grindley, G.C. (1948). The effect of knowledge of results on learning and performance: II. Some characteristics of very simple skills. *The Quarterly Journal of Experimental Psychology, 1,* 68-78.

MacPherson, S.J., Dees, V., & Grindley, G.C. (1949). The effect of knowledge of results on learning and performance: III. The influence of time intervals between trials. *The Quarterly Journal of Experimental Psychology, 1,* 167-174.

Macrae, A.W., & Holding, D.H. (1965). Method and task in motor guidance. *Ergonomics, 8,* 315-320.

Macrae, A.W., & Holding, D.H. (1966). Transfer of training after guidance or practice. *The Quarterly Journal of Experimental Psychology, 18,* 327-333.

Magill, R.A. (1973). The post-KR interval: Time and activity effects and the relationship of motor short-term memory theory. *Journal of Motor Behavior, 5,* 49-56.

Magill, R.A. (1988a). Activity during the post-knowledge of results interval can benefit motor skill learning. In O.G. Meijer & K. Roth (Eds.), *Complex movement behaviour: 'The' motor-action controversy* (pp. 231-246). Amsterdam: Elsevier.

Magill, R.A. (1988b). The many faces of practice distribution in motor learning. *Research Quarterly for Exercise and Sport, 59,* 303-307.

Magill, R.A. (1993). *Motor learning: Concepts and applications* (4th ed.). Madison, WI: Brown & Benchmark.

Magill, R.A. (in press). Knowledge is more than we can talk about: Implicit learning in motor skill acquisition. *Research Quarterly for Exercise and Sport.*

Magill, R.A., Chamberlin, C.J., & Hall, K.G. (1991). Verbal knowledge of results as redundant information for learning an anticipation timing skill. *Human Movement Science, 10,* 485-507.

Magill, R.A., & Hall, K.G. (1990). A review of the contextual interference effect in motor skill acquisition. *Human Movement Science, 9,* 241-289.

Magill, R.A., Schmidt, R.A., Young, D.E., & Shapiro, D.C. (1987). Unpublished data, University of California, Los Angeles.

Magill, R.A., & Schoenfelder-Zohdi, B. (1996). A visual model and knowledge of performance as sources of information for learning a rhythmic gymnastics skill. *International Journal of Sport Psychology, 27,* 7-22.

Magill, R.A., & Wood, C.A. (1986). Knowledge of results precision as a learning variable in motor skill acquisition. *Research Quarterly for Exercise and Sport, 57,* 170-173.

Mané, A.M., Adams, J.A., & Donchin, E. (1989). Adaptive and part-whole training in the acquisition of a complex perceptual-motor skill. *Acta Psychologica, 71,* 179-196.

Maraj, B.K.V., Elliott, D., Lee, T.D., & Pollock, B.J. (1993). Variance and invariance in expert and novice triple jumpers. *Research Quarterly for Exercise and Sport, 64,* 404-412.

Marder, E., & Calabrese, R.L. (1996). Principles of rhythmic motor pattern generation. *Physiological Reviews, 76,* 687-717.

Marsden, C.D., Merton, P.A., & Morton, H.B. (1972). Servo action in human voluntary movement. *Nature, 238,* 140-143.

Marshall, P.H., Jones, M.T., & Sheehan, E.M. (1977). The spacing effect in short-term memory: The differential attention hypothesis. *Journal of Motor Behavior, 9,* 119-126.

Marteniuk, R.G. (1973). Retention characteristics of motor short-term memory cues. *Journal of Motor Behavior, 5,* 249-259.

Marteniuk, R.G. (1974). Individual differences in motor performance and learning. *Exercise and Sport Sciences Reviews, 2,* 103-130.

Marteniuk, R.G. (1976). *Information processing in motor skills.* New York: Holt, Rinehart, and Winston.

Marteniuk, R.G. (1986). Information processes in movement learning: Capacity and structural interference effects. *Journal of Motor Behavior, 18*, 55-75.

Marteniuk, R.G., Leavitt, J.L., MacKenzie, C.L., & Athenes, S. (1990). Functional relationships between grasp and transport components in a prehension task. *Human Movement Science, 9*, 149-176.

Marteniuk, R.G., MacKenzie, C.L., & Baba, D.M. (1984). Bimanual movement control: Information processing and interaction effects. *The Quarterly Journal of Experimental Psychology, 36A*, 335-365.

Marteniuk, R.G., MacKenzie, C.L., Jeannerod, M., Athenes, S., & Dugas, C. (1987). Constraints on human arm movement trajectories. *Canadian Journal of Psychology, 41*, 365-378.

Marteniuk, R.G., & Romanow, S.K.E. (1983). Human movement organization and learning as revealed by variability of movement, use of kinematic information, and Fourier analysis. In R.A. Magill (Ed.), *Memory and control of action* (pp. 167-197). Amsterdam: Elsevier.

Martens, R., Burton, D., Vealey, R., Bump, L., & Smith, D. (1990). The development of the Competitive State Anxiety Inventory-2 (CSAI-2). In R. Martens, R.S. Vealey, & D. Burton (Eds.), *Competitive anxiety in sports* (pp. 117-190). Champaign, IL: Human Kinetics.

Martens, R., Burwitz, L., & Zuckerman, J. (1976). Modeling effects on motor performance. *Research Quarterly, 47*, 277-291.

Martens, R., & Landers, D.M. (1969). Effect of anxiety, competition and failure on performance of a complex motor task. *Journal of Motor Behavior, 1*, 1-9.

Martens, R., & Landers, D.M. (1970). Motor performance under stress: A test of the inverted-U hypothesis. *Journal of Personality and Social Psychology, 16*, 29-37.

Martin, H.A. (1970). Long-term retention of a discrete motor task. Unpublished master's thesis, University of Maryland, College Park.

Martin, J.H., & Jessell, T.M. (1991). Modality coding in the somatic sensory system. In E.R. Kandel, J.H. Schwartz, T.M. Jessell (Eds.), *Principles of neural science* (3rd ed.) (pp. 341-352). Amsterdam: Elsevier.

Massaro, D.W. (1989). *Experimental psychology: An information processing approach*. San Diego: Harcourt Brace Jovanovich.

Masson, M.E.J. (1990). Cognitive theories of skill acquisition. *Human Movement Science, 9*, 221-239.

Masters, R.S.W. (1992). Knowledge, knerves and know-how: The role of explicit versus implicit knowledge in the breakdown of a complex motor skill under pressure. *British Journal of Psychology, 83*, 343-358.

McCarthy, G., & Donchin, E. (1981). A metric for thought: A comparison of P300 latency and reaction time. *Science, 211*, 77-80.

McCloy, C.H. (1934). The measurement of general motor capacity and general motor ability. *Research Quarterly, 5* (Suppl. 5), 45-61.

McCloy, C.H. (1937). An analytical study of the stunt type test as a measure of motor educability. *Research Quarterly, 8*, 46-55.

McCracken, H.D., & Stelmach, G.E. (1977). A test of the schema theory of discrete motor learning. *Journal of Motor Behavior, 9*, 193-201.

McCullagh, P. (1993). Modeling: Learning, developmental, and social psychological considerations. In R.N. Singer, M. Murphey, & L.K. Tennant (Eds.), *Handbook of research on sport psychology* (pp. 106-126). New York: Macmillan.

McCullagh, P., & Caird, J.K. (1990). Correct and learning models and the use of model knowledge of results in the acquisition and retention of a motor skill. *Journal of Human Movement Studies, 18*, 107-116.

McCullagh, P., & Little, W.S. (1989). A comparison of modalities in modeling. *Human Performance, 2*, 107-116.

McCullagh, P., & Meyer, K.N. (1997). Learning versus correct models: Influence of model type on the learning of a free-weight squat lift. *Research Quarterly for Exercise and Sport, 68*, 56-61.

McCullagh, P., Weiss, M.R., & Ross, D. (1989). Modeling considerations in motor skill acquisition and performance: An integrated approach. *Exercise and Sport Sciences Reviews, 17*, 475-513.

McDonald, P.V., van Emmerik, R.E.A., & Newell, K.M. (1989). The effects of practice on limb kinematics in a throwing task. *Journal of Motor Behavior, 21*, 245-264.

McGeoch, J.A., & Irion, A.L. (1952). *The psychology of human learning*. New York: Longmans.

McGraw, M.B. (1935). *Growth: A study of Johnny and Jimmy*. New York: Appleton-Century.

McGraw, M.B. (1939). Later development of children specially trained during infancy: Johnny and Jimmy at school age. *Child Development, 10*, 1-19.

McGuigan, F.J. (1959). The effect of precision, delay, and schedule of knowledge of results on performance. *Journal of Experimental Psychology, 58*, 79-84.

McLeod, P. (1977). A dual task response modality effect: Support for multiprocessor models of attention. *The Quarterly Journal of Experimental Psychology, 29*, 651-667.

McLeod, P. (1980). What can probe RT tell us about the attentional demands of movement? In G.E. Stelmach & J. Requin (Eds.), *Tutorials in motor behavior* (pp. 579-589). Amsterdam: Elsevier.

McLeod, P. (1987). Visual reaction time and high-speed ball games. *Perception, 16*, 49-59.

McLeod, P., & Dienes, Z. (1993). Running to catch the ball. *Nature, 362*, 23.

McLeod, P., & Dienes, Z. (1996). Do fielders know where to go to catch the ball or only how to get there? *Journal of Experimental Psychology: Human Perception and Performance, 22*, 531-543.

McNevin, N., Magill, R.A., & Buekers, M.J. (1994). The effects of erroneous knowledge of results on transfer of anticipation timing. *Research Quarterly for Exercise and Sport, 65*, 324-329.

McPherson, S.L. (1993). Knowledge representation and decision-making in sport. In J.L. Starkes & F. Allard (Eds.), *Cognitive issues in motor expertise* (pp. 159-188). Amsterdam: Elsevier.

McPherson, S.L. (1994). The development of sport expertise: Mapping the tactical domain. *Quest, 46*, 223-240.

Meegan, D.V., & Tipper, S.P. (in press). Reaching into cluttered visual environments: Spatial and temporal influences of distracting objects. *The Quarterly Journal of Experimental Psychology.*

Melton, A.W. (Ed.) (1947). *Apparatus tests.* Washington, DC: United States Government Printing Office.

Melton, A.W. (1967). Repetition and retrieval from memory. *Science, 158*, 532.

Merkel, J. (1885). Die zeitlichen Verhaltnisse det Willensthaütigkeit. *Philosophische Studien, 2*, 73-127. (Cited in Woodworth, R.S. (1938). *Experimental psychology.* New York: Holt.)

Merton, P.A. (1953). Speculations on the servo control of movement. In G.E.W. Wolstenholme (Ed.), *The spinal cord.* London: Churchill.

Merton, P.A. (1972). How we control the contraction of our muscles. *Scientific American, 226*, 30-37.

Meyer, D.E., Abrams, R.A., Kornblum, S., Wright, C.E., & Smith, J.E.K. (1988). Optimality in human motor performance: Ideal control of rapid aimed movements. *Psychological Review, 95*, 340-370.

Meyer, D.E., Smith, J.E.K., Kornblum, S., Abrams, R.A., & Wright, C.E. (1990). Speed-accuracy tradeoffs in aimed movements: Toward a theory of rapid voluntary action. In M. Jeannerod (Ed.), *Attention and performance XIII* (pp. 173-226). Hillsdale, NJ: Erlbaum.

Meyer, D.E., Smith, J.E.K., & Wright, C.E. (1982). Models for the speed and accuracy of aimed movements. *Psychological Review, 89*, 449-482.

Meyers, J.L. (1967). Retention of balance coordination learning as influenced by extended lay-offs. *Research Quarterly, 38*, 72-78.

Michaels, C.F., & Oudejans, R.R.D. (1992). The optics and actions of catching fly balls: Zeroing out optic acceleration. *Ecological Psychology, 4*, 199-222.

Michon, J.A. (1966). Tapping regularity as a measure of perceptual motor load. *Ergonomics, 9*, 401-412.

Michon, J.A. (1967). *Timing in temporal tracking.* Soesterberg, The Netherlands: Institute for Perception, RNO-TNO.

Miller, G.A. (1956). The magical number seven, plus or minus two: Some limits on our capacity for processing information. *Psychological Review, 63*, 81-97.

Milner, A.D., & Goodale, M.A. (1993). Visual pathways to perception and action. In T.P. Hicks, S. Molotchnikoff, & T. Ono (Eds.), *Progress in brain research* (vol. 95). Amsterdam: Elsevier.

Milone, F. (1971). Interference in motor short-term memory. Unpublished master's thesis, Pennsylvania State University, University Park.

Minas, S.C. (1978). Mental practice of a complex perceptual-motor skill. *Journal of Human Movement Studies, 4*, 102-107.

Minas, S.C. (1980). Acquisition of a motor skill following guided mental and physical practice. *Journal of Human Movement Studies, 6*, 127-141.

Montagne, G., & Laurent, M. (1994). The effects of environment changes on one-handed catching. *Journal of Motor Behavior, 26*, 237-246.

Moray, N. (1970). *Attention: Selective processes in vision and hearing.* New York: Academic Press.

Morgan, C.T., & King, R.A. (1971). *Introduction to psychology* (4th ed.). New York: McGraw-Hill.

Morgan, M., Phillips, J.G., Bradshaw, J.L., Mattingley, J.B., Iansek, R., & Bradshaw, J.A.

(1994). Age-related motor slowness: Simply strategic? *Journal of Gerontology: Medical Sciences, 49,* M133-M139.

Morris, C.D., Bransford, J.D., & Franks, J.J. (1977). Levels of processing versus transfer appropriate processing. *Journal of Verbal Learning and Verbal Behavior, 16,* 519-533.

Morrissey, M.C., Harman, E.A., & Johnson, M.J. (1995). Resistance training modes: Specificity and effectiveness. *Medicine and Science in Sports and Exercise, 27,* 648-660.

Mowbray, G.H. (1960). Choice reaction times for skilled responses. *The Quarterly Journal of Experimental Psychology, 12,* 193-202.

Mowbray, G.H., & Rhoades, M.V. (1959). On the reduction of choice reaction times with practice. *The Quarterly Journal of Experimental Psychology, 11,* 16-23.

Mowrer, O.H. (1940). Preparatory set (expectancy): Some methods of measurement. *Psychological Monographs, 52* (No. 233).

Mulder, T., & Hulstijn, W. (1985). Delayed sensory feedback in the learning of a novel motor task. *Psychological Research, 47,* 203-209.

Murphy, H.H. (1916). Distribution of practice periods in learning. *Journal of Educational Psychology, 7,* 150-162.

Muybridge, E. (1887). *Animal locomotion: An electrophotographic investigation of consecutive phases of animal movements.* Philadelphia: J.B. Lippincott.

Muybridge, E. (1979). *Muybridge's complete human and animal locomotion: All 781 plates from the 1887 Animal Locomotion.* New York: Dover.

Nacson, J., & Schmidt, R.A. (1971). The activity-set hypothesis for warm-up decrement. *Journal of Motor Behavior, 3,* 1-15.

Namikas, G., & Archer, E.J. (1960). Motor skill transfer as a function of intertask interval and pretransfer task difficulty. *Journal of Experimental Psychology, 59,* 109-112.

Nashner, L., & Berthoz, A. (1978). Visual contribution to rapid motor responses during postural control. *Brain Research, 150,* 403-407.

Nashner, L.M., & McCollum, G. (1985). The organization of human postural movements: A formal basis and experimental synthesis. *Behavioral and Brain Sciences, 8,* 135-172.

Nashner, L.M., & Woollacott, M. (1979). The organization of rapid postural adjustments of standing humans: An experimental-conceptual model. In R.E. Talbott & D.R. Humphrey (Eds.), *Posture and movement* (pp. 243-257). New York: Raven.

Navon, D., & Gopher, D. (1979). On the economy of the human-processing system. *Psychological Review, 86,* 214-255.

Neiss, R. (1988). Reconceptualizing arousal: Psychobiological states in motor performance. *Psychological Bulletin, 103,* 345-366.

Neisser, U. (1967). Cognitive psychology. New York: Appleton-Century-Crofts.

Nelson, T.O. (1985). Ebbinghaus's contribution to the measurement of retention: Savings during relearning. *Journal of Experimental Psychology: Learning, Memory, and Cognition, 11,* 472-479.

Neumann, E., & Ammons, R.B. (1957). Acquisition and long-term retention of a simple serial perceptual-motor skill. *Journal of Experimental Psychology, 53,* 159-161.

Neumann, O. (1987). Beyond capacity: A functional view of attention. In H. Heuer & A.F. Sanders (Eds.), *Perspectives on perception and action* (pp. 361-394). Hillsdale, NJ: Erlbaum.

Neumann, O. (1996). Theories of attention. In O. Neumann & A.F. Sanders (Eds.), *Handbook of perception and action. Volume 3: Attention* (pp. 389-446). San Diego: Academic Press.

Newell, A., & Rosenbloom, P.S. (1981). Mechanisms of skill acquisition and the law of practice. In J.R. Anderson (Ed.), *Cognitive skills and their acquisition* (pp. 1-55). Hillsdale, NJ: Erlbaum.

Newell, K.M. (1974). Knowledge of results and motor learning. *Journal of Motor Behavior, 6,* 235-244.

Newell, K.M. (1976a). More on absolute error, etc. *Journal of Motor Behavior, 8,* 139-142.

Newell, K.M. (1976b). Motor learning without knowledge of results through the development of a response recognition mechanism. *Journal of Motor Behavior, 8,* 209-217.

Newell, K.M. (1980). The speed-accuracy paradox in movement control: Error of time and space. In G.E. Stelmach (Ed.), *Tutorials in motor behavior.* Amsterdam: Elsevier.

Newell, K.M. (1981). Skill learning. In D.H. Holding (Ed.), *Human skills.* New York: Wiley.

Newell, K.M. (1991). Motor skill acquisition. *Annual Review of Psychology, 42,* 213-237.

Newell, K.M., Antoniou, A., & Carlton, L.G. (1988). Massed and distributed practice effects: Phenomena in search of a theory? *Research Quarterly for Exercise and Sport, 59,* 308-313.

Newell, K.M., & Carlton, L.G. (1985). On the relationship between peak force and peak force variability in isometric tasks. *Journal of Motor Behavior, 17,* 230-241.

Newell, K.M., & Carlton, L.G. (1988). Force variability in isometric responses. *Journal of Experimental Psychology: Human Perception and Performance, 14,* 37-44.

Newell, K.M., Carlton, L.G., Carlton, M.J., & Halbert, J.A. (1980). Velocity as a factor in movement timing accuracy. *Journal of Motor Behavior, 12,* 47-56.

Newell, K.M., Carlton, L.G., & Hancock, P.A. (1984). Kinetic analysis of response variability. *Psychological Bulletin, 96,* 133-151.

Newell, K.M., Carlton, L.G., & Kim, S. (1994). Time and space-time movement accuracy. *Human Performance, 7,* 1-21.

Newell, K.M., Carlton, L.G., Kim, S., & Chung, C. (1993). Space-time accuracy of rapid movements. *Journal of Motor Behavior, 25,* 8-20.

Newell, K.M., Carlton, M.J., & Antoniou, A. (1990). The interaction of criterion and feedback information in learning a drawing task. *Journal of Motor Behavior, 22,* 536-552.

Newell, K.M., Carlton, M.J., Fisher, A.T., & Rutter, B.G. (1989). Whole-part training strategies for learning the response dynamics of microprocessor driven simulators. *Acta Psychologica, 71,* 197-216.

Newell, K.M., Hoshizaki, L.E.F., Carlton, M.J., & Halbert, J.A. (1979). Movement time and velocity as determinants of movement timing accuracy. *Journal of Motor Behavior, 11,* 49-58.

Newell, K.M., & McDonald, P.V. (1992). Practice: A search for task solutions. In *American Academy of Physical Education, Enhancing human performance in sport: New concepts and developments* (*The Academy papers, No. 25,* pp. 51-59). Champaign, IL: Human Kinetics.

Newell, K.M., Sparrow, W.A., & Quinn, J.T. Jr. (1985). Kinetic information feedback for learning isometric tasks. *Journal of Human Movement Studies, 11,* 113-123.

Newell, K.M., van Emmerik, R.E.A. (1989). The acquisition of coordination: Preliminary analysis of learning to write. *Human Movement Science, 8,* 17-32.

Newell, K.M., van Emmerik, R.E.A., & Sprague, R.L. (1993). Stereotypy and variability. In K.M. Newell & D.M. Corcos (Eds.), *Variability and motor control* (pp. 475-496). Champaign, IL: Human Kinetics.

Newell, K.M., & Walter, C.B. (1981). Kinematic and kinetic parameters as information feedback in motor skill acquisition. *Journal of Human Movement Studies, 7,* 235-254.

Nichols, T.R., & Houk, J.C. (1976). Improvement of linearity and regulation of stiffness that results from actions of stretch reflex. *Journal of Neurophysiology, 39,* 119-142.

Nicholson, D.E., & Schmidt, R.A. (1991). *Timing-task duration determines post-response error-detection capabilities.* Paper presented at NASPSPA annual meeting, Monterey, CA.

Nickerson, R.S., Kalikow, D.N., & Stevens, K.N. (1976). Computer-aided speech training for the deaf. *Journal of Speech and Hearing Disorders, 41,* 120-132.

Nideffer, R.M. (1976). *The inner athlete: Mind plus muscle for winning.* New York: Crowell.

Noble, C.E. (1978). Age, race, and sex in the learning and performance of psychomotor skills. In R.T. Osborne, C.E. Noble, & N. Weyl (Eds.), *Human variation: The biopsychology of age, race, and sex* (pp. 287-378). New York: Academic Press.

Norman, D.A. (1969). Memory while shadowing. *The Quarterly Journal of Experimental Psychology, 21,* 85-93.

Norman, D.A. (1976). *Memory and attention* (2nd ed.). New York: Wiley.

Norman, D.A. (1981). The categorization of action slips. *Psychological Review, 88,* 1-15.

Norman, D.A., & Bobrow, D.G. (1975). On data-limited and resource-limited processes. *Cognitive Psychology, 7,* 44-64.

Ogden, G.D., Levine, J.M., & Eisner, E.J. (1979). Measurement of workload by secondary tasks. *Human Factors, 21,* 529-548.

Osborne, R.T., Noble, C.E., & Weyl, N. (1978). *Human variation: The bio-psychology of age, race, and sex.* New York: Academic Press.

Osgood, C.E. (1949). The similarity paradox in human learning: A resolution. *Psychological Review, 56,* 132-143.

Osman, A., Kornblum, S., & Meyer, D.E. (1990). Does motor programming necessitate response execution? *Journal of Experimental Psychology: Human Perception and Performance, 16,* 183-198.

Owens, D.A. (1985). Paper presented at the Zentrum für interdisziplinäre Forschung, Universität Bielefeld, West Germany.

Paillard, J., & Amblard, B. (1985). Static versus kinetic visual cues for the processing of spatial relationships. In D. Ingle, M. Jeannerod, & D.N. Lee (Eds.), *Brain mechanisms and spatial vision* (pp. 299-330). Dordrecht: Martinus Nijhoff.

Paillard, J., & Bruchon, M. (1968). Active and passive movements in the calibration of position sense. In S.J. Freedman (Ed.), *The neuropsychology of spatially oriented behavior*. New York: Dorsey.

Parker, J.F. Jr., & Fleishman, E.A. (1960). Ability factors and component performance measures as predictors of complex tracking behavior. *Psychological Monographs, 74* (Whole No. 503).

Partridge, L.D. (1979). Muscle properties: A problem for the motor physiologist. In R.E. Talbott & D.R. Humphrey (Eds.), *Posture and movement* (pp. 189-229). New York: Raven.

Partridge, L.D. (1983). Neural control drives a muscle spring: A persisting yet limited motor theory. *Experimental Brain Research Supplementum, 7*, 280-290.

Partridge, L.D., & Benton, L.A. (1981). Muscle, the motor. In V.B. Brooks (Ed.), *Handbook of physiology: Vol. 2. Motor control* (pp. 43-106). Bethesda, MA: American Physiological Society.

Pashler, H. (1993, January-February). Doing two things at the same time. *American Scientist, 81(1)*, 48-49.

Pashler, H. (1994). Dual-task interference in simple tasks: Data and theory. *Psychological Bulletin, 116*, 220-244.

Patla, A.E. (1989). In search of laws for the visual control of locomotion: Some observations. *Journal of Experimental Psychology: Human Perception and Performance, 15*, 624-628.

Patla, A.E. (1997). Understanding the roles of vision in the control of human locomotion. *Gait & Posture, 5*, 54-69.

Patla, A.E., Frank, J.S., Allard, F., & Thomas, E. (1985). Speed-accuracy characteristics of saccadic eye movements. *Journal of Motor Behavior, 17*, 411-419.

Patla, A.E., Rietdyk, S., Martin, C., & Prentice, S. (1996). Locomotor patterns of the leading and the trailing limbs as solid and fragile obstacles are stepped over: Some insights into the role of vision during locomotion. *Journal of Motor Behavior, 28*, 35-47.

Patla, A.E., Robinson, C., Samways, M., & Armstrong, C.J. (1989). Visual control of step length during overground locomotion: Task-specific modulation of the locomotor synergy. *Journal of Experimental Psychology: Human Perception and Performance, 15*, 603-617.

Patrick, J. (1971). The effect of interpolated motor activities in short-term motor memory. *Journal of Motor Behavior, 3*, 39-48.

Paulignan, Y., Jeannerod, M., MacKenzie, C., & Marteniuk, R. (1991). Selective perturbation of visual input during prehension movements. 2. The effects of changing object size. *Experimental Brain Research, 87*, 407-420.

Paulignan, Y., MacKenzie, C., Marteniuk, R., & Jeannerod, M. (1991). Selective perturbation of visual input during prehension movements. 1. The effects of changing object position. *Experimental Brain Research, 83*, 502-512.

Pavlov, I.P. (1927). *Conditioned reflexes: An investigation of the physiological activity of the cerebral cortex.* (G.V. Anrep, Trans.). Oxford: Oxford University Press.

Payne, R.B. (1970). Functional properties of supplementary feedback stimuli. *Journal of Motor Behavior, 2*, 37-43.

Payne, R.B., & Dunman, L.S. (1974). Effects of classical predifferentiation on the functional properties of supplementary feedback cues. *Journal of Motor Behavior, 6*, 47-52.

Payne, V.G., & Isaacs, L.D. (1991). *Human motor development: A lifespan approach* (2nd ed.). Mountain View, CA: Mayfield.

Pearson, K. (1976). The control of walking. *Scientific American, 235*, 72-86.

Pélisson, D., Prablanc, C., Goodale, M.A., & Jeannerod, M. (1986). Visual control of reaching movements without vision of the limb II. Evidence of fast unconscious processes correcting the trajectory of the hand to the final position of double-step stimulus. *Experimental Brain Research, 62*, 303-311.

Pepper, R.L., & Herman, L.M. (1970). Decay and interference effects in the short-term retention of a discrete motor act. *Journal of Experimental Psychology, 83* (Monograph Supplement 2).

Perel, M. (1976). *Analyzing the role of driver/vehicle incompatibilities in accident causation using police reports* (Tech. Rep. No. DOT H5-806-509). Washington, DC: United States Department of Transportation.

Perenin, M.-T., & Vighetto, A. (1988). Optic ataxia: A specific disruption in visuomotor mechanisms I. Different aspects of the deficit in reaching for objects. *Brain, 111*, 643-674.

Peters, M. (1977). Simultaneous performance of two motor activities: The factor of timing. *Neuropsychologica, 15*, 461-464.

Peters, M. (1985). Performance of a rubato-like task: When two things cannot be done at the same time. *Music Perception, 2*, 471-482.

Peterson, L.R., & Peterson, M.J. (1959). Short-term retention of individual verbal items. *Journal of Experimental Psychology, 58*, 193-198.

Pew, R.W. (1966). Acquisition of hierarchical control over the temporal organization of a skill. *Journal of Experimental Psychology, 71*, 764-771.

Pew, R.W. (1970). Toward a process-oriented theory of human skilled performance. *Journal of Motor Behavior, 2*, 8-24.

Pew, R.W. (1974a). Human perceptual-motor performance. In B.H. Kantowitz (Ed.), *Human information processing: Tutorials in performance and cognition* (pp. 1-39). Hillsdale, NJ: Erlbaum.

Pew, R.W. (1974b). Levels of analysis in motor control. *Brain Research, 71*, 393-400.

Phillips, J.R., & Berkhout, J. (1976). *Uses of computer-assisted instruction in developing psychomotor skills related to heavy machinery operation* (Contract Rep. DAHC-19-75G0009). Alexandria, VA: US Army Research Institute.

Pigott, R.E., & Shapiro, D.C. (1984). Motor schema: The structure of the variability session. *Research Quarterly for Exercise and Sport, 55*, 41-45.

Plagenhoef, S. (1971). *Patterns of human motion: A cinematographic analysis.* Englewood Cliffs, NJ: Prentice-Hall.

Plamondon, R., & Alimi, A.M. (1997). Speed/accuracy trade-offs in target-directed movements. *Behavioral and Brain Sciences, 20*, 279-349.

Pohl, P.S., Winstein, C.J., & Fisher, B.E. (1996). The locus of age-related movement slowing: Sensory processing in continuous goal-directed aiming. *Journal of Gerontology: Psychological Sciences, 51B*, P94-P102.

Polanyi, M. (1958). *Personal knowledge: Towards a post-critical philosophy.* London: Routledge and Kegan Paul.

Polit, A., & Bizzi, E. (1978). Processes controlling arm movements in monkeys. *Science, 201*, 1235-1237.

Polit, A., & Bizzi, E. (1979). Characteristics of motor programs underlying arm movements in monkeys. *Journal of Neurophysiology, 42*, 183-194.

Pollard, R. (1986). Home advantage in soccer: A retrospective analysis. *Journal of Sport Sciences, 4*, 237-248.

Pollock, B.J., & Lee, T.D. (1992). Effects of the model's skill level on observational motor learning. *Research Quarterly for Exercise and Sport, 63*, 25-29.

Pollock, B.J., & Lee, T.D. (1997). Dissociated contextual interference effects in children and adults. *Perceptual and Motor Skills, 84*, 851-858.

Pons, T.P., Garraghty, P.E., Ommaya, A.K., Kaas, J.H., Taub, E., & Mishkin, M. (1991). Massive cortical reorganization after sensory deafferentation in adult macaques. *Science, 252*, 1857-1860.

Populin, L., Rose, D.J., & Heath, K. (1990). The role of attention in one-handed catching. *Journal of Motor Behavior, 22*, 149-158.

Posner, M.I. (1969). Reduced attention and the performance of "automated" movements. *Journal of Motor Behavior, 1*, 245-258.

Posner, M.I. (1978). *Chronometric explorations of mind.* Hillsdale, NJ: Erlbaum.

Posner, M.I., & Keele, S.W. (1969). Attentional demands of movement. *Proceedings of the 16th Congress of Applied Psychology.* Amsterdam: Swets and Zeitlinger.

Posner, M.I., & Konick, A.F. (1966). On the role of interference in short-term retention. *Journal of Experimental Psychology, 72*, 221-231.

Posner, M.I., Nissen, M.J., & Ogden, W.C. (1978). Attended and unattended processing modes: The role of set for spatial location. In H.L. Pick & I.J. Saltzman (Eds.), *Modes of perceiving and processing information* (pp. 137-157). Hillsdale, NJ: Erlbaum.

Posner, M.I., & Petersen, S.E. (1990). The attention system of the human brain. *Annual Review of Neuroscience, 13*, 25-42.

Posner, M.I., & Snyder, C.R. (1975). Attention and cognitive control. In R.L. Solso (Ed.), *Information processing and cognition.* Hillsdale, NJ: Erlbaum.

Poulton, E.C. (1950). Perceptual anticipation and reaction time. *The Quarterly Journal of Experimental Psychology, 2*, 99-112.

Poulton, E.C. (1957). On prediction in skilled movements. *Psychological Bulletin, 54*, 467-478.

Poulton, E.C. (1973). The effect of fatigue upon inspection work. *Applied Ergonomics, 4*, 73-83.

Poulton, E.C. (1974). *Tracking skill and manual control.* New York: Academic Press.

Pratt, J., & Abrams, R.A. (1994). Action-centered inhibition: Effects of distractors on movement planning and execution. *Human Movement Science, 13*, 245-254.

Pratt, J., & Abrams, R.A. (1996). Practice and component submovements: The roles of programming and feedback in rapid aimed limb movements. *Journal of Motor Behavior, 28*, 149-156.

Pratt, J., Chasteen, A.L., & Abrams, R.A. (1994). Rapid aimed limb movements: Age differences and practice effects in component submovements. *Psychology and Aging, 9,* 325-334.

Proctor, R.W., & Dutta, A. (1995). *Skill acquisition and human performance.* Thousand Oaks, CA: Sage.

Proctor, R.W., & Reeve, T.G. (Eds.) (1990). *Stimulus-response compatibility: An integrated perspective.* Amsterdam: Elsevier.

Proctor, R.W., & Van Zandt, T. (1994). *Human factors in simple and complex systems.* Boston: Allyn and Bacon.

Proteau, L. (1992). On the specificity of learning and the role of visual information for movement control. In L. Proteau & D. Elliott (Eds.), *Vision and motor control* (pp. 67-103). Amsterdam: Elsevier.

Proteau, L. (1995). Sensory integration in the learning of an aiming task. *Canadian Journal of Experimental Psychology, 49,* 113-120.

Proteau, L., Blandin, Y., Alain, C., & Dorion, A. (1994). The effects of the amount and variability of practice on the learning of a multi-segmented motor task. *Acta Psychologica, 85,* 61-74.

Proteau, L., Marteniuk, R.G., & Lévesque, L. (1992). A sensorimotor basis for motor learning: Evidence indicating specificity of practice. *The Quarterly Journal of Experimental Psychology, 44A,* 557-575.

Provins, K.A. (1958). The effect of peripheral nerve block on the appreciation and execution of finger movements. *Journal of Physiology, 143,* 55-67.

Quesada, D.C., & Schmidt, R.A. (1970). A test of the Adams-Creamer decay hypothesis for the timing of motor responses. *Journal of Motor Behavior, 2,* 273-283.

Quinn, J.T. Jr., Schmidt, R.A., Zelaznik, H.N., Hawkins, B., & McFarquhar, R. (1980). Target-size influences on reaction time with movement time controlled. *Journal of Motor Behavior, 12,* 239-261.

Quinn, J.T. Jr., & Sherwood, D.E. (1983). Time requirements of changes in program and parameter variables in rapid ongoing movements. *Journal of Motor Behavior, 15,* 163-178.

Rack, P.M.H., & Westbury, D.R. (1969). The effects of length and stimulus rate on tension in the isometric cat soleus muscle. *Journal of Physiology, 204,* 443-460.

Raibert, M.H. (1977). *Motor control and learning by the state-space model* (Tech. Rep. No. AI-TR-439). Cambridge: Massachusetts Institute of Technology, Artificial Intelligence Laboratory.

Reason, J. (1990). *Human error.* Cambridge, MA: Cambridge University.

Reason, J., & Mycielska, K. (1982). *Absent-minded? The psychology of mental lapses and everyday errors.* Englewood Cliffs, NJ: Prentice-Hall.

Redelmeier, D.A., & Tibshirani, R.J. (1997). Association between cellular-telephone calls and motor vehicle collisions. *The New England Journal of Medicine, 336,* 453-458.

Reed, E.S. (1988). Applying the theory of action systems to the study of motor skills. In O.G. Meijer & K. Roth (Eds.), *Complex movement behaviour: 'The' motor-action controversy* (pp. 45-86). Amsterdam: Elsevier.

Reeve, T.G., Dornier, L.A., & Weeks, D.J. (1990). Precision of knowledge of results: Consideration of the accuracy requirements imposed by the task. *Research Quarterly for Exercise and Sport, 61,* 284-290.

Remy, P., Zilbovicius, M., Leroy-Willig, A., Syrota, A., & Samson, Y. (1994). Movement- and task-related activations of motor cortical areas: A positron emission tomographic study. *Annals of Neurology, 36,* 19-26.

Reynolds, B., & Bilodeau, I.M. (1952). Acquisition and retention of three psychomotor tests as a function of distribution of practice during acquisition. *Journal of Experimental Psychology, 44,* 19-26.

Richardson-Klavehn, A., & Bjork, R.A. (1988). Measures of memory. *Annual Review of Psychology, 39,* 475-543.

Richter-Heinrich, E., & Miller, N. (Eds.). (1982). *Biofeedback—Basic problems and clinical applications.* Amsterdam: Elsevier.

Roberts, L.E. (1986). Is there a future for biofeedback? Paper presented at the Canadian Psychological Association Annual Meeting, Toronto.

Robinson, G.H., & Kavinsky, R.C. (1976). On Fitts' law with two-handed movement. *IEEE Transactions on Systems, Man, and Cybernetics, 6,* 504-505.

Roediger, H.L., & Craik, F.I.M. (Eds.) (1989). *Varieties of memory and consciousness: Essays in honour of Endel Tulving.* Hillsdale, NJ: Erlbaum.

Roediger, H.L., & McDermott, K.B. (1993). Implicit memory in normal human subjects. In H. Spinnler & F. Boller (Eds.), *Handbook of neuropsychology* (Vol. 8) (pp. 63-131). Amsterdam: Elsevier.

Rogers, C.A. Jr. (1974). Feedback precision and postfeedback interval duration. *Journal of Experimental Psychology, 102,* 604-608.

Rogers, D.K., Bendrups, A.P., & Lewis, M.M. (1985). Disturbed proprioception following a period of muscle vibration in humans. *Neuroscience Letters, 57,* 147-152.

Rose, D.J., & Christina, R.W. (1990). Attention demands of precision pistol-shooting as a function of skill level. *Research Quarterly for Exercise and Sport, 61,* 111-113.

Rosenbaum, D.A. (1980). Human movement initiation: Specification of arm, direction, and extent. *Journal of Experimental Psychology: General, 109,* 444-474.

Rosenbaum, D.A. (1983). The movement precuing technique: Assumptions, applications, and extensions. In R.A. Magill (Ed.), *Memory and control of action,* (pp. 231-274). Amsterdam: Elsevier.

Rosenbaum, D.A. (1991). *Human motor control.* San Diego: Academic Press.

Rosenbaum, D.A., Loukopoulos, L.D., Meulenbroek, R.G.J., Vaughan, J., & Engelbrecht, S.E. (1995). Planning reaches by evaluating stored postures. *Psychological Review, 102,* 28-67.

Rosenbaum, D.A., Marchak, F., Barnes, H.J., Vaughan, J., Slotta, J.D., & Jorgensen, M.J. (1990). Constraints for action selection: Overhand versus underhand grips. In M. Jeannerod (Ed.), *Attention and performance XIII* (pp. 321-342). Hillsdale, NJ: Erlbaum.

Rosenbaum, D.A., Meulenbroek, R.G.J., Jansen, C., Vaughan, J., & Lelivelt, A.B. (1997). Posture-based motion planning. Manuscript under review.

Rosenbaum, D.A., & Patashnik, O. (1980). Time to time in the human motor system. In R.S. Nickerson (Ed.), *Attention and performance VIII* (pp. 93-106). Hillsdale, NJ: Erlbaum.

Rosenbaum, D.A., Vaughan, J., Barnes, H.J., & Jorgensen, M.J. (1992). Time course of movement planning: Selection of handgrips for object manipulation. *Journal of Experimental Psychology: Learning, Memory, and Cognition, 18,* 1058-1073.

Rosenbaum, D.A., Weber, R.J., Hazelett, W.M., & Hindorff, V. (1986). The parameter remapping effect in human performance: Evidence from tongue twisters and finger fumblers. *Journal of Memory and Language, 25,* 710-725.

Ross, D. (1974). Interference in discrete motor tasks: A test of the theory. Unpublished doctoral dissertation, University of Michigan, Ann Arbor.

Ross, D., Bird, A.M., Doody, S.G., & Zoeller, M. (1985). Effects of modeling and videotape feedback with knowledge of results on motor performance. *Human Movement Science, 4,* 149-157.

Roth, K. (1988). Investigations on the basis of the generalized motor programme hypothesis. In O.G. Meijer & K. Roth (Eds.), *Complex motor behavior: 'The' motor-action controversy* (pp. 261-288). Amsterdam: Elsevier.

Rothstein, A.L. (1973). Effect of temporal expectancy of the position of a selected foreperiod within a range. *Research Quarterly, 44,* 132-139.

Rothstein, A.L., & Arnold, R.K. (1976). Bridging the gap: Application of research on videotape feedback and bowling. *Motor Skills: Theory Into Practice, 1,* 35-62.

Rothwell, J. (1994). *Control of human voluntary movement* (2nd ed). London: Chapman & Hall.

Rothwell, J.C., Traub, M.M., Day, B.L., Obeso, J.A., Thomas, P.K., & Marsden, C.D. (1982). Manual motor performance in a deafferented man. *Brain, 105,* 515-542.

Rubin, W.M. (1978). Application of signal detection theory to error detection in ballistic motor skills. *Journal of Experimental Psychology: Human Perception and Performance, 4,* 311-320.

Ryan, E.D. (1962). Retention of stabilometer and pursuit rotor skills. *Research Quarterly, 33,* 593-598.

Ryan, E.D. (1963). Relative academic achievement and stabilometer performance. *Research Quarterly, 34,* 185-190.

Ryan, E.D. (1965). Retention of stabilometer performance over extended periods of time. *Research Quarterly, 36,* 46-51.

Sale, D., & MacDougall, D. (1981). Specificity in strength training: A review for the coach and athlete. *Canadian Journal of Applied Sports Sciences, 6,* 87-92.

Salmela, J.H., & Fiorito, P. (1979). Visual cues in ice hockey goaltending. *Canadian Journal of Applied Sport Science, 4,* 56-59.

Salmoni, A.W., Ross, D., Dill, S., & Zoeller, M. (1983). Knowledge of results and perceptual-motor learning. *Human Movement Science, 2,* 77-89.

Salmoni, A.W., Schmidt, R.A., & Walter, C.B. (1984). Knowledge of results and motor learning: A review and critical reappraisal. *Psychological Bulletin, 95,* 355-386.

Salmoni, A.W., Sullivan, S.J., & Starkes, J.L. (1976). The attention demands of movements: A critique of the probe technique. *Journal of Motor Behavior, 8*, 161-169.

Salthouse, T.A. (1985). *A theory of cognitive aging*. Amsterdam: Elsevier.

Salthouse, T.A. (1986). Effects of practice on a typing-like keying task. *Acta Psychologica, 62*, 189-198.

Sanders, A.F. (1980). Stage analysis of reaction processes. In G.E. Stelmach & J. Requin (Eds.), *Tutorials in motor behavior* (pp. 331-354). Amsterdam: Elsevier.

Sanders, M.S., & McCormick, E.J. (1993). *Human factors in engineering and design* (7th ed). New York: McGraw-Hill.

Sanes, J.N. (1990). Motor representations in deafferented humans: A mechanism for disordered movement performance. In M. Jeannerod (Ed.), *Attention and performance XIII* (pp. 714-735). Hillsdale, NJ: Erlbaum.

Sanes, J.N., Mauritz, K.-H., Dalakas, M.C., & Evarts, E.V. (1985). Motor control in humans with large-fiber sensory neuropathy. *Human Neurobiology, 4*, 101-114.

Savelsbergh, G.J.P., & Whiting, H.T.A. (1996). Catching: A motor learning and developmental perspective. In H. Heuer & S.W. Keele (Eds.), *Handbook of perception and action. Volume 2: Motor skills* (pp. 461-501). San Diego: Academic Press.

Savelsbergh, G.J.P., Whiting, H.T.A., & Bootsma, R.J. (1991). Grasping tau. *Journal of Experimental Psychology: Human Perception and Performance, 17*, 315-322.

Savelsbergh, G.J.P., Whiting, H.T.A., & Pijpers, J.R. (1992). The control of catching. In J.J. Summers (Ed.), *Approaches to the study of motor control and learning* (pp. 313-342). Amsterdam: Elsevier.

Savelsbergh, G.J.P., Whiting, H.T.A., Pijpers, J.R., & van Santvoord, A.A.M. (1993). The visual guidance of catching. *Experimental Brain Research, 93*, 148-156.

Schellekens, J.M.H., Kalverboer, A.F., & Scholten, C.A. (1984). The micro-structure of tapping movements in children. *Journal of Motor Behavior, 16*, 20-39.

Schendel, J.D., & Hagman, J.D. (1982). On sustaining procedural skills over a prolonged retention interval. *Journal of Applied Psychology, 67*, 605-610.

Schendel, J.D., Heller, F.H., Finley, D.L., & Hawley, J.K. (1985). Use of the Weaponeer Marksmanship Trainer in predicting M16A1 rifle qualification performance. *Human Factors, 27*, 313-325.

Schendel, J.D., & Newell, K.M. (1976). On processing the information from knowledge of results. *Journal of Motor Behavior, 8*, 251-255.

Schlager, N. (Ed.) (1994). *When technology fails: Significant technological disasters, accidents and failures of the twentieth century*. Detroit: Gale Research.

Schmidt, R.A. (1967). Motor factors in coincident timing. Unpublished doctoral dissertation, University of Illinois, Urbana.

Schmidt, R.A. (1968). Anticipation and timing in human motor performance. *Psychological Bulletin, 70*, 631-646.

Schmidt, R.A. (1969a). Intra-limb specificity of motor response consistency. *Journal of Motor Behavior, 1*, 89-99.

Schmidt, R.A. (1969b). Movement time as a determiner of timing accuracy. *Journal of Experimental Psychology, 79*, 43-47.

Schmidt, R.A. (1971a). Proprioception and the timing of motor responses. *Psychological Bulletin, 76*, 383-393.

Schmidt, R.A. (1971b). Retroactive interference and amount of original learning in verbal and motor tasks. *Research Quarterly, 42*, 314-326.

Schmidt, R.A. (1972a). The case against learning and forgetting scores. *Journal of Motor Behavior, 4*, 79-88.

Schmidt, R.A. (1972b). The index of preprogramming (IP): A statistical method for evaluating the role of feedback in simple movements. *Psychonomic Science, 27*, 83-85.

Schmidt, R.A. (1972c). The index of preprogramming (IP): A statistical method for evaluating the role of feedback in simple movements. *Psychonomic Science, 27*, 83-85.

Schmidt, R.A. (1975a). *Motor skills*. New York: Harper and Row.

Schmidt, R.A. (1975b). A schema theory of discrete motor skill learning. *Psychological Review, 82*, 225-260.

Schmidt, R.A. (1976a). Control processes in motor skills. *Exercise and Sport Sciences Reviews, 4*, 229-261.

Schmidt, R.A. (1976b). Movement education and the schema theory. In E. Crawford (Ed.), *Report of the 1976 Conference June 3-8*. Cedar Falls, IA: National Association for Physical Education of College Women.

Schmidt, R.A. (1977). Schema theory: Implications for movement education. *Motor Skills: Theory Into Practice, 2*, 36-38.

Schmidt, R.A. (1980). Past and future issues in motor programming. *Research Quarterly for Exercise and Sport, 51*, 122-140.

Schmidt, R.A. (1983). On the underlying structure of well-learned motor responses: A discussion of Namikas and Schneider and Fisk. In R.A. Magill (Ed.), *Memory and control of action* (pp. 145-165). Amsterdam: Elsevier.

Schmidt, R.A. (1985). The search for invariance in skilled movement behavior. *Research Quarterly for Exercise and Sport, 56*, 188-200.

Schmidt, R.A. (1987). The acquisition of skill: Some modifications to the perception-action relationship through practice. In H. Heuer & A.F. Sanders (Eds.), *Perspectives on perception and action* (pp. 77-103). Hillsdale, NJ: Erlbaum.

Schmidt, R.A. (1988). Motor and action perspectives on motor behaviour. In O.G Meijer & K. Roth (Eds.), *Complex movement behaviour: 'The' motor-action controversy* (pp. 3-44). Amsterdam: Elsevier.

Schmidt, R.A. (1989). Toward a better understanding of the acquisition of skill: Theoretical and practical contributions of the task approach. In J.S. Skinner, C.B. Corbin, D.M. Landers, P.E. Martin, & C.L. Wells (Eds.), *Future directions in exercise and sport science research* (pp. 395-410). Champaign, IL: Human Kinetics.

Schmidt, R.A. (1989). Unintended acceleration: A review of human factors contributions. *Human Factors, 31*, 345-364.

Schmidt, R.A. (1991). Frequent augmented feedback can degrade learning: Evidence and interpretations. In J. Requin & G.E. Stelmach (Eds.), *Tutorials in motor neuroscience* (pp. 59-75). Dordrecht: Kluwer.

Schmidt, R.A. (1993). Unintended acceleration: Human performance considerations. In B. Peacock & W. Karwowski (Eds.), *Automotive ergonomics* (pp. 431-451). London: Taylor & Francis.

Schmidt, R.A. (1994). Movement time, movement distance, and movement accuracy: A reply to Newell, Carlton, and Kim. *Human Performance, 7*, 23-28.

Schmidt, R.A., & Bjork, R.A. (1992). New conceptualizations of practice: Common principles in three paradigms suggest new concepts for training. *Psychological Science, 3*, 207-217.

Schmidt, R.A., Christenson, R., & Rogers, P. (1975). Some evidence for the independence of recall and recognition in motor behavior. In D.M. Landers, D.V. Harris, & R.W. Christina (Eds.), *Psychology of motor behavior and sport II*. State College, PA: Penn State HPER Series.

Schmidt, R.A., & Gordon, G.B. (1977). Errors in motor responding, "rapid" corrections, and false anticipations. *Journal of Motor Behavior, 9*, 101-111.

Schmidt, R.A., Heuer, H., Ghodsian, D., & Young, D.E. (in press). Generalized motor programs and units of action in bimanual coordination. In M. Latash (Ed.), *Bernstein's traditions in motor control*. Mahwah, NJ: Erlbaum.

Schmidt, R.A., Lange, C., & Young, D.E. (1990). Optimizing summary knowledge of results for skill learning. *Human Movement Science, 9*, 325-348.

Schmidt, R.A., & McGown, C. (1980). Terminal accuracy of unexpectedly loaded rapid movements: Evidence for a mass-spring mechanism in programming. *Journal of Motor Behavior, 12*, 149-161.

Schmidt, R.A., McGown, C., Quinn, J.T., & Hawkins, B. (1986). Unexpected inertial loading in rapid reversal movements: Violations of equifinality. *Human Movement Science, 5*, 263-273.

Schmidt, R.A., & Nacson, J. (1971). Further tests of the activity-set hypothesis for warm-up decrement. *Journal of Experimental Psychology, 90*, 56-64.

Schmidt, R.A., & Pew, R.W. (1974). *Predicting motor-manipulative performances in the manufacture of dental appliances* (Technical Report to Heritage Laboratories). Romulus, MI: University of Michigan.

Schmidt, R.A., & Russell, D.G. (1972). Movement velocity and movement time as determiners of degree of preprogramming in simple movements. *Journal of Experimental Psychology, 96*, 315-320.

Schmidt, R.A., & Russell, D.G. (1974). Error detection in positioning responses. Unpublished manuscript, University of Michigan, Ann Arbor.

Schmidt, R.A., & Shapiro, D.C. (1986). *Optimizing feedback utilization in motor skill training* (Tech. Rep. Contract No. MDA903-85-K-0225). Alexandria, CA: U.S. Army Research Institute.

Schmidt, R.A., & Shea, J.B. (1976). A note on delay of knowledge of results in positioning responses. *Journal of Motor Behavior, 8,* 129-131.

Schmidt, R.A., & Sherwood, D.E. (1982). An inverted-U relation between spatial error and force requirements in rapid limb movements: Further evidence for the impulse-variability model. *Journal of Experimental Psychology: Human Perception and Performance, 8,* 158-170.

Schmidt, R.A., Sherwood, D.E., Zelaznik, H.N., & Leikind, B.J. (1985). Speed-accuracy trade-offs in motor behavior: Theories of impulse variability. In H. Heuer, U. Kleinbeck, & K.-H. Schmidt (Eds.), *Motor behavior: Programming, control, and acquisition* (pp. 79-123). Berlin: Springer-Verlag.

Schmidt, R.A., & White, J.L. (1972). Evidence for an error detection mechanism in motor skills: A test of Adams' closed-loop theory. *Journal of Motor Behavior, 4,* 143-153.

Schmidt, R.A., Wood, C.T., Young, D.E., & Kelkar, R. (1996). *Evaluation of the BIC J26 child guard lighter.* Technical Report, Failure Analysis Associates, Inc., Los Angeles, CA.

Schmidt, R.A., & Wrisberg, C.A. (1971). The activity-set hypothesis for warm-up decrement in a movement-speed task. *Journal of Motor Behavior, 3,* 318-325.

Schmidt, R.A., & Young, D.E. (1987). Transfer of movement control in motor learning. In S.M. Cormier & J.D. Hagman (Eds.), *Transfer of learning* (pp. 47-79). Orlando, FL: Academic Press.

Schmidt, R.A., & Young, D.E. (1991). Methodology for motor learning: A paradigm for kinematic feedback. *Journal of Motor Behavior, 23,* 13-24.

Schmidt, R.A., Young, D.E., Swinnen, S., & Shapiro, D.C. (1989). Summary knowledge of results for skill acquisition: Support for the guidance hypothesis. *Journal of Experimental Psychology: Learning, Memory, and Cognition, 15,* 352-359.

Schmidt, R.A., & Wulf, G. (1997). Continuous concurrent feedback degrades skill learning: Implications for training and simulation. *Human Factors, 39,* 509-525.

Schmidt, R.A., Zelaznik, H.N., & Frank, J.S. (1978). Sources of inaccuracy in rapid movement. In G.E. Stelmach (Ed.), *Information processing in motor control and learning* (pp. 183-203). New York: Academic Press.

Schmidt, R.A., Zelaznik, H.N., Hawkins, B., Frank, J.S., & Quinn, J.T. Jr. (1979). Motor-output vari-

ability: A theory for the accuracy of rapid motor acts. *Psychological Review, 86,* 415-451.

Schmidt, R.C., Carello, C., & Turvey, M.T. (1990). Phase transitions and critical fluctuations in the visual coordination of rhythmic movements between people. *Journal of Experimental Psychology: Human Perception and Performance, 16,* 227-247.

Schmidt, R.C., Christianson, N., Carello, C., & Baron, R. (1994). Effects of social and physical variables on between-person visual coordination. *Ecological Psychology, 6,* 159-183.

Schmidt, R.C., Shaw, B.K., & Turvey, M.T. (1993). Coupling dynamics in interlimb coordination. *Journal of Experimental Psychology: Human Perception and Performance, 19,* 397-415.

Schneider, D.M., & Schmidt, R.A. (1995). Units of action in motor control: Role of response complexity and target speed. *Human Performance, 8,* 27-49.

Schneider, K., Zernicke, R.F., Schmidt, R.A., & Hart, T.J. (1989). Changes in limb dynamics during the practice of rapid arm movements. *Journal of Biomechanics, 22,* 805-817.

Schneider, W. (1985). Training high-performance skills: Fallacies and guidelines. *Human Factors, 27,* 285-300.

Schneider, W., Dumais, S.T., & Shiffrin, R.M. (1984). Automatic processing and attention. In R. Parasuraman & R. Davies (Eds.), *Varieties of attention* (pp. 1-27). New York: Academic Press.

Schneider, W., & Fisk, A.D. (1983). Attention theory and mechanisms for skilled performance. In R.A. Magill (Ed.), *Memory and control of action* (pp. 119-143). Amsterdam: Elsevier.

Schneider, W., & Shiffrin, R.M. (1977). Controlled and automatic human information processing: I. Detection, search, and attention. *Psychological Review, 84,* 1-66.

Scholz, J.P., & Kelso, J.A.S. (1990). Intentional switching between patterns of bimanual coordination depends on the intrinsic dynamics of the patterns. *Journal of Motor Behavior, 22,* 98-124.

Scholz, J.P., Kelso, J.A.S., & Schöner, G. (1987). Nonequilibrium phase transitions in coordinated biological motion: Critical slowing down and switching time. *Physics Letters A, 123,* 390-394.

Schöner, G., Zanone, P.G., & Kelso, J.A.S. (1992). Learning as change of coordination dynamics: Theory and experiment. *Journal of Motor Behavior, 24,* 29-48.

Schutz, R. (1977). Absolute, constant, and variable error: Problems and solutions. In D. Mood (Ed.), *The measurement of change in physical education* (pp. 82-100). Boulder, CO: University of Colorado Press.

Schutz, R.W., & Roy, E.A. (1973). Absolute error: The devil in disguise. *Journal of Motor Behavior, 5*, 141-153.

Schweickert, R. (1993). Information, time, and the structure of mental events: A twenty-five-year review. In D.E. Meyer & S. Kornblum (Eds.), *Attention and performance XIV* (pp. 324-341). Cambridge, MA: Bradford.

Scully, D.M., & Newell, K.M. (1985). Observational learning and the acquisition of motor skills: Toward a visual perception perspective. *Journal of Human Movement Studies, 11,* 169-186.

Sears, T.A., & Newsom-Davis, J. (1968). The control of respiratory muscles during voluntary breathing. *Annals of the New York Academy of Sciences, 155,* 183-190.

Seibel, R. (1963). Discrimination reaction time for a 1023-alternative task. *Journal of Experimental Psychology, 66,* 215-226.

Sekiya, H., Magill, R.A., Sidaway, B., & Anderson, D.I. (1994). The contextual interference effect for skill variations from the same and different generalized motor programs. *Research Quarterly for Exercise and Sport, 65,* 330-338.

Serrien, D.J., & Swinnen, S.P. (1997a). Coordination constraints induced by effector combination under isofrequency and multifrequency conditions. *Journal of Experimental Psychology: Human Perception and Performance, 23,* 1493-1510.

Serrien, D.J., & Swinnen, S.P. (1997b). Isofrequency and multifrequency coordination patterns as a function of the planes of motion. *The Quarterly Journal of Experimental Psychology, 50A,* 386-404.

Seymour, W.D. (1954). Experiments on the acquisition of industrial skills. *Occupational Psychology, 28,* 77-89.

Shaffer, L.H. (1971). Attention in transcription skill. *The Quarterly Journal of Experimental Psychology, 23,* 107-112.

Shaffer, L.H. (1980). Analyzing piano performance: A study of concert pianists. In G.E. Stelmach & J. Requin (Eds.), *Tutorials in motor behavior* (pp. 443-455). Amsterdam: Elsevier.

Shaffer, L.H. (1984). Timing in solo and duet piano performances. *The Quarterly Journal of Experimental Psychology, 36A,* 577-595.

Shannon, C.E., & Weaver, W. (1949). *The mathematical theory of communication.* Urbana, IL: University of Illinois Press.

Shapiro, D.C. (1977). A preliminary attempt to determine the duration of a motor program. In D.M. Landers & R.W. Christina (Eds.), *Psychology of motor behavior and sport—1976* (pp. 17-24). Champaign, IL: Human Kinetics.

Shapiro, D.C. (1978). The learning of generalized motor programs. Unpublished doctoral dissertation, University of Southern California, Los Angeles.

Shapiro, D.C., & Schmidt, R.A. (1982). The schema theory: Recent evidence and developmental implications. In J.A.S. Kelso & J.E. Clark (Eds.), *The development of movement control and co-ordination* (pp. 113-150). New York: Wiley.

Shapiro, D.C., & Walter, C.B. (1982). Control of rapid bimanual aiming movements: The effect of a mechanical block. *Society for Neuroscience Abstracts, 8(2),* 733.

Shapiro, D.C., Zernicke, R.F., Gregor, R.J., & Diestel, J.D. (1981). Evidence for generalized motor programs using gait pattern analysis. *Journal of Motor Behavior, 13,* 33-47.

Shea, C.H., Guadagnoli, M.A., & Dean, M. (1995). Response biases: Tonic neck response and aftercontraction phenomenon. *Journal of Motor Behavior, 27,* 41-51.

Shea, C.H., & Kohl, R.M. (1990). Specificity and variability of practice. *Research Quarterly for Exercise and Sport, 61,* 169-177.

Shea, C.H., Kohl, R., & Indermill, C. (1990). Contextual interference: Contributions of practice. *Acta Psychologica, 73,* 145-157.

Shea, C.H., & Kohl, R.M. (1991). Composition of practice: Influence on the retention of motor skills. *Research Quarterly for Exercise and Sport, 62,* 187-195.

Shea, C.H., Shebilske, W.L., Kohl, R.M., & Guadagnoli, M.A. (1991). After-contraction phenomenon: Influences on performance and learning. *Journal of Motor Behavior, 23,* 51-62.

Shea, J.B., & Graf, R.C. (1994). A model for contextual interference effects in motor learning. In C.R. Reynolds (Ed.), *Cognitive assessment: A multidisciplinary perspective* (pp. 73-87). New York: Plenum.

Shea, J.B., & Morgan, R.L. (1979). Contextual interference effects on the acquisition, retention, and transfer of a motor skill. *Journal of Experimental Psychology: Human Learning and Memory, 5,* 179-187.

Shea, J.B., & Paull, G. (1996). Capturing expertise in sports. In K.A. Ericsson (Ed.), *The road to excellence: The acquisition of expert performance in the arts and sciences, sports, and games* (pp. 321-335). Mahwah, NJ: Erlbaum.

Shea, J.B., & Titzer, R.C. (1993). The influence of reminder trials on contextual interference effects. *Journal of Motor Behavior, 25,* 264-274.

Shea, J.B., & Upton, G. (1976). The effects on skill acquisition of an interpolated motor short-term memory task during the KR-delay interval. *Journal of Motor Behavior, 8,* 277-281.

Shea, J.B., & Wright, D.L. (1991). When forgetting benefits motor retention. *Research Quarterly for Exercise and Sport, 62,* 293-301.

Shea, J.B., & Zimny, S.T. (1983). Context effects in memory and learning movement information. In R.A. Magill (Ed.), *Memory and control of action* (pp. 345-366). Amsterdam: Elsevier.

Shea, J.B., & Zimny, S.T. (1988). Knowledge incorporation in motor representation. In O.G. Meijer & K. Roth (Eds.), *Complex movement behaviour: 'The' motor-action controversy* (pp. 289-314). Amsterdam: Elsevier.

Sheppard, D.J. (1984). *Visual and part-task manipulations for teaching simulated carrier landings* (Rep. No. 81-C-0105-9). Orlando, FL: Naval Training Equipment Center.

Sherrington, C.S. (1906). *The integrative action of the nervous system.* New Haven: Yale University Press.

Sherwood, D.E. (1988). Effect of bandwidth knowledge of results on movement consistency. *Perceptual and Motor Skills, 66,* 535-542.

Sherwood, D.E. (1990). Practice and assimilation effects in a multilimb aiming task. *Journal of Motor Behavior, 22,* 267-291.

Sherwood, D.E. (1991). Distance and location assimilation effects in rapid bimanual movement. *Research Quarterly for Exercise and Sport, 62,* 302-308.

Sherwood, D.E. (1994). Interlimb amplitude differences, spatial assimilations, and the temporal structure of rapid bimanual movements. *Human Movement Science, 13,* 841-860.

Sherwood, D.E. (1996). The benefits of random variable practice for spatial accuracy and error detection in a rapid aiming task. *Research Quarterly for Exercise and Sport, 67,* 35-43.

Sherwood, D.E., & Canabal, M.Y. (1988). The effect of practice on the control of sequential and simultaneous actions. *Human Performance, 1,* 237-260.

Sherwood, D.E., & Schmidt, R.A. (1980). The relationship between force and force variability in minimal and near-maximal static and dynamic contractions. *Journal of Motor Behavior, 12,* 75-89.

Sherwood, D.E., Schmidt, R.A., & Walter, C.B. (1988). The force/force-variability relationship under controlled temporal conditions. *Journal of Motor Behavior, 20,* 106-116.

Shiffrin, R.M., & Schneider, W. (1977). Controlled and automatic human information processing: II. Perceptual learning, automatic attending, and a general theory. *Psychological Review, 84,* 127-190.

Shik, M.L., & Orlovskii, G.N. (1976). Neurophysiology of a locomotor automatism. *Physiological Reviews, 56,* 465-501.

Shik, M.L., Orlovskii, G.N., & Severin, F.V. (1968). Locomotion of the mesencephalic cat elicited by stimulation of the pyramids. *Biofizika, 13,* 143-152.

Shirley, M.M. (1931). *The first two years (Vol. 1).* Minneapolis, MN: University of Minnesota Press.

Shumway-Cook, A., & Woollacott, M.H. (1995). *Motor control: Theory and practical applications.* Baltimore: Williams & Wilkins.

Sidaway, B., Moore, B., & Schoenfelder-Zohdi, B. (1991). Summary and frequency of KR presentation effects on retention of a motor skill. *Research Quarterly for Exercise and Sport, 62,* 27-32.

Sidaway, B., Sekiya, H., & Fairweather, M. (1995). Movement variability as a function of accuracy demand in programmed serial aiming responses. *Journal of Motor Behavior, 27,* 67-76.

Sidman, M. (1952). A note on functional relations obtained from group data. *Psychological Bulletin, 49,* 263-269.

Simon, J.R. (1969a). Reactions toward the source of stimulation. *Journal of Experimental Psychology, 81,* 174-176.

Simon, J.R. (1969b). Stereotypic reaction information processing. In L.E. Smith (Ed.), *Psychology of motor learning* (pp. 27-50). Chicago: Athletic Institute.

Simon, J.R. (1990). The effects of an irrelevant directional cue on human information processing. In R.W. Proctor & T.G. Reeve (Eds.), *Stimulus-response compatibility: An integrated perspective* (pp. 31-86). Amsterdam: Elsevier.

Simon, J.R., & Rudell, A.P. (1967). Auditory S-R compatibility: The effect of an irrelevant cue on information processing. *Journal of Applied Psychology, 51*, 300-304.

Singer, R.N. (1975). *Motor learning and human performance* (2nd ed.). New York: Macmillan.

Singer, R.N. (1980). *Motor learning and human performance* (3rd. ed.). New York: Macmillan.

Singer, R.N., & Gaines, L. (1975). Effects of prompted and trial-and-error learning on transfer performance of a serial motor task. *American Educational Research Journal, 12*, 395-403.

Singer, R.N., & Pease, D. (1976). A comparison of discovery learning and guided instructional strategies on motor skill learning, retention, and transfer. *Research Quarterly, 47*, 788-796.

Sittig, A.C. (1986). Kinesthesis and motor control. Unpublished doctoral dissertation, University of Utrecht, Holland.

Sittig, A.C., Denier van der Gon, J.J., & Gielen, C.C.A.M. (1985a). Separate control of arm position and velocity demonstrated by vibration of muscle tendon in man. *Experimental Brain Research, 60*, 445-453.

Sittig, A.C., Denier van der Gon, J.J., & Gielen, C.C.A.M. (1985b). Different control mechanisms for slow and fast human arm movements. *Neuroscience Letters, 22*, S128.

Skoglund, S. (1956). Anatomical and physiological studies of the knee joint innervation in the cat. *Acta Physiologica Scandinavica, 36* (Suppl. 124).

Slamecka, N.J., & Graf, P. (1978). The generation effect: Delineation of a phenomenon. *Journal of Experimental Psychology: Human Learning and Memory, 4*, 592-604.

Slater-Hammel, A.T. (1960). Reliability, accuracy and refractoriness of a transit reaction. *Research Quarterly, 31*, 217-228.

Small, A.M. (1990). Foreword. In R.W. Proctor & T.G. Reeve (Eds.), *Stimulus-response compatibility: An integrated perspective* (pp. v-vi). Amsterdam: Elsevier.

Smeets, J.B.J., Brenner, E., Trébuchet, S., & Mestre, D.R. (1996). Is judging time-to-contact based on 'tau'? *Perception, 25*, 583-590.

Smith, J.L. (1969). Fusimotor neuron block and voluntary arm movement in man. Unpublished doctoral dissertation, University of Wisconsin, Madison.

Smith, J.L. (1977). *Mechanisms of neuromuscular control.* Los Angeles: UCLA Printing and Production.

Smith, J.L. (1978). Sensorimotor integration during motor programming. In G.E. Stelmach (Ed.),

Information processing in motor control and learning (pp. 173-182). New York: Academic Press.

Smith, J.L., Bradley, N.S., Carter, M.C., Giuliani, C.A., Hoy, M.G., Koshland, G.F., & Zernicke, R.F. (1986). Rhythmical movements of the hindlimbs in spinal cat: Considerations for a controlling network. In M.E. Goldberger, A. Gorio, & M. Murray (Eds.), *Development and plasticity of the mammalian spinal cord* (pp. 362-374). Padova: Liviana Press.

Smith, J.L., Roberts, E.M., & Atkins, E. (1972). Fusimotor neuron block and voluntary arm movement in man. *American Journal of Physical Medicine, 5*, 225-239.

Smith, M.C. (1969). The effect of varying information on the psychological refractory period. In W.G. Koster (Ed.), *Attention and performance II.* Amsterdam: North-Holland.

Smith, P.J.K., & Davies, M. (1995). Applying contextual interference to the Pawlata roll. *Journal of Sports Sciences, 13*, 455-462.

Smith, R.E., Smoll, F.L., & Schutz, R.W. (1990). Measurement and correlates of sport-specific cognitive and somatic trait anxiety: The sport anxiety scale. *Anxiety Research, 2*, 263-280.

Smith, W.M., & Bowen, K.F. (1980). The effects of delayed and displaced visual feedback on motor control. *Journal of Motor Behavior, 12*, 91-101.

Snoddy, G.S. (1926). Learning and stability: A psychophysical analysis of a case of motor learning with clinical applications. *Journal of Applied Psychology, 10*, 1-36.

Snoddy, G.S. (1935). *Evidence for two opposed processes in mental growth.* Lancaster, PA: Science Press.

Solley, W.H. (1952). The effects of verbal instruction of speed and accuracy upon the learning of a motor skill. *Research Quarterly, 23*, 231-240.

Sonstroem, R.J., & Bernardo, P. (1982). Intraindividual pregame state anxiety and basketball performance: A reexamination of the inverted-U curve. *Journal of Sport Psychology, 4*, 235-245.

Sparrow, W.A., & Summers, J.J. (1992). Performance on trials without knowledge of results (KR) in reduced relative frequency presentations of KR. *Journal of Motor Behavior, 24*, 197-209.

Sperling, G. (1960). The information available in brief visual presentations. *Psychological Monographs, 74* (11, Whole No. 498).

Sperry, R.W. (1950). Neural basis of the spontaneous optokinetic response produced by visual inversion. *Journal of Comparative and Physiological Psychology, 43*, 482-489.

Spijkers, W., & Heuer, H. (1995). Structural constraints on the performance of symmetrical bimanual movements with different amplitudes. *The Quarterly Journal of Experimental Psychology, 48A*, 716-740.

Spijkers, W.A.C., & Lochner, P. (1994). Partial visual feedback and spatial end-point accuracy of visual aiming movements. *Journal of Motor Behavior, 26*, 283-295.

Spirduso, W.W. (1995). *Physical dimensions of aging.* Champaign, IL: Human Kinetics.

Starkes, J.L. (1987). Attention demands of spatially locating position of a ball in flight. *Perceptual and Motor Skills, 64*, 127-135.

Starkes, J.L., & Allard, F. (Eds.) (1993). *Cognitive issues in motor expertise.* Amsterdam: Elsevier.

Starkes, J.L., & Deakin, J.M. (1984). Perception in sport: A cognitive approach to skilled performance. In W.F. Straub & J.M. Williams (Eds.), *Cognitive sport psychology* (pp. 115-128). Lansing, NY: Sport Science Associates.

Starkes, J.L., Deakin, J.M., Allard, F., Hodges, N.J., & Hayes, A. (1996). Deliberate practice in sports: What is it anyway? In K.A. Ericsson (Ed.), *The road to excellence: The acquisition of expert performance in the arts and sciences, sports, and games* (pp. 81-106). Mahwah, NJ: Erlbaum.

Start, K.B. (1964). Intelligence and improvements in a gross motor skill after mental practice. *British Journal of Educational Psychology, 34*, 85-90.

Stelmach, G.E. (1969). Prior positioning responses as a factor in short-term retention of a simple motor task. *Journal of Experimental Psychology, 81*, 523-526.

Stelmach, G.E. (1974). Retention of motor skills. *Exercise and Sport Sciences Reviews, 2*, 1-31.

Stelmach, G.E., Kelso, J.A.S., & Wallace, S.A. (1975). Preselection in short-term motor memory. *Journal of Experimental Psychology: Human Learning and Memory, 1*, 745-755.

Stelmach, G.E., & Requin, J. (Eds.) (1980). *Tutorials in motor behavior.* Amsterdam: North-Holland.

Stelmach, G.E., & Requin, J. (Eds.) (1992). *Tutorials in motor behavior II.* Amsterdam: Elsevier.

Sternberg, R.J., & Wagner, R.K. (1989). Individual differences in practical knowledge and its acquisition. In P.L. Ackerman, R.J. Sternberg, & R. Glaser (Eds.), *Learning and individual differences: Advances in theory and research* (pp. 255-278). New York: Freeman.

Sternberg, S. (1969). The discovery of processing stages: Extensions of Donders' method. In W.G. Koster (Ed.), *Attention and performance II.* Amsterdam: North-Holland.

Sternberg, S., Monsell, S., Knoll, R.L., & Wright, C.E. (1978). The latency and duration of rapid movement sequences: Comparisons of speech and typewriting. In G.E. Stelmach (Ed.), *Information processing in motor control and learning* (pp. 117-152). New York: Academic Press.

Stewart, D., Cudworth, C.J., & Lishman, J.R. (1993). Misperception of time-to-collision by drivers in pedestrian accidents. *Perception, 22*, 1227-1244.

Stimpel, E. (1933). Der Wurk [The throw]. *Neue Psychologische Studien, 9*, 105-138.

Stroop, J.R. (1935). Studies of interference in serial verbal reactions. *Journal of Experimental Psychology, 18*, 643-662.

Stuart, D.G., Mosher, C.G., Gerlack, R.L., & Reinking, R.M. (1972). Mechanical arrangement and transducing properties of Golgi tendon organs. *Experimental Brain Research, 14*, 274-292.

Summers, J.J. (1975). The role of timing in motor program representation. *Journal of Motor Behavior, 7*, 229-241.

Summers, J.J. (Ed.) (1992). *Approaches to the study of motor control and learning.* Amsterdam: Elsevier.

Summers, J.J., & Pressing, J. (1994). Coordinating the two hands in polyrhythmic tapping. In S.P. Swinnen, H. Heuer, J. Massion, & P. Casaer (Eds.), *Interlimb coordination: Neural, dynamical, and cognitive constraints* (pp. 571-593). San Diego: Academic Press.

Summers, J.J., Rosenbaum, D.A., Burns, B.D., & Ford, S.K. (1993). Production of polyrhythms. *Journal of Experimental Psychology: Human Perception and Performance, 19*, 416-428.

Summers, J.J., Todd, J.A., & Kim, Y.H. (1993). The influence of perceptual and motor factors on bimanual coordination in a polyrhythmic tapping task. *Psychological Research, 55*, 107-115.

Swanson, L.R., & Lee, T.D. (1992). Effects of aging and schedules of knowledge of results on motor learning. *Journal of Gerontology: Psychological Sciences, 47*, P406-P411.

Swets, J.A. (1964). *Signal detection and recognition by human observers.* New York: Wiley.

Swift, E.J., & Schuyler, W. (1907). The learning process. *Psychological Bulletin, 4*, 307-310.

Swinnen, S.P. (1990). Interpolated activities during the knowledge-of-results delay and post-knowledge-of-results interval: Effects on performance and learning. *Journal of Experimental Psychology: Learning, Memory, and Cognition, 16,* 692-705.

Swinnen, S.P. (1992). Coordination of upper-limb movement: A neuro-dynamics account. In G.E. Stelmach & J. Requin (Eds.), *Tutorials in motor behavior II* (pp. 695-711). Amsterdam: Elsevier.

Swinnen, S.P. (1996). Information feedback for motor skill learning: A review. In H.N. Zelaznik (Ed.), *Advances in motor learning and control* (pp. 37-66). Champaign, IL: Human Kinetics.

Swinnen, S.P., Dounskaia, N., Verschueren, S., Serrien, D.J., & Daelman, A. (1995). Relative phase destabilization during interlimb coordination: The disruptive role of kinesthetic afferences induced by passive movement. *Experimental Brain Research, 105,* 439-454.

Swinnen, S.P., Heuer, H., Massion, J., & Casaer, P. (Eds.) (1994). *Interlimb coordination: Neural, dynamical, and cognitive constraints.* San Diego: Academic Press.

Swinnen, S.P., Jardin, K., & Meulenbroek, R. (1996). Between-limb asynchronies during bimanual coordination: Effects of manual dominance and attentional cueing. *Neuropsychologia, 34,* 1203-1213.

Swinnen, S.P., Schmidt, R.A., Nicholson, D.E., & Shapiro, D.C. (1990). Information feedback for skill acquisition: Instantaneous knowledge of results degrades learning. *Journal of Experimental Psychology: Learning, Memory, and Cognition, 16,* 706-716.

Swinnen, S.P., Walter, C.B., Lee, T.D., & Serrien, D.J. (1993). Acquiring bimanual skills: Contrasting forms of information feedback for interlimb decoupling. *Journal of Experimental Psychology: Learning, Memory, and Cognition, 19,* 1328-1344.

Swinnen, S.P., Walter, C.B., Pauwels, J.M., Meugens, P.F., & Beirinckx, M.B. (1990). The dissociation of interlimb constraints. *Human Performance, 3,* 187-215.

Swinnen, S.P., Walter, C. B., & Shapiro, D.C. (1988). The coordination of limb movements with different kinematic patterns. *Brain and Cognition, 8,* 326-347.

Tarpy, R.M., & Sawabini, F.L. (1974). Reinforcement delay: A selective review of the last decade. *Psychological Bulletin, 81,* 984-997.

Taub, E. (1976). Movement in nonhuman primates deprived of somatosensory feedback. *Exercise and Sport Sciences Reviews, 4,* 335-374.

Taub, E., & Berman, A.J. (1968). Movement and learning in the absence of sensory feedback. In S.J. Freedman (Ed.), *The neuropsychology of spatially oriented behavior.* Homewood, IL: Dorsey Press.

Teasdale, N., Bard, C., LaRue, J., & Fleury, M. (1993). On the cognitive penetrability of posture control. *Experimental Aging Research, 19,* 1-13.

Teasdale, N., Forget, R., Bard, C., Paillard, J., Fleury, M., & Lamarre, Y. (1993). The role of proprioceptive information for the production of isometric forces and for handwriting tasks. *Acta Psychologica, 82,* 179-191.

Telford, C.W. (1931). The refractory phase of voluntary and associative responses. *Journal of Experimental Psychology, 14,* 1-36.

Terzuolo, C.A., & Viviani, P. (1979). The central representation of learning motor programs. In R.E. Talbott & D.R. Humphrey (Eds.), *Posture and movement* (pp. 113-121). New York: Raven.

Thelen, E., & Smith, L.B. (1994). *A dynamic systems approach to the development of cognition and action.* Cambridge, MA: Bradford.

Thelen, E., & Ulrich, B.D. (1991). Hidden skills: A dynamic systems analysis of treadmill stepping during the first year. *Monographs of the Society for Research in Child Development, Serial No. 223, 56(1).*

Thomas, J.R. (1980). Acquisition of motor skills: Information processing differences between children and adults. *Research Quarterly for Exercise and Sport, 51,* 158-173.

Thomas, J.R. (1997). Motor behavior. In J.D. Massengale & R.A. Swanson (Eds.), *The history of exercise and sport science* (pp. 203-292). Champaign, IL: Human Kinetics.

Thomas, J.R., & Chissom, B.S. (1972). Relationships as assessed by canonical correlation between perceptual-motor and intellectual abilities for pre-school and early elementary age children. *Journal of Motor Behavior, 4,* 23-29.

Thomas, J.R., & French, K.E. (1985). Gender differences across age in motor performance: A meta-analysis. *Psychological Bulletin, 98,* 260-282.

Thomas, J.R., & Nelson, J.K. (1996). *Research methods in physical activity* (3rd ed.). Champaign, IL: Human Kinetics.

Thomas, J.R., Nelson, J.K., & Church, G. (1991). A developmental analysis of gender differences in health related physical fitness. *Pediatric Exercise Science, 3,* 28-42.

Thomas, J.R., Thomas, K.T., & Gallagher, J.D. (1993). Developmental considerations in skill acquisition. In R.N. Singer, M. Murphey, & L.K. Tennant (Eds.), *Handbook of research on sport psychology* (pp. 73-105). New York: Macmillan.

Thorndike, E.L. (1914). *Educational psychology.* New York: Columbia University.

Thorndike, E.L. (1927). The law of effect. *American Journal of Psychology, 39,* 212-222.

Thorndike, E.L., & Woodworth, R.S. (1901). The influence of improvement in one mental function upon the efficiency of other functions. *Psychological Review, 8,* 247-261.

Tiffin, J., & Rogers, H.B. (1943). The selection and training of inspectors. *Personnel, 22,* 3-20.

Tipper, S.P., Lortie, C., & Baylis, G.C. (1992). Selective reaching: Evidence for action-centered attention. *Journal of Experimental Psychology: Human Perception and Performance, 18,* 891-905.

Todd, J.T. (1981). Visual information about moving objects. *Journal of Experimental Psychology: Human Perception and Performance, 7,* 795-810.

Todorov, E., Shadmehr, R., & Bizzi, E. (1997). Augmented feedback presented in a virtual environment accelerates learning of a difficult motor task. *Journal of Motor Behavior, 29,* 147-158.

Tolman, E.C. (1932). *Purposive behavior of animals and men.* New York: Century.

Tränkle, U., & Deutschmann, D. (1991). Factors influencing speed and precision of cursor positioning using a mouse. *Ergonomics, 34,* 161-174.

Treisman, A.M. (1969). Strategies and models of selective attention. *Psychological Review, 76,* 282-299.

Tresilian, J.R. (1995). Perceptual and cognitive processes in time-to-contact estimation: Analysis of prediction-motion and relative judgment tasks. *Perception & Psychophysics, 57,* 231-245.

Tresilian, J.R. (1997). Correcting some misperceptions of time-to-collision: A critical note. *Perception, 26,* 229-236.

Trevarthen, C.B. (1968). Two mechanisms of vision in primates. *Psychologische Forschung, 31,* 299-337.

Trowbridge, M.H., & Cason, H. (1932). An experimental study of Thorndike's theory of learning. *Journal of General Psychology, 7,* 245-260.

Trumbo, D., Ulrich, L., & Noble, M.E. (1965). Verbal coding and display coding in the acqui-

sition and retention of tracking skill. *Journal of Applied Psychology, 49,* 368-375.

Tsutsui, S., Lee, T.D., & Hodges, N.J. (1998). Contextual interference in learning new patterns of bimanual coordination. *Journal of Motor Behavior, 30,* 151-157.

Tubbs, M.E. (1986). Goal setting: A meta-analytic examination of empirical evidence. *Journal of Applied Psychology, 71,* 474-483.

Tuller, B., & Kelso, J.A.S. (1989). Environmentally-specified patterns of movement coordination in normal and split-brain subjects. *Experimental Brain Research, 75,* 306-316.

Turner, P.E., & Raglin, J.S. (1996). Variability in precompetitive anxiety and performance in college track and field athletes. *Medicine and Science in Sports and Exercise, 28,* 378-385.

Turvey, M.T. (1977). Preliminaries to a theory of action with reference to vision. In R. Shaw & J. Bransford (Eds.), *Perceiving, acting, and knowing* (pp. 211-265). Hillsdale, NJ: Erlbaum.

Turvey, M.T. (1990). Coordination. *American Psychologist, 45,* 938-953.

Turvey, M.T., Rosenblum, L.D., Schmidt, R.C., & Kugler, P.N. (1986). Fluctuations and phase symmetry in coordinated rhythmic movements. *Journal of Experimental Psychology: Human Perception and Performance, 12,* 564-583.

Turvey, M.T., & Schmidt, R.C. (1994). A low-dimensional nonlinear dynamic governing interlimb rhythmic coordination. In S.P. Swinnen, H. Heuer, J. Massion, & P. Casaer (Eds.), *Interlimb coordination: Neural, dynamical, and cognitive constraints* (pp. 227-300). San Diego: Academic Press.

Tyldesley, D.A., & Whiting, H.T.A. (1975). Operational timing. *Journal of Human Movement Studies, 1,* 172-177.

Ulrich, R., & Wing, A.M. (1991). A recruitment theory of force-time relations in the production of brief force pulses: The parallel force unit model. *Psychological Review, 98,* 268-294.

Umiltà, C., & Nicoletti, R. (1990). Spatial stimulus-response compatibility. In R.W. Proctor & T.G. Reeve (Eds.), *Stimulus-response compatibility* (pp. 89-116). Amsterdam: Elsevier.

Underwood, B.J. (1957). Interference and forgetting. *Psychological Review, 64,* 49-60.

Underwood, B.J. (1975). Individual differences as a crucible in theory construction. *American Psychologist, 30,* 128-134.

Underwood, G., & Everatt, J. (1996). Automatic and controlled information processing: The role of attention in the processing of novelty. In O. Neumann & A.F. Sanders (Eds.), *Handbook of perception and action. Volume 3: Attention* (pp. 185-227). San Diego: Academic Press.

Vallbo, A.B. (1974). Human muscle spindle discharge during isometric voluntary contractions: Amplitude relations between spindle frequency and torque. *Acta Physiologica Scandinavica, 90,* 319-336.

Van Rossum, J.H.A. (1990). Schmidt's schema theory: The empirical base of the variability of practice hypothesis. A critical analysis. *Human Movement Science, 9,* 387-435.

Vander Linden, D.W., Cauraugh, J.H., & Greene, T.A. (1993). The effect of frequency of kinetic feedback on learning an isometric force production task in nondisabled subjects. *Physical Therapy, 73,* 79-87.

Vercher, J.L., Magenes, G., Prablanc, C., & Gauthier, G.M. (1994). Eye-head-hand coordination in pointing at visual targets: Spatial and temporal analysis. *Experimental Brain Research, 99,* 507-523.

Vereijken, B., van Emmerik, R.E.A., Whiting, H.T.A., & Newell, K.M. (1992). Free(z)ing degrees of freedom in skill acquisition. *Journal of Motor Behavior, 24,* 133-142.

Vereijken, B., Whiting, H.T.A., & Beek, W.J. (1992). A dynamical systems approach to skill acquisition. *The Quarterly Journal of Experimental Psychology, 45A,* 323-344.

Verwey, W.B., & Dronkert, Y. (1996). Practicing a structured continuous key-pressing task: Motor chunking or rhythm consolidation? *Journal of Motor Behavior, 28,* 71-79.

Vince, M.A., & Welford, A.T. (1967). Time taken to change the speed of a response. *Nature, 213,* 532-533.

Vincent, W.J. (1995). *Statistics in kinesiology.* Champaign, IL: Human Kinetics.

von Hofsten, C. (1983). Catching skills in infancy. *Journal of Experimental Psychology: Human Perception and Performance, 9,* 75-85.

von Holst, E. (1954). Relations between the central nervous system and the peripheral organs. *British Journal of Animal Behavior, 2,* 89-94.

von Holst, E. (1973). On the nature of order in the central nervous system. In R. Martin (Trans), *The selected papers of Erich von Holst. The behavioural physiology of animals and man. Volume one* (pp. 3-32). London: Methuen. (Original work published 1937)

Wade, M.G., Lindquist, R., Taylor, J.R., & Treat-Jacobson, D. (1995). Optical flow, spatial orientation, and the control of posture in the elderly. *Journal of Gerontology: Psychological Sciences, 50B,* P51-P58.

Wadman, W.J., Denier van der Gon, J.J., Geuze, R.H., & Mol, C.R. (1979). Control of fast goal-directed arm movements. *Journal of Human Movement Studies, 5,* 3-17.

Walker, N., Philbin, D.A., & Fisk, A.D. (1997). Age-related differences in movement control: Adjusting submovement structure to optimize performance. *Journal of Gerontology: Psychological Sciences, 52B,* P40-P52.

Wallace, R.J. (1971). S-R compatibility and the idea of a response code. *Journal of Experimental Psychology, 88,* 354-360.

Wallace, S.A. (1996). Dynamic pattern perspective of rhythmic movement: An introduction. In H.N. Zelaznik (Ed.), *Advances in motor learning and control* (pp. 155-194). Champaign, IL: Human Kinetics.

Wallace, S.A., & Hagler, R.W. (1979). Knowledge of performance and the learning of a closed motor skill. *Research Quarterly, 50,* 265-271.

Walsh, W.D., Russell, D.G., Imanaka, K., & James, B. (1979). Memory for constrained and preselected movement location and distance: Effects of starting position and length. *Journal of Motor Behavior, 11,* 201-214.

Walter, C.B., & Swinnen, S.P. (1990). Asymmetric interlimb interference during the performance of a dynamic bimanual task. *Brain and Cognition, 14,* 185-200.

Walter, C.B., & Swinnen, S.P. (1992). Adaptive tuning of interlimb attraction to facilitate bimanual decoupling. *Journal of Motor Behavior, 24,* 95-104.

Walter, C.B., & Swinnen, S.P. (1994). The formation and dissolution of "bad habits" during the acquisition of coordination skills. In S.P. Swinnen, H. Heuer, J. Massion, & P. Casaer (Eds.), *Interlimb coordination: Neural, dynamical, and cognitive constraints* (pp. 491-513). San Diego: Academic Press.

Walter, C.B., Swinnen, S.P., & Franz, E.A. (1993). Stability of symmetric and asymmetric discrete bimanual actions. In K.M. Newell & D.M. Corcos (Eds.), *Variability and motor control* (pp. 359-380). Champaign, IL: Human Kinetics.

Wann, J.P. (1996). Anticipating arrival: Is the tau margin a specious theory? *Journal of Experimental Psychology: Human Perception and Performance, 22,* 1031-1048.

Wann, J.P., & Nimmo-Smith, I. (1990). Evidence against the relative invariance of timing in handwriting. *The Quarterly Journal of Experimental Psychology, 42A*, 105-119.

Warren, W.H. Jr., & Whang, S. (1987). Visual guidance of walking through apertures: Body-scaled information for affordances. *Journal of Experimental Psychology: Human Perception and Performance, 13*, 371-383.

Warren, W.H. Jr., & Yaffe, D.M. (1989). Dynamics of step length adjustment during running: A comment on Patla, Robinson, Samways, and Armstrong (1989). *Journal of Experimental Psychology: Human Perception and Performance, 15*, 618-623.

Warren, W.H. Jr., Young, D.S., & Lee, D.N. (1986). Visual control of step length during running over irregular terrain. *Journal of Experimental Psychology: Human Perception and Performance, 12*, 259-266.

Weber, E. (1846). Muskelbewegung [Muscle movement]. In R. Wagner (Ed.), *Handworterbuch der Physiologie* (Vol. 3, Pt. 2, pp. 1-122). Braunschweig: Bieweg.

Weeks, D.J., & Proctor, R.W. (1990). Salient-features coding in the translation between orthogonal stimulus and response dimensions. *Journal of Experimental Psychology: General, 119*, 355-366.

Weeks, D.J., Reeve, T.G., Dornier, L.A., & Fober, G.W. (1991). Inter-criterion interval activity and the retention of movement information: A test of the forgetting hypothesis for contextual interference effects. *Journal of Human Movement Studies, 20*, 101-110.

Weeks, D.J., Zelaznik, H., & Beyak, B. (1993). An empirical note on reduced frequency of knowledge of results. *Journal of Human Movement Studies, 25*, 193-201.

Weeks, D.L., Hall, A.K., & Anderson, L.P. (1996). A comparison of imitation strategies in observational learning of action patterns. *Journal of Motor Behavior, 28*, 348-358.

Weeks, D.L., & Sherwood, D.E. (1994). A comparison of knowledge of results scheduling methods for promoting motor skill acquisition and retention. *Research Quarterly for Exercise and Sport, 65*, 136-142.

Weinberg, D.R., Guy, D.E., & Tupper, R.W. (1964). Variation of postfeedback interval in simple motor learning. *Journal of Experimental Psychology, 67*, 98-99.

Weinberg, R.S. (1994). Goal setting and performance in sport and exercise settings: A synthesis and critique. *Medicine and Science in Sports and Exercise, 26*, 469-477.

Weinberg, R.S., & Gould, D. (1995). *Foundations of sport and exercise psychology*. Champaign, IL: Human Kinetics.

Weinberg, R.S., & Ragan, J. (1978). Motor performance under three levels of trait anxiety and stress. *Journal of Motor Behavior, 10*, 169-176.

Weiss, A.D. (1965). The locus of reaction time change with set, motivation, and age. *Journal of Gerontology, 20*, 60-64.

Welch, J.C. (1898). On the measurement of mental activity through muscular activity and the determination of a constant of attention. *American Journal of Physiology, 1*, 283-306.

Welford, A.T. (1952). The 'psychological refractory period' and the timing of high-speed performance—A review and a theory. *British Journal of Psychology, 43*, 2-19.

Welford, A.T. (1968). *Fundamentals of skill*. London: Methuen.

Welford, A.T. (1984). Psychomotor performance. *Annual Review of Gerontology and Geriatrics, 4*, 237-273.

Welford, A.T., Norris, A.H., & Shock, N.W. (1969). Speed and accuracy of movement and their changes with age. *Acta Psychologica, 30*, 3-15.

Weltman, G., & Egstrom, G.H. (1966). Perceptual narrowing in novice divers. *Human Factors, 8*, 499-505.

Westling, G., & Johansson, R.S. (1984). Factors influencing the force control during precision grip. *Experimental Brain Research, 53*, 277-284.

Wetzel, M.C., & Stuart, D.G. (1976). Ensemble characteristics of cat locomotion and its neural control. *Progress in Neurobiology, 7*, 1-98.

White, R.M. Jr., & Schmidt, S.W. (1972). Preresponse intervals versus postinformative feedback intervals in concept identification. *Journal of Experimental Psychology, 94*, 350-352.

Whiting, H.T.A. (Ed.). (1984). *Human motor actions: Bernstein reassessed*. Amsterdam: Elsevier.

Whiting, H.T.A., Bijlard, M.J., & den Brinker, B.P.L.M. (1987). The effect of the availability of a dynamic model on the acquisition of a complex cyclical action. *The Quarterly Journal of Experimental Psychology, 39A*, 43-59.

Whiting, H.T.A., Gill, E.B., & Stephenson, J.M. (1970). Critical time intervals for taking in flight information in a ball-catching task. *Ergonomics, 13*, 265-272.

Wickens, C.D. (1976). The effects of divided attention on information processing in manual tracking. *Journal of Experimental Psychology: Human Perception and Performance, 2,* 1-13.

Wickens, C.D. (1980). The structure of attentional resources. In R.S. Nickerson (Ed.), *Attention and Performance VIII* (pp. 239-257). Hillsdale, NJ: Erlbaum.

Wickens, C.D. (1992). *Engineering psychology and human performance* (2nd ed.). New York: HarperCollins.

Wickens, C.D., & Baker, P. (1995). Cognitive issues in virtual reality. In W. Barfield & T.A. Furness (Eds.), *Virtual environments and advanced interface design* (pp. 514-541). New York: Oxford.

Wiener, N. (1948). *Cybernetics.* New York: Wiley.

Wightman, D.C., & Lintern, G. (1985). Part-task training for tracking and manual control. *Human Factors, 27,* 267-283.

Wightman, D.C., & Sistrunk, F. (1987). Part-task training strategies in simulated carrier landing final-approach training. *Human Factors, 29,* 245-254.

Wikswo, J.P. Jr., Gevins, A., & Williamson, S.J. (1993). The future of the EEG and MEG. *Electroencephalography and Clinical Neurophysiology, 87,* 1-9.

Wilberg, R.B. (1990). The retention and free recall of multiple movements. *Human Movement Science, 9,* 437-479.

Williams, H.G., Woollacott, M.H., & Ivry, R. (1992). Timing and motor control in clumsy children. *Journal of Motor Behavior, 24,* 165-172.

Wilson, D.M. (1961). The central nervous control of flight in a locust. *Journal of Experimental Biology, 38,* 471-490.

Wing, A.M., & Kristofferson, A.B. (1973a). The timing of interresponse intervals. *Perception & Psychophysics, 13,* 455-460.

Wing, A.M., & Kristofferson, A.B. (1973b). Response delays and the timing of discrete motor responses. *Perception & Psychophysics, 14,* 5-12.

Wing, A.M., Turton, A., & Fraser, C. (1986). Grasp size and accuracy of approach in reaching. *Journal of Motor Behavior, 18,* 245-260.

Winstein, C.J., & Garfinkel, A. (1989). Qualitative dynamics of disordered human locomotion: A preliminary investigation. *Journal of Motor Behavior, 21,* 373-391.

Winstein, C.J., Grafton, S.T., & Pohl, P.S. (1997). Motor task difficulty and brain activity: Investigation of goal-directed reciprocal aiming using positron emission tomography. *Journal of Neurophysiology, 77,* 1581-1594.

Winstein, C.J., Pohl, P.S., & Lewthwaite, R. (1994). Effects of physical guidance and knowledge of results on motor learning: Support for the guidance hypothesis. *Research Quarterly for Exercise and Sport, 65,* 316-323.

Winstein, C.J., & Schmidt, R.A. (1990). Reduced frequency of knowledge of results enhances motor skill learning. *Journal of Experimental Psychology: Learning, Memory and Cognition, 16,* 677-691.

Winter, D.A. (1990). *Biomechanics and motor control of human movement* (2nd ed.). New York: Wiley.

Witkin, H.A. (1949). Perception of body position and of the position of the visual field. *Psychological Monographs, 63* (7, Whole No. 302).

Woodworth, R.S. (1899). The accuracy of voluntary movement. *Psychological Review Monographs, 3* (Whole No. 13).

Woodworth, R.S. (1903). *Le mouvement.* Paris: Doin.

Woodworth, R.S. (1938). *Experimental psychology.* New York: Holt.

Woollacott, M.H., & Jensen, J.L. (1996). Posture and locomotion. In H. Heuer & S.W. Keele (Eds.), *Handbook of perception and action. Volume 2: Motor skills* (pp. 333-403). San Diego: Academic Press.

Woollacott, M.H., & Manchester, D.L. (1993). Anticipatory postural adjustments in older adults: Are changes in response characteristics due to changes in strategy? *Journal of Gerontology: Medical Sciences, 48,* M64-M70.

Woollacott, M.H., & Sveistrup, H. (1994). The development of sensorimotor integration underlying posture control in infants during the transition to independent stance. In S.P. Swinnen, H. Heuer, J. Massion, & P. Casaer (Eds.), *Interlimb coordination: Neural, dynamical, and cognitive constraints* (pp. 371-389). San Diego: Academic Press.

Worringham, C.J. (1992). Some historical roots of phenomena and methods in motor behavior research. In G.E. Stelmach & J. Requin (Eds.), *Tutorials in motor behavior II* (pp. 807-825). Amsterdam: Elsevier.

Worringham, C.J., Smiley-Oyen, A.L., & Cross, C.L. (1996). The neural basis of motor learning in humans. In H.N. Zelaznik (Ed.), *Advances in motor learning and control* (pp. 67-86). Champaign, IL: Human Kinetics.

Wright, C.E. (1990). Generalized motor programs: Reexamining claims of effector independence in writing. In M. Jeannerod (Ed.), *Attention and performance XIII* (pp. 294-320). Hillsdale, NJ: Erlbaum.

Wright, C.E., & Meyer, D.E. (1983). Conditions for a linear speed-accuracy trade-off in aimed movements. *The Quarterly Journal of Experimental Psychology, 35A,* 279-296.

Wright, D.L. (1991). The role of intertask and intratask processing in acquisition and retention of motor skills. *Journal of Motor Behavior, 23,* 139-145.

Wright, D.L., Li, Y., & Whitacre, C. (1992). The contribution of elaborative processing to the contextual interference effect. *Research Quarterly for Exercise and Sport, 63,* 30-37.

Wright, D.L., & Shea, C.H. (1991). Contextual dependencies in motor skills. *Memory & Cognition, 19,* 361-370.

Wright, D.L., & Shea, C.H. (1994). Cognition and motor skill acquisition: Contextual dependencies. In C.R. Reynolds (Eds.), *Cognitive assessment: A multidisciplinary perspective* (pp. 89-106). New York: Plenum.

Wright, D.L., Snowden, S., & Willoughby, D. (1990). Summary KR: How much information is used from the summary? *Journal of Human Movement Studies, 19,* 119-128.

Wrisberg, C.A. (1991). A field test of the effect of contextual variety during skill acquisition. *Journal of Teaching in Physical Education, 11,* 21-30.

Wrisberg, C.A., & Anshel, M.H. (1993). A field test of the activity-set hypothesis for warm-up decrement in an open skill. *Research Quarterly for Exercise and Sport, 64,* 39-45.

Wrisberg, C.A., & Liu, Z. (1991). The effect of contextual variety on the practice, retention, and transfer of an applied motor skill. *Research Quarterly for Exercise and Sport, 62,* 406-412.

Wrisberg, C.A., & Ragsdale, M.R. (1979). Further tests of Schmidt's schema theory: Development of a schema rule for a coincident timing task. *Journal of Motor Behavior, 11,* 159-166.

Wrisberg, C.A., & Schmidt, R.A. (1975). A note on motor learning without post-response knowledge of results. *Journal of Motor Behavior, 7,* 221-225.

Wulf, G. (1991). The effect of type of practice on motor learning in children. *Applied Cognitive Psychology, 5,* 123-134.

Wulf, G., & Lee, T.D. (1993). Contextual interference in movements of the same class: Differen-tial effects on program and parameter learning. *Journal of Motor Behavior, 25,* 254-263.

Wulf, G., Lee, T.D., & Schmidt, R.A. (1994). Reducing knowledge of results about relative versus absolute timing: Differential effects on learning. *Journal of Motor Behavior, 26,* 362-369.

Wulf, G., & Schmidt, R.A. (1989). The learning of generalized motor programs: Reducing the relative frequency of knowledge of results enhances memory. *Journal of Experimental Psychology: Learning, Memory and Cognition, 15,* 748-757.

Wulf, G., & Schmidt, R.A. (1994a). Contextual-interference effects in motor learning: Evaluating a KR-usefulness hypothesis. In J.R. Nitsch & R. Seiler (Eds.), *Movement and sport: Psychological foundations and effects. Vol. 2. Motor control and motor learning* (pp. 304-309). Sankt Augustin, Germany: Academia Verlag.

Wulf, G., & Schmidt, R.A. (1994b). Feedback-induced variability and the learning of generalized motor programs. *Journal of Motor Behavior, 26,* 348-361.

Wulf, G., & Schmidt, R.A. (1996). Average KR degrades parameter learning. *Journal of Motor Behavior, 28,* 371-381.

Wulf, G., & Schmidt, R.A. (1997). Variability of practice and implicit motor learning. *Journal of Experimental Psychology: Learning, Memory, and Cognition, 23,* 987-1006.

Wulf, G., Schmidt, R.A., & Deubel, H. (1993). Reduced feedback frequency enhances generalized motor program learning but not parameterization learning. *Journal of Experimental Psychology: Learning, Memory, and Cognition, 19,* 1134-1150.

Wulf, G., & Weigelt, C. (1997). Instructions about physical principles in learning a complex motor skill: To tell or not to tell. . . *Research Quarterly for Exercise and Sport, 68,* 362-367.

Yamanishi, J., Kawato, M., & Suzuki, R. (1980). Two coupled oscillators as a model for the coordinated finger tapping by both hands. *Biological Cybernetics, 37,* 219-225.

Yao, W., Fischman, M.G., & Wang, Y.T. (1994). Motor skill acquisition and retention as a function of average feedback, summary feedback, and performance variability. *Journal of Motor Behavior, 26,* 273-282.

Yerkes, R.M., & Dodson, J.D. (1908). The relation of strength of stimulus to rapidity of habit-formation. *Journal of Comparative Neurology and Psychology, 18,* 459-482.

Young, D.E., Cohen, M.J., & Husak, W.S. (1993). Contextual interference and motor skill acquisition: On the processes that influence retention. *Human Movement Science, 12,* 577-600.

Young, D.E. & Schmidt, R.A. (1990). Units of motor behavior: Modifications with practice and feedback. In M. Jeannerod (Ed.), *Attention and performance XIII* (pp. 763-795). Hillsdale, NJ: Erlbaum.

Young, D.E. & Schmidt, R.A. (1991). Motor programs as units of movement control. In N.I. Badler, B.A. Barsky, & D. Zeltzer (Eds.), *Making them move: Mechanics, control, and animation of articulated figures* (pp. 129-155). San Mateo, CA: Morgan Kaufmann.

Young, D.E., & Schmidt, R.A. (1992). Augmented kinematic feedback for motor learning. *Journal of Motor Behavior, 24,* 261-273.

Zaichowsky, L., & Takenaka, K. (1993). Optimizing arousal level. In R.N. Singer, M. Murphey, & L.K. Tennant (Eds.), *Handbook on research in sport psychology* (pp. 511-527). New York: Macmillan.

Zanone, P.G., & Kelso, J.A.S. (1992). Evolution of behavioral attractors with learning: Nonequilibrium phase transitions. *Journal of Experimental Psychology: Human Perception and Performance, 18,* 403-421.

Zanone, P.G., & Kelso, J.A.S. (1994). The coordination dynamics of learning: Theoretical structure and experimental agenda. In S.P. Swinnen, H. Heuer, J. Massion, & P. Casaer (Eds.), *Interlimb coordination: Neural, dynamical, and cognitive constraints* (pp. 461-490). San Diego: Academic Press.

Zavala, A., Locke, E.A., Van Cott, H.P., & Fleishman, E.A. (1965). *The analysis of helicopter pilot performance* (Tech. Rep. AIR-E-29-6/65-TR). Washington, DC: American Institutes for Research.

Zelaznik, H.N., & Hahn, R. (1985). Reaction time methods in the study of motor programming: The precuing of hand, digit, and duration. *Journal of Motor Behavior, 17,* 190-218.

Zelaznik, H.N., Hawkins, B., & Kisselburgh, L. (1983). Rapid visual feedback processing in single-aiming movements. *Journal of Motor Behavior, 15,* 217-236.

Zelaznik, H.N., Mone, S., McCabe, G.P., & Thaman, C. (1988). Role of temporal and spatial precision in determining the nature of the speed-accuracy trade-off in aimed-hand movements. *Journal of Experimental Psychology: Human Perception and Performance, 14,* 221-230.

Zelaznik, H.N., Schmidt, R.A., & Gielen, C.C.A.M. (1986). Kinematic properties of rapid aimed hand movements. *Journal of Motor Behavior, 18,* 353-372.

Zelaznik, H.N., Shapiro, D.C., & McColsky, D. (1981). Effects of a secondary task on the accuracy of single aiming movements. *Journal of Experimental Psychology: Human Perception and Performance, 7,* 1007-1018.

Zelaznik, H.N., Shapiro, D.C., & Newell, K.M. (1978). On the structure of motor recognition memory. *Journal of Motor Behavior, 10,* 313-323.

Zelaznik, H.N., Smith, A., & Franz, E.A. (1994). Motor performance of stutterers and nonstutterers on timing and force control tasks. *Journal of Motor Behavior, 26,* 340-347.

Zelaznik, H.N., & Spring, J. (1976). Feedback in response recognition and production. *Journal of Motor Behavior, 8,* 309-312.

Zernicke, R.F., & Roberts, E.M. (1978). Lower extremity forces and torques during systematic variation of non-weight bearing motion. *Medicine and Science in Sports, 10,* 21-26.

Zernicke, R.F., & Schneider, K. (1993). Biomechanics and developmental neuromotor control. *Child Development, 64,* 982-1004.

AUTHOR INDEX

Rhoades, M.V. 50, 450
Rich, S. 265, 362, 363, 434
Richardson-Klavehn, A. 55, 291, 454
Richter-Heinrich, E. 335, 454
Rietdyk, S. 110, 452
Rink, J.E. 305, 435
Ritter, B. 316, 426
Rizzolati, G. 13, 52, 441
Robazza, C. 305, 427
Roberton, M.A. 253, 438
Roberts, E.M. 135, 191, 461, 469
Roberts, L.E. 335, 454
Roberts, T.D.M. 113, 428
Robinson, C. 110, 452
Robinson, G.H. 212, 454
Robison, A.B. 178, 434
Roediger, H.L. 55, 62, 454
Rogers, C.A. Jr. 351, 455
Rogers, D.E. 11, 53-55, 147, 148, 438
Rogers, D.K. 112, 445
Rogers, H.B. 333, 464
Rogers, P. 371, 457
Rokeach, M. 257, 432
Romanow, S.K.E. 378, 379, 448
Rose, D.J. 77, 453, 455
Rosenbaum, D.A. 52-54, 80, 81, 197, 199, 224, 396, 397, 455, 462
Rosenbloom, P.S. 359, 450
Rosenblum, L.D. 219, 464
Ross, D. 290, 291, 318, 332, 336, 405, 426, 432, 448, 455
Ross, H.E. 126, 428
Rossetti, Y. 212, 432
Rossignol, S. 139, 153, 435
Roth, K. 163, 167, 455
Rothstein, A.L. 82, 332, 455
Rothwell, D. 363, 426
Rothwell, J.C. 121, 134, 136, 455
Rowan, A.K. 110, 439
Roy, E.A. 216, 433, 459
Rubin, W.M. 329, 368, 383, 455
Rudell, A.P. 52, 460
Russell, D.G. 147, 257, 368-370, 373, 398, 423, 457, 465
Rutter, B.G. 313, 451
Ryan, E.D. 256, 392, 455
Rymer, W.Z. 119, 122, 439

S
Sakata, H. 13, 441
Sale, D. 318, 455
Salmela, J.H. 257, 455
Salmoni, A.W. 14, 77, 82, 326, 329, 330, 332, 336,

341, 345-347, 349, 354, 437, 455, 456
Salthouse, T.A. 254, 377, 456
Saltiel, P. 13, 427
Samson, Y. 38, 454
Samways, M. 110, 452
Sanders, A.F. 43, 456
Sanders, M.S. 9, 43, 178, 456
Sanes, J.N. 13, 136, 456
Savelsbergh, G.J.P. 104, 106, 107, 456
Sawabini, F.L. 347, 463
Scarpa, M. 211, 436
Schellekens, J.M.H. 176, 456
Schendel, J.D. 351, 393, 407, 456
Schlager, N. 9, 456
Schmidt, R.A. 12, 14, 20, 29, 38, 54, 69, 74, 78, 80, 81, 84, 85, 90, 91, 122, 124, 127, 136, 140, 143, 147, 148, 151-153, 155, 157, 158, 163, 164, 166, 168, 176, 177, 180-182, 184, 185, 187, 188, 190, 191, 197, 199, 201, 203, 209, 210, 214, 215, 224, 226, 239, 249, 252, 266, 274, 282, 283, 289-291, 298, 301, 310, 317, 318, 326, 329, 330, 332, 335, 336, 340, 341, 345-349, 351, 353, 354, 367-371, 373, 374, 376-378, 381, 382, 388, 389, 397, 400-405, 424-426, 428, 431, 436, 439, 446, 447, 450, 451, 454-460, 463, 466-469
Schmidt, R.C. 217, 219, 223, 458, 464
Schneider, D.M. 209, 458
Schneider, K. 253, 377, 458, 469
Schneider, W. 68, 69, 362, 376, 458, 460
Schoenfelder-Zohdi, B. 289, 291, 346, 447, 460
Scholten, C.A. 176, 456
Scholz, J.P. 219-221, 442, 458
Schöner, G. 219-221, 382, 442, 458, 459
Schooler, J.W. 62, 430
Schroeder, W.H. 289, 438
Schröger, E. 63, 432
Schulman, H.G. 72, 77, 437
Schumsky, D.A. 135, 330, 331, 427, 430
Schutz, R.W. 24, 25, 87, 459, 461
Schuyler, W. 6, 462
Schweickert, R. 43, 458
Schwenkmezger, P. 87, 88, 437
Scully, D.M. 290, 459
Sears, T.A. 122, 459
Seeger, C.M. 50, 434
Seibel, R. 50, 459
Sekiya, H. 54, 310, 343, 425, 459, 460
Seng, C.N. 47, 190, 440
Serrien, D.J. 222, 334, 381, 382, 459, 463
Servos, P. 212, 436
Severin, F.V. 137, 460
Seymour, W.D. 313, 317, 459

SUBJECT INDEX

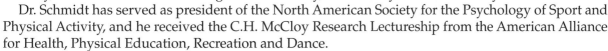

ABOUT THE AUTHORS

Richard A. Schmidt, PhD, is a principal scientist at Exponent Failure Analysis Associates, Inc., Los Angeles, and a professor of psychology at the University of California, Los Angeles. Known as one of the research leaders in motor behavior, Dr. Schmidt has nearly 30 years' experience in this area and has published widely.

The originator of "schema theory," Dr. Schmidt founded the *Journal of Motor Behavior* and was editor for 11 years. He authored the first edition of *Motor Control and Learning* in 1982 and followed up with a second edition of the popular text in 1988. He received an honorary doctorate from Catholic University of Leuven, Belgium, in recognition of his work.

Dr. Schmidt is a member of the North American Society for the Psychology of Sport and Physical Activity, the Human Factors and Ergonomics Society, and the Psychonomic Society.

Dr. Schmidt has served as president of the North American Society for the Psychology of Sport and Physical Activity, and he received the C.H. McCloy Research Lectureship from the American Alliance for Health, Physical Education, Recreation and Dance.

His leisure time activities include sailboat racing, running, and skiing.

Timothy D. Lee, PhD, is a professor in the department of kinesiology at McMaster University in Hamilton, Ontario, Canada. Since 1984 his research has been sponsored by grants from the Natural Sciences and Engineering Research Council of Canada. He has published extensively in motor behavior and psychology journals and has been an editorial board member for the *Journal of Motor Behavior* since 1992.

Dr. Lee received the Young Scientist Award from the Canadian Society for Psychomotor Learning and Sport Psychology in 1980. He also received a Senior Research Fellowship by the Dienst Onderzoekscoordinatie, Catholic University in Leuven, Belgium, in 1991-1992.

Dr. Lee is a member and past president of the Canadian Society for Psychomotor Learning and Sport Psychology, and a member of the North American Society for the Psychology of Sport and Physical Activity, the Psychonomic Society, and the Human Factors and Ergonomics Society.

His leisure time activities include hockey, golf, and music.

Related Books From Human Kinetics

Motor Behavior and Human Skill
Jan P. Piek, PhD, Editor
1998 • Hardcover • Item BPIE0675
ISBN 0-88011-675-7 • $49.00 ($73.50 Canadian)
Provides a forum for the analysis of the diverse theoretical approaches used to understand motor control.

Neurophysiological Basis of Movement
Mark L. Latash, PhD
1998 • Hardcover • 280 pp • Item BLAT0756
ISBN 0-88011-756-7 • $42.00 ($62.95 Canadian)
This textbook covers relevant information from the study of biomechanics, anatomy, control theory, and motor disorders.

Progress in Motor Control, Volume 1
Bernstein's Traditions in Movement Studies
Mark L. Latash, PhD, Editor
1998 • Hardcover • 408 pp • Item BLAT0674
ISBN 0-88011-674-9 • $49.00 ($73.50 Canadian)
Features 16 chapters by internationally known researchers. Each chapter addresses urgent problems of motor control across a spectrum of topics.

Advances in Motor Learning and Control
Howard N. Zelaznik, PhD, Editor
1996 • Hardcover • 320 pp • Item BZEL0947
ISBN 0-87322-947-9 • $42.00 ($62.95 Canadian)
Surveys the most important advances in the field, surpassing the confines of debate between proponents of the information processing and dynamical systems.

Motor Learning and Performance
From Principles to Practice
Richard A. Schmidt, PhD
1991 • Hardcover • 320 pp • Item BSCH0308
ISBN 0-87322-308-X • $38.00 ($56.95 Canadian)
Definitive introductory text helps undergraduate students apply research-based concepts for improving athletic performance and enhancing motor skill acquisition.

Motor Learning and Performance Instructor's Guide
Instructor's Guide • 1992 • Paperback • 72 pp • Item BSCH0381 • FREE to course adopters. Contact Human Kinetics for details.

To request more information or to order, U.S. customers call 1-800-747-4457, e-mail us at humank@hkusa.com, or visit our Web site at http://www.humankinetics.com/. Persons outside the U.S. can contact us via our Web site or use the appropriate telephone number, postal address, or e-mail address shown in the front of this book.

Human Kinetics
The Information Leader in Physical Activity